A CONCISE HISTORY OF

America and Its People

James Kirby Martin
University of Houston

Randy Roberts
Purdue University

Steven Mintz
University of Houston

Linda O. McMurry
North Carolina State University

James H. Jones
University of Houston
and

Sam W. Haynes
University of Texas at Arlington

 HarperCollins *CollegePublishers*

For Our Students

Executive Editor: Bruce Borland
Director of Development: Betty Slack
Cover Design: Kay Petronio
Cover Illustration: Jane Sterrett
Photo Researcher: Judy Ladendorf/Ellen Berman
Electronic Production Manager: Angel Gonzalez Jr.
Publishing Services: Ruttle, Shaw & Wetherill, Inc.
Electronic Page Makeup: Ruttle Graphics, Inc.
Printer and Binder: RR Donnelley & Sons Company
Cover Printer: RR Donnelley & Sons Company

A Concise History of America and Its People

Library of Congress Cataloging-in-Publication Data
A concise history of America and its people/James Kirby Martin . . .
    [et al.].—Single vol. ed.
    p. cm.
    Includes bibliographical references (p.) and index.
    ISBN 0-673-46780-5
    1. United States—History. I. Martin, James Kirby
E178.1.C74   1995
973—dc20   94-20138
                                                     CIP

94 95 96 97   9 8 7 6 5 4 3 2 1

Brief Contents

Detailed Contents

*At the end of each chapter are a Chronology of Key Events, a Conclusion, and Suggestions for
Further Reading.

$\mathcal{M}$aps, Charts, Figures, and Tables

$\mathcal{P}$reface

A *Concise History of America and Its People*, a newly abridged version of the full-length *America and Its People* (2nd edition), has been designed with both instructors and students of the U.S. history survey in mind. It is hoped that this text will serve the needs of teachers who require a brief overview of American history, one which will allow them to develop particular themes and issues through the use of supplemental readings such as primary sources, monographs, novels, and the like. At the same time, the authors have not lost sight of the primary task of any textbook: to engage students and hold their interest. A history text which merely synopsizes the past does so at the risk of losing the richness, color, and drama of the American experience. The challenge of the authors in *A Concise History of America and Its People*, then, has been to streamline the full-length text without compromising its effectiveness as a pedagogical tool.

In addition to retaining the style and flavor of the original, *A Concise History of America and Its People* resembles its parent in terms of organization and structure. Although more than a third shorter than the full-length text, this abridgement contains many of the distinctive and popular features of *America and Its People*. The anecdotes that open each chapter, which frame the chapter's central themes and draw students into the material, have been retained with only minor revisions. Readers will find in the abridged text more than half of the original's maps and illustrations, as well as the useful Chronology of Events at the end of each chapter. Although the Special Features section has been dropped from the format in this brief edition, some material has been rewoven into the main text, albeit in abbreviated form.

As with all books there is always room for improvement, and we have worked hard to fine-tune this new version of *America and Its People*. A number of key events have been clarified, and every effort has been made to incorporate the findings of significant recent scholarship. To improve the narrative flow and emphasize the causative effects of national affairs on American foreign policy, the sequence of chapters covering the late nineteenth century has been changed. "Imperial America," a chapter which deals with such issues as the United States' search for markets and the Spanish-American War, now follows the chapter entitled "End of the Century Crisis," which covers politics in the Gilded Age, Populism and the Panic of 1893. Whereas the second edition of the full-length text ends with the election of 1992, the final chapter (Chapter 31) of the abridged text now includes a discussion of the Clinton administration. Bibliographies at the end of each chapter have also been updated.

Most important, this abridgement of the full-length text strives to remain true to the purpose of the original: to provide students with a "people-centered" approach to the American past. By focusing on people, both the great and the ordinary, the authors endeavor to highlight the dramatic conflict among individuals and groups that has so often produced meaningful change. Both the full-length and abridged versions of *America and Its People* attempt to go beyond the study of major historical figures and their impact on national affairs; both texts seek to show how ordinary people lived their lives, and to do so in ways that students will find meaningful and relevant to their own experience. It is the authors' belief that ethnicity, gender, and race should not be treated as adjunct information, tacked onto the end of a political narrative, but rather should be presented as an integral part of American history. It is our hope that this book has succeeded in presenting a compelling, balanced, and sensitive account of a nation and its people.

The Authors

Supplements

For Instructors

Instructors Resource Manual

This extensive resource by Mark Newman of the University of Illinois at Chicago, begins with essays on teaching history through maps, film, and primary sources. Each chapter contains a synopsis, sample discussion questions, lecture supplements called "Connections and Extensions," and instructional flowcharts. The manual includes a special reproducible set of map exercises by James Conrad of Nichols College, designed to teach basic geographic literacy.

America Through the Eyes of Its People: A Collection of Primary Sources

Prepared by Carol Brown, this one-volume collection of primary documents portraying the rich and varied tapestry of American life contains documents concerning women, Native Americans, African-Americans, Hispanics, and others who helped to shape the course of U.S. history. Designed to be duplicated by instructors for student use, the documents have accompanying student exercises.

A Guide to Teaching American History through Film

Created by Randy Roberts of Purdue University, this guide provides instructors with a creative and practical tool for stimulating classroom discussions. The sections include: "American Films: A Historian's Perspective," a listing of "Films for Specific Periods of American History," "Practical Suggestions," and "Bibliography." The film listing is in a narrative form, explaining the connection between each film and the topics being studied.

Video Lecture Launchers

Prepared by Mark Newman, University of Illinois at Chicago, these video lecture launchers (each 2 to 5 minutes in duration) cover key issues in American history from 1877 to the present. The launchers are accompanied by an Instructor's Manual.

American Impressions: A CD-ROM for U.S. History

This unique, ground-breaking product for the Introduction to U.S. History course is organized in a topical/thematic framework which allows an in-depth coverage for each topic with a media-centered focus. Hundreds of photos, maps, art, graphics, and historical film clips are organized into narrated vignettes and interactive activities to create a tool for both professors and students. This first volume of a series includes: When Three Cultures Meet, The Constitution, Labor and Reform, and Democracy and Diversity: The History of Civil Rights. Each topic is explored through three major themes, Politics, Culture and Society, and Science and Health. Available for Macintosh and Windows formats.

Visual Archives of American History, 2/e

This two-sided video laserdisc explores history from a meeting of three cultures to the present and is an encyclopedic chronology of U.S. History offering hundreds of photographs and illustrations, a variety of source and reference maps—several of which are animated—plus approximately 50 minutes of video clips. For ease in planning lectures, a manual listing barcodes for scanning and frame numbers for all the content will be provided.

Transparencies

A set of over 30 map transparencies drawn from the text of *America and Its People.*

Discovering American History Through Maps and Views

Created by Gerald Danzer of the University of Illinois at Chicago, the recipient of the AHA's 1990 James Harvey Robinson Prize for his work in the development of map transparencies—this set of 140 four-color acetates is a unique instructional tool. It contains an introduction on teaching history through maps and a detailed commentary on each transparency. The collection includes cartographic and pictorial maps, views and photos, urban plans, building diagrams, and works of art.

Test Bank

This *Test Bank,* prepared by Ken Weatherbie of Del Mar College, contains over 2,000 test items, including multiple-choice, true/false and essay questions, and map exercises. The questions are keyed to topic, difficulty level, cognitive type, and relevant text page.

TestMaster Computerized Testing System

This flexible, easy-to-master computer test bank includes all the test items in the printed test bank. The *TestMaster* software allows you to edit existing questions and add your own items. Tests can be printed in several different formats and can include figures such as graphs and tables. Available for IBM and Macintosh computers.

QuizMaster

This new program enables you to design *TestMaster* generated tests that your students can take on a computer rather than in printed form. *QuizMaster* is available separately from *TestMaster* and can be obtained free through your sales representative.

Grades

A grade-keeping and classroom management software program that maintains data for up to 200 students.

For Students

Study Guide and Practice Tests

This two-volume study guide, by Ken Chiaro of Pima Community College, is designed to provide students with a comprehensive review of text material and to encourage application and critical analysis of the material. Each chapter contains a student introduction, reading comprehension and geography exercises, true-false, completion, and multiple-choice "Practice Tests."

Learning to Think Critically: Films and Myths About American History

Randy Roberts and Robert May of Purdue University use well-known films such as *Gone with the Wind* and *Casablanca* to explore some common myths about America and its past. Many widely held assumptions about our country's past come from or are perpetuated by popular films. Which are true? Which are patently not true? And how does a student of history approach documents, sources, and textbooks with a critical and discerning eye? This short handbook subjects some popular beliefs to historical scrutiny in order to help students develop a method of inquiry for approaching the subject of history in general.

Mapping American History: Student Activities

Written by Gerald Danzer of the University of Illinois at Chicago, this free map workbook for students features exercises designed to teach students to interpret and analyze cartographic materials as historical documents. The instructor is entitled to a free copy of the workbook for each copy of the text purchased from HarperCollins.

TimeLink Computer Atlas of American History

This atlas, compiled by William Hamblin of Brigham Young University, is an introductory software tutorial and textbook companion. This Macintosh program presents the historical geography of the continental United States from colonial times to the settling of the West and the admission of the last continental state in 1912. The program covers territories in different time periods, provides quizzes, and includes a special Civil War module.

$\mathcal{A}$bout the Authors

JAMES KIRBY MARTIN is a member of the Department of History at the University of Houston. A graduate of Hiram College in Ohio, he earned his Ph.D. degree at the University of Wisconsin in 1969, specializing in Early American history. His interests also include American social and military history. Among his publications are *Men in Rebellion* (1973), *In the Course of Human Events* (1979), *A Respectable Army* (1982), and *Drinking in America: A History,* rev. ed. (1987), the latter two volumes in collaboration with Mark E. Lender. Martin serves as general editor of the *American Social Experience* series, New York University Press. He recently was a senior fellow at the Philadelphia Center for Early American Studies, University of Pennsylvania, as well as scholar-in-residence at the David Library of the American Revolution, Washington Crossing, Pennsylvania. He is completing a biography of Benedict Arnold.

RANDY ROBERTS earned his Ph.D degree in 1978 from Louisiana State University. His areas of specialization include modern U.S. history and the history of American popular culture and sports. He is a member of the Department of History at Purdue University, where he recently won the Murphy Award for outstanding undergraduate teaching. His publications include *Jack Dempsey: The Manassa Mauler* (1979), *Papa Jack: Jack Johnson and the Era of White Hopes* (1983), and, in collaboration with James S. Olson, *Playing for Keeps: Sports and American Society, 1945 to the Present* (1989) and *Where the Domino Fell: America and Vietnam, 1945–1990* (1991). Roberts serves as co-editor of the *Studies in Sports and Society* series, University of Illinois Press, and is on the editorial board of the *Journal of Sports History.* His current research and writing interests include a biographical investigation of Hollywood actor John Wayne.

STEVEN MINTZ graduated from Oberlin College in Ohio before earning his Ph.D. degree at Yale University in 1979. His special interests include American social history with particular reference to families, women, children, and communities. Mintz is a member of the Department of History at the University of Houston. From 1989 to 1990 he was a visiting scholar at Harvard University's Center for European Studies, and has served as a consultant to the Smithsonian Institution's National Museum of American History. His books include *A Prison of Expectations: The Family in Victorian Culture* (1983), and, in collaboration with Susan Kellogg, *Domestic Revolutions: A Social History of American Family Life* (1988). Mintz is an editor of the *American Social Experience* series, New York University Press, and is completing a book on pre-Civil War American reform.

LINDA O. McMURRY is a member of the Department of History at North Carolina State University. She completed her undergraduate studies at Auburn University, where she also earned her Ph.D. degree in 1976. Her fields of specialization include nineteenth- and twentieth-century U.S. history with an emphasis on the African-American experience and the New South. A recipient of a Rockefeller Foundation Humanities fellowship, she has written *George Washington Carver: Scientist and Symbol* (1981), and *Recorder of the Black Experience: A Biography of Monroe Nathan Work* (1985). McMurry has been active as a consultant to public television stations and museums on topics relating to black history, and is currently completing a study of biracial organizations in the South from the Reconstruction era to World War II.

JAMES H. JONES earned his Ph.D. degree at Indiana University in 1972. His areas of specialization include modern U.S. history, the history of medical ethics and medicine, and the history of sexual behavior. A member of the Department of History at the University of Houston, Jones has been a senior fellow of the National Endowment for the Humanities, a Kennedy fellow at Harvard University, a senior research fellow at the Kennedy Institute of Ethics, Georgetown University, and a Rockefeller fellow at the University of Texas Medical Branch, Galveston. His published writings include *Bad Blood: The Tuskegee Syphilis Experiment* (1981), and he is currently finishing a book on Alfred C. Kinsey and the emergence of scientific research dealing with human sexual behavior.

SAM W. HAYNES received his B.A. from Columbia University and his Ph.D. from the University of Houston in 1988. He is the author of *Soldiers of Misfortune: The Somervell and Mier Expeditions* (1990) and the editor of Thomas Jefferson Green's memoir *Journal of the Texian Expedition Against Mier* (1993). In 1993 he received a Dobie-Paisano

Fellowship awarded by the Texas Institute of Letters. He is currently completing a biography of James K. Polk. His areas of specialization include nineteenth-century U.S. expansionism, early Texas history, and the American Southwest. He is a member of the history faculty at the University of Texas at Arlington, where he also serves as a Fellow at the Center for Greater Southwestern Studies.

Chapter *I*

The Peopling and Unpeopling of America

Each Thanksgiving Americans remember Squanto as the valued Native American friend who saved the suffering Pilgrims from starvation. Few know the other ways in which Squanto's life reflected the disastrous collision of human beings occurring in the wake of Christopher Columbus's first voyage of discovery to America in 1492. What the Europeans called the "new world" had in fact been the home of millions of people for many centuries. The tragic story of Squanto and his tribe, the Patuxets of eastern Massachusetts, vividly portrays what happened when the two cultures came into contact.

Born about 1590, Squanto acquired the values of his Algonquian-speaking elders before experiencing much contact with adventurers from overseas. Tribal fathers taught him that personal dignity came from respecting the bounties of nature and serving one's clan and village, not from acquiring material possessions. To be accepted as an adult, he had to undergo a series of trials, which included spending a harrowing winter alone in the wilderness and eating poisonous herbs. When he had demonstrated his fortitude, tribal members declared him a man.

Living among 2,000 souls in the Patuxets' principal village, Squanto may well have foreseen trouble ahead when fair-skinned Europeans started visiting the region. First there were French fishermen; more fatefully, English vessels from the Jamestown settlement in Virginia passed through in 1614. One of the captains lured 20 Indians, among them Squanto, on board his ship and, without warning, set his course for the slave market in Malaga, Spain.

Somehow Squanto avoided a lifetime of slavery. By 1617 he was in England, where he devoted himself to mastering the English tongue. When asked to serve as an interpreter and guide for yet another New England expedition, Squanto, anxious to return home, readily agreed. In 1619, when the party put in at Plymouth Bay, a shocked Squanto discovered that nothing remained of his once-thriving village, except overgrown fields and rotting human bones. As if swept away by some unnamed force, the Patuxets had disappeared from the face of the earth. Thousands of Indians had died in the Cape Cod vicinity, the victims of diseases heretofore unknown in New England and probably carried there from Europe by fishermen and explorers. When these diseases struck, the native populace, lacking antibodies, had no way of fending them off.

Squanto was living with the Pokanoket Indians when the Pilgrims stepped ashore in December 1620 at the site of his old village. The Pilgrims endured a terrible winter in which half their numbers died. Then in the early spring of 1621 a lone Indian, Samoset, appeared in Plymouth Colony. He spoke halting English and told of another who had actually lived in England. Within a week Squanto arrived and agreed to stay and

Squanto is best remembered for the assistance he gave the Pilgrims in providing the necessities of life, but his own life—and death—illustrate the tensions and problems created by contact between Native American and European cultures.

help the Pilgrims produce the necessities of life. He taught them how to grow Indian corn (maize), a crop unknown in Europe, and how to catch great quantities of fish. His efforts resulted in an abundance of food, celebrated in the first Thanksgiving feast during the fall of 1621.

The story does not have a pleasant ending. Contact with the English had changed Squanto, and he adopted some of their practices. In violation of his childhood training, he started to serve himself. As future Pilgrim Governor William Bradford recorded, Squanto told neighboring Indian tribes that the Pilgrims would make war on them unless they gave him gifts. By the summer of 1622 Squanto had become a problem for the Pilgrims, who were anxious for peace. Then he fell sick, "bleeding much at the nose," and died within a few days, another victim of some European disease.

As demonstrated by Squanto's life, white–Indian contacts did not point toward a fusing of Native American and European customs, values, and ideals. Rather, the westward movement of peoples destroyed Indian societies and replaced them with European-based communities. Native Americans experienced chaos and death when they came into contact with Europeans. By the time of the Pilgrims' arrival, the Indian population had declined by as much as 90 percent.

The First Discovery of America

The world was a much colder place 75,000 years ago. A great ice age, known as the Wisconsin glaciation, had begun. Year after year, water being drawn from the oceans formed into mighty ice caps, which in turn spread over vast reaches of land. This process dramatically lowered ocean levels. In the area of the Bering Straits, where today 56 miles of ocean separate Siberia from Alaska, a land bridge emerged, which at times may have been 1,000 miles wide. This corridor, most experts believe, provided the pathway used by early humans to enter a new world.

These people, known as Paleo-Indians, were nomads and predators. With stone-tipped spears, they hunted mastodons, woolly mammoths, giant beavers, giant sloths, and bighorn bison, as well as many smaller animals. The mammals led prehistoric men and women to America up to 30,000 or more years ago. For generations, these humans roamed Alaska in small bands, gathering seeds and berries when not hunting the big game or attacking and killing one another.

Eventually, corridors opened through the Rocky Mountains as the ice started to recede. Humans and animals trekked southward and eastward, reaching the bottom of South America and the east coast of North America by about 8000 B.C. It had been a long journey, covering thousands of miles, and in the process Paleo-Indians had become Native Americans.

The Early Americans

With the passing of time, the atmosphere began to warm as the ice age came to an end. Mammoths, mastodons, and other giant mammals did not survive the warming climate and needless overkilling. The first Americans now faced a serious food crisis. Beginning in Central America between roughly 8000 and 5000 B.C., groups of humans started cultivating plant life as an alternate food source. They soon mastered the basics of agriculture. They raked the earth with stone hoes and planted seeds that produced crops as varied as maize, potatoes, squashes, pumpkins, and tomatoes.

This agricultural revolution profoundly affected Native American life. Those who engaged in farming were no longer as nomadic. They constructed villages and ordered their religious beliefs around such elements of nature as the sun and rain. With dependable food supplies, they had more children, resulting in a population explosion. These cultures ultimately evolved into complex societies, the most sophisticated of which appeared in Central America and the Ohio and Mississippi river valleys.

Emerging before A.D. 300, the Mayas of Mexico and Guatemala built elaborate cities and temples. Their craft workers produced jewelry of gold and silver, and their merchants developed extensive trading networks. Their intellectuals devised forms of hieroglyphic writing, mathematical systems, and several calendars, one of which was the most accurate in the world at that time. After A.D. 1000 warlike peoples from the north began to conquer their cities. First came the Toltecs, then the Aztecs. The Aztecs called their principal city Tenochtitlán (the site of present-day Mexico City). At its zenith just before the Spanish conquistadores appeared in 1519, Tenochtitlán contained a population of 300,000, making it one of the largest cities in the world at that time. Although imitators of Mayan culture, the Aztecs brutally exacted tribute, both in wealth and lives, from subject tribes. Their priests reveled in human sacrifice, since Huitzilopochtli, the Aztec war god, voraciously craved human hearts. At one temple dedication, Aztec priests sacrificed some 20,000 subject peoples. Not surprisingly, these tribes hated their oppressors. Many later cooperated with the Spanish in destroying the Aztecs.

Other mighty civilizations also emerged, such as the Incas of Peru, who came into prominence after A.D. 1100. Settling in the Andes Mountains, the Incas built an extensive road system and developed a sophisticated food supply network. The Incas were even wealthier than the Aztecs. They mined gold and silver in huge quantities, which made them a special target for Spanish conquerors.

In North America the Mound Builders (Adena and Hopewell peoples) appeared in the Ohio River valley around 1000 B.C. and lasted until A.D. 700. These natives hunted and gathered food, but they obtained most of their diet from agriculture. Their merchants traded far and wide. Fascinated with death, they built elaborate burial sites, such as the Great Serpent Mound in Ohio. In time they gave way to the Temple Mound Builders (Mississippian peoples), who constructed large cities, including a huge site near Cahokia, Illinois, where as many as 75,000 people lived amid 85 large temple mounds. For unknown reasons the Mississippian culture broke apart before European contact. Remnant groups may have included the Choctaws and Creeks of Mississippi and Alabama, as well as the Natchez Indians. All but exterminated by the French in the 1730s, the Natchez were the last of the Mound Builders in North America.

Indians on the Eve of Contact

Beginning with the agricultural revolution, population in the Americas increased rapidly. Estimates vary widely, and one authority has claimed a native populace of up to 120 million persons by the 1490s. Other experts consider this estimate too high, suggesting a figure of 50 to 80 million, with 5 to 8 million inhabitants living in North America. Europe's population, by comparison, was roughly 75 million at the time of Columbus, which underscores the mistaken impression among European explorers that America was a "virgin" or "vacant" land.

The explorers encountered a world of immense cultural diversity. At the time of Columbian contact, some 550 to 650 languages were in use in Central and North America. Developing life-styles to fit their environments, native groups varied greatly. Tribes in Oregon and Washington, such as the Chinooks, did some farming, but fishing for salmon was their primary means of subsistence. In the Great Plains region, Indians such as the Arapahos and Pawnees pursued wild game within more or less fixed hunting zones. Men concentrated on bringing in meat, and women functioned as gatherers of berries and seeds. In the Southwest, the Hopi and Zuñi tribes relied upon agriculture since edible plant and animal life was scarce in their desert environment. These Indians even practiced irrigation. Perhaps they are best known for their flat-roofed, multitiered villages that the Spanish called *pueblos*.

In the East, where English explorers and settlers first made contact with Native Americans, there were dozens of small tribal groups. Southeastern natives, including Cherokees, Chickasaws, Creeks, Choctaws, and Seminoles, were more attuned to agriculture because of lengthy growing seasons. Northeastern tribes, such as the Mahicans and Micmacs, placed more emphasis upon hunting and gathering.

Eastern Woodland Indians spoke several different languages but held many cultural traits in common. Essential to their religious values was the notion of an animate universe. They considered trees, plants, and animals to be spiritually alive. Tribal *shamans,* or medicine men, communicated with these spirits and prescribed elaborate rules, or taboos, regarding the treatment of plants and animals. Indian parents, having mastered such customs, taught children like Squanto that nature contained the resources of life. Although there was intertribal trading and much gift-giving in pottery, baskets, jewelry, furs, and wampum (conch and clam shells), religious values deterred tribal members from exploiting the landscape for the sake of acquiring great personal wealth.

Eastern Woodland parents introduced their children to many other concepts. There was no individual ownership of land. Tribal boundaries consisted of geographic locales large enough to provide for basic food supplies. Although individual dignity did matter, cooperation with tribal members rather than individual competitiveness was the essential ideal, even in sports. The refinement of athletic skills also represented useful training for war. Intertribal warfare was sporadic and resulted from any number of factors, such as competition over valued hunting grounds. Festering tensions and language barriers worked against intertribal cooperation in repelling the Europeans.

Even though males served as warriors, they did not always control tribal decision making. Among the powerful Five Nations of Iroquois in central New York, tribal organization was matrilineal. Women headed individual family units that in turn formed into clans. Clan leaders were also women, and they decided which males would sit on tribal councils that considered policies regarding diplomacy and war. Among other Eastern Woodland Indians, women occasionally served as tribal *sachems* (chiefs), much to the shock of Europeans.

When European fishermen and explorers started making contact, there were 500,000 to 800,000 Indians inhabiting the region between the North Atlantic coastline and the Appalachian Mountains. The Europeans were initially curious as well as fearful, but these feelings soon gave way to expressions of contempt. Judging all people by European standards, they regarded the Indians as inferior. Native Americans looked and dressed differently. Their religious conceptions did not conform to European forms of Christianity. The men seemed lazy since women did the bulk of the farming, and there was no consuming drive to acquire personal wealth.

To make matters worse, the natives, like those of Squanto's tribe, quickly began to die in huge numbers, which further confirmed European perceptions that Indian peoples were inferior rather than merely different. These native "savages" were blocking the path of a more advanced civilization desirous of expansion, or so Europeans argued. Thus commenced what many historians have come to call the "invasion" of America.

Preparing Europe for Westward Expansion

Nearly 500 years before Columbus's first westward voyage in 1492, Europeans made their first known contacts with North America. Around A.D. 1000, the Vikings (Scandinavians) explored barren regions of the North Atlantic. Eric the Red led an expedition of Vikings to Greenland, and one of his sons, Leif Ericson, continued exploring south and westward, stopping at Baffin Island, Labrador, and Newfoundland (described as *Vinland*). There were some settlement attempts, but they did not endure.

Crusades, Commerce, and the New Learning

The Viking voyages had no long-term impact because Europe was not yet ripe for westward expansion. Nonetheless, Europeans were slowly gathering knowledge about previously unknown peoples and places. The Crusades, designed to oust the Muslim "infidels" from such Christian holy sites as Jerusalem, broadened their geographic horizons. Sanctioned by the Roman Catholic church and begun in 1095, the Crusades lasted for two centuries. Although unsuccessful in their military objectives, European warriors learned of spices that would preserve meats over long winters, fruits that would bring greater balance to diets, silk and velvet clothing, handcrafted rugs, delicate glassware, and dozens of other commodities that would make European lives more comfortable.

Italian merchants, living in independent city-states such as Venice and Genoa, took the lead in developing the Mediterranean trade. The new wealth displayed by these great merchants promoted a pervasive spirit of material acquisition. It also helped underwrite a resurgence of the arts and sciences, known as the *Renaissance.* Beginning in Italy, the Renaissance soon captivated much of Continental Europe. The new spirit of learning resulted in enhanced geographical knowledge and developments in naval science. By the mid-fifteenth century educated Europeans knew the world was not flat. Receptive to new ideas, they learned from the Muslims about the astrolabe and sextant and their uses as basic navigational instruments. Contact with the Arabs also introduced Europeans to more advanced ship and sail designs. These breakthroughs heightened prospects for worldwide exploration in the ongoing search for valuable trading commodities.

The adventures of Marco Polo underscored the new learning and exemplified its relationship to commerce and exploration. Late in the thirteenth century, this young Venetian trader traveled throughout the Orient. He recorded his findings and told of unbelievable wealth in Asian kingdoms such as Cathay (China). Around 1450, Johannes Gutenberg, a German printer, perfected movable type, making it possible to reprint limitless copies of manuscripts. The first printed edition of Marco Polo's *Journals* appeared in 1477. Merchants and explorers alike, among them Christopher Columbus, read Polo's *Journals,* which spurred them on in the prospect of gaining complete access to Oriental riches.

Nation-States Support the First Explorations

The breakdown of feudal institutions and the consolidation of feudal domains into larger, more powerful nation-states also helped make transoceanic exploration possible. The process of forming modern nation-states commenced during the fifteenth century. The marriage of Ferdinand of Aragon to Isabella of Castile in 1469 represented the beginnings of national unity in Spain. These joint monarchs hired mercenary soldiers to break the power of defiant nobles. In 1492 they also crushed the Muslims (Moors) inhabiting southern Spain, driving them as well as Jewish inhabitants out of the country. Working closely with the Roman Catholic church, Ferdinand and Isabella used the Inquisition torture chambers to break the will of others whose loyalty they doubted. By 1500 their subjects owed first allegiance to Spain, not to local manor lords.

Spain's neighbor Portugal also led the way in the process of nation-building. Consolidating his realm in the 1380s, King John I was able to support his son, Prince Henry, called "the Navigator," in the latter's efforts to learn more about the world. Henry set up a school of navigation, and with official state support he sent out ships on exploratory missions. When the crews returned, they worked to improve maps, sailing techniques, navigational procedures, and ship designs.

Initially, the emphasis was on learning, but then it shifted to a quest for valuable trade goods as Henry's mariners conquered such islands as the Azores and brought back gold, silver, and ivory from the west coast of Africa. The lure of wealth drove Portuguese sailors farther south along the African coast. Bartholomeu Dias made it to the Cape of Good Hope in 1487. Ten years later, Vasco da Gama took a small flotilla around the lower tip of Africa and on to the riches of India. Da Gama's expedition led to the development of Portugal's Far Eastern empire. None of this would have been possible without a unified Portuguese government able to tax the populace and thus sponsor Prince Henry's attempts to probe the boundaries of the unknown.

Ferdinand and Isabella were intensely aware of Portugal's triumphs when Christopher Columbus, a young mariner from the Italian city-state of Genoa, asked them to underwrite his dream of sailing west to reach the Orient. Too consumed with their struggle for internal unification, they refused him, but Columbus persisted. He had already contacted Portugal, France, and England but gained no sponsorship. Finally, Queen Isabella, less occupied with internal problems after the unification of Spain, reconsidered. She met Columbus's terms, which included 10 percent of all profits from his discoveries, and proclaimed him "Admiral of the Ocean Sea."

On August 3, 1492, Columbus and some 90 mariners set sail from Palos, Spain, in the *Niña, Pinta,* and *Santa María.* On October 12 they landed on a small island in the Bahamas, which Columbus named San Salvador (holy savior). He called the natives Indians, a misnomer that stuck, because he believed that he was near Asia (the Indies). Proceeding on, Columbus landed on Cuba, which he thought was Japan, and then on Hispaniola, where he traded for gold-laden native jewelry. In 1493 Columbus and his crew returned home to a hero's welcome and to funding for three more expeditions to America.

Explorers, Conquerors, and the Making of New Spain

A fearless explorer, Columbus turned out to be an ineffective administrator and a poor geographer. He ended up in debtors' prison, and to his dying day in 1506 he claimed he had reached Asia, not an unknown geographic entity. Geographers named the western continents after another mariner, Amerigo Vespucci, a merchant from Florence who participated in a Portuguese expedition to South America in 1501. In a widely reprinted letter, Vespucci claimed that a new world had been found, and it was his name that caught on.

Columbus's significance lay elsewhere. His 1492 venture garnered enough extractable wealth to excite the Spanish monarchs. They did not care whether Columbus had reached Asia, only that further exploratory voyages might produce unimaginable riches. Because they feared Portuguese interference, Ferdinand and Isabella moved quickly to solidify their interests. They went to Pope Alexander VI, who issued a papal bull that divided the unknown world between Portugal and Spain. In 1494 they worked out a formal agreement with Portugal in the Treaty of Tordesillas, drawing a line some 1100 miles west of the Cape Verde Islands. All undiscovered lands to the west of the demarcation line belonged to Spain. Those to the east were Portugal's.

Ferdinand and Isabella used their strong army, seasoned by its struggle for unification, to conquer the Americas. The Spanish *conquistadores* did so with relish. Befitting their crusader's ideology, they agreed to subdue the natives and, with the support of church leaders, to convert them to Roman Catholicism. Bravery and courage, these warriors believed, would bring distinction to themselves and to their nation. Further, they could gain much personal wealth, even if shared with the Crown. Gold, glory, and the gospel formed a triad of factors motivating the Spanish conquistadores, and their efforts resulted in a far-flung empire known as New Spain.

Conquistadores Overrun Native Americans

Before 1510 the Spanish confined their explorations and settlements to the Caribbean islands. Unwittingly, the conquistadores carried with them microbic weapons against the Indians. European diseases such as small-

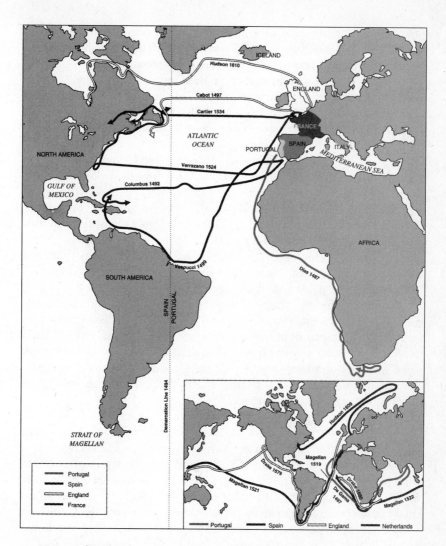

Voyages of Exploration

Except for abortive attempts by Norsemen in the late tenth century, contact between North America and Europe began at the end of the 1400s. In the 1500s settlements were founded by Spain in Mexico and Florida, and in the early 1600s France, England, Sweden, and Holland claimed territory along the Atlantic coast.

pox, typhoid, diphtheria, the measles, and various plagues and fevers took a rapid toll. In 1492, for example, more than 200,000 Indians inhabited Hispaniola. Just 20 years later, there were fewer than 30,000.

After 1510 the conquistadores moved onto the mainland. Vasco Núñez de Balboa reached Panama in 1513. He became the first European to see the Pacific Ocean, which he dutifully claimed for Spain. The same year Juan Ponce de León led a party to Florida in search of gold and a rumored fountain of youth. Although disappointed on both counts, he claimed Florida for Spain. Then in 1519 Hernando Cortés landed on the Mexican coast with 600 soldiers and marched toward Tenochtitlán, the site of modern-day Mexico City.

Aztec emperor Montezuma II offered Cortés mounds of gold and silver to keep out of Tenochtitlán, but this gesture only intensified the conquistadores' greed. They boldly marched into the city and took Montezuma prisoner. The Aztecs finally drove off Cortés's army in 1520, but less than a year later the Spaniards retook Tenochtitlán and claimed all Aztec wealth and political authority as their prize.

Cortés's stunning victory spurred on many other conquistadores, such as aggressive Francisco Pizarro. With fewer than 200 soldiers, he overwhelmed thousands of Incas in Peru, seizing the capital city of Cuzco in 1533 after hardly any fighting. Again, diseases stalked wherever Pizarro went. Showing no mercy, he executed the great chief Atahualpa and proclaimed Spain's sovereignty. By the 1550s the Spanish had conquered much of the rest of South America.

To the north, various expeditions scoured the landscape but found nothing comparable to the wealth of the Aztecs and Incas. Four hundred men under Pánfilo de Narváez began a disastrous adventure in 1528. They landed in Florida and searched the Gulf Coast region before being shipwrecked in what is now Texas. Only four men survived, one of whom, Cabeza de Vaca, wrote a tract telling of seven great cities laden with gold. His writings stimulated Hernando de Soto to investigate the lower Mississippi River valley. In 1540 another party under Francisco Vásquez de Coronado began exploring parts of New Mexico, Texas, Oklahoma, and Kansas. They were the first Europeans to see the Grand Canyon. Two years later, Spanish vessels sailed along the California coast as far north as Oregon. None of these groups ever located the fabled cities, but they advanced geographic knowledge of North America while claiming everything they came in contact with for Spain.

Constructing the Spanish Empire

To keep out intruders and to maintain order in New Spain, the Spanish Crown set up two home-based administrative agencies in Madrid. The

Columbus first landed on the Bahamian island which he named San Salvador. He described the local natives as peaceful and generous, an image that changed rapidly as *conquistadores* swept over the native populace in their rush to tap into the riches of the Americas.

House of Trade formulated economic policies and provided for annual convoys of galleons, called plate fleets, to haul American booty back to Spain. The Council for the Indies controlled all political matters in what became an autocratic, rigidly managed empire for the exclusive benefit of the parent state.

The Council for the Indies ruled through viceroys that headed four regional areas of administration. Viceroys, in turn, consulted with *audiencias* (appointed councils) on matters of local concern, but there were no popularly based representative assemblies. Normally, only pure-blooded Spaniards could influence decision making—and only if they had ties to councilors or viceroys. Those who questioned their political superiors soon learned there was little tolerance for divergent opinions.

During the sixteenth century about 200,000 Spaniards, a modest number, migrated to the Americas. Most migrants were young males looking for adventure and material riches. They did not find much of either, but some became wealthy as manor holders, ranchers, miners, and government officials. From the very outset, Spanish settlers complained about a shortage of laborers. One solution was the *encomienda* system. As *encomenderos,* or landlords, favored warriors and settlers received titles to Indian villages and the surrounding countryside as well as portions of annual crops and other forms of tribute. In exchange, the *encomenderos* were to educate the natives and instruct them in the Roman Catholic faith.

There were serious problems with the *encomienda* system. Landlords regularly abused the Indians, treating them like slave property. There was so much exploitation and death that one Dominican priest, Bartolomé de Las Casas, repeatedly begged officials in Madrid to stop such barbarities. In 1542 the Crown outlawed both the *encomienda* system and the enslavement of Indians, but this ruling did not change matters that much. Governing officials continued to award pure-blooded Spaniards vast landed estates (*haciendas*), on which Indians lived in a state of peonage, cultivating the soil and sharing their crops with their landlords (*hacendados*).

Since the native populace also kept dying off from contact with European diseases, a second solution to the labor problem was to import Africans. In 1501 the Crown authorized the first shipment of slaves to the Caribbean islands, a small beginning to what became a vast, forced migration of some ten million human beings to the Americas.

Slavery as it developed in New Spain was harsh. *Hacienda* owners and mine operators wanted only young males who could literally be worked to death, then replaced by new shiploads of Africans. On the other hand, Spanish law and Roman Catholic doctrine restrained some brutality. The Church believed that all souls should be saved, and it recognized marriage as a sacrament, meaning that slaves could wed and aspire to family life. Spanish law even permitted slaves to purchase their freedom. Such allowances were well beyond those made in future English-speaking colonies, and many blacks, particularly those who became artisans and house servants in the cities, did gain their independence.

Also easing slavery's harsh realities was the matter of skin color gradation: the lighter the skin, the greater the privileges. Since so many of the first Spanish migrants were males, they often intermarried with Indians or Africans. The mixture of skin colors in New Spain helped Africans escape some of the racial contempt experienced by blacks in English North

America, where there was less skin color variation because of legal restrictions against racial intermarriage.

Success Breeds Envy and Contempt

As Spanish authority spread north into areas that are now known as New Mexico, Arizona, and California, Franciscan, Dominican, and Jesuit friars opened missions and offered protection to natives who would accept Roman Catholic beliefs. Quite often local Indians simply incorporated Catholic doctrines into their own belief systems. When in the late 1660s and early 1670s a prolonged drought followed by a devastating epidemic ravaged Pueblos living in the upper Rio Grande valley of New Mexico, these natives openly questioned their new Catholic faith. Inspired by a native spiritual leader named Popé, they rose in rebellion in 1680 and killed or drove some 2,500 Spanish inhabitants out of New Mexico. By 1700 Spain had reconquered the region, maiming and killing hundreds of Pueblos in the process. With their numbers already in rapid decline, the Pueblos never again seriously challenged Spanish rule.

The flow of wealth from the Americas made Spain the most powerful—and envied—nation in Europe during the sixteenth century. Such success also became a source of contempt. When Las Casas, for example, wrote a book listing Spanish atrocities against the Indians, his charges became the basis of the "Black Legend," a tale that other Europeans used as a rationale for challenging Spain's New World supremacy. Spain's European rivals promised to treat Native Americans more humanely, but in reality their primary motivation was to garner a share of America's riches for themselves.

Challengers for North America: France and England

When Henry VII of England realized how successful Columbus had been, he chose to ignore the Treaty of Tordesillas and underwrote another Italian explorer, Giovanni Caboto (John Cabot), to seek Cathay (China) on behalf of the Tudor monarchy. Cabot's was the first exploratory expedition to touch North America since the Viking voyages. He landed on Newfoundland and Cape Breton Island in 1497. A second expedition in 1498 ended in disaster when Cabot was lost at sea. Still, his voyages served as the basis for English claims to North America.

Soon France joined the exploration race. In 1524 King Francis I sponsored yet another Italian mariner, Giovanni da Verrazzano, who sailed along the American coast from North Carolina to Maine. More important for later French claims, Jacques Cartier mounted three expeditions to the St. Lawrence River area, beginning in 1534, scouting as far inland as modern-day Quebec and Montreal.

The Protestant Reformation

Religious turmoil at home was one reason why the monarchs of England and France did not directly challenge Spain's supremacy in the Americas. There were too many problems at home, such as those related to religious turmoil. The Roman Catholic church had long been the wealthiest and most powerful institution in Europe. The greatest challenge to its authority came in 1517, when Martin Luther, an obscure German friar of the Augustinian order, criticized the church for what he thought were a number of unscriptural practices, particularly the selling of "indulgences" in the form of cash payments to the church to make amends for sins. As a form of penance, individuals could purchase indulgences for themselves or for others, such as deceased loved ones to assure quick journeys through purgatory to heaven.

Luther found no biblical basis for indulgences, and he despised the corrupt agents who sold them. As a professor of Scripture at the University of Wittenberg, Luther had agonized for years over the ways to earn God's grace, and he had concluded that faith was all that mattered, not ritual or good works. He insisted that people did not need priests to interpret scriptures for them but should be allowed to read the Bible for themselves in developing their own faith in God. Luther thus advocated a "priesthood of all believers" in comprehending the mysteries of Christianity. By the 1550s the doctrines of Lutheranism had taken firm hold in parts of Germany and the Scandinavian countries, often in the wake of enormous social turmoil.

Once underway, the Protestant Reformation, as the movement that Luther spawned became known, gained rapid momentum. It also took on many forms. In England, where politics rather than theology dictated the split with Rome, Henry VIII at first condemned Luther for arguing in favor of only two sacraments—baptism and communion. At the same time, Henry worried about not having a male heir to assure perpetuation of the Tudor line. In 1527 he asked Pope Clement VII to annul his marriage to Catherine of Aragon. When the pope refused, Henry severed all ties with Rome. Through a series of parliamentary acts, Henry closed monasteries and seized church property. In the 1534 Act of Supremacy he formally repudiated the pope and declared himself God's regent over England. Henceforth, all subjects would belong to the Anglican (English)

Church. The Church of England, unlike the Lutheran church, was similar to its predecessor in doctrine and ritual.

The Protestant leader whose beliefs were destined to have the greatest impact on the English colonies was John Calvin, a French lawyer who had fled to Switzerland in 1534 because of his controversial theological ideas. A brilliant and persuasive man, he soon controlled Geneva and ordered life there according to his understanding of scripture. Calvin believed God to be both all-powerful and wrathful. To avoid eternal damnation, it was necessary to gain His grace through a conversion experience denoted by accepting Jesus Christ as one's savior. However, while all had to seek, God had already predestined who would be saved and who would be damned. Since it was difficult to discern God's chosen "saints," Calvin taught that correct moral behavior according to the Bible and outward prosperity—physical and mental as well as material—represented possible signs of divine favor.

Calvin's disciples quickly spread the doctrine throughout Europe. Their numbers included founders of the German and Dutch Reformed churches, as well as Huguenots who eventually suffered from organized state persecution back in France. John Knox, another follower of Calvin, established the Presbyterian church in Scotland. In England, many Calvinists were called "Puritans." They wanted to continue Henry's reformation, but now along theological lines. Fiercely dedicated to their beliefs, they had a startling impact on the course of English history, particularly after the reign of Elizabeth I, when some of them moved to North America and others precipitated a civil war.

Defying the Supremacy of Spain

Spain's success in the Americas, combined with religious strife between Protestants and Catholics, fostered unending turmoil among European nation-states. Throughout the sixteenth century French, Dutch, and English freebooters attacked Spanish commerce or traded covertly within the Spanish empire. The most daring of the "sea dogs" were Englishmen like John Hawkins and Francis Drake. During the 1560s and 1570s Hawkins smuggled goods and raided for booty in New Spain. Drake's adventures were even more dramatic. With private financial backing, Drake attacked Spanish ports of call during the course of a three-year voyage which began in 1577. He became the first Englishman to circumnavigate the globe.

Queen Elizabeth's professions of innocence to the contrary, King Philip II of Spain suspected her of actively supporting the sea dogs. Further, he was furious with the English for giving military aid to the Protestant Dutch, who since 1567 had been fighting to free themselves from

Spanish rule. In 1588 Philip launched an armada of 130 vessels against England. The expedition ended in disaster for the Spanish when a host of English ships, most of them smaller but far more maneuverable than Philip's slow-moving galleons, appeared in the English Channel and offered battle under Drake's command. Then a fierce storm—the famous "Protestant Wind"— took over and blew the Spanish Armada to bits. The war with Spain did not officially end until 1604, but the destruction of the Armada established England's reputation as a naval power. It also demonstrated that little England, heretofore a minor kingdom, could prevail over Europe's most powerful nation, which encouraged some English subjects to press forward in securing territories in North America.

England Prepares for Westward Expansion

Besides the diminished Spanish threat, other factors helped to pave the way for England's westward expansion. None was more important than rapid population growth, which supplied a large pool of potential migrants. During the sixteenth century, England's population doubled in size, reaching four million people by the 1590s. Yet opportunities for employment or decent wages lagged behind the population explosion. The phenomenal growth of the woolen industry, for instance, forced peasants from the land as manor lords fenced in their fields to make pastures for sheep, a process known as the "enclosure movement." Meantime, cities such as London exploded in size as displaced persons poured in from the countryside and subsisted as best they could, some by working as day laborers for pitiful wages and others by begging and stealing.

Not only the uprooted peasants faced serious economic difficulties. Everyone confronted the major problem of rapid inflation. Between 1500 and 1600 the cost of goods and services spiraled upward by up to five times. The principal inflationary culprit was an overabundance of precious metal, mostly Spanish silver mined in America (seven million pounds in weight by about 1650) and then pumped into the European economy in exchange for various commodities. The money in circulation expanded more quickly than did the supply of goods or services. As a result, prices jumped dramatically.

In England even farmers owning their own land struggled to make ends meet since the cost of most necessities rose faster than what they received in the marketplace for their agricultural produce. A prolonged decline in real income on top of heavy taxes under the Tudors left many yeoman farmers destitute. In time, the abundant land of America attracted great numbers of England's failing independent farmers and permanently poor (or sturdy beggars).

The presence of so much poverty and suffering became a powerful argument for westward expansion. Besides putting beggars and other indigents back to work, colonies could serve as a source of valuable commodities. They would likewise stimulate England's shipbuilding industry and in other ways build up the power of the realm. On the other hand, Elizabeth was a tight-fisted Tudor monarch who remained unwilling to plunge vast sums of royal funds into highly speculative New World ventures. She preferred to let her favored courtiers, such as those who were currently subduing Ireland, expend their own capital and energies in searching for riches across the Atlantic Ocean.

Joining in the Invasion of America

Sir Humphrey Gilbert was a visionary who dreamed of finding a northwest passage through North America to the Orient, and who was willing to risk his personal fortune in the quest. Gilbert had other dreams as well, including the effective occupation of North America and the founding of American colonies. He appealed to Elizabeth for exclusive rights to carry out his plans, and she acceded in 1578.

The Roanoke Disaster

Gilbert did not live to see his dreams fulfilled. He disappeared in a North Atlantic storm after searching for the Northwest Passage. In 1584 his half-brother, Sir Walter Raleigh, received permission to carry on Gilbert's work. Raleigh sent out a reconnoitering party to explore the North Carolina coast and survey Roanoke Island. Then in 1585 he sponsored an expedition of 600 men. After some raiding for booty in New Spain, Raleigh's adventurers sailed north and dropped off 107 men at the chosen site.

The local Croatoan and Roanoak Indians initially welcomed the strangers, but relations quickly deteriorated as unknown diseases wreaked havoc on the native population. Warfare broke out, and the settlement had to be abandoned. Raleigh persisted, and in the summer of 1587 Governor John White and 114 others arrived on Roanoke Island. In mid-August White's daughter Elinor gave birth to Virginia Dare, the first English subject born in America. A few days later, the governor sailed back to England to obtain additional supplies. The outbreak of war with Spain delayed his return, and he did not get back to Roanoke until 1590. Nothing was left, except the word CROATOAN carved on a tree. What happened to the lost colony will never be known. No European ever saw the settlers again. Local Indians either killed or absorbed them into their tribes.

The Founding of Virginia

A few sixteenth-century English subjects did prosper in the wake of economic dislocation and spiraling inflation. Among these fortunate few were manufacturers of woolen goods and merchants who made all of Eu-

John White captured the life-style of the natives of Roanoke Island in his famous drawings.

rope a marketplace for English cloth. With their profits, these men started pooling their capital and sponsoring risky overseas business ventures by investing in *joint-stock* trading companies. Queen Elizabeth liked this model of business organization because private capital rather than royal assets would be marshaled to finance England's economic—and eventually political—expansion abroad. The Crown, of course, would share in any profits.

During the 1590s, English courtiers and merchant capitalists did not pick up on Raleigh's failed efforts. The ongoing war with Spain took precedence, and profits came easily from capturing Spanish vessels on the high seas. Once the war ended, influential merchants were anxious to pool their capital, spread the financial risk, and pursue Raleigh's patent. They took their case to the new king, the Stuart monarch James I, who willingly granted them a generous trading company charter in 1606.

In December 1606 they sent out 144 adventurers. The crossing was difficult, and 39 men died. In May 1607 the survivors located on an island some 30 miles up the James River off Chesapeake Bay. They called their settlement, really meant as a trading post, Jamestown. In its early days, Jamestown functioned as an outpost in another alien environment. The early participants were not settlers. They wanted to get in, gain access to easy forms of wealth, and get out before losing their lives.

It is amazing that Jamestown lasted at all. Many company adventurers were second and third sons of English noblemen. When Jamestown ran short of food, they still avoided agricultural work, preferring to search for gold and silver. The expedition also included valets and footmen, whose duties extended only to waiting on their aristocratic masters. Then there were goldsmiths and jewelers, plus a collection of ne'er-do-wells who apparently functioned as soldiers under gentleman officers. Hopelessly miscast for survival in the wilderness, many starved to death. Only 38 Englishmen were still alive by the early spring of 1608.

Another problem was the settlement site. Company directors had ordered the adventurers to locate on high ground far enough inland so as to go undetected by the Spanish. Jamestown Island met the second requirement, but it was a low, swampy place lying at a point on the James River where salt and fresh water mingled. The brackish water was "full of slime and filth," as one observer noted. The water could cause salt poisoning and was also a breeding ground for malaria, typhoid fever, and dysentery.

Several factors saved the Jamestown settlement. The local Indians under Powhatan, an Algonquian-speaking Pamunkey, initially offered sustenance. Powhatan had organized a confederacy of some 30 coastal tribes, numbering 20,000 people, to defend themselves against aggressive interior neighbors. Powhatan tried to stay clear of the Jamestown adventurers, but he could not help but notice their large ships, gaudy body

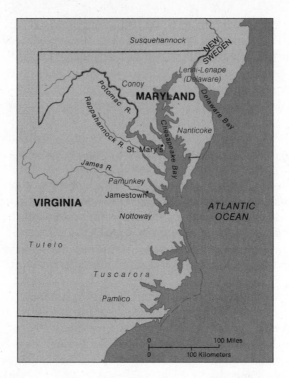

Chesapeake Settlements, 1650

armor, and noisy (though less-than-deadly) firearms. He viewed the English as potential allies in warfare with interior tribes, a faulty evaluation but one that kept him from wiping out the weakened adventurers.

At the same time, company investors in London refused to quit. They kept sending out supplies and adventurers, as many as 800 more young men plus a few women in 1608 and 1609. Upon their arrival, however, many quickly died of such diseases as malaria. Others, so debilitated from illnesses, were unable to work. They became a drain on Jamestown's precarious food supply.

At that time, the dynamic and ruthless local leadership of Captain John Smith kept the Jamestown outpost from totally collapsing. Once in Jamestown, he emerged as a virtual dictator. Smith helped save many lives by imposing discipline and forcing everyone—gentleman or servant, sick or well—to adhere to one rule: "He who works not, eats not."

In October 1609 Smith returned to England. Lacking authoritarian leadership, the adventurers experienced a tragic "starving time" during the winter of 1609–1610. Hundreds died as food supplies, described as "moldy, rotten, full of cobwebs and maggots," gave out. Only about 60 survived by eating everything from rats to snakes, and there was even an alleged instance of cannibalism. One man completely lost his mind; he murdered his wife, then "powdered [salted] her up to eat her, for which he was burned" at the stake.

Back in England, Virginia Company stockholders refused to concede defeat. By 1610 they realized that mineral wealth was an illusion but still they sent out more people. One of them, John Rolfe, experimented with local tobacco plants and produced a harsh-tasting crop. Rolfe, like the company, persisted. He procured some plants from Trinidad in the West Indies and grew a milder, more flavorful leaf. Tobacco soon became Virginia's gold and silver. The colony now had a valuable trading commodity, and settlements quickly spread along the banks of the James River. Englishmen had found an economic reason to stay in the Americas.

Dutch and French Adventurers

In the early 1600s the Spanish contented themselves with drawing wealth from their Caribbean basin empire. They did not challenge various European interlopers seeking to stake North American claims. Ultimately, Dutch settlements in New York were seized by the English, but France's efforts resulted in a Canadian empire capable of rivaling those of Spain and England.

Once fully liberated from Spanish domination at home, the Dutch grabbed at a portion of North America. In 1609 they sent out an English sea captain, Henry Hudson, to search for the Northwest Passage. Sailing up the New York waterway that bears his name, Hudson made contact with the Iroquois Indians and talked of trade in furs (broad-brimmed beaver hats were the fashion rage in Europe). The Dutch established trading stations on Manhattan Island (later called New Amsterdam) and Albany (Fort Orange) in 1624. The Iroquois did their part in delivering furs, and the colony of New Netherland took hold under the auspices of the Dutch West India Company.

Profits from furs also helped to motivate the French. In 1608 Samuel de Champlain set up an outpost at Quebec on the St. Lawrence River, and he found local Indians ready to trade. Yet only after 1663, when the Crown took control of managing the colony, did the French population in Canada grow significantly, reaching 10,000 by the 1680s. Following Champlain's lead, the French Canadians were energetic, exploring everywhere and claiming everything in sight. Few in number, they could not completely impose their cultural values on the Indians, so they established harmonious relations with dozens of different tribes. They even joined in native wars as a way of solidifying trading ties. They did use the natives for their own purposes, but they also showed respect, which paid off handsomely when their many Indian allies willingly fought beside them in a series of imperial wars that beset America beginning in 1689.

Conclusion

Except in Canada, the Europeans who explored the Americas and began colonies after 1492 acted as foreign invaders. Although a few were at first curious, they generally viewed the natives as their adversaries, describing them as "worse than those beasts which are of the most wild and savage nature." Judgments of cultural superiority seemed to justify the destruction of Native Americans.

Still, there was a "Columbian exchange" of sorts. The Indians taught the Europeans about tobacco, corn, potatoes, varieties of beans, peanuts, tomatoes, and many other crops then unknown in Europe. In return, Europeans introduced the native populace to wheat, oats, barley, and rice, as well as to grapes for wine and various melons. The Europeans also brought over domesticated animals, including horses, pigs, sheep, goats, and cattle. Horses proved to be important, particularly for Great Plains Indians, who used them in fighting against future generations of white settlers, just as tobacco production in the Chesapeake area had the unintended effect of attracting enough Europeans to end native control of that area.

Perhaps more than anything else, killer diseases served to unbalance the exchange. From the first moments of contact, great civilizations like the Aztecs and more humble groups like Squanto's Patuxets faced devastation. In some cases the Indians who survived, as in New Spain, had to accept the status of peons. Along the Atlantic coastline, survivors were drawn into the European trading network. In exchange for furs, the Indians wanted firearms to kill yet more animals whose pelts could be traded for still more guns and for alcohol to help them forget, even for a moment, what was happening to their way of life in the wake of European westward expansion.

The English would send the most settlers. They left home for various reasons. Some, like the Pilgrims, crossed the Atlantic to avoid further religious persecution. Others, such as the Puritans, sought to build a holy community that would shine as a light upon Europe. Still others, including colonists in the Chesapeake Bay area, desired land for growing tobacco. The latter group wanted laborers to help them raise their crops. Unable to enslave the Indians, they ultimately borrowed from the Spanish model and enslaved Africans. In so doing, they forced blacks to enter their settlements in chains and to become a part of a peopling and unpeopling process that helped to shape the contours of life in colonial America.

Chronology of Key Events

30,000–20,000 B.C.	First humans arrive in North America from Asia
A.D. 300–900	Mayan civilization flourishes in present-day Mexico and Guatemala
c. 900	Toltecs rise to power in the Valley of Mexico
c. 1000	Vikings reach Labrador and Newfoundland (*Vinland*)
1095	European Christians launch the Crusades to capture the Holy Lands
c. 1100	Inca civilization emerges in what is now Peru
1271	Marco Polo begins a 20-year journey to China
1420s	Portugal sends mariners to explore Africa's western coast
c. 1450	Johannes Gutenberg develops movable type, the basis of modern printing
1469	Marriage of Ferdinand and Isabella; beginning of Spanish unification
1492	Columbus makes the first of his voyages to the Americas
1494	Treaty of Tordesillas divides known world between Portugal and Spain
1497–1498	John Cabot voyages to Newfoundland and Cape Breton Island
1517	Protestant Reformation begins
1519	Conquest of the Aztec empire by Hernando Cortés and Spanish *conquistadores*
1527–1533	Anglican Reformation; Henry VIII severs ties with Roman Catholic Church
1531–1533	Conquest of the Inca empire by Francisco Pizarro
1534	Jacques Cartier explores the St. Lawrence River and claims the region for France
1585–1587	Sir Walter Raleigh sponsors Roanoke Island settlement
1607	First permanent English settlement at Jamestown established

Suggestions for Further Reading

On the pre-Columbian history of the Americas see Brian M. Fagan, *The Great Journey: The Peopling of Ancient America* (1987); and Alvin M. Josephy, Jr., ed., *America in 1492* (1991).

Useful accounts of Europe during the Age of Exploration are Charles R. Boxer, *The Portuguese Seaborne Empire* (1969); Carl Bridenbaugh, *Vexed and Troubled Englishmen, 1590–1642* (1968); Paul H. Chapman, *The Norse Discovery of America* (1981); Samuel E. Morison, *The European Discovery of America* (1971); and Wallace Notestein, *The English People on the Eve of Colonization,* (1954).

Studies of the clash of cultures in the Americas after 1492 include James Axtell, *After Columbus: Essays in the Ethnohistory of Colonial North America* (1988), *The European and the Indian* (1981), and *The Invasion Within: The Contest of Cultures in Colonial North America* (1985); William Cronon, *Changes in the Land: Indians, Colonists, and the Ecology of New England* (1983); Alfred W. Crosby, *The Columbian Exchange* (1972); Francis Jennings, *The Invasion of America: Indians, Colonialism, and the Cant of Conquest* (1975); Calvin Martin, *Keepers of the Game: Indian–Animal Relationships and the Fur Trade* (1978); and Timothy Silver, *A New Face on the Countryside: Indians, Colonists, and Slaves in the South Atlantic Forests, 1500–1800* (1990).

For information on early European efforts to colonize the Americas consult Daniel J. Boorstin, *The Americans: The Colonial Experience* (1958); Carl Bridenbaugh, *Jamestown, 1544–1699* (1980); Charles Gibson, *The Aztecs under Spanish Rule* (1964), and *Spain in America* (1966); Karen O. Kupperman, *Roanoke: The Abandoned Colony* (1984); David B. Quinn, *Set Fair for Roanoke, 1584–1606* (1985).

Useful biographies include Roland H. Bainton, *Here I Stand: Martin Luther* (1950); William J. Bouwsma, *John Calvin* (1988); Samuel E. Morison, *Christopher Columbus, Mariner* (1955); Alden T. Vaughan, *American Genesis: Captain John Smith and Virginia* (1975).

Chapter 2

Plantations and Cities upon a Hill, 1620–1700

John Punch wanted his freedom. He was a black indentured servant who joined two white servants and tried to flee Virginia in 1640, only to be caught by local residents. Brought before the Governor's council, the colony's highest court, the judges ordered the flogging of each runaway—30 lashes well laid on. Then in a telling ruling, these officials also revealed their thinking about the future status of blacks in England's North American colonies. The two whites had their terms of service extended by four years, but John Punch was sentenced to a life of slavery.

Persons of African heritage were first transported to Virginia in 1619. Since English law did not recognize human slavery, Virginia's first white settlers did not automatically assume that transplanted Africans were permanently unfree. They treated some blacks as indentured servants, a status that conveyed the prospect of personal freedom after four to seven years of laboring for someone else.

Into the 1630s some black Virginians did gain their personal freedom. Others not only owned land but held servants of African origin as well. By the 1640s, however, blacks faced a deteriorating legal status, ultimately leaving them outside the bounds of English liberty. In 1639 the new colony of Maryland guaranteed "all . . . Christians (slaves excepted)" the same "rights, liberties, . . . and free customs" as enjoyed by "any natural born subject of England." In 1643 the same assembly decreed that black women, like all adult males, would henceforth be "tithables"—those counted for local taxes because they worked in the fields. Black female servants planted, tended, and harvested tobacco crops while white female servants mainly performed household work—further evidence of discrimination based on skin color.

Between 1640 and 1670 the distinction between short-term servitude for whites and permanent, inheritable slavery for blacks became firmly fixed. In appearance and by cultural and religious tradition, Africans were not like the English. As with the "wild" Irish and Indian "savages," noticeable differences translated into assumptions of inferiority, and blacks became "beastly heathens," not quite human.

Such thinking helped justify the mixing of words like "black" and "slave," so that by the 1690s slavery in the English colonies had emerged as a caste status for blacks only. Now fully excluded from the tradition of English liberty, local law defined Africans as chattels (movable property), and their masters now had absolute control over their lives.

John Punch was among the first blacks in the Chesapeake Bay area who felt the stinging transition from servitude to slavery. He was also among the thousands of Europeans and Africans who helped settle England's North American colonies between 1620 and 1700. The societies and life-styles of these migrants had many differences, as comparisons between the founding of the northern and southern colonies demonstrate. There was, however, a common point for all migrants, regardless of status or condition; they faced a titanic struggle to survive in an alien land. Although thousands died, some 250,000 settlers inhabited England's mainland colonies by 1700, which resulted in the formation of another powerful European empire in the Americas.

From Settlements to Societies in the South

Smoking or chewing tobacco, wrote King James I, was "loathsome to the eye, hateful to the nose, harmful to the brain, and dangerous to the lungs." Despite the king's admonition, John Rolfe's experiments saved the Virginia Company—at least temporarily—by providing the struggling colony with an economic base. By the mid-1630s Virginians were selling a million pounds a year, and by the mid-1660s annual tobacco crops for export reached 15 million pounds. Virginia's climate and soil were ideal for raising tobacco. Also, new land for cultivation was plentiful, since the "stinking weed" quickly depleted the soil of its minerals. The London investors soon hailed tobacco as the savior of their venture. Other difficulties, however, cost the directors their charter, but not before company activities laid the basis for England's first enduring colony in North America.

Searching for Laborers

Life in early Virginia presented constant hardships. Migrants quickly succumbed to a variety of diseases. Survival, it seemed, depended upon "seasoning," or getting used to an inhospitable climate. Bad relations with Powhatan's Indians also caused mayhem and death, since the English and Native Americans fought in many isolated clashes. All told, the company convinced nearly 14,000 persons to attempt a new life in America, but only about 1,150 were still alive and residing in the James River area in 1624, the year the company lost its charter.

To encourage prospective laborers, company directors developed a system of indentured servitude. In theory, the system held out the opportunity of potential economic independence for England's rapidly growing numbers of landless farm servants and the urban poor. Individuals without money needed only to sign contracts in which they legally exchanged up to seven years of labor in return for passage costs. After completing their terms of service, their masters owed them "freedom dues," including clothing, farm tools, and in some cases land on which to begin anew as free persons.

The system of indentured servitude slowly took shape after 1609. At first, the company offered free passage along with shares of stock to those who signed up for seven years of labor. When terms were up, workers were to gain title to 100 acres of land as well as any stock dividends. The bait was eventual economic freedom, but even with high numbers of unemployed everywhere in England, few persons applied. Getting by marginally or facing a hangman's noose remained more attractive than an early—and often unmerciful—death in America.

Stories of brutal living conditions and high mortality rates undercut company efforts to secure a steady flow of laborers. In an effort to make settlement more attractive, the English government granted Virginia a new charter in 1618, which established a local representative assembly, the House of Burgesses. Its first deliberations took place in July 1619, a small cornerstone gathering pointing toward governments with a popular voice in England's North American colonies.

The charter also offered economic incentives. Heretofore, the company controlled all acreage, but now potential settlers could purchase land without first serving as company laborers. Fifty acres per person would be given to those who migrated or those who paid for the passage of others to Virginia. These "headrights" would permit English families with funds to relocate and get title to enough property to grow tobacco and, perhaps, prosper.

Even with these reforms, Virginia's unhealthful reputation kept families from migrating. Three-fourths of all English settlers entering seventeenth-century Virginia were indentured servants. The vast bulk of these migrants were single males under the age of 25 with no employment prospects in England. As a result, stable family life was not a characteristic of the rough-and-tumble frontier society of early Virginia.

Crushing Powhatan's Confederacy

Bickering, bloodshed, and death denoted relations with Powhatan's Indians as the English located tobacco farms along the James River. John Rolfe's marriage to Powhatan's daughter, Pocahontas, in 1614, which implied a political alliance of sorts, eased tensions, but only briefly. Rolfe soon took Pocahontas to England, where she became an instant celebrity, and both of them encouraged settlement in Virginia. Unfortunately, while preparing to return home in 1616, Pocahontas contracted smallpox or a lung disease and died.

Two years later, Powhatan also died. His more militant half-brother Opechancanough decided that slaughtering the intruders was the only means left to save his people. On Good Friday, March 22, 1622, his warriors struck everywhere. By the time the massacre was over, the Indians had killed 347 settlers, or about one-third of the English colonists, including John Rolfe. Opechancanough, however, had failed to exterminate the enemy, and in many ways the massacre was the beginning of the end for Virginia's coastal natives. White settlers, now more convinced than ever that Indians were savages, took vengeance whenever they could.

Opechancanough waited 22 years before striking again. The attack came in April 1644, and another 300 or more colonists died. The 1644 massacre was a last desperate gasp by Virginia's coastal natives. The numbers of whites were now too overwhelming for total destruction. After Opechancanough was shot to death in 1646, Confederacy chiefs signed a treaty agreeing to submit to English rule. The survivors of Powhatan's once-mighty league eventually accepted life on a reservation, as so many other remnant Indian tribes would be forced to do when Europeans pushed westward across the North American continent.

In 1624, King James I voided the debt-ridden Virginia Company's charter and declared the area a royal colony. He canceled the privilege of a local assembly and sent out his own governor, whom he authorized to rule absolutely. Virginia's planters, however, would not be denied a voice in government. To ease tensions, royal officials shrewdly called upon locally prominent men to serve as advisory councilors, and also held conventions to deal with local problems. Finally in 1639, King Charles relieved some of the pressure by permanently granting Virginians a representative assembly, thereby assuring some local participation in colony-related decision making. Unlike the Spanish and French, English subjects had refused to accept total political control by a far-off parent state. They would share in the decision making that affected their lives as colonists in America.

Proprietary Maryland and the Carolinas

The Stuart kings realized that assuring basic rights would attract more settlers, which in turn meant larger tobacco crops and more tax revenues for the Crown. Founding additional colonies, moreover, would enhance England's stature among the nations of Europe, and these same settlements could be used as dumping grounds for troublesome groups in England, such as the Puritans. Vast stretches of territory could also be granted to court favorites.

Sir George Calvert was one such favored courtier. In 1632 Charles I awarded Calvert, a Roman Catholic, title to ten million acres surrounding the northern end of Chesapeake Bay. Calvert soon died, but his son Cecilius took charge and established the colony, known as Maryland, as a haven for Roman Catholics. Maryland did not prohibit the settlement of Protestants, however, who soon represented a majority of the population. In an effort to protect the minority Catholics, Calvert proposed an Act of

Religious Toleration in 1649, which guaranteed all Christian adult males voting or officeholding rights. Although representing only a form of toleration, this act, which the assembly approved, was a key step toward liberty of conscience; yet the political bickering among Maryland's settlers continued for years to come. Regardless of the faith of early settlers, the colony soon bore a striking similarity to its Chesapeake neighbor Virginia, since Marylanders also devoted themselves to cultivating tobacco.

Meanwhile, religious warfare convulsed England. In the 1640s Puritan "Roundheads" rose up against Charles I, who had refused to let Parliament meet for several years. In 1649 the victorious Puritans beheaded Charles, and Oliver Cromwell, the leader of Puritan military forces, took political control of England as Lord Protector. Soon after Cromwell's death, Parliament invited Charles I's exiled son to reestablish the Stuart monarchy—in exchange for promises to assemble Parliament regularly and to support the Anglican church.

The restoration of Charles II in 1660 left the new king with many political debts, and in 1663 he paid off eight powerful gentlemen by awarding them title to the Carolinas—all lands lying south of Virginia and north of Spanish Florida. The new proprietors quickly set about the task of finding settlers. The Albemarle region of northeastern North Carolina developed as settlers spilled over from Virginia. Most inhabitants subsisted marginally by exporting tobacco and various timber-derived products, including pitch, tar, and potash. Focusing their efforts on settling South Carolina, the proprietors contacted small-scale English farmers on the island of Barbados, who founded Charleston (then known as Charles Town) in 1670. A steady trade in deerskins and horsehides soon developed with interior natives, but rice production eventually became the economic mainstay of the colony. By the end of the seventeenth century, English settlers in the southern colonies had constructed their lives around the exportation of cash crops, particularly tobacco and rice, supported increasingly by black slave labor. Over time the institution of slavery gave white southerners a common identity—with serious long-term consequences.

Religious Dissenters Colonize New England

English men and women migrated to North America for many reasons. Certainly the hope of economic betterment was a prime motivating factor, but in New England the initial emphasis reflected more directly on a communal desire to provide a hospitable environment for Calvinist religious values. Beginning in the 1620s New England emerged as a haven for religious dissenters of two types: separatists, such as the Pilgrims, and nonseparatists, such as the Puritans.

Separatists believed the Church of England to be so corrupt that it could not be salvaged. So as not to compromise their beliefs, their only course was to sever all ties with the Anglican church and establish their own religious communities. The intrepid band known as the Pilgrims were separatists from Scrooby Manor, a village in northeastern England. Facing official harassment, they fled to the Netherlands in 1608 but, finding life difficult there, sought a land grant to settle in America.

In September 1620 the first party of Pilgrims sailed west on the *Mayflower* under a land patent of the Virginia Company. Only one-third of the 102 migrants aboard were Pilgrims. The rest were employees of the London merchant who financed the venture. After surviving nine harrowing, storm-tossed weeks at sea, the *Mayflower* made first landfall on the northern tip of Cape Cod.

Knowing they were well to the north of Virginia territory, the Pilgrims drafted a plan of government, called the Mayflower Compact, before proceeding to the mainland in December 1620. The Compact guaranteed settlers the right to elect governing officials and a representative assembly, but only male Pilgrim "saints"—those who were church members—could vote. The Pilgrims would tolerate "strangers" in their midst and encourage them to seek God's grace—as long as they submitted to the authority of church members. In this sense the Compact was not an advanced statement of popular government; its purpose was to assure the Pilgrims full political control of Plymouth colony.

Plymouth Plantation struggled to survive; and under the effective, persistent leadership of Governor William Bradford, the settlers overcame all obstacles. Besides a deadly first winter, the Pilgrims had to reckon with no clear title to their land. In 1621 they obtained a proper patent, but it took them several years to fulfill their financial obligations to their sponsors. They did so mostly by shipping fish and furs back to England.

Slowly but surely the Pilgrim colony began to prosper. Through all of their adventures and travails, the Pilgrims never lost sight of their original purpose—freedom to worship God according to their own understanding of scriptures. Over time their numbers grew to 7,000 persons before being annexed in 1691 by the much more populous Puritan colony of Massachusetts Bay. They had endured for 70 years as the second oldest English colony in North America.

The Rise of Puritan Dissenters at Home

Far more numerous in Elizabethan England were nonseparatists who wanted to "purify" rather than separate from the Church of England. The Puritans, as these dissenters were known, have often been characterized as prudish, ignorant bigots who hated the thought of having a good time.

Modern historical research, however, has shattered this stereotype. The Puritans were reformers who, as recipients of John Calvin's legacy, took biblical matters seriously. They believed that God's word should order the steps of every person's life. What troubled them most about the Protestant Reformation in England was that it had not gone far enough. They decried the rituals and elaborate hierarchy of the Church of England. As a state-sponsored institution, the Church claimed all citizens as members, regardless of their spiritual nature. Many Anglican clergymen also seemed to lack piety, owing their positions to the influence of well-connected friends and relatives. The Puritans longed for far-reaching institutional change that would rid the Anglican church of its imperfections.

By the early 1600s the Puritans numbered in the hundreds of thousands. Their emphasis upon reading the Bible particularly appealed to literate members of the middle classes and lesser gentry. The Puritans prided themselves on hard work and the pursuit of one's "calling" as a way to glorify the Almighty. They also searched for signs that they had received God's saving grace, which all Puritans sought through a personal conversion experience. They testified in their prayer groups to these experiences—and hoped that others would agree that they had joined God's "visible saints" on earth. To be a visible saint meant that a person was fit for church membership.

King James I developed a decided distaste for religious dissenters. "I will harry them out of the land," he boldly proclaimed after becoming king of England, "or else do worse." But like Queen Elizabeth before him, James quietly endured the Puritans. He never felt secure enough in his own authority to test his will against their rapidly expanding influence. His son, Charles I, confronted the Puritans more boldly. He named William Laud, whom the Puritans considered a Roman Catholic in Anglican garb, as archbishop of the Church of England. In response, the Puritans pushed a bill through Parliament denouncing "popish" practices in church and state. Finally, Charles used his royal prerogatives to disband Parliament and tried to rule by himself between 1629 and 1640.

By the late 1620s a number of Puritans, weary of constant conflict with the Crown, decided upon an "errand into the wilderness." In 1629 they secured a joint-stock charter for the Massachusetts Bay Company. Investors knew that they were underwriting the peopling of a utopian religious experiment in America. As for King Charles, the prospect of ridding the realm of thousands of Puritans was incentive enough to give royal approval to the Bay Company charter.

Godly Mission to New England

The Puritans organized their venture carefully. They placed their settlement effort under John Winthrop, a prominent lawyer and landholder. In

1630 some 700 Puritans crowded onto 11 ships and joined Winthrop in sailing to Massachusetts. They were the vanguard of what became the *Great Migration,* or the movement of an estimated 20,000 persons to New England by 1642. These men and women did not cross the Atlantic as indentured servants but as families leaving behind the religious repression and worsening economic conditions of Charles I's England.

More than any other person, John Winthrop worked tirelessly to promote the Puritan errand. Aboard the flagship *Arbella* before landing in Massachusetts Bay, he delivered a sermon entitled "A Model of Christian Charity," in which he asserted: "We must consider that we shall be as a city upon a hill; the eyes of all people are upon us." The Puritan mission was to order human existence in the Bay Colony according to God's word. Such an example, Winthrop and other company leaders hoped, would inspire England and the rest of Europe, thereby causing the full realization of the Protestant Reformation.

Winthrop and other stockholders, once in Massachusetts, soon faced challenges to their authority. Typical was a protest in 1632 from settlers who refused to pay taxes under the "bondage" of no voice in government.

John Winthrop led the Puritans to New England, where he served several terms as governor of the Massachusetts Bay Colony.

The solution was to grant full citizenship and voting rights to male church members, or "freemen." The government of Massachusetts developed out of this arrangement. Freemen from each town sent delegates to Boston to represent local concerns in an elective assembly, the General Court. The governor, too, was elected on an annual basis, with John Winthrop holding the office almost continuously until his death in 1649. Town ministers were not eligible for political offices, so the government was not technically a theocracy. Clergymen, however, offered written advice to Winthrop and other leaders regarding religious issues, and their observations did affect political decision making.

Puritan town planners emphasized community control over individual lives. A 1635 law—later repealed—stated that inhabitants had to live within a half mile of the town church. Each family received a house lot near the village green, farmland away from the center of town, and access to pasture land and woodlots. Some towns perpetuated the European open-field system. Families gained title to strips of land in several fields and worked in common with other townspeople to bring in yearly crops. In other towns, families had all their farmland concentrated in one area.

These property arrangements reflected on English patterns of land distribution as well as the desire to promote godly behavior, especially since some first-generation settlers were not Puritans. To promote harmonious living conditions, town leaders set off lots for taverns, schools, and meetinghouses. Taverns served as community centers in which people socialized and cheerfully drank alcohol, which they believed was essential to good health. School lots satisfied concerns about education. The Puritans advocated literacy so that everyone could "understand the principles of religion and . . . laws of the country." Beginning in the 1640s, the General Court ordered each town to tax inhabitants to pay for formal schooling in reading and writing for all children. (The desire to have a learned clergy led to the founding of Harvard College in 1636.) The meetinghouse was the gathering place for town meetings and church services. It was the duty of church members to encourage non-Puritans in their midst to study the Bible, pray fervently, and seek God's grace so that they might also enjoy political and religious rights—as well as eternal salvation.

Testing the Limits of Toleration

The first generation of Puritans worked hard and prospered. Farming was the primary means of gaining a livelihood, although some coastal inhabitants took to shipbuilding, fishing, and mercantile activity. Prosperity did not stand in the way of serious internal controversies. These disagreements suggested how the Puritan system functioned on behalf of orthodoxy—and against diverse opinions—to assure adherence to the wilderness mission.

No Puritan was purer than Roger Williams. When this well-educated clergyman arrived in Boston in 1631, John Winthrop graciously welcomed him. Soon Williams received an offer to teach in the Boston church, but he refused because of rules about mandatory worship. To hold services with the unconverted in attendance was to be no purer than the Church of England. It "stinks in God's nostrils," Williams proclaimed.

So off Williams went, first to Salem and then to Plymouth Colony. Only the visible saints attended church services in Plymouth, but the Pilgrims soon dismissed Williams for his view of land ownership. He had become friendly with local Indians and had concluded that any Crown-based land patent was fraudulent—and that Puritans and Pilgrims alike were thieves because they had not purchased their land from the natives. Moving back to Salem, Williams next denounced Bay Colony leaders who meddled in church affairs. So long as churches were subject in any way to political influences, they would be as corrupt as the Church of England.

John Winthrop remained Williams's friend and kept advising him to keep his opinions to himself, but other Puritan leaders had endured enough. Orthodox adherence to the Puritan mission meant that Williams could not be tolerated. The General Court banished him in 1635. Williams fled to the Narragansett Indians from whom he eventually purchased land for a new community—Providence, Rhode Island. Partly because of his influence, the colony of Rhode Island became a center of religious toleration. Settlers there welcomed all faiths, including Judaism, and the government stayed out of matters of personal conscience. As for Williams, in his later years he became so concerned about not attempting to influence the religious beliefs of others that he rarely worshiped with anyone except his beloved wife. Personal conscience was truly sacred, he thought, which made him an advance agent for such concepts as religious freedom and separation of church and state.

Meanwhile others such as Anne Hutchinson tested the limits of orthodoxy. She was a woman of powerful mind and commanding presence who frightened leaders like John Winthrop. Hutchinson, the mother of 13 children, moved with her family to Boston in 1634, where she served as a midwife. She also spoke openly about her religious views. Hutchinson's frame of thought had a strong mystical element. Once humans experienced saving grace, she believed, God would offer direct revelation, meaning that true saints no longer needed the church or the state to help order their daily existence.

Hutchinson's ideas earned the label "Antinomian," which Puritans defined as against the laws of human governance. To Winthrop, who thought that God's revelation ended with scripture, Hutchinson appeared as an advocate of social anarchy. She was threatening to ruin the Puritan mission, since there would be no purpose to human institutions of any kind, except to control the unregenerate. In 1637 Bay Colony clergymen assembled in a synod and denounced Antinomianism as "blasphemous." Ordered to appear before the General Court, Hutchinson masterfully defended herself for two days, only to be declared guilty of sedition for dishonoring Winthrop and the other magistrates. As "a woman not fit for our society," she was banished and migrated to Rhode Island where she helped establish the community of Portsmouth.

"Hivings Out" Provoke Bloody Indian Relations

Also banished by the Bay Colony for his Antinomian views was Hutchinson's brother-in-law, John Wheelwright, who with his following went off to found Exeter, New Hampshire. Other venturesome souls had already established themselves along the coast of Maine. Massachusetts tried to maintain control of both areas, but in 1681 New Hampshire became a separate royal colony. The Bay Colony did sustain its authority over Maine by purchasing the land patents of rival claimants, and this territory remained a thinly settled appendage of Massachusetts until the granting of statehood in 1820.

Connecticut also started to emerge as a Puritan colony during the 1630s. The Reverend Thomas Hooker, who viewed John Winthrop as too dictatorial, led 100 settlers into the Connecticut River valley in May 1636. By year's end, another 700 Puritans had followed Hooker's path. The towns founded by Hooker adopted a plan of government which, while similar to that of the Bay Colony, gave voting rights to all adult male property holders, not just church members. Connecticut Puritans, however, had little interest in encouraging religious diversity; as in Massachusetts, the Congregational church dominated spiritual life.

These "hivings out" from Massachusetts, as Winthrop called them, adversely affected relations with the native populace. When Hooker's followers moved into the Connecticut River valley, they settled on land claimed by the Pequots, who decided to resist and struck at Wethersfield in April 1637, killing several people. A force of Puritans and Narragansett Indians, who hated the Pequots, retaliated a month later by surrounding and setting fire to the main Pequot village on the Mystic River. Some 400 men, women, and children died in the flames.

Warfare erupted again in the summer of 1675, when Metacomet, better known to the Puritans as King Philip, led various Indian tribes on raids along the Massachusetts-Connecticut frontier. By early 1676 all of

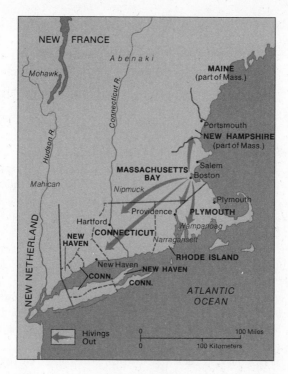

New England Colonies, 1650

New England was in chaos. Metacomet's forces even attacked towns within 20 miles of Boston. When an Indian convert shot and killed Metacomet, King Philip's War rapidly lost its momentum, but not before his warriors had leveled or done substantial damage to several towns. Some 2,000 Puritan settlers died in the war, as did about twice as many Indians, in what proved to be a futile effort to drive away the ever-expansive English. Still, King Philip's War was not the Indians' last gasp. In a few years remnant native groups began getting support from the French in Canada and once again started attacking New England's frontier towns.

Surviving in Early America

During the seventeenth century New England's population grew steadily by natural increase. Most of the 25,000 migrants crossed the ocean before the outbreak of England's civil war in the 1640s, yet by the end of the century some 93,000 colonists inhabited New England. In the Chesapeake, by comparison, as many as 100,000 persons attempted settlement, but only about 85,000 were living in Virginia and Maryland in 1700. If it had not been for the constant influx of new migrants, these two colonies might have ceased to exist.

Life and Death, North and South

The Chesapeake colonists experienced shorter, less fertile lives than their New England counterparts. In 1640, for example, Chesapeake migrants had no more than a 50 percent chance of surviving their first year in America. Hot, steamy summers fostered repeated outbreaks of malaria and typhoid fever, which, along with dysentery and poisoning from brackish drinking water, killed thousands. New England's drinking water was safer, although Puritans generally preferred home-brewed beer, and the harsher winter climate helped to kill off deadly germs. As a result, the Puritans enjoyed longer, healthier lives.

In New England 20 percent of all Puritan males who survived infancy lived into their seventies. Even with the hazards of childbirth, Puritan women lived almost as long. In Virginia and Maryland men who survived into their early twenties had reached middle age; on the average, they would not live beyond their mid-forties. For women in their early twenties, there was little likelihood of surviving beyond their late thirties. Given an average life expectancy of 50 to 55 years back in England, the Chesapeake region deserved its reputation as a human graveyard. In comparison, early New England represented a utopian health environment.

Good health among New Englanders sustained life and meant longer marriages and more children. Longevity resulted in large families, averaging seven to eight children per household. In some locales nine out of ten children survived infant diseases and grew to adulthood knowing not only their parents but their grandparents as well. Families with living grandparents were a unique characteristic of Puritan New England, reflecting life spans more typical of modern America than early modern Europe.

From a demographic perspective, then, New England families were far more stable and secure than those of the Chesapeake. Because Puritans crossed the Atlantic in family units, the ratio of women to men was more evenly balanced than in Virginia or Maryland, where most migrants were not married. Planters seeking laborers for their tobacco fields preferred young males, which skewed the sex ratio against women and retarded the development of family life. Before 1640 only one woman migrated to the Chesapeake for every six men; and as late as 1700, males still outnumbered females by a ratio of more than three to two.

A unique characteristic of Puritan New England was families with living grandparents, as illustrated in this portrait of Abigail Gerrish and her grandmother.

The system of indentured servitude also affected population patterns.
Servants could not marry until they had completed their terms. Typically,
women were in their mid-twenties before they first wed, which in combination with short adult life expectancies curbed the numbers of children
they could bear. Seventeenth-century Chesapeake families averaged only
two to three children, and a quarter of them did not survive their first year
of life. Two-thirds of all surviving children lost one parent by the age of
18, and one-third lost both. Rarely did children know grandparents. For
Chesapeake families, death was as much a daily reality as life, at least until
the early eighteenth century when disease stopped wreaking such havoc.

Roles for Men, Women, and Children

The early Puritans looked at their mission as a family undertaking, and they referred to families as "little commonwealths." Not only were families to "be fruitful and multiply," but they also served as agencies of education and religious instruction as well as centers of vocational training and social welfare. Families cared for the destitute and elderly; they took in orphans; and they housed servants and apprentices—all under one roof and subject to the authority of the father.

The Puritans carried *patriarchal* values across the Atlantic and planted them in America. New England law, reflecting its English base, subscribed to the doctrine of *coverture,* or subordinating the legal identity of women in their husbands, who were the undisputed heads of households. Unless there were prenuptial agreements, all property brought by women to marriages belonged to their mates. Husbands, who by custom and law directed their families in prayer and scripture reading, were responsible for assuring decency and good order in family life. They also represented their families in all community political, economic, and religious activities.

Wives also had major family responsibilities. "For though the husband be the head of the wife," the Reverend Samuel Willard explained, "yet she is the head of the family." It was the particular calling of mothers to nurture their children in godly living, as well as to perform many other tasks—tending gardens, brewing beer, raising chickens, cooking, spinning, and sewing—when not helping in the planting and harvesting of crops.

Most Puritan marriages functioned in at least outward harmony. If serious problems arose, local churches and courts intervened to end the turmoil. Puritan law, again reflecting English precedent, made divorce quite difficult. The process required the petitioning of assemblies for bills of separation, and the only legal grounds were bigamy, desertion, and adultery. On occasion the courts brought unruly husbands under control, as in the case of one Maine husband who brutally clubbed his wife for refusing to feed the family pig.

Family friction arose from other sources as well, some of which stemmed from the absolute control that fathers exercised over property and inheritances. If sons wanted to marry and establish separate households, they had to conform to the will of their fathers, who controlled the land. Family patriarchs normally delayed the passing of property until sons had reached their mid-twenties and selected mates acceptable to parents. Since parents also bestowed dowries on daughters as their contributions to new family units, romantic love had less to do with mate selection than parental desires to unite particular family names and estates. Puritans expected brides and grooms to learn to love one another as they went about their duty of conceiving and raising the next generation of children.

Young adults who openly defied patriarchal authority were rare. Those who did could expect to hear what one angry Bay Colony father told his unwanted son-in-law: "As you married her without my consent, you shall keep her without my help." Also unusual were instances of illegitimate children, despite the lengthy gap between puberty and marriage. As measured by illegitimate births, premarital sex could not have been that common in early New England, not a surprising finding among people living in closely controlled communities and seeking to honor the Almighty by reforming human society.

The experiences of seventeenth-century Chesapeake colonists were very different, due primarily to high death rates in combination with an unbalanced sex ratio. These conditions may have, at least temporarily, enhanced the status of some Chesapeake women, permitting single adults and widows to own and manage property and households for themselves. The fragility of life also resulted in complex family genealogies, with some households containing children from three or four marriages. In some instances local Orphans' Courts had to take charge because all adult relatives had died. Because parents did not live that long, children quite often received their inheritances by their late teens, much earlier than in New England. This advantage only meant that economic independence, like death, came earlier in life.

For indentured servants in the Chesapeake region, life was even more difficult. Planters sought to get as much labor as possible out of servants, since 40 percent died before completing their contracts. Disease was the major killer, but hard-driving planters also contributed to many early deaths. For servants who resisted their masters, local laws specified harsh penalties. Besides floggings and brandings, insubordinate servants faced extensions of service, as one unfortunate man learned after he killed three pigs belonging to his master. The court added six years to his term of service. Since servants could not marry, indentured servitude also inhibited family life, and increased the likelihood of illicit sexual activity. Quite frequently, women became the unwilling sexual partners of lustful masters or male servants. Still, the fate of female and male servants was not always abuse or death. Many survived, gained title to land, and enjoyed, however briefly, personal freedom in America.

Commercial Values and the Rise of Chattel Slavery

By 1650 there were signs that the Puritan mission was in trouble. From the outset many non-Puritan settlers, including merchants in Boston, had shunned the religious values of the Bay Colony's founders. By the 1660s children and grandchildren of the migrating generation displayed less zeal

about earning God's grace; they were becoming more like southern settlers in their eagerness to get ahead economically. By 1700 their search for
worldly prosperity even brought some New Englanders into the international slave trade.

Declension in New England

Declension, or movement away from the ideals of the Bay Colony's founding fathers, resulted in tensions between settlers adhering to the original
mission and those attracted to rising commercial values. In 1662 clergymen proposed a major compromise known as the "Half-Way Covenant."
The covenant recognized that many children were not preparing for salvation, a necessary condition for full church membership, as their parents
had done. The question was how to keep them aspiring toward a spiritual
life. The solution was halfway membership, which permitted the baptism
of the children and grandchildren of professing saints. If still in the
church, ministers and full members could continue to urge them to focus
their lives on seeking God's eternal rewards. Many communities disdained the Half-Way Covenant because of what it suggested about changing values. But with the passage of time most accepted the covenant to
help preserve some semblance of a godly society in New England.

Spreading commercial values took hold for many reasons, including
the natural abundance of the New England environment and an inability
to sustain fervency of purpose among American-born offspring who had
not personally felt the religious repression of early Stuart England. Also,
Puritans back in England, after overthrowing Charles I, generally ignored
the model society in America; this left the impression that the errand had
been futile, that no one back in Europe really cared.

The transition in values occurred gradually. In farming communities,
some families bought and sold common field strips so that all of their
landholdings were in one place, then proceeded to build homes on their
property. This was certainly a more efficient way to practice agriculture, as
well as a statement that making one's living was more important than
daily participation in village life—with its emphasis on laboring together
in God's love. In Boston and other port towns, merchants gained increasing community stature because of their wealth. By the early eighteenth
century, some of them were earning profits by participating in the African
slave trade. Their newfound status was symbolized by retinues of household servants or, more properly, slaves taken from Africa.

Clergymen disapproved of these trends. Their sermons took on the
tone of "jeremiads," modeled on the prophet Jeremiah who kept urging
Israel to return to the path of godliness. In 1679 the ministers met in a

synod and listed several problems, everything from working on the sabbath to swearing in public and sleeping during sermons. Human competitiveness and contention, they sadly concluded, were in ascendance. Worse yet, the populace, in its rush to garner worldly riches, showed little concern that Winthrop's "city upon a hill" was becoming the home of the acquisitive Yankee trader.

Stabilizing Life in the Chesapeake Region

In Maryland and Virginia there were indications by 1675 that life could be something more than brief and unkind. The death rate dropped; more children survived; the gender ratio started to balance out; and life expectancy figures rose. By the early 1700s Chesapeake residents lived well into their fifties. This was comparable to longevity estimates for England but still 10 to 15 years shorter than in New England. These patterns suggested greater family stability, as shown by longer marriages and more children; the average union now produced seven to eight offspring with five to six children surviving into adulthood.

Not only did life become more stable, but an elite group of families, controlling significant property and wealth, had begun to emerge. By 1700 the great tidewater families—the Byrds, Carters, Fitzhughs, Lees, and Randolphs among others—were making their presence felt. These gentleman-planters imitated the life-style of England's rural gentry. They constructed lavish manor houses from which they ruled over their plantation estates, dispensing hospitality and wisdom as the most important local leaders of their tobacco-producing colony.

For every great planter, there were dozens of small farmers who lacked the wealth to obtain land, slaves, and high status in society. Most eked out bare livings, yet they dreamed of the day when they, or their children, might live in the style of the planter elite. Meanwhile, they deferred to their "betters," allowing the local gentry to dominate political and social affairs.

The Beginnings of American Slavery

The system of perpetual servitude that shaped the lives of persons of African heritage like John Punch had an ancient history. Slavery had been dying out in much of Europe by the fifteenth century, but revived when Portuguese mariners made contact with sub-Saharan African peoples, some of whom were willing to barter in human flesh as well as in gold and ivory. The first Portuguese expeditions represented the small beginnings of a trade that forcibly relocated an estimated ten million Africans to the Americas during the next 350 years.

Lavish estates like Westover, built by William Byrd II, illustrate the wealth and dominance of the gentleman-planters in Virginia.

These African kingdoms thrived on elaborate regional trading networks, which the Portuguese and other Europeans, offering guns and various iron products, tapped into easily. The Portuguese found that coastal chiefs were willing to trade slaves captured in tribal wars for European firearms, which they could use when attacking interior kingdoms. A new objective of this tribal warfare became the capturing of peoples who would then be transported back to the coast and sold into slavery in exchange for yet more European goods.

Once this vicious trading cycle began, there did not seem to be any way to stop it. During the sixteenth century the Spanish and Portuguese started pouring Africans into their colonies. Decade after decade, thousands of Africans experienced the agony of being shackled in collars and ankle chains, marched in gangs to the coast, thrown into slave pens, and then packed aboard ships destined for ports of call in the Americas. One slave, Olaudah Equiano, who made the voyage during the eighteenth century, recalled the "loathsomeness of the stench" from overcrowded conditions, which made him "so sick and low" that he neither was "able to eat, nor had . . . the desire to taste anything." About 15 percent of those forced onto slave ships did not survive. For those who did, there was the frightening realization of having lost everything familiar in their lives—and not knowing what might happen next.

Shifting to Slavery in Maryland and Virginia

The English North American colonies existed at the outer edge of the African slave trade until the very end of the seventeenth century. In 1650 the population of Virginia approached 15,000 settlers, including only 500 persons of African descent. By comparison, the English sugar colony of Barbados already held 10,000 slaves, a majority of the population. English Barbadians had started to model their economy on that of other Caribbean sugar islands whereas Virginians, with a steady supply of indentured servants, had not yet made the transition to slave labor.

Factors supporting a shift, however, were present by the 1640s, as evidenced in laws discriminating against Africans and court cases involving blacks like John Punch. During the same decade, a few Chesapeake planters started to invest in Africans. Slaves cost significantly more to purchase than indentured servants, yet those who invested owned their laborers for their lifetimes and did not have to pay "freedom dues." Further, they soon discovered that Africans, having built up immunities to tropical diseases like malaria and typhoid fever, generally lived longer than white servants. Resistance to such diseases made Africans a better long-term investment, at least for well-capitalized planters.

African Slave Trade

The destinations of slaves traded between 1520 and 1810 show the heaviest concentration in Central and South America.

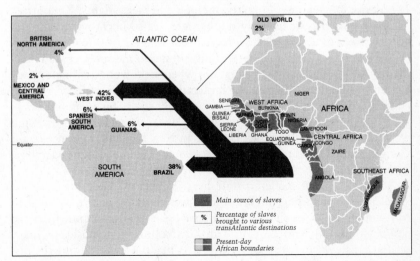

In the 1660s two additional factors encouraged the shift toward slave labor. First, Virginia legislators in 1662 decreed that slavery was an inheritable status. The law made yet unborn generations subject to slavery, a powerful incentive for risking an initial investment in human chattels. Second, the supply of new indentured servants began to shrink as economic conditions improved in England. With expanded opportunities for work, poorer citizens were less willing to risk life and limb for a chance at economic independence in America.

As a result, the slave population figures in the Chesapeake area increased dramatically. In 1750 white Virginians owned 120,000 slaves—about 40 percent of the total population. In Maryland there were 40,000 slaves— some 30 percent of the populace. Indentured servitude had become a moribund institution. White planters, great and small, now measured their wealth and status in terms of plantations and slaves owned and managed.

The World the Slaves Made

Historians once argued that slavery in English North America was harsher than the Spanish-American version. They pointed to the moderating influence of the Roman Catholic church, which mandated legal recognition of slave marriages as a sacramental right, and ancient legal precedents influencing Spanish law, which meant that slaves could earn wages for their labor in off hours and buy their freedom. Although Spanish laws may have been more humane, daily working and living conditions were not. Most slaves destined for Caribbean or South American settlements did not survive long enough to marry or enjoy other legal rights. By contrast, in North America where early deaths were not so pervasive among migrants, slaves more easily reconstructed meaningful lives for themselves.

About 90 percent of those Africans coming to the colonies labored in the South, mostly on small plantations where field work dominated their existence. There was little chance for family life, at least in the early years, because planters purchased an average of three males for every female. In addition, southern law did not recognize slave marriages—in case masters wanted to sell off some of their chattels. In New England, by contrast, the Congregational church insisted that slave marriages be recognized and respected by masters.

Southern slaves made separate lives for themselves, particularly on larger plantations where their numbers were large enough to form their own communities in the slave quarters. Here they maintained African cultural traditions and developed distinctive forms of music. In many places, female slaves managed slave quarter life, thus maintaining the matrilineal nature of African kinship ties.

Whenever possible, slaves selected mates and had large families, even if slave quarter marriages had no standing in law. As a consequence, the ratio of men to women balanced itself out over time, which in turn sped up natural population growth. Large families became a source of slave community pride. Natural increase also undercut the need to continue heavy importations of chattels. As a result, only 5 percent—399,000 persons—of all imported Africans ended up in English North America.

Such comparisons are relative. Nowhere in the Americas did slavery function in an uplifting fashion. Although blacks on large southern plantations carried on traditional cultural practices, they still had to face masters or overseers who might whip them, sell off their children, or maim or kill them if they tried to run away. Always present was the realization that whites considered them to be a subhuman species of property, which left scant room for human dignity in life beyond the slave quarters.

Conclusion

Although most blacks adapted to slavery, some remained defiant. They stole food, broke farm tools, or in a few cases poisoned their masters. In rare instances they resorted to rebellion. In September 1739 twenty slaves in the Stono River area of South Carolina rose up, seized some weapons, killed a few whites, and started marching toward Spanish Florida. Within a few days frightened planters rallied together and crushed the Stono uprising by shooting or hanging the rebels.

The South Carolina legislature soon approved a more repressive slave code, which all but restricted the movement of blacks from their home plantations. No legislator gave thought to the other possibility, which was to abandon the institution of slavery. Even though long in development, slavery now supported southern plantation agriculture and the production of such cash crops as tobacco and rice.

Just as the southern colonies had made a fateful shift from servitude to slavery, New Englanders experienced another kind of transition. Slowly but surely, they had forsaken their utopian, religiously oriented errand into the wilderness; service to mammon had replaced loyalty to God and community. The religious side would remain, but the fervor of a nobler spiritual mission was in rapid decline by 1700. Material gain was now a quality shared in common by white English colonists in America—North and South.

Prosperity, which had come after so much travail and death, promoted a sense of unlimited opportunity in profiting from the abundance of the American environment. Other realities, however, were also in the making. The colonists had learned that Crown officials now expected them to conform to new laws governing the emerging English empire.

Chronology of Key Events

1608	Pilgrims flee to Holland
1617	Virginia begins to export tobacco
1619	The first persons of African descent arrive in Virginia; first representative assembly in English North America meets in Jamestown
1620	Pilgrims cross the Atlantic Ocean on the *Mayflower* and establish a colony at Plymouth
1622	Opechancanough's Indians fail in an attempt to massacre all English settlers in Virginia
1624	New Netherland founded by the Dutch
1630	Puritans establish the Massachusetts Bay Colony
1632	Maryland becomes the first proprietary colony
1635	Roger Williams banished from Massachusetts Bay
1636	Harvard College founded
1637–1638	Anne Hutchinson convicted of heresy and banished from Massachusetts Bay
1644	Second attempted Indian massacre of Virginia settlers fails
1646	Powhatan's Confederacy accepts English rule
1649	Maryland Act of Toleration affirms religious freedom for all Christians in the colony
1660	Charles II restored to the English throne
1664	English conquer New Netherland
1675–1676	King Philip's (Metacomet's) War inflicts heavy casualties on New Englanders
1681–1682	William Penn founds Pennsylvania
1688	Glorious Revolution drives James II from England
1732	Georgia founded as haven for debtors
1739	Stono slave uprising occurs in South Carolina

Because of these imperial rules, much turmoil lay ahead for the people now inhabiting English North America.

Suggestions for Further Reading

For general surveys of family and community life in early America see David Hackett Fischer, *Albion's Seed: Four British Folkways in America* (1989); Philip Greven, *The Protestant Temperament* (1977); Nathan Huggins, *Black Odyssey: The Afro-American Ordeal in Slavery* (1977); Steven Mintz and Susan Kellogg, *Domestic Revolutions: A Social History of American Family Life* (1988); Helena M. Wall, *Fierce Communion: Family and Community in Early America* (1990).

   Useful studies of New England colonial life are Bernard Bailyn, *The New England Merchants in the Seventeenth Century* (1955); John Demos, *A Little Commonwealth: Family Life in Plymouth Colony* (1970); Stephen Foster, *The Long Argument: English Puritanism and New England Culture, 1570–1700* (1991); Philip J. Greven, Jr., *Four Generations: Colonial Andover, Massachusetts* (1970); David D. Hall, *Worlds of Wonder, Days of Judgment: Popular Religious Belief in Early New England* (1989); Perry Miller, *The New England Mind: From Colony to Province* (1953); Robert Middlekauff, *The Mathers: Three Generations of Puritan Intellectuals* (1971); Edmund S. Morgan, *The Puritan Dilemma: The Story of John Winthrop* (1958), and *Visible Saints* (1963).

   For general studies of slavery see David B. Davis, *The Problem of Slavery in Western Culture* (1966); Winthrop D. Jordan, *White Over Black* (1968). For the slave trade see Herbert S. Klein, *The Middle Passage* (1978); James Rawley, *The Transatlantic Slave Trade* (1981).

   For Southern colonial society, consult Timothy H. Breen and Stephen Innes, *"Myne Owne Ground": Race and Freedom on Virginia's Eastern Shore,* (1980); Wesley Frank Craven, *The Southern Colonies in the Seventeenth Century* (1949); Allan Kulikoff, *Tobacco and Slaves* (1986); Gloria L. Main, *Tobacco Colony: Life in Early Maryland* (1982); Edmund S. Morgan, *American Slavery, American Freedom: The Ordeal of Colonial Virginia* (1975); Darrett B. Rutman and Anita H. Rutman, *A Place in Time: Middlesex County, Virginia* (1984); Peter H. Wood, *Black Majority: Negroes in Colonial South Carolina from 1670 Through the Stono Rebellion* (1974).

Chapter *3*

Provincial America in Upheaval, 1660–1760

Hannah Dustan (1657–1736) and Eliza Lucas (1722–1793) never knew one another. Dustan lived in the town of Haverhill on the Massachusetts frontier, and Lucas spent her adult years in the vicinity of Charleston, South Carolina. Even though of different generations, both were inhabitants of England's developing North American empire. Like so many other colonists, perpetual imperial warfare affected their lives as England, France, and Spain repeatedly battled for supremacy in Europe and America between 1689 and 1763.

During the 1690s, as part of a war involving England and France, frontier New Englanders experienced devastating raids by French and Indian parties from Canada. On the morning of March 15, 1697, a band of Abenakis struck Haverhill. Hannah Dustan's husband and seven of her children saved themselves by racing for the community's blockhouse. Hannah, who had just given birth a few days before, was not so fortunate. The Abenakis captured her, as well as her baby and midwife Mary Neff.

After some discussion, the Indians killed the infant, but decided to spare Hannah and Mary along with a few other captives. The plan was to march them to the principal Abenaki village in Canada. A party of two male warriors, three women, and seven children escorted Hannah, Mary, and a young boy named Samuel Lenorson. Hannah struggled to maintain her composure as the party walked northward day after day, praying fervently for some means of escape. Just before dawn one morning, she awoke to find all her captors sound asleep. Seizing the moment, she roused Mary and Samuel, handed them hatchets, and told them to crush as many skulls as possible. Suddenly the Indians were dying, and only two, a badly wounded woman and a child, escaped.

Hannah then took a scalping knife and finished the bloody work. When she and the other captives got back to Haverhill, they had ten scalps, for which the Massachusetts General Court awarded them a bounty of £50. New Englanders hailed Hannah Dustan as a true heroine—a woman whose courage overcame the French and Indian enemies of England's empire in America. After a long and full life, Hannah Dustan died in 1736.

Two years later, George Lucas, a prosperous Antigua planter and an officer in the British army, moved to South Carolina, where he owned three rice plantations. He wanted to get his family away from the Caribbean region, since hostilities were brewing with Spain. When war required Lucas to return to military service in Antigua, he placed his 17-year-old daughter Eliza in charge of his Carolina properties. The responsibility did not faze her; she wrote regularly to her "Dear Papa" for advice, and the plantations prospered. The war, however, disrupted rice trading routes to the West Indies, and planters needed other cash crops to be sold elsewhere.

George Lucas was aware of the problem and sent Eliza seeds for indigo plants, the source of a valued deep-blue dye, to see whether indigo could be grown profitably in South Carolina. With the help of knowledgeable slaves, Eliza conducted successful experiments. In 1744 a major dye broker in England rated her product as good as the best French indigo. Just 22 years old, Eliza had pioneered a cash crop that brought additional wealth to Carolina's planters and became a major trading staple of the British empire.

Eliza ultimately married Charles Pinckney, a widower of great wealth and high social standing. In later life she took pride in the success of her children, one of whom served in the Constitutional Convention of 1787, and another represented President Washington during 1795 in negotiating an agreement that resolved western boundary questions with Spain. A heralded woman of her generation, Eliza Lucas Pinckney died at the end of the revolutionary era, nearly 140 years after the birth of Hannah Dustan.

Dustan and Pickney both lived during years of turbulence and upheaval, as England built a mighty empire in North America. Despite new imperial laws governing the lives of Americans and a series of wars with France and Spain, the colonies grew and prospered. After 1760 the colonists were in a position to question their subordinate relationship with Britain. The coming of the American Revolution cannot be appreciated without looking at the development of the British empire in America—and how that experience related to the lives of passing generations of colonists like Hannah Dustan and Eliza Lucas Pinckney.

Designing England's North American Empire

During the 1760s Benjamin Franklin tried to explain why relations between England and the colonies had turned sour. He blamed British trade policies designed to control American commerce, which had been implemented "for private advantage, under pretense of public good." The trade system, he believed, had become both oppressive and corrupt. Little more than a hundred years before, the colonists had traded as they pleased. After 1650, however, Parliament designed trade policies that exerted greater control over the activities of the American colonists.

To Benefit the Parent State

Certain key ideas underlay the new, more restrictive policies. Most important was the concept of *mercantilism* (although the term was not invented until the late eighteenth century). Mercantilist thinkers believed the world's supply of wealth was not infinite but fixed in quantity. Any nation that gained wealth automatically did so at the expense of another. In economic dealings, then, the most powerful nations always maintained a favorable balance of trade by exporting a greater value of goods than they imported. Governments controlling the most gold and silver would be the most self-sufficient and could use such wealth to stimulate internal economic development as well as strengthen military forces. This ensured not only national survival but ascendancy over other countries.

Mercantilist theory also demonstrated how colonies could best serve their parent nations. For England, the colonies could contribute to a favorable trade balance by producing such staple crops as tobacco, rice, and sugar, thus ending any need to import these goods from other countries. The American provinces, in addition, could supply valuable raw materials—for example, timber products for construction of a naval fleet. Great stands of American timber could also be fashioned into fine furniture and sold back to the colonists. Ideally, England's overseas colonies would serve as a source of raw materials and staple crops as well as a marketplace for manufactured goods.

Mercantilist reasoning affirmed the principle that the colonies existed to benefit and strengthen the parent nation. As such, provincial economic and political activities had to be closely managed. To effect these goals, Parliament passed a series of Navigation Acts (1651, 1660, 1663, and 1673), which formed the cornerstone of England's commercial relations with the colonies and the rest of the world. The acts banned foreign merchants and vessels from participating in the colonial trade; proclaimed that certain "enumerated" goods could only be shipped to England or other colonies (the first list included dyewoods, indigo, sugar, and tobacco, with furs, molasses, rice, and wood products added later); and specified that European goods destined for America had to pass through England.

Through the Navigation System, England became the central trading hub of the empire, which resulted in a great economic boom at home. After 1660 key industries like shipbuilding began to prosper as never before. By the late 1690s the English merchant fleet had outdistanced all competitors, including the Dutch.

In the colonies the Navigation Acts had mixed effects. New Englanders, taking advantage of nearby timber supplies, strengthened their economy by heavy involvement in shipbuilding. By the early 1700s Americans were constructing one-fourth or more of all English merchant vessels. In the Chesapeake Bay region, however, the enumeration of tobacco resulted in economic difficulties. By the 1660s planters were producing too much tobacco for consumption in the British Isles alone. Because of the costs of merchandising the crop through England, the price became too high to support large sales in Europe. Consequently, the glut of tobacco in England caused prices to decline, resulting in hard times and much furor among Chesapeake planters.

Seizing Dutch New Netherland

The Navigation Acts were only part of England's efforts to establish itself as an imperial power. Under Charles II, England also sought to challenge its European rivals in the Americas. A principal target was the Dutch colony of New Netherland, which served as a base for Holland's illegal trade with English settlers.

New Netherland was the handiwork of the Dutch West India Company, a joint-stock venture chartered in 1621. The company soon sent out a governor and employees to the Hudson River area to develop the fur trade with local Indians, particularly the Five Nations of Iroquois inhabiting upper New York. By 1660, New Netherland's population pushed toward 8,000, but the colony was internally weak and unstable. A series of unpopular and incompetent governors had stirred feelings of resentment among its many non-Dutch inhabitants. Denied a voice in government and freedom of worship, many settlers felt no great loyalty to Holland and its colonial administrators.

In 1664 King Charles gave his brother, James, the Duke of York, title to all Dutch lands in North America, on the obvious condition that they be conquered. James quickly organized a small invasion fleet. When the flotilla appeared before New Amsterdam in August 1664, Governor Peter Stuyvesant failed to rally the populace. With hardly an exchange of shots, New Netherland became the Duke of York's English province of New York.

James's proprietary charter had no clause mandating an assembly for his colony, but Puritans living on Long Island demanded some form of representative government. They refused to pay local taxes, arguing that they were "enslaved under an arbitrary power." The absence of a popularly based assembly for New York's colonists continued to be a source of friction. Finally, in the early 1680s James conceded the point, and an assembly met for the first time in 1683. Once he became king in 1685, however, James disallowed further assembly meetings, which was one reason for a local rebellion in 1689.

To make matters more confusing, James in 1664 turned over all his proprietary lands between the Hudson and Delaware rivers to two court favorites. Unfortunately, land patents in the eastern portion of what became the colony of New Jersey had already been offered to Puritan settlers, and questions regarding proprietary ownership plagued the colony's development for many years. Settlement proceeded slowly, with the population approaching 15,000 by 1700. Most colonists engaged in commercial farming and raised a variety of grain crops, which they marketed through New York City and Philadelphia. Because of ongoing confusion over land titles, as well as proprietary political authority, the Crown decided in 1702 that New Jersey would henceforth be a royal province.

Middle Colonies, 1685

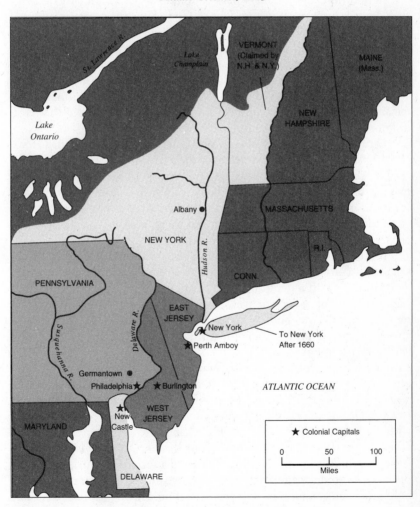

Planting William Penn's "Holy Experiment"

During the English Civil War of the 1640s a number of radical religious sects, among them the Quakers, began to appear in England. Adhering to many controversial ideas, the Quakers believed that all persons had a divine spark, or "inner light," which, when fully nurtured, allowed them to commune directly with God. Like Anne Hutchinson before them, they saw little need for human institutions. They had no ministers and downplayed the importance of the Bible, since they could order their lives according to revelation received directly from God.

In addition, the Quakers held a unique social vision. All humans, they argued, were equal in the sight of God. Thus they wore unadorned black clothing and refused to remove their broad-brimmed hats when social superiors passed by them. Women had full access to leadership positions and could serve as preachers and missionaries. Members of the sect also refused to take legal oaths, which they considered a form of swearing, and as pacifists they believed that warfare would never solve human problems. In time, Quakers became antislavery advocates, arguing that God did not hold some persons inferior because of skin color.

Early English Quakers were intensely fervent, and during the 1650s and 1660s they sent many witnesses of their faith to America. These individuals, about half of them women, fared poorly in the colonies. Puritan magistrates in Massachusetts told them of their "free liberty to keep away from us" and threw them out. Three Quakers were so persistent in coming back to Boston that officials hanged them, making them martyrs to their vision of a more harmonious world.

In 1681 Charles II gave William Penn, who had converted to the Quaker faith in the early 1660s while a student at Oxford, a land grant in America to pay off a debt owed to the estate of Penn's father. Pennsylvania, meaning Penn's woods, was a bountiful tract, and Penn wanted to make the most of it, both as a sanctuary for oppressed religious groups and as a source of personal income from quitrents (land taxes). Penn sent agents to Europe in search of settlers, offering generous land packages with low annual quitrents. He also wrote the colony's First Frame of Government, which guaranteed a legislative assembly and full freedom of religion. Determined to succeed, Penn sailed to America in 1682 to spend two years in the colony, during which time he established cordial relations with the Indians and mapped out Philadelphia.

Like the Puritans before him, Penn had a utopian vision. Unlike them, his "holy experiment" sought to mold a society in which peoples of diverse backgrounds and religious beliefs lived together harmoniously—a bold idea in an era not known for its toleration. During the next few years settlers not only from England but also from Wales, Scotland, Ireland, Holland, Germany, and Switzerland poured through the booming port of Philadelphia and then fanned out into the fertile countryside. There they established family farms, raising livestock and growing abundant grain crops, which they marketed to the West Indies and Europe. The settlers prospered, and Pennsylvania gained a reputation as "one of the best poor man's countries in the world." By the early 1700s the population exceeded 20,000.

Still, not all was perfect in the peaceable kingdom. Religious sects segregated themselves, wanting little to do with one another. Quakers dominated the government but fought endlessly over the prerogatives of power. Penn's pleas for harmony went unheeded. Equally disturbing from his point of view, settlers refused to pay quitrents, yet he kept funding the colony's development.

In his old age Penn considered the "holy experiment" a failure, concluding that peaceable kingdoms on earth lay beyond human reach. Having even endured prison for debts contracted on behalf of his colony, Penn died an embittered man in 1718. Nonetheless, peace, prosperity,

In his treaty with the Indians, William Penn sought to treat Native Americans fairly in negotiating land rights. However, Pennsylvania colonists and Penn's own officials wanted to push the native populace westward as rapidly as possible.

pluralism, and religious toleration were the hallmarks of his utopian vision. By seeking a better life for all peoples, he had infused a sense of high social purpose into the American experience.

Defying the Imperial Will: Provincial Convulsions and Rebellions

Besides standing up to the Dutch, Charles II and his advisers worked to build the emerging empire in other ways. Crown officials crossed the Atlantic to determine whether the colonists were cooperating with the Navigation System. They also sent the first customs officers to America to collect duties on enumerated goods being traded between colonies—and then to foreign ports. Increasingly, the Americans felt England's constraining hand, which in some locales helped to bring on violence.

Bacon's Bloody Rebellion in Virginia

With tobacco glutting the market in England, Virginia's economy went into a tailspin during the 1660s. The planters blamed the Navigation Acts, which stopped them from dealing directly with such foreign merchants as the Dutch; and it did not improve the planters' mood when, in 1667, Dutch war vessels captured virtually the whole English merchant fleet hauling the annual tobacco crop out of Chesapeake Bay, resulting in nearly the total loss of a year's worth of work.

The colony's economic woes were not the only problem. Some Virginians thought that their longtime royal governor, Sir William Berkeley, had become a tyrant. Berkeley handed out patronage jobs to a few preferred planters. Such favors allowed the governor to dominate the assembly and lay heavy taxes at a time when settlers were suffering economically. As a consequence, some planters lost their property, and young males just completing terms of indentured service saw few prospects for ever gaining title to land and achieving economic independence.

In 1674 Nathaniel Bacon, an ambitious and socially prominent young Englishman, arrived in Virginia. He promptly sought acceptance among Berkeley's favored friends, who controlled the lucrative Indian trade. He asked the governor for a trading license, but Berkeley denied the request, feeling that the young man had not yet proven his worth. Incensed by his rejection, Bacon started opposing Berkeley at every turn. He organized other substantial planters not favored by Berkeley, and he also appealed to Virginia's growing numbers of propertyless poor for support.

Stirrings among Indian tribes made matters worse. Far to the north in New York, the Five Nations of Iroquois had become more aggressive in their quest for furs. They started pushing other tribes southward toward Virginia, and some spilled onto frontier plantations, resulting in a few killings.

Bacon demanded reprisals, but Berkeley urged caution, noting that a war would only add to Virginia's tax burdens. Bacon asked for a military commission, stating that he would organize an army of volunteers. The governor refused, at which point Bacon charged his adversary with being more interested in protecting profits from his Indian trading monopoly than in saving settlers' lives. Bacon pulled together a force of over 1,000 men, described as "the scum of the country" by Berkeley's supporters, and indiscriminately started killing local Indians.

In response, Berkeley sent out militiamen to corral the volunteers, but Bacon's force eluded them. The governor also called a new assembly to pass reforms designed to pacify the "mutineers," but events had gone too far, and a shooting war broke out. Before the fighting ceased, Bacon's force burned Jamestown to the ground, and Berkeley fled across Chesapeake Bay.

Charles II promptly dispatched 1,000 troops from England to restore order, but by the time they arrived, Berkeley was back in control. Bacon's death from dysentery in October 1676 had already brought an end to the struggle. Royal advisers with the king's army, however, removed the aging governor from office on the grounds that his policies had helped to stir up trouble.

After 1676 the Crown started sending royal governors to Virginia with detailed instructions on managing the colony as an imperial enterprise—at times at the expense of local interests. In response, Virginia's leading gentleman-planters, previously divided into pro- and anti-Berkeley factions, settled their differences in the face of what they saw as threats to local autonomy. They rallied the people to their side, got themselves elected regularly to the House of Burgesses, and worked together to protect the colony's interests.

This fundamental recasting of political lines was an important development. No longer would rising planter elite leaders fight among themselves. They would stand united in defense of local rights and privileges, making it clear that the Crown, if it wanted harmony and stability, had to show at least some respect for the welfare of its colonists.

The Glorious Revolution Spills into America

The Crown's reactions to Bacon's Rebellion fit a larger pattern of asserting more authority over America. New England, with its independent ways, was an obvious target. The Crown revoked the Bay Colony's charter in 1684, and with the accession of James II to the throne the following year, set up an entirely new form of administration for the colonies, known as the Dominion of New England. Stretching from Nova Scotia to the Delaware River, the Dominion centralized political power in the hands of a governor and a large advisory council made up of Crown appointees. As a result, local representative assemblies would cease to exist.

From the outset the Dominion was a bad idea, perhaps made worse by naming as governor Sir Edmund Andros, a man of aristocratic bearing with impressive military credentials. Arriving in late 1686, Andros expected the Puritans to conform to the imperial will—and his autocratic rule. He announced plans to rewrite all land deeds and, then, to impose quitrents, which New Englanders had never paid. He announced import taxes to underwrite the expenses of his government, and he started prosecuting violators of the Navigation Acts.

Meanwhile, in England, James II had created an uproar by pushing royal authority too far. In defiance of England's Protestant tradition, he flaunted his Roman Catholic beliefs in public and declared that his newborn son, now next in line for the throne, would be raised a Roman Catholic. The thought of yet more religious turmoil was too much for influential English leaders to bear. In December 1688 they drove James from the realm and offered the throne to his Protestant daughter, Mary, and her Dutch husband, William of Orange. Ruling as joint monarchs, William and Mary agreed to give Parliament an equal, if not dominant, voice in Britain's political affairs.

When news of the Glorious Revolution reached Boston, local Puritan leaders went into action. Denouncing Andros and his followers as "bloody devotees of Rome,'" they seized the governor on April 18, 1689, threw him in jail, and then shipped him back to England. They did so, they insisted, to end Andros's arbitrary rule, and they asked William and Mary to restore their original corporate charter.

The coup in Massachusetts helped spark a rebellion in New York, where a volatile mix of ethnic and class tensions resulted in a violent upheaval. Jacob Leisler, a combative local merchant of German origin, took advantage of lower-class resentment toward Francis Nicholson, the Dominion's lieutenant governor, and the wealthy Dutch and English families who cooperated with his rule. When reports of the Massachusetts coup reached New York, Leisler organized a military force of 500 men and on May 31 captured Fort James that guarded New York harbor. Within a few days, Nicholson fled to England amid cries that all Dominion "popish dogs and devils" must be jailed. Leisler then set up an interim government and waited for advice from England, hoping that the new monarchs would make a permanent grant of a popularly based assembly. In addition, Leisler allowed mobs to harass and rob wealthy families.

The third colony jolted by a revolt in 1689 was Maryland, where quarrels between Roman Catholics and Protestants remained a perpetual source of tension. The proprietary governor, William Joseph, tried to contain the popish conspiracy rumors, but John Coode, a nervous local planter, organized the Protestant Association to defend Marylanders from the impending slaughter. Coode led 250 followers to St. Mary's, then Maryland's capital, where in July 1689 they removed Joseph from office, called their own assembly, and then sent representatives to England to plead for royal government.

In a chain reaction, three uprisings had occurred in the American colonies during a span of four months. Although each had its own local character, the common issue, besides the rumored Catholic conspiracy, was the question of how extensive colonial rights would be in the face of tightening imperial administration. All the colonists could do now was wait to hear from the new monarchs—and hope for the best.

New England's Witchcraft Hysteria

By the early 1690s New Englanders had lost their charter, lived under the Dominion, rebelled against Edmund Andros, and engaged in war with the hated French. These unsettled conditions may have made the populace overly suspicious and anxious about evil influences in their midst. Moreover, as New England's Puritan communities moved away from their original religious mission toward a commercial, profit-oriented society, tensions emerged which, according to some historians, manifested themselves in 1692 in an unusual form: the Salem witch trials.

Puritans, like most Europeans and colonists elsewhere, believed in witchcraft. They thought that the devil could materialize in various shapes and forms, damaging lives at will. Satan's agents included witches and wizards, women and men possessed by his evil spirits. Eighty-one New Englanders had faced accusations of practicing witchcraft before 1692, 16 of whom were put to death. These numbers were insignificant in comparison to accused witches hunted down and executed in Europe.

In 1692 the Salem area was a divided community. Salem Town, the port, was caught up in New England's commercial life, while outlying settlers around Salem Village remained quite traditional in seeking God's grace before material wealth. Resentment by the villagers was growing when, in early 1692, a few adolescent girls started having "fits." Anxious about their own lives, the girls had asked Tituba, a local slave woman from the West Indies, to tell them their fortunes. Soon thereafter the girls started acting hysterically, observers claimed, as if possessed by Satan's demons.

When asked to name possible witches, the girls did not stop with Tituba. They eventually made hundreds of accusations before a special court appointed to root the devil out of Massachusetts. With increasing frequency they pointed to prosperous citizens like those of Salem Town.

Some 50 defendants, among them Tituba, saved themselves by admitting their guilt; but 20 men and women were executed (19 by hanging and 1 by the crushing weight of stones) after steadfastly refusing to admit that they had practiced witchcraft.

By the end of the year the craze was over, probably because too many citizens of rank and influence, including the wife of the new royal governor, Sir William Phips, had been accused of doing the devil's work. In time, most participants in the Salem witchcraft trials admitted to being deluded. Although their victims could not be brought back to life, the episode stood as a cautionary reminder in the colonies about the dangers of mass hysteria. The incident also helped sustain New England's transition to a commercial society by making traditional folk beliefs—and those who espoused them—appear foolish.

Settling Anglo-American Differences

In 1691 William and Mary began to address colonial issues. As constitutional monarchs, they were not afraid of popularly based assemblies. In the case of Massachusetts they approved a royal charter that gave the Crown the authority to name royal governors and stated that all male property holders, not just church members, had the right to vote. The monarchs did not tamper with the established Congregational church, thereby reassuring old-line Puritans that conforming to the Church of England was not necessary so long as Bay Colony residents supported England's imperial aspirations. New York also gained permanent status as a royal colony in 1691, complete with a local representative assembly. Still in power, Jacob Leisler refused to step aside, which led to his arrest, trial, and execution for treason. In Maryland's case, the colony's proprietors, the Calvert family, temporarily lost political control in 1692 in favor of royal government, and shortly thereafter a Protestant assembly banned Roman Catholics from political office.

The transformation revealed a movement toward the royal model of government in which the colonies established legislative assemblies to express and defend their local concerns. Crown-appointed governors, in turn, pledged themselves to enforce the Navigation Acts and other imperial laws. So long as the colonists cooperated, they would not face autocratic forms of government. Nor would the Crown permit the kind of loose freedom of early colonial days because, in gaining basic rights the Americans also accepted responsibility for conducting their daily affairs within the imperial framework. The Glorious Revolution and its reverberations in America had made this compromise possible.

Maintaining the delicate balance between imperial intrusiveness and local autonomy was the major challenge of the eighteenth century. Until the 1760s both sides tried to make the compromise work. The Crown demonstrated its resolve by establishing the Board of Trade and Plantations in 1696 as a permanent administrative agency to advise England's leaders on colonial issues. It also mandated vice-admiralty courts in America to punish smugglers and others who violated the rules of trade.

The Board of Trade generally acted with discretion, even in recommending a few acts to restrain colonial manufacturers competing with home industries. Parliament in 1699 adopted the Woolen Act that outlawed any exportation of woolen products from America or from one colony to another. The intent was to get the colonists to buy finished woolens from manufacturers in England rather than to develop their own industry. In 1732 there was similar restrictive legislation (the Hat Act) concerning the production of beaver and felt hats. In 1750 Parliament passed the Iron Act that forbade the colonists from building new facilities or expanding old ones for the manufacture of finished iron or steel products. As a whole, this legislation had few adverse effects on the provincial economy. It simply reinforced fundamental mercantile notions regarding colonies as sources of raw materials and as markets for finished goods.

Occasionally, imperial administrators went too far, such as with the Molasses Act of 1733. In support of a thriving rum industry based mostly in New England, colonial merchants roamed the Caribbean for molasses, which cost less on French and Dutch West Indian islands. To placate British West Indian planters, Parliament tried to redirect the trade with a heavy duty (6 pence per gallon) on foreign molasses brought into the colonies. Enforcing the trade duty could have ruined the North American rum industry, but customs officers wisely ignored collecting the duty, a sensible solution to a potentially inflammatory issue.

As the eighteenth century progressed, imperial officials tried not to be overbearing. In certain instances they actually stimulated provincial economic activity by offering large cash bounties for growing such valued export commodities as the indigo originally produced by Eliza Lucas. Caught up as the empire was in warfare with France and Spain, home leaders did not want to tamper with a system that, by and large, worked. The colonists, for their part, gladly accepted what many have referred to as the "era of salutary neglect."

Maturing Colonial Societies in Unsettled Times

Besides the maintenance of stable relations with the parent state, other factors stimulated the maturing of the American provinces after 1700. Certainly the expanding population base, which saw a near doubling of numbers nearly every 20 years, strengthened the colonies, as did the pattern of widespread economic prosperity, even if not shared evenly among the populace. The important role American colonists played during a series of imperial wars also instilled a vital sense of self-confidence. By the 1760s provincial Americans took pride in what they had accomplished as subjects of the British empire in North America.

An Exploding Population Base

Between 1700 and 1760 the colonial population mushroomed from 250,000 to 1.6 million persons—and to 2.5 million by 1775. Longer lives were partly responsible for this growth, due to better health and agricultural abundance. Colonists had plentiful supplies of food. Nutritious diets led to improved overall health, making it easier for Americans to ward off virulent diseases.

Natural population increase was only one source of the population explosion. Equally significant was the introduction of non-English peoples. Between 1700 and 1775, for example, the British North American slave trade reached its peak, resulting in the involuntary entry of an estimated 250,000 Africans into the colonies. The black population grew from 28,000 in 1700 to over 500,000 in 1775, with most living as chattel slaves in the South. At least 40 to 50 percent of the African-American population increase was attributable to the booming slave trade.

Among European groups, the Scots-Irish and Germans were predominant, although a smattering of French Huguenot, Swiss, Scottish, Irish, and Jewish migrants joined the westward stream. The Scots-Irish had endured many privations. Originally Presbyterian lowlanders from Scotland, they had migrated to Ulster (Northern Ireland) in the seventeenth century at the invitation of the Crown. During the next several years they endured crop failures and huge rent increases from their English landlords. In a series of waves between 1725 and 1775 over 100,000 Scots-Irish descended upon North America. Many moved out into the southern backcountry where they squatted on open land and earned reputations as bloodthirsty Indian fighters.

Even before the first Scots-Irish wave, Germans from the area of the upper Rhine River began streaming into the Middle Colonies. Some, like Amish, Moravian, and Mennonite sectarians, were fleeing religious persecution; others were escaping crushing economic circumstances caused by overpopulation, crop failures, and heavy local taxes. By the eve of the American Revolution, some 100,000 German migrants had arrived in the colonies.

The "Europeanizing" of America

Compared to Europe, America was a land of boundless prosperity. To be sure, however, there were wide disparities in wealth, rank, and privilege that the colonists accepted as part of the natural order of life. They did so because of the pervasive influence of European values, such as the need for hierarchy and deference in social and political relations. The eighteenth century was still an era in which individuals believed in three distinct social orders—the monarchy, the aristocracy, and the "democracy" of common citizens. All persons had an identifiable place in society, fixed at birth; and to try to improve one's lot was to risk instability in the established rhythms of the universe.

Elite families set themselves apart from the rest of colonial society by imitating English aristocratic life-styles. Wealthy southern gentlemen utilized gangs of slaves to produce the staple crops that generated the income to construct lavish manor houses with elaborate formal gardens. Northern merchants built residences of Georgian design and filled them with fashionable furniture. Together, they thought of themselves as the "better sort," and they expected the "lower sort" to defer to their judgment in social and political decision making.

One characteristic, then, of the "Europeanizing" of colonial society was growing economic stratification, with extremes of wealth and poverty becoming more visible. Nevertheless, there was a large middle class, and it was still possible to get ahead in provincial America. Over 90 percent of the colonists lived in the countryside and made their livings from some form of agricultural production. By European standards, the ownership of property was widespread, yet there were also many instances of extreme poverty. Some of the worst cases were among urban dwellers, many of whom eked out the barest of livelihoods as unskilled day laborers or merchant seamen. These individuals at least enjoyed some personal freedom, which placed them above black slaves, who formed 20 percent of the population but enjoyed none of its prosperity or political rights.

With colonial wealth concentrated in fewer and fewer hands, another "Europeanizing" trend was toward the hardening of class lines. Elite families increasingly intermarried among themselves, and they spoke openly of an assumed right to serve as political stewards for the people. Although widespread property holding allowed great numbers of free white males to vote, they most often chose members of the elite to represent them in elective offices, particularly in colonial assemblies. Once elected, these stewards did constant battle with Crown-appointed governors and councilors in upper houses over the prerogatives of local decision making. In colony after colony during the eighteenth century, elite leaders insisted on the same legislative rights in their respective territorial spheres as Parliament had over all British subjects.

More often than not, royal governors had only feeble backing from the home government and lost these disputes. As a result, the provincial assemblies gained many prerogatives, including the right to initiate all money and taxation bills. Because governors depended on the assemblies for their salaries, they often approved local legislation not in the best interests of the Crown in exchange for bills appropriating their annual salaries. By the 1760s the colonial assemblies had thus emerged as powerful agencies of government.

Intellectual and Religious Awakening

Besides politics, colonial leaders were fascinated by Europe's dawning Age of Reason, also called the Enlightenment. The approach to learning was secular, based on scientific inquiry and the systematic collection of information. Leading intellectuals sought to unlock the physical laws of nature and identify laws governing human behavior. In his *Essay Concerning Human Understanding* (1690), English political thinker John Locke described the human mind as a blank sheet (*tabula rasa*) at birth waiting to be influenced by the experiences of life. If people followed the insights of reason, social and political ills could somehow be reduced or eliminated from society, and each person, as well as humankind as a whole, could advance toward greater harmony and perfection.

The key watchword of the Enlightenment was *rationalism,* meaning a firm trust in the ability of the human mind to solve earthly problems—and much less faith in the centrality of God as an active, judgmental force in the universe. Whereas John Winthrop believed that earthquakes were signs of God's wrath, his great-great-grandson, John Winthrop IV, a professor of mathematics at Harvard College in the mid-1730s, argued that movements in the earth's surface had natural causes, which he explained in scientific terms.

Benjamin Franklin became the best-known provincial student of science. In 1743 he helped found the American Philosophical Society. With the aid of a kite, Franklin performed experiments with lightning, seeking to reveal the mysteries of electrical energy. After publishing his *Experiments and Observations on Electricity* (1751), Franklin's fame spread throughout the western world.

Many religious leaders viewed Enlightenment rationalism with great suspicion. It seemed to undermine orthodox religious values by reducing God to a prime mover who had set the universe in motion only to leave humans to chart their own destiny. (This system of thought was known as Deism.) Others worried about the loss of religious faith emphasizing the need for repentance, conversion, and God's saving grace. They felt that the populace, rushing to achieve material prosperity, had become too complacent, as if affluence and good works would guarantee eternal salvation. For some clergymen, then, the time was at hand for placing a renewed emphasis on vital religious faith.

During the 1720s and 1730s in Europe and America, some ministers started holding revivals. They did so in the face of declining popular interest in formal religion, as expressed by dwindling church attendance in many locales. Through impassioned sermons delivered from their hearts, they exhorted great numbers of people to seek God's saving grace. This was the first in a succession of revivals known collectively as the Great Awakening.

In 1734 Jonathan Edwards, a Congregational minister residing in Northampton, Massachusetts, initiated a series of revival meetings aimed at the youth of this community. Edwards was a learned student of the Enlightenment who argued that experiencing God's grace was essential to the comprehension of the universe and its laws. In one sermon Edwards reminded his congregation of the "abominations of your life," vividly picturing how each member was "wallowing in sensual filthiness, as swine in mire." Appealing to the senses more than to rational inquiry, Edwards felt, was the surest way to uplift individual lives, win souls for God, and improve society as a whole.

Such local revivals did not become broad and general until after the dynamic English preacher, George Whitefield, arrived in America. Whitefield was a disciple of John Wesley, the founder of the Methodist movement in England. Possessing a booming, melodious voice and a charismatic presence, Whitefield preached with great simplicity, always stressing the essentials of God's "free gift" of grace for those seeking conversion. He made seven preaching tours to the colonies, traveled thousands of miles, delivered hundreds of sermons, and spoke to gatherings as large as 30,000. Perhaps his most dramatic tour was to New England in the autumn of 1740. In Boston over 20,000 heard him preach in a three-day period. Concluding his tour in less than a month, Whitefield left behind churches full of congregants anxious to experience conversion and bask in the glow of fellowship with God.

Concerned with reviving vital religion, the Awakening soon became a source of great contention, splitting America's religious community into "new" and "old" light camps. Many revivalists advised their flocks to shun clergymen who, while well educated in formal theology, showed no visible signs of having gained God's saving grace. Thousands paid attention, and they started breaking away from congregations where ministers were suspect.

In response, Old Light clergymen began denouncing the Awakening as a fraudulent hoax being perpetrated by unlettered fools of no theological training. In New England, orthodox Congregational ministers got their legislative assemblies to adopt anti-itinerancy laws, which barred traveling evangelists like Whitefield from preaching in their communities.

All of the turmoil had significant long-term repercussions. Those feeling a new relationship with God were less willing to submit to established authority and more determined to speak out on behalf of basic liberties. Typical were colonists in New England who had started calling themselves Baptists. They demanded the right to separate completely from the established Congregational church, to which all citizens owed taxes, and the right to support their own ministers and churches. Theirs would be a long and hard-fought campaign for an end to state-supported religion.

The liberty to worship and support whatever church one pleased was a central concern of the Awakening movement, as was a desire to see clergymen properly trained. Prior to the 1740s, there were only three colonial colleges, Harvard, William and Mary, and Yale. In demanding toleration for diverse ideas, Presbyterian revivalists set up the College of New Jersey (later Princeton) to train New Light clergymen; Baptists founded the College of Rhode Island (later Brown); and the Dutch Reformed established Queen's College (later Rutgers). In 1769 a New Light Congregational minister, Eleazar Wheelock, received a charter for Dartmouth College to carry the new birth message to Native Americans.

As the Great Awakening spread into the South, it had a variety of lasting effects. During the late 1740s and 1750s the emergence of Presbyterian congregations in Virginia called into question the authority of the established Anglican church. By the mid-1750s swelling numbers of Baptists were displaying anything but a deferential regard for the mores of Virginia's planter elite. They started demanding, for example, the "entire banishment of *dancing, gaming,* and sabbath-day diversions."

The Awakening also stimulated Protestant forms of worship among blacks. They did not forsake their African religious traditions but blended them with Christian faith in a savior who offered eternal life through God's saving grace as well as hope for triumphing over oppression in their search for human freedom.

As the Great Awakening spread through the British North American provinces, then, its proponents questioned established authority at every turn and provoked movement toward a clearer definition of fundamental human rights as well as toleration of divergent ideas. The Awakening also served to direct the colonists toward the day when Americans would naturally accept religious pluralism, as expressed in the dramatic rise of such non-state-supported denominational groups as the Baptists and Presbyterians. Greater toleration of dissenters and diverse religious ideas were hall-mark legacies of the Awakening.

None of this came easily, and some of it, especially the emphasis on the search for personal liberty and freedom of conscience, along with the questioning of established authority, may have unwittingly served to pre-dispose many colonists to the political rebellion against Great Britain that lay in the not-too-distant future. Historians have divided opinions on this matter, but most would agree that the Awakening demonstrated that American communities showed considerable strength in weathering so much divisiveness. The provinces had indeed grown up and matured dur-ing the previous 100-year period, even if the British Crown failed to ap-preciate the newfound self-confidence of its North American colonists.

International Wars Beset America

Successful participation in a series of wars involving Britain and its two North American rivals, France and Spain, also contributed to the colonists' growing self-confidence. During the seventeenth century Spain maintained its grip on Florida as well as the Gulf coast. French Canadi-ans, operating from bases in Montreal and Quebec, explored throughout the Great Lakes region and then down into the Mississippi Valley. In 1682 an expedition headed by René-Robert Cavelier, Sieur de La Salle, reached the mouth of the Mississippi River. La Salle, who dreamed of a mighty French empire west of the Appalachian Mountains, claimed the whole region for his monarch, Louis XIV.

Despite these auspicious beginnings, New France grew slowly. Con-sumed by European affairs, the French Crown did not actively encourage settlement, and as late as 1760 no more than 75,000 French subjects lived in all of Canada and the Mississippi Valley. Some were farmers or fisher-men, and most others were fur traders. On the whole, they treated Native Americans with respect, and because the French population was so small, the Indians did not worry about losing ancient tribal lands. Sound rela-tions with the Indians certainly paid off, especially after European warfare spilled over into America. The advantage of having thousands of potential allies willing to join in combat against British settlers made the French Canadians a very dangerous enemy, as events proved during the imperial wars between 1689 and 1763.

The first of the four wars, known in the colonies as King William's War (1689–1697), was a limited conflict with no major battles in Amer-ica. What made this war so frightening were bloody border clashes in-volving Indians and colonists—typical was the attack on Hannah Dus-tan's Haverhill—that resulted in some 650 deaths among the English colonists. Five years later war erupted again, this time over French claims to the Spanish throne. Known as Queen Anne's War (1702–1713) in the colonies, the Anglo-Americans found themselves dueling with Spain as well as France and their Indian allies. In terms of casualties the war was not particularly bloody for the English colonists, who lost fewer than 500 people over an 11-year period. The Treaty of Utrecht, which ended the conflict in 1713, was a virtual declaration of Britain's growing imperial might. The British realized major territorial gains, including Hudson Bay, Newfoundland, and Nova Scotia in Canada.

Britain's triumph deterred additional warfare for 26 years, but further conflict seemed inevitable. To serve as a buffer between South Carolina and Spanish Florida, the Board of Trade in 1721 called for the creation of a military colony. General James Oglethorpe, a wealthy member of Parliament, decided to pursue the idea. A true philanthropist as well as imperialist, he hoped to roll back Spanish influence in America while improving the lot of England's downcast poor, especially imprisoned debtors. In 1732 King George II issued a charter for Georgia, granting 21 trustees all the land between the Savannah and Altamaha rivers for 21 years to develop the region, after which the colony would revert to the Crown and function under royal authority.

Colonists were hard to find, largely because of the rules devised by Oglethorpe and the other trustees. To assure good order, they outlawed liquor. To promote personal industry and hard work as well as spread out settlements in an effective defensive line, they limited individual land grants to 500 acres, and they banned slavery.

As a social experiment to uplift the poor, the colony was not successful. Some migrants wanted slaves; others, referring to Oglethorpe as "our perpetual dictator," called for a popular assembly; and they all demanded alcohol. The trustees acknowledged their failure by turning Georgia back to the Crown in 1752, a year ahead of schedule. By that time, they had already conceded on the issues of slavery and strong drink. Thereafter, Georgia looked more and more like South Carolina, with large rice and indigo plantations underpinning the local economy. By 1770, the colony's populace was almost 25,000, nearly half of whom were slaves.

Meanwhile, the conflict between the major European powers continued sporadically. James Oglethorpe mounted an unsuccessful expedition against Florida in 1740, and the following year a combined British-colonial force tried unsuccessfully to capture the major Spanish port of Cartagena. In 1744, England and France came to blows again over the legitimate heir to the Austrian throne, which in its American phase the colonists called King George's War. In June 1745 a New England army achieved a brilliant victory over the French, capturing the mighty fortress of Louisbourg that guarded the entrance to the St. Lawrence River.

The triumph at Louisbourg represented for the colonists the high point of a war that cost as many as 5,000 Anglo-American lives. But in the peace settlement that ended the war, Britain returned Louisbourg to the French. In exchange it received a port in India, which the king's negotiators reasoned was of much greater value as a center for imperial trade than a fortress in the American wilderness. The colonists were furious about this action, but they were powerless to do anything except complain among themselves about their subordinate—and unappreciated—status in the empire.

Showdown: The Great War for the Empire

When war broke out again, it resulted from conflicting interests in America. In 1748 fur traders from Pennsylvania and Virginia began establishing contacts with natives in the Ohio River valley. With the boom in colonial population, leading planters in Virginia were casting a covetous eye toward the development of the Ohio River Valley. With the backing of London merchants, one group formed the Ohio Company in 1747 and two years later secured a grant of 200,000 acres from the Crown.

Determined to secure the region against encroaching Anglo-American traders and land speculators, the French in the early 1750s started constructing a chain of forts in a line running southward from Lake Erie in western Pennsylvania. By 1753 the British ministry knew of these plans and ordered colonial governors to challenge the French advance and "repel force by force" if necessary.

Virginia's Governor Robert Dinwiddie, who happened to be an investor in the Ohio Company, acted quickly. In the spring of 1754 he sent a young major of militia, George Washington, with 200 men into western Pennsylvania. Foolishly, Washington skirmished with French troops, then hastily retreated and constructed Fort Necessity. A superior French and Indian force attacked on July 3. Washington surrendered and was allowed to lead his troops back to Virginia as prisoners of war.

While Washington was preparing to defend Fort Necessity, delegates from seven colonies had gathered in Albany, New York, to plan for their defense in case of war and to secure active support from the powerful Iroquois Indian Confederacy. At this meeting, delegates Benjamin Franklin and Thomas Hutchinson proposed an intercolonial plan of government, known as the Albany Plan of Union. The idea was to have a "grand council" made up of representatives from each colony who would work with a crown official, a "president general," to plan for defense and even to tax the provinces on an equitable basis in keeping the North American colonies secure from external enemies. The plan stirred little interest at the time, since the assemblies were not anxious to share their prerogatives, especially the power of taxation, with anyone.

Home government officials ignored the Albany Plan of Union, but the Fort Necessity debacle resulted in a fateful decision to send Major General Edward Braddock, an unimaginative 60-year-old British officer who had never commanded troops in battle, to Virginia. With a combined force of 3,000 redcoats and colonial militia—Washington came along as a volunteer officer—Braddock marched toward Fort Duquesne, the site of modern-day Pittsburgh. On July 9, 1755, about eight miles from the French fort, a much smaller French and Indian force, attacking from all sides, nearly destroyed the British column, leaving two-thirds of Braddock's soldiers dead or wounded. Braddock himself sustained mortal wounds, but before he died, he stated wryly: "We shall better know how to deal with them another time."

The ensuing conflict, widely known as the Seven Years' War and later referred to in America as the French and Indian War, was a showdown between France and England. William Pitt, the king's new chief minister, viewed America as the place "where England and Europe are to be fought for." Pitt's strategic plan was to let Prussia, Britain's ally, bear the brunt of warfare in Europe, while placing the bulk of England's military resources in America with the intent of strangling New France. He also advanced a

This woodcut, displayed in the *Pennsylvania Gazette,* failed to overcome long-standing jealousies that thwarted attempts at intercolonial cooperation.

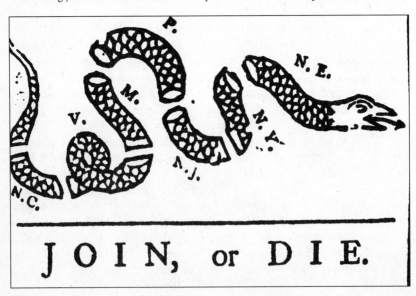

young group of dynamic officers over the heads of less capable men. It all paid off in a series of carefully orchestrated military advances that saw Quebec fall to the British in September 1759. A year later, with hardly an exchange of musket fire, Montreal surrendered to British troops.

Conclusion

The fall of the French empire in North America took place in the face of growing antagonism between British military leaders and the colonists. Americans joined provincial regiments and fought beside British redcoats, but most did not care for the experience. They found the king's regulars to be rough, crude, and morally delinquent. They viewed the king's officers as needlessly overbearing and aristocratic. They resented being treated as inferiors.

*C*hronology of Key Events

1650–1673	Navigation Acts passed to ensure that colonies trade within the emerging English empire
1664	Dutch surrender New Netherland to the English, who rename the colony New York
1676	Bacon's Rebellion takes place in Virginia
1682	La Salle claims Louisiana for France
1684	England revokes the Massachusetts Bay Colony charter
1686	Dominion of New England established
1688	Glorious Revolution drives James II from throne
1689	Rebellions occur in Massachusetts, New York, and Maryland
1692	Witchcraft scare in Salem, Massachusetts, results in execution of 20 women and men
1739–1740	Great Awakening gains momentum
1754	Albany Congress draws up plan to bring unity to the 13 colonies; George Washington defends Fort Necessity
1759	British forces capture Quebec
1763	Treaty of Paris ends the Seven Years' War

Young George Washington explained how Virginia's recruits "behaved like men, and died like soldiers" during Braddock's defeat, as compared to the British regulars, who "behaved with more cowardice than it is possible to conceive." The Americans were proud of their contributions to the triumphant British empire. They hoped that the Crown would treat them with greater respect in the days ahead. The king's chief ministers, however, believed that the colonists had done more to serve themselves than the British empire during the Seven Years' War. Because of many problems related to the war, the Crown decided to crack down on the "obstinate and ungovernable" American colonists.

Apparently the king's ministers had not learned very much from the previous 100 years of Anglo-American history. Before 1690, as the laws by which the empire operated became too restrictive, serious colonial resistance ensued. After 1690 an accommodation of differences assured the Americans basic rights and some local autonomy, so long as they supported the empire's economic and political objectives. Now more self-assertive than ever before, provincial Americans would again resist imperial plans to make them more fully subordinate to the will of the parent nation. This time they would go so far as to break the bonds of empire.

Suggestions for Further Reading

For studies of Britain's North American empire see Lawrence H. Gipson, *The British Empire Before the American Revolution*, 15 vols. (1936–1970); Michael Kammen, *Empire and Interest: The American Colonies and the Politics of Mercantilism* (1970); David S. Lovejoy, *The Glorious Revolution in America* (1972); Stephen S. Webb, *The Governors-General: The English Army and the Definition of Empire, 1569–1681* (1979).

For a general overview of North America during the late seventeenth and early eighteenth centuries see Wesley Frank Craven, *The Colonies in Transition, 1660–1713* (1968). Studies of the New England witch hysteria during this period include Paul Boyer and Stephen Nissenbaum, *Salem Possessed* (1974); John Putnam Demos, *Entertaining Satan* (1982); Carol F. Karlsen, *The Devil in the Shape of a Woman* (1987). For studies of the Middle Colonies see Patricia U. Bonomi, *A Factious People: Politics and Society in Colonial New York* (1971); Gary B. Nash, *Quakers and Politics* (1968); Robert C. Ritchie, *The Duke's Province: Politics and Society in New York* (1977); Sally Schwartz, *"A Mixed Multitude": The Struggle for Toleration in Colonial Pennsylvania* (1987). On the southern colonies see Jack P. Greene, *The Quest for Power: The Lower Houses of Assembly in the Southern Colonies, 1689–1776* (1963); Rhys Isaac, *The Transformation of Virginia,* (1982); Wilcomb E. Washburn, *The Governor and the Rebel: A History of Bacon's Rebellion* (1957). The intellectual climate in the colonies is examined in

Henry F. May, *The Enlightenment in America* (1976); Alan Heimert, *Religion and the American Mind* (1966).

On the imperial conflict in North American see Fred Anderson, *A People's Army: Massachusetts in the Seven Years' War* (1984); John E. Ferling, *Struggle for a Continent: The Wars of Early America* (1993); Francis Jennings, *Empire of Fortune: Crown, Colonies, and Tribes in the Seven Years' War* (1988; Douglas E. Leach, *Roots of Conflict: British Armed Forces and Colonial Americans* (1986), and *Arms for Empire: A Military History of the Colonies, 1607–1763* (1973).

Chapter *4*

Breaking the Bonds of Empire, 1760–1775

S amuel Adams grew up with many advantages in life. His father was a prosperous businessman who wanted his son to become a Congregational minister, so he sent him off to Harvard College. In 1740 Samuel emerged with a bachelor's degree, a reputation for free spending and excessive drinking, and little desire to become a clergyman. Enormously proud of his Puritan heritage, Adams remained a lifelong student of scripture, but his primary vocational interest was politics.

The year 1740 turned out to be disastrous for Adams's father. As a community leader he had become deeply involved in a plan to provide citizens with paper currency for local business transactions. Adams and others established a "land bank" that would lend out money to individuals who put up collateral in the form of real estate. The bank's paper money could then be used to purchase goods and services—and even pay debts as legal tender.

The directors of the Massachusetts Land Bank believed that they were performing a public service. Wealthy merchants, however, thought otherwise. They viewed such paper currencies with great skepticism. Only money properly backed by specie, such as gold or silver, they argued, could hold its value in the marketplace. They did not want to have to accept what they feared would be rapidly depreciating land-bank notes in their commercial dealings or for debts. Under the leadership of a powerful local merchant, Thomas Hutchinson, they appealed to the royal governor, who declared the land bank illegal, a position sustained in 1741 by Parliament.

With the land bank's collapse, Adams's father lost tremendous sums of money that he had invested to help underwrite the venture. He never recovered financially. When he died in 1748, he left his son a legacy of bitterness toward arbitrary royal authority and those Crown favorites, such as Thomas Hutchinson, whose actions had destroyed his family's prosperity.

Having no desire to continue his father's business, Samuel barely kept his own family in food and clothing. What little income he earned came from a number of minor political offices. In 1756 he assumed duties as a collector of local taxes for the town government, but he found it difficult to collect taxes from hard-pressed local citizens who, like himself, were struggling to make ends meet. Adams regularly accepted any good explanation—the outbreak of illness in some families and the loss of jobs in others. Boston's economy was stagnant, and unskilled workers were especially hard-pressed. As Adams was also aware, each time he did not enforce a collection he made a friend. By the early 1760s he had built up a loyal following of admirers who fervently believed that he was a good and decent man committed to protecting their interests.

Even as he earned the gratitude of Boston's ordinary citizens, Adams did not lose sight of adversaries from his past. He particularly loathed

Thomas Hutchinson, whose stature as a wealthy merchant with wide-ranging imperial connections had helped him gain a number of prominent offices. In 1758 Hutchinson secured a Crown appointment as the Bay Colony's lieutenant governor. He was already holding a local probate judgeship, was the ranking local militia officer, and was serving as an elected member of the governor's council (the upper house of the General Court). Then in 1760 he gained appointment to the post of chief judge of the superior court. His combined annual salary from these offices was around £400 sterling, ten times the amount of an average family's yearly income.

In the years ahead when Hutchinson and other royal officials in Massachusetts tried to implement imperial policies, Adams was ready to protest and resist. His allies in the streets would be the ordinary people, and they set a particularly defiant tone for the broader resistance movement throughout the 13 provinces. Whether Samuel Adams acted out of personal rancor toward Hutchinson or purely to defend American liberties was one of the secrets he carried to his grave, even as his contemporaries remembered him both in Europe and America as "one of the prime movers of the late Revolution."

The actual outbreak of the American Revolution may be traced directly to the year 1763 when British leaders began to tighten the imperial reins. The colonists protested vigorously, and communications started to break down, so much so that a permanent rupture of political affections began to take place. No one in 1763 had any idea that the developing crisis would shatter the bonds of empire, but that is exactly what happened when the American colonists, after a dozen years of bitter contention with the parent nation, finally proceeded to open rebellion in 1775.

Provoking an Imperial Crisis

In 1763 British subjects everywhere toasted the Treaty of Paris that ended the worldwide Seven Years' War. The empire had gained territorial jurisdiction over French Canada and all territory east of the Mississippi River, except for a tiny strip of land around New Orleans that France deeded to Spain. The Spanish, in turn, who also took over French territory west of the Mississippi River, had to cede the Floridas to Britain to regain the Philippines and Cuba, the latter having fallen to a combined Anglo-American force in 1762. Britain likewise made substantial gains in India. Most important from the colonists' perspective, the French "menace" had been eradicated from North America, which should have signaled a new era of imperial harmony. That was not to be the case.

N.º VII *Engrav.d for Royal American Magazine* Vol. I

M.ʳ SAMUEL ADAMS.

Samuel Adams, shown here in an engraving by Paul Revere. Adams believed that royalist leaders in Massachusetts wanted to destroy American liberties. He was a vigorous opponent of the Stamp Act, an organizer of the Sons of Liberty, and, after independence, a long-term governor of Massachusetts.

A Legacy of War-Related Problems

For the chief ministers in Great Britain under the youthful and vigorous monarch George III, who was 25 years old in 1763, the most pressing problem was Britain's national debt. During the Seven Years' War it had skyrocketed from £75 million to £137 million sterling. Advisers to the Crown worried about ways to get the debt under control, a most difficult

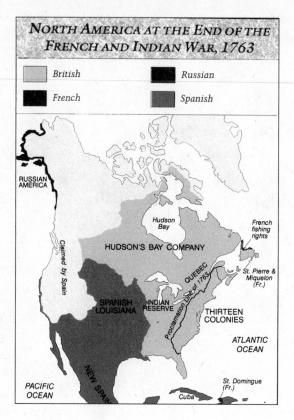

NORTH AMERICA AT THE END OF THE FRENCH AND INDIAN WAR, 1763

British
Russian
French
Spanish

RUSSIAN AMERICA

Claimed by Spain

Hudson Bay

HUDSON'S BAY COMPANY

French fishing rights

QUEBEC

St. Pierre & Miquelon (Fr.)

Proclamation Line of 1763

SPANISH LOUISIANA   INDIAN RESERVE

THIRTEEN COLONIES

ATLANTIC OCEAN

NEW SPAIN

PACIFIC OCEAN

St. Domingue (Fr.)

Cuba

North America, 1763

With the signing of the Treaty of Paris, Great Britain received almost all of France's holdings in North America.

problem considering the newly won territories that the home government now had to govern.

Closely linked to the debt issue was the matter of American smuggling activity. Many colonial merchants, eager for profits of any kind, had traded illegally with the enemy during the war. Even though the Royal Navy had blockaded French and Spanish ports in the Caribbean, traders from New England and elsewhere used various pretexts to effect business deals.

A host of issues relating to newly won territories to the north and west of the Anglo-American settlements also concerned the king's ministers. Most important, they worried about the financial burden of prolonged warfare on the frontier, should land-hungry white settlers push into Indian hunting grounds too quickly. The vacuum created by the collapse of French authority combined with fears that British officials would ignore the encroachment of white settlers on tribal lands inspired Pontiac, an Ottawa war chief, to build an alliance of several western Indian tribes.

Beginning in May 1763, Pontiac's warriors struck with a vengeance, attacking white settlements running in a southwesterly arc from New York through western Pennsylvania to Virginia. Only a severe thrashing at Bushy Run, Pennsylvania, in August 1763 turned the tide of bloody frontier warfare against the Indians, and by autumn Pontiac's allies began drifting back to their villages.

It fell to George Grenville, who became the king's chief minister in April 1763, to solve these imperial problems. Grenville held strong anti-American feelings. As he proclaimed before Parliament, "Great Britain protects America; America is bound to yield obedience." An ominous moment in Anglo-American relations was at hand. The so-called era of salutary neglect, under which the colonists had thrived in relative freedom for so many years, was about to end.

Getting Tough with the Americans

Grenville was a mercantilist in his thinking and firmly believed that the colonists had forgotten their subordinate status in the empire. In early October 1763 he issued two administrative orders designed to bring the Americans to heel. The first, known as the Orders in Council of 1763, stationed British naval vessels in American waters for the purpose of running down and seizing all colonial merchant ships suspected of illegal trading activity. The goal was to end American smuggling and to force the colonists to start paying more trade duties into royal coffers.

The second order, known as the Proclamation of 1763, dealt with the West. It addressed matters of government for the new British territories, including the temporary organization of such provinces as Quebec. It also mandated that a line be drawn from north to south along "the heads or sources of any of the rivers which fell into the Atlantic Ocean from the west and northwest." No doubt much influenced by the news of Pontiac's uprising, the ministry's notion was to stop white incursions into Indian lands. Hence, territory west of the Proclamation line was forever to be "reserved to the Indians."

The Proclamation policy may have reflected some desire for humane treatment of Native Americans; however, the cabinet was far more concerned with avoiding costly Indian wars. There were some cabinet leaders, furthermore, who did not relish the prospect of American settlements spreading too far inland from the Atlantic coastline. If the colonists built communities across the mountains and out of the reach of the imperial trading network, they would of necessity begin manufacturing all sorts of products—and might, in time, start competing with the British Isles for control of seaboard markets. From the imperial perspective, it was in the parent nation's best interest to keep the colonists to the east of the Appalachian Mountains.

The Proclamation of 1763 also related to another policy decision of momentous consequence. To keep control over both white settlers and Indians, the cabinet had already decided to maintain up to 10,000 British regulars in North America. Pontiac's uprising and the Proclamation policy determined where the redcoats were to be located, at least initially. Most would be ordered out onto the frontier, but it was unclear who would pay for these redcoats—a crucial issue, indeed.

Determined that the colonists should pay for their own defense, Grenville came up with plans to tax His Majesty's subjects in America. In April 1764 Parliament adopted the Revenue Act, usually called the Sugar Act, which placed trade duties on a number of foreign goods—coffee, indigo, sugar, and wine—regularly purchased by the colonists. It also lowered the Molasses Act duty of 1733 from six to three pence a gallon with the hope that it would be easier to collect than in the past.

Grenville projected that the Sugar Act would produce an additional £40,000 in annual revenue to assist in covering the ongoing costs of imperial administration, in this case paying for Britain's military establishment in America. From the colonists' perspective, that was exactly the problem with this legislation. As the New York assembly pointed out, the purpose was something more than merely fixing a duty that would affect the flow of commerce. In 1763 the colonists had paid only an estimated £1,800 in trade duties associated with the Navigation Acts. (It actually cost the Crown £8,000 that year to run the customs service in America.) A projected £40,000 in yearly revenue, by comparison, made it clear that the intention was to tax the Americans.

Taxation was what Grenville had most in mind, but he also had other concerns, as embodied in Parliament's adoption of the Currency Act of April 1764. This act represented an expansion of legislation directed against New England in 1751. The paper money of all colonial governments could no longer be used as legal tender in payment of private debts. Nor could provincial governments issue any new paper bills, and they were expected to retire what money they had in circulation within a reasonable time period.

Unfortunately, the colonies were in the midst of a severe postwar depression in 1764. Limiting the currency supply only worsened matters by making it yet more difficult for citizens to obtain money to conduct business—let alone pay increased taxes. If nothing else, the timing of the Currency Act was terrible; it caused the home government to appear incredibly insensitive to promoting the economic welfare of its colonies.

Parliament Endorses Direct Taxes

George Grenville really did not care about the opinions of the colonists. His major goal was to raise a substantial tax revenue in the colonies. He got what he wanted with the Stamp Act of March 1765, the capstone of his imperial program. Through the Stamp Act, Parliament asserted for the first time its full authority to lay *direct* taxes, as opposed to *indirect* (or hidden taxes, such as trade duties), on the colonists.

As such, there was nothing subtle about the Stamp Act. This legislation required Americans to pay for stamps attached to some 50 items, everything from newspapers, pamphlets, almanacs, and playing cards to port clearance papers for ships, land deeds, and wills. The price of the stamps varied according to the value of the particular items to which they were affixed. Grenville estimated that the tax would yield about £100,000 a year. All stamps would have to be paid for in hard currency, a virtual impossibility since specie continually flowed to Britain to pay for imported goods. Also, violators could be prosecuted in juryless vice-admiralty courts, as well as in regular criminal courts.

Grenville knew that the colonists would not like the Stamp Act, but he believed the time had come for Americans to pay for the benefits of being part of the mightiest empire in the western world. Grenville was not asking the colonists to help reduce the home debt, only to assist in meeting the rising costs of imperial administration. For that reason, Parliament earmarked Stamp Act revenues for maintaining the redcoats in America.

To counter arguments about taxation without representation, Grenville employed the concept of "virtual representation," maintaining that all English subjects throughout the empire—by virtue of their citizenship—enjoyed representation in Parliament. In theory, members of Parliament were to promote the public good by representing not just particular constituents but all imperial subjects in legislative decision making.

But Grenville had failed to see the whole picture. From an economic point of view, if from no other, the colonies were invaluable to the British empire. The provinces so stimulated the home economy, particularly with regard to buying manufactured goods, that a serious trade deficit had developed for the Americans. The colonists had gotten into the habit of importing much more from the British Isles than they exported in return. By the early 1770s, provincial Americans owed more than £4 million to English and Scottish creditors. This was a major reason why hard money was so difficult to come by in America. It was being drained off constantly to pay these debts.

By only looking at specific governmental costs, Grenville had missed an essential point. Provincial subjects were not just taking from the empire; they also provided a ready, indeed, captive market for British-manufactured commodities. In this sense the Americans were paying a significant price, as measured by the trade deficit, in support of the parent nation.

"Liberty, Property, and No Stamps"

Certainly the colonists were not plotting independence in 1763. They were proud to be citizens of the far-flung British empire, stretching as it did from India in the East across the globe to some 30 American colonies in the West, including such Caribbean islands as Barbados and Jamaica. With the elimination of French authority in North America, the mainland colonists were also experiencing a buoyant new sensation of freedom. Paradoxically, the reinvigorated imperial program came at the very time when the colonists, feeling great pride but needing much less government protection from across the ocean, hoped for a continuation if not an expansion of the local autonomy to which they had become accustomed. Psychologically, they were ready for anything but new imperial constraints on their lives.

Emerging Patterns of Resistance

As the Grenville program took shape, the colonists experienced various emotions. Dismay gave way to disappointment and anger. Initial reactions involved petitioning King and Parliament for a redress of grievances. By the summer of 1765 colonial protest took an extralegal turn as Americans resorted to such tactics of resistance as crowd intimidation and violence, economic boycott, and outright defiance of imperial law. The colonists no longer liked to think of themselves as Britain's children. Through their tactics of resistance they were asking to be treated more like adults. Very few British officials seemed to understand this message, which in time resulted in the full rupture of British-American relations.

The first words of protest were quite mild, expressed in a flurry of petitions and pamphlets that laid out an American position with respect to essential political rights. In reaction to the Sugar Act of 1764, the New York Assembly complained about "all impositions" by Parliament, "whether they be internal taxes, or duties paid, for what we consume." In many ways protest by pamphlet and petition was so mild in tone during 1764 that it encouraged George Grenville to pursue more comprehensive taxation plans. The intensity of American ill feeling in reaction to the Stamp Act thus shocked the home government.

First news of the Stamp Act arrived in the provinces during April 1765, which left ample time to organize effective resistance before November 1, when the Act was to take effect. Colonial protest soon became very turbulent, with Samuel Adams's Boston taking the lead in stirring up resistance.

In Massachusetts, as in many other provinces, there were a small number of royal officials favored by the parent nation's patronage. This group held the most prominent offices in colonial government, and they were known as the "royalist" or "court" political faction. Besides Lieutenant Governor and Chief Justice Thomas Hutchinson, other leading members of the royalist faction were Governor Francis Bernard, Secretary and Councilor Andrew Oliver, and Associate Justice and Councilor Peter Oliver (Andrew's younger brother). Hutchinson and the Oliver brothers were natives of New England and had all graduated from Harvard College. They were interrelated by marriage, and they were among the wealthiest citizens in America.

Even though these gentlemen were at the apex of provincial society, their opponents in the "popular" or "country" faction did not defer to them. Samuel Adams and other local leaders such as James Otis, Jr., a brilliant lawyer, viewed the likes of Hutchinson and the Oliver brothers with contempt. Adams won his first term to the Assembly in 1765 as a representative from Boston. For him personally the emerging Stamp Act crisis represented an opportunity to launch a simultaneous attack on unacceptable imperial policies and old political adversaries. The twin assault unfolded in August 1765 shortly after citizens learned that none other than Andrew Oliver was the Bay Colony's proposed Stamp Act distributor.

Protest Takes a Violent Turn

Samuel Adams did not participate directly in crowd actions. Nor did the informal popular rights governing body, known as the Loyal Nine. To help organize popular protests, Adams enlisted the aid of Ebenezer Mackintosh, a shoemaker, and Henry Swift, a cobbler, leaders of Boston's workingmen's associations. The North End and South End "leather apron" gangs were in reality fraternal organizations providing fellowship for artisans, apprentices, and common day laborers. The two groups had for many years engaged in street brawls, but now agreed to stop fighting among themselves and unite in defense of essential political liberties. In time these workers would be called the Sons of Liberty, and their cooperation proved to be a critical step in ending any implementation of the Stamp Act in Massachusetts.

On the morning of August 14, 1765, the local populace awoke to find an effigy of Peter Oliver hanging in an elm tree—later called the Liberty Tree—in the South End of Boston. That evening a crowd numbering in the thousands gathered around the tree to watch Ebenezer Mackintosh solemnly remove the effigy and exhort everyone present to join in a march through the streets. Holding the effigy high on a staff, Mackintosh and Swift led what was an orderly procession. As they marched, the people shouted: "Liberty, Property, and No Stamps."

The crowd worked its way to the local dockyards, where the Sons of Liberty ripped apart a building recently constructed by Andrew Oliver. Rumor had it that Oliver intended to store his quota of stamped paper there. Next, the crowd moved toward Oliver's stately home. Some in the crowd tore up the fence, ransacked the first floor (the Oliver family had fled), and imbibed from the well-stocked wine cellar. Others gathered on a hill behind the Oliver residence. Materials from Oliver's building as well as his wooden fence provided kindling for a huge bonfire that ultimately consumed the effigies as the working men and women of Boston cheered. By midnight this crucial crowd action was over.

Early the next morning, the thoroughly intimidated Oliver resigned. Mackintosh's crowd, rather than Crown officials, were now in control of Boston. Had Boston's Sons of Liberty and their leaders been solely concerned with rendering the Stamp Act unenforceable, they would have ceased their rioting after Oliver's resignation; however, they had other accounts to settle. A misleading rumor began to circulate through the streets claiming that Thomas Hutchinson was very much in favor of the Stamp Act, indeed had even helped to write the tax plan. As a result, the Sons of Liberty came out again on the evening of August 26. After visiting a few others, the crowd descended upon Hutchinson's palatial home, one of the most magnificent in the province. They ripped it apart. As the lieutenant governor later described the scene, "they continued their possession until daylight; destroyed, carried away, or cast into the street, everything that was in the house; demolished every part of it, except for walls, as lay in their power."

Who started the rumor remains a moot point, but Hutchinson's political enemies were well known. Further, some Bostonians may have vented their frustrations with the depressed local economy by ransacking the property of a well-placed person with imperial connections who was prospering during difficult times. Whatever the explanation, royal authority in the Bay Colony had suffered another serious blow. The mere threat of crowd violence gave Samuel Adams and his popular rights faction a powerful weapon that Hutchinson and other royalist officials never overcame.

Resistance Spreads Across the Landscape

By rendering the office of stamp distributor powerless, Boston had established a model for resistance. Colonists elsewhere were quick to act. Within the next few months distributors in Rhode Island, Maryland, and Connecticut, fearful of mob violence, resigned their commissions. By November 1 there was virtually no one foolish or bold enough to distribute stamps in America. Only Georgians experienced a short-lived implementation of the despised tax.

Crowds protesting imperial policies, in this case burning stamped documents and newspapers, were normally made up of ordinary citizens, particularly the working poor.

While the colonists employed intimidation and violence, they also petitioned King and Parliament. Assembly after assembly prepared remonstrances stating that taxation without representation was a fundamental violation of the rights of English subjects. Patrick Henry, a young and aggressive backcountry Virginia lawyer, had a profound influence on these official petitions. As a member of the Virginia House of Burgesses (lower house of the Assembly), Henry proposed a series of resolutions in mid-May 1765. The House endorsed the first four, which reiterated the no taxation without representation theme, but it rejected the fifth as too categorical a denial of Parliament's authority. Henry did not bother to present his remaining two resolutions.

Some newspapers in other provinces reprinted all seven of Henry's resolutions. The fifth stated that the Virginia Assembly held "the only exclusive right and power to lay taxes and impositions upon the inhabitants of this colony." The sixth asserted that Virginians were "not bound to yield obedience to any law" not approved by their Assembly. The seventh indicated that anyone thinking otherwise would "be deemed an enemy by His Majesty's colony."

These three resolutions read as if the Virginia burgesses had denied King and Parliament all legislative authority over the American provinces. They seemed to be advocating some form of dual sovereignty in which the American assemblies held final authority over legislative matters in America—comparable in scope to Parliament's authority over the British Isles. This was a radical concept, in fact too radical for the Virginia burgesses. Yet the reprinting of all seven of the Virginia Resolutions, as they came to be known, encouraged other assemblies to prepare strongly worded petitions during the summer and fall of 1765.

An important example of intercolonial unity was the Stamp Act Congress, attended by delegates from nine colonies. Generally speaking, cautious gentlemen of the upper ranks dominated the Stamp Act Congress. Their "declarations" on behalf of American rights had a far more conciliatory tone than the Virginia Resolutions. The delegates proclaimed their loyalty to Great Britain, but respectfully requested that Parliament relinquish its right to tax the colonies to the provincial assemblies. The Stamp Act Congress demonstrated that leaders from different colonies could meet together and agree on common principles. The Congress also suggested that unified intercolonial resistance might be possible, should events ever make that necessary.

Another, more telling blow to the Stamp Act was an intercolonial economic boycott. Merchants in New York City were the first to act. They pledged not to order British goods "of any nature, kind, or quality" unless the Stamp Act was repealed. Within a month merchants in the other principal port towns, including Boston and Philadelphia, drafted similar agreements. A trade boycott of British goods, particularly with the remnants of economic depression still plaguing the empire, was bound to win support for repeal among merchants and manufacturers in Britain.

On November 1, 1765, commerce in the colonies came to a halt. Trading vessels remained in ports because no stamped clearance papers could be obtained. Courts ceased functioning, since so many legal documents required stamps. Newspapers stopped publication, at least temporarily. For all of their bravado the Americans really did not want to defy the law. As November gave way to December, however, popular leaders began to apply various forms of pressure on more timid citizens. By the beginning of 1766 colonial business and legal activity started returning to normal, and newspaper editors commenced printing again—all in open defiance of the Stamp Act.

George Grenville thus had grossly miscalculated. Not willing to be treated as errant children, the colonists, in defending their liberties, sent petitions to Parliament, intimidated and harassed royal officials, destroyed property, cut off the importation of British goods, and, finally, openly defied the law. Americans hoped for a return to the old days of salutary neglect, but they also wondered whether the king's ministers would understand and back down in the face of such determined resistance.

Parliament Retreats

Instability in the British cabinet, as much as American protest, helped to bring about repeal of the Stamp Act. George III had never liked Grenville. In July 1765 the king asked him to step aside in favor of the Marquis of Rockingham, who was more sympathetic toward the Americans. Rockingham's political coalition was brittle, and his term as chief minister lasted just long enough to bring about repeal.

Looking for political allies, Rockingham took advantage of pressure from English traders and manufacturers who were extremely worried about the American boycott. In March 1766 Parliament repealed the Stamp Act. Home government leaders had by no means accepted colonial arguments. They insisted upon a face-saving statement designed to make it clear that King and Parliament were the supreme legislative voices of empire. In conjunction with rescinding the Stamp Act, Parliament approved the Declaratory Act, which specifically denied the claims of American assemblies to "the sole and exclusive right of imposing duties and taxes . . . in the colonies." The Declaratory Act forcefully asserted that Parliament had "full power and authority to make laws and statutes . . . , *in all cases whatsoever.*" Having repealed the Stamp Act for the sake of imperial harmony, Parliament still had the right to tax all British subjects anytime it chose. It had stated its position—and in terms irreconcilable with the stance taken by the Americans.

A Second Crisis: The Townshend Duties

What was needed in 1766 was an extended cooling-off period, but that was not to happen. The Rockingham ministry, which would have been willing to leave the colonists alone, collapsed, giving way to a new ministry headed by William Pitt, who became the Earl of Chatham. As a member of the House of Lords, Pitt let others provide for legislation in the House of Commons. One person in particular, Chancellor of the Exchequer Charles Townshend, rushed forward to fill the void in leadership. To the amazement of many, Townshend proclaimed that he knew how to tax the colonists. The result was the ill-advised Townshend duties of 1767, which renewed tension between Britain and America.

Formulating a New Taxation Scheme

Benjamin Franklin, who was in England serving as an agent for various colonies, inadvertently helped to formulate Townshend's plan. In a lengthy interview before Parliament during the repeal debates, Franklin, who was out of touch with American sentiment, stated emphatically that the colonists only objected to *direct* or "internal" taxes, such as those embodied in the Stamp Act. They did not object, he claimed, to *indirect* or "external" taxes, which may be defined as duties placed on trade goods for the purpose of gaining imperial revenue. Pointing out that Franklin was the most respected colonist of the era, Charles Townshend seized upon this distinction and came up with his taxation scheme.

In June 1767 Parliament authorized the Townshend duties, which were nothing more than import duties on a short list of trade items: British-manufactured glass, paper and lead products, painters' colors, and a three-pence-a-pound duty on tea. Townshend proclaimed that his plan would net the Crown £35,000 to £40,000 per year. In time, once the colonists got used to the idea, the list of taxable products could be lengthened. Meantime, the revenue would help defray the costs of royal governments in America.

At first, it appeared that Townshend knew what he was doing. The plan was subtle and generated very little colonial opposition. Except for tea, the duties were on luxury items, rarely used by the majority of colonists. The tea tax could be evaded by opening illicit trading connections with Dutch tea merchants—and Americans were still quite adept at the art of smuggling.

Mustering Further American Resistance

Late in 1767 John Dickinson, a Philadelphia landholder and lawyer, began publishing a series of newspaper essays, later printed as a pamphlet entitled *Letters from a Farmer in Pennsylvania*. Dickinson assailed Townshend's logic. Americans, he pointed out, had not distinguished between internal and external taxes. Certainly they had long accepted duties designed "to regulate trade" and facilitate the flow of imperial commerce. They now faced trade duties "for the single purpose" of raising revenue. Taxes disguised as trade duties, warned a most suspicious Dickinson, were "a most dangerous innovation" with the potential for turning the colonists into "abject slaves." Yet Dickinson, a man of considerable wealth who feared the destructive potential of violent crowds, urged caution in resistance; he called for the colonial assemblies merely to petition Parliament, hoping that body would listen to reason.

Parliament nonetheless viewed these arguments as seditious. It was likewise angered by the rough treatment experienced by royal customs officials, particularly in Boston where the Crown had recently located a new five-man Board of Customs Commissioners to coordinate all customs collections in America. When members of the board arrived at the end of 1767, jeering crowds greeted them at the docks. The commissioners found it virtually impossible to walk the streets or carry out their official duties without harassment.

More serious trouble erupted in Boston during June 1768 when a crowd attacked local customs collectors who had seized John Hancock's sloop *Liberty* on charges of smuggling in a cargo of Madeira wine. (Hancock, a Boston merchant, was notorious for illegal trading.) The new commissioners fled to Fort Castle William in Boston harbor for personal safety, and they asked Parliament for military protection.

Meanwhile, the Secretary for American Affairs, Lord Hillsborough, had issued orders for four regiments of British troops to proceed to Boston. When the first redcoats arrived in the fall of 1768 without serious incident, members of the royalist political faction breathed more easily and went about their duties with new courage. It looked as if crowd rule, civil anarchy, and open harassment were tactics of the past.

Samuel Adams and the popular rights faction, however, kept demanding more resistance. On August 1, 1768, they convinced an enthusiastic town meeting to accept a nonimportation boycott of British goods. New Yorkers signed a similar document a few days later. Philadelphians, bowing to the pressure of influential merchants, hoped that a petition from the Pennsylvania Assembly would change Parliament's mind. Somewhat reluctantly, they finally joined the trade boycott in February 1769. Threats of crowd action forced the merchants of Charleston, South Carolina, into line during August 1769. It had taken a year, but now all the major port towns had endorsed yet another trade boycott in defense of political liberties.

The colonists did more than boycott. In some of the port towns there was talk about producing their own manufactured goods, such as woolen cloth, in direct defiance of imperial restrictions. With the boycott in full force, wealthier citizens could no longer get the most fashionable fabrics from London, and popular leaders encouraged them to join poorer colonists in wearing homespun cloth—a sign of personal sacrifice for the cause. Some leaders urged all "genteel ladies" to master the skills of spinning and weaving.

Upper-class women, by and large, were not persuaded. They did not like the itchy feeling of homespun, and they considered spinning and weaving to be beneath their station in society. For poorer women, particularly those in the port towns, the trade boycott generated opportunities for piecemeal work in the production of homespun cloth. This meant some extra income, but there was virtually no long-term effect in improving the lot of the poor in America. Homespun was abundant, and the market price remained quite low. While wealthier women itched, complained, and worried about losing their status, poorer women were virtually donating their labor to the defense of American rights. For them the term "sacrifice" held a special meaning.

A "Bloody Massacre" in Boston

The citizens of Boston deeply resented the redcoats in their midst. Besides symbolizing political tyranny, the soldiers also competed for scarce jobs because, when not on duty, their officers allowed them to work for extra wages on a piecemeal basis. As a result, the troops made hard economic times even harder for common day laborers, semiskilled workers, and other poorer Bostonians already suffering from the prolonged economic depression besetting their community.

Throughout 1769 troop baiting by Boston's working men and women had resulted in fistfights and bloodied faces. Then on March 2, 1770, a fight broke out between off-duty redcoats and employees of a ropemaking establishment. The ugly confrontation served to inflame tempers on both sides, prompting Boston's working people to challenge the redcoats' continued presence in their community. On the evening of

March 5, crowds of day laborers, apprentices, and merchant seamen began milling about in the streets. Slowly, but without an appearance of overall direction, these groups moved toward King Street, the site of the Customs House, where a small detachment of soldiers was on guard duty.

Suddenly, angry citizens began pelting the soldiers with mud, snowballs, rocks—indeed anything that could be thrown. Captain Thomas Preston tried to steady his detachment, but one of his soldiers, fearing for his life, panicked. He leveled his musket, and a shot rang out. Ignoring Preston's orders to stop, other soldiers also fired their weapons. Before the shooting ceased, five civilians lay dead or dying, including Crispus Attucks, an unemployed mulatto merchant seaman. Bostonians would soon hail these men as martyred heroes in the struggle to defend American liberties.

Effective propaganda, such as Paul Revere's engravings of the Boston Massacre, helped increase outrage over the event. Here, the British soldiers appear to be firing without provocation into an innocent-looking crowd of citizens.

Captain Preston and his troops faced trials for murder. The court found two soldiers guilty of manslaughter; the others were judged innocent on the grounds of having been forced into a life-threatening situation by an enraged crowd of citizens. Long before these verdicts, royal officials removed the hated redcoats from Boston. In this important sense the working citizens of Boston had won at the cost of five lives. They had freed their community of British regulars and unwanted economic competition. Just as important, the "Boston Massacre" caused colonists everywhere to ask just how far King and Parliament would go to sustain their policies.

Parliament Backs Down Again

The colonists' trade boycott seriously hurt merchants and manufacturers in the British Isles. By the beginning of 1770 the Townshend program had netted only about £20,000 in revenue, a paltry sum when compared to the loss in American trade, estimated to be as high as £7 million. Once again, the colonists had found the means to force Parliament to reevaluate its position.

In January 1770 George III asked amiable Lord Frederick North to form a new cabinet and give some direction to drifting governmental affairs. North, listening to the wrath of powerful British merchants and manufacturers, moved quickly to settle differences with America. He went before Parliament on March 5, 1770, and called for repeal of the Townshend duties, except for the tax on tea, which was to stand as a face-saving, symbolic reminder of Parliament's right to tax and legislate for the Americans in all cases whatsoever. As with the Stamp Act confrontation, the colonial trade boycott of 1768-1770 most certainly had a telling effect. King and Parliament had backed off again, but it was going to be their last retreat.

The Rupturing of Imperial Relations

Lord North was a sensible leader who wanted to avoid taxation schemes and other forms of legislation that could provoke more trouble. He knew that imperial relations had been strained almost to a breaking point by too many restrictive policies thrown at the colonists in too short a time after so many years of salutary neglect. North carefully avoided challenging the Americans between 1770 and 1773. In turn, the colonial resistance movement waned. For a brief period, then, there were no new issues to stir further conflict—only old problems needing to be resolved.

When Parliament stepped away from the Townshend duties, most colonists wanted to discontinue the boycott and return to normal trade relations, despite the irritating tax on tea. They knew that the duty could be avoided by the continued smuggling of Dutch tea. Slowly, economic relations with Britain improved, and His Majesty's subjects in England and America enjoyed a brief period of mutually supportive economic prosperity.

The Necessity of Vigilance

Political relations were not so resilient. Many colonists had become very suspicious of the intentions of home government officials. Provincial leaders tried to explain what had happened since 1763 by drawing on the thoughts of England's "radical" whig opposition writers of the early eighteenth century. Men such as John Trenchard and Thomas Gordon, who had penned a series of essays known as *Cato's Letters,* had repeatedly warned about corruption in government caused by high ministerial officials lusting after power. If not somehow checked, citizens like the colonists would find themselves stripped of all liberties and living in a state of tyranny (often described as "political slavery").

What took firm hold during the 1760s was an American worldview, or ideology, that saw liberties under attack by such grasping, power-hungry leaders as George Grenville and Charles Townshend in England and their royalist puppets in America, personified by such officials as Thomas Hutchinson and Andrew Oliver. In attempting to explain what had happened, the evidence of a conspiracy seemed overwhelming. There were his Majesty's regular troops along the frontier and in Boston, and there were ships of the Royal Navy patrolling in American waters, all during peacetime. The colonists had been cut off from frontier lands, and perhaps worst of all, there had been three willful attempts to tax them, literally to deprive them of property without any voice in the decision to do so.

As never before, great numbers of colonists doubted the goodwill of the home government. Even if Lord North was behaving himself and keeping Parliament in check, many suspected that ministerial inaction was only a ploy, nothing more than a trick designed to lull Americans into a false sense of security while conspiring royal officials devised new and even more insidious plans to strip away all political rights.

Popular leaders exhorted the citizenry to be vigilant at all times. They employed various devices to ensure that the defense of liberties was not forgotten. In Boston, for example, Samuel Adams and his political lieutenants declared March 5 to be an annual commemorative holiday to honor the five fallen martyrs of the Massacre. Each year there was a large public meeting and grand oration to stir memories and to remind the populace of the possible dangers of a new ministerial assault.

Local confrontations also kept emotions stirred up. One such incident occurred in June 1772 when a Royal Navy vessel that regularly patrolled for smugglers, the *Gaspée,* ran aground off Rhode Island. A crowd disguised as Indians descended upon the stranded ship and burned it. Crown officials were furious about the *Gaspée's* destruction. They set up a royal commission of inquiry but never obtained any useful information concerning the perpetrators. The episode prompted several provincial assemblies, fearful of further threats to colonial liberties, to establish committees of correspondence to communicate with each other. These committees were soon writing back and forth regarding serious problems over tea.

The Tea Crisis of 1773

The final assault on American rights, as the colonists perceived matters, grew out of a rather inconspicuous piece of legislation known as the Tea Act of 1773. When Lord North proposed this bill, he had no idea that it would precipitate a disastrous sequence of events; in fact, he was hardly even thinking about the American provinces. His prime concern was the East India Company, a joint-stock trading venture that dated back to the early seventeenth century whose officials ruled over British interests in India.

Having prospered for years, the company was in desperate economic straits in the early 1770s. One reason was that the recent colonial boycott had cost the company its place in the American tea market. With tea warehouses bulging, company directors won important marketing concessions from Parliament in 1773. They asked to have the authority to ship tea directly from India to America (instead of via England, which added significantly to the final market price). To reduce costs further, the company proceeded to name its own tea agents in the major American ports. The net effect of these changes was to make company tea much more competitive with, if not cheaper than, smuggled Dutch blends.

Lord North thought he had found a way to get the Americans to accept the tea tax—and symbolically, at least, recognize Parliament's sovereignty. North could not imagine that the colonists would stand on principle and keep purchasing more expensive Dutch tea just to avoid the three-pence-a-pound trade duty. Suspicious Americans, however, conditioned by years of warding off undesirable imperial legislation, were looking for signs of further conspiratorial acts. A small economic saving meant nothing in the face of what appeared to be another insidious measure to reduce the colonists to a state of political slavery. Although such a worldview may seem far-fetched today, popular leaders and the general populace were thinking in confrontational terms. East India Company tea had to be resisted.

Once again, the port city of Boston became the focal point of significant protest. In early November a crowd took to the streets and tried unsuccessfully to intimidate the tea agents into resigning. When the first tea ship, the *Dartmouth,* docked in Boston later that month, the local customs collectors, fearing reprisals, fled to Fort Castle William. The local committee of correspondence, headed by Samuel Adams and his associates, put guards on the *Dartmouth* and two other tea ships entering the port within the next few days. The popular rights faction repeatedly insisted that the three tea ships be sent back to England. But Governor Thomas Hutchinson refused. Deciding that a showdown was necessary, he called upon Royal Navy vessels in the vicinity to block off the port's entrance.

On December 16 a mass meeting of local citizens took place in Old South Church. The Adams faction sent a messenger to the governor with a very clear message: remove the tea ships or else. Hutchinson refused again. Late in the day, Adams appeared before the huge gathering and reportedly shouted: "This meeting can do no more to save the country." The moment for crowd action had been proclaimed. Several dozen artisans, apprentices, and day laborers, led by Ebenezer Mackintosh, went to the docks disguised as Indians. They jumped onto the tea ships and dumped 342 chests of tea valued at £10,000 into the harbor. It took nearly three hours to complete the work of the Boston Tea Party.

Tea confrontations occurred later in other ports, but none so destructively as in Boston. Philadelphians used the threat of tar and feathers to convince local officials to send back the first tea ships to arrive there. The governor of South Carolina managed to get the tea landed, but the company product lay rotting in a warehouse and was never sold. New Yorkers had to wait until the spring of 1774 for tea ships to appear in their port. They jeered loudly at the docks, and an intelligent sea captain raised anchor and fled for the high seas. Once again, then, the Bostonians stood out for their bold defiance of imperial law.

Parliament Adopts the Coercive Acts

The Boston Tea Party shocked Lord North and other British officials. North decided that the "rebellious" Bostonians simply had to be taught a lesson, and Parliament adopted a series of legislative bills, collectively known as the Coercive Acts. Although the home government directed these laws against Massachusetts, the Coercive Acts held implications for colonists elsewhere who believed that the tyrannical parent nation was only using the Tea Party as a pretext for the final destruction of American liberties.

King George III signed the first act, known as the Boston Port Bill, into law at the end of March 1774. This act closed the port of Boston, making trade illegal until such time as local citizens paid for the tea. In May Parliament adopted the Massachusetts Government Act. This bill suspended the colony's royal charter, vastly expanded the powers of the royal governor, abolished the elective council (upper house of the General Court), and replaced that body with appointed councilors of the Crown's choosing. Town meetings could only be held with the governor's permission, except for annual spring election gatherings.

As matters turned out, Governor Hutchinson never exercised this vastly expanded authority. Dismayed by the Tea Party, he asked for a leave of absence and went to England. The Crown replaced him with General Thomas Gage, Britain's North American military commander, who held the governorship until the final disruption of royal government in the Bay Colony.

Another bill, the Administration of Justice Act, provided greater protection for customs collectors and other imperial officials in Massachusetts. If they injured or killed anyone while carrying out their duties, the governor had the right to move trials to some other colony or to England. The assumption was that local juries were too biased to render fair judgments.

Finally, in early June 1774 Parliament sanctioned an amendment to the Quartering Act of 1765. The earlier law had outlined procedures relating to the provision of housing for redcoats and had specifically excluded the use of private dwellings of any kind. The 1774 amendment gave General Gage the power to billet his troops anywhere, including unoccupied private homes, so long as the army paid fair rental rates. Parliament passed this law because Gage was bringing several hundred troops to Boston with him.

The Quebec Act, also approved in June 1774, was seen by the colonists as another piece of coercive legislation. Actually, this bill mainly concerned itself with the territorial administration of Canada by providing for a royal governor and a large appointed advisory council, but no popularly elected assembly. Roman Catholicism was to remain the established religion for the French-speaking populace. In addition, the Ohio River was to become the new southwestern boundary of Quebec.

Ever-vigilant colonial leaders viewed the Quebec Act as confirming all the worst tendencies of imperial legislation over the past decade. Parliament had denied local representative government; it had ratified the establishment of a branch of the Christian faith that was repugnant to militantly Protestant Americans, especially New Englanders; and it had wiped out the claims of various colonial governments to millions of acres of western land, in this case all of the Ohio country. The latter decision particularly infuriated well-placed provincial land speculators, among them Benjamin Franklin and George Washington, who had fixed upon this region for future development and population expansion. The Quebec Act, thousands of Americans concluded, smacked of abject political slavery.

Even without the Quebec Act, Lord North had made a tactical error by encouraging Parliament to pass so much legislation. The Port Bill punishing Boston was one thing; some Americans felt that the Bostonians had gone too far and deserved some chastisement. The rest of the Coercive Acts, however, caused widespread concern because they seemed to violate the sanctity of local political institutions, to distort normal judicial procedures, and to favor military over civil authority. For most colonists the acts resulted in feelings of solidarity with the Bostonians, which was critical to mounting yet higher levels of unified resistance.

Hurling Back the Challenge: The First Continental Congress

News of the full array of Coercive Acts provoked an outburst of intercolonial activity, the most important expression of which was the calling of the First Continental Congress. This body assembled in Philadelphia on September 5, 1774, and gentlemen of all political persuasions were there (Georgia was the only colony not represented). Among the more radical delegates were Samuel Adams and his younger cousin John, as well as Patrick Henry. George Washington was present, mostly silent in debates but firmly committed to protecting fundamental liberties. More conservative delegates were also in attendance, such as Joseph Galloway of Pennsylvania and John Jay of New York. The central question facing all the delegates was how belligerent the Congress should be. The more cautious delegates wanted to find some means of settling differences with Britain, but the radicals believed that well-organized resistance could get King and Parliament to back down yet a third time.

Accounts of the work of the First Continental Congress make clear that Samuel Adams, Patrick Henry, and others of their more radical persuasion dominated the proceedings. Although they went along with the preparation of an elaborate petition to Parliament, known as the "The Declaration of Colonial Rights and Grievances," these experienced molders of the colonial protest movement demanded much more. They drew upon the weapons of resistance that had caused Parliament to retreat before and, just in case they could not convince Parliament to repeal the Coercive Acts, they argued that Americans should begin to prepare for war.

To assure that Congress moved in the right direction, Samuel Adams and his political allies back in Massachusetts had done some careful planning. Their efforts came to light on September 9, 1774, when a convention of citizens in Suffolk County (Boston and environs) adopted a series of resolutions written by Dr. Joseph Warren, a close political associate of Adams. Once approved, Paul Revere, talented silversmith and active member of Adams's popular rights faction, mounted his horse and rode hard for Philadelphia. Revere arrived in mid-September and laid the Suffolk Resolves before Congress. Not only did these statements strongly profess American rights, but they also called for a complete economic boycott and the rigorous training of local militia companies, just in case it became necessary to defend lives, liberty, and property against the redcoats led by Thomas Gage.

Congress approved the Suffolk Resolves—and with them the initial step in organization for possible military confrontation. The delegates also committed themselves to a comprehensive plan of economic boycott, which came to be called the Continental Association. The association called for the nonimportation and nonconsumption of British goods, to be phased in over the next few months, as well as the nonexportation of colonial products if Parliament did not retreat within a year.

The association also urged every American community to establish a local committee of observation and inspection charged with having all citizens subscribe to the boycott. In reality, the association was a loyalty test. Citizens who refused to sign were about to become outcasts from the cause of liberty. The term of derision applied to them was *tory;* however, they thought of themselves as *loyalists*—maintaining their allegiance to the Crown.

The only attempt at conciliation during the first Congress came from Joseph Galloway, a wealthy Philadelphia lawyer who had long served as Pennsylvania's speaker of the house. Galloway desperately wanted to maintain imperial ties because he feared what the "common sort" of citizens might do if that attachment was irrevocably severed. Galloway drew on the Albany Plan of Union of 1754 and proposed a central government based in America that would be superior to the provincial assemblies.

Galloway's Plan of Union represented a structural alternative allowing Americans a greater voice in imperial decision making affecting the colonies, and it foreshadowed the future commonwealth organization of the British empire. But the more radical delegates called the proposal impractical and belittled it as an idea that would divert everyone from the task of the moment, which was to get Parliament to rescind the Coercive Acts.

Later, at the urging of the radicals, all references to Galloway's plan were expunged from the official minutes of Congress in favor of displaying American unity to King and Parliament. As for Galloway, he faced growing harassment as a loyalist in the months ahead and eventually fled to the British army for protection.

When the First Continental Congress ended its deliberations in late October 1774, its program was one of continued defiance, certainly not conciliation or submission. The delegates understood the course they had chosen. One of their last acts was to call for the Second Continental Congress, to convene in Philadelphia on May 10, 1775, "unless the redress of grievances, which we have desired, be obtained before that time."

As autumn 1774 gave way to another cold winter, Americans awaited the verdict of King and Parliament. Local committees of observation and inspection were busily at work encouraging—and in some cases coercing—the populace to boycott British trade goods. Local militia companies were vigorously training. Even as they prepared for war, colonists everywhere waited anxiously for the reaction of King George III, Lord

*C*hronology of Key Events

1760	George III becomes king of England
1763	Treaty of Paris ends the Seven Years' War; Pontiac leads an unsuccessful rebellion on the western frontier; Proclamation of 1763 forbids white settlement west of the Appalachian Mountains
1764	Sugar Act; Currency Act prohibits colonial governments from issuing paper money
1765	Quartering Act; Stamp Act; Stamp Act Congress
1766	Parliament repeals the Stamp Act; Declaratory Act asserts Parliament's authority to tax the colonies
1767	Townsend duties Act imposes taxes on imported glass, lead, paint, paper, and tea
1768	British troops sent to Boston
1770	Boston Massacre
1772	British naval vessel *Gaspée* burned in Rhode Island
1773	Tea Act allows East India Company to sell tea directly to American retailers; Boston Boston Tea Party ensues
1774	Coercive Acts close port of Boston; Quebec Act extends boundaries of Quebec to Mississippi and Ohio rivers; First Continental Congress in Philadelphia protests Parliamentary legislation

North, and Parliament. They would soon learn that Britain's leaders had dismissed the work of the First Continental Congress, having concluded that the parent nation could not retreat a third time.

Conclusion

In September 1774 Lord North observed: "The die is now cast, the colonies must either submit or triumph." The once harmonious relations between Britain and America had become increasingly discordant between 1763 and the end of 1774. The colonists refused to accept undesirable imperial acts, and they successfully resisted such taxation plans as the Stamp Act and the Townshend duties. In the process they came to believe firmly that ministerial leaders in England were engaging in a deep-seated plot to deprive them of their fundamental liberties. When something as inconsequential as the Townshend duty on tea precipitated yet another crisis in 1773, neither side was willing to back down. By early 1775 both sides had decided to show their resolve.

A small incident that well illustrates the deteriorating situation occurred in Boston during March 1774. At the state funeral of Andrew Oliver, the Bay Colony's most recent lieutenant governor and former stamp distributor-designate, a large gathering of ordinary citizens came out to watch the solemn procession. As Oliver's coffin was slowly lowered into the ground, these Bostonians, many of them veterans of the American resistance movement, suddenly burst into loud cheers.

Such an open expression of bad will epitomized the acute strain in British-American relations. It was almost as if the cheers were for the burial of imperial authority in America. Certainly these colonists demonstrated contempt, not pride, in their British citizenship that day. Such striking changes in attitudes, over just a few years, pointed toward the fateful clash of arms known as the War for American Independence.

Suggestions for Further Reading

Overviews of the revolutionary period include Merrill Jensen, *The Founding of a Nation, 1763–1776* (1968); James Kirby Martin, *In the Course of Human Events* (1979); Edmund S. Morgan, *The Birth of the Republic*, rev. ed. (1977); Gordon S. Wood, *The Radicalism of the American Revolution* (1992); and Esmond Wright, *Fabric of Freedom, 1763–1800*, rev. ed. (1978).

For studies of the causes of the revolution consult Bernard Bailyn, *The Ideological Origins of the American Revolution* (1967); Robert A. Becker, *Revolution, Reform, and the Politics of American Taxation, 1763–1783* (1980); Michael Kammen, *A Rope of Sand: Colonial Agents, British Politics, and the Revolution* (1968); Dirk Hoerder, *Crowd Action in Revolutionary Massachusetts* (1977); Pauline R. Maier, *From Resistance to Revolution* (1972); James Kirby Martin, *Men in Rebellion* (1973); Edmund S. and Helen M. Morgan, *The Stamp Act Crisis,* rev. ed. (1962); Gary B. Nash, *The Urban Crucible* (1979). Other valuable works include David Ammerman, *In the Common Cause: American Response to the Coercive Acts* (1974); Benjamin W. Labaree, *The Boston Tea Party* (1964).

Useful biographies of the period include Bernard Bailyn, *The Ordeal of Thomas Hutchinson* (1974); Richard R. Beeman, *Patrick Henry* (1974); John Ferling, *The First of Men: George Washington* (1988), and *John Adams* (1992); John C. Miller, *Sam Adams: Pioneer in Propaganda* (1936).

Chapter 5

The Times That Tried Many Souls, 1775–1783

Joseph Plumb Martin was a dedicated patriot soldier, one of 11,000 men and women who formed the backbone of General George Washington's Continental forces. When that army entered its Valley Forge winter campsite in December 1777, Martin recorded despondently that the soldiers' trail could "be tracked by their blood upon the rough frozen ground." The Continentals were "now in a truly forlorn condition,—no clothing, no provisions, and as disheartened as need be."

While the British army enjoyed far more comfortable quarters in Philadelphia only 20 miles away, Washington's troops constructed miserable shanties to protect them from the bitterly cold weather. Making matters more difficult was the lack of food and clothing. Martin claimed that, upon first entering Valley Forge, he went a full day and two nights without anything to eat, "save half a small pumpkin, which I cooked by placing it upon a rock, the skin side uppermost, and making fire upon it." His comrades fared no better. Within two days of moving into Valley Forge, a common grumble could be heard everywhere: "No Meat! No Meat!" By the first of January the words had become more ominous: "No bread, no soldier!"

Thus began a tragic winter of desperation for Washington's Continentals. Some 2,500 soldiers, or nearly one-fourth of the troops, perished before the army broke camp in June 1778. They died from exposure to the elements, malnutrition, and such virulent diseases as typhus and smallpox. It was not uncommon for soldiers to languish for days in their rudely constructed huts because they were too weak to drill or to go on food-hunting expeditions. Sometimes for lack of straw and blankets, they simply froze to death in their beds. To add to the woes of the camp, more than 500 of the army's horses starved to death that winter. It was impossible to bury their carcasses in the frozen ground, which only magnified the deplorable sanitation conditions and the consequent spread of disease. Under such forsaken circumstances, hundreds of soldiers deserted.

The extreme suffering at Valley Forge has usually been attributed to the severe weather and a complete breakdown of the army's supply system. In fact, weather conditions were no worse than in other years. Certainly a major reason for the deprivation at Valley Forge was widespread indifference toward an army made up of the poor, the expendable, and the unfree in American society.

Joseph Plumb Martin clearly thought this was the case. He was a young man from Connecticut, without material resources, who had first enlisted during 1776 at the very peak of patriot enthusiasm for the war. He soon learned that there were few glories in soldiering. Camp life was both dull and dangerous, given the many killer diseases that ravaged armies of the era, and battle was a frightening experience. He did not

George Washington led a bedraggled, half-starved army of 11,000 men and women into Valley Forge in December 1777.

renew his enlistment and returned to Connecticut. For a poor, landless person, economic prospects at home were not much better than serving for promises of regular pay in the Continental army. In 1777 Martin stepped forth again and agreed to enlist as a substitute.

Martin's experiences typified those of so many others who performed long-term Continental service on behalf of the cause of liberty. After an initial rush to arms in defiance of British authority in 1775, the harsh realities of military life and pitched battles dampened patriot enthusiasm to the point that by December 1776 the Continental Army all but ceased to exist. Washington's major task became that of securing enough troop strength and material support to shape an army capable of standing up time after time to British forces.

The commander-in-chief found his long-term soldiers among the poor and deprived groups of revolutionary America. Major European nations like France, Spain, and Holland eventually came to the rescue with additional troops, supplies, and vital financial support. Working together, even in the face of so much popular indifference, these allies-in-arms outlasted the mighty land and sea forces of Great Britain, making possible a generous peace settlement in 1783 that guaranteed independence for the group of former British colonies that now called themselves the 13 United States.

Reconciliation or Independence

Crown officials in England gave scant attention to the acts of the First Continental Congress because they believed that the time had come to teach the American provincials a military lesson. George III explained why. The colonists, he asserted, "have boldly thrown off the mask and avowed nothing less than a total independence of the British legislature will satisfy them." This was an inaccurate perception, but it lay behind the decision to turn the most powerful military machine in the western world, based on its record in recent wars, against the troublemakers in America and to crush resistance to British authority once and for all.

The Shooting War Starts

During the winter of 1774–1775 the king's ministers prepared for what they thought would be nothing more than a brief demonstration of military force. General Gage received "secret" orders to employ the redcoats under his command to arrest the ringleaders of rebellion; however, if the likes of Samuel Adams, John Hancock, and Joseph Warren could not be captured, then Gage was to use any methods he deemed appropriate to put an end to unrest in Massachusetts.

During February 1775 the King and Parliament authorized funds for a larger force of regular troops in America and named three high-ranking generals—William Howe, Henry Clinton, and John Burgoyne—to sail to Boston and join Gage. They also declared Massachusetts to be in a state of rebellion, which permitted redcoats to shoot down suspected rebels on sight, should that be necessary to quell opposition. Eventually this act would be applied to all 13 provinces.

General Gage received the ministry's secret orders in mid-April 1775. Being on the scene, he was not quite as convinced as his superiors about American martial weakness. Gage had repeatedly urged caution in his reports to home officials, but now there was no choice; he had to act. Because some rebel leaders had already fled to the countryside, Gage decided to send a column of regulars to Concord, a town about 20 miles northwest of Boston that also served as a storage point for patriot military supplies. Once there, the troops were to seize or destroy as much weaponry and ammunition as possible. Gage hoped this maneuver could be effected without bloodshed, fearing full-scale warfare would follow if patriot lives were lost.

At dawn on April 19, 700 British troops under Lieutenant Colonel Francis Smith passed through Lexington, five miles east of Concord. Here they encountered 70 militiamen lined up across the village green. Obviously outnumbered, the Minutemen—so-called because they had been trained to respond at a moment's notice—were not there to exchange shots, but to warn the regulars against trespassing on the property of free-born British subjects. As the redcoats came closer, a mysterious shot rang out, causing British troops to level their arms and fire. Before order was restored, eight colonists had died in what was the opening volley of the War for American Independence.

The redcoats regrouped and continued their march to Concord. Once there, a detachment moved out to cross the Old North Bridge in search of weapons and gunpowder, but was repulsed by rallying militiamen. Lieutenant Colonel Smith began to fear that his column might be cut off by onrushing citizen-soldiers, so he ordered a retreat. The rest of the day turned into a rout as an aroused citizenry fired away at the British from behind trees and stone walls. Final casualty figures showed 273 redcoats dead or wounded, as compared to 95 colonists. Lexington and Concord were clear blows to the notion of the invincibility of British arms and suggested that American citizens, when defending their own property, could and would hold their own against better-trained British soldiers.

As word of the bloodshed spread, New Englanders rallied to the patriot banner. Within days thousands of colonists poured into hastily assembled military camps surrounding Boston. Thomas Gage and his soldiers were now trapped, and they could only hope that promised reinforcements would soon reach them.

Most colonists believed that it would be only a matter of weeks before the ministry regained its senses and restored all American rights. They did not realize that Crown leaders were irrevocably committed to eradicating all colonial resistance, or that the conflict would become a long and grueling full-scale war in which the fortitude to endure would determine the eventual winner.

Moderates Versus Radicals in Congress

The shadow of Lexington and Concord loomed heavily as the Second Continental Congress convened in Philadelphia in May 1775. Despite the recent bloodshed, very few delegates had become advocates of independence. New Englanders like Samuel and John Adams were leaning that way, but the majority held out hope for a resolution of differences. By the summer of 1775 two factions had emerged in Congress: the one led by New Englanders, favoring a formal declaration of independence, and the opposing moderate faction, whose strength lay in the Middle Colonies and whose most influential leader was John Dickinson of Pennsylvania.

The two factions debated every issue with regard to possible effects on the subject of independence. The moderates remained the dominant faction into the spring of 1776, but then the weight of the spreading rebellion swung the pendulum decisively toward those favoring independence.

Early congressional wrangling centered on the organization of a Continental army. In mid-June 1775 the delegates, at the urging of the New Englanders, voted to adopt the patriot forces around Boston as a Continental military establishment. They asked the other colonies to supply additional troops and unanimously named wealthy Virginia planter George Washington to serve as commander-in-chief. Washington did have qualifications for the job, including his combat experiences during the French and Indian War. Also, he was a southerner. His presence at the head of the army was a way to involve the other colonies, at least symbolically, in what was still a localized war being fought by New Englanders.

Congressional moderates were persons caught in a bind. Although deeply concerned about American rights, they also feared independence. Like many other colonists of substantial wealth, they envisioned internal chaos in the colonies without the stabilizing influence of British rule. They also doubted whether a weak, independent American nation could long survive among aggressive European powers.

The moderates thus tried to keep open the channels of communication with the British government. Characteristic of such attempts was John Dickinson's "Olive Branch" petition, approved by Congress in July 1775. This document implored George III to intercede with Parliament and find some means to preserve English liberties in America. Like other petitions before it, the "Olive Branch" had little impact in Britain. By the autumn of 1775 the home government was already mobilizing for full-scale war.

The Expanding Martial Conflict

No matter what they tried, congressional moderates accomplished little, except in delaying a declaration of independence. The rebellion kept spreading, making a formal renunciation of British allegiance seem almost anticlimactic. On May 10, 1775, for example, citizen-soldiers seized the once-mighty fortress of Ticonderoga at the southern end of Lake Champlain. This action netted the Americans more than 100 serviceable artillery pieces that would eventually be deployed to help drive British forces from Boston.

In an effort to lure Canada into the rebellion—many hoped that Quebec Province would become the fourteenth colony—Congress approved a two-pronged invasion in the late summer of 1775. One column under General Richard Montgomery traveled down Lake Champlain and seized Montreal. The second column under Colonel Benedict Arnold proceeded on a harrowing march through the woods of Maine and finally emerged before the walls of Quebec City. On the morning of December 31, 1775, combined forces under these two commanders boldly tried to take the city but were repulsed. Montgomery lost his life, Arnold was seriously wounded, and great numbers of patriot troops were killed or captured. The rebel attempt to seize Canada had failed. This aggressive effort, however, made it increasingly difficult to argue that the colonists were only interested in defending their homes and families until political differences with Britain could be resolved.

Back in Boston, meanwhile, General Gage resumed the offensive against the New Englanders. That opportunity came on June 17, 1775, in an attack on rebel fortifications on Breed's Hill, north of Boston. As citizens watched the misnamed Battle of Bunker Hill from rooftops, the British made three separate charges, finally dislodging the patriots, who were running out of ammunition. It was the bloodiest engagement of the whole war. The British suffered 1,054 casualties—40 percent of the redcoats engaged. American casualties amounted to 411, or 30 percent.

The realization that patriot soldiers had been driven from the field undermined the euphoria that followed the rout of the redcoats at Lexington and Concord. Still, the British gained little advantage because they had failed to pursue the fleeing rebels. They remained trapped in Boston, surrounded by thousands of armed and angry colonists.

Lord Dunmore's Proclamation of Emancipation

New England and Canada did not long remain the only theaters of war. Before the end of 1775 fighting erupted in the South. In Virginia the protagonist was John Murray, Lord Dunmore, the last royal governor of the Old Dominion. In May 1774 Dunmore had dissolved the Assembly because the burgesses had called for a day of fasting and prayer in support of the Bostonians. Incensed at Dunmore's arbitrary action, Virginia's gentleman-planters started meeting in provincial conventions, acting as if royal authority no longer existed.

Dunmore resented such impudence. In June 1775 he fled Williamsburg and announced that British subjects still loyal to the Crown should join him in bringing the planter elite to its senses. Very few citizens came forward. By autumn Dunmore had concluded that planter resistance could only be broken by turning slaves against masters. On November 7, 1775, he issued an emancipation proclamation.

Dunmore hoped that Virginia's slaves would break their chains and join with him, but the plan backfired. Irate planters suppressed copies of the proclamation and spread the rumor of a royal hoax designed to lure blacks into Dunmore's camp so that he could sell them to the owners of West Indian sugar plantations. As many as 2,000 slaves took their chances and escaped to the royal standard. They became a part of Dunmore's "Ethiopian" regiment, which made the mistake of engaging Virginia militiamen in a battle at Great Bridge in December 1775. Having had no time for even the fundamentals of military training, the regiment took a drubbing. This battle ended any semblance of royal authority in Virginia. Dunmore and his followers soon retreated to a flotilla of vessels in Chesapeake Bay, and in the summer of 1776 they sailed away, leaving behind a planter class that closely guarded its human property while demanding independence from those in Britain whom it denounced as tyrants.

Resolving the Independence Question

Lord Dunmore's experiences highlighted the collapse of British political authority. Beginning in the summer of 1775, colony after colony witnessed an end to royal government. During that same summer Massachusetts moved one step further by asking the Continental Congress for permission to establish a more enduring government based on a written constitution. After ousting its royal governor, New Hampshire followed suit. These requests forced Congress to act. The delegates did so in early November, stating that the colonies might adopt "such a form of government, as . . . will best produce the happiness of the people," but only until the present dispute with Great Britain was settled.

The moderates in Congress realized that new state governments, as much if not more than a separate army, had the appearance of de facto independence. They did everything they could to prevent a total rejection of British political authority in America. Provincial assemblies in Pennsylvania, New York, Delaware, Maryland, and South Carolina also continued to balk at an irrevocable split with the mother country. Thus there was to be no resolution of the independence question before 1776.

But events were about to overwhelm the moderates. In January 1776 Thomas Paine, a recent migrant from England, published a pamphlet entitled *Common Sense,* which became an instant best-seller. In forceful language, *Common Sense* communicated a sense of urgency about moving toward independence, and it attacked congressional moderates for not being bold enough to break with the past.

Paine likewise denounced the British monarchy. He wrote: "The folly of hereditary right in Kings, is that nature disapproves it . . . by giving mankind *an ass for a lion."* *Common Sense* put severe pressure on the moderates, but they held on doggedly, hoping against hope that Great Britain would turn from its belligerent course and begin serious negotiations with Congress.

At the end of February 1776 a short, bloody battle between loyalists and patriot militia at Moore's Creek Bridge in North Carolina ended in a rout of local tories (a term of derision for those who maintained their allegiance to the Crown). North Carolina's provincial congress reversed orders to its congressional delegates and allowed them to discuss independence and vote on a plan of national government. Soon thereafter the Virginians, furious about Lord Dunmore's activities, issued similar instructions. Then leaders in Rhode Island, impatient with everyone else, boldly declared their own independence in early May. The moderates were rapidly losing their ability to block resolution of the independence question.

On June 7, 1776, Richard Henry Lee of Virginia, urging independence, presented formal resolutions to Congress which called for the creation of a national government and the formation of alliances with foreign nations in support of the war effort. Within a few days Congress established two committees, one headed by John Dickinson to produce a plan of central government and another to prepare a statement on independence. Thomas Jefferson, a tall, young, red-haired Virginian, agreed to write a draft text on independence, which the committee laid before Congress on Friday, June 28.

On Monday, July 1, John Dickinson spoke forcefully against a formal severance of ties with Great Britain. The delegates listened politely, but Dickinson was no longer in step with the mood of Congress. The next day, July 2, 12 states voted in favor of Lee's resolutions, thus technically declaring independence (New York abstained, having not yet received instructions from leaders back home).

Congress next turned to the consideration of Jefferson's draft, which one delegate in a classic understatement called "a pretty good one." The delegates made only a few changes. They deleted a controversial statement blaming the slave trade on the king as well as words repudiating friendship with the British people. By Thursday evening, July 4, 1776, everything was in place, and Congress quickly adopted Jefferson's document, a masterful explanation of the reasons why the colonists were seeking independence.

The Declaration of Independence proclaimed to the world that Americans had been terribly mistreated by the parent nation. Indeed, much of the text represents a summary list of grievances, ranging from

The Declaration of Independence came before Congress for debate on July 1,
1776, and was pronounced publicly on July 4.

misuse of a standing army and the abuse of the rights of colonial assemblies to starting an unjustified war against loyal subjects. The Declaration
also blamed George III who, by failing to control his ministers, had abandoned his role as a true servant of the people.

Much more than a list of grievances, the Declaration also gave the
revolution a clear and noble purpose. Since "all men are created equal"
and have "certain unalienable rights," which Jefferson defined as "life, liberty, and the pursuit of happiness," Americans needed to dedicate themselves to the establishment of a whole new set of political relationships
guaranteeing all citizens fundamental liberties. The great task facing the
revolutionary generation would be to institute republican forms of government, based on the rule of law and human reason.

Through Jefferson's words, the patriots of 1776 committed themselves to uplifting humanity in a world overrun by greed and petty human
ambition. None of these ideals was going to be realized, however, unless
the means could be found to defeat the huge British military force arriving in America at the very time that Congress was debating and approving
the Declaration of Independence.

Without Visible Allies: The War in the North

British officials had made a great blunder in 1775. Thinking of the colonists as "a set of upstart vagabonds, the dregs and scorn of the human species," they had woefully underestimated their opponent. Lexington and Concord drove home this reality. Although British leaders and generals continued to presume their superiority, they became far more serious about planning for the war. It was now clear that snuffing out the rebellion was a complex military assignment, given the sheer geographic size of the colonies and the absence of a strategically vital center, such as a national capital, which, if captured, would end the war. It was also clear that the use of an invading army was not the easiest way to regain the political allegiance of a people no longer placing such high value on being British subjects.

Britain's Massive Military Buildup

Directing the imperial war effort were King George, Lord North, and Lord George Germain, who became the American Secretary in 1775. Germain proved to be a surprisingly effective administrator and adept at working within England's complicated and inefficient military bureaucracy. His skills became evident in planning for the campaign of 1776—the largest land and sea offensive executed by any western nation until the Allied invasion of North Africa in 1942.

Step by step, Germain pulled the elements together. Of utmost importance was overall campaign strategy. It involved concentrating as many troops as possible on the port of New York, where great numbers of loyalists lived, then subduing the surrounding countryside as a food and supply base. Loyalists would be used to reinstitute royal government, and the king's forces would engage and destroy the rebel army. Germain believed that the American will to resist had to be shattered, and he hoped that it would take only one campaign season. The longer the rebels lasted, he argued, the greater would be their prospects for success.

Next came the matter of assembling the military forces. With the middle classes exempt from service because they were considered productive members of society, the rank and file were drawn from two sources. First, there were poorer, less productive citizens in the British Isles who would be recruited or dragooned into service. Since life in European armies was often brutal, it was not always possible to convince or coerce even the most destitute of subjects to sign enlistment papers. To ensure adequate troop strength, George III and his advisers turned to a second source, the principalities of Germany. Before the end of the war, six German states procured 30,000 soldiers, more than half from Hesse-Cassel, where the local head of state received direct cash payments from the British Crown for each soldier that he supplied. Hessians and downtrodden Britons, including many Irish subjects, thus made up the king's army.

Certainly as significant a matter as troop recruitment was military leadership. Viewing General Gage as too timid and too respectful of Americans, the king recalled him in October 1775 and named William Howe to replace him as overall commander-in-chief. William's brother Richard, Admiral Lord Howe, took charge of the naval flotilla that would carry thousands of troops to America.

Neither of the Howe brothers turned out to be hard-hitting military commanders. Politically, they identified with whig leaders in England who believed that the Americans had some legitimate grievances. They intended to move in careful steps, using the presence of so many well-trained regulars to persuade Americans to sign loyalty oaths and renounce the rebellion. In failing to achieve the strategic goal of wiping out patriot resistance in only one campaign season, the Howe brothers helped save the patriot cause from early extinction.

The Campaign for New York

Not yet aware of the scale of British mobilization, New Englanders cheered loudly in mid-March 1776 when General Howe took redcoats and loyalists in tow and fled by sea to Halifax, Nova Scotia. British control of Boston had become untenable because General Washington placed the cannons captured at Ticonderoga on Dorchester Heights overlooking the city. Howe's choice was to retreat or be bombarded into submission.

At the end of June Howe returned, sailing from Halifax to Staten Island, across the bay from Manhattan, with 10,000 soldiers. During July, even as Americans excitedly read their Declaration of Independence, more and more British troops appeared, another 20,000 by mid-August. Including seamen under Admiral Howe's command, the British had some 43,000 well-supplied, well-trained, and well-armed combatants. By comparison, George Washington had 28,000 troops on his muster rolls, but only 19,000 present and fit for duty. To make matters worse, the bulk of his army lacked good weapons or supplies and was deficient in training and discipline.

The decision to defend New York, which the Continental Congress insisted upon and to which Washington acceded, was one of the great rebel blunders of the war. Completely outnumbered, the American commander unwisely divided his soldiers between Manhattan and Brooklyn

Heights on Long Island. They took a severe beating in defending Brooklyn Heights, but Lord Howe allowed them to escape across the East River. Learning from this mistake, Washington would never place his troops in so potentially disastrous a position again.

The Howe brothers moved along indecisively through the rest of the campaign season. Every time they had the advantage, they failed to destroy the rebel army. Washington retreated into New Jersey, and by early December what remained of his army had crossed the Delaware River into Pennsylvania.

Saving the Cause at Trenton

Increasingly dispirited, hundreds of half-starving, battle-wearied patriot troops deserted. Others, ravaged by disease or wounded in battle, were left along the way with the hope of receiving decent treatment from their pursuers. Having virtually destroyed his prey, William Howe ordered his troops into winter camps and returned to New York City. He ignored his charge to end the rebellion in one campaign season, fully satisfied that mopping-up operations could be easily conducted in the spring of 1777.

George Washington assessed his desperate position and decided upon a bold counterstroke. The success of this maneuver might save his army; defeat would surely ruin it. With muster rolls showing only 6,000 troops, he divided his soldiers into three groups and tried to recross the icy Delaware River on Christmas evening. Their targets were British outposts in New Jersey. Of the three contingents, only Washington's near-frozen band of 2,400 soldiers accomplished this daring maneuver.

At dawn they reached Trenton, capturing almost 1,000 unsuspecting Hessians, who were still groggy with liquor from their Christmas celebration. Within another few days the elated Americans again outdueled British units at Princeton. In these two engagements Washington had done much more than just regain lost ground. He had saved the Continental Army from virtual extinction. Never again during the war would the British come so close to total victory—and all because of a failure to annihilate Washington's shattered forces when the opportunity was there. William Howe never seemed to understand this mistake. He relaxed in his winter quarters in New York and gloried in the knighthood awarded him for his victory at Brooklyn Heights.

Another error British military commanders committed was their unwillingness to make use of the king's friends in America. An estimated 20 percent of the populace, these loyal subjects stood ready to fight the rebels to assure a continuation of British rule. Before the war was over an estimated 50,000 loyalists enlisted, but royal commanders did not really take advantage of them. The official attitude seemed to be that loyalists were just colonists, a part of the "rude" American rabble.

On the rebel side, the Trenton and Princeton victories did not result in a revived outpouring of popular support for Washington's army. Thomas Paine begged the populace to rally at this moment of deep despair. "These are the times that try men's souls," Paine stated forcefully. "The summer soldier and the sunshine patriot will, in this crisis, shrink from the service of his country; but he that stands it now, deserves the love and thanks of man and woman."

The Real Continentals

One of the greatest problems facing Washington and the Continental Congress after 1776 was sustaining the rebel army's troop strength. In May 1777 the commander-in-chief only had 10,000 soldiers, of which 7,363 were present and fit for duty. This number increased substantially during the summer and fall, although only an estimated 11,000 Continentals entered Valley Forge. For the remainder of the war Washington's core of regulars rarely was more sizable. At times, as few as 5,000 soldiers stood with him.

After 1776 the rank and file of the Continental Army came to be made up of economically hard-pressed and unfree citizens. The bulk of Washington's long-term Continentals were young (ranging in age from

Northern Theater of War, 1775–1778

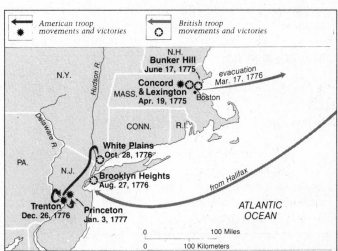

their early teens to mid-twenties), landless, and unskilled. Also well represented were indentured servants and slaves who stood as substitutes for their masters in return for guarantees of personal freedom at the war's end.

In 1777 Massachusetts became the first state to authorize the enlistment of blacks—both slaves and freemen. Rhode Island soon followed suit by raising two black regiments. Southern states were far more reluctant to allow slaves to substitute for their masters. Maryland and Virginia ultimately did so, which caused one patriot general to query why so many "sons of freedom" seemed so anxious "to trust their all to be defended by slaves." Add to these groups captured British soldiers and deserters, particularly Hessians and Irishmen, as well as tories and criminals who were often given a choice between military service or the gallows, and a composite portrait of the real Continental Army begins to emerge.

Eighteenth-century armies also accepted women in the ranks. Like their male counterparts, they were invariably living on the margins of society. These women must be differentiated from so-called camp followers—those who marched along with their husbands or were prostitutes. Women in service performed various functions, ranging from caring for the sick and wounded, cooking, and mending clothes to scavenging battlefields for clothing and equipment and burying the dead. On occasion they became directly involved in combat.

Whether male or female, a unifying characteristic of Washington's post-1776 Continentals was poverty and, in many cases, lack of personal freedom. In their social profile, they looked very much like their counterparts in the British army. As a group, they repeatedly risked their lives in return for promises of food, clothing, pay, and even land on which to make a decent living after the war. Their dreams of future prosperity depended upon the success of the rebellion, and that is one reason why they willingly endured, even though the far more prosperous civilian populace ignored their privation at such encampments as Valley Forge.

Rescuing the Patriots: Toward Global Conflict

The struggles of the American rebels did not go unobserved in European diplomatic circles. France and Spain, in particular, hoped that the rebellion would succeed. Territorial losses sustained during the Seven Years' War had swung the European balance of power decisively in Britain's favor. For France, post-1763 disagreements between Britain and America represented an opportunity to deflate the puffed-up British lion. Losing the colonies would weaken Britain immeasurably. French statesmen had little interest in fostering American political liberties. They hoped only to advance France's future while exacting revenge on an old and despised enemy.

France Offers Covert Assistance

Before 1775, the French sent spies to America to report on events, and when possible to help stir up ill will toward Britain. Once the war started, France provided covert assistance to the rebels while maintaining a public stance of disinterested neutrality. If the rebels demonstrated their long-term resolve and proved worthy in combat, then France would enter the war and help crush the British.

Secret French aid, which came in the form of cash subsidies and loans, strengthened the rebel cause immeasurably, thus helping the patriots to endure until the French government came out publicly against Great Britain. To promote American interests, the Continental Congress sent a three-person delegation to Paris which included Benjamin Franklin. Already well known among French intellectuals because of his electrical experiments, the aging Philadelphian became a popular celebrity. With his simple dress, witty personality, worldly charm, and shrewd mind, he embodied the ideals of republicanism. Working closely with the astute French foreign minister, the Comte de Vergennes, Franklin played his role well in helping secure a formal alliance with Britain's long-time enemy.

The British Seize Philadelphia

The home government's plan for 1777 was to send an army under "Gentleman Johnny" Burgoyne south from Canada through the Lake Champlain corridor. In turn, Howe was to move troops up the Hudson River, eventually linking with Burgoyne at Albany. Called the Hudson Highlands strategy, the goal was to cut off New England from the rest of the colonies before sweeping eastward to reconquer the very region that had been the seedbed of rebellion.

Sir William Howe, however, had ideas of his own about campaign strategy. He favored going after and destroying the main Continental Army. During June 1777 he tried to lure Washington into a major battle in New Jersey, but the American commander refused the bait. At this juncture Howe made a decision that may have cost Britain the war. All but abandoning the primary campaign goal of joining up with Burgoyne, he resolved to seize Philadelphia, hoping at the same time to catch and crush Washington's Continentals as they moved into eastern Pennsylvania to protect the rebel capital.

On September 11 the British mauled the Continentals at Brandywine Creek, southwest of Philadelphia, but the engagement did not destroy the rebel army. Within another two weeks Sir William proudly led his troops into Philadelphia; yet except for the establishment of comfortable winter quarters, the British commander had accomplished nothing of consequence. Although another patriot attack on British troops at Germantown on October 4 ended in failure, the Continental Congress had already moved westward to York, Pennsylvania. Howe's capture of the rebel's capital had been a hollow quest—and had cost the British dearly.

Capturing Burgoyne's Army at Saratoga

The 1777 British descent from Canada had been planned carefully, at least on paper. The army of General Burgoyne, strengthened by hundreds of Indians who had joined the British to put an end to colonial settlers' seizure of tribal lands, moved southward in mid-June. The main column of nearly 8,000 pushed into Lake Champlain and drove the rebels from Fort Ticonderoga in early July. A second column of 1,700 under Colonel Barry St. Leger proceeded up the St. Lawrence River and onto Lake Ontario, before sweeping south toward Fort Schuyler at the western end of the Mohawk Valley. St. Leger's troops were to act as a diversionary force. Soon they had 750 desperate rebel defenders of Fort Schuyler under siege. Seemingly, nothing could stop these two columns, which were to converge again in Albany.

After seizing Ticonderoga, Burgoyne became more tentative about his southward movement. Like William Howe in 1776, he did not take his colonial opponents seriously enough. The rebels blocked Burgoyne's path by cutting down trees, ripping up bridges, and moving boulders into fording points on streams. Soon the British advance had been slowed to less than a mile a day.

Meanwhile, St. Leger's diversionary force was running into trouble. Militiamen in the Mohawk Valley tried to break through to Fort Schuyler. On August 6, 1777, they clashed with St. Leger's loyalists and Indians at the bloody Battle of Oriskany. St. Leger's victory was only temporary. Upon hearing rumors of thousands of rebel soldiers moving rapidly toward Fort Schuyler, the Indians, satiated with the bloodshed at Oriskany, quickly broke camp and fled, leaving the British colonel no alternative but to retreat back into Canada.

Oriskany was the beginning of the end for the once-mighty Iroquois nation, whose tribes were now hopelessly divided and consuming each other in combat. When war chieftain Joseph Brant (Thayendanegea) of the Mohawks led numerous bloody frontier raids for the British, a Continental Army expedition under General John Sullivan marched into central New York during 1779 and destroyed every Iroquois village it came upon. After the war was over, the more aggressive Iroquois migrated north to Canada or west into the Ohio country, where they fought to keep out white frontiersmen; others, less militant, moved quietly onto reservations in western New York.

Burgoyne had now lost his diversionary force. He suffered yet another major setback on August 16 when New Hampshire militiamen overwhelmed some 900 Hessians who were out raiding for supplies near Bennington, Vermont. With little prospect of relief from New York City, Burgoyne's army was now all but entrapped some 30 miles north of Albany along the Hudson River. In two desperate battles (September 19 and October 7) the British force tried to find a way around the well-entrenched rebels, but the brilliant field generalship of Benedict Arnold inspired the Americans to victory. It was all over for Burgoyne, and at Saratoga he surrendered to General Horatio Gates on October 17, 1777.

Losing an army at Saratoga was an unnecessary disaster for Britain, caused primarily by William Howe's unwillingness to work in concert with Burgoyne and follow through on the Hudson Highlands strategy. The victory was a major triumph for the Americans. It convinced Vergennes that it was now safe for France to commit publicly to the rebel cause.

On February 6, 1778, the French government signed two treaties with the American commissioners. The Treaty of Amity and Commerce recognized American independence and encouraged the development of trading ties. The Treaty of Alliance established a military pact between the two allies should hostilities break out between France and Britain. On March 20 King Louis XVI formally greeted the American commissioners at court and announced that the new nation had gained France's diplomatic recognition. In June 1778 a naval battle in the English Channel between British and French warships resulted in formal declarations of war by both powers.

The World Turned Upside Down

When George Washington learned about the French alliance in May 1778, he declared a holiday for "rejoicing throughout the whole army." There was much to celebrate. The Americans had survived the winter, and they had also benefited from the rigorous field training of Baron Friedrich von Steuben, a pretended Prussian nobleman who had volunteered to teach the soldiery how to fight in a more disciplined fashion. With the announcement of open, direct aid from France, which would include land troops and naval reinforcements, the prospects for actually beating the British now appeared considerably brighter.

Revamping British Strategy

The alliance with France changed the fundamental character of the War for Independence. British officials realized that they were no longer just contending with upstart rebels in America. They were getting themselves ensnared in a world war. France, with its well-trained army and highly mobile navy, had the ability to strike British territories anytime and anywhere it chose. The British military problem became even more complex in 1779 when Spain joined the war, hoping to regain the Rock of Gibraltar. Then in late 1780 the British declared war on the Netherlands, partly so that they could capture the Dutch Caribbean island of St. Eustatius, a major source of war supplies for the American patriots.

The dawning reality of world war threatened the British empire with major territorial losses across the globe. One result was a redesigned war plan—the Southern strategy—for reconquering the rebellious American provinces. The assumption was that His Majesty's troops could no longer be massed against the American rebels; instead, they would have to be dispersed to threatened points, such as islands in the West Indies, and later Gibraltar.

The first step came in May 1778 when General Sir Henry Clinton, who had taken over as North American commander from a discredited William Howe, received orders to evacuate Philadelphia. In June Clinton's troops retreated to New York City, narrowly averting a disastrous defeat by Washington's pursuing Continentals at Monmouth Court House (June 28) in central New Jersey. Clinton was to hang on as best he could at the main British base, but he would have to accept a reduction in forces for campaigning elsewhere. The process of dispersal began during the autumn of 1778. Clinton avoided major battles with Washington's army in the North while he slowly implemented the Southern strategy.

Lord George Germain mistakenly assumed that loyalists existed in far greater numbers in the South than they actually did. The idea was to employ bands of armed loyalists, who would operate in conjunction with a main redcoat army to subdue all rebels, beginning in Georgia and then moving in carefully planned steps northward. When any previously rebel-dominated region had been fully secured, royal government would be reintroduced. Ultimately, the whole South would be brought back into the British fold, opening the way for eventual subjugation of the North. The Southern strategy required patience as well as careful nurturing of loyalist sentiment. Both seemed possible when a detachment of 3,500 redcoats quickly reconquered Georgia in December 1778.

Until the French alliance, the South was a secondary theater of war, although there had been sporadic fighting between loyalists and rebel militia. White-Indian relations were bloodier. Both sides maneuvered for the favor of the most powerful Indian nations. In the summer of 1776 the Cherokees attacked frontier settlements from Virginia to South Carolina, killing settlers who had unwisely moved onto traditional tribal hunting grounds. They were soon beaten back with equal ferocity by North Carolina and Virginia militiamen. The Cherokees agreed to forswear further assistance to the British, and the other major tribes, seeing what had happened, took little part in events after 1778.

The most serious setback for the American cause in the South came in 1780 when Sir Henry Clinton led an expedition by sea against Charleston, South Carolina. There General Benjamin Lincoln, with just 3,000 Continental regulars and a smattering of militia, found himself completely outnumbered and trapped when part of Clinton's force moved inland and cut off escape routes. Facing prospects of extermination, Lincoln surrendered without much of a fight on May 12.

Clinton's victory at Charleston was a second major advance in the Southern strategy. The British commander sailed back to New York in high spirits, leaving behind Charles, Lord Cornwallis, to secure all of South Carolina. Clinton had ordered Cornwallis to move forward with care, making sure that loyalist partisans always had firm control of territory behind his advancing army. Ironically, Cornwallis was one of the few aggressive British generals in America. His desire to rush forward and get on with the fight helped undermine the Southern strategy.

At first, Cornwallis's boldness reaped dividends. After learning about the fall of Charleston, the Continental Congress ordered Horatio Gates, now known as the "hero of Saratoga," to proceed south and check Cornwallis. Gates botched the assignment completely. He gathered troops, mostly raw militiamen, in Virginia and North Carolina, then hastily rushed his soldiers into the British lair. Early on the morning of August 16, 1780, Cornwallis's force intercepted Gates's column near Camden, South Carolina. Not only did the American troops lack training, but bad provisions had made them ill. Cornwallis's army devastated the rebels in yet another crushing American defeat in the South.

The Tide of War Turns at Last

During 1780 everything seemed to go wrong for the patriot cause. Besides major setbacks in the South, officers and soldiers directly under Washington's command were increasingly restive about long-overdue wages and inadequate supplies. In July 1780 the officers threatened mass resignations unless Congress did something—and speedily. In September a frustrated Benedict Arnold switched his allegiance back to the British. By the end of the year Continental army troop strength fell below 6,000. Then, as the new year dawned, Washington faced successive mutinies among his hardened veterans in the Pennsylvania and New Jersey lines. The Continental Army seemed to be disintegrating.

Quite simply, it looked as if the British were winning the endurance contest of wills. At no time during the war, except for those dark days just before Washington's counterstrike at Trenton, had the rebel cause appeared more forlorn. What could not be seen was that British successes in the South moved the redcoats toward a far greater failure. Encouraged by its victories, General Cornwallis's army overreached itself. After Camden, Cornwallis started pushing toward North Carolina. His left wing under Major Patrick Ferguson, whose soldiers were mostly loyalists, repeatedly shot down or hanged patriots who fell in their path. Pursued by growing numbers of frontiersmen grimly determined to protect their homesteads and families, Ferguson fell back to Kings Mountain in northern South Carolina. He calculated that he and his 1,100 followers could withstand any assault from atop the promontory. On October 7, 1780, frontier militia units attacked from all sides. Ferguson fell mortally wounded; the rest of his column was killed, wounded, or captured; and the frontiersmen hanged nine of Ferguson's loyalists as a warning to others who might fight for the king.

His left wing destroyed, Cornwallis was unable to bring all of South Carolina under British control. Whenever royal troops moved to a new locale, rebel guerrilla bands under such leaders as "Swamp Fox" Francis Marion emerged from their hiding places and wreaked vengeance on tory sympathizers. Once again, the British had not effectively protected citizens favorably disposed toward them, which in combination with the debacle at Kings Mountain cut deeply into the reservoir of loyalist support available to Cornwallis.

Like his fellow officers, Cornwallis held Americans in contempt, believing that it was only a matter of time until superior British arms would destroy the rebels. However, he did not bargain on facing the likes of General Nathanael Greene, who replaced Gates as the Southern Department commander. When Greene arrived in North Carolina he found very few troops available for duty, while the "appearance" of those in camp, he stated despondently, "was wretched beyond description."

Greene was a military genius. Violating the military maxim of concentrating troop strength, he decided to divide his soldiers into three groups. One rebel column headed by General Daniel Morgan lured the British into a trap at Hannah's Cowpens in western South Carolina on January 17, 1781. Only 140 of the some 1,100 British soldiers escaped being killed, captured, or wounded. Meanwhile, Cornwallis relentlessly pursued Greene, who kept retreating before him. Finally, on March 15, 1781, the rebels squared off for battle at Guilford Courthouse in central North Carolina. Cornwallis gained a technical victory, but sustained heavy casualties; his troops were exhausted, and the rebels were still very much in the field.

Franco-American Triumph at Yorktown

Cornwallis retreated to the seacoast to rest his army, then decided to take over British raiding operations in Virginia, which had begun in January

Southern Theater of War, 1780–1781

1781 under turncoat Benedict Arnold. In storming northward, Cornwallis totally abandoned the Southern strategy. Nathanael Greene was now free to reassert full patriot authority in the states south of Virginia.

Back in New York, Sir Henry Clinton fumed. He wanted to discipline his subordinate but lacked the courage. Instead, he sent Cornwallis orders in July to establish a defensive base and to refrain from conducting any offensive operations. Reluctantly, Cornwallis selected Yorktown, with easy access to Chesapeake Bay.

At this juncture everything fell into place for the Americans. Upon learning that a French naval fleet would be making its way north from the West Indies, Washington, in concert with French troops under the Comte de Rochambeau, started marching his soldiers south, leaving only enough troops behind in New York to keep Clinton tied down. In early September the French fleet, after dueling with British warships, took control of Chesapeake Bay, thus sealing off any escape for Cornwallis's army. As the month came to a close, some 7,800 French troops and 9,000 Continentals and militiamen surrounded the British army of 8,500 at Yorktown. Cornwallis wrote Clinton: "If you cannot relieve me very soon you must expect to hear the worst."

Using traditional siege tactics, Washington and Rochambeau squeezed Cornwallis into submission. It did not take long. On October 17 a lone British drummer marched toward the Franco-American lines with a white flag showing. Two days later the British force laid down its arms, while its musicians played an appropriate song, "The World Turned Upside Down." The surrender at Yorktown was an emotional scene. A second British army had been captured in America, and the question now was whether Great Britain still had the resolve to continue the war.

A Most Generous Peace Settlement

It was not the great Franco-American victory at Yorktown alone that brought the British to the peace table. It was the accumulation of wounds being inflicted by the Americans and their European allies, with Yorktown the most damaging, that forced the home ministers into peace negotiations.

As early as 1778 Britain had felt the effects of world war. Daring American seaman John Paul Jones conducted raids along the English and Scottish coasts, while French and Spanish warships were soon attacking British vessels at will in the English Channel. French warships threatened British possessions in the West Indies. France and Spain were about to launch a major expedition against Gibraltar. In the spring of 1781 a Spanish force under Bernardo de Gálvez captured a sizable British garrison at Pensacola, Florida, and the British soon experienced setbacks as far away as India. The allies had demonstrated that they could carry the war anywhere, suggesting the prospect of disastrous consequences for the powerful British empire.

In March 1782 Lord North's ministry collapsed, and a new cabinet opened negotiations in France with designated American peace commissioners Benjamin Franklin, John Adams, and John Jay. On November 30, 1782, the representatives agreed to preliminary peace terms. The other belligerents also started coming to terms, largely because the naval war had turned against France and Spain and British troops had saved Gibraltar. All parties signed the final peace accords at Paris on September 3, 1783.

The major European powers now recognized the independence of the 13 rebellious colonies. Further, the peace settlement established the Mississippi River as the western boundary line of the new nation. Britain returned Florida to Spain. Although the American commissioners had tried and failed to gain Canada, they had obtained title to the vast reserve of Indian territory lying between the Appalachian Mountains and the Mississippi River. All told, effective bargaining by the American peace commissioners gave the former colonists a huge geographic base on which to build their new republic.

The peace settlement was significant in several other respects. The treaty was silent about the rights of Indians, whose interests the British ignored, despite repeated promises during the war to protect the lands of Native Americans who joined the king's cause. Britain recognized American fishing rights off the coast of eastern Canada, thus sustaining a major New England industry. The British demanded that prewar debts be paid in full to its merchants (few actually were) and insisted upon the complete restoration of the rights and property of loyalists. The American commissioners agreed to have Congress make such a recommendation to the states (which they generally ignored). The peace treaty, then, both established American independence and laid the groundwork for future conflict.

Conclusion

The Americans came out remarkably well in 1783. They emerged victorious not only in war but at the peace table as well. The young republic had endured over its parent nation, Great Britain, and, with invaluable assistance from foreign allies, particularly France, had earned its freedom from European monarchism and imperialism. On the other hand, it was far from certain whether the United States could sustain its independence or have much of a future as a nation, given the many internal problems facing the 13 sovereign states.

Chronology of Key Events

1775	First military clashes between British troops and Colonists at Lexington and Concord; Second Continental Congress meets in Philadelphia; George Washington given command of Continental Army.
1776	Thomas Paine publishes *Common Sense;* Declaration of Independence adopted; British rout rebel soldiers in vicinity of New York City; British defeated at Battle of Trenton
1777	British forces seize Philadelphia; General Burgoyne surrenders at Saratoga
1778	Franco-American alliance; British troops conquer Savannah, Georgia
1779	Spain joins the war against Britain
1780	British capture Charleston; Battle of Camden, South Carolina, Battle of Kings Mountain; the Dutch enter the war against Britain
1781	British defeated at Hannah's Cowpens; Guilford Courthouse ends in a draw; British surrender at Yorktown, Virginia
1783	Treaty of Paris ends the War for American Independence

Among those who did not cheer heartily at the prospect of peace were the officers and soldiers of the Continental Army. They had made great personal sacrifices and had every reason to be proud of their accomplishments; however, they deeply resented the lack of civilian support that had plagued them throughout the long conflict. Even in leaving the service, wrote Private Joseph Plumb Martin, they were "turned adrift like old worn-out horses" without just financial compensation for their services. Still, they had the personal satisfaction of knowing that their pain and suffering had sustained the vision of a bright and glorious future for the infant United States, but only if revolutionary Americans resolved their own political differences—especially those relating to the implanting of republican ideals in institutions of government.

Suggestions for Further Reading

For an overview of the revolutionary war consult Don Higginbotham, *The War of American Independence* (1971); John R. Alden, *The American Revolution, 1775–1783* (1954). See also Marcus Cunliffe, *George Washington: Man and Monument,* rev. ed. (1982); James Kirby Martin, ed., *Ordinary Courage: The Revolutionary War Adventures of Joseph Plumb Martin* (1993).

On daily life on the eve of the Revolution see Robert A. Gross, *The Minutemen and Their World* (1976). On the composition of the Continental Army and its role in revolutionary society see James Kirby Martin and Mark Edward Lender, *A Respectable Army: The Military Origins of the Republic* (1982); Charles Royster, *A Revolutionary People at War* (1979). The military side of the revolution is examined in William M. Fowler, Jr., *Rebels under Sail: The American Navy During the Revolution* (1976); Ira Gruber, *The Howe Brothers and the American Revolution* (1972); W. Robert Higgins, ed., *The Revolutionary War in the South* (1979); Lee Kennett, *The French Forces in America, 1780–1783* (1977); Piers Mackesy, *The War for America, 1775–1783* (1964); Dave R. Palmer, *The Way of the Fox: American Strategy in the War for America* (1975).

On the diplomacy of the Revolution see Samuel F. Bemis, *The Diplomacy of the American Revolution,* rev. ed. (1957); Jonathan R. Dull, *A Diplomatic History of the American Revolution* (1985). On the Confederation period consult H. James Henderson, *Party Politics in the Continental Congress* (1974); Merrill Jensen, *The Articles of Confederation* (1940); Jackson Turner Main, *The Sovereign States* (1973); Jack N. Rakove, *The Beginnings of National Politics* (1979).

Chapter **6**

Securing the Republic and Its Ideals, 1776–1789

Nancy Shippen was a product of Philadelphia's best lineage. Although she was born in 1763, the political turmoil leading to rebellion did not affect her early life. As a privileged daughter in an upper-class family, it was her duty to blossom into a charming woman, admired for her beauty and social graces, rather than develop her intellect. Her education consisted of the refinement of skills that would please and entertain—dancing, cultivating her voice, playing musical instruments, painting on delicate china, and producing pieces of decorative needlework.

Three hundred miles away in Boston, Phillis Wheatley was also reckoning with the American Revolution. Her life had been very different from Nancy's. Born on Africa's West Coast around 1753, she had been snatched from her parents by slave catchers. At the Boston slave market, Mrs. Susannah Wheatley, looking for a young female slave to train in domestic service, noticed her. In Phillis the Wheatley family got much more; their new slave yearned to express her thoughts and feelings through poetry.

Conventional wisdom dictated that slaves should not be educated. Exposure to reading and writing might make them resentful, perhaps even rebellious. Sensing Phillis's talents, the Wheatley family defied convention. She mastered English and Latin, even preparing translations of ancient writings. By 1770 some of her poems had been published, followed in 1773 by a collection entitled *Poems on Various Subjects, Religious and Moral.*

Little as Phillis Wheatley and Nancy Shippen had in common, they lived during an era in which men thought of all women, regardless of their rank in society, as second-class human beings. In the case of Phillis, she carried the additional burden of being black in an openly racist society. Like other women in revolutionary America, they could only hope that the ideals of human liberty might someday apply to them.

For Nancy Shippen there were two male tyrants in her life. The first was her father, who in 1781 forced her into marriage with the son of one of New York's most powerful and wealthy families. The man she truly loved had only "honorable expectations" of a respectable income, so her father, to whom she legally belonged until marriage, insisted that she wed the second tyrant in her life—her husband Henry Beckman Livingston.

The marriage was a disaster, most likely because Henry was a known philanderer. Nancy eventually took her baby daughter and moved back to her family. She wanted full custody of the child, who by law was the property of her husband. Henry made it clear that he would never give up his legal rights to his daughter, should Nancy embarrass him in public by seeking a divorce. Even if she had defied him, divorces were very hard to get because they involved proving adultery or desertion.

Although they were from diverse cultures, Phillis Wheatley and Nancy Shippen were considered second-class citizens because they were women.

To keep actual custody of her daughter, Nancy accepted her entrapment. Several years later Henry relented and arranged for a divorce, but by that time Nancy's spirit was broken. This former belle of Philadelphia society lived on unhappily in hermitlike fashion until her death in 1841. Having been so favored at birth, her adult years were a personal tragedy, primarily because of her legal dependence on the will of men.

Phillis Wheatley, by comparison, enjoyed some personal freedom before she died in 1784. Emancipated upon the death of her owners, Phillis married a free black man and bore him three children. But the family was poor, and there was scant time for poetry. It was very difficult for free

blacks to get decent jobs, and Phillis struggled each day to help her family avoid destitution. She lived long enough to see slavery being challenged in the North; but she died knowing that African Americans, even when free, invariably faced discrimination based on race, forcing families like hers to exist on the margins of revolutionary society.

The experiences of Phillis Wheatley and Nancy Shippen raise basic questions about the character of the Revolution. Did the cause of liberty really change the lives of Americans? If it was truly a movement to end tyranny, secure human rights, and ensure equality of opportunity, then why did individuals like Wheatley and Shippen benefit so little? A major reason was that white, adult males of property and community standing put greater emphasis on setting up an independent nation between 1776 and 1789 than on securing human rights. Still, the ideology of liberty could not be denied. Primarily, the revolutionary era saw the creation of a new nation and the articulation of fundamental ideals regarding human freedom and dignity—ideals that have shaped the course of American history.

Establishing New Republican Governments

Winning the war and working out a favorable peace settlement represented two of three crucial elements that made for a successful rebellion. The third factor centered on the formation of stable governments. Everyone agreed that a monarchical system, indeed any form capable of producing political tyranny, was unacceptable. A second point of consensus was that governments should be republican in character. Sovereignty, or ultimate political authority, previously residing with King and Parliament, should be vested in the people. After all, political institutions presumably existed to serve them. As such, citizens should be governed by laws, and laws should be the product of collective deliberations of representatives elected by the citizenry.

Defining the core ideals of republicanism—popular sovereignty, rule by law, and legislation by elected representatives—was not a source of disagreement. Yet revolutionary leaders argued passionately about the organization and powers of new governments, both state and national, as well as the extent to which basic political rights should be put into practice. At the heart of the argument was the concept of *public virtue:* whether citizens were capable of subordinating their self-interest to the greater good of the whole community. Although some leaders answered in the affirmative, others did not. Their trust or distrust of the people directly affected how far they were willing to go in implementing republican ideals.

Leaders who believed that citizens could govern themselves and not abuse public privileges for private advantage were in the vanguard of political thinking in the western world. As such, they may be called radicals. On the other hand, more cautious, elitist revolutionary leaders feared what the masses might do without the restraints of central political authority. These leaders remained attached to traditional notions of hierarchy and deference in social and political relationships. They still thought that the "better sort" of citizens should be the stewards who guided the people. They wanted a strong central government to replace King and Parliament, a government controlled by more cautious revolutionaries in the interests of national political stability.

People Victorious: The New State Governments

In the wake of collapsing British authority during 1775 and 1776, radical and cautious revolutionaries squared off in constitutional conventions.

Their heated debates produced several new state constitutions by the end of 1777, plus a plan of national government written by the Continental Congress. Although the state constitution-makers varied in their commitment, free, white, adult male citizens (about 20 percent of the total population) gained expanded voting and officeholding rights. The movement clearly was toward greater popular participation in governmental decision making.

Pennsylvanians produced the most democratic of the first state constitutions. All white male citizens, with or without property, could now vote for legislators, who served in an annually elected unicameral, or one-chamber, assembly. By comparison, Maryland's constitution-framers were much less trusting. They maintained a three-tiered structure of government, reminiscent of the king and two houses of Parliament. Potential voters had to meet modest property-holding requirements. Those elected to the lower house had to own at least a 50-acre freehold farm while election to the upper house and governorship was restricted to the wealthiest members of society. In Pennsylvania ordinary citizens could control their own political destiny, but in Maryland the "better sort" were to act as stewards for the people, hence continuing the tradition of deferential politics.

The other state constitutions varied between these two extremes. Those of New Hampshire, North Carolina, and Georgia were more like Pennsylvania. New York, Virginia, and South Carolina resembled the Maryland plan more closely. Delaware and New Jersey were in the middle.

Only New Jersey defined the electorate without regard to gender. Its 1776 constitution gave the vote to "all free inhabitants" meeting minimal property qualifications. This permitted some women to vote. Since all property in marriage belonged to husbands, New Jersey had technically extended franchise rights only to widows and spinsters (very few divorced women were to be found anywhere in America). Nonetheless, great numbers of married women went to the polls regularly. Although the experiment worked, this concept proved too radical for the customary male-dominated political culture of revolutionary America, and in 1807 New Jersey disenfranchised females.

Because of the first state constitutions, male citizens with more ordinary family backgrounds, less personal wealth, and a greater diversity of occupations began to gain greater access to political offices after the Revolution started. Neither as well-educated nor as well-to-do as in the past, these leaders were, as one Virginian noted in 1776, "the people's men (and the people in general are right)." Radical leaders throughout the states heartily endorsed these sentiments.

The Articles of Confederation

In June 1776 the Continental Congress called for a plan of national government. John Dickinson, the well-known reluctant revolutionary who refused to vote for independence, took the lead. Concerned about losing the stabilizing influence of British authority, Dickinson proposed a muscular plan of central government to be called the Articles of Confederation for "THE UNITED STATES OF AMERICA," in which the states would have little actual authority.

The radical revolutionaries who dominated Congress in late 1776 and 1777 did not like this plan. They feared power too far removed from the people. After all, they had rebelled against a distant government that they had perceived as tyrannical. When Congress finally completed revisions of the Articles of Confederation in November 1777, the delegates made sure that the states retained their sovereignty. At most, the central government could coordinate activities among the states. It could manage the war, but it did not even have taxation authority to support that effort. If Congress needed money (it obviously did), it could "requisition" the states. The states, however, could decide for themselves whether they would send funds to Congress. As a testament to the sovereignty of the 13 states, each had to ratify the Articles before this plan could go into full operation.

Fundamentally penniless and powerless, the Confederation government represented the optimistic view that a virtuous citizenry did not require the constraining hand of central authority. This bold vision—fully in line with the rejection of King and Parliament as a far distant, autocratic central government—pleased radicals like Samuel Adams, Thomas Paine, and Thomas Jefferson. Cautious revolutionaries still harbored grave doubts, and events over the next few years convinced them that the first constitutional settlement had all but doomed the experiment in republicanism to failure.

Crises of the Confederation

The young American republic had to face many immediate challenges. These included ratifying the Articles of Confederation, establishing a national domain west of the Appalachians, finding some means to pay for the war, achieving stable diplomatic relations with foreign powers, and guarding against domestic insurrections.

Over time, those who advocated a strong central government formed an informal political bloc, since known as the *nationalists*. With each passing year the nationalists became more and more frustrated by the Confederation. Finally, in 1787 they overwhelmed their opposition by pressing for and getting a new plan of national government.

Struggle to Ratify the Articles

Given the wartime need for national unity in the face of a common enemy, Congress asked each state to approve the Articles of Confederation quickly. Overcoming much indifference, 12 states had finally ratified by January 1779—but Maryland still held out.

The propertied gentlemen who controlled Maryland's revolutionary government objected to one specific provision in the Articles. Although Dickinson's draft had designated all lands west of the Appalachian Mountains as a *national domain,* belonging to all of the people for future settlement, the final version left these lands in the hands of states having sea-to-sea clauses in their colonial charters. Maryland, having a fixed western boundary, had no such western claim; nor did Rhode Island, New Jersey, Pennsylvania, or Delaware.

Maryland's leaders simply refused to be cut off from western development. Many had invested in land companies trying to gain title to large parcels of western territory, and they stood to make substantial profits if the national Congress would recognize these claims. The Maryland assembly adamantly refused ratification unless the landed states turned over their charter titles to Congress. Virginia, which had the largest claim, including the vast region north of the Ohio River that came to be known as the "Old Northwest," faced the most pressure. Forsaking local land speculators for the national interest, the Virginia Assembly broke the deadlock in January 1781 by agreeing to cede its claims to Congress.

If self-interest had not been involved, ratification would have followed quickly; however, greedy Maryland leaders still held out. They pronounced Virginia's grant unacceptable because of a condition not permitting Congress to award lands on the basis of Indian deeds. Fortunately for the republic, the war intervened. In early 1781, with the British raiding in the Chesapeake Bay region, Marylanders became quite anxious about their defense. Congressional leaders urged ratification in exchange for promises of Continental military support. All but cornered, the Maryland Assembly reluctantly gave in and approved the Articles of Confederation.

Contention over Financing the War

From the very first, financial problems plagued the new central government. Under the Articles, Congress had no power of taxation; it repeatedly asked the states to pay a fair proportion of war costs. The states, also hard-pressed for funds, rarely sent in more than 50 percent of their requisitions. Meantime, soldiers like Joseph Plumb Martin endured shortages of food, clothing, camp equipment, and pay.

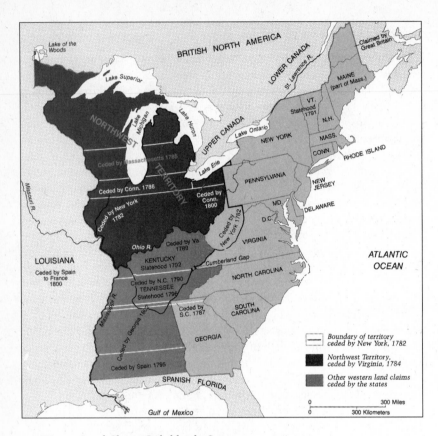

Western Land Claims Ceded by the States

The battle over conflicting state claims to western lands was a major issue
facing the Continental Congress.

The lack of tax revenues forced Congress to resort to various expedient measures to meet war costs. Between 1775 and 1780 it issued some
$220 million in paper money. Lacking any financial backing, these "Con-
tinentals" became so worthless by 1779 that irate army officers complained that "four months' pay of a private [soldier] will not procure his
wretched wife and children a single bushel of wheat." In addition, Congress, largely to get military supplies, issued interest-bearing certificates of
indebtedness. Without any means to pay interest, these notes, which also
circulated as money, rapidly lost value. If it had not been for financial assistance from allies like France and the Netherlands, the war effort might
well have floundered.

Deeply disturbed by these conditions, many nationalists in the Continental Congress acted forcefully to institute financial reform. Their leader was the wealthy Philadelphia merchant, Robert Morris, sometimes called the "financier of the Revolution." His assistant superintendent, Gouverneur Morris (no relation), a wealthy New Yorker then practicing law in Philadelphia, was also critical to shaping the events that lay ahead.

At the urging of the nationalists, congressional delegates approved the Impost Plan of 1781. It called for import duties of five percent on all foreign trade goods entering the United States, the revenues to belong to Congress. These funds could be used to pay the army, to back a stable national currency, and, ultimately, to meet foreign loan obligations. Because the plan involved giving Congress taxation authority, the delegates recommended it in the form of an amendment to the Articles. Amendments required the approval of all 13 states.

Reluctant as they were to share taxation powers with the central government, many state leaders agreed with Robert Morris. By the fall of 1782, 12 states had ratified. Only Rhode Island voted against ratification. Once again, one state had blocked the will of the other 12.

In this crucial matter the nationalists had allies. Most prominent were disgruntled officers in the Continental Army. Rarely had the soldiers been paid, for Congress lacked a fixed source of revenue to meet its obligations to its fighting men and women. After a group of high-ranking officers learned about Rhode Island's decision, they sent a menacing petition to Congress, insisting upon five years of full pay in lieu of promised half-pay pensions when mustering out of the service. They warned of "fatal effects" if their demands were not met.

Threatened Military Coup: The Newburgh Conspiracy

For years Continental officers and soldiers alike had been complaining about the ungenerous treatment they received from revolutionary leaders and civilians. Convinced that the general populace had lived well at home while the army endured privation, sickness, and death in the field, they spoke with impassioned feelings about the absence of citizen virtue. As one officer bluntly wrote: "I hate my countrymen." Personal sacrifice for the good of the whole community, it seemed to the Continentals, had been exacted only from those with the fortitude to fulfill the obligation of long-term military service.

After the British surrender at Yorktown, Washington moved 11,000 troops north to Newburgh, New York. From this campsite near the Hudson River, the Continental Army waited for peace terms and kept its eye on British forces in New York City. As peace negotiations dragged on, officers and soldiers worried about being demobilized without back pay and promised pensions.

When the congressional nationalists received the officers' hotly worded petition, they were more pleased than alarmed. They soon devised a scheme to use these threats to extort taxation authority from the states. If need be, they would encourage the army to go back into the field and threaten the civilian populace with a military uprising. The danger, of course, was that the army might get out of control, seize the reins of government, and push the revolution toward some form of military dictatorship.

Washington refused to cooperate in a military coup directed at the states and the people. Perhaps better than anyone in revolutionary America, he understood that military power had to remain subordinate to civilian authority, or the republic would never be free. Robert Morris and other congressional nationalists found General Horatio Gates, who dreamed of replacing Washington at the head of the army, much more receptive to their scheme, but without Washington's support the Newburgh conspiracy collapsed.

Nonetheless, dissension in the ranks, and dissatisfaction with the central government, continued unabated. After leaving the army one angry group of Pennsylvania Continentals marched on Philadelphia in June 1783. They surrounded Independence Hall where Congress held its sessions and refused to leave until they received back pay. The frightened delegates asked the Pennsylvania government for protection, but state officials turned down their request. Thoroughly humiliated by armed soldiers and a state government that would not defend them, the delegates first moved to Princeton, New Jersey, then to Annapolis, Maryland, and finally to New York City. The delicate fabric of the new nation seemed to be unraveling.

Drifting Toward Disunion

Despite the Paris peace settlement and the final removal of British troops, most citizens engaged in another battle beginning in late 1783—this one against a hard-hitting economic depression. Farmers in New England reeled from the effects of new British trade regulations which in essence turned the Navigation System against the independent Americans. The Orders in Council of 1783 prohibited the sale of many American agricultural products in the British West Indies, formerly a key market for New England goods, and required many commodities to be conveyed to and from the islands in British vessels. The orders represented a serious blow to New England's agricultural, shipping, and shipbuilding trades. Making matters even worse, merchants in all the states had purchased large quantities of British goods at war's end, only to discover they could not sell these commodities to citizens feeling the effects of the depression.

The central government could do little. It did send John Adams to Britain in 1785 as the first minister from the United States. Adams, however, made no headway in getting British officials to back off from the Orders in Council. He dejectedly reported to Congress that "they rely upon our disunion" to avoid negotiations.

Some merchants, primarily from the Middle Atlantic states, were anxious to break free of Britain's economic hold. An opportunity presented itself in 1784 when John Jay, Congress's newly appointed secretary for foreign affairs, started negotiations with Don Diego de Gardoqui, Spain's first minister to the United States. Spain, concerned that Americans, now streaming into the trans-Appalachian west, would in time covet its territory beyond the Mississippi, had closed that river to American commerce. Attempting to assuage possible bad feelings, Gardoqui offered an advantageous commercial treaty. Jay and a number of powerful merchants from the Middle Atlantic states saw merit in the Spanish proposal. They viewed southwestern development as a potential threat to eastern economic dominance. When Jay reported on his discussions to Congress in the summer of 1786, tempers flared. The southern states voted as a bloc against any such treaty, which ended the Jay-Gardoqui negotiations. But southerners and westerners still suspected that Jay and his eastern merchant allies would not hesitate to abandon them altogether for petty commercial gains.

Daniel Shays's Rebellion

Postwar economic conditions were so bad in several states that citizens began demanding tax relief from their governments. In western Massachusetts desperate farmers complained about huge property tax increases by the state government to pay off its war debt. Taxes on land rose by more than 60 percent in the period 1783–1786, exactly when a depressed postwar economy meant that farmers were getting little income from the sale of excess agricultural goods.

Local courts, in the absence of tax payments, started to seize the property of men like Daniel Shays, a revolutionary war veteran. Viewing their plight in terms of tyranny, the farmers of western Massachusetts believed that they had the right to break the chains of oppression, just as they had done in resisting British rule a few years before. This time, however, the enemy was their own state government.

In late August 1786 an estimated 1,000 farmers poured into Northampton and shut down the county court. This crowd action represented the first of many such closures. By popular mandate citizens would no longer permit judges to seize property or condemn people to debtors' prison as the penalty for not paying taxes. Frightened state leaders in Boston hastily organized an army to deal with the crisis.

The insurrection soon fizzled. On January 25, 1787, Shays and his followers attacked the federal arsenal at Springfield, but were driven off. In early February the army pursued the western rebels through a driving snowstorm and routed them at Petersham. These setbacks, along with tax relief from the assembly and amnesty for the leaders of the rebellion, ended the uprising.

Shays's Rebellion, however, held broader significance. Only a strong central government, nationalists believed, could save the republic from internal chaos. The nationalists now intensified their campaign for a new constitutional settlement, one designed to bring the self-serving sovereign states and the people under control.

Human Rights and Social Change

The years between 1776 and 1787 were not just a time of mounting political confrontation between nationalists and localists. The period also witnessed the establishment of many fundamental human rights. When Thomas Jefferson penned his famous words, "all men are created equal," he informed George III that kings were not superior to the people by some assumed right of birth. Jefferson went on to say that all human beings had "certain unalienable rights," or rights literally beyond governmental control. Republican governments had the responsibility to respect and guarantee these rights, including "life, liberty, and the pursuit of happiness" for all citizens.

At the same time Americans had waged civil war against Britain to preserve property rights. Tyrannical governments, for example, threatened property through taxation without representation. In trying to protect property rights while expanding human rights, revolutionary leaders learned that the two could clash. They found it much easier to guarantee human rights when property rights, such as those relating to the ownership of slaves, were not also at stake. Thus there were some striking contradictions in efforts to enshrine greater freedom for all inhabitants in revolutionary America.

In Pursuit of Religious Freedom

Since the days of the Great Awakening, dissenter religious groups had expressed opposition to established churches in the colonies. The Baptists were particularly outspoken. They wanted official toleration and an end to taxes used exclusively for state-supported churches. In 1786 Virginia passed its Statute of Religious Freedom, which not only provided for the separation of church and state, but guaranteed complete freedom of conscience. Jefferson would later be labeled an atheist for his efforts on behalf of this legislation, but for him the statute was just as significant as the Declaration of Independence, and he had these sentiments engraved on his tombstone.

Disestablishment quickly followed in other states, particularly in the South where the Anglican church (soon to become the Episcopal Church) had been dominant. In New England, only Rhode Islanders, following in the tradition of Roger Williams, had enjoyed full latitude in worship. With the Revolution the cause of religious freedom started to move forward in other New England states. Lawmakers began letting citizens decide which local church to support with their tax monies. This development represented a partial victory for individuals who preferred worshipping as Baptists or Presbyterians. However, dissenters still had to accept Congregationalism as the established state church; complete separation of church and state did not occur in New England until the early nineteenth century.

Freedom of religion was one among a number of fundamental rights to make headway during the revolutionary era. Several states adopted bills of rights similar to Virginia's, guaranteeing freedom of speech, assembly, and the press, as well as trials by jury. Other states started revising their legal codes, making penalties for crimes less harsh. Such feudal practices as primogeniture and entail (passing and committing property only to eldest sons through the generations) were abolished. Running through all these acts was the republican assumption that citizens should have the opportunity to lead productive lives, uninhibited by laws violating personal conscience or denying the opportunity to acquire property.

The Propertyless Poor and the West

For many Americans gaining property remained only a dream. At least 20 percent of the population lived at the poverty level or below, eking out precarious existences as unskilled laborers. Indeed, wealth was more unevenly distributed in 1800 than it had been in 1750. One reason for the increased concentration of wealth in fewer hands was the policy of state governments regarding the seizure of loyalist property. Anxious to obtain a source of wartime revenue, states sold these holdings, worth milllions, to the highest bidders. This practice favored men of wealth with investment capital and worked against any substantial redistribution of property.

Another missed opportunity lay with the enormous trans-Appalachian frontier awaiting development. Washington's Continental soldiers, who ranked among the poorest members of revolutionary society, had been promised western lands for long-term service. When they mustered out in 1783, they received land warrant certificates. In order to survive, most veterans soon exchanged these paper certificates for the bare necessities of life. As a result, very few were ever able to begin anew in the Ohio country, once military tracts had been set aside and surveyed.

Still, western lands remained a source of hope for economically downtrodden soldiers and civilians alike. In 1775 explorer Daniel Boone blazed open the "Wilderness Road" to Kentucky, which contained a population of 74,000 fifteen years later. Newly formed white settlements in Kentucky and Tennessee soon created pressures to open territory north of the Ohio River. After ceding the Old Northwest to the United States in 1783, however, the British did not abandon their military posts there. To maintain the lucrative fur trade, they bolstered the Indians with a steady supply of firearms. Whites foolish enough to venture north of the Ohio River rarely survived, and the region remained closed to large numbers of westward-moving settlers well into the 1790s.

Despite the British and Indians, Congress was eager to open the Ohio country. With this goal in mind the delegates approved three land ordinances. The 1784 Ordinance provided for territorial government and guaranteed settlers that they would not remain in permanent colonial status. When enough people (later specified at 60,000) had moved in, a constitution could be written, state boundaries set, and admission to the union as a full partner would follow. The 1785 Ordinance called for orderly surveying of the region. Townships of six miles square were to be laid out in gridlike fashion, containing 36 sections of 640 acres each. Proceeds from the sale of the sixteenth section were to be used to finance public education. The Northwest Ordinance of 1787 refined governmental arrangements, gave a bill of rights to prospective settlers, and proclaimed slavery forever banned north of the Ohio River. In providing for orderly development and eventual statehood, the land ordinances may well have been the most significant legislation of the Confederation-period Congress.

Even so, the ordinances were not fully enlightened. Congress, in its desperate search for revenue, viewed the Old Northwest as a source of long-term income. The smallest purchase individual settlers could make was 640 acres, priced at $1.00 per acre, and there were to be no purchases on credit. Families of modest means, let alone poorer ones, could not meet such terms. To survive, the poorest western settlers had no alternative but to squat on uninhabited land until they were driven off.

Women Appeal for Fundamental Liberties

Like the poor, women experienced little success in improving their lot during the revolutionary era. By law and social practice, women were legally dependent on men, as the case of Nancy Shippen so vividly illustrated. What held the greatest promise for women, at least for those of middling and affluent status, was the ideology of republicanism, which directly influenced family life by offering a broadened definition regarding the role of mothers. Patriot leaders repeatedly asserted that the republic would founder without virtuous citizens. Hence it became a special trust for mothers to implant strong moral character and civic virtue in their children, especially their sons, so that they would uphold the obligations of disinterested citizenship for the good of the nation.

The concept of "republican motherhood" had potentially liberating qualities. It became the calling of republican mothers to manage the domestic sphere of family life, just as husbands were to take responsibility for the family's economic welfare. This duty reduced traditional male dominance in all family matters. Elevating the role of women in family life may also have affected the nature of courtship by putting more emphasis upon affection than on parental control in the making of marriages. However, the immediate effect of this emerging tendency should not be exaggerated, as Nancy Shippen's experiences indicate.

If women were to be responsible for instilling proper values in future generations, they needed more and better schooling. During the 1780s and 1790s some states started taxing citizens for the support of elementary education. Massachusetts broke new ground in 1789 by requiring its citizens to pay for female as well as male elementary education. In addition, these two decades saw the opening of many new private schools, which offered more advanced education to daughters of well-to-do families in subjects traditionally reserved for males, such as mathematics, science, and history.

Still, the emphasis in expanding opportunities for middle- and upper-class women was upon service to the family and the republic, not on individual development. Most men in revolutionary America resisted further change for women. Although republican motherhood offered higher status, most men still thought of women as a form of property whose existence should be devoted to masculine welfare and happiness.

The Question of Race

Revolutionary ideology placed a premium on such terms as *liberty* and *equality.* Almost everyone recognized that it was inconsistent to use such terms while holding 500,000 African Americans (one-fifth of the population in 1776) in perpetual bondage. For generations, colonial Americans had taken slavery for granted, as if it were part of the natural order of life. All of the talk about liberty and political slavery during the 1760s and 1770s began to undermine this unquestioning attitude, so much so that even slaveholding patriots like Patrick Henry asked whether the institution was not "repugnant to humanity . . . and destructive to liberty?" Some revolutionary leaders decisively answered "yes."

In 1774 Philadelphians, among them Benjamin Franklin, organized an abolition society. Pressure from this group and from antislavery Quakers resulted in Pennsylvania becoming the first state (1780) to declare human bondage illegal. Soon other northern states followed, modeling their emancipation laws on Pennsylvania's, which specified that children born to slave mothers had to be set free by the age of 28. By 1800 slavery was a dying institution in the North.

Many revolutionary leaders hoped that the drive to abolish slavery would also extend into the South. During the 1780s there were some positive signs. After 1783 only South Carolina and Georgia were still involved in the international slave trade. States such as Maryland, Delaware, and Virginia passed laws making it easier for planters to manumit (free) individual slaves. George Washington was one of a few wealthy planters who took advantage of Virginia's manumission law. He referred to slavery as a "misfortune" that sullied revolutionary ideals, and in his will he made provision for the liberation of his slaves.

Washington, as in most other ways, was unusual. Far more typical was Thomas Jefferson. In his *Notes on the State of Virginia* (1785) Jefferson called slavery "a perpetual exercise" in "the most unremitting despotism," but he could not bring himself to free his own slaves. His chattels formed the economic base of his way of life. Their labor gave him the time that he needed for politics and, ironically, the time to work so persuasively on behalf of human liberty.

Support for his life-style was not the only reason Jefferson held back. He was representative of his times in believing blacks to be inherently inferior to whites. In his *Notes* he made a number of comparisons of ability detrimental to blacks, such as in the category of reasoning power (Jefferson scoffed at the poems of Phillis Wheatley, which he described as "below the dignity of criticism"). He thought, too, that the emancipation of all blacks would result in racial war. Thus, a man who labored so diligently for human rights in his own lifetime remained in bondage to the racist concepts of his era.

Negative racial attitudes were the norm in revolutionary America, as the growing number of freed blacks learned again and again. Because of the general abolition and individual manumission movements, the free black population approached 60,000 by 1790 and 108,000 by 1800 (11 percent of the total African-American population). Like the some 5,000 black Continental Army veterans, Phillis Wheatley, and George Washington's former slaves, these individuals repeatedly had to struggle to survive in a hostile society.

Slave Concentration, 1790

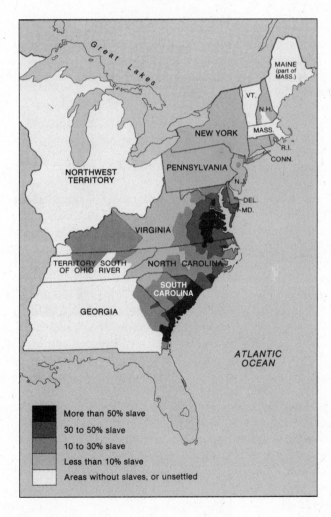

Many free blacks moved to the large northern port towns, where slavery was a fading threat. They built their own neighborhoods, and skilled workers opened shops to serve one another. Other urban free blacks performed domestic service at low wages for well-to-do white families, but they did so as free persons with the opportunity to fashion independent lives for themselves. Free African Americans also established their own churches, such as the African Methodist Episcopal Church, founded by Richard Allen in Philadelphia in 1786. African Baptist and African Presbyterian denominations also developed in the northern port towns, and these churches provided opportunities for formal education, since black children were rarely welcome in white schools.

Whether in the North or the South, the reality more often than not was open discrimination. As a group, free African Americans responded by providing for one another and believing in a better day when revolutionary ideals regarding human freedom and liberty would have full meaning in their lives. In this sense they still had much in common with their brethren in slavery.

Second New Beginning, New National Government

In 1787 many revolutionary leaders were more concerned about internal political stability than securing human rights. With all the talk of breaking up the Confederation, with Shays's Rebellion not yet completely quelled, and with the states arguing endlessly about almost everything, political leaders believed that matters of government should take primacy, or the republican experiment might be forever lost. Certainly the nationalists felt this way, and they were pushing hard for a revision of the first constitutional settlement.

In September 1786 representatives from five states met briefly in Annapolis, Maryland, to discuss pressing interstate commercial problems. Those present included such strong nationalists as Alexander Hamilton, John Dickinson, and James Madison. Since so few states were represented, the delegates abandoned their agenda in favor of an urgent plea asking all the states to send delegates to a special constitutional convention.

This time the states responded, largely because of the specter of civil turmoil associated with Shays's Rebellion. Twelve states—Rhode Island refused to participate—named 74 delegates, 55 of whom would attend the Constitutional Convention in Philadelphia. As the Continental Congress instructed the delegates in February 1787, their purpose was to revise the Articles of Confederation, making them "adequate to the exigencies . . . of the union." Some nationalists, however, had other ideas. They wanted a whole new plan of national government. Their ideas would dominate the proceedings from beginning to end, and their determination produced the Constitution of 1787.

The Framers of the Constitution

The men who gathered in Philadelphia were successful lawyers, planters, and merchants of education, wealth, and wide-ranging accomplishments, not ordinary citizens. They represented particular states, but most of them thought in national terms, based on experiences like serving in the Continental Congress and the Continental Army. They feared for the future of the republic, unless someone did something—and soon—to strengthen the weak central government as a means of containing the selfishness of particular states. Having for years been frustrated by the Revolution's first constitutional settlement, they seized the opportunity for change and made the most of it.

Among those present during the lengthy proceedings, which stretched from May 25 to September 17, was the revered George Washington, who served as the convention's president. Other notable leaders included James Madison, Alexander Hamilton, Gouverneur and Robert Morris, and John Dickinson. Benjamin Franklin, at 81, was the oldest delegate. He offered his finely tuned diplomatic tact in working out compromises that kept the proceedings moving forward.

Although the delegates disagreed vehemently, they never let differences over particular issues deflect them from their main purpose—to find the constitutional means for an enduring republic. The Constitution was not perfect, as Benjamin Franklin stated on the last day of the convention, but it did bring stability and energy to national government— and it has endured.

A Document Constructed by Compromises

If the nationalists had been doctrinaire, their deliberations would have collapsed. They held fast to their objective—providing for a strong central government—but were flexible about ways to achieve their goal. Thus they were able to compromise on critical issues. The first great points of difference dealt with the structure of government and whether states should be represented equally or according to population distribution. The eventual compromise required the abandonment of the Articles of Confederation.

Slight of build and reserved, James Madison of Virginia has been called the "father of the Constitution." He worked out a proposed plan of national government, then made arrangements to have it presented by Edmund Randolph, a more adept public speaker and Virginia's governor, at the outset of the convention. This strategy worked, and the delegates gave the "Virginia Plan" their undivided attention. The plan outlined a

James Madison, a strong nationalist, has been called the "father of the Constitution" for his plan of national government. He became the nation's fourth president.

three-tiered structure with an executive branch and two houses of Congress. Madison also envisioned a separate judicial branch.

Delegates from the less populous, smaller states objected. Under the Virginia Plan representatives to the two chambers of Congress would be apportioned to the states according to population, whereas under the Articles, each state, regardless of population, had an equal voice in national government. For such delegates as lawyer William Paterson of New Jersey, the latter practice ensured that the interests of the smaller states would not be sacrificed to those of the more populous, larger states. Thus Paterson countered with his "New Jersey Plan" on June 15. It retained equal voting in a unicameral national legislature, and it also vested far greater authority, including the powers of taxation and regulation of interstate and foreign commerce, in the central government.

On June 19 the delegates voted to adopt a three-tiered structure, but they did not resolve the question of how the states should be represented in the two new legislative branches. For several days it appeared as if the convention had reached an impasse, and some delegates were threatening to leave.

With Franklin and others calling for harmony, the delegates finally hammered out a settlement. Central to the "Great Compromise," which saved the convention from dissolving, was an agreement providing for proportional representation in the lower house (favoring the more populous states) and equality of representation in the upper house (favoring the less populous states). In the upper house each state would have two senators. Although the senators could vote independently of each other, they could also operate in tandem to protect state interests.

Having passed this crucial hurdle, the convention turned to other issues, not the least of which was slavery. Delegates from the Deep South wanted guarantees that would prevent any national tampering with their chattel property. Some northerners, however, including those who had supported abolition in their states, preferred constitutional restrictions on slavery. For a while, it looked as if there would be no compromise, but in the end both sides made concessions for the sake of union. By mutual agreement, the Constitution neither endorsed nor condemned slavery, nor can the word be found in the text. It did guarantee southerners that slaves would count as "three-fifths" of white persons for purposes of determining representation in the lower house. Although this meant more congressional seats for the South, direct taxes would be based on population, including "three-fifths of all other persons." Thus the South would pay more in taxes. The delegates also agreed that there would be no national legislation against the importation of slaves from abroad until at least 1808.

Although these clauses gave implicit recognition to slavery, it should be noted that the Northwest Land Ordinance of 1787, adopted by the Continental Congress in New York at the same time, forever barred slavery north of the Ohio River. The timing has led some historians to conclude that inhibiting the spread of slavery was also part of the compromise, representing a major concession to northern interests. The North-South Compromise kept the convention and the republic together by temporarily mollifying most delegates on an extremely divisive issue. Still, chattel slavery was so inconsistent with the ideals of human liberty that the problem could not be sidestepped for long.

A third set of issues provoking compromise had to do with the office of president. Nobody seemed sure what range of authority the national executive should have, how long the term of office should be, or how the president should be elected. By early September the delegates, fatigued by endless debates and extremely hot weather during three months of meetings, settled these questions quickly. The office of the president was potentially powerful. Besides serving as commander-in-chief of military forces, the incumbent could fashion treaties with foreign powers, subject to ratification by a two-thirds vote of the Senate. The president could veto congressional legislation, which both houses of Congress could only override with two-thirds majorities. Congress, in turn, had an important check on the president. It could impeach the executive if presidential powers were abused. Four years seemed like a reasonable term of office, and reelection would be possible.

To help insulate the president from manipulation by public opinion, the delegates made the office indirectly elective. They did so by creating the electoral college. Each state would have the same number of electors as representatives and senators. In states that permitted popular voting for the presidency, citizens would cast ballots for electors who favored particular candidates. In turn the electors would meet and each vote for the person they favored. The candidate with a majority of electoral college votes would become president. The person with the second highest total would become vice president. Should the electors fail to reach a majority decision, the election would be turned over to the House of Representatives, where each state would have one vote in choosing a president.

The subject of the presidency might have been more contentious had no person of George Washington's universally acclaimed stature been on the scene. Washington was the one authentic popular hero and symbol of national unity to emerge from the Revolution, and the delegates were already thinking of him as the first president. Since he was so fully trusted as a firm apostle of republican principles who had disdained the mantle of a military dictator, defining the mode of election and powers of the national executive were not insurmountable tasks.

The Ratification Struggle

Thirty-nine delegates affixed their signatures to the proposed Constitution on September 17, 1787. The delegates who signed knew there would be significant opposition because their plan cut so heavily into state authority. Before finishing their deliberations, they made the shrewd move of agreeing that only nine states needed to ratify the Constitution—through special state conventions rather than through state legislatures—to allow the new central government to commence operations. The nationalists were not going to let one or two states destroy months of work—and what they viewed as the best last hope for a languishing republic.

In another astute move, the nationalists started referring to themselves as *Federalists,* and they disarmed their opponents by calling them *Antifederalists.* Actually, the Antifederalists were the real federalists; they wanted to continue the confederation of sovereign states, and they sought to keep power as close as possible to the people, mostly in the hands of state governments. This confusion in terminology may have gotten some local Federalist candidates elected to state ratifying conventions, thus helping to secure victory for the Constitution.

The nationalists were also very effective in explaining the Convention's work. The essence of their argumentation appeared in *The Federalist Papers,* a series of 85 remarkably cogent newspaper essays written by James Madison, Alexander Hamilton, and John Jay on behalf of ratification in New York. Under the pseudonym "Publius," they discussed various aspects of the Constitution and tried to demonstrate how the document would ensure political stability and provide enlightened legislation.

The new government, they asserted, had been designed to protect the rights of all citizens. No one self-serving faction, whether representing a minority or majority of citizens, could take power completely and deprive others of their liberties and property. The Constitution would check and balance willful interest groups because basic powers would be divided among the various branches of government. And the system was truly federal, they argued, because much decision-making authority remained with the states as a further protection against power-hungry, self-serving factional interest groups.

Beyond these advantages, the Constitution embodied the principle of representative republicanism, as Madison explained in his famous *Federalist No. 10* essay. Large election districts for the House of Representatives would make it more difficult for factions to manipulate elections, enabling citizens of true merit to get elected and to enact laws beneficial for citizens everywhere.

The nationalists admitted that they were overturning the first constitutional settlement of 1776. The new emphasis on a strong central government was necessary, they believed, because the people had failed the test of public virtue. They had shown more interest in their individual welfare, for instance, than in making material or personal sacrifices to support the Continental war effort. They had formed into troublesome factions like the Maryland land speculators and the Massachusetts rebel followers of Daniel Shays, all to the detriment of the republic's political stability.

The nationalists, now expecting to function as the country's political stewards, did not repudiate the concept of popular sovereignty. Rather, they enshrined it in such concepts as representative republicanism. The people were to have a political voice, in the abstract at least. Their representatives, supposedly detached from selfish concerns, could now more easily check narrow interests inhibiting stable national development.

The Antifederalists viewed this new settlement with grave alarm. One writer feared that the Constitution would support "in practice a *permanent* ARISTOCRACY" of self-serving, wealthy citizens. Leading Antifederalists, among them Samuel Adams, Patrick Henry, and Richard Henry Lee, still had negative images of the distant British government, too far removed from the people to be checked in any effective way. Having rebelled against what they perceived as the tyranny of the British imperial government, they were not anxious to approve a plan for a new central government with enough power to threaten the states and the people with yet more political tyranny. They preferred life under the Articles of Confederation.

The Antifederalists failed to deflect nationalist momentum, even though there would be close calls in some ratifying conventions, such as in Massachusetts, New York, and Virginia. The well-organized nationalists were always ready to counter Antifederalist complaints. When there were objections about the absence of a national bill of rights guaranteeing each citizen fundamental liberties, they promised that the first Congress would prepare one. When there were cries for a second convention that would not overturn but modify the Articles of Confederation, they argued that the new government should first be given a chance. If it did not work, the nationalists stated, they would support another convention.

When the New Hampshire convention voted to ratify on June 21, 1788, the necessary nine states had given their approval. The two large states of Virginia and New York were still not in the fold, however, so everyone hesitated. Promises of a bill of rights helped bring the Virginia convention around in a close vote (89 yeas to 79 nays) on June 25. A month later, after much skillful Federalist maneuvering, the dominant

Antifederalists in New York conceded enough votes for ratification to occur by the slim margin of 30 yeas to 27 nays. Somewhat belatedly, North Carolina ratified the constitution in November 1789. Rhode Island, which had refused to participate in the Constitutional Convention, ratified the document by a close vote in 1790 only after the United States threatened to sever commercial ties.

Conclusion

In 1776 those radical revolutionaries who believed in a virtuous citizenry had sought to expand popular participation in government. By and large they succeeded. This first constitutional settlement proved to be unsatisfactory, however, largely because the weak central government under the

*C*hronology of Key Events

1775	Daniel Boone blazes the "Wilderness Road" to Kentucky; Lord Dunmore calls for the emancipation of Virginia's slaves
1775–1777	Several states adopt new state constitutions
1776–1777	Congress drafts the Articles of Confederation
1780	Pennsylvania becomes the first state to provide for the emancipation of slaves
1781	Articles of Confederation ratified by all the states
1783	Newburgh Conspiracy fails to produce a military coup
1784	Land Ordinance of 1784 guarantees western settlers territorial government
1785	Land Ordinance of 1785 provides for the survey and sale of western lands
1786	Virginia adopts Jefferson's Statute of Religious Freedom separating church and state; Shays's Rebellion; Annapolis Convention calls for a national constitutional convention
1787	Northwest Ordinance bars slavery north of the Ohio River; Constitutional Convention convenes in Philadelphia
1787–1788	Constitution ratified by eleven states

Articles of Confederation lacked the authority to support even the mini-mal needs of the new nation. Blaming the states and the people, the na-tionalist leaders produced a second constitutional settlement in 1787 by drafting a plan for a more powerful central government. It was to be above the people and the states, strong enough to establish and preserve national unity and stability.

The new republic began functioning in 1789. Yet the full potential of republican ideals had yet to be realized. Notions regarding each Ameri-can's right to enjoy life, liberty, happiness, and property in an equalitarian society fell far short of full implementation. Women remained second-class citizens, and the bonds of slavery still manacled most African Amer-icans. Even with the opening of the trans-Appalachian West, which came at the expense of thousands of Native Americans, poorer citizens found it difficult to gain access to farmland on which they could provide for them-selves and secure their personal prosperity. Nonetheless, the years between 1776 and 1789 had witnessed a revolution in human expectations. The foundations of what would one day be a system of political democracy had been laid.

Suggestions for Further Reading

Valuable overviews of the early national period include Merrill Jensen, *The New Nation, 1781–1789* (1950); Forrest McDonald, *E Pluribus Unum: The Forma-tion of the American Republic, 1776–1790* (1965); and Gordon S. Wood, *The Creation of the American Republic, 1776–1787* (1969).

On the crises that beset the Confederation see E. James Ferguson, *The Power of the Purse* (1961); David Szatmary, *Shays's Rebellion* (1980).

On the social impact of the American Revolution consult David Brion Davis, *The Problem of Slavery in the Age of Revolution* (1975); Philip S. Foner, *Labor and the American Revolution* (1977); Sylvia R. Frey, *Water from the Rock: Black Resistance in a Revolutionary Age* (1991); J. Franklin Jameson, *The Ameri-can Revolution Considered as a Social Movement* (1926); Linda Kerber, *Women of the Republic* (1980); Mary Beth Norton, *Liberty's Daughters: The Revolutionary Experience of American Women, 1750–1800* (1980); and Laurel Thatcher Ulrich, *A Midwife's Tale: The Life of Martha Ballard* (1990).

For important studies of the Philadelphia convention, see Charles A. Beard, *An Economic Interpretation of the Constitution of the United States* (1913); Forrest McDonald, *We the People: The Economic Origins of the Constitution* (1958), and *Novus Ordo Seclorum: The Intellectual Origins of the Constitution* (1985). For in-sights into the opponents of the Constitution, see Jackson T. Main, *The Antifed-eralists* (1961). See also Robert Rutland, *James Madison, the Founding Father* (1987); Jack N. Rakove, *James Madison and the Creation of the American Repub-lic* (1990).

Chapter *7*

Shaping the New Nation, 1789–1800

The United States was the first nation in history to institute a periodic national census. Since 1790, the country has tried to count each man, woman, and child every ten years. The first census asked just six simple questions, yet when supplemented with other statistical information, it provides a treasure chest of information about the social and economic life of the American people.

Taking the nation's first census was an extraordinarily difficult challenge. The nation's sheer physical size—stretching across 867,980 square miles—made it impossible to conduct an accurate count. Many people refused to speak to census takers; some because they feared that this was a step toward enactment of new taxes, others because they felt that the Bible prohibited census taking. To make matters worse, census takers were abysmally paid, receiving just $1 for every 150 rural residents and $1 for every 300 city dwellers counted. Indeed, the pay was so low that one judge found it difficult to find "any person whatever" to take the census.

What was the United States like in 1790? According to the first census, the United States contained just 3,929,214 people, about half living in the northern states, half in the South. At first glance, the population seems quite small (it was only about a quarter the size of England's and a sixth the size of France's). But it was growing extraordinarily rapidly. Just 1.17 million in 1750, the population would pass five million by 1800.

The 1790 census revealed a nation still overwhelmingly rural in character. In a population of nearly four million, only two cities had more than 25,000 people. Yet the urban population, while small, was growing extremely rapidly, especially in the West, where frontier towns like Louisville started to sprout.

In 1790, most Americans still lived on the Atlantic coast. Nevertheless, the West was the most rapidly growing part of the nation. During the 1790s, the population of Kentucky and Tennessee increased nearly 300 percent, and by 1800, Kentucky had more people than five of the original 13 states.

The first census also revealed an extraordinarily youthful population, with half the people under the age of 16. Exceptionally diverse, three-fifths of the white population was English in ancestry and another fifth was Scottish or Irish. The remainder was of German, Dutch, French, Swedish, or other background. A fifth of the entire population was African-American.

Records indicate that the American economy was still quite undeveloped. There were fewer than 100 newspapers in the entire country; three banks (with total capital of less than $5 million); three insurance companies; and 75 post offices. And yet the United States was perched on the edge of an extraordinary decade of growth.

Over the next ten years, American society made tremendous economic advances. During the 1790s, states chartered almost ten times more corporations, banks, and transportation companies than during the 1780s. Exports climbed from $29 million to $107 million; cotton production rose from 3,000 bales to 73,000 bales. The number of patents issued increased from just three in 1790 to 44 in 1800. Altogether, 11 mechanized mills were built in the country during the 1790s, laying the foundations of future economic growth.

In 1800, as in 1790, the United States remained a nation of farms, plantations, and small towns, of yeomen, slaves, and artisans. Nevertheless, the nation was undergoing far-reaching social and economic transformations. Improvements in education and culture were particularly striking. Between 1783 and 1800, Americans founded 17 new colleges and a large number of female academies.

For the young United States, the last years of the eighteenth century were a period of rapid demographic and economic growth. They were also years of crucial political developments. During this period the United States adopted a bill of rights protecting individual liberties, enacted a financial program securing the nation's credit, and created its first political parties. It was during this dramatic era that the United States established a strong and vigorous national government.

Putting the New National Government into Operation

The United States was the first modern nation to achieve independence through a successful revolution against colonial rule. Although many colonies in the nineteenth and twentieth centuries followed the example of the United States in winning independence through revolution, few were as successful in subsequently developing politically and economically. Even the United States, however, struggled to establish itself in its first decade under the Constitution.

The new nation faced severe economic and foreign policy problems. A huge debt remained from the Revolutionary War, and paper money issued during the war was virtually worthless. Along with these pressing economic problems were foreign threats to the new nation's independence. In violation of the peace treaty of 1783 ending the Revolutionary War, Britain continued to occupy forts in the Old Northwest, and Spain refused to recognize the new nation's southern and western boundaries. In 1790, economic problems, domestic political conflict, and foreign policy issues challenged the new nation in its efforts to establish a stable republic.

Setting Up a New Government

The first task facing American leaders was to establish the machinery of government. The new United States government consisted of nothing more than 75 post offices, a large debt, a small number of unpaid clerks, and an army of just 46 officers and 672 soldiers. There was no federal court system, no navy, and no system for collecting taxes.

It fell to Congress to take the initial steps toward putting the new national government into operation. To raise revenue, it passed a tariff on imported goods and an excise tax on liquor. To encourage American shipping, it imposed duties on foreign vessels. To provide a structure for the executive branch of government, it created departments of State, Treasury, and War. By the Judiciary Act of 1789, Congress organized a federal judiciary, which consisted of a Supreme Court with six justices, a district court in each state, and three appeals courts.

To strengthen popular support for the new government, Congress also approved a Bill of Rights for the Constitution. These first ten amendments guaranteed the rights of free press, free speech, and religion; the right to peaceful assembly; and the right to petition government. The Bill of Rights also ensured that the national government could not infringe on the right to trial by jury. In an effort to reassure Antifederalists that the powers of the new government were limited, the tenth amendment "reserved to the States respectively, or to the people" all powers not specified in the Constitution.

Defining the Presidency

The Constitution provided only a broad outline of the office and powers of the president. Important issues that would profoundly affect future generations of Americans remained unsettled. It would be up to George Washington, as the first president, to define the office, and to establish many precedents regarding the president's relationship with the other branches of government. It was unclear, for example, whether the president was to personally run the executive branch or, instead, act like a constitutional monarch and delegate responsibility to the vice president and executive officers, called the "cabinet." Washington favored a strong and active role for the president. Modeling the executive branch along the lines of a general's staff, Washington consulted his cabinet officers and listened to them carefully, but he made the final decisions, just as he had done while serving as commander-in-chief.

The relationship between the executive and legislative branches was also uncertain. Should a president, like Britain's prime minister, personally appear before Congress to defend administration policies? Should the Senate have sole power to dismiss executive officials? The answers to such questions were not clear. Washington insisted that the president could dismiss presidential appointees without the Senate's permission. A bitterly divided Senate approved this principle by a single vote.

With regard to foreign policy, Washington tried to follow the literal words of the Constitution, which stated that the president should negotiate treaties with the advice and consent of the Senate. He appeared before the Senate in person to discuss a pending Indian treaty. The senators, however, refused to provide immediate answers and referred the matter to a committee. "This defeats every purpose of my coming here," Washington declared. In the future he negotiated treaties first and then sent them to the Senate for ratification.

The most difficult task that the president faced was deciding whom to nominate for public office. For secretary of war, Washington nominated Henry Knox, an old military comrade, who had held a similar position under the Articles of Confederation. As postmaster general, he named Samuel Osgood of Massachusetts, who carried out his tasks in a single room with the help of two clerks. For attorney general, he tapped fellow Virginian Edmund Randolph, and John Jay as chief justice of the Supreme Court. He nominated a fellow Virginian, Thomas Jefferson, to the State Department. He named his former aide-de-camp, the 34-year-old Alexander Hamilton, to head the Treasury Department.

Alexander Hamilton's Financial Program

The most pressing problems facing the new government were economic. As a result of the Revolution, the federal government had acquired a huge debt: $54 million including interest. The states owed another $25 million. Paper money issued under the Continental Congresses and the Articles of Confederation was worthless. Foreign credit was unavailable.

Ten days after Alexander Hamilton became treasury secretary, Congress asked him to report on ways to solve the nation's financial problems. Hamilton, a man of strong political convictions, immediately realized that he had an opportunity to create a financial program that would embody his political principles.

Hamilton believed that the nation's stability depended on an alliance between the government and citizens of wealth and influence. No society could succeed, he maintained, "which did not unite the interest and credit of rich individuals with those of the state." Unlike Thomas Jefferson, Hamilton doubted the capacity of common people to govern themselves. "The people are turbulent and changing," he maintained, "they seldom judge or determine right."

To keep the masses in check, Hamilton favored a strong national government. Born in the British West Indies, Hamilton never developed the

George Washington's first cabinet consisted of Secretary of War Henry Knox, Secretary of the Treasury Alexander Hamilton, Secretary of State Thomas Jefferson, and Attorney General Edmund Randolph.

intense loyalty to a state that was common among many Americans of the time. He wanted to create a unified nation and a powerful federal government, intending to use government fiscal policies to strengthen federal power at the expense of the states and "make it in the immediate interest of the moneyed men to co-operate with government in its support."

The paramount problem facing Hamilton was the huge national debt. In 1790, the national debt totaled about $79 million. Hamilton argued that it was vital for the nation to fund these debts in order to establish the credit of the federal government. He proposed in his "Report on the Public Credit" (1790) that the government assume the entire indebtedness—principal and interest—of the federal government and the states.

This proposal ignited a firestorm of controversy, since states like Maryland, Pennsylvania, North Carolina, and Virginia had already paid off their war debts. They saw no reason why they should be taxed by the federal government to pay off the debts of states like Massachusetts and South Carolina. Others opposed the scheme because it would provide enormous profits to speculators who had bought bonds from Revolutionary War veterans for as little as 10 or 15 cents on the dollar. Many of these financial speculators were associates of Hamilton or members of Congress who knew that Hamilton's report would recommend full payment of the debt.

For six months a bitter debate raged in Congress. The nation's future seemed in jeopardy until a compromise orchestrated by James Madison and Thomas Jefferson secured passage of Hamilton's plan. In exchange for southern votes in Congress, Hamilton promised his support for locating the future national capital on the banks of the Potomac River, the border between two southern states, Virginia and Maryland.

Hamilton's debt program was a remarkable success. Funding and assumption of the debt created pools of capital for business investment and firmly established the credit of the United States abroad. By demonstrating Americans' willingness to repay their debts, he made America a good credit risk attractive to foreign investors. European investment capital started pouring into the new nation in large amounts.

Hamilton's next objective was to create a Bank of the United States, modeled after the Bank of England, to issue currency, collect taxes, hold government funds, regulate the nation's financial system, and make loans to the government and private borrowers. This proposal, like his debt scheme, unleashed a storm of protest.

One criticism directed against the bank was that it threatened to undermine the nation's republican values. Banks—and the paper money they issued—would simply encourage speculation, stock-jobbing and corruption. The bank was also opposed on constitutional grounds. Adopting a position known as "strict constructionism," Thomas Jefferson and James Madison charged that a national bank was unconstitutional since the Constitution did not specifically give Congress the power to create a bank. Other grounds for criticism were that the bank would subject America to foreign influences (because foreigners would have to purchase a high percentage of the bank's stock) and give a propertied elite disproportionate influence over the nation's fiscal policies (since private investors would control the bank's board of directors). Worse yet, the bank would increase the public debt, which, in turn, would add to the nation's tax burden. Under Hamilton's plan, the bank would raise capital by selling stock to private investors. Investors could pay for up to three-quarters of the bank stock they purchased with government bonds of indebtedness. The burden of financing the bank, therefore, would ultimately rest on the public treasury.

Hamilton responded to the charge that a bank was unconstitutional by formulating the doctrine of "implied powers." He argued that Congress did have the power to create a bank since the Constitution granted the federal government authority to do anything "necessary and proper" to carry out its constitutional functions (in this case its fiscal duties). This represented the first attempt to defend a "loose" interpretation of the Constitution.

In 1791 Congress passed a bill creating a national bank for a term of 20 years. The first Bank of the United States, like Hamilton's debt plan, was a great success. It helped regulate the currency of private banks. It provided a reserve of capital on which the government and private investors drew. It helped attract foreign investment to the credit-short new nation. In 1811, however, the jealousy of private commercial banks convinced Congress to allow the bank, which was chartered for a maximum of 20 years, to expire.

The final step in Hamilton's economic program was a proposal to aid the nation's infant industries. In his *Report on Manufactures* (1791), Hamilton argued that the nation's long-term interests "will be advanced, rather than injured, by the due encouragement of manufactures." Through high tariffs designed to protect American industry from foreign

The National Bank of the United States, which opened in Philadelphia in 1791, was a key part of Alexander Hamilton's economic plan for a strong central government.

competition, government bounties and subsidies, and internal improvements of transportation, he hoped to break Britain's manufacturing hold on America.

Opposition to Hamilton's proposal came from many quarters. Many Americans feared that the proposal would excessively cut federal revenues by discouraging imports. Shippers worried that the plan would reduce foreign trade. Farmers feared the proposal would lead foreign countries to impose retaliatory tariffs on American agricultural products.

The most eloquent opposition came from Thomas Jefferson, who believed that the growth of manufacturing threatened the values of an agrarian way of life. Hamilton's industrial vision of America's future directly challenged Jefferson's ideal of a nation of freehold farmers, tilling the fields, communing with nature, and maintaining personal freedom by virtue of land ownership. Manufacturing, Jefferson believed, should be left to European cities, which were cesspools of human corruption. Like slaves, factory workers would be manipulated by their masters, who not only would deny them satisfying lives but also would make it impossible for them to think and act as independent citizens.

Congress rejected most of Hamilton's proposals to aid industry. Nevertheless, the debate over Hamilton's plan carried with it fateful consequences. Fundamental disagreements had arisen between Hamiltonians and Jeffersonians over the federal government's role, constitutional interpretation, and distinct visions of how the republic should develop. To resolve these fundamental differences, Americans would create modern political parties—parties the writers of the Constitution neither wanted nor planned for.

The Birth of Political Parties

When George Washington assembled his first cabinet, there were no national political parties in the United States. In selecting cabinet members, he paid no attention to partisan labels and simply chose the individuals he believed were best qualified to run the new nation. Similarly, the new Congress had no party divisions. In all the states except Pennsylvania, politics was not waged between parties but, rather, between impermanent factions built around leading families, political managers, ethnic groups, or such interest groups as debtors and creditors.

By the time Washington retired from the presidency in 1797, the nature of the American political system had radically changed. The first president devoted part of his "Farewell Address" to denouncing "the baneful effects of the Spirit of Party," which had come to dominate American politics. Local and state factions had given way to two competing national parties, known as the Federalists and the Republicans. They nominated political candidates, managed electoral campaigns, and represented distinctive outlooks or ideologies. By 1796, the United States had produced its first modern party system. These political parties breathed new life into the concept of popular sovereignty, by making the people the ultimate arbiters in American political life.

The framers of the Constitution had not prepared their plan of government with political parties in mind. They associated parties with the interest groups that dominated the British government and hoped that in the United States the "better sort of citizens," rising above popular self-interest, would debate key issues and reach a harmonious consensus regarding how best to legislate for the nation's future.

Yet despite a belief that parties were evil and posed a threat to enlightened government, political factions gradually coalesced into political parties during Washington's first administration. To build support for his financial programs, Alexander Hamilton relied heavily on government patronage. Of 2,000 federal officeholders appointed between 1789 and 1801, two-thirds were Federalist party activists, who used positions as postmasters, tax collectors, judges, and customs house officials to favor the interests of the Federalists. By 1794 Hamilton's faction and its opponents had evolved into the first national political parties in history capable of nominating candidates, coordinating votes in Congress, staging public meetings, organizing petition campaigns, and disseminating propaganda.

Hamilton's opponents struck back. Madison and his ally Thomas Jefferson saw in Hamilton's program an effort to establish the kind of corrupt patronage society that existed in Britain, with a huge public debt, a standing army, high taxes, and government-subsidized monopolies. Hamilton's aim, declared Jefferson, was to assimilate "the American government to the form and spirit of the British monarchy."

World Events and Political Polarization

World events intensified partisan divisions. On July 14, 1789, 20,000 French men and women stormed the Bastille, a hated royal fortress, marking the beginning of the French Revolution. For three years France experimented with a constitutional monarchy. Then in 1792, the revolution took a violent turn. In August, Austrian and Prussian troops invaded France to put an end to the revolution. French revolutionaries responded by deposing King Louis XVI and placing him on trial. He was found guilty and, in January 1793, beheaded. France declared itself a republic and launched a reign of terror against counterrevolutionary elements in the population. A general war erupted in Europe pitting revolutionary France against a coalition of European monarchies, led by Britain. With two brief interruptions, this war would last 23 years.

Many Americans reacted enthusiastically to the overthrow of the king and the creation of a French republic. The French people appeared to have joined America in a historic struggle against royal absolutism and aristocratic privilege. More cautious men of privilege expressed horror at the cataclysm sweeping France. The French Revolution, they feared, was not merely a rebellion against royal authority, but a mass assault against property and Christianity. Conservatives urged President Washington to support England in its war against France.

Washington believed that involvement in the European war would weaken the new nation before it had firmly established its own independence. He proposed to keep the country "free from political connections with every other country, to see them independent of all, and under the influence of none." The president, however, faced a problem. During the War for American Independence, the United States had signed an alliance with France. Washington took the position that while the United States should continue to make payments on its war debts to France, it should refrain from directly supporting the new French Republic. In April 1793 he issued a proclamation of neutrality, stating that the "conduct" of the United States would be "friendly and impartial toward the belligerent powers."

1793 and 1794: Years of Crisis

During 1793 and 1794 a series of explosive new controversies further divided the followers of Hamilton and Jefferson. Washington's administration confronted a French effort to entangle America in its war with England, armed rebellion in western Pennsylvania, Indian uprisings, and the threat of war with Britain. These controversies intensified party spirit and promoted an increase in voting along party lines in Congress.

In April 1793, "Citizen" Edmond Charles Genêt, minister of the French Republic, arrived in the United States. His mission was to persuade American citizens to join in France's "war of all peoples against all kings." Genêt proceeded to pass out military commissions as part of a plan to attack Spanish New Orleans, and letters authorizing Americans to attack British commercial vessels. Washington regarded these activities as clear violations of U.S. neutrality, and demanded that France recall its hot headed minister. Fearful of continued political turmoil at home, Genêt requested and was granted political asylum, bringing his ill-fated mission to an end. However, the Genêt affair did have an important effect—it intensified party feeling. From Vermont to South Carolina, citizens organized Democratic-Republican clubs to celebrate the triumphs of the French Revolution. Hamilton suspected that these societies really existed to stir up grass-roots opposition to the Washington administration. Jefferson hotly denied these accusations, but the practical consequence was to further divide followers of Hamilton and Jefferson.

Political polarization was further intensified by the outbreak of popular protests in western Pennsylvania against Hamilton's financial program. To help fund the nation's war debt, Congress in 1791 passed Hamilton's proposal for a whiskey excise tax. Frontier farmers objected to the tax on whiskey as unfair. On the frontier, because of high transportation costs, the only practical way to sell surplus corn was to distill it into whiskey. Thus, frontier farmers regarded a tax on whiskey in the same way as American colonists had regarded Britain's stamp tax.

By 1794 western Pennsylvanians had had enough. Like the Shaysites of 1786, they rose up in defense of their property and the fundamental right to earn a decent living. Some 7,000 frontiersmen marched on Pittsburgh to stop collection of the tax. Determined to set a precedent for the federal government's authority, Washington gathered an army of 15,000 militiamen to disperse the rebels. In the face of this overwhelming force, the uprising collapsed. Two men were convicted of treason, but later pardoned by the president. The new government had proved that it would enforce laws enacted by Congress.

Thomas Jefferson viewed the Whiskey Rebellion from quite a different perspective. He saw the fiendish hand of Hamilton in putting down what he called a rebellion that "could never be found." Further, Jefferson claimed, Hamilton had used the army to stifle legitimate opposition to unfair government policies.

The year 1794 also brought a crisis in America's relations with Britain. For a decade, Britain had refused to evacuate forts in the Old Northwest as promised in the treaty ending the Revolution. Control of those forts impeded white settlement of the Great Lakes region and allowed the British to monopolize the fur trade. Frontiersmen believed that British officials at those posts sold firearms to the Indians and incited uprisings against white settlers. War appeared imminent when British warships stopped 300 American ships carrying food supplies to France and to France's overseas possessions, seized their cargoes, and forced seamen suspected of deserting from British ships into the British navy.

Washington acted decisively to end the crisis. He first moved to end the Indian threat. He called upon Revolutionary War veteran Anthony Wayne to clear the Ohio country of Indians. On August 20, 1794, Wayne's soldiers overwhelmed the resisting Indians at the Battle of Fallen Timbers in northwestern Ohio. Wayne later met with representatives of the Miami Confederacy and negotiated the Treaty of Greenville. Under

President Washington is reviewing the troops at Fort Cumberland, Maryland.
These troops formed part of the force of 15,000 militiamen Washington
assembled to disperse the Whiskey Rebellion in western Pennsylvania, a protest
against the whiskey excise tax.

this agreement, Native Americans ceded much of the present state of
Ohio in return for cash, presents, and a promise that the federal government would treat the Indian nations fairly in land dealings.

The president next sent Chief Justice John Jay to London to seek a
negotiated settlement with the British. The United States's strongest bargaining chip was a threat to join an alliance of European trading nations
to resist British trade restrictions. Alexander Hamilton may have undercut
Jay by secretly informing the British minister that the United States
would not join the alliance.

Jay secured the best agreement he could under the circumstances.
Britain agreed to evacuate its forts on American soil, and promised to
cease harassing American shipping (provided the ships did not carry con-
traband to Britain's enemies). Britain additionally agreed to pay damages
for the ships it had seized and to permit the United States to trade with
India and to carry on restricted trade with the British West Indies. But Jay
failed to win concessions on a host of other American grievances, such as
British incitement of the Indians, and Britain's routine searching of American ships for escaping deserters.

As a result of the debate over Jay's Treaty, the first party system fully emerged. Publication of the terms of the treaty unleashed a storm of protest from the emerging Jeffersonian Republicans. Republican newspapers and pamphlets denounced the treaty as craven submission to British imperial power and wealthy commercial, shipping, and trading interests. In Philadelphia a mob hanged Jay in effigy; in New York angry crowds pelted Alexander Hamilton with stones.

Washington never anticipated the wave of outrage that greeted his decision to sign the treaty. Republicans accused him of forming an Anglo-American alliance, and they made his last years in office miserable by attacking him for conducting himself like a "tyrant." They sought to kill the treaty in the House of Representatives by refusing to appropriate the funds necessary to carry out the treaty's terms unless the president submitted all documents relating to the treaty negotiations. Washington refused to comply with the House's request for information, thereby establishing the principle of executive privilege. This precedent gives the chief executive authority to withhold information from Congress on grounds of national security. In the end, fear that rejection of the Jay Treaty would result in disunion or war convinced the House to approve the needed appropriations.

Washington's popularity returned within a few months when he was able to announce that a treaty had been negotiated with Spain opening up the Mississippi River to American trade. Spain, fearing joint British and American action against its American colonies, recognized the Mississippi River as the new nation's western boundary and the 31st parallel (the northern border of Florida) as America's southern boundary. Pinckney's Treaty (1795)—also known as the Treaty of San Lorenzo—also granted Americans the right to navigate the Mississippi River as well as the right to export goods, duty free, through New Orleans, which was still a Spanish city.

Washington Decides to Retire

President Washington was now in a position to retire gracefully. He had avoided war, crushed the Indians, pushed the British out of western forts, established trade with selected parts of Asia, and opened the Northwest Territory to settlement. In his Farewell Address, published in a Philadelphia newspaper in 1796, Washington warned his countrymen against the growth of partisan divisions. In foreign affairs, he warned against long-term alliances. Declaring the "primary interests" of America and Europe to be fundamentally different, he argued that "it is our true policy to steer clear of permanent alliance with any portion of the foreign world."

A New President and New Challenges

Washington's decision to retire set the stage for one of the most critical presidential elections in American history. The election of 1796 was the first in which voters could choose between competing political parties; it was also the first election in which candidates were nominated for the vice presidency. It was a critical test of whether the nation could transfer power through a contested election.

The Federalists chose John Adams, the first vice president, as their presidential candidate, and the Republicans selected Thomas Jefferson. In an effort to attract southern support, the Federalists named Thomas Pinckney of South Carolina as Adams's running mate. The Republicans, hopeful of attracting votes in New York and New England, chose Aaron Burr of New York as their vice-presidential nominee.

Both parties turned directly to the people, rallying supporters through the use of posters, handbills, and rallies. For the first time in American history, the mass of people became directly involved in a presidential election. Republicans portrayed their candidate as "a firm Republican" while they depicted his opponent as "the champion of rank, titles, and hereditary distinctions." Federalists countered by condemning Jefferson as the leader of a "French faction" intent on undermining religion and morality.

In the popular voting, Federalists drew support from New England; commercial, shipping, manufacturing, and banking interests; Congregational and Episcopalian clergy; professionals; and farmers who produced for markets. Republicans attracted votes from the South and from smaller planters; backcountry Baptists, Methodists, and Roman Catholics; small merchants, tradesmen, and craftsmen; and subsistence farmers.

John Adams won the election, despite backstage maneuvering by Alexander Hamilton, who disliked Adams intensely. Hamilton developed a complicated scheme to elect Thomas Pinckney, the Federalist candidate for vice president. Under the electoral system originally set up by the Constitution, each presidential elector was allowed to vote twice, with the candidate who received the most votes becoming president, while the candidate who came in second was elected vice president. According to Hamilton's plan, southern electors would drop Adams's name from their ballots, while still voting for Pinckney. Thus Pinckney would receive more votes than Adams and be elected president. When New Englanders learned of this plan, they dropped Pinckney from their ballots, ensuring that Adams won the election. When the final votes were tallied, Adams received 71 votes, only three more than Jefferson. As a result, Jefferson became vice president.

The Presidency of John Adams

The new president was a 61-year-old Harvard-educated lawyer who had been an early leader in the struggle for independence. Short, bald, overweight, and vain (he was known, behind his back, as "His Rotundity"), Adams had found the vice presidency extremely frustrating. He complained to his wife Abigail: "My country has contrived for me the most insignificant office that ever the invention of man contrived or his imagination conceived."

His presidency also proved frustrating. He had failed to win a decisive electoral mandate and was saddled with the opposition leader as his vice president. He faced intense opposition within his own party and continuing problems from France throughout his four years in office. He avoided outright war with France, but he destroyed his political career. He suggested for his epitaph: "Here lies John Adams, who took upon himself the responsibility of the peace with France, in the year 1800."

The Quasi-War with France

A decade after the Constitution was written, the United States faced its most serious international crisis: an undeclared naval war with France. In the Jay Treaty, France perceived an American tilt toward Britain, especially in the provision permitting the British to seize French goods from American ships in exchange for financial compensation. France retaliated by launching an aggressive campaign against American shipping, particularly in the West Indies, capturing hundreds of vessels flying the United States flag.

Adams attempted to negotiate with France, but the French government refused to receive the American envoy and suspended commercial relations. Adams then called Congress into special session. Determined not to permit the United States to be "humiliated," he recommended that Congress arm American merchant ships, purchase new naval vessels, fortify harbors, and expand the artillery and cavalry. To pay for it all, Adams recommended a series of new taxes. By a single vote, a bitterly divided House of Representatives authorized the president to arm American merchant ships, but it postponed consideration of the other defense measures.

Adams then sent three commissioners to France to try to negotiate a settlement. Charles Maurice de Talleyrand, the French foreign minister, continually postponed official negotiations. In the meantime, three emissaries of the French minister (known later simply as X, Y, and Z) said that the only way the Americans could see the minister was to pay a bribe of

$250,000 and provide France with a $10 million loan. The indignant American commissioners refused. When word of the "XYZ affair" became known in the United States, it aroused a popular demand for war. The popular slogan was "millions for defense, but not one cent for tribute." The Federalist-controlled Congress authorized a standing army of 20,000 troops, a 30,000 man reserve army, and created the nation's first navy department. It also unilaterally abrogated America's 1778 treaty with France.

Adams named George Washington commanding general of the United States army, and, at Washington's insistence, designated Alexander Hamilton second in command. During the winter of 1798, 14 American warships backed by some 200 armed merchant ships captured some 80 French vessels and forced French warships out of American waters and back to bases in the West Indies. But the president refused to ask Congress for an official declaration of war. This is why this conflict is known as the quasi-war.

Despite intense pressure to declare war against France or to seize territory belonging to France's ally Spain, President Adams succeeded in averting full-scale war and achieving a peaceful settlement. Early in 1799, with the backing of moderate Federalists and Republicans, Adams proposed reestablishing diplomatic relations with France. When more extreme Federalists refused to go along with the plan, Adams threatened to resign and leave the presidency in the hands of Vice-President Jefferson.

In 1800, after seven months of wearisome negotiations, diplomats worked out an agreement known as the Convention of 1800. The agreement freed the United States from its alliance with France; in exchange, America forgave $20 million in damages caused by the illegal seizure of American merchant ships during the 1790s.

Adams kept the peace, but at the cost of a second term as president. The more extreme Federalists reacted furiously to the negotiated settlement. Hamilton vowed to destroy Adams: "If we must have an enemy at the head of Government, let it be one whom we can oppose, and for whom we are not responsible."

The Alien and Sedition Acts

During the quasi war the Federalist-controlled Congress attempted to suppress political opposition and stamp out sympathy for revolutionary France by enacting four laws in 1798 known as the Alien and Sedition acts. The Naturalization Act lengthened the period necessary before immigrants could receive citizenship from 5 to 14 years. The Alien Act gave the president the power to imprison or deport any foreigner believed to be dangerous to the United States. The Alien Enemies Act allowed the president to deport enemy aliens in time of war. Finally, the Sedition Act made it a crime to attack the government with "false, scandalous, or malicious" statements or writings. Adams, bitterly unhappy with the "spirit of falsehood and malignity" that threatened to undermine loyalty to the government, signed the measures.

The Alien acts were so broadly written that hundreds of foreign refugees fled to Europe fearing detention. But it was the Sedition Act that produced the greatest fear within the Republican opposition. Federalist prosecutors and judges used the Sedition Act to attack leading Republican newspapers, securing indictments against 25 people, mainly Republican editors and printers. Ten people were eventually convicted, one a Republican Congressman from Vermont.

Republicans accused the Federalists of conspiring to subvert fundamental liberties. In Virginia the state legislature adopted a resolution written by James Madison that advanced the idea that states have the right to determine the constitutionality of federal law, and pronounced the Alien and Sedition acts unconstitutional. Kentucky's state legislature went even further, adopting a resolution written by Thomas Jefferson that declared the Alien and Sedition acts "void and of no force." The Kentucky resolution raised an issue that would grow increasingly important in American politics in the years before the Civil War: Did states have the power to declare acts of Congress null and void? In 1799, however, no other states were willing to go as far as Kentucky and Virginia.

With the Union in danger, violence erupted. In the spring of 1799, German settlers in eastern Pennsylvania rose up in defiance of federal tax collectors. President Adams called out federal troops to suppress the so-called Fries Rebellion. The leader of the rebellion, an auctioneer named John Fries, was captured, convicted of treason, and sentenced to be hanged. Adams followed Washington's example in the Whiskey Rebellion and pardoned Fries, but Republicans feared that the Federalists were prepared to use the nation's army to suppress dissent.

The Revolution of 1800

In 1800 the young republic faced another critical test: Could national leadership pass peacefully from one political party to another? Once again, the nation had a choice between John Adams and Thomas Jefferson. But this election was more than a contest between two men; it was also a real party contest for control of the national government. Deep substantive and ideological issues divided the two parties. Federalists feared that Jefferson would reverse all the accomplishments of the preceding 12 years. A Republican president, they thought, would overthrow the Constitution by returning power to the states, dismantling the army and navy, and overturning Hamilton's financial system.

The Republicans charged that the Federalists, by creating a large standing army, imposing heavy taxes, and using federal troops and the federal courts to suppress dissent, had shown contempt for the liberties of the American people. They worried that the Federalists' ultimate goal was to centralize power in the national government and involve the United States in the European war on the side of Britain.

The contest was one of the most vigorous in American history and emotions ran high. Jefferson's Federalist opponents called him an "atheist in religion, and a fanatic in politics." They claimed he was a drunkard, an enemy of religion, and the father of numerous mulatto children. Jefferson's supporters responded by charging that President Adams was a warmonger, a spendthrift, and a monarchist who longed to reunite Britain with its former colonies.

The election was extremely close. The Federalists won all of New England's electoral votes, while the Republicans dominated the South and West. The final outcome hinged on the results in New York. Rural New York supported the Federalists, and Republican fortunes therefore depended on the voting in New York City. There, Jefferson's running mate, Aaron Burr, had created the most successful political organization the country had yet seen. Burr organized rallies, established ward committees, and promoted loyal supporters for public office. Burr's efforts paid off; Republicans won a majority in New York's legislature, which gave the state's 12 electoral votes to Jefferson and Burr.

Jefferson appeared to have won by a margin of eight electoral votes. But a complication soon arose. Because each Republican elector had cast one ballot for Jefferson and one for Burr, the two men received exactly the same number of electoral votes. Under the Constitution, the election was now thrown into the Federalist-controlled House of Representatives. Instead of emphatically declaring that he would not accept the presidency, Burr refused to say anything. So the Federalists faced a choice: they could help elect the hated Jefferson, or they could throw their support to the opportunistic Burr. Hamilton disliked Jefferson, but he believed he was a far more honorable man than Burr, whose "public principles have no other spring or aim than his own aggrandizement."

On February 17, 1801, after six days of balloting and 36 ballots, the House of Representatives finally elected Thomas Jefferson the third president of the United States. And as a result of the election, Congress adopted the Twelfth Amendment to the Constitution, which provides for separate ballots for president and for vice president.

Conclusion

In 1789 it was an open question whether the Constitution was a workable plan of government. It was still unclear if the new nation could establish a strong and vigorous national government or win the respect of foreign nations. For a decade, the new nation battled threats to its existence. It faced bitter party conflict, threats of secession, and foreign interference with American shipping and commerce.

*C*hronology of Key Events

1789	First session of Congress meets; Electoral College names George Washington the first president; Washington selects the first cabinet; Federal Judiciary Act establishes federal court system; French Revolution begins
1790	Congress adopts Hamilton's proposal to fund the national debt at full value and to assume all state debts
1791	Bank of the United States established; Congress adopts excise tax on distilled liquors; Bill of Rights becomes part of the Constitution
1793	Washington issues Neutrality Proclamation; Citizen Genêt affair
1794	Jay's Treaty; Whiskey Rebellion; Battle of Fallen Timbers
1795	Treaty of Greenville opens Ohio to white settlement; Pinckney Treaty negotiated with Spain
1796	Washington's Farewell Address
1797	John Adams inaugurated as second president
1798	XYZ Affair; undeclared naval war with France begins; Alien and Sedition acts; Virginia and Kentucky resolutions declare Alien and Sedition acts unconstitutional
1800	Washington, D.C. becomes nation's capital; Convention of 1800
1801	House of Representatives elects Thomas Jefferson as third president

By any standard, the new nation's achievements were impressive. During the first decade under the Constitution, the country adopted a bill of rights, protecting the rights of the individual against the power of the central and state governments; enacted a financial program that secured the government's credit and stimulated the economy; and created the first political parties that directly involved the enfranchised segment of the population in national politics. In the face of intense partisan conflict, the United States became the first nation to transfer political power peacefully from one party to another as a result of an election. A nation, strong and viable, had emerged from its baptism by fire.

Suggestions for Further Reading

For an overview of the Federalist period consult Stanley M. Elkins and Eric McKitrick, *The Age of Federalism* (1993); John C. Miller, *The Federalist Era* (1960). See also Leonard D. White, *The Federalists* (1948).

Important biographies of George Washington include Marcus Cunliffe, *George Washington: Man and Monument* (1958); James Thomas Flexner, *George Washington*, 4 vols. (1965–1972). For further information on the Washington administration consult Harry Ammon, *The Genêt Mission* (1973); Thomas P. Slaughter, *The Whiskey Rebellion* (1986). See also Jacob E. Cooke, *Alexander Hamilton* (1982). On John Adams see Ralph Adams Brown, *The Presidency of John Adams* (1975).

The rise of the two-party system is examined in John F. Hoadley, *Origins of American Political Parties* (1986). For more on the Jeffersonian ideology see Joyce Appleby, *Capitalism and a New Social Order: The Republican Vision of the 1790s* (1984); Lance Banning, *The Jeffersonian Persuasion* (1978); Daniel Sisson, *The American Revolution of 1800* (1974).

Chapter 8

The Jeffersonians in Power, 1800–1815

On the morning of June 18, 1804, a visitor handed a package to the former Treasury secretary Alexander Hamilton. Inside was a newspaper clipping and a terse three-sentence letter. The clipping said that Hamilton had called Vice President Aaron Burr "a dangerous man, and one who ought not to be trusted with the reins of government." It went on to say that Hamilton had "expressed" a "still more despicable opinion" of Burr—apparently a bitter personal attack on Burr's public and private morality, not merely a political criticism. The letter, signed by Burr, demanded a "prompt and unqualified" denial or an immediate apology.

Hamilton and Burr had sparred verbally for decades. Hamilton regarded Burr as an unscrupulous man, and had worked to defeat him in Burr's race for governor of New York earlier in the year. When, after three weeks, Hamilton had failed to respond to his letter satisfactorily, Burr insisted that they settle the dispute according to the code of honor.

Shortly after 7 o'clock on the morning of July 11, 1804, Burr and Hamilton met on the wooded heights of Weehawken, New Jersey, a customary dueling ground directly across the Hudson River from New York. Hamilton's son Philip had died there in a duel in 1801.

Hamilton's second handed Burr one of two pistols equipped with hairspring triggers. After he and Burr took their positions ten paces apart, Hamilton raised his pistol on the command to "Present!" and fired. His shot struck a tree a few feet to Burr's side. Then Burr fired. His shot struck Hamilton in the right side and passed through his liver. Hamilton died the following day.

The states of New York and New Jersey wanted to try Burr for murder; New Jersey actually indicted him. The vice president fled through New Jersey by foot and wagon to Philadelphia, then took refuge in Georgia and South Carolina, until the indictments were quashed and he could finish his term in office.

The Jeffersonian era—the period stretching from 1800 to 1815—was rife with conflict, partisan passion, and larger-than-life personalities. On the domestic front, a new political party, the Republicans, came to office for the first time and a former vice president was charged with treason against his country. The era was also marked by foreign policy challenges. Pirates, operating from bases on the coast of North Africa, harassed American shipping and enslaved American sailors. Britain and France interfered with American shipping. Finally, the United States once again waged war with Britain, the world's strongest power. These developments raised profound questions: Could the country peacefully transfer political power from one party to another? Could the country preserve political stability? And most important of all, could the nation preserve its neutral rights and national honor in the face of grave threats from Britain and France?

In 1800, Aaron Burr ran as Jefferson's vice-presidential candidate. Burr's effective campaigning tactics and efficient political machine in New York helped bring victory to the Republican party.

Jefferson Takes Command

Thomas Jefferson's goal as president was to restore the principles of the American Revolution. In his view, a decade of Federalist party rule had threatened republican government. Not only had the Federalists levied oppressive taxes, stretched the provisions of the Constitution, and established a bastion of wealth and special privilege in the creation of a national bank, they also had subverted civil liberties and expanded the powers of the central government at the expense of the states. A new revolution was necessary, "as real a revolution in the principles of our government as that of 1776 was in its form." What was needed was a return to basic republican principles.

Beginning with his very first day in office Jefferson sought to demonstrate his administration's commitment to republican principles. At noon, March 4, 1801, Jefferson, clad in clothes of plain cloth, walked from a nearby boarding house to the new United States Capitol in Washington. Without ceremony, he entered the Senate chamber and took the presidential oath of office. In his inaugural address Jefferson sought to allay fear that he planned a Republican reign of terror. "We are all Republicans," he said, "we are all Federalists." Echoing George Washington's

Farewell Address, he asked his listeners to set aside partisan and sectional differences. He also laid out the principles that would guide his presidency: a frugal, limited government; reduction of the public debt; respect for states' rights; encouragement of agriculture; and a limited role for government in peoples' lives. He committed his administration to repealing oppressive taxes, slashing government expenses, cutting military expenditures, and paying off the public debt.

Restoring Republican Government

Thomas Jefferson, the nation's third president, was a man of many talents. Though best known for his political accomplishments, he was also an architect, inventor, philosopher, planter, scientist, and talented violinist. Jefferson was an extremely complex man, and his life was filled with apparent inconsistencies. An idealist who repeatedly denounced slavery, the "Apostle of Liberty" owned 200 slaves when he wrote the Declaration of Independence and freed only five slaves at the time of his death. A vigorous opponent of all forms of human tyranny and staunch defender of human equality, he adopted a patronizing attitude toward women, declaring that their proper role was to "soothe and calm the minds of their husbands." And yet Jefferson remains this country's most eloquent exponent of democratic principles. A product of the Enlightenment, Jefferson was a stalwart defender of political freedom, equality, religious freedom, and intellectual freedom. He was convinced that the yeoman farmer, who worked the land, provided the backbone of democracy. He popularized the idea that a democratic republic required an enlightened and educated citizenry and that government had a duty to assist in the education of a meritocracy based on talent and ability.

As president, Jefferson strove to return the nation to republican values. Through his personal conduct and public policies he sought to return the country to the principles of democratic simplicity, economy, and limited government. He took a number of steps designed to rid the White House of aristocratic customs that had prevailed during the administrations of Washington and Adams. He introduced the custom of having guests shake hands instead of bowing stiffly; he also placed dinner guests at a round table, so that no individual would have to sit in a more important place than any other. In an effort to discourage a "cult of personality," he refused to sanction public celebrations of his birthday declaring, "The only birthday I ever commemorate is that of our Independence, the Fourth of July." Jefferson refused to ride in an elegant coach or host formal dinner parties and balls. Instead, he invited small groups of senators and representatives to dinner and wore clothes made of homespun cloth.

Jefferson believed that presidents should not try to impose their will on Congress, and consequently he refused to initiate legislation or to veto congressional bills on policy grounds. Convinced that presidents Washington and Adams had acted like British monarchs by personally appearing before Congress and requesting legislation, Jefferson simply sent Congress written messages. It would not be until the presidency of Woodrow Wilson that another president would publicly address Congress and call for legislation.

Jefferson's commitment to republican simplicity was matched by his stress on economy in government. His ideal was "a wise and frugal Government, which shall . . . leave [Americans] free to regulate their own pursuits of industry and improvement." He slashed army and navy expenditures, cut the budget, eliminated taxes on whiskey, houses, and slaves, and fired all federal tax collectors. He reduced the army to 3,000 soldiers and 172 officers, the navy to 6 frigates, and foreign embassies to 3—in Britain, France, and Spain. His budget cuts allowed him to cut the federal debt by a third, despite the elimination of all internal taxes.

Jefferson did not conceive of government in entirely negative terms. Convinced that ownership of land and honest labor were the firmest bases of political stability, Jefferson convinced Congress to cut the price of public lands and to extend credit to purchasers in order to encourage landownership and rapid western settlement. A firm believer in the idea that America should be the "asylum" for "oppressed humanity," he persuaded Congress to reduce the residence requirement for citizenship from 14 to 5 years. In the interest of protecting civil liberties, he allowed the Sedition Act to expire in 1801, freed all people imprisoned under the act, and refunded their fines.

In one area Jefferson felt his hands were tied. He considered the Bank of the United States "the most deadly" institution to republican government. But Hamilton's bank had been legally chartered for 20 years and Jefferson's secretary of the Treasury, Albert Gallatin, said that the bank was needed to provide credit for the nation's growing economy. So Jefferson allowed the bank to continue to operate, but he weakened its influence by distributing the federal government's deposits among 21 state banks.

Contemporaries were astonished by the sight of a president who had renounced all the practical tools of government: an army, a navy, and taxes. Jefferson's actions promised, said a British observer, "a sort of Millennium in government." Jefferson's goal was, indeed, to create a new kind of government, a republican government wholly unlike the centralized, corrupt, patronage-ridden one against which Americans had rebelled in 1776.

Reforming the Federal Government

Jefferson thought that one of the major obstacles to restoring republican government was the 3,000 Federalist officeholders. Of the first 600 political appointees named to federal office by presidents Washington and Adams, all but six were Federalists. Even after learning of his defeat, Adams appointed Federalists to every vacant government position. The most dramatic postelection appointment was naming John Marshall, a Federalist, chief justice of the Supreme Court.

Jefferson was committed in principle to the idea that government office should be filled on the basis of merit, not political connections. Only government officeholders guilty of malfeasance or incompetence should be fired. Nothing more should be asked of government officials, he felt, than that they be honest, able, and loyal to the Constitution. Jefferson wholly rejected the idea that a victorious political party had a right to fill public offices with loyal party supporters.

Although many Republicans felt that Federalists should be replaced by loyal Republicans, Jefferson declared that he would remove only "midnight" appointees who had been named to office by President Adams after he learned of his electoral defeat. Nevertheless, Jefferson fired relatively few Federalists. During his first two years in office, he replaced just one-third of all government officials.

War on the Judiciary

When Thomas Jefferson took office, not a single Republican served as a federal judge. In Jefferson's view, the Federalists had turned the federal judiciary into a branch of their political party and intended to use the courts to frustrate Republican plans. The first major political battle of Jefferson's presidency involved his effort to weaken Federalist control of the federal judiciary.

The specific issue that provoked Republican anger was the Judiciary Act of 1801, which was passed by Congress five days before Adams's term expired. The law created 16 new federal judgeships, positions which President Adams promptly filled with Federalists. Even more damaging, from a Republican perspective, the act strengthened the power of the central government by extending the jurisdiction of the federal courts over such issues as bankruptcy and land disputes, which were previously the exclusive domain of state courts. Finally, the act reduced the number of Supreme Court justices effective with the next vacancy, delaying Jefferson's opportunity to name a new Supreme Court justice.

Jefferson's supporters in Congress repealed the Judiciary Act of 1801, but the war over control of the federal courts continued. One of Adams's "midnight appointments" to a judgeship was William Marbury, a loyal Federalist. Although approved by the Senate, Marbury never received his letter of appointment from Adams. When Jefferson became president, Marbury demanded that the new secretary of state, James Madison, issue the commission. Madison refused and Marbury sued, claiming that under section 13 of the Judiciary Act of 1789, the Supreme Court had the power to issue a court order that would compel Madison to give him his judgeship.

The case threatened to provoke a direct confrontation between the judiciary on the one hand and the executive and legislative branches of the federal government on the other. If the Supreme Court ordered Madison to give Marbury his judgeship, the secretary of state was likely to ignore the Court, and Jeffersonians in Congress might try to limit the high court's power.

In his opinion in *Marbury* v. *Madison* John Marshall, the new chief justice of the Supreme Court, ingeniously expanded the court's power without directly provoking the Jeffersonians. Marshall conceded that Mar-

John Marshall, the fourth chief justice of the United States, expanded the Court's power in *Marbury v. Madison* by establishing the right of judicial review. He thus gave the federal courts the power to determine the constitutionality of federal laws and congressional acts.

bury had a right to his appointment but ruled the Court had no authority to order the secretary of state to act, since the section of the Judiciary Act that gave the Court the power to issue an order was unconstitutional.

Marbury v. *Madison* was a landmark in American constitutional history. The decision firmly established the power of the federal courts to review the constitutionality of federal laws and to invalidate acts of Congress when they are found to conflict with the Constitution. This power, known as *judicial review,* provides the basis for the important place that the Supreme Court occupies in American life today.

Marshall's decision in *Marbury* v. *Madison* intensified Republican party distrust of the courts. Impeachment, Jefferson and his followers believed, was the only way to be rid of federal judges they considered unfit or overly partisan, and make the courts responsive to the public will. Federalists responded by accusing the administration of endangering the independence of the federal judiciary.

Three weeks before the Court handed down its decision in *Marbury* v. *Madison,* congressional Republicans launched impeachment proceedings against Federal District Judge John Pickering of New Hampshire. An alcoholic who may have been insane, Pickering was convicted and removed from office.

On the day of Pickering's conviction, the House voted to impeach Supreme Court Justice Samuel Chase, a staunch Federalist. From the bench, he had openly denounced equal rights and universal suffrage and accused the Jeffersonians of atheism and being power hungry. Undoubtedly, Chase was guilty of unrestrained partisanship and injudicious statements. An irate President Jefferson called for Chase's impeachment.

Chase was put on trial for holding opinions "hurtful to the welfare of the country." But the real issue was whether Chase had committed an impeachable offense, since the Constitution specified that a judge could only be removed from office for "treason, bribery, or other high crimes" and not for partisanship or judicial misconduct. In a historic decision that helped to guarantee the independence of the judiciary, the Senate voted to acquit Chase. Although a majority of the Senate found him guilty, seven Republicans broke ranks and denied Jefferson the two-thirds majority needed for a conviction.

Chase's acquittal had momentous consequences for the future. If the Jeffersonians had succeeded in removing Chase, they would probably have removed other Federalist judges from the federal bench. However, since Chase's acquittal, no further attempts have ever been made to remove federal judges solely on the grounds of partisanship or to reshape the federal courts through impeachment. Despite the Republicans' active hostility toward an independent judiciary, the Supreme Court had emerged as a vigorous third branch of government.

International Conflict

In his inaugural address Thomas Jefferson declared that his fondest wish was for peace. "Peace is my passion," he repeatedly insisted. As president, however, he was unable to realize his wish. Like Washington and Adams before him, Jefferson faced the difficult task of preserving American independence and neutrality in a world torn by war and revolution.

The Barbary Pirates

Jefferson's first major foreign policy crisis came from the "Barbary pirates" who preyed on American shipping off the coast of North Africa. The conflict began in 1785, when Algerian pirates boarded an American merchant schooner sailing off the coast of Portugal, took its 21-member crew to Algeria, and enslaved them. During the next eight years, 100 more hostages were seized from American ships. Congress agreed to pay a ransom for their release, and by 1800 one-fifth of all federal revenues went to the North African states as tribute.

Early in Jefferson's first term, he refused to pay additional tribute demanded by the North African states. Determined to end the humiliating demands, he sent warships to the Mediterranean to enforce a blockade of Tripoli. The result was a protracted conflict with Tripoli, which lasted until 1805. Tripoli eventually agreed to make peace, though the United States continued to pay other Barbary states until 1816.

The Louisiana Purchase

At the same time that conflict raged with the Barbary pirates, a more serious crisis loomed on the Mississippi River. In 1795, Spain granted western farmers the right to ship their produce down the Mississippi River to New Orleans, where their cargoes of corn, whiskey, and pork were loaded aboard ships bound for the east coast and foreign ports. In 1800, Spain secretly ceded the Louisiana territory to France, and closed the port of New

Barbary States

Thomas Jefferson's first foreign policy crisis occurred when he refused to pay tribute to the Barbary States for the release of hostages captured by Algerian pirates. Instead, he sent eight ships to enforce a blockade of Tripoli.

Orleans to American farmers. Westerners, left without a port from which to export their goods, exploded with anger. Many demanded war.

The prospect of French control of the Mississippi alarmed Jefferson. Spain had held only a weak and tenuous grip on the Mississippi, but France was a much stronger power. Jefferson feared the establishment of a French colonial empire in North America blocking American expansion. The United States appeared to have only two options: diplomacy or war.

The president sent James Monroe to join Robert Livingston, the American minister to France, with instructions to purchase New Orleans and as much of the Gulf Coast as they could for $2 million. Circumstances played into American hands when 100,000 slaves rose up in revolt in the French colony of Haiti. In 1800, France sent troops to crush the insurrection, but they met a determined resistance led by a former slave named Toussaint L'Ouverture. Then, they were wiped out by mosquitoes carrying yellow fever. Without Haiti, which he regarded as the centerpiece of an American empire, French ruler Napoleon Bonaparte had little interest in keeping Louisiana.

Two days after Monroe's arrival, the French finance minister unexpectedly announced that France was willing to sell not just New Orleans but all of Louisiana Province, a territory extending from Canada to the Gulf of Mexico and westward as far as the Rocky Mountains. The American negotiators agreed on a price of $15 million, or about 4 cents an acre.

Since the Constitution did not give the president specific authorization to purchase land, Jefferson considered asking for a constitutional amendment empowering the government to acquire territory. In Congress Federalists bitterly denounced the purchase, fearing that the creation of new western states would weaken the influence of their party. In the end Jefferson, fearing that Napoleon might change his mind, simply sent the agreement to the Senate, which ratified it. "The less said about any constitutional difficulty, the better," he stated. In a single stroke, Jefferson had doubled the size of the country.

To gather information about the geography, natural resources, wildlife, and peoples of Louisiana, President Jefferson dispatched an expedition led by his private secretary Meriwether Lewis and William Clark, a Virginia-born military officer. For two years Lewis and Clark led some 30 soldiers and ten civilians up the Missouri River as far as present-day central North Dakota and then west to the Pacific.

Disunionist Conspiracies

Anger over the acquisition of Louisiana led some Federalists to consider secession as a last resort to restore their party's former dominance. One group of Federalist congressmen plotted to establish a "Northern Confederacy," which would consist of New Jersey, New York, the New England

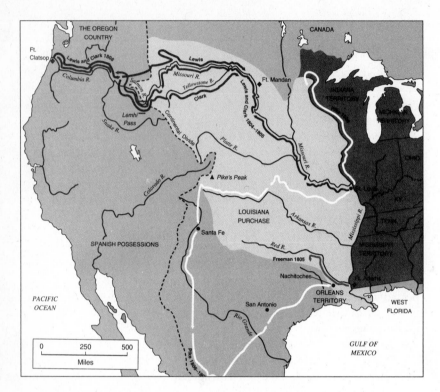

The Louisiana Purchase and Route of Lewis and Clark

No one realized how much territory Jefferson had acquired through the Louisiana Purchase until Lewis and Clark explored the far West.

states, and Canada. Alexander Hamilton repudiated this scheme, and the conspirators turned to Vice President Aaron Burr. In return for Federalist support in his campaign for the governorship of New York, Burr was to swing New York into the Northern Confederacy. Burr was badly beaten, in part because of Hamilton's opposition. Incensed and irate, Burr challenged Hamilton to the duel described at the beginning of this chapter.

Because of the duel, Burr was now a ruined politician and a fugitive from the law. The Republican party stripped away his control over political patronage in New York. His fortunes at their lowest point, the desperate Burr became involved in a conspiracy for which he would be put on trial for treason.

During the spring of 1805 Burr traveled to the West, where he and James Wilkinson, military governor of Louisiana, hatched an adventurous scheme. It is still uncertain what the conspirators' goal was, since Burr, in his efforts to attract support, told different stories to different people.

Spain's minister believed that Burr planned to set up an independent nation in the Mississippi Valley. Others reported that he planned to seize Spanish territory in what is now Texas, California, and New Mexico. The British minister was told that for $500,000 and British naval support, Burr would separate the states and territories west of the Appalachians from the rest of the Union and create an empire with himself as its head.

In the fall of 1806 Burr and some 60 conspirators traveled down the Ohio River toward New Orleans to assess possibilities and perhaps to incite disgruntled French settlers to revolt. Wilkinson, recognizing that the scheme was doomed to failure, decided to betray Burr. He wrote a letter to Jefferson describing a "deep, dark, wicked, and widespread conspiracy, . . . to seize on New Orleans, revolutionize the territory, and carry an expedition against Mexico."

Burr fled, but was finally apprehended in the Mississippi Territory. He was then taken to the Richmond, Virginia, circuit court, where, in 1807, he was tried for treason. Jefferson, convinced that Burr was a dangerous man, wanted a conviction regardless of the evidence. Chief Justice Marshall, who presided over the trial, was equally eager to discredit Jefferson. Ultimately, Burr was acquitted. The reason for the acquittal was the Constitution's very strict definition of treason as "levying war against the United States" or "giving . . . aid and comfort" to the nation's enemies. In addition, each overt act of treason had to be attested to by two witnesses. The prosecution was unable to meet this strict standard, and as a result of Burr's acquittal, few future cases of treason have ever been tried in the United States.

Was Burr guilty of conspiring to destabilize the United States and separate the West by force? Probably not. The prosecution's case rested largely on the unreliable testimony of coconspirator James Wilkinson, who was a spy in the pay of Spain while also a U.S. army commander and governor of Louisiana. What, then, was the purpose of Burr's mysterious scheming? It appears likely that the former vice president was planning a filibuster expedition—an unauthorized military attack—on Mexico, which was then controlled by Spain. The dream of creating a western republic appealed to many early nineteenth-century Americans—especially to those who feared that a European power might seize Spain's New World colonies unless America launched a preemptive strike. To the end of his life, Burr denied that he had plotted treason against the United States.

The Eagle, the Tiger, and the Shark

In 1804 Jefferson was easily reelected, carrying every state except Connecticut and Delaware. He received 162 electoral votes to only 14 for his Federalist opponent, Charles C. Pinckney. Although his second term began, he later wrote, "without a cloud on the horizon," storm clouds soon gathered as a result of renewed war in Europe. Jefferson faced the difficult challenge of keeping the United States out of the European war, while defending the nation's rights as a neutral.

In May 1803, just two weeks after Napoleon sold Louisiana to the United States, France declared war on Britain. As part of his overall strategy to bring Britain to its knees, Napoleon instituted the "Continental System," a policy of economic warfare which closed European ports to British goods and ordered the seizure of any neutral vessel that carried British goods or stopped in a British port. Britain retaliated in 1807 by issuing Orders in Council, which required all neutral ships to land at a British port to obtain a trading license and pay a tariff. Britain threatened to seize any ship that failed to obey the Orders in Council. By 1807, France had seized 500 ships and Britain nearly 1,000.

United States shipping was caught in the crossfire. The most outrageous violation of America's neutral rights was the British practice of impressment. The British navy desperately needed sailors. Unable to procure sufficient volunteers, the British navy resorted to seizing—impressing—men on streets, in taverns, and on British merchant ships. When these efforts failed to muster sufficient men, the British began to stop foreign ships and remove seamen alleged to be British subjects. By 1811, nearly 10,000 American sailors had been forced into the British Navy, although an undetermined number were actually deserters from British ships who made more money sailing on U.S. ships.

Outrage over impressment reached a fever pitch in 1807 when the British man-of-war *Leopard* fired three broadsides at the American naval frigate *Chesapeake,* which had refused to allow British officers to search the American ship for Royal Navy deserters. The blasts killed three American sailors. British authorities then boarded the American ship and removed four seamen, only one of whom was really a British subject.

"Dambargo"

In a desperate attempt to stave off war, for which it was ill prepared, and win respect for America's neutral rights, the United States imposed an embargo on foreign trade. Convinced that American trade was vital to European industry, Jefferson persuaded Congress in late 1807 to adopt a policy of "peaceable coercion": a ban on all foreign shipping and exports.

Jefferson regarded the embargo as an idealistic experiment—a moral alternative to war. Jefferson was not a doctrinaire pacifist, but he had long advocated economic coercion as an instrument of diplomacy. Now he had a chance to put his ideas into practice.

The embargo was an unpopular and costly failure. It hurt the American economy far more than the British or French, and resulted in widespread smuggling. Without the European export market, warehouses were crammed with huge stockpiles of unsold grain and cotton. Farm prices fell sharply. Shippers also suffered. Without the lucrative wartime trade, harbors filled with idle ships and nearly 30,000 sailors found themselves jobless. The embargo resuscitated the Federalist party, which regained power in several New England states and made substantial gains in the congressional elections of 1808.

Jefferson believed that Americans would cooperate with the embargo out of a sense of patriotism. Instead, evasions of the act were widespread, and smuggling flourished, particularly through Canada. Pressure to abandon the embargo mounted, and early in 1809, just three days before Jefferson left office, Congress repealed the embargo. In effect for 15 months, the embargo exacted no political concessions from either France or Britain. But it had produced economic hardship, evasion of the law, and political dissension at home.

The problem of American neutrality now fell to Jefferson's handpicked successor, James Madison. "The Father of the Constitution" was small in stature and frail in health. A quiet and scholarly man, who secretly suffered from epilepsy, Madison brought a keen intellect and a wealth of experience to the presidency. As Jefferson's secretary of state, he had kept the United States out of the Napoleonic wars, and was committed to using economic coercion to force Britain and France to respect America's neutral rights.

In 1809, Congress replaced the failed embargo with the Non-Intercourse Act, which reopened trade with all nations except Britain and France. Violations of American neutrality continued, and a year later Congress replaced the Non-Intercourse Act with a new measure, Macon's Bill No. 2. This policy reopened trade with France and Britain. It stated, however, that if either Britain or France agreed to respect America's neutral rights, the United States would immediately stop trade with the other nation. Napoleon seized on this new policy in an effort to entangle the United States in his war with Britain. In the summer of 1810 he announced repeal of all French restrictions on American trade. Even though France continued to seize American ships and cargoes, President Madison snapped at the bait. In early 1811, he cut off trade with Britain and recalled the American minister.

For 19 months, the British went without American trade, but gradually economic coercion worked. Food shortages, mounting unemployment, and increasing inventories of unsold manufactured goods led the British to end its trade restrictions (though not the British Navy's policy of impressment). But it was too late; President Madison had already asked Congress for a declaration of war. A divided House and Senate concurred. The House voted to declare war on Britain by a vote of 79 to 49; the Senate by a vote of 19 to 13.

A Second War of Independence

Why did the United States declare war on Britain in 1812? Resentment at British interference with American rights on the high seas was certainly the most loudly voiced grievance. British trade restrictions, impressment of thousands of American seamen, and British blockades humiliated the country and undercut America's national honor and neutral rights.

But if British harassment of American shipping was the primary motivation for war, why then did the pro-war majority in Congress come largely from the South, the West, and the frontier, and not from northeastern shipowners and sailors? The vote to declare war on Britain divided along sharp regional lines. Representatives from western, southern, and frontier states voted 65 to 15 for war, while representatives from New England, New York, and New Jersey, states with strong shipping interests, voted 34 to 14 against war.

Northeastern Federalists and a handful of Republicans from coastal regions of the South regarded war with Britain as a grave mistake. The United States, they insisted, could not hope to challenge British supremacy on the seas and the government could not finance a war without bankrupting the country. Southerners and westerners, in contrast, were eager to avenge British actions that mocked American sovereignty on land and sea. Many southerners and westerners blamed British trade policies for depressing agricultural prices and producing an economic depression. War with Britain also offered another incentive: the possibility of clearing western lands of Indians by removing the Indians' strongest ally—the British. And finally, many westerners and southerners had their eye on expansion, viewing war as an opportunity to add Canada and Spanish-held Florida to the United States.

Weary of Jefferson and Madison's patient and pacifistic policy of economic coercion, voters swept 63 out of 142 representatives from Congress in 1810 and replaced them with young Republicans that Federalists dubbed "War Hawks." These second-generation Republicans avidly supported national expansion and national honor. These young Republicans elected Henry Clay, a representative from frontier Kentucky, Speaker of the House on his very first day in Congress. Clay then assigned other young Republicans, such as John C. Calhoun, a freshman representative from South Carolina, to key House committees.

Staunchly nationalist and rabidly anti-British, eager for territorial expansion and economic growth, the young Republicans regarded the Napoleonic Wars in Europe as an unparalleled opportunity to defend national honor, assert American interests, and conquer Canada and Florida.

Further contributing to their pro-war fervor was the belief that the British incited frontier Indian attacks. Anti-British feeling soared in November 1811, when General William Henry Harrison precipitated a fight with an Indian alliance led by the Shawnee Prophet, Tenskwatawa, at Tippecanoe Creek in Indiana. More than 60 American soldiers were killed and 100 were wounded. Since British guns were found on the battlefield, young Republicans concluded that the British were responsible for the incident.

Early Defeats

Although Congress voted strongly in favor of war, the country entered the conflict deeply divided. Not only would many New Englanders refuse to subscribe to war loans, some merchants would actually ship provisions that Britain needed to support its army, which was fighting Napoleon in

At the Battle of Tippecanoe, U.S. troops led by General William Henry Harrison routed the smaller force of Native Americans under the Shawnee prophet, Tenskwatawa.

Europe. Moreover, the United States was woefully unprepared for war. The army consisted of fewer than 7,000 soldiers and the navy was grotesquely overmatched.

The American strategy called for a three-pronged invasion of Canada and heavy harassment of British shipping. The attack on Canada, however, was a disastrous failure. At Detroit, 2,000 American troops surrendered to a much smaller British and Indian force. An attack across the Niagara River, near Buffalo, resulted in 900 American prisoners of war when the New York State militia refused to provide support. Along Lake Champlain a third army retreated into American territory after failing to cut undefended British supply lines. By the end of 1812, British forces controlled key forts in the Old Northwest, including Detroit and Fort Dearborn, the future site of Chicago. The only consolation for the Americans was a string of naval victories in single-ship encounters.

In 1813 America suffered new failures. In January, an American army advancing toward Detroit was defeated and captured in the swamps west of Lake Erie. Then, in April, Americans staged a raid across Lake Ontario to York (now Toronto). American soldiers set fire to the two houses of the provincial parliament, an act that brought retaliation in the burning of Washington, D.C., by the British. A plan to capture Montreal in the fall of 1813 also ended without an attack.

Only a series of unexpected victories at the end of the year raised American spirits. On September 10, 1813, America won a major naval victory at the Battle of Lake Erie. There, Oliver Hazard Perry successfully engaged six British ships. Though Perry's flagship, the *Lawrence,* was disabled in the fighting, he went on to capture the British fleet. He reported his victory with the stirring words, "We have met the enemy and they are ours."

The Battle of Lake Erie was America's first major victory of the war. It forced the British to abandon Detroit and retreat toward Niagara. On October 5, 1813, Major General William Henry Harrison overtook the retreating British army and their Indian allies at the Thames River. He won a decisive victory in which the Indian leader Tecumseh was killed, thereby ending the fighting strength of the northwestern Indians.

The Tide Turns

In early 1814, prospects for an American victory dimmed. In the spring, Britain defeated Napoleon in Europe, freeing 18,000 veteran British troops to participate in an invasion of the United States. The British planned to invade the United States at three points: upstate New York across the Niagara River and Lake Champlain, the Chesapeake Bay, and New Orleans.

At Niagara, however, a small American army stopped the British advance, and on Lake Champlain American naval forces commanded by Thomas Macdonough placed British supply lines in jeopardy, forcing 11,000 British troops to retreat into Canada. Outnumbered more than three to one, American forces had halted Britain's invasion from the north.

In a second attempt to invade the United States, Britain landed 4,000 soldiers on the Chesapeake Bay coast. But no one knew if the British planned to march first on Baltimore or on Washington, D.C. The answer was Washington, where untrained soldiers lacking uniforms and standard equipment were protecting the capital.

The result was utter chaos. On August 24, 1814, the British humiliated the nation by capturing and burning Washington, D.C. President Madison and his wife Dolly were forced to flee the capital, carrying with them many of the nation's treasures, including the Declaration of Independence and Gilbert Stuart's portrait of George Washington. For 72 hours, the president was forced to hide in the Virginia and Maryland countryside. The British arrived so soon after the president fled that the officers dined on a White House meal that had been prepared for the Madisons and 40 invited guests.

Britain's next objective was Baltimore. To reach the city, British warships had to pass the guns of Fort McHenry, which was manned by 1,000 American soldiers. On September 13, 1814, British warships began a 25-hour bombardment of the fort.

All through the night British cannons fired on Fort McHenry. At dawn on September 14, Francis Scott Key, a young lawyer detained on a British ship, saw the flag still waving over the fort's ramparts. The Americans had repulsed the British attack, with only four soldiers killed and 24 wounded. Key was so moved by the American victory that he wrote the words to "The Star-Spangled Banner" on the back of an envelope. The song was destined to become the young nation's national anthem.

The country still faced grave threats in the South. In 1813, the Creek Indians, encouraged by the British, had attacked American settlements in what are now Alabama and Mississippi. Frontiersmen from Georgia, Mississippi, and Tennessee, led by Major General Andrew Jackson, retaliated and succeeded in defeating the Creeks in March 1814, at the battle of Horseshoe Bend in Alabama. When the Creek War ended, Jackson proceeded to cut British supply lines in the South. He knew that Spain, supposedly neutral, had allowed Britain to use the Florida port of Pensacola as a base of operations for a planned invasion of New Orleans. In a week Jackson marched from Mobile, Alabama, to Pensacola and seized the city, forcing the British to delay their invasion.

But, on January 8, 1815, the British fleet and a battle-tested 10,000-man army finally attacked New Orleans in an attempt to seize control of the mouth of the Mississippi River. To defend the city, Jackson assembled a ragtag army, including French pirates, Choctaw Indians, western militia, and freed slaves. Although British forces outnumbered Americans by more than two to one, American artillery and sharpshooters stopped the invasion. American losses totaled only 8 dead and 13 wounded, while British casualties were 2,036, with almost 400 soldiers killed.

Ironically, American and British negotiators in Ghent, Belgium, had signed the peace treaty ending the War of 1812 two weeks earlier. Britain, convinced that the American war was so difficult and costly that nothing would be gained from further fighting, agreed to return to the conditions that existed before the war. Left unmentioned in the peace treaty were the issues over which Americans had fought the war—impressment, naval blockades, or the British Orders in Council.

The War's Significance

Although often treated as unimportant, a minor footnote to the bloody European war between France and Britain, the War of 1812 was crucial for the United States. First, it effectively destroyed the Indians' ability to resist American expansion east of the Mississippi. Native Americans were crushed in the North by General William Henry Harrison and in the South by General Andrew Jackson. Abandoned by their British allies, the Indians made the best treaties they could. Reluctantly, they ceded most of their lands north of the Ohio River and in southern and western Alabama to the U.S. government.

Second, the war strengthened America's position relative to Spain in the South and Southwest. It allowed the United States to rewrite its boundaries with Spain and solidify control over the lower Mississippi River and the Gulf of Mexico. Although the United States did not succeed in conquering Canada or defeating the British empire, it had fought the world's strongest power to a stalemate. Spain recognized the significance of this fact, and in 1819 Spanish leaders abandoned Florida and agreed to an American boundary running clear to the Pacific Ocean.

Third, the Federalist party never recovered from its opposition to the war. Many Federalists believed that the War of 1812 was really fought to help Napoleon in his struggle against Britain, and they had opposed the war by refusing to pay taxes, boycotting war loans, and refusing to furnish troops. In December 1814, delegates from New England gathered in Hartford, Connecticut, where they recommended a series of constitutional amendments to restrict the power of Congress to wage war, regulate commerce, and admit new states. The delegates also supported a one-term presidency (in order to break the grip of Virginians on the office) and abolition of the three-fifths compromise (which increased the political clout of the South), and talked of seceding if they did not get their way. The proposals of the Hartford Convention became public knowledge at the same time as the terms of the Treaty of Ghent and the American victory in the Battle of New Orleans. Euphoria over the war's end led many people to brand the Federalists as traitors. The party never recovered from this stigma and disappeared from national politics.

*C*hronology of Key Events

1801	John Marshall becomes chief justice; House of Representatives elects Thomas Jefferson as the third president; Jefferson sends eight ships to enforce a blockade of Tripoli
1802	Judiciary Act of 1801 repealed
1803	*Marbury* v. *Madison* upholds principle of judicial review; Jefferson purchases Louisiana from France
1804	Lewis and Clark expedition in Louisiana; Aaron Burr kills Alexander Hamilton in a duel; impeachment of federal district Judge John Pickering and Supreme Court Justice Samuel Chase
1807	Aaron Burr charged with treason; U.S. frigate *Chesapeake* attacked by British; Embargo Act
1809	Embargo Act repealed; James Madison sworn in as fourth president; Non-Intercourse Act prohibits trade with Britian and France
1810	Macon's Bill No. 2 reopens trade with Britian and France
1811	William Henry Harrison routs Indians led by Tenskwatawa in Battle of Tippecanoe
1812	War against Britain declared; Americans surrender Detroit to British
1813	Battle of Lake Erie; Battle of the Thames
1814	Battle of Horseshoe Bend; British burn Washington, D.C.; British fleet defeated on Lake Champlain; Hartford Convention; Treaty of Ghent ends war of 1812
1815	Jackson defeats British at Battle of New Orleans

Conclusion

Between 1800 and 1815 the Jeffersonian Republicans increased the nation's size, opened new lands to western settlement, and won international respect for American independence. In a climate of war and revolution, the new nation acquired Louisiana and the Southeast, defeated powerful Indian confederations in the Northwest and South, and evicted British troops from American soil. What emerged from this period was a strong, confident, and united nation.

Suggestions for Further Reading

For an overview of the Jeffersonian era consult Merrill Peterson, *Thomas Jefferson and the New Nation* (1970). Other valuable biographies of Thomas Jefferson include Fawn M. Brodie, *Thomas Jefferson: An Intimate History* (1974); Noble E. Cunningham, Jr., *In Pursuit of Reason: The Life of Thomas Jefferson* (1987); Dumas Malone, *Jefferson and His Time,* 6 vols. (1948–1981); Forrest McDonald, *The Presidency of Thomas Jefferson* (1976); Robert W. Tucker and David C. Hendrickson, *Empire of Liberty: The Statecraft of Thomas Jefferson* (1990); Robert M. Johnstone, Jr., *Jefferson and the Presidency* (1978);

For more on Jeffersonian republicanism consult Drew McCoy, *The Elusive Republic: Political Economy in Jeffersonian America* (1980), and *The Last of the Fathers: James Madison and the Republican Legacy* (1989); Merrill Peterson, *The Jefferson Image in the American Mind* (1960); Leonard D. White, *The Jeffersonians* (1951); James S. Young, *The Washington Community, 1800–1828* (1966).

For information on the Federalists during the Jeffersonian period see David H. Fischer, *The Revolution of American Conservatism* (1965); Linda K. Kerber, *Federalists in Dissent* (1970); Shaw Livermore, *The Twilight of Federalism* (1962).

The War of 1812 is examined in R. David Edmunds, *Tecumseh and the Quest for Indian Leadership* (1984); Donald R. Hickey, *The War of 1812* (1989); Regionald Horsman, *The Causes of the War of 1812* (1962); Ralph Ketcham, *James Madison* (1971); J. C. A. Stagg, *Mr. Madison's War* (1983).

Chapter **9**

Nationalism, Economic Growth, and the Roots of Sectional Conflict, 1815–1824

As the year 1810 began, Francis Cabot Lowell, a 36-year-old Boston importer, was bitterly discouraged. His health was failing and, as a result of war between Britain and France, his importing business was in ruins. Uncertain about which way to turn, he decided to travel abroad. While overseas, he discovered his life's calling. In Britain, he marveled at textile factories at Manchester. Although it was illegal to export textile machinery or plans, Lowell carefully studied the power looms and secretly made sketches of the designs.

Upon his return to Boston in 1813, Lowell constructed textile machinery superior to any he had seen in England. The next year, in Waltham, Massachusetts, he and two associates built the world's first factory able to convert raw cotton into cloth by power machinery under one roof.

To staff his new textile mill, Lowell chose a labor force different from that found in any previous factory. Determined to avoid the misery of England's textile mills, Lowell recruited his labor force from among the daughters of New England farmers, who agreed to work in Lowell's mill for two or three years as a way of earning a dowry or an independent income. Because spinning and weaving had long been performed by women in the home, and because young women were willing to work for half or a third of the wages of young men, they seemed to offer a perfect solution to the factory's labor needs.

To break down the prejudice against factory work as degrading and immoral, the company announced that it would employ only women of good moral character. It threatened to fire any employee guilty of smoking, drinking, lying, swearing, or any other immoral conduct. The company required employees to attend church and provided boardinghouses where mill girls lived under the careful supervision of housekeepers of impeccable character. Within a few years, the new factory was overwhelmed with job applicants.

The opening of the Boston Manufacturing Company's textile mill in 1814 marked a symbolic beginning to a new era in the nation's history. For Americans, the end of the War of 1812 unleashed a surge of nationalism, dramatic industrial growth, and rapid expansion to the West. In the years ahead, the United States would undergo an economic transformation, symbolized by improvements in transportation and agriculture, rapid urban growth, and many technological innovations.

Paradoxically, it was during these years of nationalism and growth that sectional and political conflicts were exacerbated. Westward expansion, the rapid growth of industry in the North, and the strengthening of the federal government created problems that dominated American political life for the next 40 years.

The Growth of American Nationalism

Early in the summer of 1817, as a conciliatory gesture toward the Federalists who had opposed the War of 1812, James Monroe, the nation's fifth president, embarked on a goodwill tour through the Northeast and Midwest. Everywhere Monroe went, citizens greeted him warmly, holding parades and banquets in his honor. In Federalist Boston, a crowd of 40,000 welcomed the Republican president. John Quincy Adams expressed amazement at the acclaim with which the president was greeted: "Party spirit has indeed subsided throughout the Union to a degree that I should have thought scarcely possible."

A Federalist newspaper, reflecting on the end of party warfare and the renewal of national unity, called the times the "Era of Good Feelings." The phrase accurately describes the period of James Monroe's presidency, which, at least in its early years, was marked by a relative absence of political strife and opposition. With the collapse of the Federalist party, the Jeffersonian Republicans dominated national politics. Reflecting a new spirit of political unity, the Republicans adopted many of the nationalistic policies of their former opponents, establishing a second national bank, a protective tariff, and improvements in transportation.

To the American people, James Monroe was the popular symbol of the Era of Good Feelings. A dignified and formal man, Monroe was the last president to don the fashions of the eighteenth century. He wore his hair in a powdered wig and favored knee breeches, long white stockings, and buckled shoes. His political values, too, were those of an earlier day. Like George Washington, Monroe worked to eliminate party and sectional rivalries by his attitudes and behavior. He hoped for a country without political parties, governed by leaders chosen on their merits. So great was his popularity that he won a second presidential term by an electoral college vote of 231 to 1. A new era of national unity appeared to have dawned.

Neo-Hamiltonianism

Traditionally, the Republican party stood for limited government, states' rights, and a strict interpretation of the Constitution. By 1815, however, the party had adopted former Federalist positions on a national bank, protective tariffs, a standing army, and national roads.

In a series of policy recommendations to Congress at the end of the War of 1812, President Madison revealed the extent to which Republicans had adopted Federalist policies. He called for a program of national economic development directed by the central government, which included the creation of a second Bank of the United States to provide for a stable currency, a protective tariff to encourage industry, a program of internal improvements to facilitate transportation, and a permanent 20,000-man army. In subsequent messages, he recommended an extensive system of roads and canals, new military academies, and establishment of a national university in Washington.

Old-style Republicans, who clung to the Jeffersonian ideal of limited government, dismissed Madison's proposals, but his nationalistic program found enthusiastic support among the new generation of political leaders. Convinced that inadequate roads, the lack of a national bank, and dependence on foreign imports had nearly resulted in a British victory in the war, these young leaders were eager to use the federal government to promote national economic development. Henry Clay, John C. Calhoun, and Daniel Webster were the principal leaders of the second generation of American political life—the period stretching from the War of 1812 to almost the eve of the Civil War. Each was destined to become the preeminent spokesman of his region—Clay of the West, Calhoun of the South, Webster of the North.

The leader of this group of younger politicians was Henry Clay, a Republican from Kentucky. Clay was one of the "War Hawks" who had urged President Madison to wage war against Britain. After the war, Clay became one of the strongest proponents of an active federal role in national economic development. He used his position as Speaker of the House to advance an economic program that he later called the "American System." According to this plan, the federal government would erect a high protective tariff to keep out foreign goods, stimulate the growth of industry, and create a large urban market for western and southern farmers. Revenue from the tariff, in turn, would be used to finance internal improvements of roads and canals to stimulate the growth of the South and West.

Another leader of postwar nationalism was John C. Calhoun, a Republican from South Carolina. Calhoun, like Clay, entered Congress in 1811, and later served with distinction as secretary of war under Monroe and as vice president under both John Quincy Adams and Andrew Jackson. Later, Calhoun became the nation's leading exponent of states' rights, but at this point he seemed to John Quincy Adams "above all sectional and factious prejudices more than any other statesman of this Union with whom I have ever acted."

The other dominant political figure of the era was Daniel Webster. Nicknamed "the Godlike Daniel" for his magnificent speaking style, Webster argued 168 cases before the Supreme Court. When he entered Congress as a Massachusetts Federalist, he opposed the War of 1812, the

Eager to use the federal government to promote economic development, young politicians like Henry Clay of Kentucky (left) and John C. Calhoun of South Carolina (right) supported a protective tariff to stimulate industry, a national bank to promote economic growth, and federally funded aid for transportation.

creation of a second national bank, and a protectionist tariff. But, later in his career, after industrial interests supplanted shipping and importing interests in the Northeast, Webster became a staunch defender of the national bank and a high tariff, and perhaps the nation's strongest exponent of nationalism and most vigorous critic of states' rights. His argument that the United States was not only a union of states but a union of people would later be developed by Abraham Lincoln.

The severe financial problems created by the War of 1812 led to a wave of support for the creation of a second national bank. The demise of the first Bank of the United States just before the war had left the nation ill equipped to deal with the war's financial demands. To finance the war effort, the government borrowed from private banks at high interest rates. As demand for credit rose, the private banks issued bank notes greatly exceeding the amount of gold or silver that they held. One Rhode Island bank issued $580,000 in notes backed up by only $86.48 in gold and silver. The result was high inflation. Prices jumped 40 percent in just two years.

In 1816 Congress voted by a narrow margin to charter a second Bank of the United States for 20 years and give it the privilege of holding government funds without paying interest for their use. Supporters of a second national bank argued that it would provide a safe place to deposit government funds and a convenient mechanism for transferring money between states. Supporters also claimed that a national bank would promote monetary stability by regulating private banks. A national bank would strengthen the banking system by refusing to accept the notes issued by overspeculative private banks and ensuring that bank notes were readily exchangeable for gold or silver. Opposition to a national bank came largely from private banking interests and traditional Jeffersonians, who considered a national bank to be unconstitutional and a threat to republican government.

The War of 1812 provided tremendous stimulus to American manufacturing. It encouraged American manufacturers to produce goods previously imported from overseas. By 1816, 100,000 factory workers, two-thirds of them women and children, produced more than $40 million worth of manufactured goods a year. Capital investment in textile manufacturing, sugar refining, and other industries totaled $100 million.

Following the war, however, cheap British imports flooded the nation, threatening to undermine local industries. Congress responded to the flood of imports by continuing a tariff to protect America's infant industries from low-cost competition. With import duties ranging from 15 to 30 percent on cotton, textiles, leather, paper, pig iron, wool, and other goods, the tariff promised to protect America's growing industries from foreign competition. Shipping and farming interests, on the other hand, opposed the tariff on the grounds that it would make foreign goods more expensive to buy and would provoke foreign retaliation.

Conquering Space

Prior to 1812 westward expansion had proceeded slowly. Most Americans were nestled along the Atlantic coastline. In 1800 more than two-thirds of the new nation's population still lived within 50 miles of the Atlantic seaboard, and the center of population rested within 18 miles of Baltimore. Only two roads cut across the Allegheny Mountains, and no more than half a million pioneers had moved as far west as Kentucky, Tennessee, Ohio, or the western portion of Pennsylvania. Cincinnati was a town of 15,000 people; Buffalo and Rochester, New York did not yet exist. Thomas Jefferson estimated in 1803 that it would be a thousand years before settlers occupied the region east of the Mississippi.

The end of the War of 1812 unleashed a rush of pioneers to Indiana, Illinois, Ohio, northern Georgia, western North Carolina, Alabama, Mississippi, Louisiana, and Tennessee. Congress quickly admitted five states to the Union: Louisiana in 1812, Indiana in 1816, Mississippi in 1817, Illinois in 1818, and Alabama in 1819. Pioneers demanded cheaper land and clamored for better transportation to move goods to eastern markets.

Farmers demanded that Congress revise legislation to make it easier to obtain land. Originally, Congress viewed federal lands as a source of revenue, and public land policies reflected that view. Under a policy adopted in 1785 and reaffirmed in 1796, the federal government only sold land in blocks of at least 640 acres. Although the minimum allotment was reduced to 320 acres in 1800, federal land policy continued to retard sales and concentrate ownership in the hands of a few large land companies and wealthy speculators.

In 1820 Congress sought to make it easier for farmers to purchase homesteads in the West by selling land in small lots suitable for operation by a family. Congress reduced the minimum allotment offered for sale from 320 to 80 acres. The minimum price per acre fell from $2 to $1.25. The second Bank of the United States encouraged land purchases by liberally extending credit. The result was a boom in land sales. For a decade, the government sold approximately a million acres of land annually.

Westward expansion also created a demand to expand and improve the nation's roads and canals. In 1808, Albert Gallatin, Thomas Jefferson's Treasury secretary, proposed a $20 million program of canal and road construction. As a result of state and sectional jealousies and charges that federal aid to transportation was unconstitutional, the federal government funded only a single turnpike, the National Road, at this time stretching from Cumberland, Maryland, to Wheeling, Virginia (later West Virginia), but much later extending westward from Baltimore through Ohio and Indiana to Vandalia, Illinois.

In 1816 John C. Calhoun introduced a new proposal for federal aid for road and canal construction. "Let us," he exclaimed, "bind the republic together with a perfect system of roads and canals. Let us conquer space." Narrowly, Calhoun's proposal passed. But on the day before he left office, Madison vetoed the bill on constitutional grounds.

Despite this setback, Congress did adopt major parts of the nationalist neo-Hamiltonian economic program. It had established a second Bank of the United States to provide a stable means of issuing money and a safe depository for federal funds. It had enacted a tariff to raise duties on foreign imports and guard American industries from low-cost competition. It had also instituted a new public land policy to encourage western settlement. In short, Congress had translated the spirit of national pride and unity that the nation felt after the War of 1812 into a legislative program that placed the national interest above narrow sectional interests.

Judicial Nationalism

The decisions of the Supreme Court also reflected the nationalism of the postwar period. With John Marshall as chief justice, the Supreme Court acquired greater prestige and independence. When Marshall took office, in the last days of John Adams's administration in 1801, the Court met in the basement of the Capitol and was rarely in session for more than six weeks a year. Since its creation in 1789, the Court had only decided 100 cases.

In a series of critical decisions, the Supreme Court greatly expanded its authority. As previously noted, *Marbury* v. *Madison* established the Supreme Court as the final arbiter of the Constitution and its power to declare acts of Congress unconstitutional. *Fletcher* v. *Peck* (1810) declared the Court's power to void state laws. *Martin* v. *Hunter's Lessee* (1816) gave the Court the power to review decisions by state courts.

After the War of 1812, Marshall wrote a series of decisions that further strengthened the powers of the national government. *McCulloch* v. *Maryland* (1819) established the constitutionality of the second Bank of the United States and denied to states the right to exert independent checks on federal authority. The case involved a direct attack on the second Bank of the United States by the state of Maryland, which had placed a tax on the bank notes of all banks not chartered by the state.

In his decision, Marshall dealt with two fundamental questions. The first was whether the federal government had the power to incorporate a bank. The answer to this question, the Court ruled, was yes because the Constitution granted Congress implied powers to do whatever was "necessary and proper" to carry out its constitutional powers—in this case, the power to manage a currency. The second question raised was whether a state had the power to tax a branch of the Bank of the United States. In answer to this question, the Court said no. The Constitution, the Court asserted, created a new government with sovereign power over the states. "The power to tax involves the power to destroy," the Court declared, and the states do not have the right to exert an independent check on the authority of the federal government.

During this period the Supreme Court also encouraged economic competition and development. In *Dartmouth* v. *Woodward* (1819), the Court served to promote business growth by denying states the right to alter or impair contracts unilaterally. The case involved the efforts of the New Hampshire legislature to alter the charter of Dartmouth College, which had been granted by George III in 1769. The Court held that a charter was a valid contract protected by the Constitution and that states do not have the power to alter contracts unilaterally. In *Gibbons* v. *Ogden* (1824), the Court broadened federal power over interstate commerce. The Court overturned a New York law that had awarded a monopoly over steamboat traffic on the Hudson River, ruling that the Constitution had specifically given Congress the power to regulate commerce.

Under John Marshall, the Supreme Court became the final arbiter of the constitutionality of federal and state laws. The Court's role in shifting sovereign power from the states to the federal government was an important development. It would become increasingly difficult in the future to argue that the union was a creation of the states, that states could exert an independent check on federal government authority, or that Congress's powers were limited to those specifically conferred by the Constitution.

Defending American Interests in Foreign Affairs

The War of 1812 stirred a new nationalistic spirit in foreign affairs. This spirit resulted in a decision to end the raids by the Barbary pirates on American commercial shipping in the Mediterranean. For 17 years the United States had paid tribute to the ruler of Algiers. In March 1815 Captain Stephen Decatur and a fleet of ten ships sailed into the Mediterranean, where they captured two Algerian gunboats, towed the ships into Algiers harbor, and threatened to bombard the city. As a result, all the North African states agreed to treaties releasing American prisoners without ransom, ending all demands for American tribute, guaranteeing that American commerce would not be interfered with, and providing compensation for American vessels that had been seized.

After successfully defending American interests in North Africa, Monroe acted to settle old grievances with the British. Britain and the United States had left a host of issues unresolved in the peace treaty ending the War of 1812, including disputes over boundaries, trading and fishing rights, and rival claims to the Oregon region. The two governments moved quickly to settle these issues. The Rush-Bagot Agreement, signed with Great Britain in 1817, removed most military ships from the Great Lakes. In 1818, Britain granted American fishermen the right to fish in eastern Canadian waters, agreed to the 49th parallel as the boundary between the United States and Canada from Minnesota to the Rocky Mountains, and consented to joint occupation of the Oregon region.

The critical foreign policy issue facing the United States after the War of 1812 was the fate of Spain's crumbling New World empire. Many of Spain's colonies had taken advantage of the turmoil in Europe during the Napoleonic Wars to fight for their independence. Florida, however, was still under Spanish control. Pirates, fugitive slaves, and Native Americans used Florida as a sanctuary and as a jumping-off point for raids on settlements in Georgia. In December 1817, to end these incursions, Monroe authorized General Andrew Jackson to lead a punitive expedition against the Seminole Indians in Florida. Jackson attacked the Seminoles, destroyed their villages, and overthrew the Spanish governor. He also court-martialed and executed two British citizens whom he accused of inciting the Seminoles to commit atrocities against Americans.

Jackson's actions provoked a furor in Washington. Secretary of War John C. Calhoun and other members of Monroe's cabinet urged the president to reprimand Jackson for acting without specific authorization. In Congress, Henry Clay called for Jackson's censure. Secretary of State Adams, however, saw in Jackson's actions an opportunity to wrest Florida from Spain.

Instead of apologizing for Jackson's conduct, Adams declared that the Florida raid was a legitimate act of self-defense. Adams informed the Spanish government that it would either have to police Florida effectively or cede it to the United States. Convinced that American annexation was inevitable, Spain ceded Florida to the United States in the Adams-Onis Treaty of 1819. In return, the United States agreed to honor $5 million in damage claims by Americans against Spain, and renounced, at least temporarily, its claims to Texas.

At the same time, European intervention in the Pacific Northwest and Latin America threatened to become a new source of anxiety for American leaders. In 1821, Russia claimed control of the entire Pacific coast from Alaska to Oregon and closed the area to foreign shipping. This development coincided with rumors that Spain, with the help of its European allies, was planning to reconquer its former colonies in Latin America. European intervention threatened British as well as American interests. Not only did Britain have a flourishing trade with Latin America, which would decline if Spain regained its New World colonies, but it also occupied the Oregon region jointly with the United States. In 1823, British Foreign Minister George Canning proposed that the United States and Britain jointly announce their opposition to further European intervention in the Americas.

Monroe initially regarded the British proposal favorably. But his secretary of state, John Quincy Adams, opposed a joint Anglo-American declaration. Secure in the knowledge that the British would use their fleet to support the American position, Adams convinced President Monroe to make an independent declaration of American policy. In his annual message to Congress in 1823, Monroe outlined the principles that have become known as the Monroe Doctrine. He announced that the Western

Hemisphere was henceforth closed to any further European colonization, declaring that the United States would regard any attempt by European nations "to extend their system to any portion of this hemisphere as dangerous to our peace and safety." European countries with possessions in the hemisphere—Britain, France, the Netherlands, and Spain—were warned not to attempt expansion. Monroe also said that the United States would not interfere in internal European affairs.

For the American people, the Monroe Doctrine was the proud symbol of American hegemony in the Western Hemisphere. Unilaterally, the United States had defined its rights and interests in the New World. During the first half of the nineteenth century the United States lacked the military power to enforce the Monroe Doctrine and depended on the British navy to deter European intervention in the Americas, but the nation had clearly warned the European powers that any threat to American security would provoke American retaliation.

The Roots of American Economic Growth

At the beginning of the nineteenth century the United States was an overwhelmingly rural and agricultural nation. Most Americans lived on farms or in villages with fewer than 2,500 inhabitants. The nation's population was small and scattered over a vast geographical area—just 5.3 million in 1800, compared to Britain's 15 million and France's 27 million. Transportation and communications had changed little over the previous half century. A coach ride between Boston and New York took three days. South of the Mason-Dixon line, except for a single stagecoach that traveled between Charleston and Savannah, there was no public transportation of any kind.

American houses, clothing, and agricultural methods were surprisingly primitive. Fifty miles inland, half the houses were log cabins, lacking even glass windows. Farmers planted their crops in much the same way as their parents and grandparents. Few farmers practiced crop rotation or used fertilizers or drained fields. They made plows out of wood, allowed their swine to run loose, and left their cattle outside except on the coldest nights.

Manufacturing was also still quite backward. In rural areas, farm families grew their own food, produced their own soap and candles, wove their own blankets, and constructed their own furniture. The leading manufacturing industries—iron-making, textiles, and clothes-making—employed only about 15,000 people in mills or factories.

After the War of 1812, however, the American economy grew at an astonishing rate. The twenty-five years that followed Andrew Jackson's victory at New Orleans represented a critical period for the nation's future economic growth, during which the United States overcame a series of obstacles that had stood in the way of sustained economic expansion. Improved transportation, rapid urbanization, increased farm productivity, and technological innovation transformed a rural, agricultural nation into one of the world's industrial leaders.

Accelerating Transportation

At the outset of the nineteenth century the lack of reliable, low-cost transportation was a major barrier to American industrial development. The stagecoach, slow and cumbersome, was the main form of transportation. Twelve passengers, crowded along with their bags and parcels, traveled at just four miles an hour. In Connecticut and Massachusetts, Sunday travel was still forbidden by law.

Wretched roads plagued travelers. Larger towns had streets paved with cobblestones, but most roads were simply dirt paths left muddy and rutted by rain. The presence of tree stumps in the middle of many roads posed a serious obstacle to carriages. Charles Dickens aptly described American roads as a "series of alternate swamps and gravel pits."

In 1791 builders first inaugurated a new era in transportation with the construction of a 66-mile-long turnpike between Philadelphia and Lancaster, Pennsylvania. This stimulated a craze for toll road construction. By 1811, 135 private companies in New York had invested $7.5 million in 1,500 miles of road. By 1838, Pennslyvania had invested $37 million to build 2,200 miles of turnpikes.

Despite the construction of turnpikes, the cost of transporting freight over land remained high. Because water transportation was cheaper, farmers often shipped their produce down the Mississippi, Potomac, or Hudson rivers by flatboat or raft. Unfortunately, water transportation was slow and few vessels were capable of going very far upstream. The trip downstream from Pittsburgh to New Orleans took a month; the trip upstream against the current took four months. Steam power offered the obvious solution, and inventors built at least 16 steamships before Robert Fulton successfully demonstrated the commercial practicality of steam navigation. In 1807, he sailed a 160-ton side-wheeler, the *Clermont,* 150 miles from New York City to Albany in only 32 hours. "Fulton's folly," as critics called it, opened a new era of faster and cheaper water transportation.

Water transportation was further revolutionized by the building of canals. In 1825 the state of New York opened the Erie Canal, which connected the Great Lakes to the Atlantic Ocean. The canal was a stupendous engineering achievement. Three thousand workers, using hand

In 1807, Robert Fulton demonstrated the feasibility of steam travel by
launching his 160-ton-side-wheeler, the *Clermont,* on the Hudson River.

labor, toiled for eight years to build the canal. They built 84 locks, each
15 feet wide and 90 feet long, to raise or lower barges 10 feet at a time.

Built almost entirely with state and local funding, "Clinton's
Ditch"—named after the Erie canal's chief backer, Governor DeWitt
Clinton—sparked an economic revolution. Before the canal was built, it
cost $100 and took 20 days to transport a ton of freight from Buffalo to
New York City. After the canal was opened, the cost fell to $5 a ton and
transit time was reduced to 6 days.

The success of the Erie Canal led other states to embark on expensive
programs of canal building. Pennsylvania spent $10 million to build a
canal between Philadelphia and Pittsburgh. The states of Illinois, Indiana,
and Ohio launched projects to connect the Ohio and Mississippi rivers to
the Great Lakes. By 1840, 3,326 miles of canals had been dug at a cost of
$125 million.

Cities like Baltimore and Boston, which were unable to reach the
West with canals experimented with the railroad, a novel form of transportation. Early railroads suffered from nagging engineering problems
and vociferous opposition. Brakes were wholly inadequate, consisting of
wooden blocks operated by a foot pedal. Boilers exploded so frequently
that passengers had to be protected by bales of cotton. Engine sparks set
fire to fields and burned unprotected passengers. Vested interests, including turnpike and bridge companies, stagecoaches, ferries, and canals,
sought laws to prohibit trains from carrying freight.

Nonetheless, it quickly became clear after 1830 that railroads were
destined to become the nation's chief means of moving freight. During the

1830s, construction companies laid down 3,328 miles of track, roughly equal to all the miles of canals in the country. With an average speed of ten miles an hour, railroads were faster than stagecoaches, canalboats, and steamboats, and, unlike water-going vessels, could travel in any season.

The transportation revolution sharply reduced the cost of shipping goods to market and stimulated agriculture and industry. New roads, canals, and railroads speeded the pace of commerce and strengthened ties between the East and West.

Transforming American Law

The growth of an industrial economy in the United States required a shift in American law. At the beginning of the nineteenth century, American law was rooted in concepts that reflected the values of a slowly changing, agricultural society. The law presumed that goods and services had a just price, independent of supply and demand. Courts forbade many forms of competition and innovation in the name of a stable society. Courts and judges legally protected monopolies and prevented lenders from charging high rates of interest. The law allowed property owners to sue for damages if a mill built upstream flooded their land or impeded their water supply. After 1815, however, the American legal system favored economic growth, profit, and entrepreneurial enterprise.

By the 1820s courts, particularly in the Northeast, had begun to abandon many traditional legal doctrines that stood in the way of a competitive market economy. Courts dropped older doctrines that assumed that goods and services had an objective price, independent of supply and demand. Courts also rejected many usury laws, and increasingly held that only the market could determine interest rates or prices or the equity of a contract.

To promote rapid economic growth, courts and state legislatures gave new powers and privileges to private firms. Companies building roads, bridges, canals, and other public works were given the power to appropriate land; private firms were allowed to avoid legal penalties for fires, floods, or noise they caused on the grounds that the companies served a public purpose. Courts also reduced the liability of companies for injuries to their own employees, ruling that an injured party had to prove negligence or carelessness on the part of an employer in order to collect damages. The legal barriers to economic expansion had been struck down.

Early Industrialization

The United States lagged far behind Europe in the practical application of science and technology. There was probably just one steam engine in regular operation in the United States in 1800, one hundred years after simple engines had first been used in Europe. Inventors often failed because they were unable to finance their projects or persuade the public to use their inventions. The inadequate state of higher education also slowed technological innovation. At the beginning of the nineteenth century, Harvard, the nation's most famous college, graduated just 39 men a year, no more than it had graduated in 1720. All the nation's libraries put together contained barely 50,000 volumes.

By the 1820s, however, the United States had largely overcome resistance to technological innovation, with literally hundreds of inventors and amateur scientists transforming European ideas into practical technologies. Their inventions inspired in Americans a boundless faith in technology. Early American technology was pioneered largely by self-taught amateurs, whose zeal led them to create inventions that trained European scientists did not attempt. As early as the 1720s it was known that electricity could be conducted along a wire to convey messages, but it was not until 1844 that an American named Samuel F. B. Morse demonstrated the practicality of the telegraph and devised a workable code for sending messages. A Frenchman built the first working steamship in 1783, but it was 24 years later that Robert Fulton produced the first commercially successful steamship. The first real steam engine was invented by an Englishman in 1699, but it was an American named Oliver Evans who in 1805 produced a light and powerful steam engine with high-pressure cylinders.

In the 1820s and 1830s America became the world's leader in adopting mechanization, standardization, and mass production. Manufacturers began to adopt labor-saving machinery that allowed workers to produce more goods at lower costs. The single most important figure in the development of this system was Eli Whitney, the inventor of the cotton gin. In 1798, Whitney persuaded the U.S. government to award him a contract for 10,000 muskets. Until then, rifles had been manufactured by skilled artisans, who made individual parts by hand and then carefully fitted the pieces together. At the time Whitney made his offer, the federal arsenal at Springfield, Massachusetts, was capable of producing only 245 muskets in two years. Whitney's idea was to develop precision machinery that would allow a worker with little manual skill to manufacture identical gun parts that would be interchangeable from one gun to another.

Other industries soon adopted the system. As early as 1800 manufacturers of wooden clocks began to use interchangeable parts. Makers of sewing machines used mass production techniques as early as 1846, and the next year manufacturers mechanized the production of farm machinery.

Innovation was not confined to manufacturing. During the years following the War of 1812, American agriculture underwent a transformation nearly as profound and far-reaching as the revolution taking place in industry. No longer cut off from markets by the high cost of transportation, farmers began to grow larger crop surpluses and to specialize in cash crops. A growing demand for cotton for England's textile mills led to the introduction of long-staple cotton from the West Indies into the islands and lowlands of Georgia and South Carolina. Eli Whitney's invention of the cotton gin in 1793—which permitted an individual to clean 50 pounds of short-staple cotton in a single day, 50 times more than could be cleaned by hand—made it practical to produce the crop in the South. Other cash crops raised by southern farmers included rice, sugar, flax for linen, and hemp for rope fibers. In the Northeast, the growth of mill towns and urban centers created a growing demand for hogs, cattle, sheep, corn, wheat, wool, butter, milk, cheese, fruit, vegetables, and hay to feed horses.

As production for the market increased, farmers began to demand improved farm technology. An improved cast-iron plow replaced the conventional wooden plow, allowing a farmer to double the acreage he could put into cultivation. Prior to the introduction in 1803 of the cradle scythe—a rake used to cut and gather up grain and deposit it in even piles—a farmer could not harvest more than half an acre a day. The horse rake—a device introduced in 1820 to mow hay—allowed a single farmer to perform the work of eight to ten men. The invention in 1836 of a mechanical thresher, used to separate the wheat from the chaff, helped to cut in half the man-hours required to produce an acre of wheat.

By 1830 the roots of America's future industrial growth had been firmly planted. Back in 1807, the nation had just 15 or 20 cotton mills, containing approximately 8,000 spindles. By 1831 the number of spindles in use totaled nearly a million and a quarter. Factory production had made household manufacture of shoes, clothing, textiles, and farm implements obsolete. The United States was well on its way to becoming one of the world's leading manufacturing nations.

The Growth of Cities

At the beginning of the nineteenth century the United States was a nation of farms and rural villages. Only four cities had populations with more than 10,000 inhabitants. Boston, which in 1800 contained just 25,000 inhabitants, looked much as it had prior to the Revolution. Its streets, still paved with cobblestones, were unlighted at night. New York City's entire police force, which only patrolled the city at night, consisted of two captains, two deputies, and 72 assistants.

During the 1820s and 1830s the nation's cities grew at an extraordinary rate. The urban population increased sixty percent a decade, five times as fast as that of the country as a whole. In 1810, New York City's population was less than 100,000. Two decades later it was more than 200,000.

The chief cause of the increase was the migration of sons and daughters away from farms and villages. The growth of commerce drew thousands of farm children to the cities to work as bookkeepers, clerks, and salespeople. The expansion of factories demanded thousands of laborers, mechanics, teamsters, and operatives. The need of rural areas for services available only in urban centers also promoted the growth of cities, particularly in the West. Farmers needed their grain milled and their livestock butchered; tobacco growers needed their crop cured and marketed.

Pittsburgh's growth illustrates these processes at work. Frontier farmers needed products made of iron, such as nails, horseshoes, and farm implements. Pittsburgh lay near western Pennsylvania's coal fields. Because it was cheaper to bring the iron ore to the coal supply for smelting than to transport the coal to the side of the iron mine, Pittsburgh became a major iron producer. Iron foundries and blacksmith shops proliferated. So did glass factories, which required large amounts of fuel to provide heat for glassblowing. As a result, Pittsburgh's population tripled between 1810 and 1830.

As urban areas grew, many problems were exacerbated, including the absence of clean drinking water, the pressing need for cheap public transportation, and, most important, poor sanitation. Sanitation problems led to heavy urban mortality rates and frequent typhoid, dysentery, typhus, cholera, and yellow fever epidemics.

Most city dwellers used outdoor privies, which emptied into vaults and cesspools that sometimes leaked into the soil and contaminated the water supply. Kitchen wastes were thrown into ditches; refuse was thrown into trash piles by the side of the streets. Every horse deposited as much as 20 pounds of manure and urine on city streets each day. To help remove the garbage and refuse, many cities allowed packs of dogs, goats, and pigs to scavenge freely.

Although elite urbanites were beginning to enjoy some amenities, such as indoor toilets, which began to appear around 1815, many of the cities' poorest inhabitants lived in slums. On New York's lower east side, men, women, and children were crowded into damp, unlighted, ill-ventilated cellars with 6 to 20 persons living in a single room. Despite growing public awareness of the problems of slums and urban poverty, conditions remained unchanged for several generations.

The Growth of Political Factionalism and Sectionalism

The Era of Good Feelings began with a burst of nationalistic fervor. The economic program adopted by Congress, including a national bank and a protective tariff, reflected the growing feeling of national unity. The Supreme Court promoted the spirit of nationalism by establishing the principle of federal supremacy. Industrialization and improvements in transportation also added to the sense of national unity by contributing to the nation's economic strength and independence and by linking the West and the East together.

But this same period also witnessed the emergence of growing factional divisions in politics, including a deepening sectional split between the North and South. A severe economic depression between 1819 and 1822 provoked bitter division over questions of banking and tariffs. Geographic expansion exposed latent tensions over the morality of slavery and the balance of economic power. It was during the Era of Good Feelings that the political issues arose that would dominate American politics for the next 40 years.

The Panic of 1819

In 1819 a financial panic swept across the country. The growth in trade that followed the War of 1812 came to an abrupt halt. Unemployment mounted, banks failed, mortgages were foreclosed, and agricultural prices fell by half. Investment in western lands collapsed. The downswing spread like a plague across the country. In Cincinnati bankruptcy sales occurred almost daily. In Lexington, Kentucky, factories worth half a million dollars were idle. One economist estimated that 3 million people, one-third of the nation's population, were adversely affected by the panic.

The panic had several causes, including a dramatic decline in cotton prices, a contraction of credit by the Bank of the United States designed to curb inflation, an 1817 congressional order requiring hard-currency payments for land purchases, and the closing of many factories due to foreign competition.

The panic unleashed a storm of popular protest. Many debtors agitated for "stay laws" to provide relief from debts as well as the abolition of debtors' prisons. Manufacturing interests called for increased protection from foreign imports, but a growing number of southerners believed that high protective tariffs, which raised the cost of imported goods and reduced the flow of international trade, were the root of their troubles. Many people clamored for a reduction in the cost of government and pressed for sharp reductions in federal and state budgets. Others, particularly in the South and West, blamed the panic on the nation's banks and particularly the tight-money policies of the Bank of the United States.

By 1823 the panic was over, but it had made a lasting imprint on American politics. The panic led to demands for the democratization of state constitutions, an end to restrictions on voting and officeholding, and heightened hostility toward banks and other "privileged" corporations and monopolies. The panic also exacerbated tensions within the Republican party and aggravated sectional tensions as northerners pressed for higher tariffs while southerners abandoned their support of nationalistic economic programs.

The Missouri Crisis

In the midst of the panic a crisis over slavery erupted with stunning suddenness. It was, Thomas Jefferson wrote, like "a firebell in the night." The crisis was ignited by the application of Missouri for statehood, and it involved the status of slavery west of the Mississippi River.

East of the Mississippi, the Mason-Dixon line and the Ohio River formed a boundary between the North and South. States south of this line were slave states; states north of this line had either abolished slavery or adopted gradual emancipation policies. West of the Mississippi, however, no clear line demarcated the boundary between free and slave territory.

Representative James Tallmadge, a New York Republican, provoked the crisis in February 1819 by introducing an amendment to restrict slavery in Missouri as a condition of statehood. The amendment prohibited the further introduction of slaves into Missouri and provided for emancipation of all children of slaves at the age of 25. Voting along ominously sectional lines, the House approved the Tallmadge Amendment, but the amendment was defeated in the Senate.

Southern and northern politicians alike responded with fury. Southerners condemned the Tallmadge proposal as part of a northeastern plot to dominate the government. They declared the United States to be a union of equals, claiming that Congress had no power to place special restrictions upon a state. Talk of disunion and civil war was rife. Northern politicians responded with equal vehemence. Northern leaders argued that national policy, enshrined in the Northwest Ordinance, committed the government to halt the expansion of the institution of slavery. They warned that the extension of slavery into the West would inevitably increase the pressures to reopen the African slave trade. Mass meetings convened in a number of cities in the Northeast. Never before had passions over the issue of slavery been so heated or sectional antagonisms so overt.

Compromise ultimately resolved the crisis. In 1820, the Senate narrowly voted to admit Missouri as a slave state. To preserve the sectional balance, it also voted to admit Maine, which had previously been a part of Massachusetts, as a free state, and to prohibit the formation of any further slave states from the territory of the Louisiana Purchase north of the 36° 30' north latitude. Henry Clay then skillfully steered the Missouri compromise through the House, where a handful of antislavery representatives, fearful of the threat to the Union, threw their support behind the proposals.

Although compromise had been achieved, it was clear that sectional conflict had not been resolved, only postponed. Southerners won a victory in 1820, but they paid a high price. While many states would eventually be organized from the Louisiana Purchase area north of the compromise line, only two (Arkansas and part of Oklahoma) would be formed from the southern portion. If the South was to defend its political power against an antislavery majority, it had but two options in the future. It would ei-

Missouri Compromise

The agreement reached in the Missouri Compromise temporarily settled the argument over slavery in the territories.

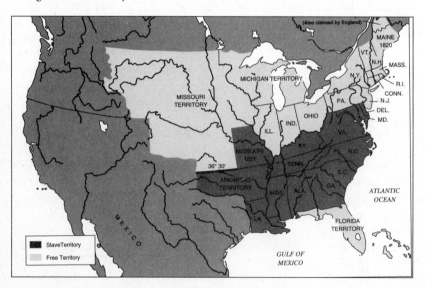

ther have to forge new political alliances with the North and West, or it would have to acquire new territory in the Southwest. The latter would inevitably reignite northern opposition to the further expansion of slavery. Thus the Era of Good Feelings ended on a note of foreboding.

Conclusion

The Era of Good Feelings came to a formal close on March 4, 1825, the day that John Quincy Adams was inaugurated as the nation's sixth president. Adams, who had served eight years as his predecessor's secretary of state, believed that James Monroe's terms in office would be regarded by future generations of Americans as a "golden age." In his inaugural address he spoke with pride of the nation's achievements since the War of 1812. A strong spirit of nationalism pervaded the nation and the country stood united under a single political party, the Republicans. The nation had settled its most serious disputes with England and Spain, extended its boundaries to the Pacific, asserted its diplomatic independence, encour-

*C*hronology of Key Events

1807	Robert Fulton's *Clermont* demonstrates practicality of steam-powered navigation
1814	Boston Manufacturing Company's textile mill opens
1815	Congress declares war on Algiers
1816	Congress charters Second Bank of the United States; James Monroe elected fifth president
1818	General Andrew Jackson invades Florida; Rush-Bagot Agreement establishes U.S.–Canadian boundary
1819	Panic of 1819; Adams-Onis Treaty; *Dartmouth* v. *Woodward*; *McCulloch* v. *Maryland*
1820	Missouri Compromise prohibits slavery in the northern half of Louisiana Purchase; Monroe reelected
1823	Monroe Doctrine issued, opposes European colonization or interference in the Americas
1825	Erie Canal opens

aged the wars for national independence in Latin America, developed a strong manufacturing system, and had begun to create a system of transportation adequate to a great nation.

The Era of Good Feelings marked a period of dramatic growth and intense nationalism, but it also witnessed the emergence of new political divisions as well as growing sectional animosities. The period following the War of 1812 brought rapid growth to cities, manufacturing, and the factory system in the North, while the South's economy remained centered around slavery and cotton. These two great sections were developing along diverging lines. Whether the spirit of nationalism or the spirit of sectionalism would triumph was the great question that would dominate American politics over the next four decades.

Suggestions for Further Reading

For an overview of the period see William Barney, *The Passage of the Republic* (1987); John R. Howe, *From the Revolution Through the Age of Jackson* (1973); John Mustfield, *The New Nation, 1800–1845* rev. ed. (1982).

For American economic development after 1815 consult Alfred D. Chandler, Jr., *The Visible Hand* (1977); Paul W. Gates, *The Farmer's Age* (1960); Carter Goodrich, *Government Promotion of American Canals and Railroads* (1960); David Hamer, *New Towns in the New World* (1990); David A. Hounshell, *From the American System to Mass Production* (1984); Glenn Porter and Harold C. Livesay, *Merchants and Manufacturers* (1971); Peter Temin, *Causal Factors in American Economic Growth in the Nineteenth Century* (1975).

On American foreign policy during this period see Samuel F. Bemis, *John Quincy Adams and the Foundations of American Foreign Policy* (1949); Ernest R. May, *The Making of the Monroe Doctrine* (1975); Frederick W. Merk, *The Monroe Doctrine and American Expansionism* (1966).

Significant biographies include Harry Ammon, *James Monroe: The Quest for National Identity* (1971); Leonard Baker, *John Marshall: A Life in Law* (1974); Richard Current, *Daniel Webster and the Rise of National Conservatism* (1955); Mary W. M. Hargreaves, *The Presidency of John Quincy Adams* (1985); *John Marshall: Defender of the Constitution* (1981); Barbara M. Tucker, *Samuel Slater and the Origins of the American Textile Industry* (1984).

Chapter *10*

Power and Politics in Jackson's America

It was, without a doubt, one of the most exciting, colorful, and dirty presidential campaigns in American history. In 1840 William Henry Harrison, a military hero best known for fighting an alliance of Indians at the Battle of Tippecanoe in 1811, challenged the Democratic incumbent, Martin Van Buren, for the presidency.

Harrison's campaign began on May 4 when a huge procession, made up of an estimated 75,000 people, marched through the streets of Baltimore to celebrate Harrison's nomination by the Whig party convention. Although Harrison was college-educated and brought up on a plantation with a work force of some 200 slaves, his Democratic opponents had already dubbed him the "log cabin" candidate, who was happiest on his backwoods farm sipping hard cider. In response, Harrison's supporters enthusiastically seized on this image and promoted it in a number of colorful ways. They distributed barrels of hard cider, passed out campaign hats and placards, and mounted eight log cabins on floats.

Harrison's campaign brought many innovations to the art of electioneering. For the first time a presidential candidate spoke out on his own behalf. Previous candidates had chosen to let others speak for them. Harrison's backers also coined the first campaign slogans: "Tippecanoe and Tyler Too," and "Van, Van is a used up man." They staged log cabin raisings, including the erection of a 50-by-100-foot cabin on Broadway in New York City. They sponsored barbecues and mass rallies attended by thousands of people.

While defending their man as the "people's" candidate, Harrison's backers heaped an unprecedented avalanche of personal abuse on his Democratic opponent. The Whigs accused President Van Buren of eating off of golden plates and lace tablecloths, and drinking French wines. Whigs in Congress denied Van Buren an appropriation of $3,665 to repair the White House lest he turn the executive mansion into a "palace as splendid as that of the Caesars." The object of this rough and colorful kind of campaigning was to convince voters that the Democratic candidate harbored aristocratic leanings, while Harrison truly represented the people.

The Harrison campaign provided a number of effective lessons for future politicians, most notably an emphasis on symbols and imagery over ideas and substance. Fearful of alienating voters and dividing the Whig party, the political convention that nominated Harrison agreed to adopt no party platform. Harrison himself said nothing during the campaign about his principles or proposals. He closely followed the suggestion of one of his advisers that he run on his military record and offer no indication "about what he thinks now, or what he will do hereafter."

The new campaign techniques produced an overwhelming victory. In 1840 voter turnout was the highest it had ever been in a presidential election: nearly 80 percent of eligible voters cast ballots. The log cabin candidate for president won 53 percent of the popular vote and a landslide victory in the electoral college.

Political Democratization

In 1821 American politics was still largely dominated by deference. Competing political parties were nonexistent and voters generally deferred to the leadership of local elites or leading families. Political campaigns tended to be relatively staid affairs. Direct appeals by candidates for support were considered in poor taste. Election procedures were, by later standards, quite undemocratic. Most states imposed property and taxpaying requirements on the white adult males who alone had the vote, and conducted voting by voice. Presidential electors were generally chosen by state legislatures. Given the fact that citizens had only the most indirect say in the election of the president, it is not surprising that voting participation was generally extremely low, amounting to less than 30 percent of adult white males.

Between 1820 and 1840 a revolution took place in American politics. In most states, property qualifications for voting and officeholding were repealed, and voting by voice was largely eliminated. Direct methods of selecting presidential electors, county officials, state judges, and governors replaced indirect methods. Because of these and other political innovations, voter participation skyrocketed. By 1840 voting participation had reached unprecedented levels. Nearly 80 percent of adult white males went to the polls.

A new two-party system, made possible by an expanded electorate, replaced the politics of deference to and leadership by elites. By the mid-1830s two national political parties with marked philosophical differences, strong organizations, and wide popular appeal competed in virtually every state. Professional party managers used partisan newspapers, speeches, parades, rallies, and barbecues to mobilize popular support. Our modern political system had been born.

The Expansion of Voting Rights

The most significant political innovation of the early nineteenth century was the abolition of property qualifications for voting and officeholding. Hard times resulting from the panic of 1819 led many people to demand an end to these restrictions. In New York, for example, fewer than two adult males in five could legally vote for senator or governor. Under a state constitution approved in 1821 all adult white males were allowed to vote, so long as they paid taxes or had served in the militia. Five years later, an amendment to the state's constitution eliminated the taxpaying and militia qualifications, thereby establishing universal white manhood suffrage. By 1840 universal white manhood suffrage had largely become a reality. Only three states—Louisiana, Rhode Island, and Virginia—still restricted the suffrage to white male property owners and taxpayers.

In order to encourage popular participation in politics, most states also instituted statewide nominating conventions, opened polling places in more convenient locations, extended the hours that polls were open, and eliminated the earlier practice of voting by voice. This last reform did not truly institute the secret ballot, which was only adopted beginning in the 1880s, since voters during the mid-nineteenth century usually voted with

Extension of Male Suffrage

Some states and territories reserved the suffrage to white male property holders and taxpayers, while other permitted an alternative such as a period of residence.

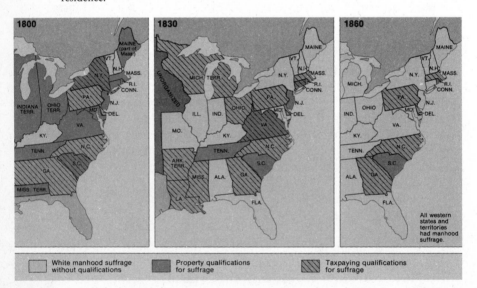

straight-ticket paper ballots prepared by the political parties themselves. Each party had a different colored ballot, which voters deposited in a publicly viewed ballot box, so that those present knew who had voted for which party. By 1824 only six of the nation's 24 states still chose presidential electors in the state legislature, and eight years later the only state still to do so was South Carolina, which continued this practice until the Civil War.

In addition to removing property and tax qualifications for voting and officeholding, states also reduced residency requirements for voting. Immigrant males were permitted to vote in most states if they had declared their intention to become citizens. During the nineteenth century 22 states and territories permitted immigrants who were not yet naturalized citizens to vote. States also allowed voters to choose presidential electors, governors, and county officials.

While universal white manhood suffrage was becoming a reality, restrictions on voting by blacks and women remained in force. Only one state, New Jersey, had given unmarried women property holders the right to vote following the Revolution, but the state rescinded this right at the same time it extended suffrage to all adult white men. Most states also explicitly denied the right to vote to free blacks. By 1858 free blacks were eligible to vote in just four northern states: New Hampshire, Maine, Massachusetts, and Vermont.

Popular Attacks on Privilege

The democratic impulse that swept the country in the 1820s was also apparent in widespread attacks on special privilege and aristocratic pretension. Established churches, the courts, and the legal and medical professions all saw their elitist status diminished.

The judiciary was made more responsive to public opinion through the election, rather than the appointment, of judges. To open up the legal profession, many states dropped formal training requirements to practice law. Some states also abolished training and licensing requirements for physicians, allowing unorthodox "herb and root" doctors, including many women, to compete freely with established physicians.

The surge of democratic sentiment had an important political consequence: the breakdown of deferential politics. During the first quarter of the nineteenth century local elites lost much of their influence. They were replaced by professional politicians. In the 1820s political innovators such as Martin Van Buren, the son of a tavernkeeper, and Thurlow Weed, a newspaper editor in Albany, New York, devised new campaign tools, such as torchlight parades, subsidized partisan newspapers, and nominating conventions. These political bosses and manipulators soon discovered that the most successful technique for arousing popular interest in politics was to attack a privileged group or institution that had used political influence to attain power or profit.

The "Anti-Masonic party" was the first political movement to win a widespread popular following using this technique. In the mid-1820s a growing number of people in New York and surrounding states had come to believe that members of the fraternal order of Freemasons, who seemed to monopolize many of the region's most prestigious political offices and business positions, had used their connections to enrich themselves. They noted, for instance, that Masons held 22 of the nation's 24 governorships. By 1830 the Anti-Mason movement had succeeded in capturing half the vote in New York state and had gained substantial support throughout New England.

The Rebirth of Parties

The first years of the new republic had given rise to two competing political parties, the Federalists and the Republicans. The first party system, unlike the kinds of political parties Americans are familiar with today, tended to have a strong sectional character, with the Federalists dominant in New England and the Republicans dominant elsewhere.

After the War of 1812 the nation reverted to a period of one-party government in national politics. The decline of the Federalist party created the illusion of national political unity, but appearances were deceptive. Without the discipline imposed by competition with a strong opposition party, the Republican party began to fragment into cliques and factions.

During James Monroe's presidency the Republican party disintegrated as a stable national organization. Following his overwhelming victory in 1816, Monroe sought to promote the ideal expressed by George Washington in his Farewell Address: a nation free of partisan divisions. Like Washington, he appointed rival factional leaders, such as John Quincy Adams and John C. Calhoun, to his cabinet. He refused to use federal patronage to strengthen the Republican party. He also took the position that Congress, not the president, was the best representative of the public will, and therefore should define public policy.

The absence of a strong leader, however, led to the fragmentation of the Republican party during Monroe's administration. Factional and sectional rivalries grew increasingly bitter and party machinery fell into disuse.

Birth of the Second Party System

Over time, local and personal factions began to coalesce into a new political party system. Three critical factors contributed to the creation of the second party system. The first was the financial panic of 1819 and the subsequent depression. The panic resulted in significant political differences over such issues as debt relief, banking and monetary policy, and tariffs. Farmers, particularly in the South and West, demanded enactment of stay laws to postpone repayment of debts. Many artisans and farmers blamed banks for causing the panic by printing an excess of worthless paper money. They demanded that bank notes be replaced by hard money, gold and silver coinage. These groups often disagreed with pro-business interests, which called for the extension of credit, higher tariffs to protect infant industries, and government-financed transportation improvements to reduce the cost of trade.

A second source of political division was southern alarm over the slavery debates in Congress in 1819 and 1820. Many southern leaders feared that the Missouri crisis might spark a realignment in national politics along sectional lines. Anxiety over the slavery debates induced many southerners to seek political alliances with the North. As early as 1821, Old Republicans in the South—those who opposed high tariffs, a national bank, and federally funded internal improvements—had begun to form a loose alliance with Senator Martin Van Buren of New York and the Republican party faction he commanded, the Albany Regency.

The third major source of political division was the selection of presidential candidates. The "Virginia dynasty" of presidents, a chain that had begun with George Washington and included Thomas Jefferson, James Madison, and James Monroe, was at its end by 1824. Traditionally, the Republican party's candidate was selected by a caucus of the party's members in Congress. At the 1824 caucus the members met in closed session and chose William Crawford, Monroe's secretary of the Treasury, as the party's choice. Not all Republicans, however, supported this method of nominating candidates, and therefore refused to participate.

When Crawford suffered a stroke and was left partially disabled, four other candidates emerged: Secretary of State John Quincy Adams, the son of the nation's second president and the only candidate from the North; John C. Calhoun, who had little support outside of his native South Carolina; Henry Clay, the Speaker of the House; and General Andrew Jackson, the hero of the Battle of New Orleans and victor over the Creek and Seminole Indians.

In the election of 1824 Jackson received the greatest number of votes both at the polls and in the electoral college, followed (in electoral votes) by Adams, Crawford, and then Clay. But he failed to receive the constitutionally required majority of the electoral votes. As provided by the Twelfth Amendment of the Constitution, the election was therefore thrown into the House of Representatives, which was required to choose from among the top three vote-getters in the electoral college. There, Henry Clay persuaded his supporters to vote for Adams, commenting acidly that he did not believe "that killing two thousand five hundred Englishmen at New Orleans" was a proper qualification for the presidency. Adams was elected on the first ballot.

The Philadelphia *Observer* charged that Adams had made a secret deal to obtain Clay's support. Three days later, Adams's nomination of Clay as secretary of state seemed to confirm the charges of a "corrupt bargain." Jackson was outraged, since he could legitimately argue that he was the popular favorite. The general exclaimed, "The Judas of the West has closed the contract and will receive the thirty pieces of silver."

The Presidency of John Quincy Adams

John Quincy Adams was one of the most brilliant and well-qualified men ever to occupy the White House. A deeply religious, intensely scholarly man, he read biblical passages at least three times a day—once in English, once in German, and once in French. He was fluent in seven foreign languages, including Greek and Latin. During his brilliant career as a diplomat and secretary of state, he negotiated the treaty that ended the War of 1812, acquired the Floridas, and conceived the Monroe Doctrine.

But Adams lacked the political skills and personality necessary to create support for his program. Like his father, Adams lacked personal warmth. His adversaries mockingly described him as a "chip off the old iceberg."

Adams's problems as president did not arise exclusively from his temperament. His misfortune was to serve as president at a time of growing partisan divisions. The Republican party had now split into two distinct camps. Adams and his supporters, known as National Republicans, favored a vigorous role for the central government in promoting national economic growth, while the Jacksonian Democrats demanded a limited government and strict adherence to laissez-faire principles.

As the only president to lose both the popular vote and the electoral vote, Adams faced hostility from the start. Jackson and his supporters accused the new president of "corruptions and intrigues" to gain Henry Clay's support. Acutely aware of the fact that "two-thirds of the whole people [were] averse" to his election as president, Adams promised in his inaugural address to make up for this with "intentions upright and pure, a heart devoted to the welfare of our country." A staunch nationalist,

Adams proposed an extraordinary program of federal support for science and economic development that included a national university, astronomical observatories ("lighthouses of the skies"), federal funding of roads and canals, and exploration of the country's territory—all to be financed by a high tariff.

Adams's advocacy of a strong federal government and a high tariff enraged defenders of slavery and states' rights advocates who clung to traditional Jeffersonian principles of limited government and strict construction of the Constitution. They feared that any expansion of federal authority might set a precedent for interference with slavery. Adams met with further frustration because he was unwilling to adapt to the practical demands of politics. Adams made no effort to use his patronage powers to build support for his proposals, and refused to fire federal officeholders who openly opposed his policies. During his entire term in office he removed just 12 incumbents, and these only for gross incompetence. He justified his actions by saying that he did not want to make "government a perpetual and intermitting scramble for office."

Adams's Indian policies also cost him supporters. Although he, like his predecessor Monroe, wanted to remove the southern Indians to the area west of the Mississippi River, he believed that the state and federal governments had a duty to abide by Indian treaties and to purchase, not merely annex, Indian lands. Adams's decision to repudiate and renegotiate a fraudulent treaty that stripped the Georgia Creek Indians of their land outraged land-hungry southerners and westerners.

Even in the realm of foreign policy, his strong suit prior to the presidency, Adams encountered difficulties. To strengthen ties with Latin America, he sent delegates to a Pan-American conference in Central America, but his representatives arrived too late to take part. His attempts to peacefully acquire Texas from Mexico failed, as did his efforts to persuade Britain to permit more American trade with the British West Indies.

The "American System" and the "Tariff of Abominations"

President Adams was committed to using the federal government to promote national economic development. His program included a high protective tariff to promote industry, the sale of public lands at low prices to encourage western settlement, federally financed transportation improvements, expanded markets for western grain and southern cotton, and a strong national bank to regulate the economy.

Adams's secretary of state, Henry Clay, called this economic program the "American system" because it was supposed to promote growth in all parts of the country. But the program infuriated southerners who believed that it favored northeastern industrial interests at their region's expense. Southerners particularly disliked a protective tariff, since it raised the cost of manufactured goods, which they did not produce.

Andrew Jackson's supporters in Congress sought to exploit the tariff question in order to embarrass Adams and help Jackson win the presidency in 1828. They framed a bill, which became known as the Tariff of Abominations, to win support for Jackson in Kentucky, Missouri, New York, Ohio, and Pennsylvania while weakening the Adams administration in New England. The bill raised duties on iron, hemp, and flax (which would benefit westerners), while lowering the tariff on woolen goods (to the detriment of New England textile manufacturers).

The Tariff of Abominations created a political uproar in the South, where it was denounced as unconstitutional and discriminatory. The tariff, southerners insisted, was essentially a tax on their region to assist northern manufacturers. South Carolina expressed the loudest outcry against the tariff. At a public meeting in Charleston, protesters declared that a tariff was designed to benefit "one class of citizens [manufacturers] at the expense of every other class." Some South Carolinians called for revolutionary defiance of the national government.

Vice President John C. Calhoun, a skilled logician well versed in political philosophy, offered a theoretical framework for southern discontent. Retreating from his early nationalistic position, Calhoun anonymously published the "South Carolina Exposition," an essay that advanced the principle of "nullification." A single state, Calhoun maintained, might overrule or "nullify" a federal law within its own territory, until three-quarters of the states had upheld the law as constitutional. In 1828 the state of South Carolina decided not to implement this doctrine but rather to wait and see what attitude the next president would adopt toward the tariff.

The Election of 1828

"J. Q. Adams who can write" squared off against "Andy Jackson who can fight" in the election of 1828, one of the most bitter campaigns in American history. Jackson's followers repeated the charge that Adams was an "aristocrat" who had obtained office as a result of a "corrupt bargain." The Jackson forces also alleged that the president had used public funds to buy personal luxuries and had installed gaming tables in the White House.

Adams's supporters countered by digging up an old story that Jackson had begun living with his wife before she was legally divorced from her first husband (which was technically true, although neither Jackson nor his wife Rachel knew her first husband was still living). They called the general a slave trader, a gambler, and a backwoods buffoon who could not spell more than one word out of four correctly.

The Jackson campaign in 1828 was the first to appeal directly for voter support through a professional political organization. Skilled political leaders, like Martin Van Buren of New York, Amos Kendall of Kentucky, and Thomas Ritchie of Virginia, created a vast network of pro-Jackson newspapers, which pictured the general as the "candidate of the people." Jackson supporters set up an extensive network of campaign committees and subcommittees to organize mass rallies, parades, and barbecues, and to erect hickory poles, Jackson's symbol.

For the first time in American history a presidential election was the focus of public attention, and voter participation increased dramatically. Twice as many voters cast ballots in the election of 1828 as in 1824, four times as many as in 1820. As in most previous elections, the vote divided along sectional lines. Jackson swept every state in the South and West and Adams won the electoral votes of every state in the North except Pennsylvania and part of New York.

Contemporaries interpreted Jackson's resounding victory as a triumph for political democracy. Jackson supporters called the vote a victory for the "farmers and mechanics of the country" over the "rich and well born." Even Jackson's opponents agreed that the election marked a watershed in the nation's political history, signaling the beginning of a new democratic age. One Adams supporter said bluntly, "a great revolution has taken place."

Andrew Jackson: The Politics of Egalitarianism

Supporters of Adams regarded Jackson's victory with deep pessimism. A justice of the Supreme Court declared, "The reign of King 'Mob' seems triumphant." But enthusiasts greeted Jackson's victory as a great triumph for the people. At the inaugural, a cable that was stretched in front of the east portico of the Capitol to keep back the throngs snapped under the

Table 10.1

Election of 1828			
Candidate	*Party*	*Popular Vote*	*Electoral Vote*
Andrew Jackson	Democratic	642,553	178
John Q. Adams	National Republican	500,897	83

pressure of the surging crowd. As many as 20,000 well-wishers attended a White House reception to honor the new president, muddying rugs, breaking furniture, and damaging china and glassware.

In certain respects, Jackson was truly a self-made man. Born in 1767 in a frontier region along the North and South Carolina border known as the Waxhaws, he was the first president to be born in a log cabin. Orphaned at an early age, he had volunteered to fight in the American Revolution when he was 13.

Jackson soon rose from poverty to a career in law and politics. Although he would later gain a reputation as the champion of the common people, in Tennessee he was allied by marriage, business, and political ties to the state's elite and against the yeomanry. As a land speculator, cotton planter, and attorney, he accumulated a large personal fortune and acquired more than 100 slaves. His candidacy for the presidency was initially promoted by speculators, creditors, and elite leaders in Tennessee who hoped to exploit Jackson's popularity in order to combat antibanking sentiment and fend off challenges to their dominance of state politics.

Twenty thousand people attended a reception for President Jackson at the White House, trampling rugs, breaking furniture, and damaging china.

Rotation in Office

Few presidents have aroused as much controversy as Andrew Jackson. In office, Jackson greatly enhanced the power and prestige of the presidency. Whereas each member of Congress represented a specific regional constituency, only the president, Jackson declared, represented all the people of the United States. Jackson convinced many Americans that their votes mattered. He espoused a political ideology of "democratic republicanism" that stressed the common people's virtue, intelligence, and capacity for self-government. He also expressed a deep disdain for the "better classes," which claimed a "more enlightened wisdom" than common men and women.

Endorsing the view that a fundamental conflict existed between working people and the "nonproducing" classes of society, Jackson and his supporters promised to remove any impediments to the ordinary citizen's opportunities for economic improvement. According to the Jacksonians, inequalities of wealth and power were the direct result of monopoly, favoritism, and special privileges, which made "the rich richer and the powerful more potent." Only free competition in an open marketplace would ensure that wealth would be distributed in accordance with each person's "industry, economy, enterprise, and prudence." The goal of the Jacksonians was to remove all obstacles that prevented farmers, artisans, and small shopkeepers from earning a greater share of the nation's wealth.

Nowhere was the Jacksonian ideal of openness made more concrete than in Jackson's theory of rotation in office, known as the "spoils system." In his first annual message to Congress, Jackson defended the principle that public offices should be rotated among party supporters in

Known as a champion of the common people, President Jackson greatly expanded the powers of the presidency.

order to help the nation achieve its republican ideals. Performance in public office, Jackson maintained, required no special intelligence or training, and rotation in office would ensure that the federal government did not develop a class of corrupt civil servants set apart from the people. His supporters advocated the spoils system on practical political grounds, viewing it as a way to reward political party loyalists and build a stronger party organization. As Jacksonian Senator William Marcy of New York proclaimed, "To the victor belongs the spoils."

The spoils system opened government positions to many of Jackson's supporters, but it was neither as new nor as democratic as it appeared. During his first 18 months in office, Jackson replaced fewer than 1,000 of the nation's 10,000 civil servants on political grounds, and fewer than 20 percent of federal officeholders were removed during his administration. Moreover, many of the men Jackson appointed to office had backgrounds of wealth and social eminence. Further, Jackson did not originate the spoils system. By the time he took office, a number of states, including New York and Pennsylvania, practiced political patronage.

Clearing the Land of Indians

The first major political controversy of Jackson's presidency involved Indian policy. At the time Jackson took office, 125,000 Native Americans still lived east of the Mississippi River. The key issues were whether these Indian tribes would be permitted to block white expansion and whether the U.S. government and its citizens would abide by previously made treaties.

Since Jefferson's presidency, two conflicting Indian policies, assimilation and removal, had governed the treatment of Native Americans. The assimilation policy encouraged Indians to adopt white American customs and economic practices. The government provided financial assistance to missionaries in order to Christianize and educate Native Americans and convince them to adopt single-family farms. Proponents defended assimilation as the only way Native Americans would be able to survive in a white-dominated society. By the 1820s the Cherokees had demonstrated an ability to adapt to changing conditions while maintaining their tribal heritage. Sequoyah, a leader of these people, had developed a written alphabet. Soon the Cherokees opened schools, established churches, built roads, operated printing presses, and even adopted a constitution.

The other policy—removal—was first suggested by Thomas Jefferson as the only way to ensure the survival of Indian cultures. The goal of this policy was to encourage the voluntary migration of Indians westward to tracts of land where they could live free from white harassment. As early as 1817 James Monroe declared that the nation's security depended on rapid settlement along the southern coast, and that it was in the best interests of Native Americans to move westward. In 1825 he set before Congress a plan to resettle all eastern Indians on tracts in the West where whites would not be allowed to live.

After initially supporting both policies, Jackson favored removal as the solution to the controversy. This shift in federal Indian policy came partly as a result of a dispute between the Cherokee nation and the state of Georgia. The Cherokee people had adopted a constitution asserting sovereignty over their land. The state responded by abolishing tribal rule and claiming that the Cherokees fell under its jurisdiction. The discovery of gold on Cherokee land triggered a land rush, and the Cherokee nation sued to keep white settlers from encroaching on its territory. In two important cases, *Cherokee Nation* v. *Georgia* in 1831 and *Worcester* v. *Georgia* in 1832, the Supreme Court ruled that states could not pass laws conflicting with federal Indian treaties and that the federal government had an obligation to exclude white intruders from Indian lands. Angered, Jackson is said to have exclaimed: "John Marshall has made his decision; now let him enforce it."

The primary thrust of Jackson's removal policy was to encourage Indian tribes to sell all tribal lands in exchange for new lands in Oklahoma and Arkansas. Such a policy, the president maintained, would open new farm land to whites while offering Indians a haven where they would be free to develop at their own pace.

During the winter of 1831 the Choctaw became the first tribe to walk the "Trail of Tears" westward. Promised government assistance failed to arrive, and malnutrition, exposure, and a cholera epidemic killed many members of the Indian nation. Then, in 1836, the Creek suffered the hardships of removal. About 3,500 of the tribe's 15,000 members died along the westward trek. Those who resisted removal were bound in chains and marched in double file.

Emboldened by the Supreme Court decisions declaring that Georgia law had no force on Indian territory, the Cherokees resisted removal. The federal government bribed a faction of the tribe to leave the land in exchange for transportation costs and $5 million, but most Cherokees held out until 1838, when the army evicted them from their land. All told, 4,000 of the 15,000 tribal members died along the trail to Indian territory in what is now Oklahoma.

A number of other tribes also organized resistance against removal. In the Old Northwest, the Sauk and Fox Indians fought the Black Hawk War to recover ceded tribal lands in Illinois and Wisconsin. The Indians claimed that when they had signed the treaty transferring title to their land, they had not understood the implications of the action. The United

States army and the Illinois state militia ended the resistance by wantonly killing nearly 500 Sauk and Fox men, women, and children who were trying to retreat across the Mississippi River. In Florida the military spent seven years putting down Seminole resistance at a cost of $20 million and 1,500 casualties, and even then succeeding only after kidnapping a Seminole leader during peace talks.

By twentieth-century standards Jackson's Indian policy was both callous and inhumane. Despite the semblance of legality—94 treaties were signed with Indians during Jackson's presidency—Indian migrations to the West almost always occurred under the threat of government coercion. The federal government probably lacked the resources and military means necessary to protect the eastern Indians from encroaching whites, even had it wanted to do so. By the 1830s a growing number of missionaries and humanitarians agreed with Jackson that Indians needed to be resettled westward for their own protection. Removal failed in large part because of the nation's commitment to limited government and its lack of experience with social welfare programs. Contracts for food, clothing, and transportation were awarded to the lowest bidders, many of whom failed to fulfill their contractual responsibilities. The tragic outcome was readily foreseeable.

The problem of preserving native cultures in the face of an expanding nation was not confined to the United States. Jackson's removal policy can only be properly understood when seen as part of a broader process: the political and economic conquest of frontier regions by expanding nation states. During the early decades of the nineteenth century European nations were penetrating into many frontier areas, including the steppes of Russia, the plains of Argentina, the veldt of South Africa, the outback of Australia, and the American West. In each of these regions national expansion was justified on the grounds of strategic interest (to preempt settlement by other powers) or in the name of opening valuable land to white settlement and development. And in each case expansion was accompanied by the removal or wholesale killing of native peoples.

Sectional Disputes over Public Lands and Nullification

Bitter sectional disputes arose during Jackson's presidency over public lands and the tariff. After the Revolutionary War the federal government owned one-quarter billion acres of public land; the Louisiana Purchase added another half billion acres to the public domain. These public lands constituted the federal government's single greatest source of public revenue.

In 1820, to promote the establishment of farms, Congress encouraged the rapid sale of public land by reducing the minimum land purchase from 160 to just 80 acres, at a price of $1.25 per acre. Still, a variety of groups favored even easier terms for land sales. Squatters, for example, who violated federal laws that forbade settlement prior to the completion of public surveys, pressured Congress to adopt preemption acts that would permit them to buy the land they occupied at the minimum price of $1.25 when it came up for sale. Urban workingmen demanded free homesteads for any American who would settle the public domain. Transportation companies, which built roads, canals, and later railroads, called for grants of public land to help fund their projects.

In Congress two proposals—"distribution" and "graduation"—competed for support. Under the distribution proposal, which was identified with Henry Clay, Congress would distribute the proceeds from the sale of public lands to the states, which would use the funds to finance transportation improvements. Senator Thomas Hart Benton of Missouri offered an alternative proposal, graduation. He proposed that Congress gradually reduce the price of unsold government land and, finally, give away land that remained unpurchased.

At the end of 1829 a Connecticut senator proposed a cessation of public land sales. This transformed the debate over public lands into a sectional battle over the nature of the union. Senator Benton denounced the proposal as a brazen attempt by manufacturers to keep laborers from settling the West, fearing that westward migration would reduce the size of the urban work force and therefore raise their wage costs.

Benton's speech prompted Robert Y. Hayne, a supporter of John C. Calhoun, to propose an alliance of southern and western interests based on a low tariff and cheap land. Affirming the principle of nullification, he called on the two sections to unite against attempts by the northeast to strengthen the powers of the federal government.

Daniel Webster of Massachusetts answered Hayne in one of the most famous speeches in American history. The United States, Webster proclaimed, was not simply a compact of the states. It was a creation of the people, who had invested the Constitution and the national government with ultimate sovereignty. If a state disagreed with an action of the federal government, it had a right to sue in federal court or seek to amend the Constitution, but it had no right to nullify a federal law. Such action would inevitably lead to anarchy and civil war. It was delusion and folly to think that Americans could have "Liberty first and Union afterwards," Webster declared. "Liberty and Union, now and forever, one and inseparable."

Jackson revealed his position on the questions of states' rights and nullification at a Jefferson Day dinner on April 13, 1830. Fixing his eyes on Vice President John C. Calhoun, the president expressed his sentiments with this toast: "Our Union: It must be preserved." Calhoun responded to Jackson's challenge and offered the next toast: "The Union, next to our liberty, most dear. May we always remember that it can only be preserved by distributing equally the benefits and burdens of the Union."

Relations between Jackson and Calhoun had grown increasingly strained. Jackson had learned that when Calhoun was secretary of war under Monroe he had called for Jackson's court-martial for his conduct during the military occupation of Florida in 1818. Jackson was also angry because Mrs. Calhoun had snubbed the wife of Secretary of War John H. Eaton, because Mrs. Eaton was the twice-married daughter of a tavern-keeper. Because Jackson's own late wife Rachel had been snubbed by society, the president had empathy for young Peggy Eaton. In 1831 Jackson reorganized his cabinet and forced Calhoun's supporters out. The next year Calhoun became the first vice president to resign his office, when he became a senator from South Carolina.

In 1832, in an effort to conciliate the South, Jackson proposed a lower tariff. Revenue from the existing tariff (together with the sale of public lands) was so high that the federal debt was quickly being paid off; in fact on January 1, 1835, the United States Treasury had a $440,000 surplus. The new tariff adopted in 1832 was somewhat lower than the Tariff of 1828 but still maintained the principle of protection. In protest, South Carolina's fiery "states' righters" declared both the Tariff of 1832 and the Tariff of 1828 null and void. To defend nullification, the state legislature voted to raise an army.

Jackson responded by declaring nullification illegal, and then asked Congress to empower him to use force to execute federal law. Congress promptly enacted a Force Act. Privately, Jackson threatened to "hang every leader . . . of that infatuated people, sir, by martial law, irrespective of his name, or political or social position." He also dispatched a fleet of eight ships and a shipment of 5,000 muskets to Fort Pinckney, a federal installation in Charleston harbor.

In Congress, Henry Clay, the "great compromiser" who had engineered the Missouri Compromise of 1820, worked feverishly to reduce South Carolina's sense of grievance. "He who loves the Union must desire to see this agitating question brought to a termination," he said. In less than a month he persuaded Congress to enact a compromise tariff with lower levels of protection. South Carolinians backed down, rescinding the ordinance nullifying the federal tariff.

South Carolina's anxiety had many causes. By 1831 declining cotton prices and growing concern about the future of slavery had turned the state from a staunch supporter of economic nationalism into the nation's most aggressive advocate of states' rights. Increasingly, economic grievances fused with concerns over slavery. In 1832 the Palmetto State was one of just two states whose population was made up of a majority of slaves. By that year events throughout the hemisphere made South Carolinians desperately uneasy about the future of slavery. In 1831 and 1832 militant abolitionism had erupted in the North, slave insurrections had occurred in Southampton County, Virginia, and Jamaica, and Britain was moving to emancipate all slaves in the British Caribbean.

By using the federal tariff as the focus of their grievances, South Carolinians found an ideal way of debating the question of state sovereignty without debating the morality of slavery. Following the Missouri Compromise debates, a slave insurrection led by Denmark Vesey had been uncovered in Charleston in 1822. By 1832 South Carolinians did not want to stage debates in Congress that might bring the explosive slavery issue to the fore and possibly incite another slave revolt.

The Bank War

Although the tariff was important, the major political issue of Jackson's presidency was his war against the second Bank of the United States. To understand this battle, the nature of the banking system at the time Jackson assumed the presidency must be understood. It was completely different than it is today. At that time, the federal government coined only a limited supply of hard money and printed no paper money at all. The principal source of circulating currency—of paper bank notes—was private commercial banks (of which there were 329 in 1829), chartered by the various states. These private, state-chartered banks supplied the credit necessary to finance land purchases, business operations, and economic growth. The notes they issued were promises to pay gold or silver, but they were backed by a limited amount of precious metal and they fluctuated greatly in value.

In 1816 the federal government had chartered the second Bank of the United States partly in an effort to control the notes issued by state banks. By demanding payment in gold or silver, the national bank could discipline overspeculative private banks. But the very idea of a national bank was unpopular for various reasons. Many people blamed it for causing the Panic of 1819. Others resented its political influence. For example, Senator Daniel Webster was both the bank's chief lobbyist and a director of the bank's Boston branch. Wage earners and small businesspeople blamed it for economic fluctuations and loan restrictions. Private banks resented its privileged position in the banking industry.

In 1832 Henry Clay, Daniel Webster, and other Jackson opponents in Congress, seeking an issue for that year's presidential election, passed a bill rechartering the second Bank of the United States. The bank's charter was not due to expire until 1836, but Clay and Webster wanted to force

Jackson to take a clear pro-bank or antibank position. Jackson had frequently attacked the bank as an agency through which speculators, monopolists, and other seekers of economic privilege cheated honest farmers and mechanics. Now his adversaries wanted to force him either to sign the bill for recharter, alienating voters hostile to the bank, or veto it, antagonizing conservative voters who favored a sound banking system.

Jackson vetoed the bill in a forceful message that condemned the bank as a privileged "monopoly" created to make "rich men . . . richer by act of Congress." The bank, he declared, was "unauthorized by the Constitution, subversive of the rights of the States, and dangerous to the liberties of the people." In the presidential campaign of 1832 Henry Clay tried to make an issue of Jackson's bank veto, but Jackson swept to an easy second-term victory, defeating Clay by 219 electoral votes to 49.

Jackson interpreted his reelection as a mandate to undermine the bank still further. In September 1833 he ordered his Treasury secretary to divert federal revenues from the Bank of the United States to selected state banks, which came to be known as "pet" banks. The secretary of the Treasury and his successor resigned rather than carry out the president's order. It was only after Jackson appointed a second new secretary that his order was implemented. Jackson's decision to divert federal deposits from the national bank prompted his adversaries in the Senate to formally censure the president's actions as arbitrary and unconstitutional. The bank's president, Nicholas Biddle, responded to Jackson's actions by reducing loans and calling in debts. Over the span of six months the bank reduced loans by nearly $10 million in an attempt to pressure Jackson to approve a new charter. "The Bank . . . is trying to kill me," Jackson declared, "but I will kill it."

Jackson's decision to divert funds drew strong support from many conservative businesspeople who believed that the bank's destruction would increase the availability of credit and open up new business opportunities. Jackson, however, hated all banks, and believed that the only sound currencies were gold and silver. Having crippled the Bank of the United States, he promptly launched a crusade to replace all bank notes with hard money. In the Specie Circular of 1836 Jackson prohibited payment for public lands with anything but gold or silver. That same year, in another antibanking measure, Congress voted to deprive pet banks of federal deposits. Instead, nearly $35 million in surplus federal funds to the states was distributed to help finance internal improvements.

To Jackson's supporters, the presidential veto of the bank bill was a principled assault on a bastion of wealth and special privilege. His efforts to curtail the circulation of bank notes was an attempt to rid the country of a tool used by commercial interests to exploit farmers and working men and women. To his critics, the veto was an act of economic ignorance that destroyed a valuable institution that promoted monetary stability, eased the long-distance transfer of funds, provided a reserve of capital on which other banks drew, and helped regulate the bank notes issued by private banks. Jackson's effort to limit the circulation of bank notes was a misguided act of a president who failed to understand the role of a banking system in a modern economy.

The effect of Jackson's banking policies remains a subject of debate. Initially, land sales, canal construction, cotton production, and manufacturing boomed following Jackson's decision to divert federal funds from the bank. At the same time, however, state debts rose sharply and inflation increased dramatically. Prices climbed 28 percent in just three years. Then in 1837, just after the election of Jackson's successor Democrat Martin Van Buren, a deep financial depression struck the nation. Cotton prices fell by half. In New York City 50,000 people were thrown out of work and 200,000 lacked adequate means of support. Mobs in New York broke into the city's flour warehouse. From across the country came "rumor after rumor of riot, insurrection, and tumult." Not until the mid-1840s would the country fully pull out of the depression.

Who was to blame for the Panic of 1837? One school of thought holds Jackson responsible, arguing that his banking policies removed a vital check on the activities of state-chartered banks. Freed from the regulation of the second Bank of the United States, private banks rapidly expanded the volume of bank notes in circulation, contributing to the rapid increase in inflation. Jackson's Specie Circular of 1836, which sought to curb inflation by requiring that public land payments be made in hard currency, forced many Americans to exchange paper bills for gold and silver. Many private banks lacked sufficient reserves of hard currency and were forced to close their doors, triggering a financial crisis.

Another school of thought blames the panic on factors outside of Jackson's control. A surplus of cotton on the world market caused the price of cotton to drop sharply, throwing many southern and western cotton farmers into bankruptcy. Meanwhile, in 1836, Britain suddenly raised interest rates, which drastically reduced investment in the American economy and forced a number of states to default on loans from foreign investors.

If Jackson's policies did not necessarily cause the panic, they certainly made recovery more difficult. Jackson's handpicked successor, Martin Van Buren, responded to the economic depression in an extremely doctrinaire way. A firm believer in the Jeffersonian principle of limited government, Van Buren refused to provide government aid to business. Fearful that the federal government might lose funds it had deposited in private banks, Van Buren convinced Congress in 1840 to adopt an independent treasury system. Under this proposal federal funds were locked up in subtreasuries, depriving the banking system of hard currency that might have aided recovery.

The Jacksonian Court

Presidents' judicial appointments represent one of their most enduring legacies. In his two terms as president Andrew Jackson appointed five of the seven justices on the Supreme Court. To replace Chief Justice John Marshall, who died in 1835, Jackson selected his Treasury secretary, Roger B. Taney, who would lead the court for nearly three decades. Under Taney, the Court broke with tradition, and sought to extend Jacksonian principles of promoting individual opportunity by removing traditional restraints on competition in the marketplace. The Taney Court upheld the doctrine of limited liability for corporations and provided legal sanction to state subsidies for canals, turnpikes, and railroads. Taken together, the decisions of the Taney Court played a vital role in the emergence of the American system of free enterprise.

One case in particular, that of *Charles River Bridge* v. *Warren Bridge,* raised an issue fundamental to the nation's future economic growth: whether state-granted monopolies would be allowed to block competition from new enterprises. In 1828 the state of Massachusetts chartered a company to build a toll-free bridge connecting Boston and neighboring Charlestown. The owners of an existing toll bridge sued, claiming that their 1785 charter included an implied right to a monopoly.

In its decision, the Court ensured that monopolistic privileges granted in the past would not be allowed to interfere with public welfare. The Court held that contracts conferred only explicitly stated rights. The decision epitomized the ideals of Jacksonian democracy: a commitment to removing artificial barriers to opportunity and an emphasis upon free competition in an open marketplace.

Jackson's Legacy

Andrew Jackson was one of the nation's most resourceful and effective presidents. In the face of hostile majorities in Congress, he carried out his most important policies, affecting banking, internal improvements, Native Americans, and tariffs. As president, Jackson used the veto power more often than all previous presidents combined during the preceding 40 years, and used it in such a way that he succeeded in representing himself as the champion of the people against special interests in Congress. In addition, his skillful use of patronage and party organization and his successful manipulation of public symbols helped create the nation's first modern political party with truly national appeal.

And yet, despite his popular appeal, Jackson's legacy is a matter of great dispute among historians. His Indian policies continue to arouse passionate criticism, while his economic policies, contrary to his reputation as the president of the common man, did little to help small farmers, artisans, and working people. In fact, his policies actually weakened the ability of the federal government to regulate the nation's economy. Indeed, many historians now believe that slaveholders—not small farmers or working people—benefited most. His Indian policies helped to open new lands for slaveowners, and his view of limited government forestalled federal interference with slavery.

Rise of a Political Opposition

Although it took a number of years for Jackson's opponents to coalesce into an effective national political organization, by the mid-1830s the Whig party, as the opposition came to be known, was able to battle the Democratic party on almost equal terms throughout the country. The party was formed in 1834 as a coalition of National Republicans, Anti-Masons, and disgruntled Democrats, who were united by their hatred of "King Andrew" Jackson and his "usurpations" of congressional and judicial authority. The party took its name from the seventeenth-century British Whigs, who had defended English liberties against the usurpations of pro-Catholic Stuart Kings.

In 1836 the Whigs mounted their first presidential campaign. The party ran three regional candidates against Martin Van Buren: Daniel Webster, the senator from Massachusetts; Hugh Lawson White, who had appeal in the South; and William Henry Harrison, who fought an Indian alliance at the Battle of Tippecanoe and appealed to the West. The party strategy was to throw the election into the House of Representatives, where the Whigs would unite behind a single candidate. Van Buren easily defeated all his Whig opponents, winning 170 electoral votes to just 73 for his closest rival.

The emergence of Martin Van Buren as Jackson's successor resulted in a major defection of southerners and conservative Democrats to the Whig party. Unlike the southern slave-owning Jackson, Van Buren was a "Yankee" from New York, and many southerners feared that he could not be trusted to protect slavery. As a result, the Whigs carried Georgia, Kentucky, Maryland, and Tennessee.

Ironically, as president, Van Buren supported a congressional rule—known as the Gag Rule—which quashed debate over antislavery petitions in the House of Representatives. His independent treasury scheme combined with his staunch opposition to any federal interference in the economy lured Calhoun and the southern nullifiers back to the Democratic party. Conversely, his attacks on paper money and his scheme to remove federal funds from the private banking system alienated many conservative Democrats who threw their support to the Whigs.

Following his strong showing in the election of 1836, William Henry Harrison received the united support of the Whig party in 1840. Benefiting from the Panic of 1837 and from a host of colorful campaign innovations, Harrison easily defeated Van Buren by a vote of 234 to 60 in the electoral college.

Unfortunately, the 68-year-old Harrison caught cold while delivering a two-hour inaugural address in the freezing rain. Barely a month later, he died of pneumonia, the first president to die in office. His successor, John Tyler of Virginia, was an ardent defender of slavery, a staunch advocate of states' rights, and a former Democrat, whom the Whigs had nominated in order to attract Democratic support to the Whig ticket.

A firm believer in the principle that the federal government should exercise no powers other than those expressly enumerated in the Constitution, Tyler rejected the entire Whig legislative program, which called for the reestablishment of a national bank, an increased tariff, and federally funded internal improvements.

The Whig party was furious. To protest Tyler's rejection of the Whig political agenda, all members of the cabinet but one resigned. Tyler had become a president without a party. "His Accidency" vetoed nine bills during his four years in office, frustrating Whig plans to recharter the national bank and raise the tariff, while simultaneously distributing proceeds of land sales to the states. In 1843 Whigs in the House of Representatives made Tyler the subject of the first serious impeachment attempt, but the resolutions were defeated by a vote of 127 to 83.

Curiously, it was during Tyler's administration that the nation's new two-party system achieved full maturity. Prior to Tyler's ascension to office, the Whig party had been a loose conglomeration of diverse political factions unable to agree on a party platform. Tyler's presidency increased unity among Whigs who found common cause in their opposition to his policies. On important issues four-fifths of all Whig members of Congress regularly voted together. At the same time, the Whigs created an elaborate network of party newspapers in all parts of the country. Never before had party identity been so high or partisan sentiment so strong.

Who Were the Whigs?

The Jacksonians made a great effort to to persuade voters to identify their own cause with Thomas Jefferson and their Whig opponents with Alexander Hamilton. In spite of Democratic charges to the contrary, however, the Whigs were not simply a continuation of the Federalist party. Like the Democrats, the Whigs drew support from all parts of the nation. Indeed, the Whigs often formed the majority of the South's representatives in Congress. Like the Democrats, the Whigs were a coalition of sectional interests, class and economic interests, and ethnic and religious interests.

Democratic voters tended to be small farmers, residents of less-prosperous towns, and the Scots-Irish and Catholic Irish. Whigs tended to be educators and professionals, manufacturers, business-oriented farmers, British and German Protestant immigrants, upwardly aspiring manual laborers, free blacks, and active members of Presbyterian, Unitarian, and Congregational churches. The Whig coalition included supporters of Henry Clay's American System, states' righters, religious groups alienated by Jackson's Indian removal policies, and bankers and businesspeople frightened by the Democrats' antimonopoly and antibank rhetoric.

Whereas the Democrats stressed class conflict, Whigs emphasized the harmony of interests between labor and capital, the need for humanitarian reform, and leadership by men of talent. The Whigs also idealized the "self-made man," who starts "from an humble origin, and from small beginnings rise[s] gradually in the world, as a result of merit and industry." Finally, the Whigs viewed technology and factory enterprise as forces for increasing national wealth and improving living conditions.

In 1848 and 1852 the Whigs tried to repeat their successful 1840 presidential campaign by nominating military heroes for the presidency. The party won the 1848 election with General Zachary Taylor, an Indian fighter and hero of the Mexican War, who had never cast a vote in a presidential election. Like Harrison, Taylor confined his campaign speeches to uncontroversial platitudes. "Old Rough and Ready," as he was known, died after just sixteen months in office. Then, in 1852, the Whigs nominated another Indian fighter and Mexican War hero, General Winfield Scott, who carried just four states for his dying party. Scott was the last Whig nominee to play an important role in a presidential election.

Conclusion

A political revolution occurred in the United States between 1820 and 1840. Property qualifications for voting and officeholding were abolished, voting by voice was eliminated, voter participation increased, and a new party system emerged. Unlike America's first political parties, the Federalists and Republicans, the Jacksonian Democrats and the Whigs were parties with grass-roots organization and support in all parts of the nation.

Andrew Jackson, the dominant political figure of the period, spelled out the new democratic approach to politics. In the name of eliminating special privilege and promoting equality of opportunity, he helped institute the national political nominating convention, defended the spoils system, destroyed the second Bank of the United States, and opened

*C*hronology of Key Events

1820	Land Act reduces price of public land to $1.25 an acre
1825	House of Representatives elects John Quincy Adams as sixth president
1828	South Carolina Exposition; Congress passes Tariff of Abominations; Andrew Jackson elected seventh president
1830	Indian Removal Act; Webster-Hayne debate
1832	Jackson vetoes second Bank of the United States recharter bill;
1833	Congress adopts "Compromise Tariff" lowering tariff rates and "Force Bill" authorizing Jackson to enforce federal law in South Carolina
1835	Roger B. Taney succeeds John Marshall as Chief Justice
1836	Specie Circular; Martin Van Buren elected eighth president
1837	Panic of 1837; *Charles River Bridge* v. *Warren Bridge*
1840	Independent Treasury Act; William Henry Harrison elected ninth president
1841	John Tyler becomes tenth president on death of Harrison

millions of acres of Indian lands to white settlement. A strong and determined leader, Jackson greatly expanded the power of the presidency. No matter how one evaluates his eight years in the White House, there can be no doubt that he left an indelible stamp on the nation's highest office; indeed, on a whole epoch in American history.

Suggestions for Further Reading

General surveys of the Jacksonian era include Edward Pessen, *Jacksonian America: Society, Personality, and Politics,* rev. ed. (1978); Arthur M. Schlesinger, Jr., *The Age of Jackson* (1945); Harry L. Watson, *Liberty and Power* (1990).

Biographies of Andrew Jackson include James C. Curtis, *Andrew Jackson and the Search for Vindication* (1976); Robert Remini, *Andrew Jackson and the Course of American Freedom* (1981), and *Andrew Jackson and the Course of American Democracy* (1984). See also Marvin Meyers, *The Jacksonian Persuasion* (1957); John W. Ward, *Andrew Jackson: Symbol for an Age* (1955).

On Jackson's banking and economic policies, see Bray Hammond, *Banks and Politics in America: From the Revolution to the Civil War* (1957); Peter Temin, *The Jacksonian Economy* (1969). Other aspects of Jackson's presidency are examined in Daniel Feller, *Public Lands in Jacksonian Politics* (1984); Ronald Satz, *American Indian Policy in the Jacksonian Era* (1975).

Significant biographies of Jackson's opponents are Irving H. Bartlett, *Daniel Webster* (1978); John Niven, *John C. Calhoun and the Price of Union* (1988); Robert Remini, *Henry Clay* (1991).

On the emergence of the second party system, see Richard Hofstadter, *The Idea of a Party System* (1969); Richard P. McCormick, *The Second American Party System* (1966). The political ideologies of the two parties are examined in Lee Benson, *The Concept of Jacksonian Democracy* (1961); Daniel Walker Howe, *The Political Culture of the American Whigs* (1979). See also W. P. Vaughn, *The Antimasonic Party in the United States* (1983).

Chapter ***II***

Reforming American Society

Many early nineteenth-century New Yorkers feared that their city was being overwhelmed by crime. In one highly publicized incident a little girl was stabbed to death over a penny she had begged. In another incident in 1849, 30 people died and another 100 were injured in a riot outside the city's Astor Place Opera House. Declared the city's mayor: "This city is infested by gangs of hardened wretches" who "patrol the streets making night hideous and insulting all who are not strong enough to defend themselves." Between 1814 and 1835 New York City's population doubled, but reports of crime increased fivefold.

Poverty and crime appeared to be epidemic. Young girls, dressed in rags, tried to support themselves by selling toothpicks. An estimated 10,000 prostitutes plied their trade, brazenly standing outside of fashionable hotels or strolling through theaters. Gangs, bearing such names as the Plug Uglies, Dead Rabbits, and the Bowery B'hoys, prowled the city streets, stealing from warehouses, junk shops, and private residences.

Critics decried a "carnival of murder." In 1857 six men were shot or stabbed in barroom brawls in a single night. In response to the apparent upsurge in crime, fearful citizens armed themselves, carrying guns and night sticks for their defense when they went outside at night. For added protection, many homeowners installed iron bars over their ground-floor windows.

During the decades before the Civil War, newspapers were filled with reports of crime, vice, and violence in the growing cities of the North, in the slave South, and on the frontier. Incidents of crime and violence led many Americans to ask how a free society could maintain stability and moral order. Americans sought to answer this question through religion, education, and social reform.

The Reform Impulse

The first half of the nineteenth century witnessed an enormous effort to improve society through reform. Reformers launched unprecedented campaigns to assist the handicapped, rehabilitate criminals and prostitutes, outlaw alcohol, guarantee women's rights, and abolish slavery. Our modern systems of free public schools, prisons, and hospitals for the infirm and the mentally ill are all legacies of this first generation of American reform. What factors gave rise to the reform impulse and why was it unleashed with such vigor in pre–Civil War America?

Sources of the Reform Impulse

The reformers had many different reasons for wanting to change American society. Some people turned to reform as a way of imposing order;

others were motivated by a religious vision of creating a godly society on earth. Still others viewed reform as a way of spreading the values associated with the Protestant ethic: sobriety, punctuality, self-discipline, and personal responsibility.

During the first decades of the nineteenth century America's revolutionary heritage, Enlightenment philosophy, and religious zeal all contributed to a spirit of optimism, a sensitivity to human suffering, and a boundless faith in humankind's capacity to improve social institutions. The Declaration of Independence, with its emphasis on natural rights, liberty, and equality, led reformers to view their efforts as a continuation of political struggles begun during the Revolution. The philosophy of the Enlightenment, with its belief in the people's innate goodness and its rejection of the inevitability of poverty and ignorance, was another important source of reform. By providing a more favorable moral and physical environment through the application of reason, reform could overcome social problems and antisocial behavior.

Religion further strengthened the reform impulse. Almost all the leading reformers were devoutly religious men and women, who wanted to deepen the nation's commitment to Christian principles. Two trends in religious thought—religious liberalism and evangelical revivalism—strengthened reformers' zeal. Religious liberalism was an emerging form of humanitarianism that rejected the harsh Calvinist doctrines of original sin and predestination. Its preachers stressed the basic goodness of human nature and each individual's capacity to follow the example of Christ.

William Ellery Channing was America's leading exponent of religious liberalism. In 1815 Channing's beliefs became the basis for American Unitarianism. The new religious denomination stressed individual freedom of belief, and a united world under a single God. Channing's beliefs stimulated many reformers to work toward improving the conditions of the physically handicapped, the criminal, the pauper, and the enslaved.

Second Great Awakening

The evangelical revivalism that swept the country in the early nineteenth century was also a source of the reform impulse. This great religious fervor came to be called the Second Great Awakening. Evangelical leaders urged their followers to repent their sins and reject selfishness and materialism. To the revivalists, sin was not a metaphysical abstraction. Luxury, high living, indifference to religion, preoccupation with worldly and commercial matters—all these were denounced as sinful. If men and women did not seek God through Christ, the nation would face divine retribution. Evangelical revivals helped instill a belief that Americans had been chosen by God to lead the world toward "a millennium of republicanism."

Charles Grandison Finney, the "father of modern revivalism," led revivals throughout the Northeast. Despite his lack of formal theological training, Finney was remarkably successful in converting souls to Christ. He prayed for sinners by name; he held meetings that lasted night after night for a week or more; he set up an "anxious bench" at the front of the meeting, where the almost-saved could receive special prayers. He also encouraged women to actively participate in revivals. Finney's message was that anyone could experience a redemptive change of heart and a resurgence of religious feeling. If only enough people converted to Christ, Finney told his listeners, the millennium would arrive within three years.

Revival meetings attracted both frontier settlers and city folk, slaves and masters, farmers and shopkeepers. The revivals had their greatest appeal among isolated farming families on the western and southern frontier, among upwardly mobile merchants, shopkeepers, artisans, and skilled laborers in the expanding commercial and industrial towns of the North. They drew support from social conservatives who feared that America would disintegrate into a state of anarchy without the influence of evangelical religion, and also enlisted followers among poorer whites and slaves in the South. Above all, revivals attracted large numbers of young women, who took an active role in organizing meetings, establishing church organizations, and editing religious publications.

Moral Reform

The earliest reformers wanted to persuade Americans to adopt more godly personal habits. They set up associations to battle profanity and Sabbath breaking, to place a Bible in every American home, to provide religious education for the children of the poor, and to curb the widespread heavy use of hard liquor. By discouraging drinking, gambling, and encouraging observance of the Sabbath, reformers hoped to "restore the government of God."

The most extensive moral reform campaign was against drinking, which had long been an integral part of American life. Many people believed that downing a glass of whiskey before breakfast was conducive to good health. Easily affordable to even the poorest Americans—a gallon of whiskey cost 25 cents in the 1820s—consumption had risen markedly since the beginning of the century.

Reformers sought to alter the cultural norms that encouraged alcohol consumption by identifying liquor as the cause of a wide range of social, family, and personal problems. Many middle-class women blamed alcohol for the abuse of wives and children and the squandering of family resources. Many businesspeople identified drinking with crime, poverty, and inefficient, unproductive employees.

Americans turned to revival meetings in times of social and economic upheaval. These meetings, which stressed new birth conversions, could last for days.

The stage was clearly set for the appearance of an organized movement against liquor. In 1826 the nation's first formal national temperance organization was born: the American Society for the Promotion of Temperance. Led by socially prominent clergy and laypeople, the new organization called for total abstinence from distilled liquor.

By 1835 an estimated 2 million Americans had taken the "pledge" to abstain from hard liquor. Temperance reform drew support from many southerners and westerners who were otherwise indifferent or hostile to reform. Their efforts helped reduce annual per capita consumption of alcohol from seven gallons in 1830 to just three gallons a decade later. In addition, a campaign to restrict the manufacture and sale of alcohol culminated in the nation's first statewide prohibition law in Maine in 1851.

The sudden arrival of hundreds of thousands of immigrants heightened the concerns of temperance reformers. Between 1830 and 1860 nearly two million Irish arrived in the United States along with an additional 893,000 Germans. Increasingly, the alleged heavy drinking of immigrants was regarded as a problem demanding government action.

Social Reform

The nation's first reformers tried to improve the nation's moral and spiritual values by distributing Bibles and religious tracts, promoting observance of the Sabbath, and curbing drinking. Beginning in the 1820s a new phase of reform—social reform—spread across the country, directed at such problems as crime, illiteracy, poverty, and disease. Reformers sought to solve these problems by creating new institutions to deal with them—including prisons, public schools, and asylums for the deaf, the blind, and the mentally ill.

The Problem of Crime in a Free Society

Prior to the American Revolution punishment for crimes generally involved some form of corporal punishment, ranging from the death

As early as the 1820s, urban slums like New York City's Five Points began to appear. These areas of poverty, crime, filth, and violence attracted beggars, pimps, prostitutes, and hoodlums.

penalty for serious crimes to public whipping, confinement in stocks, and branding for lesser offenses. Jails were used as temporary confinement for criminal defendants awaiting trial or punishment. Conditions in these early jails were abominable. Debtors were confined with hardened criminals, and offenders of both sexes and of all ages were confined in large groups in cramped cells.

During the pre–Civil War decades reformers began to view crime as a social problem—a product of environment and parental neglect—rather than the result of original sin or human depravity. Revulsion over the spectacle of public punishment led to the rapid construction of penal institutions in which the "disease" of crime could be quarantined and inmates could be gradually rehabilitated in a controlled environment. Two rival prison systems competed for public support. After constructing Auburn Prison, New York State authorities adopted a system in which inmates worked in large workshops during the day and slept in separate cells at night. Convicts had to march in lockstep and refrain from speaking or even looking at each other. In Pennsylvania's Eastern State Penitentiary, constructed in 1829, authorities placed even greater stress on the physical isolation of prisoners. Every prison cell had its own exercise yard, work space, and toilet facilities. Under the Pennsylvania plan prisoners lived and worked in complete isolation from each other. Called "penitentiaries" or "reformatories," these new prisons reflected the belief that hard physical labor and solitary confinement might encourage introspection and instill habits of discipline that would rehabilitate criminals.

The legal principle that a criminal act should only be legally punished if the offender was fully capable of distinguishing between right and wrong opened the way to one of the most controversial aspects of American jurisprudence—the insanity defense. The question arose dramatically in 1835 when a deranged Englishman named Richard Lawrence walked up to President Andrew Jackson and fired two pistols at him at a distance of six feet. Incredibly, both guns misfired, and Jackson was unhurt. The court found Lawrence insane and not subject to criminal prosecution; instead, he was confined for treatment of his mental condition.

Another major effort was a movement to outlaw capital punishment. Prior to the 1830s most states reduced the number of crimes punishable by death and began to perform executions outside of public view, lest the public be stimulated to acts of violence by the spectacle of hangings. In 1847 Michigan became the first modern jurisdiction to outlaw the death penalty and was soon followed by Rhode Island and Wisconsin.

Imprisonment for debt also came under attack. As late as 1816 an average of 600 residents of New York City were in prison at any one time for failure to pay debts. More than half owed less than $50. Imprisoned debtors were, of course, unable to work and therefore unable to pay off their debts. Increasingly, reformers regarded imprisonment as irrational. Beginning with New York State in 1817, states eliminated the practice of jailing people for trifling debts. Subsequently other states forbade the jailing of women for debt.

The Struggle for Educational Opportunity

Of all the ideas advanced by antebellum reformers, none was more original than the principle that all American children should be educated to their fullest capacity at public expense. Prior to the 1840s apprenticeship had been a major form of education, and formal schooling was largely limited to those who could afford to pay. Reformers viewed education as the key to individual opportunity and the creation of an enlightened and responsible citizenry. They also believed that public schooling could be an effective weapon in the fight against juvenile delinquency and an essential ingredient in the education and assimilation of immigrants.

Horace Mann of Massachusetts, the nation's leading educational reformer, led the fight for government support for public schools. As a state legislator, Mann took the lead in establishing a board of education, and his efforts resulted in a doubling of state expenditures on education. He was also successful in winning state support for teacher training, an improved curriculum in schools, grading of pupils by age and ability, and a lengthened school year. He was also partially successful in curtailing the use of corporal punishment. In 1852 Massachusetts adopted the first compulsory school attendance law in American history. By 1860 almost one third of the high schools in the United States were located in Massachusetts.

Support for public schools transcended class lines. It came not only from conservatives but also from working people. Public schools were largely the result of local efforts around the country and were most successful in the Northeast and later in the Midwest.

Such educational opportunities, however, were not available to all. Most northern cities specifically excluded blacks from their public school systems; cities like New York and Boston consigned black children to inferior segregated schools. Women and religious minorities also experienced discrimination. Many public school teachers showed an anti-Catholic bias by using texts that portrayed the Catholic church as a threat to republican values and by reading biblical passages from the Protestant version of the scriptures. Beginning in New York City in 1840, Catholics decided to establish a separate system of parochial schools in which children would receive a religious education as well as training in the arts and sciences. For women, education beyond the level of handicrafts and basic reading and writing was largely confined to separate female academies and seminaries for the affluent.

In higher education a few institutions opened their doors to blacks and women. In 1833 Oberlin College became the nation's first coeducational college. Three colleges for blacks were established before the Civil War, and a few other institutions began to admit small numbers of black students. In 1837 Mount Holyoke, the first women's college, was established to train teachers and missionaries. A number of western universities also admitted women.

The reform impulse was evident in other changes in higher education. At the beginning of the nineteenth century most colleges offered their students, who usually enrolled between the ages of 12 and 15, only a narrow training in the classics designed to prepare them for the ministry. During the 1820s and 1830s colleges broadened their curricula to include the study of history, literature, geography, modern languages, and the sciences. The entrance age was also raised and the requirements demanded of students were broadened.

The number of colleges also increased. Most of the new colleges, particularly in the South and West, were church-affiliated, but several states established state universities. Prior to the Civil War 16 states provided some financial support to higher education, and in New York City by the 1850s an education, from elementary school to college, was available tuition free.

Asylums for Society's Outcasts

A number of reformers devoted their attention to the problems of the mentally ill, the deaf, and the blind. In 1841 Dorothea Dix, a 39-year-old former schoolteacher, volunteered to give religious instruction to women incarcerated in the East Cambridge, Massachusetts, House of Correction. She was horrified to find mentally ill inmates dressed in rags and confined to a single dreary room without any source of heat. Shocked by what she saw, she embarked on a lifelong crusade to reform the treatment of the mentally ill. After a two-year secret investigation of every jail and almshouse in Massachusetts, Dix issued a report to the state legislature. The mentally ill, she found, were brutally treated and mixed indiscriminately with paupers and hardened criminals. Dix then carried her campaign for state-supported asylums nationwide, persuading more than a dozen state legislatures to improve institutional care for the insane.

Through the efforts of such reformers as Thomas Gallaudet and Samuel Howe, institutions to care for the deaf and blind began to appear. Thomas Hopkins Gallaudet established in 1817 the nation's first school in Hartford, Connecticut, to teach deaf-mutes to read and write, read lips, and communicate through hand signals. Samuel Gridley Howe accomplished for the blind what Gallaudet achieved for the deaf. He founded the country's first school for the blind in Boston and produced printed materials with raised type.

Radical Reform

The initial thrust of reform—moral reform—was to rescue the nation from infidelity and intemperance. A second line of reform, social or humanitarian reform, sought to alleviate such sources of human misery as crime, cruelty, disease, and ignorance. A third line of reform, radical reform, sought national regeneration by eliminating slavery and racial and sexual discrimination.

The Rise of the Antislavery Movement

In the early nineteenth century the emancipation of slaves in the northern states and the prohibition against the African slave trade generated optimism that slavery was dying. Congress in 1787 had barred slavery from the Old Northwest, the region north of the Ohio River to the Mississippi River. The number of slaves freed by their masters had risen dramatically in the upper South during the 1780s and 1790s, and more antislavery societies had been formed in the South than in the North. At the present rate of progress, predicted one religious leader in 1791, within 50 years it will "be as shameful for a man to hold a Negro slave, as to be guilty of common robbery or theft."

By the early 1830s, however, the development of the Cotton Kingdom proved that slavery was not on the road to extinction. Despite the end of the African slave trade, the slave population had continued to grow, climbing from 1.5 million in 1820 to over 2 million a decade later.

A widespread belief that blacks and whites could not coexist and that racial separation was necessary encouraged futile efforts at deportation and overseas colonization. In 1816 a group of prominent ministers and politicians formed the American Colonization Society to resettle free blacks in West Africa, encourage planters voluntarily to emancipate their slaves, and create a group of black missionaries who would spread Christianity in Africa. During the 1820s Congress helped fund the cost of transporting free blacks to Africa—first to Sierra Leone and then, beginning in 1822, to Liberia. It soon became apparent that colonization was a wholly impractical solution to the nation's slavery problem. Each year the nation's slave population rose by roughly 50,000, but in 1830 the American Colonization Society succeeded in persuading just 259 free blacks to migrate to Liberia, bringing the total number of blacks colonized in Africa to just 1,400.

The movement condemning colonization and northern discrimination against African Americans was initially led by free blacks. As early as 1817 more than 3,000 members of Philadelphia's black community staged a protest against colonization. In 1829 David Walker, a free black owner of a secondhand clothing store in Boston, issued the militant pamphlet *Appeal to the Colored Citizens of the World.* The appeal threatened insurrection and violence if calls for the abolition of slavery and improved conditions for free blacks were not realized. The next year some 40 black delegates from eight states held the first of a series of annual conventions that denounced slavery and called for an end to discriminatory laws in the northern states.

The idea of abolition received impetus from William Lloyd Garrison. In 1829 the 25-year-old white Bostonian added his voice to the outcry against colonization, denouncing it as a cruel hoax designed to promote the racial purity of the northern population while doing nothing to end slavery in the South. Instead, he called for "immediate emancipation." By "immediate" he meant the immediate and unconditional release of slaves from bondage without compensation to slaveowners.

Garrison founded *The Liberator,* a militant abolitionist newspaper that was the country's first publication to demand an immediate end to slavery. On the front page of the first issue he defiantly declared: "I will not equivocate—I will not excuse—I will not retreat a single inch—AND I WILL BE HEARD."

Within four years 200 antislavery societies had appeared in the North. They had mounted a massive propaganda campaign to proclaim

The Liberator sought immediate freedom for slaves, without compensation to their owners.

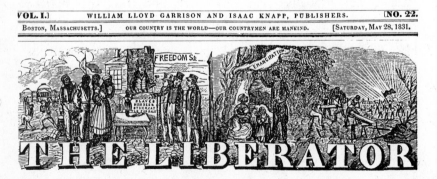

William Lloyd Garrison, the symbol of radical abolitionism, sought immediate freedom for slaves, without compensation to their owners.

the sinfulness of slavery. These societies distributed a million pieces of abolitionist literature and sent 20,000 tracts directly to the South. They avoided concrete proposals for emancipation, however, fearful of becoming embroiled in debates over the details of specific plans.

Abolitionists attacked slavery on several grounds. Slavery was illegal because it violated the principles of natural rights to life and liberty embodied in the Declaration of Independence. Justice, said Garrison, required that the nation "secure to the colored population . . . all the rights and privileges that belong to them as men and as Americans." Slavery was sinful because slaveholders, in the words of abolitionist Theodore Weld, had usurped "the prerogative of God." Slavery also encouraged sexual immorality and undermined the institutions of marriage and the family. Not only did slave masters sexually abuse and exploit slave women, abolitionists charged, but in some older southern states, such as Virginia and Maryland, they bred slaves for sale to the more recently settled parts of the Deep South.

Antislavery agitation provoked a harsh public reaction in both the North and the South. Mobs led by "gentlemen of property and standing" attacked the homes and businesses of abolitionist merchants, destroyed abolitionist printing presses, disrupted antislavery meetings, and attacked black neighborhoods. During antiabolitionist rioting in Philadelphia in October 1834, a white mob destroyed 45 homes in the city's black community. A year later a Boston mob dragged Garrison through the streets and almost lynched him before authorities removed him to a city jail for his own safety. In 1837 the abolitionist movement acquired its first martyr when an antiabolitionist mob in Illinois set fire to the printing business of the Reverend Elijah P. Lovejoy, then shot him as he fled the building.

Division in the Antislavery Movement

The violent response produced division within the antislavery movement. At the 1840 annual meeting of the American Anti-Slavery Society in New York, abolitionists split over such questions as women's right to participate in the administration of the organization and the advisability of nominating abolitionists as independent political candidates. Garrison won control of the organization, and his opponents promptly walked out. From this point on, no single organization could speak for abolitionism.

One group of abolitionists looked to politics as the answer to ending slavery and founded political parties, such as the Liberty party, for that purpose. The Liberty party, founded in 1840 under the leadership of Arthur and Lewis Tappan, wealthy New York City businessmen, and James G. Birney, a former slaveholder, called on Congress to abolish slavery in the District of Columbia, end the interstate slave trade, and cease admitting new slave states to the Union. The party also sought the repeal of local and state laws in the North, which discriminated against free blacks. The Liberty party nominated Birney for president in 1840 and again in 1844, and although it gathered less than 7,100 votes in its first campaign, it polled some 62,000 votes four years later and captured enough votes in Michigan and New York to deny Henry Clay the presidency.

In 1848 antislavery Democrats and Whigs merged with the Liberty party to form the Free Soil party. Unlike the Liberty party, which was dedicated to the abolition of slavery and equal rights for blacks, the Free Soil party narrowed its demands to the abolition of slavery in the District of Columbia and exclusion of slavery from the federal territories. The Free Soilers also wanted a homestead law to provide free land for western settlers, high tariffs to protect American industry, and federally sponsored internal improvements.

Other abolitionists, led by Garrison, took a more radical direction, advocating civil disobedience and linking abolitionism to such other reforms as women's rights, world government, and international peace. Garrison and his supporters established the New England Non-Resistance Society in 1838. Members refused to vote or hold public office. In 1854 Garrison attracted notoriety by publicly burning a copy of the Constitution, which he called "a covenant with death and an agreement with Hell" because it acknowledged the legality of slavery.

African Americans played a vital role in the abolitionist movement, staging protests against segregated churches, schools, and public transportation. In New York and Pennsylvania free blacks launched petition drives for equal voting rights. Northern blacks also had a pivotal role in the "underground railroad," which provided escape routes for southern slaves through the northern states and into Canada. African-American churches offered sanctuary to runaways, and black "vigilance" groups in cities like New York and Detroit offered physical resistance to slave catchers.

Fugitive slaves, such as Harriet Tubman, advanced abolitionism by publicizing the horrors of slavery. Their firsthand tales of whippings and separation from spouses and children combated the notion that slaves were content under slavery and undermined belief in racial inferiority. Tubman risked her life by making 19 trips into slave territory in order to free as many as 300 slaves. Slaveholders posted a reward of $40,000 for the capture of the "Black Moses."

Frederick Douglass was the most famous fugitive slave and black abolitionist. The son of a Maryland slave woman and an unknown white father, Douglass was separated from his mother and sent to work on a plantation when he was six years old. At the age of 20 he escaped from slavery by borrowing the papers of a free black sailor. In the North, Douglass became the first runaway slave to speak out on behalf of the antislavery cause. Although he initially allied himself with William Lloyd Garrison, Douglass later started his own newspaper, *The North Star,* and supported political action against slavery.

By the 1850s many blacks had become pessimistic about defeating slavery. Colonizationist sentiment appeared among African Americans. In the 15 months following passage of the federal Fugitive Slave Law in 1850, some 13,000 free blacks fled the North for Canada. In 1854 the National Emigration Convention was created to investigate possible sites for black colonization in Haiti, Central America, and West Africa.

Other blacks argued in favor of violence. Black abolitionists in Ohio adopted resolutions encouraging slaves to escape and called on their fellow citizens to violate any law that "conflicts with reason, liberty and justice, North or South." By the late 1850s a growing number of free blacks had concluded that it was just as legitimate to use violence to secure the freedom of the slaves as it had been to establish the independence of the American colonies.

Over the long run, the fragmentation of the antislavery movement worked to the advantage of the cause. Henceforth, northerners could support whichever form of antislavery best reflected their views. Moderates could vote for political candidates with abolitionist sentiments without

Harriet Tubman, a fugitive slave who led 19 raids into slave territory, was a strong proponent of abolitionism. In 1841 Frederick Douglass gained public notice by giving a powerful speech against slavery. He opposed not only slavery but all forms of racial discrimination.

being accused of radical Garrisonian views or of advocating violence for redress of grievances.

The Birth of Feminism

The women's rights movement was a major legacy of radical reform. At the outset of the century women experienced political, social, and legal discrimination. Women were prohibited from voting or holding office in every state; they had no access to higher education and were excluded from professional occupations. American law was guided by the principle that a wife had no legal identity apart from her husband. She could not be sued, nor could she bring a legal suit, make a contract, or own property. She was not permitted to control her own wages or gain custody of her children in case of separation or divorce, and under many circumstances she was even deemed incapable of committing crimes.

Broad social and economic changes, such as the development of a market economy and a decline in the birthrate, opened employment opportunities for women. Instead of bearing children at two-year intervals after marriage, as was the general case throughout the colonial era, early nineteenth-century women bore fewer children and ceased childbearing at younger ages. More women were postponing marriage or not marrying at all; unmarried women gained new employment opportunities as "mill girls" and elementary school teachers; and a growing number of women achieved prominence as novelists, editors, teachers, and leaders of church and philanthropic societies.

While there were many improvements in the status of women during the first half of the century, women still lost political and economic status when compared with men. As the franchise was extended to larger and larger numbers of white males, including large groups of recent immigrants, the gap in political power between women and men widened. Even though women made up a core of supporters for many reform movements, men excluded them from positions of decision making and relegated them to separate female auxiliaries. Women also lost economic status as production shifted away from the household to the factory and workshop. During the late eighteenth century the need for a cash income led women and older children to engage in a variety of household industries, such as weaving and spinning. Increasingly, in the nineteenth century these tasks were performed in factories and mills.

The fact that changes in the economy tended to confine women to a sphere separate from men had important implications for reform. Since women were believed to be uncontaminated by the competitive struggle for wealth and power, many argued that they had a duty—and the capacity—to exert an uplifting moral influence on American society.

Catharine Beecher and Sarah J. Hale helped lead the effort to expand women's roles through moral influence. Beecher, the eldest sister of Harriet Beecher Stowe, was one of the nation's most prominent educators before the Civil War. A woman of many talents and strong leadership, she spearheaded the campaign to convince school boards that women were suited to serve as schoolteachers. Hale edited the nation's most popular women's magazines, the *Ladies' Magazine* and *Godey's Lady's Book.*

Both Beecher and Hale worked tirelessly for women's education (Hale helped found Vassar College). They gave voice to the grievances of women: the abysmally low wages paid in the needle trades, the physical hardships endured in the nation's shops and mills (where women worked 14 hours a day), and the minimizing of women's intellectual aspirations. Even though neither woman supported full equal rights, they were important transitional figures in the emergence of feminism. Each significantly broadened society's definition of "women's sphere" and assigned women vital social responsibilities: to shape the character of children, to morally uplift husbands, and to promote causes of "practical benevolence."

Catalyst for Women's Rights

A public debate over the proper role of women in the antislavery movement, especially their right to lecture to audiences composed of both sexes, led to the first organized movement for women's rights. By the mid-1830s more than a hundred female antislavery societies had been created, and women abolitionists were circulating petitions, editing abolitionist tracts, and organizing antislavery conventions. A key question was whether women abolitionists would be permitted to lecture to "mixed" audiences of men and women.

Angelina Grimké and her sister Sarah—two sisters from a wealthy Charleston, South Carolina, slaveholding family—were the first women to break the restrictions and widen women's sphere through their writings and lectures. In 1837 Angelina gained national notoriety by lecturing against slavery to audiences that included men as well as women. Sarah Grimké followed with a pamphlet entitled *Letters on the Equality of the Sexes and the Condition of Women,* one of the first modern statements of feminist principles. She denounced the injustice of lower pay and denial of equal educational opportunities for women. Her pamphlet expressed outrage that women were "regarded by men, as pretty toys or as mere instruments of pleasure," and taught to aspire to no higher goal than marriage. Men and women, she concluded, should not be treated differently, since both were endowed with inherent natural rights.

In 1848 Lucretia Mott and Elizabeth Cady Stanton organized the first women's rights convention in history. The convention was held in July 1848 at Seneca Falls, New York. Participants drew up a Declaration of Sentiments, modeled on the Declaration of Independence, that opened with the phrase "All men and women are created equal." Among the resolutions adopted by the convention, only one was not ratified unanimously—that women be granted the right to vote.

By midcentury women's rights conventions had been held in every northern state. Despite public ridicule, female reformers contributed to important, if limited, advances against discrimination. They succeeded in gaining adoption of Married Women's Property Laws in a number of states, granting married women full control over their own income and property. A New York law passed in 1860 gave women joint custody over children and the right to sue and be sued, and several states adopted permissive divorce laws.

Utopian Communities

Between the 1820s and 1840s hundreds of "utopian communities" were founded by individuals who believed in the perfectability of the social and political order. The characteristics of these communities varied widely. Although most were short-lived, these communities sought to provide blueprints for a perfectionist vision of an ideal society.

One group, popularly known as the Shakers, believed that the millennium was at hand and that the time had come for people to totally renounce sin. By 1800 there were 12 Shaker colonies. These communities placed Shaker men and women on a level of sexual equality and both sexes served as elders and deacons. Aspiring to live like the early Christians, the Shakers adopted communal ownership of property and a way of life emphasizing simplicity. The two most striking characteristics of the Shaker communities were their dances and abstinence from sexual relations. The Shakers believed that religious fervor should be expressed through the head, heart, and mind, and their ritual religious practices included shaking, shouting, and dancing. Viewing sexual intercourse as the basic cause of human sin, the Shakers also adopted strict rules concerning celibacy. They attempted to replenish their membership by admitting volunteers and taking in orphans.

Another utopian effort was Robert Owen's experimental community at New Harmony, Indiana, which reflected the influence of Enlightenment ideas. Owen, a paternalistic Scottish industrialist, was deeply troubled by the social consequences of the industrial revolution. Inspired by the idea that people are shaped by their environment, Owen purchased a site in Indiana where he sought to establish common ownership of property and abolish religion. At New Harmony the marriage ceremony was reduced to a single sentence and children were raised outside of their natural parents' home. The community lasted just three years, from 1825 to 1828.

Some 40 utopian communities were inspired by the French theorist Charles Fourier, who hoped to eliminate poverty through the establishment of scientifically organized cooperative communities called "phalanxes." In each phalanx profits were divided according to the amount of money members had invested, their skill, and their labor. Women received equal job opportunities and equal pay, equal participation in decision making, and the right to speak in public assemblies. Although one Fourier community lasted for 18 years, most were unsuccessful.

In 1841 George Ripley, a former Unitarian clergyman, established the Brook Farm community near Boston in an attempt to substitute ideals of "brotherly cooperation," harmony, and spiritual fulfillment for the "selfish competition," class division, and alienation that increasingly characterized the larger society. "Our ulterior aim is nothing less than Heaven on Earth," declared one community member. Brook Farm's residents, who never numbered more than 200, supported themselves by farming, teaching, and manufacturing clothing.

Perhaps the most notorious and successful experimental colony was John Humphrey Noyes's Oneida Community in New York. Noyes believed that the final millennium would only occur when people strove to become perfect through an "immediate and total cessation from sin." In 1848 he established a perfectionist community that practiced communal ownership of property and "complex marriage." Complex marriage involved the marriage of each member of the community to every member of the opposite sex. Exclusive emotional or sexual attachments were forbidden, and sexual relations were arranged through an intermediary in order to protect a woman's individuality and give her a choice in the matter. After the Civil War the community conducted experiments in eugenics, the selective control of mating in order to improve the hereditary qualities of children. Oneida flourished in its original form until 1880.

Artistic and Cultural Ferment

During the early nineteenth century Europeans treated American culture with contempt. They charged that America was too commercial and materialistic, too preoccupied with money and technology, to produce great art and literature. "In the four quarters of the globe," asked one English critic, "who reads an American book? or goes to an American play? or looks at an American picture or statue?"

In fact, the decades preceding the American Civil War are among the most creative in all of American cultural and intellectual history, producing some of this nation's greatest poets, novelists, and philosophers.

At the beginning of the nineteenth century many Americans wondered whether their country's infant democracy was capable of producing great works of art. The United States had few professional writers or artists. In part, the United States lacked a large class of patrons to subsidize the arts. It possessed few magazines and only a single art museum. Above all, America seemed to lack the traditions out of which artists and writers could create great works. In 1837 Ralph Waldo Emerson urged Americans to cast off their "long apprenticeship to the learning of other lands," abandon subservience to English models, and create distinctly American forms of art rooted in the facts of American life.

Even before Emerson's call for a distinctly American culture, a number of authors had already begun to create literature emphasizing native scenes and characters. Washington Irving (1783–1859), who was probably the first American to support himself as a man of letters, demonstrated the possibility of creating art out of native elements in his classic tales "Rip Van Winkle" (1819) and "The Legend of Sleepy Hollow" (1820).

The poet Henry Wadsworth Longfellow was even more successful in transforming American legends into the stuff of art and reaching a broad popular audience. His narrative poems dramatizing scenes from America's past made such figures as Paul Revere, Miles Standish, John Alden, Priscilla Mullins, and Hiawatha household names.

James Fenimore Cooper was another successful mythmaker. In *The Spy* (1821) and *The Pioneers* (1823) Cooper created one of the most enduring archetypes in American culture. His hero, the frontiersman Natty Bumppo (also known as Hawkeye, Leather stocking, and the Pathfinder) was an American knight errant at home in the wilderness. He became the prototype not only for future trappers and scouts, but also for countless cowboys, detectives, and superheroes found in popular American fiction and film. Part of Natty Bumppo's appeal was that he gave expression to many of the misgivings early nineteenth-century Americans felt about the cost of progress. An acute social critic, Cooper railed against the destruction of the natural environment, the violence directed at American Indians, and the rapaciousness and materialism of an expansive American society.

American Transcendentalism

Some intellectuals, many of them young New Englanders of Unitarian background, found liberal religion too formal and rationalistic to meet their spiritual and emotional needs. Known as Transcendentalists, they believed that logic and reason were incapable of explaining the fundamental mysteries of human existence. Where, then, could people find answers to life's fundamental problems? The deepest insights, the Transcendentalists believed, were to be found within the human individual, through intuition.

The Transcendentalists shared a common outlook: a belief that each person contains infinite and godlike potentialities; an emphasis on emotion and the senses over reason and intellect; and a glorification of nature as a creative, dynamic force in which people could discover their true selves and commune with the supernatural. Like the romantic artists and poets of Europe, they emphasized the individual, the subjective, the imaginative, the personal, the emotional, and the visionary.

The central figure in Transcendentalism was Ralph Waldo Emerson. Trained, like his father, to be a liberal Unitarian minister, Emerson found his parents' faith unsatisfying. Unitarian theology and ritual, he wrote, was "corpse-cold"; it was the "thin porridge or cold tea" of genteel Bostonians. Emerson's life was marked by personal tragedy and illness—his father died when he was a boy; his first wife died after less than two years of marriage; his firstborn son died at the age of five; a brother went insane. Consequently, Emerson could never believe that logic and reason offered answers to life's mysteries.

Appalled by the complacency, provinciality, and materialism of Boston's elite, the 29-year-old Emerson resigned as minister of the prestigious Second Church of Boston in 1832. Convinced that no external answers existed to the fundamental problems of life, he decided to look inward.

In his essays and public lectures Emerson distilled the essence of the new philosophy: All people contain seeds of divinity, but society, traditionalism, and lifeless religious institutions thwart the fulfillment of these potentialities. In his essay "Nature" (1836) Emerson asserted that God's presence is immanent within both humanity and nature and can best be sensed through intuition rather than through reason. In his essay "Self-Reliance" (1841) he called on his readers to strive for true individuality in the face of intense social pressures for conformity.

Although Emerson himself was not an active reformer, his philosophy inspired many reformers far more radical than he. His stress on the individual, his defense of nonconformity, and his vocal critique of the alienation and social fragmentation that had accompanied the growth of cities and industry led others to try to apply the principles of Transcendentalism to their personal lives and to society at large.

Henry David Thoreau was one of the Transcendentalists who strove to realize Emersonian ideals in his personal life. Thoreau, like Emerson, felt nothing but contempt for social conventions. In March 1845 the 28-year-old Thoreau, convinced that his life was being frittered away by details, walked into the woods near Concord, Massachusetts, to live alone. He put up a cabin near Walden Pond as an experiment—to see if it was possible for a person to live truly free and uncommitted:

> I went into the woods because I wished to live deliberately, to front
> only the essential facts of life, and see if I could not learn what it had
> to teach, and not, when I came to die, discover that I had not lived.

The aim of his experiment was to break free from the distractions and artificialities of life, to shed himself of needless obligations and possessions, and to establish an original relationship with nature. His motto was "simplify, simplify."

During his 26 months at Walden Pond he constructed his own cabin, raised his own food, observed nature, explored his inner self, and kept a 6,000-page journal. He also spent a night in jail for refusing to pay taxes as a protest against the Mexican War. This incident led him to write the classic defense of nonviolent direct action, "Civil Disobedience."

A Literary and Artistic Renaissance

Emerson's 1837 plea for Americans to cease imitating Europeans, speak with their own voices, and create art drawn from their own experiences coincided with an extraordinary burst of literary creativity. Nathaniel Hawthorne,

Herman Melville, Edgar Allan Poe, Harriet Beecher Stowe, and Walt Whitman, like Emerson and Thoreau, produced literary works of the highest magnitude, yet in their own time many of their greatest works were greeted with derision, abuse, or indifference. It is a tragic fact that with the sole exception of Harriet Beecher Stowe, none of pre–Civil War America's greatest writers was able to earn more than a modest income from his or her books.

During his lifetime Edgar Allan Poe received far more notoriety from his legendary dissipation—he died an alcoholic at age 40—than from his poetry or short stories. Sorely underappreciated by contemporaries, Poe invented the detective novel; edited the *Southern Literary Messenger,* one of the country's leading literary journals; wrote incisive essays on literary criticism; and produced some of the most masterful poems and frightening tales of horror ever written. Poe said that his writing style consisted of "the ludicrous heightened into the grotesque; the fearful coloured into the horrible; the witty exaggerated into the burlesque; the singular wrought into the strange and mystical."

Nathaniel Hawthorne, the author of *The Scarlet Letter* (1850), more than any other early nineteenth-century American writer, challenged society's faith in science, technology, progress, and humanity's essential goodness. Many of his greatest works project nineteenth-century concerns—about women's roles, sexuality, and religion—on to seventeenth-century Puritan settings. Some of his stories examine the hubris of scientists and social reformers who dare to tamper with the natural environment and human nature.

Herman Melville, author of *Moby Dick* (1851), had little formal education and claimed that his intellectual development did not begin until he was 25. Part of a New York literary circle called Young America, Melville dreamed of creating a novel as vast and energetic as the nation itself. In *Moby Dick* he produced such a masterwork. Based on the tale of a gigantic white whale that sank a whaling ship, *Moby Dick* combined whaling lore and sea adventure into an epic drama of human hubris, producing an allegory that explores what happens to a people who defy divine limits. Tragically, neither *Moby Dick* nor Melville's later works found an audience. Melville died in utter obscurity, and his literary genius was only rediscovered in the 1920s.

Walt Whitman was a carpenter's son with only five years of schooling. Emerson considered him to be the very ideal of the native American poet, but most reviewers reacted scornfully to his collection of poems, *Leaves of Grass,* deeming it "trashy, profane & obscene" for its sexual frankness. Unconventional in style—Whitman invented "free verse" rather than use conventionally rhymed or regularly metered verse—the volume stands out as a landmark in the history of American literature for its celebration of the diversity, the energy, and the expansiveness of pre–Civil War America.

If Americans could produce literary masterpieces, were they also capable of creating visual art that would rival that of Europe? Although the last half of the eighteenth century witnessed the appearance of a number of talented portrait painters, most were simply skilled craftspeople who devoted most of their time to painting houses, furniture, or signs. Perhaps the biggest obstacle to the development of the visual arts was the fact that the revolutionary generation associated art with luxury, corruption, sensual appetite, and aristocracy. Commented one person: "When a people get a taste for the fine arts, they are ruined."

During the early nineteenth century, however, artists succeeded in overcoming public hostility toward the visual arts. One way artists gained a degree of respectability was through historical painting. The American public hungered for visual representations of the great events of the American Revolution, and works such as John Trumbull's Revolutionary War battle scenes and his painting of the Declaration of Independence (1818) fed the public's appetite. Romantic landscape paintings also attracted a large popular audience. Portrayals of the American landscape by such artists as Thomas Cole and the Hudson River school, Albert Bierstadt, and Frederick Church evoked a sense of the immensity, power, and grandeur of nature, which had not yet been completely tamed by an expansive American civilization.

Popular Culture

Existing alongside these literary and artistic achievements was a vibrant popular culture. One important aspect of a common culture was the mass-circulation newspaper. After the Revolution most newspapers were subsidized by political parties, which used them as mouthpieces to promote their views. But with the development in the 1830s of the steam printing press, which dramatically cut printing costs and speeded production, the modern mass-circulation newspaper emerged. Journalistic pioneers, like James Gordon Bennett of the New York *Herald,* introduced features that we still associate with the daily newspaper, including crime stories, gossip columns, and sports pages. To increase circulation, the New York *Sun* relied on sensationalism and even hoaxes, practices that were soon copied by its rivals. Along with the modern newspaper came magazines. By 1850 magazines began to appeal to almost every imaginable audience, with the proliferation of children's magazines, scientific journals, literary reviews, women's magazines, religious periodicals, and comics.

American literary tastes were extremely varied. The middle class tended to read sentimental domestic tales, like Susan Warner's *The Wide, Wide World,* one of the most popular mid-nineteenth century novels; sentimental love poetry by authors like Lydia Sigourney, or morally high-minded adventure tales, like Richard Henry Dana, Jr.'s *Two Years Before the Mast* (1840) or historian Francis Parkman's *The Oregon Trail* (1847). Less well educated Americans favored dime novels (which usually sold for a nickel), which often dealt with such topics as frontier adventure, pirate tales, and urban crime.

Pseudoscience also captured the popular fancy during the decades before the Civil War. During the early nineteenth century science was advancing so rapidly that it was difficult to distinguish authentic scientific discoveries from hoaxes. Before the Civil War Americans were fascinated by a variety of pseudosciences, including phrenology (which linked human character to the shape and bumps of a person's head), animal magnetism (the belief in a universal electrical fluid influencing physics and even human psychology), mesmerism (the control of a hypnotized person by a medium), and spiritualism (direct communication with spirits of the deceased through trance visions or seances).

Another distinctive feature of pre–Civil War popular culture was the minstrel show. The first uniquely American entertainment form, the minstrel show provided comedy, music, dance, and novelty acts to audiences hungry for entertainment. Offering humor that ranged from comedy skits to slapstick and one-liners—often mocking pompous politicians and pretentious professionals—the minstrel shows also introduced many of America's most enduring popular songs, including "Turkey in the Straw" and "Dixie."

Minstrel shows popularized the songs of Stephen Foster, the most popular American composer of the mid-nineteenth century. Foster wrote more than 200 songs during his lifetime, mainly sentimental ballads and love songs (such as "Old Folks at Home," "My Old Kentucky Home," and "Beautiful Dreamer") and uptempo, rhythmic comic songs (such as "Camptown Races" and "Oh! Susanna").

Reflecting the racism of the broader society, minstrel shows presented a denigrating portrayal of black Americans. Racial stereotypes were the minstrel shows' stock in trade. Actors wore grotesque makeup, spoke in ludicrous dialects, and presented plantation life in a highly romanticized manner.

Conclusion

The first half of the nineteenth century witnessed the rise of the first secular movements in history to educate the deaf and blind, care for the mentally ill, extend equal rights to women, and abolish slavery. Inspired by the revolutionary ideals of the Declaration of Independence and the Bill of Rights, the Enlightenment faith in reason, and liberal and evangelical religious principles, educational reformers created a system of free public education, prison reformers constructed specialized institutions to reform criminals, temperance reformers sought to end the drinking of liquor, and utopian socialists established ideal communities to serve as models of a better world.

*C*hronology of Key Events

1776	First Shaker community in America founded near Albany, New York
1817	American Colonization Society founded
1818	Washington Irving publishes *Rip Van Winkle*
1825	Charles Finney leads his first religious revivals; Robert Owen founds New Harmony community in Indiana
1826	American Society for the Promotion of Temperance founded
1829	David Walker issues *Appeal to the Colored Citizens of the World*
1831	William Lloyd Garrison begins publishing *The Liberator,* militant abolistionist newspaper
1833	American Anti-Slavery Society formed; New York *Sun,* the first penny newspaper, published
1837	Emerson presents his address on the "American Scholar"; abolitionist Elijah P. Lovejoy killed by a proslavery mob in Illinois
1840	James G. Birney runs for president as Liberty party candidate; Sarah Grimké publishes *Letters on the Equality of the Sexes and the Condition of Women*
1841	Dorothea Dix begins crusade on behalf of the mentally ill; Brook Farm founded
1848	Seneca Falls convention on women's rights held in New York; Free Soil party receives ten percent of presidential vote
1850	Nathaniel Hawthorne publishes *The Scarlet Letter*
1851	Herman Melville publishes *Moby Dick*
1852	Massachusetts adopts the first compulsory education law
1854	Henry David Thoreau publishes *Walden*
1855	Walt Whitman publishes *Leaves of Grass*

The Civil War largely brought an end to the era of optimistic, perfectionist reform. The grim violence of the war shattered the pre–Civil War reformers' confidence in the "perfectability of man" and sparked a reaction against the emotionalism and utopian idealism of pre–Civil War reform. Although a large number of abolitionists continued to fight for black equality and many feminists moved from women's rights to the fight for women's suffrage, a period of retrenchment set in during the 1870s and 1880s, when counterreformers reversed many of the accomplishments of prewar reformers by restoring capital punishment and making divorce laws more stringent.

Still, many of the goals of the antebellum reformers would live on. The pre–Civil War reformers' spirit of hope and their willingness to question established customs and institutions would survive as a source of inspiration for later proponents of penal reform, women's rights, labor unions, and racial justice.

Suggestions for Further Reading

Valuable overviews of the reform impulse in the antebellum period are Robert H. Abzug, *Cosmos* (*rumbling; American Reform and the Religious Imagination* (1994); and Ronald Walters, *American Reformers* (1978). For more on the Second Great Awakening see Whitney R. Cross, *The Burned Over District* (1950); Keith J. Hardman, *Charles Grandison Finney* (1987); Paul Johnson, *A Shopkeeper's Millennium* (1978).

Moral reform issues are examined in Clifford S. Griffin, *Their Brothers' Keepers* (1960); Mark E. Lender and James Kirby Martin, *Drinking in America*, rev. ed. (1987); W. J. Rorabaugh, *The Alcoholic Republic* (1979); Ian R. Tyrell, *Sobering Up: From Temperance to Prohibition in Antebellum America* (1979). On social reform see Jonathan Messerli, *Horace Mann* (1972); Raymond A. Mohl, *Poverty in New York* (1971); David Rothman, *The Discovery of the Asylum* (1971).

On the early feminist movement consult Lois Banner, *Elizabeth Cady Stanton* (1980); Nancy F. Cott, *The Bonds of Womanhood* (1977); Carl N. Degler, *At Odds* (1980); Sara Evans, *Born for Liberty* (1989); Mary P. Ryan, *Womanhood in America*, 3d ed. (1983); Nancy Woloch, *Women and the American Experience* (1984).

The antislavery movement is examined in Benjamin Quarles, *Black Abolitionists* (1969); P. J. Staudenraus, *The African Colonization Movement* (1961); James B. Stewart, *Holy Warriors: The Abolitionists and American Slavery* (1976).

On American intellectuals and literary achievements during the antebellum period see Paul F. Boller, Jr., *American Transcendentalism* (1974); Lawrence Buell, *New England Literary Culture* (1986). On popular culture see Lawrence Levine, *Highbrow/Lowbrow: The Emergence of Cultural Hierarchy in America* (1988).

Chapter *12*

The Divided North, the Divided South

In the early 1790s slavery appeared to be a dying institution. Slave imports into the New World were declining and slave prices were falling because the crops grown by slaves—tobacco, rice, and indigo—did not generate enough income to pay for their upkeep. In Maryland and Virginia planters were replacing tobacco, a crop grown by a slave labor force, with wheat and corn, which was not. At the same time, leading Southerners, including Thomas Jefferson, denounced slavery as a source of debt, economic stagnation, and moral dissipation. A French traveler reported that people throughout the South "are constantly talking of abolishing slavery, of contriving some other means of cultivating their estates."

Then Eli Whitney of Massachusetts gave slavery a new lease on life. In 1792, just after graduating from Yale, Whitney traveled south in search of employment as a schoolteacher. While visiting a plantation near Savannah, Georgia, Whitney became intrigued with the problems encountered by southern planters in successfully producing green seed, short-staple cotton. The booming textile industry had created a high demand for the crop, but it could not be marketed until the seeds had been extracted from the cotton boll, a laborious and time-consuming process.

From a slave known only as Sam, Whitney learned that a comb could be used to remove seeds from cotton. In just ten days Whitney devised a way of mechanizing the comb. Within a month Whitney's cotton engine (gin for short) could separate fiber from seeds faster than 50 people working by hand.

Whitney's invention revitalized slavery in the South. In two years the price of slaves doubled. By 1825 field hands, who brought $500 apiece in 1794, were worth $1,500. As the price of slaves rose, so too did the number of slaves. During the first decade of the nineteenth century the number of slaves in the United States increased by 33 percent.

As the institution of slavery expanded in the South, it declined in the North. In 1780 Pennsylvania adopted the first emancipation law in the New World. Judicial decisions freed slaves in Massachusetts and New Hampshire, and other northern states passed gradual emancipation acts. By the early nineteenth century the new republic was fatefully divided into a slave section and a free section.

A Divided Culture

By 1860 most Americans believed that the Mason-Dixon line divided the nation into two distinctive cultures: a commercial North and an agrarian South. Many factors contributed to this sense of sectional difference. Diction, work habits, diet, and labor systems distinguished the two regions. One section depended on slave-based agriculture; the other emphasized

While seeking employment in the South, Yankee schoolteacher Eli Whitney developed a simple machine for separating cotton from its seeds. The "cotton gin" met the increasing demand for cotton and breathed new life into the institution of slavery.

commercial agriculture based on family farms and a developing industrial sector resting on wage labor.

The population of the North was more than 50 percent greater than in the South. Urbanization was far more advanced, as thousands of European immigrants flocked to northern cities. In addition, commerce, financial institutions, manufacturing, and transportation were more developed. In contrast, the South had more primitive transportation facilities. Cities were smaller and fewer in number. Most important of all, a third of the South's population lived in slavery.

Despite these differences, the pre–Civil War North and the South were in certain respects strikingly similar. Both sections were predominantly rural. Both had booming economies and were engaged in speculation and trade. Both were rapidly expanding westward. Both enacted democratic political reforms and voted for the same national political parties. Nevertheless, most Americans thought of their nation as divided into two halves, a commercial civilization and an agrarian civilization, each operating according to entirely different sets of values.

The Emergence of a New Industrial Order in the North

By 1860, even though the North remained predominantly a rural agricultural society, profound and far-reaching changes had taken place. Commercial agriculture had replaced subsistence agriculture. Household production had been supplanted by centralized manufacturing outside the home. And nonagricultural employment had begun to overtake agricultural employment. By 1860, nearly half of the North's population made a living outside of the agricultural sector.

These economic transformations were all aspects of the industrial revolution, a revolution that affected every aspect of life. It raised living standards, transformed the work process, and relocated hundreds of thousands of people across oceans and from rural farms and villages to fast-growing industrial cities.

The most obvious consequence of this revolution was an impressive increase in wealth, per capita income, and commercial, middle-class job opportunities. Between 1800 and 1860 output increased 12-fold, and purchasing power doubled. New middle-class jobs proliferated. Increasing numbers of men found work as agents, bankers, brokers, clerks, merchants, professionals, and traders. Living standards rose sharply, at least for the rapidly expanding middle class. By 1860 many urban middle-class families had central heating, indoor plumbing, and wall-to-wall carpeting.

Although the industrial revolution brought many material benefits, critics decried its negative consequences. Labor leaders deplored the bitter suffering of factory and sweatshop workers, the breakdown of craft skills, the vulnerability of urban workers to layoffs and economic crises, and the maldistribution of wealth and property. Conservatives lamented the disintegration of an older household-centered economy in which husbands, wives, and children had labored together. Southern writers argued that the North's growing class of free laborers were slaves of the marketplace, suffering even more insecurity than the South's chattel slaves, who were provided for in sickness and old age.

During the early nineteenth century the industrial revolution transformed northern society, altering the way people worked and lived and contributing to growing sectional differences between the North and South. How and why did the industrial revolution occur when it did? What were its consequences? How did it fuel sectional antagonisms?

The Transformation of the Rural Countryside

In 1790 most families in the rural North produced most of what they needed to live. Instead of using money to purchase necessities, families entered into complex exchange relationships with relatives and neighbors and used barter to acquire the goods they needed. To supplement their meager incomes, farm families often did piecework for shopkeepers and craftsmen. In the late eighteenth century these "household industries" provided work for thousands of men, women, and children in rural areas. Shopkeepers or master craftspeople supplied farm families with raw materials and paid them piece rates to produce such items as linens and farm utensils.

Between 1790 and the 1820s a new pattern emerged. Subsistence farming gave way to commercial agriculture as farmers increasingly began to grow cash crops for sale, using the proceeds to buy goods produced by others. In New Hampshire farmers raised sheep for wool; in western Massachusetts they began to fatten cattle and pigs for sale to Boston; in eastern Pennsylvania they specialized in dairy products.

The household industries that had once employed thousands of rural women and children also began to decline during this period. They were replaced by manufacturing in city shops and factories. New England farm families began to buy their shoes, furniture, and sometimes even their clothes ready-made. Small rural factories closed their doors, and village artisans who produced for local markets found themselves unable to compete against cheaper city-made goods. As local opportunities declined, many long-settled farm areas suffered sharp population losses, as thousands of young people left the fields for cities.

The Disruption of the Artisan System of Labor

In the late eighteenth century the North's few industries were small. Skilled craftspeople, known as *artisans* or *mechanics,* performed most manufacturing in small towns and larger cities. Such crafts as blacksmithing, bootmaking, carriage building, and leather working were performed by hand in a small shop or home.

The artisan class was divided into three subgroups. At the highest level were self-employed master craftspeople. They were assisted by skilled journeymen, who owned their own tools but lacked the capital to set up their own shops, and by apprentices, teenaged boys who typically served a three-year term in exchange for training in a craft.

The first half of the nineteenth century witnessed the decline of the artisan system of labor. The independent artisans of earlier years gave way to an increasingly industrial economy of wage laborers and salaried employees. Skilled tasks, previously performed by artisans, were divided and subcontracted out to less expensive unskilled laborers. Small shops were replaced by factories, which made the relationship between employer and employee increasingly impersonal. Many masters abandoned their supervisory role to foremen and contractors and substituted unskilled teenaged boys for journeymen. Words like *employer, employee, boss,* and *foreman*—descriptive of the new relationships—began to be widely used.

Between 1790 and 1850 the work process, especially in the building trades, printing, and such rapidly expanding consumer manufacturing industries as tailoring and shoemaking, was radically reorganized. The older household-based economy, in which assistants lived in the homes of their employers, gradually disappeared. Young men moved out of rooms in their master's home into hotels and boardinghouses in distinct working-class neighborhoods. The older view that each worker should be attached to a particular master, who would supervise his behavior and assume responsibility for his welfare, declined. The older paternalistic view was replaced by a new conception of labor as a commodity, like cotton, that could be acquired or disposed of according to the laws of supply and demand.

The Introduction of the Factory System

In 1789 Samuel Slater, who had just finished an apprenticeship in a Derbyshire textile mill, emigrated to the United States. He obtained a job as manager of a mill in Pawtucket, Rhode Island, which opened a year later. Although the little factory had only 19 empoyees, it was among the first to consolidate manufacturing operations under a single roof, thus marking the beginning of the modern factory system.

For an inexpensive and reliable work force Slater and other factory owners turned to child labor. During the early phases of industrialization textile mills and other factories had a ravenous appetite for cheap teenage laborers. In many mechanized industries, from a quarter to over half of the work force was made up of young men or women under the age of 20.

During the first half of the nineteenth century unmarried women made up a majority of the work force in cotton textile mills and a substantial minority of workers in factories manufacturing ready-made clothing, hats, and shoes. Unlike farmwork or domestic service, employment in a mill offered female companionship and an independent income. Wages were twice what a woman could make as a seamstress, tailor, or schoolteacher. Furthermore, most mill girls viewed the work as only temporary before marriage. Most worked in the mills fewer than four years, and frequently interrupted their stints in the mill for several months at a time with trips back home.

By the 1830s increasing competition among textile manufacturers caused deteriorating working conditions that drove native-born women out of the mills. Employers cut wages, lengthened the workday, and required mill workers to tend four looms instead of just two. Hannah Borden, textile worker from Fall River, Massachusetts, was required to have her loom running at 5 A.M. She was given an hour for breakfast and a half hour for lunch. Her workday ended at 7:30 P.M. For a 6-day work week she received between $2.50 and $3.50.

The mill girls militantly protested these conditions. In 1834 and again in 1836 they went out on strike. During the 1840s fewer and fewer native-born women were willing to work in the mills. Increasingly, employers replaced them with a new class of permanent factory operatives: immigrant women from Ireland.

The Rise of Organized Labor

By the 1820s a growing number of journeymen were organizing to protest employer practices. Unlike their counterparts in Britain, American journeymen did not protest against the introduction of machinery into the workplace. Instead, they vehemently protested wage reductions, declining standards of workmanship, and the increased use of unskilled and semiskilled workers. Journeymen charged that manufacturers had reduced "them to degradation and the loss of that self-respect which had made the mechanics and laborers the pride of the world." They insisted that they were the true producers of wealth and that manufacturers, who did not engage in manual labor, were unjust expropriators of wealth.

In an attempt to raise wages, restrict hours, and reduce competition from unskilled workers, skilled journeymen formed the nation's first labor unions. In larger eastern cities like Boston, New York, and Philadelphia, as well as in smaller western cities like Cincinnati, Louisville, and Pittsburgh, they formed local trade unions and city trades' assemblies. House carpenters, handloom weavers, combmakers, shoemakers, and printers formed national societies to uphold uniform wage standards. In 1834 journeymen established the National Trades' Union, the first organization of American wage earners on a national scale. By 1836 union membership had climbed to 300,000.

Despite bitter employer opposition, some gains were made. In 1842, in the landmark case *Commonwealth* v. *Hunt,* the Massachusetts supreme court established a new precedent by recognizing the right of unions to exist. In addition to establishing the nation's first labor unions, journeymen also formed political organizations, known as Working Men's parties. Working men and women published at least 68 labor papers, and they agitated for

During the 1830s, rapid inflation and mounting competition for jobs
encouraged growth of unions. By the late 1830s, an estimated 300,000
American workers were union members.

free public education, reduction of the workday, and abolition of capital
punishment, state militias, and imprisonment for debt. Following the Panic
of 1837, land reform was one of labor's chief demands. One hundred sixty
acres of free public land for those who would actually settle the land was the
demand, and "Vote Yourself a Farm" became the popular slogan.

Labor's greatest success was a campaign to establish a ten-hour workday in most major northeastern cities. In 1835 carpenters, masons, and
stonecutters in Boston staged a seven-month strike in favor of a ten-hour
day. Quickly, the movement spread to Philadelphia, where carpenters,
bricklayers, and blacksmiths went on strike. Textile workers in Paterson,
New Jersey, were the first factory operatives to strike for a reduction in
work hours. Soon, women textile operatives in Lowell added their voices
to the call for a ten-hour day, contending that such a law would "lengthen
the lives of those employed, by giving them a greater opportunity to
breathe the pure air of heaven" as well as provide "more time for mental
and moral cultivation."

In 1840 the federal government introduced a ten-hour workday on public works projects. In 1847 New Hampshire became the first state to adopt a ten-hour day law. It was followed by Pennsylvania in 1848. Both states' laws, however, included a clause that allowed workers to agree voluntarily to work more than a ten-hour day. Despite the limitations of these state laws, agitation for a ten-hour day did result in a reduction in the average number of hours worked, to approximately 11.5 by 1850.

At the same time, however, the quickening pace of commerce dramatically increased demand for unskilled workers, who earned extremely low incomes and led difficult lives. Frequent unemployment compounded the problems of the unskilled. In Massachusetts upward of 40 percent of all workers were out of a job for part of a year, usually for four months or more. Fluctuations in demand, inclement weather, interruptions in transportation, technological displacement, fire, injury, and illness all could leave workers jobless.

Typically, a male laborer earned just two-thirds of his family's income. The other third was earned by wives and children. Many married women performed work in the home, such as embroidery and making artificial flowers, tailoring garments, or doing laundry. The wages of children were critical for a family's standard of living. Children under the age of 15 contributed 20 percent of the income of many working-class families.

Immigrants: The New Working Class

At the beginning of the nineteenth century only about 5,000 immigrants arrived in the United States each year. During the 1830s, however, immigration climbed sharply as 600,000 immigrants poured into the country. This figure jumped to 1.7 million in the 1840s, when harvests all across Europe failed, and reached 2.6 million in the 1850s. Most of these immigrants came from Germany, Ireland, and Scandinavia, pushed from their homelands by famine, eviction from farm lands by landlords, political unrest, and the destruction of traditional handicrafts by factory enterprises. Attracted to the United States by the prospects of economic opportunity and political and religious freedom, many dispossessed Europeans braved the voyage across the Atlantic.

During the summer of 1845 a "blight of unusual character" devastated Ireland's potato crop, the basic staple in the Irish diet. Famine and disease soon spread through the Irish countryside. Observers reported seeing children crying with pain and looking "like skeletons, their features sharpened with hunger and their limbs wasted, so that there was little left but bones, their hands and arms." Masses of bodies were buried without coffins, a few inches below the soil. Over the next ten years 750,000 Irish

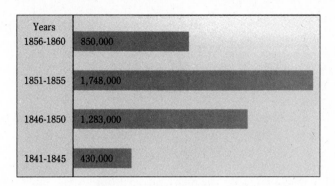

Total immigration, 1840–1860

died and another 2 million left their homeland for Great Britain, Canada, and the United States.

By the 1850s the Irish comprised half the population of Boston and New York, and German immigrants made up a significant proportion of the populations in Cincinnati, Milwaukee, and St. Louis. The new immigrants found employment in construction work, domestic service, factories, foundries, and mining. As early as 1855 German and Irish immigrants constituted 96 percent of New York City's shoemakers and tailors.

The Divided North

During the decades preceding the Civil War it was an article of faith among Northerners that their society offered unprecedented economic equality and opportunity, free of rigid class divisions and glaring extremes of wealth and poverty.

In fact, the percentage of wealth held by those at the top of the economic hierarchy appears to have increased substantially before the Civil War. The first stages of industrialization and urbanization in the North, far from diminishing social inequality, actually widened class distinctions and intensified social stratification. At the top of the social and economic hierarchy was an elite class of families, linked together by intermarriage, membership in exclusive social clubs, and residence in exclusive neighborhoods, as rich as the wealthiest families of Europe. At the bottom were the working poor—immigrants, casual laborers, free blacks, widows, and orphans—who might be thrown out of work at any time. These poor, propertyless, unskilled laborers comprised a vast floating population, which trekked from city to city in search of work.

Between these two extremes were family farmers and a rapidly expanding urban middle class. This was a highly mixed group which ranged from prosperous entrepreneurs and professionals to hard-pressed journeymen, who found their skills increasingly obsolete.

Does this mean that the pre–Civil War North was not the fluid, "egalitarian" society that Jacksonians claimed? The answer is a qualified no. In the first place, the North's richest individuals, unlike Europe's aristocracy, were not ostentatiously rich; they were a working class, engaged in commerce, finance, manufacturing, real estate, and the professions. Even more important, wealthy Northerners publicly rejected the older Hamiltonian notion that the rich and well-born were superior to the masses of people. During the early decades of the nineteenth century wealthy Northerners shed the wigs, knee breeches, ruffled shirts, and white-topped boots that had symbolized high social status in colonial America and began to dress like other men, signaling their acceptance of an ideal of social equality.

Above all, it was the North's relatively high rates of economic and social mobility that gave substance to a widespread belief in equality of opportunity. Although few rich men were truly "self-made," there were many dramatic examples of upward mobility and countless instances of more modest climbs up the ladder of success. Even at the bottom of the economic hierarchy, prospects for advancement increased markedly after 1850. During the 1830s and 1840s less than one unskilled worker in ten managed in the course of a decade to advance to a white-collar job. After 1850 the percentage doubled. The sons of unskilled laborers were even more likely to advance to skilled or white-collar employment. Even the poorest unskilled laborers often were able to acquire a house and a savings account.

It was the reality of economic mobility that convinced the overwhelming majority of Northerners that they lived in a uniquely open society, in which differences in wealth or status were the result of hard work and ambition.

Southern Distinctiveness

Pre–Civil War Americans regarded Southerners as a distinct people, who possessed their own values and way of life. It was widely though mistakenly believed that the North and South had originally been settled by two distinct groups of immigrants, each with its own ethos. Northerners were said to be the descendants of seventeenth-century English Puritans, while Southerners were the descendants of England's country gentry. In the eyes of many pre–Civil War Americans this contributed to two distinct kinds of Americans: the aggressive, individualistic, money-grubbing Yankee and the southern cavalier. According to the popular stereotype, the cavalier, unlike the Yankee, was violently sensitive to insult, indifferent to money, and preoccupied with honor.

The Old South: Images and Realities

During the three decades before the Civil War popular writers created a stereotype, now known as the "plantation legend," that described the South as a land of aristocratic planters, beautiful southern belles, poor white trash, faithful black household servants, and superstitious field-hands. In the eyes of many Northerners, uneasy with their increasingly urban, individualistic commercial society, the culture of the South seemed to have many things absent from the North—a leisurely pace of life, a clear social hierarchy, and an indifference to money.

Despite the strength of the plantation stereotype, the South was, in reality, a diverse and complex region. Though Americans today often associate the Old South with cotton plantations, large parts of the South were unsuitable for plantation life. In the mountainous regions of eastern Tennessee and western Virginia few plantations and few slaves were to be found. Nor did southern farms and plantations devote their efforts exclusively to growing cotton or other cash crops, such as rice and tobacco. Unlike the slave societies of the Caribbean, which produced crops exclusively for export, the South devoted much of its energy to raising food and livestock.

The white South's social structure was much more complex than the popular stereotype of proud aristocrats disdainful of honest work and ignorant, vicious, exploited poor whites. The Old South's intricate social hierarchy included many small slave owners and relatively few large ones.

Actually, large slaveholders were extremely rare. In 1860 just 11,000 Southerners—three-quarters of one percent of the white population—owned more than 50 slaves; just 2,358 owned as many as 100 slaves. However, although large slaveholders were few in number, they owned most of the South's slaves. Over half of all slaves lived on plantations with 20 or more slaves and a quarter lived on plantations with more than 50 slaves.

Slave ownership was relatively widespread. In the first half of the nineteenth century one-third of all southern white families owned slaves, and a majority of white southern families either owned slaves, had owned them, or expected to own them. Few slave owners led lives of leisure or refinement. The average slave owner lived in a log cabin rather than a mansion and was a farmer rather than a planter. The average holding varied between four and six slaves, and most slaveholders possessed no more than five.

White women in the South, despite the image of the hoop-skirted southern belle, suffered under heavier burdens than their northern counterparts. They married earlier, bore more children, and were more likely to die young. They lived in greater isolation and had less access to the company of other women. Their education was briefer and much less likely to result in opportunities for independent careers.

The plantation legend was misleading in still other respects. Slavery was neither dying nor was it unprofitable. In 1860 the South was richer than any country in Europe except England. The southern economy generated enormous wealth and was critical to the economic growth of the entire United States. Prior to the Civil War the South grew 60 percent of the world's cotton, provided over half of all U.S. export earnings, and furnished 70 percent of the cotton consumed by the British textile industry. Cotton exports paid for a substantial share of the capital and technology that laid the basis for America's industrial revolution. In addition, precisely because the South specialized in agricultural production, the North developed a variety of business that provided services for the southern states, including textile and meat processing factories, and financial and commercial facilities.

Impact of Slavery on the Southern Economy

Although slavery was highly profitable, it had a negative impact on the southern economy. It impeded the development of industry and cities and contributed to high debts, soil exhaustion, and a lack of technological innovation.

The South, like other slave societies, did not develop urban centers for commerce, finance, and industry on a scale equal to those found in the North. Southern cities were small because they failed to develop diversified economies. Unlike the cities of the North, southern cities rarely became processing or finishing centers and southern ports rarely engaged in international trade. Their primary functions were to market and transport cotton or other agricultural crops, supply local planters and farmers with such necessities as agricultural implements, and produce the small number of manufactured goods, such as cotton gins, needed by farmers.

An overemphasis on slave-based agriculture led Southerners to neglect industry and transportation improvements. As a result, manufacturing and transportation lagged far behind the North's. In 1860 the North had approximately 1.3 million industrial workers compared to the South's 110,000, and northern factories manufactured nine-tenths of the industrial goods produced in the United States.

The South's transportation network was primitive by northern standards. Most southern railroads served primarily to transport cotton to southern ports, where the crop could be shipped on northern vessels to northern or British factories for processing.

Southern states kept taxation and government spending at much lower levels than in the North. As a result, Southerners lagged far behind Northerners in their support for public education. Illiteracy was widespread. In 1850 20 percent of all southern white adults could not read or write, while the illiteracy rate in New England was less than half of one percent during the same period.

Because large slaveholders owned most of the region's slaves, wealth was more stratified than in the North. In the deep South the middle class held a relatively small proportion of the region's property, but wealthy planters owned a very significant portion of the productive lands and slave labor.

There are indications that during the last decade before the Civil War slave ownership was increasingly concentrated in fewer and fewer hands. As soil erosion and exhaustion diminished the availability of cotton land, scarcity and heavy demand forced the price of land and slaves to rise beyond the reach of most, and in newer cotton-growing regions yeomen farmers were pushed off the land as planters expanded their holdings. During the 1850s the percentage of the total white population owning slaves declined significantly. By 1860 the proportion of white slaveholders had fallen from about one-third to one-fourth. As slave and land ownership grew more concentrated, a growing number of whites were forced by economic pressure to leave the land and move to urban centers.

Growth of a Distinctive Southern Identity

Beginning in the 1830s the South developed a new and aggressive "nationalism" that was rooted in its sense of distinctiveness and its perception that it was ringed by enemies. The South began to conceive of itself more and more as the true custodian of America's revolutionary heritage. Southern travelers who ventured into the North regarded it as a "strange and distant land" and expressed disgust with its vice-ridden cities and its grasping materialism.

At the same time, southern intellectuals began to defend slavery as a positive good. After 1830 white Southerners stopped referring to slavery as a necessary evil. Instead, they argued that it was a beneficial institution that created a hierarchical society superior to the leveling democracy of the North. By the late 1840s a new, more explicitly racist rationale for slavery had emerged.

With the emergence of militant abolitionism in the North, sharpened by slave uprisings in Jamaica and Virginia, the South began to see itself as surrounded by enemies. Southern leaders responded aggressively. Prior to the 1830s southern statements on slavery had been defensive; afterward, they were defiant.

In the 1840s a growing number of southern ministers, journalists, and politicians began to denounce the North's form of capitalism as exploitative. Southern writers like George Fitzhugh argued that slavery was a beneficent institution that permitted the development of an upper class devoted to high intellectual pursuits. The champions of slavery maintained that the South's hierarchical society was superior to the individualistic, materialistic civilization of the North in which abolitionism, feminism, and labor unrest indicated that the social order was disintegrating.

During the 1840s a growing number of Southerners defended slavery on explicitly racial grounds. In doing so, they drew on new pseudoscientific theories of racial inferiority. Some of these theories came from Europe, which was seeking justification for imperial expansion over nonwhite peoples in Africa and Asia. Other racist ideas were drawn from northern scientists, who claimed that blacks and whites were separate species.

The Decline of Antislavery Sentiment in the South

During the eighteenth century the South was unique among slave societies in its openness to antislavery ideas. In Delaware, Maryland, and North Carolina Quakers freed more than 1,500 slaves and sent them out of state. Scattered Presbyterian, Baptist, and Methodist ministers condemned slavery as a sin "contrary to the word of God." As late as 1827, the number of antislavery organizations in the South actually outnumbered those in the free states by at least four to one.

The South's historical openness to antislavery ideas ended in the 1830s. Southern religious sects that had expressed opposition to slavery in the late eighteenth century modified their antislavery beliefs. State law and public opinion stifled debate and forced conformity to proslavery arguments. Southern state legislatures adopted a series of laws suppressing criticism of the institution. Louisiana in 1830 made it a crime to make any statement that might produce discontent or insubordination among free blacks. Six years later Virginia made it a felony for any member of an abolition society to come into the state and for any citizen to deny the legality of slavery. The silent pressure of public opinion limited public discussion of the slavery question. An "iron curtain" against the invasion of antislavery propaganda was erected.

Nonetheless, many white Southerners felt genuine moral doubts about slavery. For the most part, however, these doubts were directed into efforts to reform the institution by converting slaves to Christianity, revising slave codes to make them less harsh, and making slavery conform to the ideal depicted in the Old Testament.

During the early nineteenth century the southern states enacted new codes regulating the punishment of slaves and setting minimum standards for maintenance. State legislatures defined killing a slave with malice as murder and made dismemberment and some other cruel punishments illegal. Three states forbade the sale of young slave children from their parents, and four states permitted slaves to be taught to read and write.

Many of the new laws went unenforced, but they suggest that a new code of values and behavior was emerging. Paternalism was the defining characteristic of this new code. According to this new ideal, slaveholding was "a duty and a burden" carrying strict moral obligations. A humane master of a plantation was supposed to show concern for the spiritual and physical well-being of his slaves.

These minimal efforts to reform slavery were, however, accompanied by tighter restrictions on other aspects of slave life. Private manumissions were made illegal. Southern states instituted the death penalty for any slaves involved in plotting a rebellion. Most states prohibited slaves from owning firearms, placed tight restrictions on slave funerals, and barred black preachers from conducting religious services unless a white person was present. In order to restrict contact between free blacks and slaves, a number of southern states required manumitted slaves to leave the state. Other restrictive laws quarantined vessels containing black sailors and imprisoned those who stepped on shore.

Southern Nationalism

Seeking to free their region from cultural and economic dependence on the North, southern "nationalists" sought to insulate the South from the corrupting commercial and industrial values of the North. This desire for regional independence took many forms, all of which stressed the distinctiveness of southern culture.

The 1830s and 1840s saw attempts to promote southern economic self-sufficiency, to create southern-oriented educational and religious institutions, and to develop a distinctive southern literature. Beginning in 1837 southern leaders held the first of a series of commercial conventions in an attempt to diversify their economy. Other southern nationalists strove to create educational institutions, arguing that the South had to create its own institutions of higher learning in order to protect the young from antislavery ideas. Regional independence was also called for in religion. Due in large part to a fear of antislavery agitation, southern Baptists,

Methodists and Presbyterians sought to sever their denominational affili-ations with northern churches. Southerners also called for a distinctive and peculiarly southern literature. More than 30 periodicals were founded with the word "Southern" in their title, all intended to "breathe a South-ern spirit, and sustain a strictly Southern character."

By the early 1850s a growing number of aggressive Southerners had moved beyond earlier calls for cultural and economic separatism. Militant nationalists called for the reopening of the slave trade and the annexation of new slave territories in Latin America and the Caribbean.

In a bid to acquire new lands for slavery a filibustering expedition was launched from New Orleans in 1851 to secure Cuba for the South. After this failed, extreme southern nationalists supported the efforts of William Walker, "the gray-eyed man of destiny," to extend slave labor into Latin America. In 1853, with considerable southern support, Walker raised a private army and unsuccessfully invaded Mexico. Two years later he launched the first of three invasions of Nicaragua. On his final foray in 1860 he was taken prisoner by a British officer, handed over to Honduran authorities, and, at the age of 36, executed by a firing squad. The only practical effect of these schemes was to arouse northern opinion against an aggressive southern slaveocracy.

Slavery

The primary distinguishing characteristic of the South was its dependence on slave labor. During the decades before the Civil War 4 million black Americans, one-third of the South's population, labored as slaves.

In general, slaves were overworked, poorly clad, inadequately housed, and received the minimum of medical care. Debt, the death of a master, or merely the prospect of economic gain frequently tore slave husbands from wives and slave parents from children. And yet, as brutal and de-structive as the institution of slavery was, slaves were not defenseless or emasculated victims. Slaves were able to sustain ties to their African past and to maintain a separate life. Through religion, folklore, music, and family life as well as more direct forms of resistance, slaves were able to sustain a vital culture supportive of human dignity.

The Legal Status of Slaves

Every southern state enacted a slave code that defined the slave owners' power and the slaves' status as property. The codes stated that a slave, like a domestic animal, could be bought, sold, and leased. A master also had the right to compel a slave to work. The codes prohibited slaves from owning property, testifying against whites in court, or making contracts. Slave marriages were not recognized by law. Under the slave codes, slavery was lifelong and hereditary, and any child born to a slave woman was the property of her master.

The slave codes gave slaves limited legal rights, but their primary purpose was to enforce discipline. In order to refute abolitionist contentions that slavery was unjust and inhumane, southern legislators adopted statutes regulating slaves' hours of labor and establishing certain minimal standards for slave upkeep. Most states also defined the wanton killing of a slave as murder, prohibited cruel and unusual punishments, and extended to slaves accused of capital offenses the right to trial by jury and legal counsel. Whipping, however, was not regarded by southern legislatures as a cruel punishment, and slaves were prohibited from bringing suit to seek legal redress for violations of their rights.

The main goal of the slave codes, however, was to regulate slaves' lives. Slaves were forbidden to strike whites or use insulting language toward white people, hold a meeting without a white person present, visit whites or free blacks, or leave plantations without permission. The laws prohibited whites and free blacks from teaching slaves to read and write, gambling with slaves, or supplying them with liquor, guns, or poisonous

Slavery's worst evil was that it reduced people to the status of property. Under slavery, slaves could be bought, sold, leased, and traded from their families.

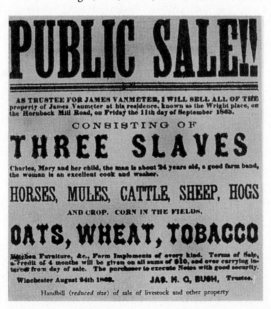

PUBLIC SALE!!

AS TRUSTEE FOR JAMES VANMETER, I WILL SELL ALL OF THE property of James Vanmeter at his residence, known as the Wright place, on the Hornback Mill Road, on Friday the 11th day of September 1865.

CONSISTING OF

THREE SLAVES

Charles, Mary and her child, the man is about 24 years old, a good farm hand, the woman is an excellent cook and washer.

HORSES, MULES, CATTLE, SHEEP, HOGS

AND CROP. CORN IN THE FIELDS,

OATS, WHEAT, TOBACCO

Kitchen Furniture, &c., Farm Implements of every kind. Terms of Sale, a credit of 4 months will be given on all sums of $10, and over carrying interest from day of sale. The purchaser to execute Notes with good security.

Winchester August 24th 1862.   JAS. H. O. BUSH, Trustee.

Handbill (reduced size) of sale of livestock and other property drugs. Most of the time, authorities loosely enforced these legal restrictions, but whenever fears of slave uprisings spread, enforcement tightened.

Slave Labor

Slaves performed all kinds of work. During the 1850s half a million slaves lived in southern towns and cities, where they were hired out by their owners as skilled artisans or laborers. Many other slaves were engaged in construction of roads and railroads. Most slaves, to be sure, were field hands, but even on plantations not all slaves were menial laborers. Some worked as blacksmiths or carpenters; others were domestic servants; and still others held managerial posts. At least two-thirds of the slaves worked under the supervision of black foremen of gangs, called drivers. Not infrequently they managed the whole plantation in the absence of their masters.

For most slaves, slavery meant backbreaking field work on small farms or larger plantations. Solomon Northrup, a free black who was kidnapped and enslaved for 12 years on a Louisiana cotton plantation, wrote a graphic description of the work regimen imposed on slaves: "The hands are required to be in the cotton field as soon as it is light in the morning, and, with the exception of ten or fifteen minutes, which is given them at noon to swallow their allowance of cold bacon, they are not permitted to be a moment idle until it is too dark to see, and when the moon is full, they often times labor till the middle of the night." Even then, the slaves' work was not over; it was still necessary to feed swine and mules, cut wood, and pack the cotton. At planting time or harvest time work was even more exacting, as planters required slaves to stay in the fields 15 or 16 hours a day.

To maximize productivity, slave owners assigned each hand a specific set of tasks throughout the year. During the winter field slaves ginned and pressed cotton, cut wood, repaired buildings and fences, and cleared fields. In the spring and summer field hands plowed and hoed the land, killed weeds, and planted and cultivated crops. In the fall slaves picked, ginned, and packed cotton, shucked corn, and gathered peas. Elderly slaves cared for children, made clothes, and prepared food.

Labor on large plantations was as rigidly organized as in a factory. Under the gang system, which was widely used on cotton plantations, field hands were divided into plow gangs and hoe gangs, each commanded by a driver. Under the task system, mainly used on rice plantations, each hand was given a specific daily work assignment.

Because slaves had little direct incentive to work hard, slave owners combined a variety of harsh penalties with positive incentives. Some masters denied disobedient slaves passes or forced them to work on Sundays or holidays. Other planters confined disobedient hands to private or public jails. Chains and shackles were widely used to control runaways. Whipping was a key part of the system of discipline and motivation. On one Louisiana plantation at least one slave was lashed every four-and-a-half days. In his diary Bennet H. Barrow, a Louisiana planter, recorded flogging "every hand in the field," breaking his sword on the head of one slave, shooting another in the thigh, and cutting another with a club "in 3 places very bad."

But physical pain alone was not enough to elicit hard work. To stimulate productivity, some masters gave slaves small garden plots and permitted them to sell their produce. Others distributed gifts of food or money at the end of the year. Still other planters awarded prizes, holidays, and year-end bonuses to particularly productive slaves. One Alabama master permitted his slaves to share in the profits of the crops.

Material Conditions of Slave Life

Deprivation and physical hardship were the hallmarks of life under slavery. It now seems clear that the material conditions of slave life may have been even worse than those of the poorest, most downtrodden free laborers in the North and in Europe. Although the slaves' material conditions improved greatly in the nineteenth century, slaves were still much more likely than southern or northern whites to die prematurely, suffer malnutrition or dietary deficiencies, or lose a child in infancy.

The slaves' diet was monotonous and unvaried, consisting largely of cornmeal, salt pork, and bacon. Only rarely did slaves drink milk or eat fresh meat or vegetables. This diet provided enough bulk calories to ensure that slaves had sufficient strength and energy to work as productive field hands, but it did not provide adequate nutrition. As a result, slaves were small for their age, suffered from vitamin and protein deficiencies, and were victims of such ailments as beriberi, kwashiorkor, and pellagra.

Plantation records reveal that over half of all slave babies died during their first year of life—a rate twice that of white babies. Although slave children's death rate declined after the first year of life, it remained twice the white rate. Poor nutrition and high rates of infant and child mortality contributed to a short average life expectancy—just 21 or 22 years compared to 40 to 43 years for whites.

The physical conditions in which slaves lived were appalling. Lacking privies, slaves had to urinate and defecate in the cover of nearby bushes. Lacking any sanitary disposal of garbage, they were surrounded by decaying food. Chickens, dogs, and pigs lived next to the slave quarters, and in consequence animal feces contaminated the area. Such squalor contributed to high rates of dysentery, typhus, diarrhea, hepatitis, typhoid fever, and intestinal worms.

Slave quarters were cramped and crowded. The typical cabin—a single, windowless room, with a chimney constructed of clay and twigs and a floor made up of dirt or planks resting on the ground—ranged in size from 10 × 10 feet to 21 × 21 feet. These small cabins were often quite crowded, containing five, six, or more occupants. On some plantations slaves lived in single-family cabins; on others, two or more shared the same room. On the largest plantations unmarried men and women were sometimes lodged together in barracks-like structures.

Slave Family Life

Slavery severely strained black family life. Slave sales frequently broke up slave families. During the Civil War nearly 20 percent of ex-slaves reported that an earlier marriage had been terminated by "force." The sale of children from parents was even more common. Over the course of a lifetime, the average slave had a fifty-fifty chance of being sold at least once and was likely to witness the sale of several members of his immediate family.

Even in instances in which marriages were not broken by sale, slave husbands and wives often resided on separate farms or plantations and were owned by different individuals. On large plantations one slave father in three had a different owner than his wife and could visit his family only at his master's discretion. On smaller holdings divided ownership occurred even more frequently. The typical farm and plantation were so small that it was difficult for many slaves to find a spouse at all. As one ex-slave put it, men "had a hell of a time getting a wife during slavery."

Other obstacles stood in the way of an independent family life. Living accommodations undermined privacy. Many slaves had to share their single-room cabins with relatives and other slaves who were not related to them. On larger plantations food was cooked in a common kitchen and young children were cared for in a communal nursery while their parents worked in the fields. Even on model plantations children between the ages of seven and ten were taken from their parents and sent to live in separate cabins.

Slavery imposed rigid limits on the authority of slave parents. Nearly every slave child went through an experience similar to one recalled by a young South Carolina slave named Jacob Stroyer. Jacob was being trained as a jockey. His trainer beat him regularly, for no apparent reason. Jacob appealed to his father for help, but his father simply said to work harder, "for I cannot do anything for you." When Jacob's mother argued with the trainer, she was whipped for her efforts. From this episode, Jacob learned a critical lesson: The ability of slave parents to protect their own children was sharply limited.

Of all the evils associated with slavery, abolitionists most bitterly denounced the sexual abuse suffered by slave women. Abolitionists claimed that slaveholders adopted deliberate policies to breed slaves for sale in the lower South and sexually exploited slave women. Some masters did indeed take slave mistresses and concubines. One slave, Henry Bibb, said that a slave trader forced Bibb's wife to become a prostitute.

Planters also sought to increase slave birthrates through a variety of economic incentives. Many slaveholders gave bounties in the form of cash or household goods to mothers who bore healthy children and increased rations and lightened the workload of pregnant and nursing women.

And yet, despite the constant threat of sale and family breakup, African Americans managed to forge strong family ties and personal relationships. Although southern law provided no legal sanction for slave marriages, most slaves established de facto arrangements that were often stable over long periods of time. In spite of frequent family disruption, a majority of slaves grew up in families headed by a father and a mother. Nuclear family ties stretched outward to an involved network of extended kin. In large measure because of the strength and flexibility of kinship ties, black Americans were able to resist the psychologically debilitating effects of slavery.

Contrary to what early nineteenth-century abolitionists charged, the sexual life of slaves was not casual or promiscuous nor did slave women become mothers at a particularly early age. Some slave women, like some white women, engaged in premarital intercourse and bore children outside of marriage. But most slave women settled into a long-lasting monogamous relationship in their early twenties, which lasted, unless broken by sale, until the wife or her husband died.

Slave Cultural Expression

Notwithstanding the harshness and misery of slave life, slaves developed a distinctive culture. Even under the weight of slavery blacks developed a vital religion, music, and folklore. Through their families, their religion, and their cultural traditions, they were able to fashion an autonomous culture and community, beyond the direct control of their masters.

During the late eighteenth and early nineteenth centuries slaves embraced Christianity, but they molded and transformed it to meet their own needs. Their religious beliefs were a mixture of African traditions and Christianity. From their African heritage they brought a hopeful and optimistic view of life, which contrasted sharply with evangelical Protestantism's emphasis on human sinfulness. In Protestant Christianity the slaves found an emphasis on love and the spiritual equality of all people that strengthened their ties to other blacks. Many slaves fused the concepts of Moses, who led his people to freedom, and Jesus, who suffered on behalf of all humankind, into a promise of deliverance in this world.

A major form of black religious expression was the spiritual. Slave spirituals, like "Go Down Moses" with its refrain "let my people go," indicated that slaves identified with the history of the Hebrew people, who had been oppressed and enslaved, but achieved eventual deliverance.

In addition to the spiritual, another major form of slave cultural expression was folklore. Slave folktales were much more than amusing stories; slaves used them to comment on the whites around them and to convey everyday lessons for living. Among the most popular slave folktales were the Brer Rabbit tales, derived from similar African stories, which told of powerless animals who achieve their will through wit and guile rather than power and authority. These tales taught slave children how they had to function in a white-dominated world and held out the promise that the powerless would eventually triumph over the strong.

Slave Resistance

It was a basic tenet of the proslavery argument that slaves were docile, contented, faithful, and loyal. In fact, there is no evidence that the majority of slaves were contented. One scholar has identified more than 200 instances of attempted insurrection or rumors of slave resistance between the seventeenth century and the Civil War. And many slaves who did not directly rebel made their masters' lives miserable through a variety of indirect protests against slavery, including sabotage, stealing, malingering, murder, arson, and infanticide.

Four times during the first 31 years of the nineteenth century slaves attempted major insurrections. In 1800 a 24-year-old Virginia slave named Gabriel Prosser, who was a blacksmith, led a march of perhaps 50 armed slaves on Richmond. The plot failed when a storm washed out the road to Richmond, giving the Virginia militia time to arrest the rebels. White authorities executed Prosser and 25 other conspirators.

In 1811 in southern Louisiana, between 180 and 500 slaves, led by Charles Deslondes, a free mulatto from Haiti, marched on New Orleans, armed with axes and other weapons. Slave owners retaliated by killing 82 blacks and placing the heads of 16 leaders on pikes.

In 1822 Denmark Vesey, a former West Indian slave who had been born in Africa, bought his freedom and moved to Charleston, South Carolina. There he devised a conspiracy to take over the city on a summer Sunday when many whites would be vacationing outside the city. Using his connections as a leader in the African Church of Charleston, Vesey drew support from skilled black artisans, as well as from field slaves. Before the revolt could take place, however, a domestic slave of a prominent Charlestonian informed his master. The authorities proceeded to arrest 131 blacks and hang 37.

The most famous slave revolt took place nine years later in Southampton County in southern Virginia. On August 22, 1831, Nat Turner, a Baptist preacher, led a small group of fellow slaves into the home of his master Joseph Travis and killed the entire Travis household. By August 23 Turner's force had increased to between 60 and 80 slaves and had killed more than 50 whites. The local militia counterattacked and killed about 100 blacks. Twenty more slaves, including Turner, were later executed. Turner's revolt sparked a panic that spread as far south as Alabama and Louisiana.

Slave uprisings were much less frequent and less extensive in the American South than in the West Indies or Brazil. Outright revolts did not occur more often because the chances of success were minimal and the consequences of defeat catastrophic.

The conditions that favored revolts elsewhere were absent in the South. In Jamaica, blacks outnumbered whites ten to one, whereas in the South whites were a majority in every state except Mississippi and South Carolina. In addition, slaveholding units in the South were much smaller than in other slave societies in the Western Hemisphere. Half of all U.S. slaves worked in units of 20 or less; in contrast, many sugar plantations in Jamaica had more than 500 slaves. Finally, southern slaves had few havens to which to escape. The major exception was the swamp country in Florida where black "maroons" joined with Seminole Indians in resisting the U.S. army.

Recognizing that open resistance would be futile or even counterproductive, many plantation slaves expressed their opposition to slavery in a variety of subtle ways. Most day-to-day resistance took the form of breaking tools, feigning illness, doing shoddy work, stealing, and running away. These acts of resistance were apt to occur when a master or overseer overstepped customary bounds. Through these acts, slaves tried to establish a right to proper treatment.

Free Blacks

In 1860 488,000 black Americans were *not* slaves. After the American Revolution, slave owners freed thousands of slaves, and countless others emancipated themselves by running away. In Louisiana a large free black Creole population had emerged under Spanish and French rule, and in

South Carolina a Creole population had arrived from Barbados. The number of free blacks in the Deep South increased rapidly with the arrival of thousands of light-colored refugees from the black revolt in Haiti.

Free blacks varied greatly in status. Most lived in poverty, but in a few cities, such as New Orleans, Baltimore, and Charleston, free blacks worked as skilled craftsmen. In the lower South a few free blacks achieved high occupational status and actually bought slaves of their own. One of the wealthiest free blacks was William Ellison, the son of a slave mother and a white planter. As a slave apprenticed to a skilled artisan, Ellison had learned how to make cotton gins, and at the age of 26 bought his freedom with his overtime earnings. At his death in 1861 he had acquired the home of a former South Carolina governor, a shop, lands, and 63 slaves worth more than $100,000.

Free people of color occupied an uneasy middle ground between the dominant whites and the masses of slaves. Legally, courts denied them the right to serve on juries or to testify against whites. Some, like William Ellison, distanced themselves from those black people who remained in slavery and even bought and sold slaves. Others identified with slaves and poor free blacks and took the lead in establishing separate black churches.

In addition to the more than 250,000 free blacks who lived in the South, another 200,000 free blacks lived in the North. Although free blacks comprised no more than 3.8 percent of the population of any northern state, they faced intense legal, economic, and social discrimination, which kept them desperately poor. All but four states—New Hampshire, Maine, Massachusetts, and Vermont—denied them the right to vote.

In the North as well as the South most free blacks faced economic hardship and substandard living conditions. Free blacks in both regions suffered from heightened discrimination and competition from white immigrants in both the skilled trades and such traditional occupations as domestic service. On the eve of the Civil War the plight of free blacks worsened. South Carolina debated the reenslavement of free blacks, prompting almost 3,000 to emigrate to the North.

Conclusion

In the late 1850s the North and South had become in the eyes of many Americans two distinct civilizations, each having its own distinctive set of values and ideals: one increasingly urban and industrial, the other committed to slave labor. Although the two sections shared many of the same ideals, ambitions, and prejudices, they had developed along diverging lines. In increasing numbers, Northerners identified their society with

Chronology of Key Events

1790	Samuel Slater opens the nation's first textile mill in Pawtucket, Rhode Island
1793	Eli Whitney obtains a patent for the cotton gin
1801	Gabriel Prosser's slave insurrection uncovered
1806	Journeymen shoemakers in New York stage one of the nation's first labor strikes
1811	Charles Deslondes's slave insurrection in southern Louisiana suppressed
1822	Denmark Vesey's slave rebellion uncovered in South Carolina
1831	Nat Turner rebellion
1832	Virginia legislature defeats proposal to abolish slavery
1834	National Trades' Union organized; Massachusetts mill girls stage their first strike
1837	Panic of 1837
1840	Ten-hour day established for federal employees
1842	Massachusetts supreme court, in *Commonwealth* v. *Hunt,* recognizes unions' right to exist
1845	Irish Potato Famine

progress and believed that slavery was an intolerable obstacle to innovation, self-improvement, and commercial and economic growth. A growing number of Southerners, in turn, regarded their rural and agricultural society as the true embodiment of republican values. The great question before the nation was whether it could continue to exist half slave, half free.

Suggestions for Further Reading

For information on the antebellum North and the rise of industrialization see Thomas Dublin, *Women at Work: The Transformation of Work and Community in Lowell, Massachusetts,* (1979); Philip Taylor, *The Distant Magnet: European*

Emigration to the U.S.A. (1971); Stephan Thernstrom, *Poverty and Progress, Social Mobility in a Nineteenth Century City* (1964); Anthony F. C. Wallace, *Rockdale: The Growth of an American Village in the Early Industrial Revolution* (1978); Sean Wilentz, *Chants Democratic* (1984).

Studies focusing on the southern slaveocracy include William J. Cooper, Jr., *South and the Politics of Slavery* (1978); William J. Cooper, Jr. and Thomas E. Terrill, *The American South* (1990); Eugene D. Genovese, *The Political Economy of Slavery* (1965), and *The World the Slaveholders Made* (1969); Robert E. May, *The Southern Dream of a Caribbean Empire* (1973).

Valuable studies on the culture of slaves and free blacks are Ira Berlin, *Slaves Without Masters: The Free Negro in the Antebellum South* (1974); John W. Blassingame, *The Slave Community: Plantation Life in the Antebellum South,* rev. ed. (1979); John B. Boles, *Black Southerners* (1983); Eugene D. Genovese, *From Rebellion to Revolution: Afro-American Slave Revolts in the Making of the Modern World* (1979), and *Roll, Jordan, Roll: The World the Slaves Made* (1974); Leon Litwack, *North of Slavery: The Negro in the Free States* (1961); Stephen B. Oates, *The Fires of Jubilee: Nat Turner's Fierce Rebellion* (1975).

Chapter *13*

Surge to the Pacific

Early in April 1846, 87 pioneers led by George Donner, a well-to-do 62 year-old farmer, set out from Illinois, for California. As this group of pioneers headed westward, they never imagined the hardship and tragedy that awaited them. Like many emigrants, they were ill prepared for the dangerous trek. The pioneers' 27 wagons were loaded not only with necessities but with fancy foods and liquor and such luxuries as built-in beds and stoves.

In Wyoming the party decided to take a shortcut, having read in a guidebook that pioneers could save 400 miles by cutting south of the Great Salt Lake. At first the trail was "all that could be desired," but soon huge boulders, arid desert, and dangerous mountain passes slowed the expedition to a crawl. During one stretch, the party traveled only 36 miles in 21 days. In late October the Donner party reached the eastern Sierra Nevada Mountains and prepared to cross Truckee Pass, the last remaining barrier before they arrived in California's Sacramento Valley. They climbed the high Sierra ridges in an attempt to cross the pass, but early snows blocked their path.

Trapped, the party built crude tents covered with clothing, blankets, and animal hides, which were soon buried under 14 feet of snow. The pioneers intended to slaughter their livestock for food, but many of the animals perished in 40-foot snowdrifts. To survive, the Donner party was forced to eat mice, their rugs, and even their shoes. In the end, surviving members of the party escaped starvation only by eating the flesh of those who died.

Finally, in mid-December, 17 men and women made a last-ditch effort to cross the pass to find help. They took only a six-day supply of rations, consisting of finger-sized pieces of dried beef—two pieces a person per day. During a severe storm two of the group died. The surviving members of the party "stripped the flesh from their bones, roasted and ate it, averting their eyes from each other, and weeping." More than a month passed before seven frostbitten survivors reached an American settlement. By then, the rest had died and two Indian guides had been shot and eaten.

Relief teams immediately sought to rescue the pioneers still trapped near Truckee Pass. The situation that the rescuers found was unspeakably gruesome. Thirteen were dead. Surviving members of the Donner party were delirious from hunger and overexposure. One survivor was found in a small cabin next to a cannibalized body of a young boy. Of the original 87 members of the party, only 47 survived.

It took Americans a century and a half to expand as far west as the Appalachian Mountains, a few hundred miles from the Atlantic coast. It took another 50 years to push the frontier to the Mississippi River. By 1830 fewer than 100,000 pioneers had crossed the Mississippi.

Margaret Reed was one of only 47 survivors of the original party of 87 pioneers to reach California.

Only a small number of explorers, fur trappers, traders, and mission-aries had ventured far beyond the Mississippi River. These trailblazers drew a picture of the American West as a land of promise, a paradise of plenty, filled with fertile valleys and rich land. During the 1840s tens of thousands of Americans began the process of settling the West beyond the Mississippi River. Thousands of families chalked GTT ("Gone to Texas") on their gates or painted "California or Bust" on their wagons and joined the trek westward. By 1850 pioneers had pushed the edge of settlement all the way to Texas, the Rocky Mountains, and the Pacific Ocean.

Opening the West

Before the nineteenth century, mystery shrouded the Far West. Mapmak-ers knew very little about the shape, size, or topography of the land west of the Mississippi River. French, British, and Spanish trappers, traders, and missionaries had traveled the Upper and Lower Missouri River and the British and Spanish had explored the Pacific coast, but most of western North America was an unknown.

The popular conception of the West was largely a mixture of legend and guesswork. Even educated people like Thomas Jefferson, believed that the West was populated by primeval beasts and that only a single ridge of mountains, known as the "Stony Mountains," needed to be crossed before one could see the Pacific Ocean.

Pathfinders

In 1803 President Thomas Jefferson appointed Meriwether Lewis and William Clark to explore the Missouri and Columbia rivers as far as the Pacific. As a politician interested in the rapid settlement and commercial development of the West, Jefferson wanted Lewis and Clark to establish American claims to the region west of the Rocky Mountains, gather information about furs and minerals in the region, and identify sites for trading posts and settlements. The president also instructed the expedition to collect information covering the diversity of life in the West, ranging from climate, geology, and plant growth to fossils of extinct animals and Indian religions, laws, and customs.

In 1806 the year that Lewis and Clark returned from their 8,000-mile expedition, a young army lieutenant named Zebulon Pike left St. Louis to explore the southern border of the Louisiana Territory, just as Lewis and Clark had explored the territory's northern portion. Traveling along the Arkansas River, Pike saw the towering peak that bears his name. He and his party then traveled into Spanish territory along the Rio Grande and Red River. Pike's description of the wealth of Spanish towns, primarily Chihuahua and Santa Fe, in the Southwest brought some American traders to the region.

Pike's report of his expedition, published in 1810, helped to create one of the most influential myths about the Great Plains: This region was nothing more than a "Great American Desert," a treeless and waterless land of dust storms and starvation. "Here," wrote Pike, is "barren soil, parched and dried up for eight months of the year . . . [without] a speck of vegetation." This image of the West as a region of savages, wild beasts, and deserts received added support from another government-sponsored expedition, one led by Major Stephen H. Long in 1820 in search of the source of the Red River. Long's report described the West as "wholly unfit for cultivation, and . . . uninhabitable by a people depending upon agriculture for their subsistence." This report helped implant the image of the

"Great American Desert" even more deeply in the American mind, retarding western settlement for a generation.

The view of the West as a dry, barren wasteland was not fully offset until the 1840s when another government-sponsored explorer, John C. Frémont, nicknamed "The Pathfinder," mapped much of the territory between the Mississippi Valley and the Pacific Ocean. His glowing descriptions of the West as a paradise of plenty captivated the imagination of many midwestern families who, by the 1840s, were eager for new lands to settle.

Mountain Men

Traders and trappers were more important than government explorers in opening the West to white settlement. Trappers and traders were the first U.S. citizens to exploit the West economically. They trapped beaver and bartered with Indians for pelts. They blazed the great westward trails through the Rockies and Sierra Nevada and stirred the popular imagination with stories of redwood forests, geysers, and fertile valleys in California, Oregon, and other areas west of the Rocky Mountains. The men also undermined the ability of the western Indians to resist white incursions by encouraging intertribal warfare and making Indians dependent on American manufactured goods. They killed off animals that provided a major part of the Indian hunting and gathering economy, distributed alcohol, and spread disease.

When Lewis and Clark completed their expedition, they brought back reports of rivers and streams in the northern Rockies teeming with beaver and otter. Fur traders and trappers quickly followed in their footsteps. Starting in 1807, keelboats ferried fur trappers up the Missouri River. By the mid-1830s these "mountain men" had marked out the overland trails that would lead pioneers to Oregon and California.

The Rocky Mountain Fur Company played a central role in the opening of the western fur trade. Instead of buying skins from the Indians, the company inserted ads in St. Louis newspapers asking for white trappers willing to go to the wilderness. In 1822 it sent a hundred trappers out along the upper Missouri River. Three years later the company introduced the "rendezvous" system, under which trappers met once a year at an agreed-upon meeting place to barter pelts for supplies. "The rendezvous," wrote one participant, "is one continued scene of drunkenness, gambling, and brawling and fighting, as long as the money and the credit of the trappers last."

At the same time that mountain men searched for beaver in the Rockies and along the Columbia River, other groups trapped furs in the Southwest, then part of Mexico. In 1827 Jedediah Smith and a party of 15 trappers, after nearly dying of thirst, discovered a westward route to California.

It led across the burning Mojave Desert and the San Bernardino Mountains to the Pacific Coast. Jim Beckwourth, a black mountain man who was the son of a Virginia slave, also discovered a pass through the Sierra Nevada that became part of the overland trail to California.

The western fur trade lasted only until 1840, when the last annual rendezvous was held. Beaver hats for gentlemen went out of style in favor of silk hats, bringing the romantic era of the mountain man, dressed in a fringed buckskin suit, to an end. Fur-bearing animals had been trapped out, and profits from trading, which amounted to as much as 2,000 percent during the early years, fell steeply. Instead of hunting furs, some trappers became scouts for the United States Army or pilots for the wagon trains that were beginning to carry pioneers to Oregon and California.

Trailblazing

The Santa Fe and Oregon trails were the two principal routes to the Far West. William Becknell, an American trader, opened the Santa Fe Trail in 1821. Ultimately, the trail tied the New Mexican Southwest economically to the rest of the United States and hastened American penetration of the region.

Western Trails

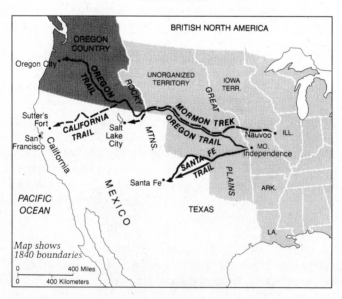

The Santa Fe Trail served primarily commercial functions. From the early 1820s until the 1840s an average of 80 wagons and 150 traders used the Santa Fe Trail each year. Mexican settlers in Santa Fe purchased cloth, hardware, glass, and books. On their return east, American traders carried Mexican blankets, beaver pelts, wool, mules, and silver. By the 1830s traders had extended the trail into California, with branches reaching Los Angeles and San Diego. By the 1850s and 1860s more than 5,000 wagons a year took the trail across long stretches of desert, dangerous water crossings, and treacherous mountain passes. The Santa Fe Trail made the Spanish southwest economically dependent on the United States and first brought Americans into the areas that became Arizona, California, and New Mexico.

In 1811 and 1812 fur trappers marked out the Oregon Trail, the longest and most famous pioneer route in American history. This trail crossed about 2,000 miles from Independence, Missouri, to the Columbia River country of Oregon. During the 1840s 12,000 pioneers traveled the trail's entire length to Oregon.

Travel on the Oregon Trail was a tremendous test of human endurance. The journey by wagon train took six months. Settlers encountered prairie fires, sudden blizzards, and impassable mountains. Cholera and other diseases were common; food, water, and wood were scarce. Only the stalwart dared brave the physical hardship of the westward trek.

Spanish and Indian America

When Americans ventured westward, they did not enter virgin land. Large parts of the Far West were already occupied by Indians and Mexicans, who had lived in the region for hundreds of years and established their own distinctive ways of life.

Hispanic America

Between 1528 and 1800 Spain established imperial claims and isolated outposts in an area extending from present-day Montana to Mexico and from California to the Mississippi River. Half a century before the first English colonists arrived at Jamestown, Spain had permanent settlements in the Far West, founded partly as a way to keep out other European powers. Then, in the late sixteenth century, Spain planted a colony in New Mexico and a century later built the first settlements in what is now Arizona and Texas. In the late eighteenth century fears of British and Russian occupation of the Pacific Coast led Spain also to establish outposts in California.

The Spanish clergy, particularly Jesuits and Franciscans, played a critical role in settling the Southwest, using the mission system. Their missions were designed to spread Christianity among, and establish control over, native populations. In some areas, they forced Indians to live in mission communities where the priests taught them weaving, blacksmithing, candle-making, and leather-working, and forced them to work in workshops, orchards, and fields for long hours. The missions were most successful in New Mexico (despite an Indian revolt in 1680) and California, and far less successful in Arizona and Texas.

Mission life reached its peak in California, an area that Spain did not begin to colonize until 1769. In the mid-eighteenth century Spain learned that Russian seal hunters and traders were moving south from Alaska into California. Determined to halt the Russian advance, Spanish authorities established a string of missions and presidios (military forts) along the Pacific coast. Between 1769 and 1823 Spain established 21 missions in California, extending from San Diego northward to Sonoma.

By the early nineteenth century, however, resistance to colonial rule in Spanish America was growing. In 1810 Miguel Hidalgo y Costilla, a Mexican priest, led a revolt which, although short-lived, represented the beginning of Mexico's struggle for independence. Mexican independence was finally achieved in 1821. The War of Independence marked the beginning of a period of far-reaching change in the Southwest. Among the most important consequences of the collapse of Spanish rule was the opening of the region to American economic penetration. Mexican authorities in New Mexico and Arizona allowed American traders to bring American goods into the area and trappers to hunt for beaver. Texas and California were also opened up to American commerce and settlement. By 1848 Americans made up about half of California's non-Indian population.

Mexican independence also led to the demise of the mission system in California. After the revolution the missions were "secularized"—broken up and their property sold or given away to private citizens. In 1833–1834 the Mexican government confiscated California mission properties and exiled the Franciscan friars. As a result, mission properties fell into private hands. By 1846 mission land and cattle had largely passed into the hands of 800 private landowners called rancheros, who controlled 8 million acres of land in units (ranchos) ranging in size from 4,500 to 50,000 acres. The ranchos were run like feudal estates, and the Indians who worked on the estates had a status similar to that of slaves. Indeed, the death rate of Indians who worked on ranchos was twice as high as the rate among southern slaves, and by 1848 one-fifth of California's Indian population had died.

After it won its independence from Spain, Mexico secularized the missions and divided land into ranchos. This painting shows a Mexican *ranchero*.

Western Indians

In 1840, before large numbers of pioneers and farmers crossed the Mississippi, at least 300,000 Indians lived in the Southwest, on the Great Plains, in California, and on the northwest Pacific Coast. The Native American population was divided into more than 200 tribes. Their life-styles ranged from nomadic hunting and gathering to sedentary farming. Their social organization was equally diverse, each tribe having its own language, religious beliefs, kinship patterns, and system of government.

The best-known of the western Indians are the 23 Indian tribes—including the Cheyenne and Sioux—who lived on the Great Plains and hunted buffalo, antelope, deer, and elk for subsistence. For many present-day Americans, the Plains Indians, riding on horseback, wearing a war-bonnet, and living in a tepee, are regarded as the typical American Indians. In fact, however, the Plains Indians first acquired the horse from the Spanish in the sixteenth century. Not until the middle of the eighteenth century did these tribes have a large supply of horses and not until the early to mid-nineteenth century did most Plains Indians have firearms.

South and west of the Plains, in the huge arid region that is now Arizona and New Mexico, sophisticated farmers, like the Hopi, Zuni, and other Pueblo groups, coexisted with nomadic hunters and gatherers, like the Apache and Navajo. In the Great Basin, the harsh barren region between the Sierra Nevada and the Rocky Mountains, food was so scarce that nations like the Paiutes and the Gosiutes subsisted on berries, nuts, roots, insects, and reptiles.

More than 100,000 Indians still lived in California when the area was acquired by the United States in 1848. Most of these people occupied small villages during the winter but moved during the rest of the year gathering wild plants and seeds, hunting small game, and fishing in the rivers.

The large number of tribes living along the northwest Pacific Coast developed an elaborate social hierarchy based on wealth and descent. These people found an abundant food supply in the sea, coastal rivers, and forests. They took salmon, seal, whale, and otter from the coastal waters and hunted deer, moose, and elk in the forests.

Contact with white traders, trappers, and settlers caused a dramatic decline in Indian populations. In California, disease and deliberate campaigns of extermination killed 70,000 Indians between 1849 and 1859. In the Great Basin, impoverished Gosiutes and Paiutes were shot by trappers for sport. In Texas, the Karankawas and many of the other original tribes of the area largely disappeared. Further west, Comanche, Kiowa, and Apache warriors bitterly resisted white encroachment on their land. Tribes in the Pacific Northwest and the northern Plains struggled desperately to slow the arrival of whites along the Oregon Trail. The Nez Percé and Flathead Indians expelled American missionaries from their tribal lands, and the Snake, Cheyenne, Shasta, and Rogue River Indians tried futilely to cut emigrant routes. The federal government employed the army to protect settlers and attack the western Indians and forced the cession of 147 million acres of tribal lands to the United States between 1853 and 1857.

Settling the Far West

During the early 1840s thousands of pioneers headed westward toward California and Oregon. In 1841 the first party of 69 pioneers left Missouri for California, led by an Ohio schoolteacher named John Bidwell. The members of the party knew little about western travel: "We only knew that California lay to the west." The hardships the party endured were nearly unbearable. They were forced to abandon their wagons and eat their pack animals. American pioneering of the Far West had begun. During the next 25 years some 350,000 more made the trek along the overland trails.

The rugged pioneer life was not a new experience for most of these early western settlers. Most of the pioneers who migrated to the Far West came from the states that border the Mississippi River—Missouri, Arkansas, Louisiana, and Illinois—which had only recently acquired statehood. Either they or their parents had already moved several times before reaching the Mississippi Valley.

Life on the Trail

For many families, the great spur for emigration was economic; the financial depression of the late 1830s, accompanied by floods and epidemics in the Mississippi Valley, forced many to pull up stakes and head west. Said one woman: "We had nothing to lose, and we might gain a fortune." Most settlers traveled in family units. Even single men attached themselves to family groups.

At first, pioneers tried to maintain the rigid sexual division of labor that characterized early nineteenth-century America. Men drove the wagons and livestock, stood guard duty, and hunted buffalo and antelope for extra meat. Women got up before dawn, collected wood and "buffalo chips" (animal dung used for fuel), hauled water, kindled campfires, kneaded dough, and milked cows. The demands of the journey forced a blurring of gender-role distinctions for women who, in addition to domestic chores, performed many duties previously reserved for men. They drove wagons, yoked cattle, and loaded wagons. Some men even did things such as cooking, previously regarded as women's work.

Accidents, disease, and sudden disaster were ever-present dangers. Diseases such as typhoid, dysentery, and mountain fever killed many pioneers. Emigrant parties also suffered devastation from buffalo stampedes, prairie fires, and floods. Pioneers buried at least 20,000 emigrants along the Oregon Trail.

Still, despite the hardships of the experience, few emigrants ever regretted their decision to move west. As one pioneer put it: "Those who crossed the plains . . . never forgot the ungratified thirst, the intense heat and bitter cold, the craving hunger and utter physical exhaustion of the trail. . . . But there was another side. True they had suffered, but the satisfaction of deeds accomplished and difficulties overcome more than compensated and made the overland passage a thing never to be forgotten."

Manifest Destiny

In 1845 John L. O'Sullivan, editor of the *Democratic Review,* referred in his magazine to America's "manifest destiny to overspread the continent allotted by Providence for the free development of our yearly multiplying millions." One of the most influential slogans ever coined, *manifest destiny* expressed the romantic emotion that led Americans to risk their lives to settle the Far West.

The idea that America had a special destiny to stretch across the continent motivated many people to migrate west and encouraged men and women to dream big dreams. "We Americans," wrote Herman Melville, one of this country's greatest novelists, "are the peculiar, chosen people—the Israel of our time." Aggressive nationalists invoked the idea to justify Indian removal, war with Mexico, and American expansion into Cuba and Central America. More positively, the idea of manifest destiny inspired missionaries, farmers, and pioneers, who dreamed only of transforming plains and fertile valleys into farms and small towns.

Gone to Texas

In 1822, when the first caravan of American traders traversed the Santa Fe Trail and the first hundred fur trappers searched the Rocky Mountains for beaver, a small number of Americans followed trails to another frontier—Texas.

American settlement in Texas began with the encouragement of first the Spanish, and then Mexican, governments. In the summer of 1820 Moses Austin, a bankrupt 59-year-old Missourian, asked Spanish authorities for a large Texas land tract that he would promote and sell to American pioneers. The following year the Spanish government gave him permission to settle 300 families in Texas. Spain welcomed the Americans for two reasons—to provide a buffer against illegal U.S. settlers, who were creating problems in east Texas even before the grant was made to Austin, and to help develop the land, since only 3,500 native Mexicans had settled in Texas (which was part of the Mexican state of Coahuila y Tejas).

Moses Austin soon died, but his son Stephen carried out his dream to colonize Texas. By 1824 he had attracted 272 colonists to Texas and persuaded the new government of Mexico that encouragement of American immigration was the best way to develop the area. To promote colonization, Mexico in 1825 gave land agents (called *empresarios*) 67,000 acres of land for every 200 families they brought to Texas. Mexico imposed two conditions on land ownership: Settlers had to become Mexican citizens and they had to convert to Roman Catholicism. By 1830 there were 16,000 Americans in Texas.

As the Anglo population swelled, Mexican authorities grew increasingly suspicious of the growing American presence in Texas, and in 1827 the government sent General Manuel de Mier y Terán to investigate the situation. In his report Terán warned that unless the Mexican government took timely measures, American settlers in Texas were certain to rebel. Differences in language and culture, Terán believed, had produced bitter enmity between the colonists and native Mexicans. The colonists, he noted, refused to learn the Spanish language, maintained their own separate schools, and conducted most of their trade with the United States. They complained bitterly that they had to travel more than 500 miles to reach a Mexican court and resented the efforts of Mexican authorities to deprive them of the right to vote.

To reassert its authority over Texas, the Mexican government reaffirmed its constitutional prohibition against slavery throughout Mexico, established a chain of military posts occupied by convict soldiers, levied customs duties, restricted trade with the United States, and decreed an end to further American immigration. These actions might have provoked Texans to revolution. But in 1832 General Antonio López de Santa Anna became Mexico's president. Colonists hoped that he would make Texas a self-governing state within the Mexican republic, separate from the much more populous Coahuila, thereby eliminating any reason for rebellion. Once in power, however, Santa Anna proved to be far less liberal than many Americans had believed. In 1834 he overthrew Mexico's constitutional government, abolished state governments, and made himself dictator. When Stephen Austin went to Mexico City to try to settle the Texans' grievances, Santa Anna imprisoned him in a Mexican jail for a year.

On November 3, 1835, American colonists adopted a constitution and organized a temporary government but voted overwhelmingly against declaring independence. A majority of colonists hoped to attract the support of Mexican liberals in a joint effort to depose Santa Anna and to restore power to the state governments, hopefully including a separate state of Texas.

While holding out the possibility of compromise, the Texans prepared for war. The provisional government elected Sam Houston, a former Tennessee governor and close friend of Andrew Jackson, to lead whatever military forces he could muster. In the middle of 1835 scattered local outbursts erupted against Mexican rule. Then a band of 300 to 500 Texans captured Mexico's military headquarters in San Antonio. The Texas Revolution was underway.

Soon the ominous news reached Texas that Santa Anna himself was marching north with 7,000 soldiers to crush the revolt. In actuality, Santa

Anna's army was not particularly impressive; it was filled with raw recruits and included many Indian troops who spoke and understood little Spanish. When Houston learned that Santa Anna's initial goal was to recapture San Antonio, he ordered San Antonio abandoned. But Texas rebels decided to defend the town and made their stand at an abandoned Spanish mission, the Alamo. The Texans were led by William Travis and Jim Bowie and included the frontier hero David Crockett.

For 12 days Mexican forces laid siege to the Alamo. At 5 A.M., March 6, Mexican troops scaled the mission's walls. By 8 A.M., the fighting was over. One hundred eighty-three defenders lay dead, including several Mexicans who had fought for Texas independence.

Two weeks after the defeat at the Alamo, James Fannin and his men surrendered to Mexican forces near Goliad with the understanding that they would be treated as prisoners of war. Instead, Santa Anna ordered more than 350 Texans shot.

These defeats, however, had an unexpected side effect. They gave Sam Houston time to raise and train an army. Volunteers from the American South flocked to his banner. On April 21 his army of less than 800 men surprised and utterly defeated Santa Anna's army as it camped out on the San Jacinto River, east of present-day Houston. The next day Houston's army captured Santa Anna himself and forced him to sign a treaty granting Texas its independence, a treaty that was never ratified by the Mexican government because it was acquired under duress.

For most Mexican settlers in Texas, defeat meant that they would be relegated to second-class social, political, and economic positions. The new Texas constitution denied citizenship and property rights to those who failed to support the revolution. All persons of Hispanic ancestry were considered in the "denial" category unless they could prove otherwise. Consequently, many Mexican landowners fled the region.

Texas grew rapidly, following independence. In 1836 5,000 immigrants arrived in Texas, boosting its population to 30,000. By 1847 its population had reached 140,000. The region also grew economically. Although cotton farming dominated the Texas economy, cattle were becoming an increasingly important industry. Many Mexican landowners abandoned cattle after the Texas Revolution, and, by the 1840s, large numbers of wild cattle roamed the range. By 1850 the first American cowboys were driving 60,000 cattle a year to New Orleans and California.

The Texas Question

Texas had barely won its independence when it decided to become a part of the United States. A referendum held soon after the Battle of San Jacinto showed Texans favoring annexation by a vote of 3,277 to 93.

The annexation question became one of the most controversial issues in American politics in the late 1830s and early 1840s. The issue was not Texas but slavery. The admission of Texas to the Union would upset the sectional balance of power in the U.S. Senate, just as the admission of Missouri had threatened 15 years earlier. President Andrew Jackson, acutely conscious of the opposition to admitting Texas as a slave state, agreed only to recognize Texan independence. In 1838 John Quincy Adams, now a member of the House of Representatives, staged a 22-day filibuster that successfully blocked annexation. It appeared that Congress had settled the Texas question. For the time being, Texas would remain an independent republic.

At this point, proslavery Southerners began to popularize a conspiracy theory that would eventually bring Texas into the Union as a slave state. In 1841 John Tyler, an ardent defender of slavery, succeeded to the presidency on the death of William Henry Harrison. Tyler and his secretary of state, John C. Calhoun, argued that Great Britain was scheming to annex Texas and transform it into a haven for runaway slaves. According to this theory, British slave emancipation in the West Indies had been a total economic disaster, and the British now hoped to undermine slavery in the American South by turning Texas into a British satellite state. In fact, British abolitionists, but not the British government, were working to convince Texas to outlaw slavery in exchange for British foreign aid. Sam Houston did his part to excite the fears of Americans by conducting highly visible negotiations with the British government. If the United States would not annex Texas, Houston warned, Texas would seek the support of "some other friend." In the spring of 1844 Calhoun hammered out an annexation treaty with Texas diplomats, but the agreement failed to gain the required two-thirds majority for Senate ratification.

The Texas question became the major political issue in the presidential campaign of 1844. James K. Polk, the Democratic candidate, was a strong supporter of annexation, and his victory encouraged Tyler to attempt to annex Texas again in the waning months of his administration. This time Tyler submitted the measure in the form of a resolution, which required only a simple majority of both houses. Congress narrowly approved the resolution in 1845, making Texas the twenty-eighth state.

Webster-Ashburton Treaty

During the decades before the Civil War the border between the United States and British America was the scene of constant tensions. In 1837 many Americans viewed an insurrection in eastern Canada as an opportunity to annex the country. Americans who lived near the Canadian border

aided the rebels, and in one incident several hundred western New Yorkers crossed into Canada and staged an abortive attack on a band of British
soldiers. After British forces suppressed the uprising, New Yorkers provided safe haven for the insurrection's leaders. When the rebels began to
launch raids into Canada from western New York State, Canadian officials crossed the U.S. border, killed a Canadian rebel, and burned an
American ship, the *Caroline,* which had supplied the rebels. When Americans demanded an apology and reparations, Canadian officials refused.
Almost immediately, another dispute erupted over the Maine boundary as
American and Canadian lumberjacks and farmers battled for possession
of northern Maine and western New Brunswick.

The Webster-Ashburton Treaty of 1842 settled these controversies.
The treaty awarded the United States most of the disputed territory in
Maine and New Brunswick, and adjusted the Canadian-United States
boundary between Lake Superior and Lake of the Woods. The Webster-
Ashburton Treaty left one major border controversy unresolved: the
Canadian-American boundary in the Pacific Northwest.

Oregon

Disputes between the United States and Britain over the "Oregon" country emerged early in the nineteenth century. In 1810 John Jacob Astor, an
American who had made a fortune in the Great Lakes fur trade, decided
to open a trading post, named Astoria, at the mouth of the Columbia
River. He hoped the post would secure a monopoly over the western fur
trade, and then ship the furs to eager customers in China. The venture
proved unsuccessful, however, and for nearly two decades the fur trade
was dominated by the British Hudson's Bay Company.

As British fur traders expanded their activities in the Pacific Northwest, American politicians grew alarmed that Britain would gain sovereignty over the region. American diplomats moved quickly to try to solidify American claims to Oregon. Spain, Russia, Britain, and the United
States all claimed rights to the Pacific Northwest. In 1818 British and
American negotiators agreed that nationals of both countries could trade
in the region; this agreement was renewed in 1827. In 1819 the United
States persuaded Spain to cede its claims to Oregon to the United States,
and two years later Secretary of State John Quincy Adams warned Russia
that the United States would oppose any Russian attempts to occupy the
territory.

The rapid influx of a large number of land-hungry Americans into
Oregon in the mid-1840s forced Britain and the United States to decide
the status of Oregon. In the presidential election of 1844 the Democratic

party demanded the "re-occupation" of Oregon and annexation of the entire Pacific Northwest coast up to the edge of Russian-held Alaska, which was fixed at 54° 40'. This demand helped James K. Polk win the presidency in 1844.

In truth, Polk had little desire to go to war with Britain. Furthermore, he believed that the northernmost portions of the Oregon country were unsuitable for agriculture. Therefore, in 1846—despite the expansionist slogan "54° 40' or fight"—he readily accepted a British compromise on the boundary dispute to extend the existing United States-British American boundary along the 49th parallel from the Rocky Mountains to the Pacific Ocean.

The Mormon Frontier

Pioneers migrated to the West for a variety of reasons. Some were driven westward by the hope of economic and social betterment, others by a restless curiosity and an urge for adventure. The Mormons moved west for an entirely different reason—to escape religious persecution.

Oregon Country, Pacific Northwest Boundary Dispute

The United States and Great Britain nearly came to blows over the disputed boundary in Oregon.

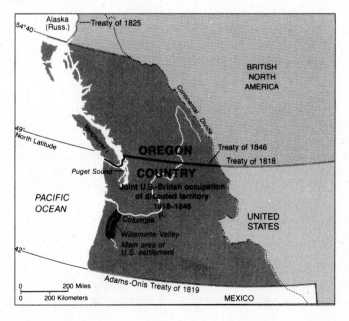

The Mormon church had its beginnings in upstate New York in 1823. Joseph Smith, the son of a farmer, claimed to have received divine revelations that told him of the existence of a set of buried golden plates that contained a lost section from the Bible describing a tribe of Israelites that had lived in America. Smith also claimed to have unearthed the golden plates, and four years later, with the aid of magic stones, translated them into English. The messages on the plates were later published as the *Book of Mormon.*

By the 1830s Smith had attracted several thousand followers from rural areas of the North and the frontier Midwest. The converts to Mormonism were usually small farmers and tradesmen who had been displaced by the growing commercial economy and who were repelled by the rising tide of liberal religion and individualism in early nineteenth-century America.

Because Joseph Smith said that he conversed with angels and received direct revelations from the Lord, local authorities threatened to indict him for blasphemy. He and his followers responded by moving to Ohio, then to Missouri. There, proslavery mobs attacked the Mormons, accusing them of inciting slave insurrection. They burned several Mormon settlements and seized Mormon farms and houses. Fifteen thousand Mormons fled Missouri after the governor proclaimed them enemies who "had to be exterminated, or driven from the state."

In 1839 the Mormons resettled along the east bank of the Mississippi River in Nauvoo, Illinois, which soon grew into the second largest city in the state. Both Illinois Whigs and Democrats eagerly sought support among the Mormons. In exchange for their votes the state legislature awarded Nauvoo a special charter that made the town an autonomous city-state, complete with its own 2,000-man militia.

But trouble arose again. In 1844 a dissident group within the church published a newspaper denouncing the practice of polygamy and attacking Joseph Smith for trying to become "king or lawgiver to the church." On Smith's orders, city officials destroyed the dissidents' printing press. Under the protection of the Illinois governor, Smith and his brother were then confined to a jail cell in Carthage. A mob of citizens broke into Smith's cell, shot him and his brother, and threw their bodies out of a second-story window.

Why did the Mormons seem so menacing? Many individualistic Americans felt threatened by the communalism of the Mormon church. By voting as their elders told them to and controlling land as a bloc, the Mormons seemed to have an unfair advantage in the struggle for wealth and power. Mormonism was also denounced as a threat to fundamental social values. Protestant ministers railed against it as a threat to Christianity since Mormons insisted that the *Book of Mormon* was Holy Scripture, equal in importance to the Bible. The Mormons were also accused of corrupt moral values. Before the church changed its rules in 1890, the Mormons practiced polygamy, which they saw as an effort to reestablish the patriarchal Old Testament family. Polygamy also served an important social function by absorbing single or widowed women into Mormon communities. Contrary to popular belief, it was not widely practiced. Altogether, only 10 to 20 percent of Mormon families were polygamous and nearly two-thirds involved a man and two wives.

After the murder of Joseph Smith, the Mormons decided to migrate across a thousand miles of unsettled prairie, plains, and arid desert in search of a new refuge. In 1846 a new leader, Brigham Young, led the Mormons to the Great Salt Lake. As governor of the Mormon state of Deseret and later as governor of Utah, Young oversaw the building of Salt Lake City and 186 other Mormon communities, developed church-owned businesses, and established the first cooperative irrigation projects.

Early nineteenth-century American society attached enormous importance to individualism, secularism, monogamous marriage, and private property, and the Mormons were believed to threaten each of these values. But, in a larger sense, the Mormons' aspirations were truly American. They sought nothing less than the establishment of the Kingdom of God on earth—a dream that was, of course, not new in this country. In seeking to build God's kingdom the Mormons were carrying on a quest that had been begun by their Puritan ancestors two centuries before.

The Mexican War

When Brigham Young led the Mormons west, he was seeking a homeland outside the boundaries of the United States. But even before he arrived at the Great Salt Lake during the summer of 1847, Utah as well as California, Nevada, and parts of Arizona, Colorado, New Mexico, and Wyoming, became part of the United States as a result of the war with Mexico.

Why War?

Fifteen years before the United States was plunged into Civil War, it fought a war against Mexico that added half a million square miles of territory to the United States. Not only was it the first American war fought almost entirely outside the United States, it was also the first American war to be reported, while it happened, by daily newspapers. It was also a controversial war that bitterly divided American public opinion. Finally, it was the war that gave young officers such as Ulysses S. Grant, Robert E. Lee, Thomas ("Stonewall") Jackson, William Tecumseh Sherman, and George McClellan their first experience in a major conflict.

The underlying cause of the Mexican War was the inexorable movement of American pioneers into the Far West. As Americans marched westward, they moved into land claimed by Mexico, and inevitably Mexican and American interests clashed.

The immediate reason for the conflict was the annexation of Texas in 1845. Despite its defeat at San Jacinto in 1836, Mexico refused to recognize Texan independence and warned the United States that annexation would be tantamount to a declaration of war. In early 1845 when Congress voted to annex Texas, Mexico cut diplomatic relations, but took no further action.

The Mexican War was the nation's first war to be reported in newspapers while it happened.

Polk told his commanders to prepare for the possibility of war. He ordered American naval vessels in the Gulf of Mexico to position themselves outside Mexican ports. Secretly, he warned the Pacific fleet to prepare to seize ports along the California coast in the event of war. Anticipating a possible Mexican invasion of Texas, he dispatched American forces in Louisiana to Corpus Christi.

Peaceful settlement of the two countries' differences still seemed possible. In the fall of 1845 the president sent John Slidell as "envoy extraordinary and minister plenipotentiary" to Mexico City with a proposal to resolve the disputes peacefully. The most significant controversies concerned Texas's boundary and the Mexican government's failure to compensate American citizens for losses incurred during Mexico's years of political turmoil. Slidell was authorized to cancel the damage claims and pay $5 million in reparations if the Mexicans agreed to recognize the Rio Grande as the southwestern boundary of Texas (earlier, the Spanish government had defined the Texas boundary as the Nueces River, 130 miles north of the Rio Grande). No Americans lived between the Nueces and the Rio Grande, although many Hispanics lived in the region.

Polk not only wanted to settle the boundary and claims disputes, he also wanted to acquire Mexico's two northwestern provinces, New Mexico and California. He directed Slidell to offer up to $5 million for the province of New Mexico—which included Nevada and Utah and parts of four other states—and up to $25 million for California.

Polk was anxious to acquire California because in mid-October 1845 he had been led to believe that Britain was on the verge of making California a protectorate. It was widely believed that Mexico had agreed to cede California to Britain as payment for outstanding debts. Immediate preventive action seemed necessary. Polk therefore instructed his consul in Monterey to encourage Californians to agitate for annexation by the United States. He also dispatched a young Marine Corps lieutenant, Archibald H. Gillespie, to California, apparently to foment revolt against Mexican authority.

The Mexican government, already incensed over the annexation of Texas, refused to negotiate. The Mexican president, José Herrera, refused to receive Slidell and ordered his leading commander, General Mariano Paredes y Arrillaga, to assemble an army and reconquer Texas. Paredes proceeded to topple Herrera's government and declared himself president. But he also refused to receive Slidell.

The failure of Slidell's mission led Polk to order Brigadier General Zachary Taylor to march 3,000 troops from Corpus Christi, Texas, to "defend the Rio Grande." Late in March of 1846 Taylor and his men set up camp along the Rio Grande, directly across from the Mexican city of Matamoros, on a stretch of land claimed by both Mexico and the United States.

On April 25 a Mexican cavalry force crossed the Rio Grande and clashed with a small American squadron, forcing the Americans to surrender after the loss of several lives. Polk used this episode as an excuse to declare war. "Hostilities may be considered to have commenced," Taylor wrote to President Polk.

Hours before he received word of the skirmish on May 9, Polk and his cabinet had already decided to press for war with Mexico. On May 11 Polk asked Congress to acknowledge that a state of war already existed. "Mexico," the president announced, "has passed the boundary of the United States, has invaded our territory and shed American blood upon the American soil." Congress responded with a declaration of war.

The Mexican War was extremely controversial. Its supporters blamed Mexico for the hostilities because it had severed relations with the United States, threatened war, refused to receive an American emissary, or to pay the damage claims of American citizens. Opposition leaders denounced the war as an immoral land grab by an expansionistic power against a weak neighbor that had been independent barely two decades. The war's critics claimed that Polk deliberately provoked Mexico into war by ordering American troops into disputed territory. A Delaware senator declared that ordering Taylor to the Rio Grande was "as much an act of aggression on our part as is a man's pointing a pistol at another's breast."

Critics argued that the war was an expansionist power play dictated by an aggressive southern slaveocracy intent on acquiring more land for cotton cultivation and more slave states to better balance the northern free states in the U.S. Senate. "Bigger pens to cram with slaves," was the way poet James Russell Lowell put it. Others blamed the war on expansion-minded Westerners who were hungry for land, and on eastern trading interests, which dreamed of establishing "an American Boston or New York" in San Francisco to increase trade with Asia. Mexicans denounced the war as a brazen attempt by the United States to seize Mexican territory.

The War

American strategy was based on a three-pronged attack. Colonel Stephen Kearny had the task of securing New Mexico, while naval forces under Commodore John D. Sloat blockaded the California coast and General Zachary Taylor invaded Mexico.

Kearny easily accomplished his mission. In less than two months he marched his 1,700-man army more than a thousand miles. On August 18, 1846, he occupied Santa Fe and declared New Mexico's 80,000 inhabitants American citizens. In California, American settlers in the Sacramento Valley, fearful that Mexican authorities were about to expel them, revolted even before reliable reports of the outbreak of war reached the area. The so-called Bear Flag Rebellion soon came to an end, and by January 1847 U.S. naval forces under Commodore Robert F. Stockton and an expeditionary force under Captain John C. Frémont had brought the region under American control. Meanwhile, the main U.S. army under Taylor's command had taken Matamoros, and by late September captured Monterrey, Mexico's largest northern city.

Although the American invasion of Mexico's northernmost provinces was completely successful, the Mexican government did not surrender. In June 1846 Colonel A. W. Doniphan led 856 Missouri cavalry volunteers 3,000 miles across mountains and desert into the northern Mexican province of Chihuahua. He occupied El Paso and then captured the capital city of Chihuahua. Further south, 6,000 volunteers under the command of Zachary Taylor held their ground against a Mexican force of 15,000 at the battle of Buena Vista on February 22 and 23, 1847.

Despite an impressive string of American victories, Mexico still refused to negotiate. Switching strategy, Polk ordered General Winfield Scott to invade central Mexico from the sea, march inland, and capture Mexico City. On March 9, 1847, the Mexicans allowed an American force of 10,000 men to land unopposed at Veracruz on the Gulf of Mexico. Scott's army then began to march on the Mexican capital. On April 18, at a mountain pass near Jalapa, a 9,000-man American force met 13,000 Mexican troops and in bitter hand-to-hand fighting, forced the Mexicans to flee. As Scott's army pushed on toward Mexico City, it stormed a Mexican fortress at Contreras and then routed a large Mexican force at Churubusco on August 19 and 20. For two weeks, from August 22 to September 7, Scott observed an armistice to allow the Mexicans to consider peace proposals. When the negotiations failed, Scott's 6,000 remaining men attacked El Molino del Rey and stormed Chapultepec, a fortified castle guarding Mexico City's gates.

Despite the capture of their capital, the Mexicans refused to surrender. Hostile crowds staged demonstrations in the streets, and snipers fired shots and hurled stones and broken bottles from the tops of flat-roofed Mexican houses. To quell the protests, General Scott ordered the streets "swept with grape and cannister" and artillery "turned upon the houses whence the fire proceeded." Outside the capital, belligerent civilians attacked army supply wagons, and guerrilla fighters harassed American troops.

War Fever and Antiwar Protests

During the first few weeks following the declaration of war a frenzy of pro-war hysteria swept the country. Two hundred thousand men responded

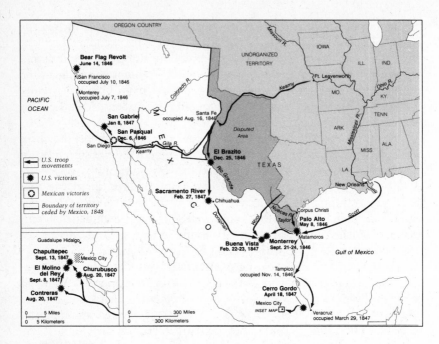

Mexican War

The Mexican War would increase the nation's size by one-third.

to a call for 50,000 volunteers. Novelist Herman Melville observed, "a military ardor pervades all ranks. . . . Nothing is talked about but the halls of the Montezumas." In New York placards bore the slogan "Mexico or Death." Many newspapers, especially in the North, declared that the war would benefit the Mexican people by bringing them the blessings of democracy and liberty. The *Boston Times* said that an American victory "must necessarily be a great blessing" because it would introduce "the reign of law where license has existed for a generation."

In Philadelphia 20,000 turned out for a pro-war rally, and in Cincinnati 12,000 celebrated Zachary Taylor's victories with cannon salutes, parades, and speeches. In Tennessee 30,000 men volunteered for 3,000 positions as soldiers, prompting one applicant to complain that it was "difficult even to purchase a place in the ranks." The war was particularly popular in the West. Of the 69,540 men who were accepted for service, more than 40,000 were from the western states.

But from the war's very beginning, a small but highly visible group of intellectuals, clergymen, pacifists, abolitionists, and Whig and Democratic politicians denounced the war as brutal aggression against a "poor, feeble, distracted country." Abolitionist William Lloyd Garrison's militant newspaper, the *Liberator,* expressed open support for the Mexican people: "Every lover of Freedom and humanity throughout the world must wish them the most triumphant success."

Most Whigs supported the war—in part because two of the leading American generals, Zachary Taylor and Winfield Scott, were Whigs, and in part because they remembered that opposition to the War of 1812 had destroyed the Federalist party. But many prominent Whigs, from the South as well as the North, openly expressed opposition. Thomas Corwin of Ohio denounced the war as merely the latest example of American injustice to Mexico. Daniel Webster, a frequent Whig presidential candidate, mockingly described the conflict as a "war of pretexts"—the pretext that Mexico had refused to receive an American emissary, had refused to pay Americans financial claims, and had invaded American territory.

A freshman Whig congressman from Illinois named Abraham Lincoln lashed out against the war, calling it immoral, proslavery, and a threat to the nation's republican values. One of Lincoln's constituents branded him "the Benedict Arnold of our district," and he was denied renomination by his own party.

As newspapers informed their readers about the hardships and savagery of life on the front, public enthusiasm for the war began to wane. The war did not turn out to be the romantic exploit that Americans envisioned. Troops complained that their food was "green with slime;" their meat, they said, would stick "if thrown against a smooth plank." Diarrhea, amoebic dysentery, measles, and yellow fever ravaged American soldiers. Seven times as many Americans died of disease and exposure as died of battlefield injuries. Of the 90,000 Americans who served in the war, only 1,721 died in action. Another 11,155 died from disease and exposure to the elements.

Public support for the war was further eroded by reports of brutality against Mexican civilians. After one of their members was murdered, the Arkansas volunteer cavalry surrounded a group of Mexican peasants and began an "indiscriminate and bloody massacre of the poor creatures." A young lieutenant named George G. Meade reported that volunteers in Matamoros robbed the citizens, stole their cattle, and killed innocent civilians "for no other object than their own amusement." If only a tenth of the horror stories were true, General Winfield Scott wrote, it was enough "to make Heaven weep, & every American of Christian morals blush for his country."

During wartime the party in power has often lost support. The Mexican War was no exception. In the congressional election of 1846, which took place half a year after the outbreak of war, the Democrats lost control of the House of Representatives to the Whigs.

Peace

Difficult negotiations followed the war. After American troops entered the Mexican capital, Santa Anna, the Mexican president, resigned and the Mexican Congress retreated to a provincial capital to try to reorganize. Not until mid-November 1847 was a new civilian government able to gain control over the country and name a peace negotiator.

As Americans waited impatiently for a final peace settlement, they grew increasingly divided over their war aims. Ultra-expansionists, who drew support from such cities as Baltimore, New York, and Philadelphia as well as from the West, wanted the United States to annex all of Mexico. Many Southerners, led by John C. Calhoun, called for a withdrawal to the Rio Grande. They opposed annexation of any territory below the Rio Grande because they did not want to extend American citizenship to Mexicans. Most Democratic party leaders, however, wanted to annex at least the one-third of Mexico south and west of the Rio Grande.

Then suddenly on February 22, 1848, word reached Washington that a peace treaty had been signed. On February 2, 1848, Nicholas Trist, a Spanish-speaking State Department official, signed the Treaty of Guadalupe Hidalgo, ending the Mexican War. Trist had actually been ordered home two months earlier by Polk, but he had continued negotiating anyway, fearing that his recall would be "deadly to the cause of peace."

According to the treaty, Mexico ceded to the United States only those areas that Polk had originally sought to purchase. Mexico ceded California, Nevada, Utah, New Mexico, and parts of Arizona, Colorado, Kansas, and Wyoming to the United States for $15 million and the assumption of $3.25 million in debts owed to Americans by Mexico. The treaty also settled the Texas border dispute in favor of the United States, placing the Texas-Mexico boundary at the Rio Grande.

Ultra-expansionists called on Polk to throw out the treaty, but a war-weary public wanted peace. Polk quickly submitted the treaty to the Senate, which ratified it overwhelmingly. The war was over.

The War's Significance

The story of America's conflict with Mexico tends to be overshadowed by the story of the Civil War, which began only a decade and a half later. In fact, the conflict had far-reaching consequences for the nation's future. It increased the nation's size by a third, but it also created deep political divisions that threatened the country's future.

The most significant result of the Mexican War was to reignite the question of slavery in the western territories—the very question that had divided the country in 1819. Even before the war had begun, philosopher

Ralph Waldo Emerson had predicted that the United States would "conquer Mexico, but it will be as the man who swallows the arsenic which will bring him down in turn. Mexico will poison us." The war convinced a growing number of Northerners that southern slave owners had precipitated the war in order to open new lands to slavery and acquire new slave states. And most significant of all, the war weakened the party system and made it increasingly difficult for congressional leaders to prevent the issue of slavery from dominating congressional activity.

Political Crisis of the 1840s

Prior to the Mexican War, the major political issues that divided Americans were questions of tariffs, banking, internal improvements, and land. Political positions on these issues largely divided along party lines. After the outbreak of war with Mexico a new issue began to dominate American politics—the extension of slavery in the western territories. Public opinion began to polarize and party cohesion began to break down as party factional and sectional divisions grew more important than traditional party coalitions.

The question of slavery burst into the public spotlight one summer evening in 1846. Congressman David Wilmot, a Pennsylvania Democrat, introduced an amendment, known as the Wilmot Proviso, to a war appropriations bill. The proviso forbade slavery in any territory acquired from Mexico. Throughout the North, thousands of workingmen, mechanics, and farmers feared that free workers would be unable to compete successfully against slave labor. "If slavery is not excluded by law," said one northern congressman, "the presence of the slave will exclude the laboring white man."

Southerners denounced the Wilmot Proviso as "treason to the Constitution." Polk tried to quiet the debate between "Southern agitators and Northern fanatics" by assuring moderate Northerners that slavery could never take root in the arid southwest, but his efforts were to no avail. With the strong support of westerners, the amendment passed the House twice, but was defeated in the Senate. Although the Wilmot Proviso did not become law, the issue it raised—the extension of slavery into the western territories—continued to contribute to the growth of political factionalism.

Meanwhile, at the very moment that Congress was debating the Wilmot Proviso, another sectional dispute flared up over the tariff. In 1846 President Polk persuaded Congress to enact the Walker Tariff, a low tariff that delighted Southerners, but infuriated Northerners who favored tariff protection for industry.

Growing sectional tensions were also evident in the founding of the Free Soil party in 1848. This sectional party opposed the westward expansion of slavery and favored free land for western homesteaders. Much more popular than the Liberty party, an earlier antislavery political party, the Free Soil party drew support from dissident New England Whigs (known as "conscience" Whigs because of their opposition to slavery), antislavery New York Democrats, and former members of the Liberty party. Under the slogan "free soil, free speech, free labor, and free men," the party nominated Martin Van Buren as its presidential nominee in 1848 and polled 291,000 votes. This was enough to split the Democratic vote and throw the election to Whig candidate Zachary Taylor.

Up until the last month of 1848, the debate over slavery in the Mexican cession seemed academic. Most Americans thought of the newly acquired territory as a wasteland filled with "broken mountains and dreary desert." Then, in his farewell address, Polk electrified Congress with the news that gold had been discovered in California—and suddenly the question of slavery was inescapably important.

The Gold Rush

On January 24, 1848, less than ten days before the signing of the peace treaty ending the Mexican War, James W. Marshall, a 36-year-old carpenter and handyman, noticed several bright bits of yellow mineral near a sawmill in California's Sacramento Valley that he was building for John A. Sutter, a Swiss-born rancher. The yellow mineral was gold.

On March 15 a San Francisco newspaper, the *Californian,* printed the first account of Marshall's discovery. Within two weeks the paper had lost its staff and was forced to shut down its printing press. In its last edition it told its readers: "The whole country, from San Francisco to Los Angeles . . . resounds with the sordid cry of Gold! Gold! Gold! while the field is left half-planted, the house half-built, and everything neglected but the manufacture of picks and shovels."

In 1849 80,000 men arrived in California—half by land and half by ship around Cape Horn or across the Isthmus of Panama. Only half were Americans; the rest came from Europe, Latin America, and China. Soldiers deserted; sailors jumped ship; husbands left wives; apprentices ran away from their masters; farmers and businesspeople deserted their livelihoods. Within a year California's population had swollen from 14,000 to 100,000.

The gold rush transformed California from a sleepy society into one that was wild, unruly, ethnically diverse, and violent. In San Francisco alone there were more than 500 bars and 1,000 gambling dens. There were a thousand murders in San Francisco during the early 1850s, but only one conviction. "Forty-niners" slaughtered Indians for sport, drove Mexicans from the mines on penalty of death, and sought to restrict the immigration of foreigners, especially the Chinese. Since the military government was incapable of keeping order, leading merchants formed vigilance committees, which attempted to rule by lynch law and the establishment of "popular" courts.

The gold rush era in California lasted less than a decade. By the mid-1850s the lone miner who prospected for gold with a pick, a shovel, and a washpan was already an anachronism. Mining companies using heavy machinery replaced the individual prospector. Systems of dams exposed whole river bottoms. Drilling machines drove shafts 700 feet into the earth. Hydraulic mining machines blasted streams of water against mountainsides. The romantic era of California gold mining had come to a close.

*C*hronology of Key Events

1803	Louisiana Purchase
1804	Lewis and Clark Expedition
1810	Mexican War for Independence begins; John Jacob Astor attempts to plant a trading post in Oregon
1811–1812	Fur trappers mark out the Oregon Trail
1818	United States and Britain agree to joint occupation of Oregon
1821	Mexico gains independence from Spain; first American traders traverse the Santa Fe Trail; Stephen Austin founds American colony in Texas
1830	Joseph Smith, Jr., founds Church of Jesus Christ of Latter-Day Saints
1835–36	Texas Revolution
1838	John Quincy Adams's filibuster defeats move to annex Texas
1841	First party of pioneers leaves Missouri for California
1844	Joseph Smith, Jr., assassinated at Carthage, Illinois
1845	Texas admitted as twenty-eighth state
1846	The United States declares war on Mexico; Britain and the United States divide Oregon along 49th parallel; Donner party becomes trapped in Sierra Nevada; Brigham Young leads the Mormons to the Great Salt Lake Valley
1848	Gold discovered in California; Treaty of Guadalupe Hidalgo
1849	Gold Rush begins

Conclusion

By 1860 the gold rush was over. Prospectors had found more than $350 million worth of gold. Certainly, some fortunes were made, but few struck it rich. Even James W. Marshall, who discovered the first gold bits, and John A. Sutter, on whose ranch gold was discovered, died penniless.

By 1850 the American flag flew over an area that stretched from sea to sea. In the span of just five years, the United States had increased in size by a third and acquired an area that now includes the states of Arizona, California, Colorado, Idaho, Nevada, New Mexico, Oregon, Texas, Utah, Washington, and Wyoming.

The exploration and settlement of the Far West is one of the great epics of nineteenth-century history. But America's dramatic territorial expansion also created severe problems. In addition to providing the United States with its richest mines, greatest forests, and most fertile farm land, the Far West intensified the sectional conflict between the North and South and raised the fateful and ultimately divisive question of whether slavery would be permitted in the western territories. Could democratic political institutions resolve the question of slavery in the western territories? That question would dominate American politics in the 1850s.

Suggestions for Further Reading

For general overviews of the period, see Ray A. Billington, *Westward Expansion,* 5th ed. (1982); and Richard White, *"Its Your Misfortune and None of My Own"* (1991). Valuable studies focusing on various aspects of Manifest Destiny are Norman A. Graebner, *Empire on the Pacific* (1955); Thomas R. Hietala, *Manifest Design: Anxious Aggrandizement in Late Jacksonian America* (1985); Reginald Horsman, *Race and Manifest Destiny* (1981); Robert Johannsen, *To the Halls of the Montezumas* (1985); Albert K. Weinberg, *Manifest Destiny* (1935). Biographies of James K. Polk include Paul H. Bergeron, *The Presidency of James K. Polk* (1987); and Charles Sellers, *James K. Polk: Continentalist* (1966).

For studies of the settlement of the trans-Mississippi west during the antebellum period consult William Cronon, *Nature's Metropolis: Chicago and the Great West* (1991); Sandra L. Myres, *Westering Women and the Frontier Experience* (1982); John Unruh, *The Plains Across* (1979). On the borderlands see David J. Weber, *The Mexican Frontier* (1982). For studies on Texas, see Sam W. Haynes, *Soldiers of Misfortune* (1990); Paul D. Lack, *The Texas Revolutionary Experience* (1992).

Chapter *14*

The House Divided

Early in 1864 a New York economist named John Smith Dye published a book entitled *The Adder's Den or Secrets of the Great Conspiracy to Overthrow Liberty in America*. In his volume Dye set out to prove that for more than 30 years a ruthless Southern "slave power" had engaged in a deliberate, systematic plan to subvert civil liberties, undermine the Constitution, and extend slavery into the western territories.

In Dye's eyes, the entire history of the United States was the record of repeated Southern plots to expand slavery. An arrogant "slave power," he maintained, had entrenched slavery in the Constitution, caused financial panics to sabotage the Northern economy, dispossessed Indians from their native lands, and fomented revolution in Texas and war with Mexico in order to expand the South's slave empire. Most important of all, he insisted, the Southern slaveocracy had secretly assassinated two presidents by poison and unsuccessfully attempted to murder three others.

According to Dye, this campaign of assassination began in 1835 when John C. Calhoun, outraged by Andrew Jackson's opposition to states' rights, encouraged a deranged man named Richard Lawrence to kill Jackson. This plot failed when Lawrence's pistols misfired. Six years later, Dye argued, a successful attempt was made on William Henry Harrison's life. After he refused to cooperate in a Southern scheme to annex Texas, Harrison died of symptoms resembling arsenic poisoning. This left John Tyler, a strong defender of slavery, in the White House.

The next president to die at the hands of the slave power, according to Dye, was Zachary Taylor, who had opposed the extension of slavery into California. Just 16 months after taking office Taylor was stricken by acute gastroenteritis, caused, claimed Dye, by arsenic poisoning. He was succeeded by Vice President Millard Fillmore, who was more sympathetic to the Southern cause. Just three years later, Dye maintained, another attempt was made on a president's life. The slave power considered Franklin Pierce, a New Hampshire Democrat, unreliable. On the way to his inauguration Pierce's railroad car derailed and rolled down an embankment. The president and his wife escaped injury, but their 12-year-old son was killed. In the future, Pierce toed the Southern line.

In 1857, Dye claimed, yet another attempt was made to kill a president. James Buchanan, a Pennsylvania Democrat, had won his party's nomination in the face of fierce Southern opposition, and, in Dye's view, the slaveocracy wanted to remind Buchanan who was in charge. At a Washington banquet shortly before Buchanan's inauguration, Southern agents sprinkled arsenic on the lump sugar used by Northerners to sweeten their tea. Because Southerners drank coffee and used granulated sugar, no Southerners were injured. But, according to Dye, 60 Northerners were poisoned, including the president, and 38 died. Frightened by this near bout with death, Buchanan proved to be a reliable tool of the slave power.

No credible evidence supports any of Dye's sensational allegations. Yet even if his charges were without foundation, Dye was not alone in interpreting events in conspiratorial terms. His book *The Adder's Den* was only one of the most extreme examples of conspiratorial charges that had been made by abolitionists since the late 1830s. By the 1850s a growing number of Northerners had come to believe that an aggressive Southern slave power had seized control of the federal government and threatened to subvert republican ideals. At the same time, an increasing number of Southerners had begun to believe that antislavery radicals dominated Northern politics and would "rejoice" in the race war and racial amalgamation that would surely follow emancipation.

During the 1850s the American political system was incapable of containing the sectional disputes that had smoldered for more than half a century. One major political party—the Whigs—collapsed. Another—the Democrats—split into Northern and Southern factions. With the breakdown of the party system the issues raised by slavery exploded. The bonds that had bound the country for more than seven decades began to unravel.

The Crisis of 1850

In 1849 an expedition of Texas slave owners and their slaves arrived in the California gold fields. As curious prospectors looked on, the Texans staked out claims and put their slaves to work panning for gold. White miners, who considered it unfair that they should have to compete with slave labor, were outraged. They held a mass meeting and resolved "that no slave or Negro should own claims or even work in the mines." They ordered the Texans out of the gold fields within 24 hours.

Three days later the white miners elected a delegate to a convention that had been called to frame a state constitution and to apply for admission to the Union. At the convention, the miners' delegate proposed that "neither slavery nor involuntary servitude" should ever "be tolerated" in California. The convention adopted his proposal unanimously.

California's application for admission to the Union as a free state in 1849 raised the question that would dominate American politics during the 1850s: Would slavery be allowed to expand into the West or would the West remain free soil? It was the issue of slave expansion—and not the morality of slavery—that would make antislavery a respectable political position in the North, polarize public opinion, and initiate the chain of events that would lead the United States to civil war.

California's application for statehood made slavery's expansion an unavoidable political issue. Southerners feared that California's admission as a free state would upset the sectional balance of power. The free states already held a commanding majority in the House of Representatives because they had a much greater population than did the slave states. Therefore the political power of proslavery Southerners depended on maintaining a balance of power in the Senate. Since the Missouri Compromise, Congress had paired the admission of a free state and a slave state. If California was admitted as a free state, there would be 16 free states and only 15 slave states. The sectional balance of power in the Senate would be disrupted, and the South feared that it would lose its ability to influence political events.

The instability of the Democratic and Whig parties, and the growing political power of Northern opponents of slave expansion, further dimmed chances of a peaceful compromise. When the Thirty-first Congress convened in December 1849, neither the Democrats nor the Whigs had a stable majority. Southern Whigs were deserting their party in droves, and Northern and Southern Democrats were badly split.

In the North and Midwest opponents of the westward expansion of slavery made striking gains, particularly within the Democratic party. Coalitions of Democrats and Free Soilers elected congressmen determined to prevent Southern expansion. Every Northern state legislature except Iowa's asserted that Congress had the power and duty to exclude slavery from the territories.

Southern hotspurs talked openly of secession. Senator Robert Toombs of Georgia declared that if the North deprived the South of the right to take slaves into California and New Mexico, "I am for disunion." Such bold talk inched the South closer to secession.

The South's Dilemma

Why were the South's political leaders so worried about whether slavery would be permitted in the West when geography and climate made it unlikely that slavery would ever prosper in the area? The answer lies in the South's growing awareness of its minority status in the Union, of the elimination of slavery in many other areas of the Western Hemisphere, and of the decline of slavery in the upper South. For more and more Southerners, the region's future depended on whether the West was opened or closed to slavery.

By 1850 New World slavery was confined to Brazil, Cuba, Puerto Rico, a small number of Dutch colonies, and the American South. British slave emancipation in the Caribbean in 1833 had been followed by an intensified campaign to eradicate the international slave trade. In areas like

Brazil and Cuba, slavery could not long survive once the slave trade was cut off because the slave populations of these countries had a skewed sex ratio and were unable to naturally reproduce their numbers. Only in the American South could slavery survive without the Atlantic slave trade.

Exacerbating Southern fears about slavery's future was a sharp decline in slavery in the upper South. The South's leaders feared that in the future the upper South would soon become a region of free labor. By midcentury, the South's slave owners faced a further dilemma. Within the region itself, slave ownership was increasingly concentrated in fewer and fewer hands. The desire to ensure the support for slavery among poorer whites led some Southerners to agitate for reopening the African slave trade, believing that nonslaveholding Southerners would only support the institution if they had a chance to own slaves themselves. But most Southern leaders believed the best way to perpetuate slavery was through westward expansion, and they wanted concrete assurance that Congress would not infringe on the right to take slaves into the western territories. Without such a guarantee, declared an Alabama politician, "THIS UNION CANNOT STAND."

Slave Concentration, 1860/The Cotton Kingdom

As shown here, northern African Americans were providing escape routes for slaves along the Underground Railroad. Slave-owning Southerners feared that the end of slavery would reduce their economic and political status in the Union.

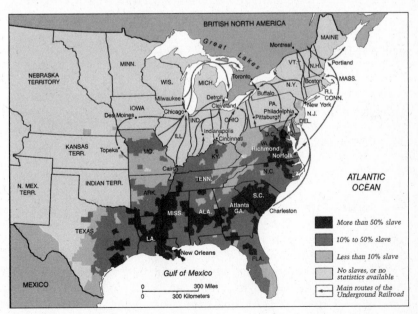

The Compromise of 1850: The Illusion of Sectional Peace

Ever since David Wilmot had proposed in 1846 that slavery be prohibited from any territory acquired from Mexico, opponents of slavery had argued that Congress possessed the power to regulate slavery in all of the territories. Ardent proslavery Southerners vigorously disagreed. Politicians had repeatedly but unsuccessfully tried to work out a compromise. One simple proposal had been to extend the Missouri Compromise line to the Pacific Ocean, excluding slavery north of 36° 30' latitude but permitting it south of that line. This proposal attracted the support of moderate Southerners but generated little support outside the region. Another proposal, supported by two key Democratic senators, Lewis Cass of Michigan and Stephen Douglas of Illinois, was known as "squatter sovereignty" or "popular sovereignty." It declared that the people actually living in a territory should decide whether or not to allow slavery.

Henry Clay, the aging statesman known as the "Great Compromiser" for his efforts on behalf of the Missouri Compromise and the Compromise Tariff of 1832 (which resolved the nullification crisis), once again appealed to Northerners and Southerners to place national patriotism ahead of sectional loyalties. He believed that compromise could only be effective if it addressed all the issues dividing the two regions. He proposed that California be admitted as a free state; that territorial governments be established in New Mexico and Utah without any restrictions on slavery; that Texas relinquish its claim to land in New Mexico in exchange for federal assumption of Texas's unpaid debts; that Congress enact a stringent and enforceable fugitive slave law; and that the slave trade—but not slavery—be abolished in the District of Columbia.

Clay's proposal ignited an eight-month debate in Congress and led John C. Calhoun to threaten Southern secession. On March 4, 1850, Calhoun offered his response to Clay's compromise proposal. Calhoun was dying of tuberculosis and was too ill to speak publicly, so his speech was read by a colleague. He warned the North that the only way to save the Union was to "cease the agitation of the slave question," concede "to the South an equal right" to the western territories, return runaway slaves, and accept a constitutional amendment that would protect the South against Northern violations of its rights. In the absence of such concessions, Calhoun argued, the South's only option was to secede.

Three days later Daniel Webster, the North's most spellbinding orator, abandoned his previous opposition to the expansion of slavery into the western territories and threw his support behind Clay's compromise. The 68-year-old Massachusetts Whig called on both sides to resolve their differences in the name of patriotism. The North, he insisted, could afford to be generous because climate and geography ensured that slavery would never be profitable in the western territories. He concluded by warning his listeners that "there can be no such thing as a peaceable secession." Webster's speech provoked a storm of outrage from Northern opponents of compromise, but it did have one important effect. It reassured moderate Southerners that powerful interests in the North were committed to compromise.

Still, opposition to compromise was fierce. Whig President Zachary Taylor argued that California, New Mexico, Oregon, Utah, and Minnesota should all be admitted to statehood before the question of slavery was addressed—a proposal that would have given the North a ten-vote majority in the Senate. William H. Seward, the New York senator, speaking for the opponents of slave expansion, denounced the compromise as conceding too much to the South and proclaimed that there was a "higher law" than the Constitution, a law that demanded an end to slavery. At the same time, many Southern extremists bristled at the idea of admitting California as a free state. In July, Northern and Southern senators opposed to the very idea of compromise joined ranks to defeat a bill that would have admitted California to the Union and organized New Mexico and Utah without reference to slavery.

Compromise appeared to be dead. A bitterly disappointed Henry Clay left Washington, his efforts apparently for nought. Then with unexpected suddenness the outlook abruptly changed. On the evening of July 9, 1850, President Taylor died of gastroenteritis. Taylor's successor was Millard Fillmore, a 50-year-old New Yorker, who was an ardent supporter of compromise.

In Congress leadership in the fight for a compromise passed to Stephen Douglas, a Democratic senator from Illinois. An arrogant and dynamic leader, 5 foot 4 inches in height, with a massive head, bushy eyebrows, and a booming voice, Douglas was known as the "Little Giant." Douglas abandoned Clay's strategy of gathering all issues dividing the sections into a single "omnibus" bill. Instead, he introduced Clay's proposals one at a time. In this way, he was able to gather support from varying coalitions of Whigs and Democrats and Northerners and Southerners on each issue.

As finally approved, the compromise admitted California as a free state, allowed the territorial legislatures of New Mexico and Utah to settle the question of slavery in those areas, provided for the return of runaway slaves, abolished the slave trade in the District of Columbia, and gave Texas $10 million to abandon its claims to territory in New Mexico east of the Rio Grande.

The Fugitive Slave Law

The most divisive element in the Compromise of 1850 was the Fugitive Slave Law, which permitted any black to be sent south solely on the affidavit of anyone claiming to be his or her owner. As a result, free blacks were in danger of being placed in slavery. The law also stripped runaway slaves of such basic legal rights as the right to a jury trial and the right to testify in one's own defense. The law further stipulated that accused runaways stand trial in front of special commissioners, not a judge or a jury, and that the commissioners be paid $10 if a fugitive was returned to slavery but only $5 if the fugitive was freed—a provision that many Northerners regarded as a bribe to ensure that any black accused of being a runaway would be found guilty. And finally, the law required all U.S. citizens and U.S. marshals to assist in the capture of escapees. Anyone who refused to aid in the capture of a fugitive, interfered with the arrest of a slave, or tried to free a slave already in custody was subject to a heavy fine and imprisonment.

The Fugitive Slave Law kindled widespread outrage in the North and converted thousands of Northerners to the free soil doctrine that slavery should be barred from the western territories. "We went to bed one night old-fashioned, conservative, compromise, Union Whigs," wrote a Massachusetts factory owner, "and waked up stark mad Abolitionists." Efforts to enforce the law resulted in abuses that repelled many Northern moderates. Riots directed against the law broke out in many cities. In Boston federal marshals and 22 companies of state troops were needed to prevent a crowd from storming a courthouse to free a fugitive named Anthony Burns.

Eight Northern states attempted to invalidate the law by enacting "personal liberty" laws that forbade state officials from assisting in the return of runaways and extended the right of jury trial to fugitives. Southerners regarded these attempts to obstruct the return of runaways as a violation of the Constitution and federal law.

The free black communities of the North responded defiantly to the 1850 law. Northern blacks provided about 1,500 fugitive slaves with sanctuary along the Underground Railroad to freedom. Others established vigilance committees to protect blacks from hired kidnappers who were searching the North for runaways. And 15,000 free blacks, convinced that they could never achieve equality in America, emigrated to Canada, the Caribbean, and Africa after the adoption of the federal law.

One Northern moderate who was repelled by the fugitive slave law was Harriet Beecher Stowe. In 1852 she published *Uncle Tom's Cabin,* the single most powerful attack on slavery ever written. Stowe had learned about slavery while living in Cincinnati, Ohio, across from slaveholding Kentucky. Her book awakened millions of Northerners to the moral evil of slavery. Southerners denounced Stowe as a "wretch in petticoats," but in the North the book sold a million copies in 16 months. No novel has ever exerted a stronger influence on American public opinion. Legend has it that when President Lincoln met Mrs. Stowe during the Civil War, he said, "So this is the little woman who made this big war."

Disintegration of the Party System

As late as 1850 the two-party system was, to all outward appearances, still healthy. Every state, except for South Carolina, had two effective political parties. Both the Democratic party and the Whigs were able to attract support in every section and in every state in the country. Voter participation was extremely high, and in presidential elections neither party was able to gain more than 53 percent of the popular vote. Then, in the space of just five years, the two-party system began to disintegrate in response to two issues: massive foreign immigration and the reemergence of the issue of the expansion of slavery.

The Know-Nothings

The most momentous shift in party sentiment in American history took place in the early 1850s following the rise of a party vigorously opposed to immigrants and Catholics. This party, which was known as the American party or Know-Nothing party, crippled the Whig party, weakened the Democratic party, and made the political system incapable of resolving the growing crisis over slavery.

Hostility toward immigrants and Catholics had deep roots in American culture. The Protestant religious revivals of the 1820s and 1830s stimulated a "No Popery" movement. Prominent Northern clergymen accused the Catholic Church of conspiring to overthrow democracy and subject the United States to Catholic despotism. Popular fiction offered graphic descriptions of priests seducing women during confession and nuns cutting unborn infants from their mothers' wombs and throwing them to dogs. Anti-Catholic sentiment culminated in mob rioting and in the burning of churches and convents. In 1834, for example, a Philadelphia mob rampaged through Irish neighborhoods, burning churches and houses.

A massive wave of immigration from Ireland and Germany after 1845 led to a renewed outburst of antiforeign and anti-Catholic sentiment. Between 1846 and 1855, more than three million foreigners arrived in America. In cities such as Chicago, Milwaukee, New York, and St. Louis immigrants actually outnumbered native-born citizens. Nativists—ardent opponents of immigration—capitalized on deep-seated Protestant antagonism toward Catholics, working-class fear of economic competition from cheaper immigrant labor, and resentment among native-born Americans of the growing political power of foreigners. Nativists charged that Catholics were responsible for a sharp increase in poverty, crime, and drunkenness and were subservient to a foreign leader, the pope.

To native-born Protestant workers, the new immigrants posed a tangible economic threat. Economic slumps in 1851 and 1854 resulted in severe unemployment and wage cuts. Native workers blamed Irish and German immigrants for their plight. The immigrants also posed a political threat. Concentrated in the large cities of the eastern seaboard, Irish and German immigrants voted as blocs and quickly built up strong political organizations.

One example of anti-Catholic hostility was the formation of a secret fraternal society made up of native-born Protestant workingmen. Called "The Order of the Star Spangled Banner," it soon formed the nucleus of a new political party known as the Know-Nothing or the American party. The party received its name from the fact that when members were asked about the workings of the party, they were supposed to reply, "I know nothing."

By 1855 the Know-Nothings had captured control of the legislatures in New England except in Vermont and Maine and were the dominant opposition party to the Democrats in New York, Pennsylvania, Maryland, Virginia, Tennessee, Georgia, Alabama, Mississippi, and Louisiana. In the presidential election of 1856 the party supported Millard Fillmore and won more than 21 percent of the popular vote and 8 electoral votes. In Congress the party had 5 senators and 43 representatives. Between 1853 and 1855 the Know-Nothings replaced the Whigs as the nation's second largest party.

By 1856, however, the Know-Nothing party was already in decline. Many Know-Nothing officeholders were relatively unknown men with little political experience. In the states where they gained control, the Know-Nothings proved unable to enact their legislative program, which included a 21-year residency period before immigrants could become citizens and vote, a limitation on political officeholding to native-born Americans, and restrictions on the sale of liquor.

After 1855 the Know-Nothing party was supplanted in the North by a new and explosive sectional party, the Republicans. By 1856 Northern workers felt more threatened by the Southern slave power than by the pope and Catholic immigrants. At the same time, fewer and fewer Southerners were willing to support a party that ignored the question of the expansion of slavery. As a result, the Know-Nothing party rapidly dissolved.

Nevertheless, the Know-Nothings left an indelible mark on American politics. The Know-Nothing movement eroded loyalty to the national political parties, helped destroy the Whig party, and undermined the capacity of the political system to contain the divisive issue of slavery.

Young America

For nearly four years following the Compromise of 1850, agitation over the question of the expansion of slavery abated. Most Americans were weary of the continuing controversy and turned their attention away from politics to focus instead on railroads, cotton, and trade. The early 1850s were dominated by dreams of greater American influence abroad—in areas such as Asia, the Caribbean, and Central America. Majestic clipper ships raced from New York to China in as few as 104 days. Steamship and railroad promoters launched ambitious schemes to build transit routes across Central America to link California and the Atlantic Coast. In 1853 Commodore Matthew Perry sailed into Tokyo Bay with two steam frigates and two sailing ships, thereby ending Japan's era of isolation from the Western world. The whole world appeared to be opening up to American influence.

Franklin Pierce, a New Hampshire Democrat elected as the nation's fourteenth president in 1852, tried to unite the country with an aggressive program of foreign expansion called "Young America." He sought to annex Hawaii, expand American influence in Honduras and Nicaragua, and acquire new territory from Mexico and Spain. He announced that his administration would not be deterred "by any timid forebodings of evil" raised by the slavery question. But each effort to expand the country's boundaries only provoked new sectional disputes because any acquisition would have posed the question of its status with regard to slavery.

Pierce was the first "doughface" president. He was, in the popular phrase, "a Northern man with Southern principles." Many Northerners suspected that Pierce's real goal was the acquisition of new territory for slavery. This suspicion was first raised in 1853, when the president instructed James Gadsden, his minister to Mexico, to purchase Mexican territory to provide a route for a southern transcontinental railroad.

Cuba was the next object of Pierce's ambitions. Southern slaveholders coveted Cuba's 300,000 slaves. Other Americans wanted to free Cuba's white population from Spanish rule. In 1854 Pierce instructed his ambassador to Spain to offer $130 million for Cuba, but Spain refused the offer. That same year, at a meeting in Ostend, Belgium, three of Pierce's diplomatic ministers sent a dispatch, later titled the Ostend Manifesto, to the secretary of state, urging the seizure of Cuba if Spain continued to refuse to sell the island. The Ostend Manifesto outraged Northerners, who regarded it as a brazen attempt to expand U.S. slavery in defiance of Spain's sovereign rights.

The Kansas-Nebraska Act

In 1854, less than four years after the Compromise of 1850, a piece of legislation was introduced in Congress that revived the issue of the expansion of slavery, shattered all illusions of sectional peace, and reordered the political landscape by destroying the Whig party, dividing the Democratic party, and creating the Republican party. Ironically, the author of this legislation was Senator Stephen A. Douglas, the very man who had pushed the earlier compromise through Congress.

As chairman of the Senate Committee on Territories, Douglas proposed that the area west of Iowa and Missouri—which had been set aside as a permanent Indian reservation—be organized as the Nebraska Territory and opened to white settlement. Douglas had sought to achieve this objective since 1844, but Southern congressmen had objected because Nebraska was located in the northern half of the Louisiana Purchase where the Missouri Compromise prohibited slavery. In order to forestall Southern opposition, Douglas's original bill ignored both the Missouri Compromise and the status of slavery in the Nebraska Territory. It simply provided that Nebraska, when admitted as a state, could enter the Union "with or without slavery," as its "constitution may prescribe."

Southern senators, however, demanded that Douglas add a clause specifically repealing the Missouri Compromise and stating that the question of slavery would be determined on the basis of popular sovereignty. For reasons still in dispute, Douglas relented to Southern pressure. In its final form Douglas's bill created two territories, Kansas and Nebraska, and declared that the Missouri Compromise was "inoperative and void." With solid support from Southern Whigs and Southern Democrats and the votes of half of the Northern Democratic congressmen, the measure passed. On May 30, 1854, President Pierce signed the measure into law.

Why did Douglas risk reviving the slavery question? His critics accused him of yielding to the Southern pressure because of his presidential ambitions and a desire to enhance the value of his holdings in Chicago real estate and western lands. They charged that the Illinois senator's chief interest in opening up Kansas and Nebraska was to secure a right of way for a transcontinental railroad that would make Chicago the transportation center of mid-America.

Douglas's supporters, on the other hand, pictured him as a statesman laboring for western development and a sincere believer in popular sovereignty as a solution to the problem of slavery in the western territories. Douglas had long insisted that the democratic solution to the slavery issue was to allow the people who actually settled a territory to decide whether slavery would be permitted or forbidden. Popular sovereignty, he believed, would allow the nation to "avoid the slavery agitation for all time

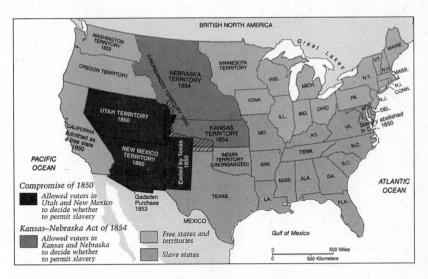

Compromise of 1850/Kansas-Nebraska Act

to come." Moreover, he believed that because of climate and geography slavery could never be extended into Kansas and Nebraska anyway.

In order to understand why Douglas introduced the Kansas-Nebraska Act, it is important to realize that by 1854 political and economic pressure to organize Kansas and Nebraska had become overwhelming. Midwestern farmers agitated for new land. A southern rail route had been completed through the Gadsden Purchase in December 1853, and promoters of a northern route for a transcontinental railroad viewed territorial organization as essential. Missouri slaveholders, already bordered on two sides by free states, believed that slavery in their state was doomed if they were surrounded by a free territory. All wanted to see the region opened to settlement.

Revival of the Slavery Issue

Neither Douglas nor his Southern supporters anticipated the extent and fury of Northern opposition to the Kansas-Nebraska Act. Douglas predicted that the "storm will soon spend its fury," but it did not subside. Northern Free-Soilers regarded the Missouri Compromise line as a "sacred compact" that had forever excluded slavery from the northern half of the Louisiana Purchase. Now they feared that under the guise of popular sovereignty, the Southern slave power threatened to spread slavery across the entire western frontier.

No single piece of legislation ever passed by Congress had more far-reaching political consequences. The Kansas-Nebraska Act brought about nothing less than a dramatic realignment of the two-party system. Conservative Whigs abandoned their party and joined the Democrats, while Northern Democrats with free-soil sentiments repudiated their own elected representatives.

The chief beneficiary of these defections was a new political organization, the Republican party. A combination of diverse elements, the Republican party stood for the belief that slavery must be barred from the western territories. It contained antislavery radicals, Free-Soilers, Whigs, Jacksonian Democrats, nativists, and antislavery immigrants.

In the fall of 1854 the new party contested congressional elections for the first time and won 46 seats in the House of Representatives. It included a number of men, like William H. Seward of New York, who believed that blacks should receive civil rights including the right to vote. But the new party also attracted many individuals, like Ohio senator Salmon P. Chase and Abraham Lincoln, who favored colonization as the only workable solution to slavery. Despite their differences, however, all of these groups shared a conviction that the western territories should be saved for free labor. "Free labor, free soil, free men," was the Republican slogan.

The Gathering Storm

Because the Kansas-Nebraska Act stated that the future status of slavery in the territories was to be decided by popular vote, both antislavery Northerners and proslavery Southerners competed to win the region for their section. Since Nebraska was too far north to attract slave owners, Kansas became the arena of sectional conflict. For six years, proslavery and antislavery factions fought in Kansas as popular sovereignty degenerated into violence.

"Bleeding Kansas" and "Bleeding Sumner"

Across the drought-stricken Ohio and Mississippi valleys, thousands of land-hungry farmers hoped to stake a claim to part of Kansas's 126,000 square miles of territory. Along with these pioneers came a small contingent of settlers whose express purpose was to keep Kansas free soil. Even before the 1854 act had been passed, the New England Emigrant Aid Company was promoting the emigration of antislavery New Englanders to Kansas to "vote to make it free." By the summer of 1855 more than 9,000 pioneers—mainly midwestern Free-Soilers—had settled in Kansas.

Slaveholders from Missouri expressed alarm at the activities of the Emigrant Aid Society. In response, they formed "Social Bands" and "Sons of the South" to "repel the wave of fanaticism which threatens to break upon our border." One Missouri lawyer told a cheering crowd that he would hang any "free soil" emigrant who came into Kansas.

Competition between proslavery and antislavery factions reached a climax on May 30, 1855, when Kansas held territorial elections. Although only 1,500 men were registered to vote, 6,000 ballots were cast, many of them by proslavery "border ruffians" from Missouri. As a result, a proslavery legislature was elected, which passed a series of laws protecting the "peculiar institution" in Kansas.

Free-Soilers called the election a fraud and held their own "Free State" convention which drew up a constitution that not only prohibited slavery in Kansas but also barred free blacks from the territory. Like the Free-Soilers who settled California and Oregon, most Northerners in Kansas wanted the territory to be free and white.

When Congress convened in January 1856, it was confronted by two rival governments in Kansas. President Pierce threw his support behind the proslavery legislature and asked Congress to admit Kansas to the Union as a slave state.

Violence broke out between Northern and Southern settlers over rival land claims, town sites, railroad routes—and, most dangerous of all, the question of slavery. In one episode, when a proslavery grand jury indicted several members of the Free-Soil Topeka government for high treason, 800 proslavery men marched into Lawrence, Kansas, to arrest the leaders of the antislavery government. The posse burned the local hotel, looted a number of houses, destroyed two antislavery printing presses, and killed one man.

On May 19, 1856—two days before the "sack of Lawrence"—Senator Charles Sumner of Massachusetts began a two-day speech in which he denounced "The Crime Against Kansas." In his speech Sumner charged that there was a Southern conspiracy to make Kansas a slave state. He proceeded to argue that a number of Southern senators, including Senator Andrew Butler of South Carolina, stood behind this conspiracy. Launching into a bitter personal diatribe, Sumner accused Senator Butler of taking "the harlot, Slavery," for his "mistress."

Two days later Butler's nephew, Congressman Preston Brooks of South Carolina, entered a nearly empty Senate chamber determined to "avenge the insult to my State." Sighting Sumner at his desk, Brooks charged at him and began striking the Massachusetts senator over the head with a cane. He swung so hard that the cane broke into pieces.

Although it would take Sumner three years to recover from his injuries and return to his Senate seat, he promptly became a martyr to the cause of freedom in the North, where a million copies of his "Crime

Clutching a pen in one hand and a copy of his "Crime Against Kansas" speech in the other, Senator Charles Sumner attempts to defend himself against an attack by South Carolina Congressman Preston Brooks.

Against Kansas" speech were distributed. In the South, Brooks was hailed as a hero. Merchants in Charleston bought the congressman a new cane, inscribed "Hit him again." A vote to expel Brooks from Congress failed because every Southern representative but one voted against the measure. Instead, Brooks was censured. He promptly resigned his seat and was immediately reelected.

The episode had repercussions in strife-torn Kansas. John Brown, a devout Bible-quoting Calvinist who believed that he had a personal responsibility to overthrow slavery, announced that the time had come "to fight fire with fire" and "strike terror in the hearts of proslavery men." The next day, in reprisal for the "sack of Lawrence" and the assault on Sumner, Brown and six companions dragged five proslavery men and boys from their beds at Pottawatomie Creek, split open their skulls with a sword, cut off their hands, and laid out their entrails.

A war of revenge erupted in Kansas. Columns of proslavery Southerners ransacked free farms while they searched for Brown and the other "Pottawatomie killers." Armed bands looted enemy stores and farms. At Osawatomie, proslavery forces attacked John Brown's headquarters, leaving a dozen men dead. John Brown's men killed four Missourians, and proslavery forces retaliated by blockading the free towns of Topeka and Lawrence. Before it was over, guerrilla warfare in Kansas would leave 200 dead.

The Election of 1856

The presidential election of 1856 took place in the midst of Kansas's civil war. President Pierce hoped for renomination to a second term in office, but Northern indignation over the Kansas-Nebraska Act led the Democrats to seek out a less controversial candidate. Northern and western Democrats succeeded in winning the nomination for James Buchanan, a 65-year-old Pennsylvania bachelor. The dying Whig party and the Southern wing of the Know-Nothing party nominated former President Millard Fillmore.

The Republican party held its first national convention in Philadelphia in June, nominating the dashing young explorer and soldier John C. Frémont for president. Frémont was a romantic figure who had led more than a dozen major explorations of the Rocky Mountains and Far West. After accepting the Republican nomination, he declared that Kansas should be admitted to the Union as a free state. This was his only public utterance during the entire 1856 campaign. A few weeks later the Northern wing of the Know-Nothing party threw its support behind Frémont.

The election was one of the most bitter in American history and the first in which voting divided along rigid sectional lines. The Democratic strategy was to picture the Republican party as a hotbed of radicalism. Democrats called the Republicans the party of disunion and described Frémont as a "black abolitionist" who would destroy the Union. Republicans responded by accusing the Democrats of being accomplices in a conspiracy to extend slavery.

Although Buchanan garnered only 45 percent of the popular vote, because of the presence of Fillmore he narrowly carried five Northern states, giving him a comfortable margin of victory in the electoral college. Buchanan won 174 electoral college votes to 114 for Frémont and 8 for Fillmore.

The election showed how polarized the nation had become. The South, except for Maryland, voted solidly Democratic. Frémont did not receive a single vote south of the Mason-Dixon line. At the same time, the northernmost states were solidly Republican.

In their first presidential campaign the Republicans had made an extraordinarily impressive showing. Eleven free states voted for Frémont. If only two more states had voted in his favor, the Republicans would have won the election.

The Supreme Court Speaks

In his inaugural address Buchanan declared that "the great object of my administration will be to arrest . . . the agitation of the slavery question in the North." He then predicted that a forthcoming Supreme Court decision would once and for all settle the controversy over slavery in the western territories. Two days after Buchanan's inauguration, the high court handed down its decision.

On March 6, 1857, the Supreme Court finally decided a question that Congress had evaded for decades: whether Congress had the power to prohibit slavery in the territories. Repeatedly, Congress had declared that this was a constitutional question that the Supreme Court should settle. Now, for the first time, the Supreme Court offered its answer.

The case originated in 1846, when a Missouri slave, Dred Scott, sued to gain his freedom. Scott argued that while he had been the slave of an army surgeon, he had lived for four years in Illinois, a free state, and Wisconsin, a free territory, and that his residence on free soil had erased his slave status. By a 7-2 margin the Court ruled that Dred Scott had no right to sue in federal court, that the Missouri Compromise was unconstitutional, and that Congress had no right to exclude slavery from the territories. All nine justices rendered separate opinions, but Chief Justice Taney delivered the opinion that expressed the position of the Court's majority. His opinion represented a judicial defense of the most extreme proslavery position.

The chief justice made two sweeping rulings. The first was that Dred Scott had no right to sue in federal court because neither slaves nor free blacks were citizens of the United States. At the time the Constitution was adopted, the chief justice wrote, blacks had been "regarded as beings of an inferior order" with "no rights which the white man was bound to respect."

Second, Taney declared that any law excluding slaves from the territories was a violation of the Fifth Amendment prohibition against the seizure of property without due process of law. The Missouri Compromise was unconstitutional, the Court declared, because it prohibited slavery north of 36° 30'.

In a single decision the Court sought to resolve all the major constitutional questions raised by slavery. It declared that the Declaration of Independence and the Bill of Rights were not intended to apply to black Americans. It stated that the Republican party platform—barring slavery from the western territories—was unconstitutional. And it ruled that Stephen Douglas's doctrine of "popular sovereignty"—which stated that territorial governments had the power to prohibit slavery—was also unconstitutional.

Republicans reacted with scorn. Radical abolitionists called for secession. Many Republicans—including an Illinois politician named Abraham Lincoln—regarded the decision as part of a slave power conspiracy to legalize slavery throughout the United States.

The Dred Scott decision was a major political miscalculation. In its ruling, the Supreme Court sought to solve the slavery controversy once and for all. Instead the Court intensified sectional strife, undercut possible compromise solutions to the divisive issue of the expansion of slavery, and weakened the moral authority of the judiciary.

The Lecompton Constitution: "A Swindle and a Fraud"

Late in 1857 President Buchanan faced a major test of his ability to suppress the slavery controversy. In September proslavery forces in Kansas met in Lecompton, the territorial capital, to draft a constitution that would bring Kansas into the Union as a slave state. Recognizing that a proslavery constitution would be defeated in a fair election, proslavery delegates offered voters a referendum on whether they preferred "the constitution with slavery" or "the constitution without slavery." In either case, however, the new constitution guaranteed slave ownership as a sacred right. Free-Soilers boycotted the election and, as a result, "the constitution with slavery" was approved by a 6,000 vote margin.

President Buchanan—afraid that the South would secede if Kansas were not admitted to the Union as a slave state—accepted the proslavery Lecompton constitution as a satisfactory application of the principle of popular sovereignty. He then demanded that Congress admit Kansas as the sixteenth slave state.

After a rancorous debate, the Senate passed a bill that admitted Kansas as a slave state under the Lecompton constitution. But the House of Representatives rejected this measure and instead substituted a compromise, which allowed Kansans to vote on the proslavery constitution. As a thinly veiled bribe to encourage Kansans to ratify the document, the bill offered Kansas a huge grant of public land if it approved the Lecompton constitution. While federal troops guarded the polls, Kansas voters overwhelmingly rejected the proslavery constitution.

The bloody battle for Kansas had come to an end. Free-Soilers took control of the territorial legislature and repealed Kansas's territorial slave code. Stripped of any legal safeguards for their slave property, most Kansas slave owners quickly left the territory. When the federal census was taken in 1860, just two slaves remained in Kansas.

But the nation would never be the same. To antislavery Northerners, the Lecompton controversy showed that the slave power was willing to subvert democratic processes in an attempt to force slavery on a free people. In Kansas, they charged, proslavery forces had used violence, fraud, and intimidation to expand the territory open to slavery. To the more extreme opponents of slavery in the North, the lesson was clear. The only way to preserve freedom and democratic procedures was to destroy slavery and the slave power through force of arms.

Crisis of the Union

By 1858, a growing number of Northerners were convinced that two fundamentally antagonistic societies had evolved in the nation, one dedicated to freedom, the other opposed. They had come to believe that their society was locked in a life and death struggle with a Southern society dominated by an aggressive slave power, which had seized control of the federal government and imperiled the liberties of free people. Declared the *New York Tribune:* "We are not one people. We are two peoples. We are a people for Freedom and a people for Slavery. Between the two, conflict is inevitable."

At the same time, an increasing number of Southerners expressed alarm at the growth of antislavery and anti-Southern sentiment in the North. They were convinced that Republicans would not only insist on halting slavery's expansion but would also seek to undermine the institution where it already existed. As the decade closed, the dominant question of American political life was whether the nation's leaders could find a peaceful way to resolve the differences separating the North and South.

The Lincoln-Douglas Debates

The critical issues dividing the nation—slavery versus free labor, popular sovereignty, and the legal and political status of African Americans—were brought into sharp focus in a series of debates during the 1858 election campaign for U.S. senator from Illinois. The campaign pitted a little-known lawyer from Springfield named Abraham Lincoln against Senator Stephen A. Douglas, the front-runner for the Democratic presidential nomination in 1860. (Senators, at the time, were elected by state legislators, and Douglas and Lincoln were actually campaigning for candidates from their party for the state legislature.)

The contest received intense national publicity. One reason for the public attention was that the political future of Stephen Douglas was at stake. Douglas had openly broken with the Buchanan administration over the proslavery Lecompton constitution and had joined with Republicans to defeat the admission of Kansas to the Union as a slave state. Many wondered if Douglas would now assume the leadership of the Free-Soil movement.

The public knew little about the man the Republicans selected to run against Douglas. Lincoln had been born in 1809 and had grown up on the wild Kentucky and Indiana frontier. At the age of 21 he moved to Illinois where he worked as a clerk in a country store, became a local postmaster and a lawyer, and served four terms in the lower house of the Illinois General Assembly. A Whig in politics, Lincoln was elected in 1846 to the U.S. House of Representatives, but his stand against the Mexican War had made him too unpopular to win reelection. After the passage of the Kansas-Nebraska Act in 1854 Lincoln reentered politics, and in 1858 the Republican party nominated him to run against Douglas for the Senate.

Lincoln accepted the nomination with the famous words: " 'A house divided against itself cannot stand.' I believe this Government cannot endure permanently half slave and half free." He did not believe the Union would fall, but he did predict that it would cease to be divided. Lincoln proceeded to argue that Stephen Douglas's Kansas-Nebraska Act and the Supreme Court's Dred Scott decision were part of a conspiracy to make slavery lawful "in all the States, old as well as new—North as well as South."

For four months Lincoln and Douglas crisscrossed Illinois, traveling nearly 10,000 miles and participating in seven face-to-face debates before crowds of up to 15,000. During the course of the debates Lincoln and Douglas presented two sharply contrasting views of the problem of slavery. Douglas argued that slavery was a dying institution that had reached its natural limits and could not thrive where climate and soil were inhospitable. He asserted that the problem of slavery could be resolved if it was treated as a local problem. Lincoln, on the other hand, regarded slavery as a dynamic, expansionistic institution, hungry for new territory. He argued that if Northerners allowed slavery to spread unchecked, slave owners would make slavery a national institution and would reduce all laborers, white as well as black, to a state of virtual slavery.

The sharpest difference between the two candidates involved the issue of African Americans' legal rights. Douglas was unable to conceive of blacks as anything but inferior to whites, and he was unalterably opposed to Negro citizenship. "I want citizenship for whites only," he declared. Lincoln said that he, too, was opposed to granting free blacks full legal rights. But he insisted that black Americans were equal to Douglas and "every living man" in their right to life, liberty, and the fruits of their own labor.

At Freeport, Illinois, Lincoln asked Douglas to reconcile the Supreme Court's Dred Scott decision, which denied Congress the power to exclude slavery from a territory, with popular sovereignty. Could the residents of a territory "in any lawful way" exclude slavery prior to statehood? Douglas replied by stating that the residents of a territory could exclude slavery by refusing to pass laws protecting slaveholders' property rights. "Slavery cannot exist a day or an hour anywhere," he declared, "unless it is supported by local police regulations."

Any way he answered, Douglas was certain to alienate Northern Free-Soilers or proslavery Southerners. The Dred Scott decision had given slave owners the right to take their slavery into any western territories. Now Douglas said that territorial settlers could exclude slavery, despite what the Court had ruled. Douglas won reelection, but his cautious statements antagonized Southerners and Northern Free-Soilers alike.

Although Lincoln failed to win a Senate seat, his battle with Stephen Douglas had catapulted him into the national spotlight and made him a serious presidential possibility in 1860. As Lincoln himself noted, his defeat was "a slip and not a fall."

Harpers Ferry

Up until the Kansas-Nebraska Act, abolitionists were averse to the use of violence. Opponents of slavery hoped to use moral suasion and other peaceful means to eliminate slavery. But by the mid-1850s the abolitionists' aversion to violence had begun to fade. In 1858 William Lloyd Garrison complained that his followers were "growing more and more warlike." On the night of October 16, 1859, violence came and John Brown was its instrument.

Brown's plan was to capture the federal arsenal at Harpers Ferry, Virginia (now West Virginia), and arm slaves from the surrounding countryside. His long-range goal was to drive southward into Tennessee and Alabama, raiding federal arsenals and inciting slave insurrections. Failing that, he hoped to ignite a sectional crisis that would destroy slavery.

At eight o'clock Sunday evening, October 16, John Brown led a raiding party of approximately 21 men into Harpers Ferry, where they captured the lone night watchman and cut the town's telegraph lines. Encountering no resistance, Brown's men seized the federal arsenal, an armory, and a rifle works. Brown then sent out several detachments to round up hostages and liberate slaves.

But Brown's plans soon went awry. As news of the raid spread, angry townspeople and local militia companies cut off Brown's escape routes and trapped his men in the armory. Twice Brown sent men carrying flags of truce to negotiate. On both occasions, drunken mobs, yelling "Kill them, Kill them," gunned the men down. Two days later U.S. Marines commanded by Colonel Robert E. Lee arrived in Harpers Ferry. Brown and his men took refuge in a fire engine house and battered holes through the building's brick wall to shoot through. Colonel Lee's marines stormed the engine house and rammed down its doors. Five of Brown's party escaped, ten were killed, and seven, including Brown himself, were taken prisoner.

A week later John Brown was put on trial in a Virginia court, even though his attack had occurred on federal property. He was found guilty of treason, conspiracy, and murder, and was sentenced to die on the gallows.

On December 2 Brown was hanged, a martyr to his cause. Across the North church bells tolled, flags flew at half-mast, and buildings were draped in black bunting. Ralph Waldo Emerson compared Brown to Jesus Christ and declared that his death had made "the gallows as glorious as the cross."

As Robert E. Lee's marines broke through the brick walls of John Brown's stronghold at Harper's Ferry, Brown "felt the pulse of his dying son with one hand and held his rifle with the other, and commanded his men with the utmost composure."

Prominent Northern Democrats and Republicans, including Stephen Douglas and Abraham Lincoln, spoke out forcefully against Brown's raid and his tactics. Lincoln expressed the views of the Republican leadership when he denounced Brown's raid as an act of "violence, bloodshed, and treason" that deserved to be punished by death. But Southern whites refused to believe that politicians like Lincoln and Douglas represented the true opinion of most Northerners. These men condemned Brown's "invasion," observed a Virginia senator, "only because it failed."

Conclusion

For 40 years the debate over the extension of slavery had divided North and South. National leaders had tried on several occasions to reach a permanent, workable solution to the problem, without success. With the collapse of the Whigs and the rise of the Republicans, the nation's first sectional party, the American political process could no longer contain the fierce antagonisms and mutual distrust which separated the two regions.

In 1859 John Brown's raid convinced many white Southerners that a majority of Northerners wished to free the slaves and incite a race war.

Chronology of Key Events

1850   Compromise of 1850

1852   Harriet Beecher Stowe publishes *Uncle Tom's Cabin*

1853   Gadsden Purchase from Mexico

1854   Ostend Manifesto; Commodore Matthew Perry negotiates a treaty opening Japan to American trade; Kansas-Nebraska Act reignites sectional controversy over slavery; "Bleeding Kansas" begins; Republican party formed

1856   "Sack of Lawrence;" "Bleeding Sumner"—Congressman Preston Brooks of South Carolina beats Senator Charles Sumner of Massachusetts; John Brown's raid on Pottawatomi Creek, Kansas

1857   Dred Scott decision

1858   Kansas voters reject the Lecompton constitution; Lincoln-Douglas debates

1859   John Brown's raid at Harpers Ferry

Southern extremists, known as "fire-eaters," told large crowds that John Brown's attack on Harpers Ferry was "the first act in the grand tragedy of emancipation, and the subjugation of the South in bloody treason." After Harpers Ferry, Southerners increasingly believed that secession and creation of a slaveholding confederacy were now the South's only options. A Virginia newspaper noted that there were "thousands of men in our midst who, a month ago, scoffed at the idea of a dissolution of the Union as a madman's dream, but who now hold the opinion that its days are numbered." The final bonds that had held the Union together had come unraveled.

Suggestions for Further Reading

Good overviews of the period include William W. Freehling, *The Road to Disunion: Secessionists at Bay* (1990); Michael Holt, *The Political Crisis of the 1850s* (1978); David M. Potter, *The Impending Crisis* (1976). See also Kenneth M. Stampp, *America in 1857* (1990).

For analyses of Southern attitudes on the eve of the Civil War see William J. Cooper, *Liberty and Slavery* (1983); David Brion Davis, *The Slave Power Conspiracy and the Paranoid Style* (1970). For information on Northern attitudes consult Eric Foner, *Free Soil, Free Labor, Free Men* (1970); William E. Gienapp, *Origins of the Republican Party* (1987).

For information on the Dred Scott Case see Don E. Fehrenbacher, *The Dred Scott Case* (1978). On foreign policy, see P. B. Wiley and Korogi Ichiro, *Yankees in the Lands of the Gods* (1990); Robert E. May, *The Southern Dream of a Caribbean Empire* (1974). Good biographical studies include Robert W. Johannsen, *Stephen A. Douglas* (1973); Stephen B. Oates, *To Purge This Land with Blood: A Biography of John Brown,* 2d ed., (1984).

Chapter *15*

A Nation Shattered by Civil War, 1860–1865

L ooking eastward from Sharpsburg into the mountains of western Maryland, General Robert E. Lee uttered the fateful words: "We will make our stand." Behind him was the Potomac River and to his front was Antietam Creek. Having invaded Union territory in early September 1862, Lee dispersed his Army of Northern Virginia, some 50,000 strong, across the countryside to capture strategic points and to rally the citizens of this border, slaveholding state behind the Confederate cause. Now he issued orders for his troops to reassemble with all haste at Sharpsburg. A major battle was in the making. General George B. McClellan's Army of the Potomac, numbering nearly 100,000 soldiers, was rapidly descending upon Lee's position.

Early on the morning of September 17 the great battle began. As the day progressed, Union forces attacked in five uncoordinated waves, which allowed Lee to maneuver his heavily outnumbered troops from point to point to meet each assault. As darkness fell, the Confederates still held their lines. Lee knew, however, that if McClellan attacked again the next morning, the Southern army might well be annihilated.

Among those rebel troops who marched into Maryland was 25-year-old Thomas Jefferson Rushin. He had grown up secure in his social station as the second son of Joel Rushin, a prospering west Georgia cotton planter who owned 21 slaves. Anxious to show that Southern gentlemen would never shrink from battle in defense of their way of life, he enlisted in Company K of the Twelfth Georgia Volunteers in June 1861. At 5:30 A.M. on September 17, 1862, Sergeant Rushin waited restlessly north of Sharpsburg—where the first Union assault occurred.

As dawn beckoned, Rushin and his comrades first heard skirmish fire, then the booming of cannons. Out in an open field they soon engaged Yankee troops appearing at the edge of a nearby woods. The Twelfth Georgia Volunteers stood their ground until they pulled back at 6:45 A.M. By the time that order came, 62 Georgians lay dead or wounded, among them the lifeless body of Thomas Jefferson Rushin.

At 9:00 A.M. General Ambrose E. Burnside's Union soldiers prepared to cross a stone bridge over Antietam Creek. On the other side was sharply rising ground, on top of which troops in gray waited, ready to shoot at any person bold enough to venture onto what became known as Burnside Bridge.

The Eleventh Connecticut Volunteers were among those poised for the advance. Included in their number was 18-year-old Private Alvin Flint, Jr., who had enlisted a few months before in Company D. He was from Hartford where his father, Alvin, Sr., worked in a papermaking factory. Flint's departure from home was sorrowful because his mother had

The human toll of the Civil War was overwhelming for contemporaries and remains so for later generations. Thomas Jefferson Rushin (left) and Alvin Flint, Jr. (right), were young casualties at the Battle of Antietam.

just died of consumption. A few weeks later he received word that his younger sister had succumbed to the same disease.

Flint's own sense of foreboding must have been overwhelming as he charged toward the bridge. In an instant, he became part of the human carnage, as minié balls poured down from across the bridge. Bleeding profusely from a mortal wound, he died before stretcher-bearers could reach him.

Flint never knew that his father and younger brother had recently joined another Connecticut regiment. By January, the two remaining Flints also would be dead, the victims of typhoid fever.

With 23,000 dead and wounded soldiers, Antietam turned out to be the bloodiest one-day action of the Civil War. And before the slaughter ended in 1865, total casualties reached 1.2 million people, including 620,000 dead—more than the total number of United States troops who lost their lives in World Wars I and II combined. Back in April 1861 when the Confederates fired on Fort Sumter, no one foresaw such carnage. No one imagined bodies as "thick as human leaves" decaying in fields around Sharpsburg, or how "horrible" looking would be "the faces of the dead."

The coming of the Civil War could be compared to a time bomb ready to explode. The fundamental issue was slavery and the question of whether the "peculiar institution" would be allowed to spread across the American landscape. Southerners feared that Northern leaders would use federal authority to declare slavery null and void throughout the land. Invoking the principle of states' rights, the South voted to secede. The North, in response, went to war to save the Union. Lurking in the background was the issue of permitting the continued existence of slavery. The carnage of the war settled the matter. A few days after Antietam, President Abraham Lincoln announced the Emancipation Proclamation, which transformed the Civil War into a struggle to end slavery—and the way of life it supported—as a means of destroying Confederate resistance and preserving the federal Union.

From Secession to Full-Scale War

On April 23, 1860, the Democratic party gathered in Charleston, South Carolina, to select a presidential candidate. No nominating convention faced a more difficult task. The delegates argued bitterly among themselves. In a rehearsal of what was to come, many Southern delegates left the convention. The breaking up of the Democratic party cleared the way for Lincoln's election, which in turn provoked the secession of seven Southern states by February 1861.

Electing a New President

Even before the Democratic convention met, there was evidence that the party was crumbling. Early in 1860 Jefferson Davis of Mississippi introduced a series of resolutions in the U.S. Senate calling for federal protection of slavery in all western territories. More extreme "fire-eaters," such as William L. Yancey of Alabama, not only embraced Davis's proposal but announced that he and others would leave the convention if the party did not defend their inalienable right to hold slaves and nominate a Southerner for president. Playing to cheering galleries in Charleston, the center of secessionist sentiment, delegates from eight Southern states walked out after the convention rejected an extreme proslavery platform.

Those who remained tried to nominate a candidate, but after dozens of ballots no one received a two-thirds majority. So the delegates gave up and agreed to reconvene in Baltimore in another six weeks. But that convention also failed to produce a consensus. Finally, in two separate meetings, Northern delegates named Stephen A. Douglas as their candidate while Southern delegates chose John C. Breckinridge of Kentucky.

To confuse matters further, a short-lived party, the Constitutional Union, emerged. This coalition of former Whigs, Know-Nothings, and pro-Union Democrats nominated John Bell of Tennessee. The party enjoyed support among moderates in the border states, enabling Bell to draw votes away from both Douglas and Breckinridge and making it easier for the sectional Republican party to carry the election.

When the Republicans gathered in Chicago in mid-May, they were very optimistic, especially with the Democrats hopelessly divided. Delegates constructed a platform that included high tariffs in an appeal to gain the support of Northern manufacturers and a homestead law in a bid to win the backing of citizens wanting free farmland. On the slave expansion issue there was no hint of compromise, although the platform did not call for an end to the institution of slavery in states where it already existed. To help ensure victory, Republican party regulars rejected front-runner William H. Seward, a strong antislavery advocate, in favor of Abraham Lincoln, a relative unknown.

According to custom, Lincoln stayed at home during the campaign and let others speak for him. His supporters inflamed sectional tensions by bragging that slavery would never survive their candidate's presidency. As a result, the 1860 presidential campaign took place in a lightning-charged atmosphere of threats and fears bordering on hysteria. Rumors of slave revolts, town burnings, and the murder of women and children swept the South. In one Alabama town a mob hanged a stranger, thinking him to be an abolitionist.

On election day, November 6, 1860, Lincoln won only 39.9 percent of the popular vote, but he received 180 electoral college votes, 57 more than the combined total of his opponents. The vote was purely sectional; Lincoln's name did not appear on the ballots of ten Southern states. Even when totaling all the popular votes against him, Lincoln still would have won in the electoral college by 17 votes because he carried the most populous states—all in the North. His election dramatically demonstrated to Southerners their minority status.

Secession Rends the Union

Lincoln told one friend during the campaign that Southerners "have too much good sense, and good temper, to attempt the ruin of the govern-

Table 15.1

Election of 1860			
Candidate	*Party*	*Popular Vote*	*Electoral Vote*
Abraham Lincoln	Republican	1,865,593	180
John C. Breckinridge	Democratic Southern	848,356	72
Stephen A. Douglas	Democratic Northern	1,382,713	12
John Bell	Constitutional Union	592,906	39

ment." He explained to others that he would support a constitutional amendment protecting slavery where it already existed, but Southerners believed otherwise. Convinced that a Republican administration would seek to abolish slavery, South Carolina's legislature unanimously called for a secession convention. On December 20, 1860, the delegates voted unanimously to leave the Union. The rationale had long since been developed by John C. Calhoun. State authority was superior to that of the nation, and as sovereign entities, states could leave the Union as freely as they had joined.

By early February 1861 the Deep South states of Georgia, Florida, Alabama, Mississippi, Louisiana, and Texas had also voted in favor of secession. Representatives from the seven states first met in Montgomery, Alabama, on February 8 and proclaimed a new nation, the Confederate States of America. They elected Jefferson Davis provisional president and wrote a plan of government, which, except for emphasizing states' rights, they modeled on the federal Constitution. The Confederate constitution limited the president to a single six-year term, required a two-thirds vote of Congress to admit new states or enact appropriations bills, and forbade protective tariffs and government funding of internal improvements.

Some Northerners believed that the South should be allowed to "depart in peace." Senator John J. Crittenden of Kentucky proposed another alternative: to enshrine the old Missouri Compromise line of 36° 30' in a constitutional amendment that would also promise no future restrictions on slavery where it existed. Neither idea appealed to Lincoln. Secession was unconstitutional, he maintained, and appeasement, especially any plan endorsing the spread of slavery, was unacceptable.

President-elect Lincoln decided to do nothing until after his inauguration. He continued to hope that pro-Unionist sentiment in the South would win out over secessionist feelings. Also, eight slave states remained in the Union; controversial statements might have pushed some or all of them into the Confederate camp. Lincoln would make his moves prudently, indeed so carefully that some leading Republicans misread him as an inept fool. William Seward, his future secretary of state, even politely offered to run the presidency on Lincoln's behalf.

Lincoln Takes Command

On March 4 Lincoln took the oath of office as the nation's sixteenth president. His inaugural address contained a powerful but simple message: the Union was "perpetual," and secession was illegal. To resist federal authority was "insurrectionary." As president, he would support the Union by maintaining possession of federal properties in the South. Then Lincoln appealed to the Southern people: "We are not enemies, but friends." And he warned: "In your hands, my dissatisfied countrymen, and not in mine, is the momentous issue of civil war. . . . You can have no conflict without yourselves being the aggressors."

Even as he spoke, Lincoln knew that the seceding states had taken possession of all federal military installations within their borders—with the principal exceptions of Fort Sumter, guarding the entrance to Charleston harbor, and Fort Pickens at Pensacola. The next day Lincoln received an ominous report. Major Robert Anderson, in command of Fort Sumter, was running out of provisions and would have to abandon his position within six weeks unless resupplied.

Realizing that he had overestimated the extent of pro-Union feeling in the South, Lincoln ordered the navy to take provisions to Fort Sumter. Just before the expedition left, he sent a message to South Carolina's governor, notifying him that "if such attempt be not resisted, no effort to throw in men, arms, or ammunition, will be made." It was up to the rebels, from the president's point of view, to decide whether they wanted war.

Knowing that help for the Union garrison was on the way, Confederate General P. G. T. Beauregard ordered the cannonading of Fort Sumter. The firing commenced at 4:30 A.M. on April 12, 1861. Thirty-four hours later Major Anderson surrendered. On April 15 Lincoln announced that an "insurrection" existed and called for 75,000 volunteers to put down the Southern rebellion. The Civil War had begun.

An Accounting of Resources

The firing on Fort Sumter caused both jubilation and consternation. Most citizens thought that a battle or two would quickly end the conflict, so they rushed to enlist, not wanting to miss the action. The emotional outburst was particularly strong in the South where up to 200,000 enthusiasts tried to join the fledgling Confederate military machine. Several thousand had to be sent home because it was impossible to muster them into the service in so short a time with even the bare essentials of war—uniforms, weapons, camp equipment, and food rations.

Professional military men like Lieutenant Colonel Robert E. Lee, who had experienced combat in the Mexican War, were less enthusiastic. "I see only that a fearful calamity is upon us," he wrote. Lee was anxious "for the preservation of the Union," but he felt compelled to defend the "honor" of Virginia, should state leaders vote for secession.

Virginians seceded (April 17) in direct response to Lincoln's declaration of an insurrection. By late May, North Carolina, Tennessee, and Arkansas had also voted to leave the Union. In all, 11 states containing a population of nearly 9 million people, including 3.5 million slaves, proclaimed their independence. On the other hand, four slaveholding states bordering the North—Delaware, Maryland, Kentucky, and Missouri—equivocated about secession. Lincoln understood that sustaining the loyalty of the border states was critical. Besides making it more difficult for the Confederates to carry the war into the North, their presence gave the Union, with 23 million people, a major asset should there be a prolonged military struggle.

Secession

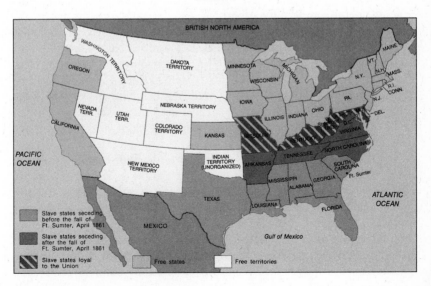

The North possessed overwhelming advantages going into the war. The value of Northern property was twice that of the South; the banking capital advantage was ten to one, and it was eight to one in investment capital. The North could easily underwrite the production of war goods, whereas the South would have to struggle, given its scarce capital resources and an industrial capacity far below that of the North. By other crucial resource measures, such as railroad mileage, representing the capacity to move armies and supplies easily, the Union was far ahead of the Confederacy. The North had 22,000 miles of track, as compared to 9,000 for the South. In 1860 U.S. manufacturers produced 470 locomotives, only 17 of which were built in the South. That same year the North produced 20 times as much pig iron, 17 times the clothing, and 32 times as many firearms.

With this imbalance, it is incredible that the South performed so well in the early stages, and that the North fared so poorly. Among the Southern assets, at least in 1861, was sheer geographic size. As long as the Confederacy maintained a defensive military posture, the North would have to demonstrate an ability to win more than an occasional battle. It would have to conquer a massive region, and this factor alone emboldened Southern leaders. In analogies alluding to the American Revolution, they discussed how the British, with superior resources, had failed to reconquer the colonies. If Southerners maintained their resolve, something more likely to happen when soldiers were defending homes and families, nothing, it appeared, could extinguish their desire for national independence.

In addition, the South held an initial advantage in generalship. Mature senior commanders like Albert Sidney Johnston, Joseph E. Johnston, and Robert E. Lee quickly gravitated to the top of the new Confederate command structure. The Union structure, however, was already in place, with the aging hero of the Mexican War, 74-year-old Winfield Scott, serving as general-in-chief in April 1861. Men like Ulysses S. Grant and William Tecumseh Sherman, who would later win renown as Union generals, were not even in the service at the outset of the war. It would take Grant and Sherman time to work through the pack of lackluster military professionals in line ahead of them.

Then there was the matter of civilian leadership. At the outset the South appeared to have the advantage. Jefferson Davis, the Confederacy's new president, possessed superb qualifications. Besides being a wealthy slaveholder, he had a West Point education, had fought in the Mexican War, had served in Congress, and had been Franklin Pierce's secretary of war. Davis proved to be a hardworking but ineffective administrator. He would not delegate authority and became tangled up in details; he surrounded himself with weak assistants; he held strong opinions on all subjects; and he was invariably rude to those who disagreed with him. Perhaps worst of all, he was not an inspirational leader, something the South desperately needed after war weariness set in.

Abraham Lincoln, by comparison, lacked the outward demeanor of a cultured gentleman. He had little formal schooling; he had spent an impoverished childhood in Kentucky and Indiana before moving to Illinois and succeeding as a country lawyer; he had served only one term in Congress; and he had virtually no military experience, except for brief duty as a militia captain during the Black Hawk War. But Northerners soon found that Lincoln viewed himself as a man of the people, eager to do anything necessary to save the Union. They saw him bear up under savage criticism. Even those who disagreed with him came to admire his ability to reflect and think through the implications of proposed actions—then move forward decisively. Lincoln emerged as an inspirational leader in the North's drive for victory.

"Forward to Richmond!" and "On to Washington!"

War hysteria was pervasive after Fort Sumter, and Southerners and Northerners alike exuded confidence. The populace clearly wanted a fight. Throughout the North the war cry was "Forward to Richmond!," referring to the Virginia city 100 miles south of Washington that had been selected as the permanent capital of the Confederacy. Throughout the South anyone shouting "On to Washington!" could expect to hear cheering voices in return. The land between the two capitals soon became a major combat zone, and the bloodshed began after President Lincoln, bowing in mid-July to pressure for a demonstration of Union superiority in arms, ordered General Irvin McDowell and 30,000 half-trained "Billy Yanks" to engage General P. G. T. Beauregard and his "Johnny Rebs," who were gathering at sleepy Manassas Junction, lying near a creek called Bull Run 25 miles southwest of the federal capital.

The Battle of Bull Run (First Manassas) occurred on Sunday, July 21. Citizens of Washington packed picnic lunches and went out to observe the engagement. Because the battlefield soon became shrouded in smoke, they saw little except Union soldiers finally breaking off and fleeing past them in absolute panic for their lives. Bull Run had its glorious moments, such as when Virginians under Thomas J. Jackson held onto a key hill, despite a crushing federal assault. This earned Jackson his nickname, "Stonewall," and he became the South's first authentic war hero. There were no heroes for the North. As Union troops straggled back into Washington, they "looked pretty well whipped." Bull Run, with 2,700 Union and 2,000 Confederate casualties, proved to Lincoln that the warring sections were in for a long-term struggle.

Planning the Union Offensive

Bull Run showed the deficiencies of both sides. Union troops had not been trained well enough to stand the heat of battle. The Confederates were so disorganized after sweeping their adversaries from the field that they could not take advantage of the rout and strike a mortal blow at Washington. Lincoln now realized, too, that he had to develop a comprehensive strategy—a detailed war plan—to break the Southern will of resistance. Also, he needed to find young, energetic generals who could organize Union forces and guide them to victory. Devising a war strategy proved to be much easier than locating military leaders with the capacity to execute those plans.

Civil War, 1861–1862

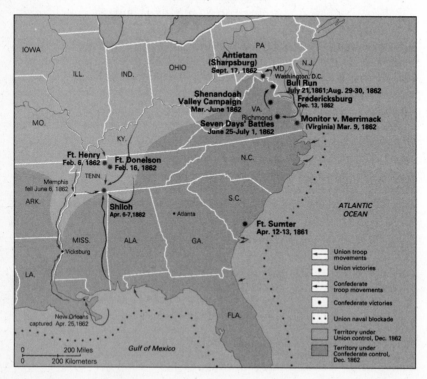

Well before Bull Run, Lincoln turned to Winfield Scott for an overall strategic design, and the general came up with the "Anaconda Plan"— which like the snake was intended to squeeze the resolve out of the Confederacy. The three essential coils included a full naval blockade of the South's coastline to cut off shipments of war goods and other supplies from Europe; a campaign to gain control of the Mississippi River, thereby splitting the Confederacy into two parts; and a placement of armies at key points to ensure that Southerners could not wiggle free.

Lincoln liked certain features of the strategic plan. He ordered the blockade, a seemingly impossible assignment, given a southern coastline stretching for 3,550 miles and containing 189 harbors and navigable rivers. In early 1861 the U.S. Navy had only 7,600 seamen and 90 warships, 21 of which were unusable. But with a burst of energy under Secretary Gideon Welles, the navy ultimately grew to 650 vessels and 100,000 sailors. Lincoln's "paper blockade," as detractors called it, became more effective with each passing month, and it also was a political success. Neutral powers generally respected the blockade, which seriously hampered Southern efforts to gain essential war matériel from abroad.

Lincoln also concluded that splitting the Confederacy was critical. He ordered Generals Henry W. Halleck, headquartered in St. Louis, and Don Carlos Buell, based in Louisville, to build great armies for the western theater. The president likewise worked with the Navy Department to devise the means to gain control of the Mississippi River. The latter effort resulted in the risky campaign of Captain David G. Farragut, whose fleet captured New Orleans on April 25, 1862. Farragut's triumph was a major first step in cutting the South apart and crippling dreams of independence.

The third aspect of the Anaconda Plan, Lincoln thought, was naive. Fort Sumter convinced him that the slaveholding elite had too strong a grip on the Southern populace to expect any significant rallying of pro-Unionists. Nor should armies sit on the sidelines or train endlessly and wait for a decisive battle. After Bull Run Lincoln got Congress to authorize the enlistment of 500,000 additional volunteer troops, far beyond the number recommended by Scott.

For a man with no formal training in military strategy, Lincoln was way ahead of the generals immediately surrounding him. As he explained to one of them, "we have the *greater* numbers," and if "superior forces" could strike "at *different* points at the *same* time," breakthroughs would occur. Lincoln's thinking pointed toward unrestrained total war, implying the complete destruction of the South, if need be, to save the Union. What the former militia captain needed were ranking officers of like mind. Lincoln hoped that he found such a person in George B. McClellan.

Yankee Reverses and Rebel Victories

George McClellan was a man of great bravado who had finished second in his West Point class and written a book on the art of war. Skilled at organizing and training troops, he was also an inspiring leader. With his usual brashness McClellan told Lincoln: "I can do it all." Unfortunately, the cocksure commander was incapable of using effectively what he had built.

Lincoln gave McClellan everything necessary to do the job. Not only did the president name him commander of the Army of the Potomac, which at peak strength numbered 150,000 troops, but he made him general-in-chief after Winfield Scott retired in the fall of 1861. The problem was McClellan's unwillingness to move his showcase force into combat. When Lincoln called for action, McClellan demanded more soldiers. The rebels, he claimed from spy reports, had 220,000 troops at Manassas Junction—the actual number was closer to 36,000. To counter this mythical force, McClellan wanted at least 273,000 men before entering the field. Lincoln, convinced that only crushing victories on several fronts could break the Confederate will, believed that McClellan had contracted a bad case of "the slows."

To give McClellan his due, his approach to the war was different from Lincoln's. He intended to maneuver his army but avoid large battles. He wanted to save soldiers' lives, not expend them, and he thought that he could threaten Southerners into submission by getting them to realize the futility of standing up to so superior a force—and so brilliant a general in command.

In March 1862, McClellan finally began the Peninsula campaign, transporting his army down through Chesapeake Bay to the peninsula formed by the York and James rivers, about 75 miles southeast of Richmond. In May his army moved forward at a snail's pace, which allowed the Confederates time to mass 70,000 troops before him. By the end of the month his advance units were approaching the outskirts of Richmond. Rebel forces under Joseph E. Johnston struck the main Union army near the Chickahominy River on May 31 and June 1. The Battle of Seven Pines cost a total of 10,000 casualties, among them a seriously wounded General Johnston.

Johnston's misfortune opened the way for Robert E. Lee to assume command of the Army of Northern Virginia. Lee called in "Stonewall" Jackson's corps from the Shenandoah Valley and went after the Union army aggressively. McClellan all but panicked. Insisting that his army now faced 200,000 rebels (the number was 90,000), he retreated after two inconclusive fights north of the Chickahominy. What ensued was the Battle of the Seven Days (June 25–July 1) in which combined casualties reached 30,000, two-thirds sustained by the Confederates. Still, Lee's offensive punches prevailed—and saved Richmond. McClellan soon boarded his troops on waiting transport ships and returned to Washington.

At first, Robert E. Lee was an adviser to Jefferson Davis. Then, on June 1, 1862, Davis appointed him to command the Confederate Army of Northern Virginia. After the war, Lee encouraged reconciliation between the North and South.

The aggressive Lee, meantime, sensed other opportunities. In defending Richmond the rebels had abandoned their advanced post at Manassas Junction. A Union force numbering 45,000 under General John Pope had moved into position there. Having just come in from the western theater, Pope was as blind to danger as McClellan was cautious. Lee, once sure of McClellan's decision to retreat, wheeled about and rushed northward toward Pope.

Dividing his force in half, Lee sent Jackson's corps in a wide, looping arc around Pope. On August 29 Jackson began a battle known as Second Bull Run (Second Manassas). When Pope turned to face Jackson, Lee hit him from the other side. The battle raged for another day and ended with Union troops again fleeing for Washington.

Lee led his victorious troops into Maryland in early September, toward another rendezvous with McClellan. The two armies met at Antietam on September 17, the bloodiest day of the war. Despite a numerical advantage, the Union army never got its punches coordinated, and could manage no better than a draw. Two days later Lee's army retreated back into Virginia.

Federal Breakthrough in the West

In the West the Union offensive fared much better. Brigadier General Ulysses S. Grant devised a plan to cut through the rebel defensive line, which was under the command of General Albert Sidney Johnston, thus opening states like Tennessee to full-scale invasion. In February 1862 Grant launched a successful land and river offensive against Forts Henry and Donelson, two rebel strongholds guarding the Tennessee and Cumberland rivers in northwestern Tennessee.

After breaking the Confederate line, Grant's army of 40,000 poured into Tennessee, following after Johnston, who retreated all the way to Corinth in northern Mississippi. Cautioned by General Halleck "to strike no blow until we are strong enough to admit no doubt of the result," Grant settled his army in at Pittsburg Landing, 25 miles north of Corinth along the Tennessee River—with advanced lines around a humble log church bearing the name Shiloh. There he waited for reinforcements. Flushed with confidence, Grant did not bother to order a careful posting of picket guards.

When Johnston received additional troops under General Beauregard, he decided to attack. At dawn on April 6, 40,000 rebels overran Grant's outer lines, and for two days the battle raged before the Federals drove off the Confederates. The Battle of Shiloh (Pittsburg Landing) resulted in 20,000 combined casualties. General Johnston died the first day from a severe leg wound, which cost the South a valued commander. Grant, so recently hailed as a war hero, now faced severe criticism for not having secured his lines. Some even claimed that he was drunk when the rebels first struck, undercutting—at least for the moment—thoughts of elevating him to higher command.

Ulysses S. Grant was criticized for his command tactics early in the war, but Lincoln remained supportive of him throughout. Grant later became the eighteenth president of the United States.

To and From Emancipation: The War on the Home Front

Keeping up morale—and the will to endure at all costs—was a major challenge for both sides, once citizens at home accepted the reality of a long and bloody conflict. Issues threatening to erode popular resolve were different in the North and the South. How civilian leaders handled these problems had a direct bearing on the outcome of the conflict; and Northern leaders, drawing on greater resources, proved more adept at finding solutions designed to keep up morale while breaking the Southern will to continue the war.

An Abundance of Confederate Shortages

With their society lacking an industrial base, Southern leaders understood the need for securing material aid from Europe, just as the American colonists had received foreign support to sustain their rebellion against Britain. Secessionists thought that Europe's dependence on cotton would assure them unofficial assistance, if not diplomatic recognition as an independent nation. "Cotton," predicted the *Charleston Mercury,* "would bring England to her knees." It did not. There was already a glut in the European marketplace, and textile manufacturers after 1861 turned to Egypt, India, and Brazil as sources for new supplies of cotton.

Despite concerted diplomatic efforts, Great Britain and other European nations officially ignored the Confederacy. What secessionists had not fully considered was that European countries were just as dependent on Northern grain crops to help feed their populace. In addition, nations like Britain, having long since abandoned slavery, had serious moral qualms about publicly recognizing a slave power.

The Confederacy, however, received small amounts of secret aid from Europe. By 1865 blockade runners brought an estimated 600,000 European-produced weapons into Southern ports, and in 1862 English shipyards built two commerce raiders, the *Florida* and *Alabama,* before protests from the Lincoln administration ended such activity. The Richmond government also received about $710 million in foreign loans, secured by promises to deliver cotton; but the tightening Union naval blockade made the exportation of cotton difficult, discouraging further European loans because of the mounting risk of never being paid back.

From the very outset Union naval superiority was a critical factor in isolating the South. The Confederacy simply lacked the funds to build a fleet of any consequence, which allowed the Union navy to dominate the sea lanes. The effects of cutting the South off from external support were profound. By the spring of 1862 citizens at home were experiencing many shortages—and getting mad about it. Such common items as salt, sugar, and coffee had all but disappeared, and shoes and clothing were at a premium. In 1863 bread riots broke out in several Southern cities, including Richmond. Shortages abetted rapid inflation, as did the overprinting of Confederate dollars. Between 1861 and 1865 prices spiraled upward on the average of 7,000 percent.

Most Southerners, in trying to comprehend so many difficulties, blamed their central government. When the Confederate Congress enacted a conscription act in 1862—the first draft law in U.S. history—because of rapidly declining enlistments, many Southerners accused their government of trampling on the principle of states' rights, the very issue that had caused them to secede. Moreover, the draft law allowed individuals to purchase substitutes, and, with rapid inflation, avoiding service became a wealthy man's prerogative. When the central government in October 1862 exempted from the draft all those managing 20 or more slaves, ordinary citizens started referring to the contest as "a rich man's war and a poor man's fight."

Directing the Northern War Effort

Although Abraham Lincoln focused most of his energies on military matters, he did not neglect other vital areas, including diplomatic relations and domestic legislation. His foreign policy was designed to keep European nations from supporting the Confederacy, and his domestic goal was to maintain high levels of popular support for the war effort. Lincoln was successful on both counts, but he took many risks, the most dramatic being his announcement of an emancipation proclamation.

Unlike Jefferson Davis, Lincoln delegated authority whenever he could. In foreign affairs he relied heavily on Secretary of State William Seward, whom European leaders came to regard as hotheaded but effective. There were some intense diplomatic moments, such as in November 1861 when the U.S. warship *San Jacinto* intercepted a British packet vessel, the *Trent,* and seized two Confederate envoys, James M. Mason and John Slidell, who were on their way to the courts of Europe. England vehemently protested such an overt violation of maritime law—stopping and searching neutral vessels on the high seas. Lincoln smoothed matters over by apologizing for the *Trent* affair and releasing the envoys from jail.

A few months later Seward received reports that English shipyards were completing two ironclad ram vessels for the Confederacy. This time the United States threatened serious repercussions, and British officials confiscated the ironclads, thus averting another crisis. With Europe maintaining a posture of neutrality the North could fully focus its energies on defeating the South.

Also helping the Yankee cause was wartime prosperity, which Lincoln and a Republican-dominated Congress tried to sustain. In 1862 Congress passed the Homestead Act, which granted 160 acres free to individuals who agreed to farm that land for at least five years; the Morrill Land Grant Act, which offered huge parcels of public land to states that established agricultural colleges; and the Pacific Railway Act, which laid the basis for constructing a transcontinental railroad after the war. Further, to protect the North's manufacturing interests from foreign competition, the Republican Congress approved tariff acts that raised import duties nearly 50 percent.

Under the watchful eye of Treasury Secretary Salmon P. Chase, the government likewise resorted to various expedients to finance the war effort. In 1861 Congress approved a modest income tax with rates that only fell on the wealthy. The government also taxed the states, borrowed heavily (around $2.2 billion), and issued "greenbacks," a currency that, like Confederate dollars, had no backing in gold or silver but held its value because of slowly growing confidence in the Union war effort.

Historians have debated whether the economic boom in the North generated by the Civil War sped up the process of industrialization in the United States. By some measures, such as the annual rate of economic growth during the 1860s, the war injured the economy, if destruction of property in the South is included. By the war's end in 1865 two-fifths of all Southern livestock had been killed; more than half of the Confederacy's farm machinery had been destroyed; and countless plantations and family farms had been ruined. In the North, by comparison, per capita commodity output rose by 56 percent during the decade of the 1860s, and the amount of working capital to underwrite business activity increased by 50 percent. Entrepreneurs, John D. Rockefeller and Andrew Carnegie among them, made monumental profits from war contracts. Their newfound capital base and methods of large-scale business organization certainly foreshadowed the rapid postwar transition to a full-scale industrial economy.

The intense level of governmental activity resulted in charges that Lincoln's true purpose was to become a dictator. These accusations started soon after Fort Sumter when the new president, acting by himself since Congress was not then in session, declared an insurrection and began a military buildup. Shortly thereafter, secessionist-minded Marylanders attacked Yankee troops moving through Baltimore. To quell such turbulence, Lincoln suspended the writ of habeas corpus in Maryland and ordered the arrest of leading advocates of secession.

In a federal circuit court case, *Ex Parte Merryman*, Supreme Court Chief Justice Roger B. Taney proclaimed Lincoln's action in Maryland illegal by arguing that only Congress had the authority to suspend writs of habeas corpus in times of rebellion. Lincoln ignored Taney's ruling, and John Merryman, one of those arrested, languished in a military prison with no set trial date on vague charges of having incited Marylanders to secede from the Union.

During the war Lincoln authorized the arrest of some 14,000 dissidents and had them jailed without any prospect for trials. He was careful, however, not to go after his political opponents, particularly leading members of the Democratic party. The president worked to have open and fair elections, operating on a distinction between legitimate dissent in support of the nation and willful attempts to subvert the Union. Most agree that Lincoln, given the tense wartime climate, showed sensitivity toward basic civil rights. At the same time he clearly tested the limits of presidential powers.

Issuing the Emancipation Proclamation

Abraham Lincoln believed fervently in the ideals of the Declaration of Independence, which gave Americans "the right to rise" out of poverty, as he described his own experience, and "get through the world respectably." Although he believed that chattel slavery was inconsistent with the ideals of the American Revolution, as president he had promised not to interfere with the institution in the Southern states. When the fighting commenced, he seemed to move with indecisive steps toward emancipation. His only war aim, he claimed well into the spring of 1862, was to save the Union. When in August 1861 General John C. Frémont, then heading federal military operations in Missouri, declared an end to slavery in that state, the president not only rescinded the proclamation but removed Frémont from command.

For a man who despised slavery, Lincoln held back in resolving the emancipation question for many reasons. First, he did not want to drive slaveholding border states like Missouri into the Confederacy. Second, he worried about pervasive racism; white Northerners had willingly taken up arms to save the Union, but he wondered whether they would keep fighting to liberate the black population. Third, if he moved too fast, he reasoned, he might lose everything, including the Union itself, should Northern peace advocates seize upon popular fears of emancipation and create an overwhelming demand to stop the fighting in favor of Southern independence. Fourth, he had personal doubts as to whether blacks and whites could ever live together harmoniously in freedom.

By the summer of 1862 Lincoln had finally made up his mind. The death toll, he now reasoned, had become too great; all the maiming and killing had to have some larger purpose, transcending the primary war aim of preserving the Union. For Lincoln the military contest had become a test to see whether the republic, at long last, had the capacity to live up to the ideals of the American Revolution, which could only be determined by announcing the Emancipation Proclamation.

Lincoln knew he was gambling with Northern morale at a time when Union victories were all but nonexistent, when enlistments were in decline, and when war weariness had set in. He was aware that racists would spread their poison far and wide. So the president waited for the right moment, such as after an important battlefield triumph, to quiet his critics who would surely say that emancipation was a desperate measure designed to cover up presidential mismanagement of the war.

As a shrewd politician, Lincoln began to prepare white Northerners for what was coming. He explained in late August: "If I could save the Union without freeing *any* slave, I would do it; and if I could save it by freeing *all* the slaves, I would do it; and if I could save it by freeing some and leaving others alone, I would also do that." Thus avoiding the pronouncement of high ideals in public, the president decided to treat his assault on slavery as a war measure designed to ensure total military victory.

On September 22, 1862, five days after the Battle of Antietam, Lincoln announced his preliminary Emancipation Proclamation, which called upon Southerners to lay down their arms and return to the Union by year's end or to accept the abolition of slavery. Getting no formal response, on January 1, 1863, he declared all slaves in the Confederacy "forever free," although slavery could continue to exist in the four Union border states—to assure a united front against the rebels.

Emancipation Tests Northern Resolve

In the Confederacy the planter elite played on traditional racist themes and used the proclamation to rally white citizens wavering in their resolve. Here was proof, shouted planter leaders, that every indignity the South had suffered was part of a never-ending abolitionist plot to stir up slave rebellions and "convert the quiet, ignorant black son of toil into a savage incendiary and brutal murderer."

Reaction to the proclamation in the North varied widely. With Democrats in Congress calling for Lincoln's impeachment, some cabinet members urged the president to reconsider. Republicans also feared repercussions in the upcoming November elections. They did lose seats, but they still controlled Congress, despite the efforts of many Democrats to smear "Black Republican" candidates. Certainly, too, frustration with so many battlefield reverses, as much as news of the proclamation, hurt Republican candidates at the polls.

On the other hand, many criticized Lincoln for not going far enough. Abolitionists chided him for failing to eradicate slavery in all the states. Foreign opinion generally applauded Lincoln, although a few commentators made caustic remarks about a curious new "principle" that no American would henceforth be allowed to own slaves "unless he is loyal to the United States."

Northern blacks, however, were jubilant. Frederick Douglass stated: "We shout for joy that we live to record this righteous decree." Up until this point blacks had found the war frustrating. Federal officials had blocked their attempts to enlist. Not wanting to stir up racial violence, Lincoln had danced around the issue. Most early black enlistments were in the navy. Finally in 1862 Secretary of War Edwin M. Stanton, with the president's backing, called for the enlistment of blacks—North and South. In a model program, Colonel Thomas W. Higginson, a radical abolitionist, worked with former slaves in the Sea Island region of South Carolina, an area under Union control, to mold them into a well-trained regiment. Higginson's troops fought effectively, demonstrating that blacks could master the art of war.

No regiment proved that more dramatically than the 54th Massachusetts Infantry. Like all other black regiments, the 54th trained separately from white units and received its commands from white officers. On July 18, 1863, the 54th, Massachusetts led by Robert Gould Shaw, the 25-year-old scion of a prominent antislavery family, launched an early evening assault against Fort Wagner, a major bastion protecting Charleston harbor for the Confederacy. Eventually repulsed after fierce fighting, the 54th experienced more than a 40 percent casualty rate. Shaw, who was shot dead in the charge, became a martyred war hero in the North.

Before the war ended, 179,000 blacks, most of them former slaves, served in the Union army, and another 29,000 were in the navy. Some 44,000 died fighting to save the Union and to defend the prize of freedom for African Americans. Twenty-four blacks received the Congressional Medal of Honor for extraordinary bravery in battle. Among them was Sergeant William H. Carney of the 54th Massachusetts, whose citation praised him for grabbing the regimental flag after its bearer was shot down and leading the troops forward into the outer works of Fort Wagner. Carney, a runaway slave from Virginia, then planted the flag and engaged in hand-to-hand combat. Severely wounded, he reluctantly retreated with flag in hand, not suspecting that he would become the first black Medal of Honor recipient in the Civil War—and American history.

Despite the Emancipation Proclamation, African Americans received lower military pay until protests ended such discrimination in 1864; and they quite often drew menial work assignments, such as digging latrines and burying the dead after battle. Emancipation, blacks soon realized, was just the beginning of an awesome struggle that lay ahead—beyond the Civil War—to overcome the prejudice and hatred that had locked them in slavery for over two centuries.

Breaking Confederate Resistance, 1863–1865

During the spring of 1863 Union war sentiment sagged to a new low point. Generals kept demanding more troops; yet with the exception of black enlistees, there were few new volunteers. Congress faced up to reality in March and passed a Conscription Act, which provided for the drafting of males between the ages of 20 and 45. Draftees could buy exemptions for $300—an average wage for half a year—or hire substitutes. All told, federal conscription produced 166,000 soldiers, roughly three-fourths of whom were substitutes.

Conscription infuriated many Northerners, particularly day laborers who lacked the income to buy their way out of the service. Riots took place in several cities, and the worst were in New York where Irish workers, sensing a plot to force them into the Union army so that newly freed slaves would get their jobs, vented their rage in mid-July 1863. The rampaging started when workers assaulted a building in which a draft lottery was taking place. For a week the streets were not safe, particularly for blacks, who in a few cases were beaten to death or hanged by roaming mobs. Only the intervention of federal troops ended the New York draft riots, but not before 100 or more persons had died.

The Tide Turns: Gettysburg and Vicksburg

After the Battle of Antietam, Lincoln had had enough of McClellan's cautious tactics. He named Ambrose E. Burnside to head the eastern army. Burnside did not have "the slows." He rushed his troops south and, on December 13, 1862, foolishly engaged Lee in a frontal assault at Fredericksburg, Virginia. His force outnumbered Lee's by a ratio of three to two; but Burnside's casualties that day were nearly 11,000, as compared to under 5,000 for the Army of Northern Virginia.

Shattered by the defeat, Burnside offered strong hints to Lincoln about finding a replacement. Lincoln accommodated him and elevated "Fighting Joe" Hooker, whose ambitions to command the Army of the Potomac were well known. Moving south in late April 1863, Hooker got 75,000 troops across the Rappahannock River and quickly squared off with Lee's Confederates in early May in what became a bloody brawl known as the Battle of Chancellorsville. The intense action resulted in a combined casualty count of 21,000 before Hooker pulled back across the

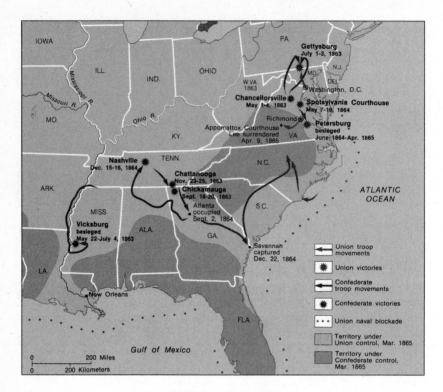

Civil War, 1863–1865

Rappahannock on the evening of May 5. "Stonewall" Jackson, shot accidentally by his own pickets during the engagement, died a few days later, costing General Lee and the South an authentic military genius. As for Hooker, the embarrassment of Chancellorsville soon brought to an end his command of the Army of the Potomac.

At this juncture, Lee asked Jefferson Davis for permission to lead his troops northward into Pennsylvania. There they could disrupt rail traffic, live off the land, and, most important, try to win a battle so overwhelming that Lincoln would be forced to consider peace terms favorable to the Confederacy. During June, Lee executed his plan. Late in the month Lincoln asked George G. Meade, a lackluster but competent general, to assume command of the Army of the Potomac, and on July 1, 1863, the two armies squared off against each other just west of a small Pennsylvania town called Gettysburg.

The Battle of Gettysburg, lasting three days, was the bloodiest engagement of the war, with combined casualties of more than 50,000. On the third day, hoping that he could split and rout his adversary, Lee massed soldiers under General George E. Pickett for an assault on the center of the Union line. Some 13,000 rebels charged across a mile of open, gradually rising fields, but were thrown back with 7,000 casualties. Late the next day Lee retreated, his army battered but not yet broken. Nonetheless, Gettysburg was a decisive battle. Never again would Lee have the troop strength to carry the war into enemy territory.

Meanwhile, in the western theater, the South suffered another major setback. After repeated attempts to seize Vicksburg, the Confederacy's last major stronghold on the Mississippi, from the north, General Grant had moved 75,000 troops south through eastern Arkansas into Louisiana, then swept east across the Mississippi River and slowly turned west in a wide arc, securing his lines against rebel marauders along the way. By late May, Grant had Vicksburg under siege, and his artillery bombarded that city and its defenders for six weeks. Reduced to living in caves and eating rats, Confederate troops and local citizens held on valiantly until they could take no more. On July 4, 1863, the day after Pickett's Charge, Grant accepted Vicksburg's surrender. Union forces had finally severed the Confederacy.

With these triumphs the war had turned against the South. Still, the combat was far from over, as Lincoln knew only too well as he rode a train to Gettysburg to dedicate a national memorial cemetery before a large crowd in November 1863. At Gettysburg he urged all citizens to "resolve that these dead shall not have died in vain;. . . and that government of the people, by the people, for the people, shall not perish from the earth."

Crushing Blows from Grant and Sherman

Vicksburg revived Grant's tarnished reputation, and after Union forces suffered an embarrassing defeat at the Battle of Chickamauga in northwestern Georgia on September 19–20, 1863, Lincoln named him overall commander of western forces. Grant quickly restored federal fortunes in the campaign to capture Chattanooga, Tennessee (November 1863). Now it was possible to plunge an army into Georgia to cut away at the heart of the Confederacy.

Early in 1864 Lincoln decided to name Grant general-in-chief. Vowing to end the war in a year, Grant planned to pursue the enemy deep inside the Confederacy, destroying all property that could be used to support the rebel armies. The general-in-chief called upon his old ally, General William Tecumseh Sherman, now commanding western forces, to march to Atlanta and destroy key Southern railheads there. As Sherman proceeded, he was to challenge the Confederate Army of Tennessee under General Joseph E. Johnston, now recovered from wounds suffered in defending Richmond back in the spring of 1862.

Grant and Sherman began operations in May 1864. Grant moved south across the Rappahannock River and engaged Lee in the Battle of the Wilderness (May 5–6). Union forces took a beating, but instead of retreating they rolled southeastward in what became the month-long campaign for Virginia. Again and again Johnny Rebs and Billy Yanks clashed at such places as Spotsylvania Court House (May 7–19) and Cold Harbor (June 1–3), within a few miles of Richmond. Finally, the two exhausted armies settled along siege lines at Petersburg, 20 miles southeast of the Confederate capital, with Grant waiting for Lee's army to disintegrate.

There had been nothing quite like the Virginia campaign before. Grant started with 120,000 soldiers, and half of them were casualties by early June. By the time Lee reached the Petersburg trenches in mid-June, his army had been reduced by more than a third to 40,000.

In the North, Peace Democrats called Grant a "butcher," but the general-in-chief, with Lincoln's backing, held tight to the war plan. Winning was now only a matter of time since the president, as the manager of the Union's superior resources, could supply more troops. The South, however, had no manpower left to give. Of an estimated 1.2 million white males between the ages of 16 and 50, some 90 percent had already seen Confederate military service; the comparable figure for the North was 40 percent.

In late 1864 Jefferson Davis admitted the South's need for new manpower when he called for the conscription of slaves. The Richmond government in March 1865 mandated the enlistment of 300,000 slaves; but by that time it was too late for Southerners "to gain our independence," as a Georgian noted with irony, "by the valor of our slaves." The war was over before black regiments could be organized.

If the Confederacy had any hope for survival in the fall of 1864, it centered on the upcoming presidential election. The Republicans, calling themselves the National Union party, renominated Lincoln in June with a new vice-presidential running mate, Andrew Johnson, a Democrat who had served as Tennessee's Union war governor after Grant's invasion of that state in early 1862. The Democrats nominated General George B. McClellan, running on a platform promising a negotiated end to the war, even if that meant independence for the Confederacy—a position McClellan himself thought too extreme to support. A despairing Lincoln, looking at the horrible casualty figures in Virginia, feared repudiation at the polls by a populace too sickened by the carnage to let him finish the fight.

Lincoln's pessimism proved groundless. He had not counted on General Sherman, moving slowly toward Atlanta in the face of stout rebel resistance. News of the capture of this major Confederate railroad and manufacturing center thrilled Northerners. The South was obviously in serious trouble. Voters gave Lincoln a resounding victory. On November 8, 1864, he received 55 percent of the popular vote and 212 electoral college votes, as compared to just 21 for McClellan.

Total War Forces Surrender

In the eighteenth century warfare rarely affected the whole populace. Armies were small, and combat could be conducted in war zones away from population centers. By comparison, the Civil War touched nearly every American life. Families gave fathers and sons to the armed services; and women assumed the management of farms or moved to the cities and took jobs to keep factories going in the production of war goods. Hundreds of women on both sides became nurses, and they fought to save thousands of lives. Dorothea Dix, superintendent of Union army nurses, and Clara Barton, who later founded the American Red Cross (1881), endured incredible personal privation to comfort those in pain. For the Confederacy, Sally L. Tompkins ran a clean, well-managed hospital in Richmond, Virginia.

In forcing an end to all the suffering and killing, General Sherman, after taking Atlanta, proposed to march his troops eastward to Savannah, Georgia, then north toward Grant's army in Virginia. Before year's end his soldiers cut a swath through Georgia 60 miles wide, and then in January 1865 they entered South Carolina, which they thought of as "the birth place of Dark Treason" against the Union. In systematic fashion Sherman's army broke the Southern capacity to keep fighting by burning and leveling everything in sight.

As word of Sherman's devastating march reached Lee's troops in the Petersburg trenches, they deserted in droves, wanting to get back home to protect their loved ones. By late March Lee's army had fewer than 35,000 troops, compared to Grant's total of 115,000. The situation was all but hopeless, so the Confederate commander ordered a retreat to the west. Grant's soldiers moved quickly to encircle the disintegrating rebel army, and on April 9, 1865, Lee met with Grant and surrendered at Appomattox. Grant graciously allowed the Confederates to keep their horses—they had to give up their arms—so that they could more easily plow their fields and plant crops after returning home. Lee's surrender served as a signal to other Confederate commanders to lay down their arms. The Civil War, at long last, had ended.

Conclusion

At noon on Good Friday, April 14, 1865, a crowd gathered to watch Major General Robert Anderson raise over Fort Sumter the very same U.S. flag that he had surrendered four years before. A genuinely moved Anderson said: "I thank God that I have lived to see this day." Then he hoisted up the "weather-beaten, frayed, and shell-torn old flag" as Union

*C*hronology of Key Events

1860	Abraham Lincoln elected sixteenth president; Crittenden Compromise fails; South Carolina secedes
1861	Six Deep-South States secede; Confederate States of America formed; Fort Sumter falls to Confederates; South wins First Battle of Bull Run (First Manassas)
1862	Union victory at Battle of Shiloh; Confederacy adopts a draft law; Homestead Act; Morrill Act; South wins Battle of the Seven Days and Second Battle of Bull Run (Second Manassas); Union victory at Battle of Antietam (Sharpsburg); Lincoln issues preliminary Emancipation Proclamation; Battle of Fredericksburg results in Southern victory
1863	Lincoln suspends habeas corpus for draft resisters; Battle of Gettysburg; siege of Vicksburg ends with Union victory; New York City draft riots occur
1864	Virginia campaign; siege of Petersburg begins; Sherman marches through Georgia
1865	Lee surrenders at Appomattox; John Wilkes Booth assassinates Lincoln; Andrew Johnson becomes seventeenth president

naval vessels out in Charleston harbor fired their cannons in salute. Citizens at the fort wept and cheered, realizing that the national tragedy was finally over, a tragedy that had forever sealed the fate of secession. The states, while far from reunited, would continue together as a nation.

Just a few hours later another shot rang out, this time in the nation's capital. John Wilkes Booth, a Confederate sympathizer and racist fanatic, gained access to the presidential box at Ford's Theater and assassinated the president at point-blank range. The next morning, four years to the day after he had declared an insurrection and called up federal troops, Lincoln died at the age of 56.

In his last days Lincoln felt the elation of knowing that a war begun to preserve the Union had achieved its objective. He took pride in the elimination of slavery from the American landscape, which he called the "act" that would put "my name . . . into history." Lincoln had also started to speak openly of citizenship for blacks as part of his reconstruction plans. Even as the American people mourned his passing, they too turned to the difficult task of how best to bring the South—defeated, destroyed, but still with a resolute streak of defiance—back into the nation.

Suggestions for Further Reading

Three valuable surveys of the Civil War are Shelby Foote, *The Civil War,* 3 vols. (1958–1974); James M. McPherson, *Battle Cry of Freedom* (1988); Allan Nevins, *The War for the Union,* 4 vols. (1959–1971).

Specialized military studies of the Civil War include Michael C. C. Adams, *Our Masters the Rebels* (1978); Joseph T. Glatthaar, *Partners in Command: Relationships Between Leaders in the Civil War* (1993); Paddy Griffith, *Battle Tactics of the Civil War* (1989); Gerald F. Linderman, *Embattled Courage: Combat in the American Civil War* (1987); Charles Royster, *The Destructive War: Sherman, Jackson, and the Americans* (1991); Steven E. Woodworth, *Jefferson Davis and His Generals: The Failure of Confederate Command in the West* (1990). The lives of common soldiers are the focus of Bell I. Wiley, *The Life of Johnny Reb* (1943), and *The Life of Billy Yank* (1952). On the role of African Americans during the war consult Joseph T. Glatthaar, *Forged in Battle: The Civil War Alliance of Black Soldiers and White Officers* (1990).

On the politics of the war effort, see LaWanda Cox, *Lincoln and Black Freedom* (1981); Paul D. Escott, *After Secession: Jefferson Davis* (1978); Eric Foner, *Politics and Ideology in the Age of the Civil War* (1980); Mark E. Neely, Jr., *The Fate of Liberty: Abraham Lincoln and Civil Liberties* (1991).

On the home front and American society during the conflict see Iver Bernstein, *The New York City Draft Riots* (1990); Randall C. Jimerson, *The Private Civil War: Popular Thought During the Sectional Conflict* (1988); Phillip Shaw Paludan, *"A People's Contest"* (1988); George C. Rable, *Civil Wars: Women and the Crisis of Southern Nationalism* (1989).

Valuable biographies of the period include Douglas S. Freeman, *R. E. Lee: A Biography,* 4 vols. (1934–1935); William S. McFeely, *Grant: A Biography* (1981); Stephen W. Sears, *George B. McClellan* (1988).

Chapter *16*

The Nation Reconstructed: North, South, and the West, 1865–1877

A s Thomas Pinckney approached El Dorado, his plantation in South Carolina, he felt a quiver of apprehension. Pinckney, a captain in the defeated Confederate army, had stayed the night with neighbors before going to reclaim his land. "Your negroes sacked your house," they reported. "They got it in their heads that the property of whites belongs to them." Pinckney remembered the days when he had been met with cheerful greetings from his slaves; now he was welcomed with an eerie silence. In the house, a single servant seemed genuinely glad to see him, but she pleaded ignorance as to the whereabouts of the other freed persons. He lingered about the house until after the dinner hour. Still no one appeared, so he informed the servant that he would return in the morning.

The next day Pinckney returned and summoned his former slaves. Their sullen faces reflected their defiant spirits. Pinckney told them, "I do not wish to interfere with your freedom. But I want my old hands to work my lands for me. I will pay wages." The freed persons remained silent as he gave further reassurances. Finally one responded. They would never again work for a white man, he told his former master. Pinckney seemed confused and asked how they expected to support themselves and where they would go. They quickly informed him that they intended to stay and work the land themselves.

Pinckney had no intention of allowing his former slaves to lay claim to his property. He joined with his neighbors in an appeal to the Union commander at Charleston, who sent a company of troops. The freed persons still refused to work under his terms, so Pinckney denied them access to food and supplies. Soon his head plowman begged food for his hungry family, claiming he wanted to work. Slowly, other former slaves drifted back. "They had suffered," he later recalled, "and their ex-master had suffered with them."

All over the South this scenario was acted out with variations, as former masters and slaves sought to define their new relationships. Whites tried to keep the freed persons a dependent labor source; African Americans struggled to win as much independence as possible. At the same time the other sections of the nation faced similar problems of determining the status of heterogeneous populations whose interests were sometimes in conflict with the majority. The war had reaped a costly harvest in lives and property, but at the same time it accelerated the modernization of the economy and society. Western expansion forced Americans to deal with the often hostile presence of the Plains Indians; the resumption of large-scale immigration raised issues of how to adapt to a society made up of many different ethnic and religious groups. Complicating these issues were unresolved questions about federal authority, widespread racial prejudice in both North and South, and strongly held beliefs in the sanctity of property rights.

Reconstruction offered an opportunity to balance conflicting interests with justice and fairness. In the end, however, the government was unwilling to establish ongoing programs and permanent mechanisms to protect the rights of minorities. As on Pinckney's plantation, economic power usually became the determining factor in establishing relationships. Authorities sacrificed the interests of both African Americans and the Indians of the West to the goals of national unity and economic growth. Yet in the ashes of failure were left two cornerstones on which the future could be built—the Fourteenth and Fifteenth Amendments to the Constitution.

Postwar Conditions and Issues

The war had exacted a heavy price on Americans, but its costs were not borne equally. Many segments of the Northern economy were stimulated by wartime demands and had benefited from federal programs enacted to aid industrial growth. Virtually exempt from the devastation of the battlefield, the North built railroads and industries and increased agricultural production. At the same time torn-up Southern rails were twisted around trees, Southern factories were put to the torch, and Southern farmland lay choked with weeds.

In 1865 Southerners were still reeling from the bitter legacy of total war. General Philip Sheridan announced that after his troops had finished in the Shenandoah Valley even a crow would have to carry rations to fly over the area. One year after the war Carl Schurz noted that along the path of Sherman's march the countryside still "looked for many miles like a broad black streak of ruin and desolation." Southern cities suffered the most. Much of what was not destroyed was confiscated, and emancipation divested Southerners of another $2 billion to $4 billion in assets. The decline of Southern wealth has been estimated at more than 40 percent during the four years of war.

The War's Impact on Individuals

Returning soldiers and their wives had to reconstruct relationships disrupted by separation—and the assumption of control by the women on farms and plantations. Southerners worried about how to meet their obligations, since Confederate currency and bonds were now worthless. Many white Southerners also feared that the end of slavery would bring a nightmare of black revenge, rape, and pillage unless whites retained social control.

For four million former slaves, emancipation had come piecemeal, following the course of the Northern armies. It was not finalized until the ratification of the Thirteenth Amendment in December 1865. By then most border states had voluntarily adopted emancipation, but the amendment destroyed the remnants of slavery in Delaware and Kentucky. Most slaves waited patiently for the day of freedom, continuing to work the plantations but speaking up more boldly. Sometimes the Yankees came, proclaimed them free, and then left them to the mercy of their masters. Most, therefore, reacted cautiously in testing the limits of their new freedom.

Many African Americans had to leave their plantations, at least for a short time, to feel liberated. A few were not sure about the meaning of freedom and thought they would never have to work again. Soon, most learned they had gained everything—and nothing. As Frederick Douglass noted, the freed person "was free from the individual master but a slave of society. He had neither money, property, nor friends. He was free from the old plantation, but he had nothing but the dusty road under his feet. . . . He was turned loose, naked, hungry, and destitute to the open sky."

The wartime plight of homeless and hungry blacks as well as whites impelled Congress to take unprecedented action, establishing on March 3, 1865, the Freedmen's Bureau within the War Department. The bureau was to provide "such issues of provisions, clothing, and fuel" as were needed to relieve "destitute and suffering refugees and their wives and children." Never before had the national government assumed responsibility for relief. Feeding and clothing the population had not been deemed its proper function. Considered a drastic measure warranted only by civil war, the bureau was to operate for only a year.

The bureau was more than a relief agency. It had its own courts to deal with land and labor disputes. Agents in every state provided rations and medical supplies and helped to negotiate labor contracts between former slaves and landowners. The quality of the service rendered to the freed persons depended on the ability and motivation of the individual agents. Some courageously championed the freed persons' cause; others sided with the former masters. One of the most lasting benefits of the Freedmen's Bureau was the schools it established, frequently in cooperation with such Northern agencies as the American Missionary Association. During and after the war, African Americans of all ages flocked to these schools. The freed persons shrewdly recognized the keys to the planters' power—land, literacy, and the vote. The white South legally denied all three to African Amerians in slavery, and many former slaves were determined to have them all.

During the war General Sherman had been plagued with swarms of freed persons following his army, and in January 1865 he issued an order setting aside a strip of abandoned coastal lands from Charleston, South Carolina, to Jacksonville, Florida, for the exclusive use of freed blacks who were to be given title to 40-acre lots. Three months later the bill establishing the Freedmen's Bureau gave the agency control of thousands of acres of abandoned and confiscated lands to be rented to former slaves for three-year periods with an option to buy at a later date. By June 1865, 40,000 African Americans were cultivating land. In the Sea Islands and elsewhere they proved they could succeed as independent farmers. Yet land reform was not a popular cause among whites. Although a few congressmen continued to advocate land confiscation and redistribution, most freed persons never realized the dream of "forty acres and a mule."

Unresolved Issues

At war's end many questions remained unanswered. The first of these concerned the status of the former slaves. They were indeed free, but were

Former slaves realized that education was one key to real freedom and flocked to schools opened by the Freedmen's Bureau, the American Missionary Association, and various religious and human rights groups.

they citizens? The Dred Scott decision had denied citizenship to all African Americans. Even if it were decided that they were citizens, what rights were conferred by that citizenship? Would they be segregated as free blacks in the antebellum North had often been? Also, citizenship did not automatically convey suffrage rights; women were proof of that. Were the freed persons to be given the ballot? Racial prejudice as well as constitutional and partisan questions complicated these weighty matters.

The Constitution had been severely tested by civil war, and many felt it had been twisted by the desire to save the Union. Once the emergency was over, how were constitutional balance and limits to be restored? Except during the terms of a few strong presidents, Congress had been the most powerful branch of government during the nation's first 70 years. Lincoln had assumed unprecedented powers, and Congress was determined to regain its ascendency. The ensuing battle directly influenced Reconstruction policies and their implementation.

Secession was dead, but what about states' rights? Almost everyone agreed that a division of power between the national and state governments was crucial to the maintenance of freedom. The fear of centralized tyranny remained strong. There was reluctance to enlarge federal power into areas traditionally controlled by the states, even though action in some of those areas was essential to craft the kind of peace many desired. Hesitation to reduce states' rights produced timid and compromised solutions to such issues as suffrage. Also of concern was federal action in the realm of social welfare, a new and controversial role for the national government.

Another constitutional question concerned the status of the former Confederate states and how they were to be readmitted to the Union. There was no constitutional provision for failed secession, and many people debated whether the South had actually left the Union. Southerners and their Democratic party sympathizers now argued that the states had never legally separated from the rest of the nation, thus denying validity to the Confederacy in order to quickly regain their place in the Union. Extremists on the other side—Radical Republicans—insisted that the South had reverted to the status of conquered territory, forfeiting all rights as states. Lincoln and others believed that the Confederate states had remained in the Union but had forfeited their rights. This constitutional hairsplitting grew out of a struggle between the executive and legislative branches to determine which had the power to readmit the states and on what terms. It also reflected the hostility of some Northerners toward the "traitorous rebels" and the unwillingness of some Southerners to accept the consequences of defeat.

Affecting all these questions was partisan politics. The Republican party had very few adherents in the South. Its continued existence was dubious in the face of the probable reunion of the Northern and Southern wings of the Democratic party. Paradoxically, the political power of the

South, and in turn the Democratic party, was increased by the abolition of slavery. As freed persons, all African Americans would be counted for representation; as slaves only three-fifths of them had been counted. Thus the Republican party's perceived need to make itself a national party also influenced the course of Reconstruction.

Presidential Reconstruction

Early in the conflict questions regarding the reconstruction of the nation were secondary to winning the war—without victory there would be no nation to reconstruct. Nonetheless, Lincoln had to take some action as Union forces pushed into the South. Authority had to be imposed in the reclaimed territory, so the president named military governors for Tennessee, Arkansas, and Louisiana in 1862 after federal armies occupied most of those states. Lincoln also began formulating plans for civilian governments for those states and for other Confederate areas once they came under the control of Union forces.

Lincoln's Plan

Called the 10 percent plan, Lincoln's provisions were incredibly lenient. Rebels could receive presidential pardon by merely swearing their future allegiance to the Union and their acceptance of the end of slavery. Only a few people were excluded from pardons: Confederate military and civilian officers; United States judges, congressmen, and military officers who had resigned their posts to serve the Confederacy. Nevertheless, Lincoln did not require the new state governments to bar such people from future voting or officeholding. Moreover, after only 10 percent of the number who had voted in 1860 had taken the oath of allegiance, a state could form a civilian government. When such states produced a constitution outlawing slavery, Lincoln promised to recognize them as reconstructed. He did not demand any provisions for protecting black rights or allowing black suffrage.

The president's generosity outraged Radical Republicans, such as Representative Thaddeus Stevens of Pennsylvania and Senator Charles Sumner of Massachusetts. They thought the provisions did not adequately punish Confederate treason, restructure Southern society, protect the rights of African Americans, or aid the Republican party. The Radicals were in a minority, but Lincoln's leniency also dismayed many moderate Republicans. They shared the Radical view that Reconstruction was a congressional, not a presidential, function.

Congress then drew up a plan of its own: the Wade-Davis Bill. Its terms were much more stringent, yet not unreasonable. A majority, rather than 10 percent, of each state's voters had to declare their allegiance to form a government. Only those taking "ironclad" oaths of their past Union loyalty were allowed to participate in the making of new state constitutions. Barely a handful of high-ranking Confederates, however, were to be permanently barred from political participation. The only additional requirement imposed by Congress was the repudiation of the Confederate debt; Northerners did not want Confederate bondholders to benefit from their "investment in treason" at the cost to northern taxpayers. Congress would determine when a state had met these requirements.

A constitutional collision was postponed by Lincoln's pocket veto of the bill and his assassination on April 14, 1865. His successor, Andrew Johnson, was a Tennessee Democrat and Unionist. Of humble origins and illiterate until adulthood, he was the only Southerner to remain in the Senate after his state seceded. As with the Radical wing of the Republican party Johnson hated the planter class, but it was their aristocratic domination of the South, not their slaveholding, that he disliked. He was a firm believer in black inferiority and did not support the Radical aim of black legal equality. He also advocated strict adherence to the Constitution and strongly supported states' rights.

Johnson's Plan

In the end Johnson did not reverse Lincoln's lenient policy. Congress was not in session when Johnson became president so he had about eight months to pursue policies without congressional interference. He issued his own proclamation of amnesty in May 1865 and issued about 13,000 pardons. The most important aspect of the pardons was Johnson's claim that they restored all rights, including property rights. Thus many freed persons with crops in the ground suddenly found their masters back in charge—a disillusioning first taste of freedom that foreclosed further attempts at widespread land redistribution.

Johnson also announced plans for the reconstruction of North Carolina—a plan that was to set the pattern for all Southern states. A native Unionist was named provisional governor with the power to call a constitutional convention elected by loyal voters. Omitting Lincoln's 10 percent provision, Johnson did eventually require ratification of the Thirteenth Amendment, repudiation of Confederate debts, and state constitutional provisions abolishing slavery and renouncing secession. He also recommended limited suffrage for African Americans, primarily to stave off congressional attempts to give the vote to all black males.

The presidential plan fell short of the Radicals' hopes, but many moderates might have accepted it had the South complied with the letter

Andrew Johnson was the only president of the United States to be impeached. His successful defense centered on the legitimate uses of his executive powers.

and the spirit of Johnson's proposals. Instead, Southerners seemed determined to ignore their defeat. The state governments, for the most part, met the minimum requirements, but their apparent acceptance grew out of a belief that very little had actually changed. Thus Southerners proceeded to show almost total disregard for Northern sensibilities. Presenting themselves, like prodigal sons, for admission to Congress were four Confederate generals, six Confederate cabinet officials, and as the crowning indignity, Confederate Vice President Alexander H. Stephens. Most Northerners were not exceedingly vindictive. Still, the North wanted signs of change and indications of repentence by the former rebels.

Black Codes in the South

At the very least, Northerners expected adherence to the abolition of slavery, but the South was blatantly forging new forms of bondage. African Americans were to be technically free, but Southern whites expected them to work and live as they had before emancipation. To accomplish this purpose, the new state governments enacted a series of laws known as the Black Codes. This legislation granted certain rights denied to slaves. Freed persons had the right to marry, own property, sue and be sued, and testify in court. However, Black Codes in all states prohibited racial inter-marriage, and some forbade freed persons from owning certain types of property, such as alcoholic beverages and firearms. Most so tightly re-stricted black legal rights that they were practically nonexistent. Black Codes imposed curfews on African Americans, segregated them, and out-lawed their right to congregate in large groups.

The Black Codes also sought to fashion a labor system as close to slavery as possible. Some laws required that African Americans obtain spe-cial licenses for any job except agricultural labor or domestic service. Most mandated the signing of yearly labor contracts, which sometimes required African Americans to call the landowner "master" and allowed withhold-ing wages for minor infractions. Mississippi even prohibited black owner-ship or rental of land. Mandatory apprenticeship programs took children away from their parents, and vagrancy laws allowed authorities to arrest blacks and use them on chain gangs or rent them out to planters for as long as a year at a time.

Most Northerners would not have insisted on black equality or suf-frage, but the South had regressed too far. Some Black Codes were virtually identical to the old slave codes, with the word *negro* substituted for *slave*. At the same time, reports of white violence against blacks filtered back to Washington. As a result, Congress refused to seat the representatives and senators from the former Confederate states when it reconvened in De-cember 1865 and instead proceeded to investigate conditions in the South.

Congressional Reconstruction

To discover what was really happening in the South, Congress established the Joint Committee on Reconstruction, which conducted inquiries and interviews that provided graphic and chilling examples of white repres-sion and brutality toward African Americans. Prior to the committee's final report, even moderates came to believe that action was necessary. In early 1866 Congress passed a bill to extend the life of the Freedmen's Bu-reau, but Johnson vetoed it, claiming that the bureau was constitutional only as a wartime measure. Congress then passed the Civil Rights Act, granting citizenship to all persons born in the United States. Once again, Johnson used his veto power to kill a bill that he deemed both unconsti-tutional and unwise. This time, however, Congress overrode the veto. It then passed a slightly revised Freedmen's Bureau bill in July and enacted it over Johnson's veto. Even though the South had ignored much of John-son's advice, such as granting limited suffrage to blacks, the president stubbornly held to his conviction that reconstruction was complete and labeled his congressional opponents as "traitors."

Johnson's language did not create a climate of cooperation. Congress did not care about the constitutional questions that he raised and his chal-lenge to congressional authority. Determined to establish an alternate program of reconstruction, Congress drafted the Fourteenth Amendment. Undoubtedly the most significant legacy of Reconstruction, the first arti-cle of the amendment defined citizenship and its basic rights. Every per-son born in the United States and subject to its jurisdiction was declared a citizen. The amendment also forbade any state from abridging the rights of citizenship or from depriving any person of "due process of law." Al-though 100 years would pass before its provisions were enforced as in-tended, the amendment has been interpreted to mean that states as well as the federal government are bound by the Bill of Rights—an important constitutional change that paved the way for the civil rights decisions and laws of the twentieth century.

The amendment did not require black suffrage but reduced the "basis of representation" proportionately for those states not allowing it. Former Confederate leaders were also barred from holding office unless pardoned by Congress—not the president. Finally, neither Confederate war debts nor compensation to former slaveholders were ever to be paid. Congress adopted the amendment, in June 1866 and then sent it to the states for ratification.

President Johnson bristled at this assault on his perceived powers and urged the Southern states not to ratify the amendment. All but Tennessee decided to take his advice and wait for further congressional action. John-son took to the campaign trail, urging voters to oust the Radicals in the 1866 congressional elections. He met with heckling and humiliation dur-ing his "swing around the circle." The campaign was vicious, character-ized by appeals to racial prejudice by the Democrats and charges of Democratic treason by the Republicans. The Republicans won over-whelming victories, which they interpreted as a mandate for congressional reconstruction.

"Radical" Reconstruction

The election results along with Southern intransigence finally gave the Radicals the upper hand. In 1867 Congress passed the Military Recon-struction Act that raised the price of readmission. This act declared all ex-isting "Johnson governments," except Tennessee's, void and divided the

South into five military districts headed by military governors who were to be granted broad powers. Following the ratification of a new state constitution that provided for black suffrage, elections were to be held and the state would be required to ratify the Fourteenth Amendment. When that amendment became part of the Constitution and Congress approved the new state constitutions, the states would be granted representation in Congress once again.

Obviously, Johnson disliked the congressional plan; he vetoed it, only to see his veto overridden. Nevertheless, as commander-in-chief he reluctantly appointed military governors, and by the end of 1867 elections had been held in every state except Texas. Because many white Southerners boycotted the elections, the South came under the control of Republicans supported by Union forces. In a way, however, Southerners had brought more radical measures upon themselves by their inflexibility.

Congress realized the plan it had enacted was unprecedented and subject to challenge by the other two branches of government. To check Johnson's power, Congress also passed the Tenure of Office Act, which required Senate consent for the removal of any official whose appointment had required the Senate's confirmation. It was meant in part to protect Secretary of War Edwin M. Stanton, who supported the Radicals.

When the president attempted to remove Stanton, the House of Representatives voted to impeach Johnson. In the Senate trial that followed radical prosecutors argued that Johnson had committed "high crimes and misdemeanors" and asserted that a president could be removed for political reasons, even without being found legally guilty of crimes—a position James Madison had supported during the drafting of the Constitution.

The vote for conviction fell one short of the required two-thirds majority, when seven Republicans broke ranks and voted against conviction. This action set the precedent that a president must be guilty of serious misdeeds to be removed from office. The outcome was a political blow to the Radicals, costing them some support. On the other hand, Johnson's brush with impeachment did make him more cooperative for the last months of his presidency.

Black Suffrage

In the 1868 presidential election the Republicans won with Ulysses S. Grant, whose Civil War victories made his name a household word. His slogan, "Let us have peace," was appealing, but his election was less than a ringing endorsement for Radical policies. The military hero who had seemed invincible barely won the popular vote in several key states.

While a few Radicals had long favored black suffrage, only after the Republicans' electoral close call in 1868 did the bulk of the party begin to consider a suffrage amendment. Many were swayed by the political certainty that the black vote would be theirs and might give them the margin of victory in future close elections. Others were embarrassed by the hypocrisy of forcing black suffrage on the South while only 7 percent of Northern African Americans could vote. Still others believed that granting African Americans the vote would relieve whites of any further responsibility to protect black rights.

Suffrage supporters faced many objections to such an amendment. One was based on the lack of popular support. At that time only seven Northern states granted blacks the right to vote, and, since 1865, referendum proposals for black suffrage in eight states had been voted down. The amendment was so unpopular that, ironically, it could never have won adoption without its ratification by the Southern states, where black suffrage already existed. A more serious challenge was the question of whether Congress could legislate suffrage at all. Before Reconstruction the national government had never taken any action regarding the right to vote; suffrage had been considered not a right but a privilege which only the states could confer.

The issue of an amendment guaranteeing black suffrage also raised the question of whether women should be granted the franchise. As leaders of the Women's Loyal League, Elizabeth Cady Stanton and Susan B. Anthony had both worked hard for the adoption of the Thirteenth Amendment, only to be rewarded by inclusion of the word *male* in the Fourteenth Amendment of the Constitution—the first time that word appears. Some women, such as Lucy Stone of the American Woman Suffrage Association, accepted the plea of longtime women's suffrage supporter Frederick Douglass that it was the "Negro's hour," and worked for ratification. Anthony, however, vowed to "cut off this right arm of mine before I will ever work for or demand the ballot for the Negro and not the woman." Such differences played a role in splitting the women's movement in 1869 between those working for a national suffrage amendment and those who concentrated their efforts on the state level. Anthony and Stanton founded the National Woman Suffrage Association to fight for a constitutional amendment and other feminist reforms. Others became disillusioned with that approach and established the American Woman Suffrage Association, which focused on obtaining suffrage on a state-by-state basis.

Actually, women did not lose much by not being included in the Fifteenth Amendment. To meet the various objections, compromise was necessary. The resulting amendment did not grant the vote to anyone. It merely stated that the vote could not be denied "on account of race, color, or previous condition of servitude." Suffrage was still essentially to be controlled by the states, and other bases of exclusion would not be deemed unconstitutional. These loopholes would eventually allow white Southerners to make a mockery of the amendment.

Although congressional reconstruction was labeled "radical," compromise and caution had prevailed. What Congress did *not* do is as important as what it did. It did not even guarantee the right to vote. There was only one execution for war crimes and only Jefferson Davis was imprisoned for more than a few months. For all but a handful, ex-Confederates were not permanently barred from voting or holding office. Most local Southern governments were undisturbed. Land as well as rights were restored to former rebels, eliminating the possibility of extensive land redistribution. The only attempt by the national government to meet the basic needs of African-American citizens was the temporary Freedmen's Bureau—justified only as an emergency measure. The cautious nature of Reconstruction doomed it as an opportunity to provide means for the protection of minority rights.

Such congressional moderation reflected the spirit of the age. Long-cherished beliefs in the need for strict construction of the Constitution and in states' rights presented formidable barriers to truly radical changes. Property rights were considered sacrosanct—even for "traitors." Cherished ideals of self-reliance and the conviction that a person determined his or her own destiny led many to believe that African Americans should take care of themselves.

Tainting every action was the widespread racist conviction that African Americans were not equal to whites. Many Northerners were more concerned with keeping blacks in the South than with abstract black rights. Even Radical Representative George Julian admitted to his Indiana constituents, "the real trouble is that *we hate the negro*. It is not his ignorance that offends us, but his color."

The plan for Reconstruction evolved fitfully, buffeted first one way and then another by the forces of the many unresolved issues at war's end. If permanent changes were very limited, nonetheless precedents had been set for later action, and for a brief time congressional reconstruction brought about the most democratic governments the South had ever seen—or would see for another hundred years.

Reconstruction in the South

Regardless of the specific details hammered out in Washington, any dictated peace would probably have been unpalatable to Southern whites. They were especially leery of any action that seemed to threaten white supremacy. Most Southerners condemned the Freedmen's Bureau, believing that its agents were partial to African Americans. Actually there was great diversity in the background and goals of bureau agents. Some were idealistic young New England men and women who came south to aid in the transition to freedom. Others were army officers whose first priority was to maintain order, often by siding with the landowners.

The results of bureau actions were mixed in regard to conditions for African Americans. The agents helped to negotiate labor contracts that African Americans had to sign to obtain rations. Frequently the wages were well below the rate at which slaves had been hired out by their owners before the war. Although money was scarce at the time, these contracts helped to keep African Americans on the farm—someone else's farm. On the other hand, between 1865 and 1869 the bureau issued over 21 million rations, of which about 5 million went to whites. The bureau also operated more than 40 hospitals, opened hundreds of schools, and accomplished the herculean task of resettling some 30,000 people displaced by the war. The agency showed that the federal government could establish and administer a massive relief program, as it would again do during the depression of the 1930s.

Carpetbaggers, Scalawags, and Black Republicans

After the passage of the Reconstruction Acts in 1867, Republican officeholders joined bureau agents in directing the course of Reconstruction. Northerners who came to the South during or after the war and became engaged in politics were called "carpetbaggers" by resentful Southerners. They supposedly arrived with a few meager belongings in their carpetbags, which they would fill with their ill-gotten gains from looting an already devastated South. Probably what most infuriated whites was the carpetbaggers' willingness to cooperate with African Americans. Native whites accused the carpetbaggers of cynically exploiting the freed persons for their own gain.

White Southerners who voted for Republicans were labeled "scalawags." The term had been used previously as a synonym for a loafer or rascal. Such men were said to have "sold themselves for office" and become a "subservient tool and accomplice" of the carpetbaggers. Some scalawags were members of the old commercial elite of bankers and merchants who, as former Whigs, favored the economic policies of the Republican party. The majority of Southern white Republican voters were yeoman farmers and poor whites from areas where slavery had been unimportant. They had long resented planter domination and had opposed secession.

Northerners who engaged in politics in the South before or after the war were called carpetbaggers. This cartoon shows Ulysses S. Grant and Union soldiers propping up carpetbag rule with bayonets, while the "Solid South" staggers under the weight.

Most detested by white Southerners were the black Republicans. They loathed the prospect of African Americans in authority. They feared that the former slaves would exact payment for their years of bondage. Democrats also knew that racism was their best rallying cry to regain power. Whites claimed that ignorant freed persons, incapable of managing their own affairs, were allowed to run the affairs of state with disastrous results.

Such myths persisted for a long time. Southern whites had determined even before Reconstruction began that it would be "the most galling tyranny and most stupendous system of organized robbery that is to be met with in history." The truth was, as black leader W. E. B. Du Bois later wrote, "There is one thing that the white South feared more than negro dishonesty, ignorance, and incompetency, and that was negro honesty, knowledge, and efficiency." To a surprising degree they got what they most feared.

Black voters were certainly as fit to vote as the millions of illiterate whites enfranchised by Jacksonian democracy. Black officials as a group were as qualified as their white counterparts. In South Carolina two-thirds of them were literate, and in all states most of the acknowledged leaders were well educated and articulate. They usually had been members of the Northern or Southern free black elite or part of the slave aristocracy of skilled artisans and household slaves. Hiram Revels, a U.S. senator from Mississippi, was the son of free blacks who had sent him to college in the North. James Walker Hood, the presiding officer of the North Carolina constitutional convention of 1867, was a Pennsylvania native and an African Methodist Episcopal missionary. Some, such as Francis Cardoza of South Carolina, were the privileged mulatto sons of white planters. Cardoza had been educated in Scottish and English universities. During Reconstruction 14 such men served in the U.S. House of Representatives and two in the Senate. By 1901, six others were elected to the House, before Southern black political power was effectively demolished.

In a historic first, seven African Americans were elected to the Forty-first and Forty-second Congresses. Between 1869 and 1901, two African Americans became senators and 20 served in the House.

Even if black Republicans had been incompetent, they could hardly be held responsible for the perceived abuses of so-called black reconstruction. Only in South Carolina did African Americans have a majority of the delegates to the constitutional convention provided for by the Reconstruction Acts. Neither did they dominate the new governments; only for a two-year period in South Carolina did blacks control both houses of the legislature. When the vote was restored to ex-Confederates, African Americans comprised only one-third of the voters of the South, and only in two states did they have a majority.

Actually, carpetbaggers dominated most Republican governments. They accounted for less than one percent of the party's voters but held a third of the offices. Their power was especially obvious in the higher offices. Over half of all Southern Republican governors and almost half of the Republican congressmen and senators were former Northerners. Although some carpetbaggers did resemble their stereotypes, most did not. Many had come south before black enfranchisement and could not have predicted political futures based on black votes. Most were Union veterans; some brought with them much-needed capital for local investments. A few came with a sense of mission to educate blacks and reform Southern society.

Since African Americans constituted only a third of the population and carpetbaggers less than one percent, those two groups had to depend on the votes of a sizable number of native white Southerners to obtain political offices in some regions of the South. To win the scalawags' vote (most of whom were poor whites) the Republicans appealed to class interests, playing on traditional lower-class resentment of the planter aristocracy. Many Southerners, won over by campaign promises of debtor relief, accepted such arguments and joined African Americans to put Republicans into office. The coalition, however, was always shaky, given the racism of poor whites. The scalawags actually represented a swing vote that finally moved toward the Democratic party of white supremacy later in the 1870s.

Character of Republican Rule

While the coalition lasted, the Republican governments became the most democratic that the South had ever had. More people could vote for more offices; all remaining property requirements for voting and officeholding were dropped; representation was made fairer through reapportionment; and more offices became elective rather than appointive. Salaries for public officials made it possible to serve without being wealthy. Most important, universal male suffrage was enacted with the support of black legislators. Ironically, by refusing to deny Southern whites what had been denied to them—the vote—African Americans sowed the seeds of their own destruction.

The Republican state constitutions, which brought the South firmly into the mainstream of national reform, often remained in effect years after the end of Reconstruction. Legislatures abolished automatic imprisonment for debt and reduced the use of the death penalty. More institutions for the care of the indigent, orphans, mentally ill, deaf, and blind were established. Tax structures were overhauled, reducing head taxes and increasing property taxes to relieve somewhat poorer taxpayers. At the same time, Southern railroads, harbors, and bridges were rebuilt.

Black legislators had the most success in laying the foundations for public education. Antebellum provisions for public schools below the Mason-Dixon line were meager to nonexistent. In every state African Americans were among the main proponents of state-supported schools, but most accepted segregated facilities as necessary compromises. Some black parents did not even desire integration; they believed their children could not flourish in environments tainted by white supremacy. By 1877 some 600,000 blacks were in schools, but only the University of South Carolina and the public schools of New Orleans were integrated.

As desirable as many of the new social services were, they required money and money was scarce. The war had destroyed not only railroads and bridges but also much of the Southern tax base. The necessary tax increases were unpopular, as were soaring state debts. Both were blamed on corruption, with some justification. Louisiana Governor Henry C. Warmouth netted some $100,000 during a year in which his salary was only $8,000. One black man was paid $9,000 to repair a bridge with an original cost of only $500. Contracts for rebuilding and expanding railroads, subsidies to industries, and bureaucracies for administering social services offered abundant opportunities for graft and bribery.

When these scandals came to light, Southern whites were quick to point an accusing finger at freed persons who, they claimed, were unfit for positions of authority. Actually, although African Americans received a large share of the blame, they received little of the profit. A smaller percentage of blacks than whites were involved in the scandals. Also the corruption that the Democrats denounced at every turn was rather meager in comparison to the shenanigans of some Democratic regimes in the North. In the aftermath of the war an orgy of national corruption seemed to infect both political parties.

Black and White Adaptation

The "tyranny" that so distressed Southern whites did not include wholesale disfranchisement or confiscation of their lands. Just as the ex-slaves on Thomas Pinckney's plantation had learned, freed persons everywhere soon realized that the economic power of whites had diminished little. If anything, land became more concentrated in the hands of a few. In one Alabama county the richest 10 percent of landowners increased their share of landed wealth from 55 to 63 percent between 1860 and 1870. Some African Americans, usually through hard work and incredible sacrifice, were able to obtain land. The percentage of blacks who owned property increased from less than 1 to 20 percent. Indeed, African Americans seemed to fare better than poor whites, for whom the percentage of land ownership dropped from 80 to 67 percent.

Most poor blacks and whites worked on someone else's land as sharecroppers. Under this system, landowners gave tenants a plot of land to work in return for a share of the crops. African Americans preferred the sharecropping system because working in gangs as contract and wage laborers under white supervision smacked too much of slavery. Anxious to obtain as much autonomy as possible, some freed persons hitched mule teams to their old slave cabins and carried them off to their assigned acres.

Sharecropping at first seemed to be a good bargain for African Americans. Receiving a half share of the crops they produced, they were making more for working less. Fewer family members worked and black men labored shorter hours; as a group African Americans worked one-third fewer hours than under slavery.

But sharecropping proved to be disastrous for most blacks and poor whites. They needed more than land to farm; they also required seeds, fertilizers, and provisions to live on until they harvested their crops. To obtain these necessities they often borrowed against their share of the crops. Falling crop prices, high credit rates, and, in later years, laws favoring creditors left many to harvest a growing burden of debt with each crop.

If most freedmen did not win economic freedom, they benefited from freedom in other ways. Since it was no longer illegal to learn to read and write, African Americans pursued education with much zeal. A growing number also sought higher education. Between 1860 and 1880 over 1,000 African Americans earned college degrees. Some went north to college, but most attended one of the 13 Southern colleges established by the American Missionary Association or by black and white churches with the assistance of the Freedmen's Bureau. Such schools as Howard University and Fisk University were a permanent legacy of Reconstruction.

African Americans were also able to enjoy and expand their rich cultural heritage. Religion was a central focus for most, just as it had been in slavery. Church membership in such antebellum denominations as the African Methodist Episcopal soared. In essence, black Christians declared their religious independence, and their churches became centers of political and social activities as well as religious ones.

The very changes that gave African Americans hope during Reconstruction distressed poor whites. Black political equality rankled them, but much more serious was their own declining economic status. As their land ownership decreased, more whites became dependent on sharecropping and low-wage jobs, primarily in the textile industry.

Ironically, although nearly everyone perceived poor whites as the group most hostile to blacks, the two shared many aspects of a rich Southern cultural heritage. In religion and recreation their experiences were similar. At camp meetings and revivals poor whites practiced a highly emotional religion, just as many black Southerners did. Both groups spun yarns and sang songs that reflected the perils of their existence and provided folk heroes. They also shared many superstitions as well as useful folk remedies. Race, however, was a potent wedge between them that upper-class whites frequently exploited for their own political and economic goals.

Planters no longer dominated the white elite; sharecropping turned them and others into absentee landlords. The sons of the old privileged families joined the growing ranks of lawyers, railroad entrepreneurs, bankers, industrialists, and merchants. In some ways, the upper and middle classes began to merge, but in many places the old elite and their children still enjoyed a degree of deference and political leadership. Their hostility toward African Americans was not as intense, largely because they possessed means of control. When their control slipped, however, they also became strident racists.

Violent White Resistance

Large numbers of whites of all classes engaged in massive resistance to Reconstruction. In 1866 some young men in Pulaski, Tennessee, organized the Ku Klux Klan, which began as a social club with all the trappings of fraternal orders—secret rituals, costumes, and practical jokes. They soon learned that their antics intimidated African Americans; thenceforth the Klan grew into a terrorist organization, copied all over the South under various names. A major goal of the Klan was to intimidate Republican voters and restore Democrats to office. In South Carolina, when blacks working for a scalawag began to vote, Klansmen visited the plantation and "whipped every nigger man they could lay their hands on." The group's increasing lawlessness alarmed many people and led to congressional action. The Klan was broken up by three Enforcement Acts that gave the president the right to suspend habeas corpus against "armed combinations" interfering with any citizen's right to vote. In 1871 Grant did so in nine South Carolina counties. Disbanding the Klan, however, did little to decrease Southern violence or the activities of similar terrorist groups.

Some black Southerners were probably never allowed to vote freely. At the peak of Reconstruction, fewer than 30,000 federal troops were stationed in the entire South, hardly enough to protect the rights of 4.5 million African Americans. As troops were being withdrawn, Democrats sought to regain control of their states. Without secret ballots landowners could threaten sharecroppers with eviction for "improper" voting. In addition to economic intimidation, violence against freed persons escalated in most states as the Democrats increased their political power. When victory seemed close, Democrats justified any means to "redeem" the South and rid it of Republican influence. In six heavily black counties in Mississippi such tactics proved highly successful, reducing Republican votes from more than 14,000 in 1873 to only 723 in 1876. Beginning with Virginia and Tennessee in 1869, by 1876 all but three states—Louisiana, Florida, and South Carolina—had Democratic "Redeemer" governments. The final collapse of Reconstruction became official the following year with the withdrawal of federal troops from the three unredeemed states.

Reconstruction in the North and West

In the end, the South could be said to have lost the war but won the peace. After 1877 Southern whites found little resistance to their efforts to forge new institutions to replace both the economic benefits and racial control of slavery. By 1910 they had devised a system of legalized repression that gave whites many of the benefits of slavery without all the responsibilities. Surely this pattern was not what the North had envisioned after Appomattox in 1865; nonetheless, as the years passed, civil rights for African Americans ceased to become a Northern priority. A shifting political climate, economic hard times, increasing preoccupation with other issues, and continued racism combined to make most Northerners retreat from any responsibility for the protection of black rights.

Northern Shifts in Attitudes

When Grant won the presidency in 1868, the voters had chosen a war hero who had no political record or experience. They voted not so much for a program, but for Grant's campaign slogan: "Let us have peace." The victorious general proved to be a poor choice. Politically inexperienced, haunted by a fear of failure, and socially insecure, Grant was too easily influenced by men of wealth and prestige. He made some dismal appointments and remained loyal to individuals who did not merit his trust. The result was a series of national political scandals. Grant was not personally involved, but his close association with the perpetrators blemished both his and his party's image. The first major scandal involved the Crédit Mobilier, a dummy construction company used to milk money from railroad investors in order to line the pockets of a few insiders, including Vice President Schuyler Colfax and a number of other prominent Republicans. Later, bribes and kickback schemes surfaced that involved Indian trading posts, post office contracts, and commissions for tax collection. Such revelations as well as the corruption in some Southern Republican governments did little to enhance the public image of the party, and Democrats were quick to make corruption a major issue in both the North and the South.

In the 1872 presidential election disenchantment with the Grant administration prompted a group calling themselves Liberal Republicans to form a separate party and nominate their own candidate, *New York Tribune* editor Horace Greeley. Among Greeley's campaign pledges was a more moderate Southern policy. Even with the Democrats also nominating Greeley, Grant easily won reelection, but Republican dominance was slipping. That year the Democrats captured the House and made gains in the Senate, following further revelations of Republican corruption.

At least as detrimental to Republican political fortunes was a depression that followed the panic of 1873, which resulted from overinvestment in railroads and risky financial deals. Lasting six years, the depression was the most serious economic downturn the nation had yet experienced. Whatever their cause, depressions usually result in "voting the rascals out." Yet economic distress had an even wider impact on Reconstruction. People's attention became focused on their pocketbooks rather than on abstract ideals of equality and justice. Economic scrutiny brought such issues as currency and tariffs to the forefront. As the depression deepened, many questioned Republican support for "sound money" backed by gold and the retirement of the legal-tender "greenback" paper money that had been issued during the war.

Those greenbacks had increased the money supply needed to finance postwar economic expansion. Yet many Republicans were suspicious of any money not backed by specie—that is, gold or silver. One of the last actions of the Republican-controlled Congress was to pass the Resumption Act of 1875. This bill provided for the gradual redemption of greenbacks in gold. The resulting deflation favored creditors over debtors because debtors were forced to repay loans with money that was worth more than when they borrowed it. Many Americans, especially farmers, were already in debt, and deflation coupled with a depression brought economic distress.

Actually, the panic of 1873 brought into clearer focus the vast changes occurring in the North during Reconstruction. The United States was experiencing the growing pains of economic modernization and westward expansion, the effects of which, such as the completion of the first transcontinental railroad in 1869, overshadowed Reconstruction-related issues. By the late 1870s the Republican party had foresaken its reformist past to become a protector of railroad and business interests rather than a guarantor of basic rights.

Racism and American Indians

The major reason for the decline of Reconstruction was the pervasive belief in white supremacy. There could be little determination to secure equal rights for those who were considered unequal in all other respects. Reconstruction represented a failed opportunity to resolve justly the status of one minority, and the climate of racism almost ensured failure for others as well. Westward expansion not only diverted attention from Reconstruction but also raised the question of what was to be done about the Plains Indians. They, too, were considered inferior to whites. Although Reconstruction at first offered hope to African Americans, for the American Indian hope was fading.

In the end, African Americans were oppressed; Native Americans were exterminated or pushed onto shrinking reservations. Because most Africans, like Europeans, depended on agriculture rather than hunting, they adapted more easily to agricultural slavery. Black labor was valuable, if controlled; Indians stood as barriers to expansion.

When settlers first began moving onto the Great Plains, they encountered about 250,000 Plains Indians and 13 million buffalo. Some tribes, including the Zuñi, Hopi, Navaho, and Pawnee, had fixed settlements and depended on gardening and farming. Such tribes as the Sioux, Apache, and Cheyenne, however, were nomadic hunters who followed the buffalo herds over vast tracts of land.

Cultural differences caused misunderstandings between settlers and Native Americans and ultimately led to conflict. Among Anglo-Americans capitalism fostered competition and frontier living promoted individualism. On the other hand, Plains Indians lived in tribes based on kinship ties. As members of an extended family that included distant cousins, Indians were taught to place the welfare of the group over the interests of the individual. The emphasis within a tribe was on cooperation rather than competition. Some tribes might be richer than others, but there was seldom a large gap between the rich and the poor within a tribe.

The two cultures' widely divergent forms of political organization also caused problems. Among the Indian tribes, power as well as wealth was usually shared. Chiefs seldom had much individual power, but were generally religious and ceremonial leaders. Whites incorrectly believed that an Indian chief could make decisions and sign treaties that would be considered legal and binding by fellow tribal members.

Another major cultural difference between the newly arriving settlers and the Plains tribes was their attitude toward the land. Most Indians had no concept of private property. They refused to draw property lines and borders because of how they viewed the place of people in the world. Whites tended to see land, plants, and animals as resources to be exploited. Indians, on the other hand, stressed the unity of all life. Most of the Plains Indians believed that land could be utilized, but never owned. The idea of owning land was as absurd as owning the air people breathed. As Chief Joseph of the Nez Percé tribe said, "The earth and myself are of one mind." Thus people were not meant to dominate the rest of nature; they were a part of it.

Although some tribes could coexist peacefully with settlers, nomadic Indians had a way of life that was incompatible with miners, railroad developers, cattle ranchers, and farmers. Most had no desire for assimilation; they merely wanted to be left alone. To Anglo-Americans the Indians were barriers to expansion. They agreed with Theodore Roosevelt that the West was not meant to be "a game reserve for squalid savages." Thus U.S. Indian policy focused on getting more territory for white settlement. Prior to Reconstruction the federal government signed treaties that divided land between Indians and settlers and restricted the movement of each on the lands of the other. Frequently Indian consent was fraudulently obtained, and white respect for Indian land depended on how desirable it was for settlement.

During the Civil War, Sioux, Cheyenne, and Arapaho warriors rejected the land cessions made by their chiefs. Violence against settlers erupted as frontier troop strength was reduced to fight the Confederacy. The war also provided an excuse to nullify previous treaties and pledges with the tribes resettled in Oklahoma by Andrew Jackson's Indian removal. Some Native Americans did support the Confederacy, but all suffered the consequences of Confederate defeat. Settlers moved into the most desirable land, pushing the Indians farther south and west. Some Indians began to resist.

In 1864 the territorial governor of Colorado persuaded most of the warring Cheyennes and Arapahoes to come to Fort Lyon on Sand Creek, promising them protection. Colonel J. M. Chivington's militia, however, attacked an Indian camp flying a white flag and the American flag and killed hundreds of Indian men, women, and children. The following year Congress established a committee to investigate the causes of conflict. Its final report in 1867 led to the creation of an Indian Peace Commission charged with negotiating settlements. At two conferences in 1867 and

1868 Indian chiefs were asked to restrict their tribes to reservations in the undesirable lands of Oklahoma and the Black Hills of the Dakotas in return for supplies and assistance from the government.

Most Indians did not consider the offer very generous, but those who refused to acquiesce soon found that resistance was futile. Railroads had penetrated the West, bringing in both settlers and federal troops more rapidly. The destruction of the buffalo herds by hunters was a particularly important factor in the subjugation of the Indian tribes. These herds played a crucial role in most Plains Indians' culture—providing almost all the basic necessities. Indians ate the buffalo meat, made clothing and tepees out of the hides, used the fats for cosmetics, fashioned the bones into tools, made thread from the sinews, and even burned dried buffalo droppings as fuel. Without the buffalo, most Indians became dependent on the federal government for food and clothing, and submitted peacefully to the new reservation policy.

In 1874 gold was discovered in the Black Hills Indian reservation in the present-day Dakotas. The area suddenly became tempting to whites, and miners began pouring into lands guaranteed to the Indians only five years before. In June 1876 federal troops were sent in to crush an uprising of Chief Sitting Bull's Sioux warriors and their Cheyenne allies. Instead, the warring tribes won their greatest victory against white encroachment when Indians overwhelmed and killed Lieutenant Colonel George A. Custer and 264 men at Little Bighorn. The battle had little long-term effect, however, except to strengthen white resolve in dealing with the "Indian problem."

The treatment of both Indians and African Americans would be justified by the increasingly virulent racism of whites, which was given "scientific" support by scholars of the late nineteenth century. One point was clear by 1876: Northerners who believed that the only good Indian was a dead Indian could hardly condemn Southern whites for their treatment of African Americans.

Final Retreat from Reconstruction

By 1876, fewer Americans championed black rights than had at the close of the Civil War. Some of the old abolitionist Radicals had grown tired of what had become a protracted and complex situation. Radical Republicans such as Thaddeus Stevens and Charles Sumner, who had labored to guarantee civil rights for African Americans, were dead. By 1876, all the elements were present for a national retreat on Reconstruction: the distraction of economic distress, a deep desire for unity among whites, the respectability of racism, a frustrated weariness with black problems by former allies, a growing conservatism on economic and social issues, a changing political climate featuring a resurgence of the Democratic party, and finally a general public disgust with the failure of Reconstruction.

The presidential election of that year sealed the fate of Reconstruction and brought this chapter in American history to a close.

Corruption was a major issue in the 1876 election. The Democrats chose Samuel J. Tilden, a New Yorker whose claim to fame was breaking up the notorious Boss Tweed Ring in New York City. The Republicans nominated Rutherford B. Hayes, a man who had offended few, largely by doing little. The election itself was so riddled with corruption and violence that no one can ever know what would have happened in a fair election. Tilden won the popular vote and led Hayes in undisputed electoral votes 184 to 165. However, 185 votes were needed for election, and 20 votes were disputed—19 of them from Louisiana, Florida, and South Carolina. These were the only Southern states still under Republican rule with the backing of federal troops. In each, rival election boards sent in different returns.

With no constitutional provision for such an occurrence, the Republican Senate and Democratic House established a special commission to decide which returns were valid. Composed of eight Republicans and seven Democrats, the Electoral Commission proceeded to vote along party lines, and gave all the disputed votes to Hayes. Democrats were outraged, and a constitutional crisis seemed in the making if a united Democratic front in the House voted to reject the commission's findings.

A series of agreements between Hayes's advisers and Southern Democratic congressmen averted the crisis. In what came to be called the "Compromise of 1877," Hayes agreed to support federal aid for Southern internal improvements, especially a transcontinental railroad. He also promised to appoint a Southern Democrat to his cabinet and to allow Southern Democrats a say in the allocation of federal offices in their region. Most important, however, was his pledge to remove the remaining federal troops from the South. In return, Southern Democrats promised to protect black rights and to support the findings of the Electoral Commission. On March 2 the House declared Hayes the presidential winner by an electoral vote of 185 to 184. After taking office, Hayes removed the

Table 16.1

Election of 1876				
Candidate	Party	Uncontested Electoral Vote	Popular Vote	Electoral Vote
Ruthford B. Hayes	Republican	165	4,034,311	185
Samuel J. Tilden	Democratic	184	4,288,546	184
Peter Cooper	Greenback	—	75,973	—

troops, and the remaining Republican governments in the South soon collapsed.

Scholars once considered the Compromise of 1877 an important factor in the end of Reconstruction. Actually, its role was more symbolic than real; it merely buried the corpse. The battle for the Republican party's soul had been lost by its abolitionist faction well before the election of 1876. The Democratic party had never sought to extend or protect black rights. The Supreme Court began to interpret the Fourteenth and Fifteenth Amendments very narrowly, stripping them of their strength. Thus one by one many African-American rights were lost during the next four decades.

Conclusion

As the Civil War ended, many unresolved issues remained. The most crucial involved the status of former slaves and of the former Confederate states. The destinies of both were inextricably intertwined. Anything

Chronology of Key Events

1863	Lincoln proposes 10 percent plan for Reconstruction
1864	Lincoln vetoes Wade-Davis Bill; Sand Creek Massacre
1865	Freedmen's Bureau established; Lincoln assassinated; Andrew Johnson becomes seventeenth president; Thirteenth Amendment ratified, abolishing slavery
1866	Civil Rights Act
1867	Reconstruction Act divides South into five military districts
1868	President Johnson impeached; Fourteenth Amendment, guaranteeing citizenship to African Americans, ratified; Ulysses S. Grant elected eighteenth president
1870	Fifteenth Amendment ratified, outlaws exclusion from voting on basis of race
1870–71	Ku Klux Klan Acts passed
1876	Custer defeated at Little Bighorn
1877	Compromise of 1877; Rutherford B. Hayes becomes nineteenth president

affecting the status of one influenced the fate of the other. Quick read-mission of the states with little change would doom black rights. En-forced equality of African Americans under the law would create turbu-lence and drastic change in the South. This difficult problem was further complicated by constitutional, economic, and political considerations, ensuring that the course of Reconstruction would be chaotic and contra-dictory.

Presidential Reconstruction under both Lincoln and Johnson favored rapid reunification and white unity more than changes in the racial struc-ture of the South. The South, however, refused to accept a meaningful end to slavery, as the Black Codes blatantly demonstrated. Congressional desire to reestablish legislative supremacy and the Republican need to build a national party combined with this Southern intransigence to unite Radical and moderate Republicans in the need to protect black rights and to restructure the South. What emerged from congressional recon-struction were Republican governments that expanded democracy and enacted needed reforms which many Southern whites deeply resented. At the core of that resentment was not disgust over incompetence or corrup-tion but hostility to black political power in any form.

Given the pervasiveness of racial prejudice, what was remarkable was not that the Freedmen's Bureau, the constitutional amendments, and the civil rights legislation failed to produce permanent change but that these actions were taken at all. Cherished ideas of property rights, limited gov-ernment, and self-reliance, as well as an almost universal belief in black in-feriority, virtually guaranteed that the experiment would fail. The first na-tional attempt to resolve fairly and justly the question of minority rights in a pluralistic society was abandoned in less than a decade. Indians, blacks, and women saw the truth of the Alabama planter's words of 1865: "Poor elk—poor buffaloe—poor Indian—poor Nigger—this is indeed a white man country." Nevertheless, less than a century later, seeds planted by the Reconstruction era amendments would finally germinate, flower, and be harvested.

Suggestions for Further Reading

Effective overviews of the Reconstruction period are Eric Foner, *Reconstruction: America's Unfinished Revolution* (1988); Leon Litwack, *Been in the Storm So Long* (1979); James McPherson, *Ordeal by Fire* (1982); Kenneth M. Stampp, *The Era of Reconstruction* (1965).

For information on the Johnson and Grant presidencies see Michael Les Bene-dict, *The Impeachment of Andrew Johnson* (1973); William S. McFeely, *Grant: A Biography* (1981); Eric McKitrick, *Andrew Johnson and Reconstruction* (1960).

Conditions in the South during Reconstruction are examined in Stephen J. DeCanio, *Agriculture in the Postbellum South* (1974); Herbert G. Gutman, *The Black Family in Slavery and Freedom* (1976); Thomas Holt, *Black over White* (1977); Jay R. Mandle, *The Roots of Black Poverty* (1978); Michael Perman, *The Road to Redemption: Southern Politics, 1869–1879* (1984); George C. Rable, *But There Was No Peace* (1984); James Roark, *Masters Without Slaves* (1977).

On the West during the Reconstruction period see Robert F. Berkhofer, *The White Man's Indian* (1978); Eugene H. Berwanger, *The West and Reconstruction* (1981); Francis Paul Prucha, *American Indian Policy in Crisis* (1975); Wilcomb E. Washburn, *The Indian in America* (1975).

Chapter *17*

Emergence as an Economic Power

On a cold winter's night in December 1900, 75 of the richest, most influential American businessmen gathered in New York for a dinner to honor Charles Schwab, president of Carnegie Steel Company. Seated to the honoree's right was J. P. Morgan, the powerful investment banker and consolidator of industry. In his after-dinner speech, Schwab predicted a bright future of low prices and stability for the steel industry, to be ushered in by the formation of a scientifically integrated firm—one that combined all phases of the industry from the production of raw steel to the manufacture of finished products.

Morgan did not miss the point of the speech. Previously, Carnegie Steel had limited its operations to making raw steel, while Morgan and others had been busily creating trusts among the producers of such finished steel products as tubes and wire. Trusts were attempts to unite smaller competing firms in order to control the market and raise prices. Trusts often used their combined power to put remaining competitors out of business. The steel products trusts, however, had a problem. Andrew Carnegie, whose company was the largest supplier of raw steel, hated trusts. Deciding to beat the the trusts at their own game, he joined several informal arrangements to fix prices, known as "pools," only to sabotage them from within. Morgan and his cohorts soon realized that depending on Carnegie for raw steel would doom their consolidation schemes. Consequently, in July 1900 three steel products companies canceled all their contracts with Carnegie, determined to produce their own steel or buy it from others—and put Carnegie out of business.

Carnegie, however, refused to surrender. By continuing his policy of spending money to make money, Carnegie knew he could produce superior products at cheaper prices. He decided to pay no dividends on common stock and began plans to build a $12 million tube plant.

The antiquated and scattered plants of his competitors would have been no match for Carnegie's new ones. Few promoters doubted one steel executive's assertion that Carnegie could "have driven entirely out of business every steel company in the United States." Carnegie, however, wanted to retire. Schwab's speech was aimed at producing a bargain, not a war. After the dinner and into the night Morgan fired questions at Schwab. Finally, in the early hours of the next day Morgan said, "Well, if Andy wants to sell, I'll buy. Go find his price."

When Schwab approached Carnegie about selling his steel empire, Carnegie listened. The following day they met again, at which time Carnegie handed him a slip of paper with his asking price of $480 million written in pencil. When Schwab gave Morgan the offer, he replied, "I accept the price." A few days later Morgan stopped by Carnegie's office to congratulate him "on being the richest man in the world."

The transaction was a good deal for both men. Carnegie had his millions to endow libraries and anything else that struck his fancy. Morgan founded United States Steel Corporation. A colossus even among the existing giants of American industry, it was capitalized at $1.4 billion, a figure three times larger than the annual budget of the federal government.

The fates of Carnegie and Morgan reflected the momentous changes that took place after the Civil War. Moving from the ranks of second-rate industrial powers, by 1900 the nation was the leader—with a manufacturing output exceeding the combined total of Great Britain, France, and Germany. As Andrew Carnegie exclaimed in 1886, "The old nations of the earth creep on at a snail's pace; the Republic thunders past with the rush of an express."

Many yardsticks supported his assertion. Between 1870 and 1914 railroad mileage increased from 53,000 to 250,000—more than the combined mileage of the rest of the world. Land under agricultural production doubled; the gross national product was six times larger; the amount of manufactured goods per person tripled.

The rapidity of change produced chaotic conditions, which led to new managerial styles and finally to economic consolidation and the rise of supercorporations like United States Steel. The forces of economic modernization swept through all sections and all segments of the economy. The results were profound alterations of the social order that touched virtually every aspect of American life.

America: Land of Plenty

The phenomenal growth which the American economy experienced during the last quarter of the nineteenth century was built on the foundations laid during the antebellum period. Industrial development, the abundance of land and people, technological breakthroughs, and a favorable business climate had all been characteristic of the United States on the eve of the Civil War.

Mineral and Geographic Possibilities

Explorers and early settlers in what would become the United States were disappointed not to find the same abundance of gold and silver that had enriched their Spanish neighbors to the south. Only in the nineteenth century did Americans begin to realize the vast wealth that their expansion had brought. Most spectacular was the discovery of gold in California in the late 1840s. It sparked frenzied prospecting all through the West.

Each new discovery led to "rushes," creating mining towns almost overnight. Between 1850 and the 1880s thousands of men and women of almost every ethnic background helped create makeshift social institutions whenever and wherever strikes were made.

After living weeks or months at subsistence level, many miners went home poorer than when they had started. While a few did strike it rich, inefficient mining methods quickly exhausted the easily obtainable supplies of precious metals. Extracting ore from beneath the ground and in veins of quartz was expensive. It required large capital investments best raised by mining syndicates, frequently financed by eastern and European investors, which bought prospectors' claims for a fraction of their value.

As mining became an organized business, its focus moved to less exotic but more useful minerals such as copper, lead, talc, zinc, quartz, and oil, which fed the growing demands of the industrializing East. By the 1880s mining no longer represented easy riches for pioneering individuals; it had become an integrated part of the nation's modern, industrial economy. Emerging basic industries such as steel, petroleum, and electric power depended on large supplies of various minerals, which seemed to become available as needed. Sometimes new deposits were found; other times new uses for minerals spurred the mining of known deposits.

Iron, which had been widely used prior to the war for plows and other implements, was limited by its lack of durability. Then Andrew Carnegie and others employed new technology to produce large quantities of relatively cheap and durable steel. The availability of steel opened new manufacturing vistas, and between 1870 and 1900 the output of steel grew from 850,000 tons to over 10.5 million tons.

The same pattern characterized the mining of other minerals. Copper, at first mainly used for household products, became a key ingredient in such new fields as oil refining, electrical generation and conduction, and telephone communications. Most went into the miles and miles of wiring that electrified the cities. Similarly, the spectacular rise of the coal industry was generated by the increased use of coal-burning steam engines to power machinery and locomotives. As late as 1869 almost half of all power used in manufacturing came from waterwheels; by 1900 coal-burning steam engines supplied 80 percent of such power.

Even more dramatic was the rise of the petroleum industry. Many people were aware of large oil reserves in Pennsylvania, which seeped into streams and springs. Early demand was mainly limited to such uses as patent medicines of dubious value. Encouraged by reports that petroleum could be developed as a lighting source and lubricating oil, Pennsylvania businessman George Bissell funded drilling efforts, and in 1859 his employee, Edwin L. Drake, tapped the first oil well in Titusville, Pennsylvania. Oil was soon being used to lubricate machine parts, and by the 1870s about 20 million barrels were being produced annually. When refined into kerosene, it could also be used for illumination and cooking. During the late nineteenth century kerosene lamps and stoves were common features in American homes.

Growing demand led to the search for "liquid gold" in the Southwest. In 1901 a well shot a 160-foot stream of oil into the air at Spindletop, Texas. New sources thus became available for the development of the gasoline engine in the twentieth century. Abundant natural resources and technology often interacted—each shaping the evolution of the other.

Technological Change

Seldom has a single generation experienced such rapid change as in the late nineteenth century. Technology dramatically transformed much of people's lives. Bewildering as the changes sometimes were, the public generally welcomed new inventions with wide-eyed wonder. Across the country, thousands greeted the completion of the first transcontinental railway at Promontory Point, Utah, in 1869. Awed sightseers crammed expositions celebrating "progress," such as the 1876 Philadelphia Centennial Exposition, where visitors saw for the first time the Corliss engine, bicycles, the typewriter, the elevator, Alexander Graham Bell's telephone, and even the "floor covering of the future"—linoleum. At the 1893 World's Columbian Exposition in Chicago everything was powered by electricity, and many of the miracles of 1876 had become commonplace "necessities."

The impact of new inventions was enormous. Whereas only 276 inventions had been recorded during the Patent Office's first decade in the 1790s, during the single year of the Columbian Exposition 22,000 patents were issued. Offices became mechanized with the invention of the typewriter in 1867 and the development of a practical adding machine in 1888. Numerous inventions such as George Westinghouse's airbrake, which made longer, faster trains possible, revolutionized railroad transportation. Later, electric streetcars profoundly changed the character of urban development by accelerating the move to the suburbs.

Along with transportation changes, communications innovations welded a collection of communities into a unified nation. Links with the rest of the world also increased when an Atlantic telegraphic cable was completed in 1866. New inventions in the field of printing made popular newspapers with wide circulations a reality—along with mass advertising. Photographic advances culminated in George Eastman's hand-held Kodak camera in 1888. However, few, if any, inventions rivaled the importance of the telephone—more than one and one-half million were installed by 1900.

Increasingly, new inventions such as the telephone relied on cheap and efficient sources of electricity. Here the name of Thomas Edison stands above the rest. Beginning his career at an early age by peddling candy and newspapers on trains, Edison soon became a telegrapher and invented various improvements. The success of his ideas convinced him to go into the "invention business." Establishing a research lab at Menlo Park, New Jersey, in 1876, he invented the phonograph, the incandescent light bulb, as well as hundreds of other devices such as a better telephone, the dictaphone, the mimeograph, the dynamo, motion pictures, and electric transmission. With backing from banker J. P. Morgan, he created the first electric company in 1882 in New York City and formed the Edison General Electric Company in 1888 to produce light bulbs.

As in all research, Edison followed a number of blind alleys, but his only serious mistake was the choice of direct electrical current. This decision limited the range of transmission to a radius of about two miles. George Westinghouse's development of an alternating current system in 1886 soon supplanted direct current, forcing even Edison's companies to make the switch.

While a handful of inventors struck it rich, inventions often paved the way to vast fortunes for such entrepreneurs as Carnegie. The success of most of the captains of industry came from their effective exploitation of new technology. Carnegie utilized such advances as the Bessemer and open-hearth processes to produce cheap and plentiful steel. In like manner,

In his Menlo Park, New Jersey, laboratory, Thomas Edison aimed at practicality in his inventions. He eventually obtained over 1,000 patents. Here he is listening to his phonograph in 1888.

John D. Rockefeller built his industrial empire on new oil refining methods, and Gustavus Swift's meat-packing operation depended on the invention of the refrigerated railroad car. Eventually machine-made, interchangeable parts revolutionized every industry engaged in mass production.

Population Patterns and the New Industrial Work Force

Population changes and growth played an important role in the expanding economy. By the 1890s farmers became a minority for the first time, and by 1900 six out of every ten Americans made their living outside of agriculture. Although technology produced machines that displaced many skilled craftspeople and farmers, employment rose. For example, despite a tremendous increase in agricultural productivity, the needs of a rapidly expanding population created so many new markets that the agricultural work force still grew by 50 percent.

At the same time, nonagricultural employment rose 300 percent. Those not engaged in farming increasingly concentrated in the cities. Between 1860 and 1900 urban residents increased from 6 million to 24 million. This growing urbanization was essential to the expansion of industry—both feeding it and being fed by it.

Some economic historians contend that of all the factors spurring industrial growth none was more important than the rise of an American mass market. The urban population boom and the transportation revolution made mass consumerism possible by creating markets unparalleled in vastness and accessibility.

Mass markets would not have inevitably led to mass production without the public's acceptance of standardized goods. Several factors made Americans more receptive than Europeans to such products. Class distinctions, though not absent, were more blurred and became increasingly so with the availability of ready-made clothing. Also, physical mobility broke down many of the local loyalties so prevalent in Europe. Such factors created opportunities that modern mass advertising exploited. By 1900, $90 million was being spent annually to convince Americans of the advantages of specific brand names; modern advertising had embarked on its unending mission to shape the tastes of the public.

Advertising increased demand for many products, creating more industrial jobs for urban consumers. The dramatic expansion of this industrial work force was fed mainly by massive migration to the cities, rather than by the natural increase of the urban population. Four-fifths of the 18 million new city residents moved there; approximately half of them were migrants from rural America. They came to cities for a variety of reasons.

One was an increasing surplus of young men and women in the country-side. Rural birthrates remained high while mechanization decreased the number of hands needed to produce a crop. Such surpluses naturally "pushed" people from rural areas, but the cities also "pulled" them with the promise of more excitement, variety, and modern conveniences. Urban jobs also paid more; in 1890 clerical workers averaged $848 a year, more than three times as much as farm laborers.

Internal migration alone could not supply the enormous demand for industrial labor. Even before the Civil War native-born Americans could no longer be lured in sufficient numbers to work in factories. Rural white Americans more frequently joined the growing ranks of white-collar workers. Because of the persistent notions of black inferiority, rural African Americans, who would have gladly worked in factories, were passed over in favor of foreign workers. Thus, in 1890 only seven percent of black males held factory jobs, and as late as 1900 about 90 percent of African Americans remained in the South—the least urbanized section of the nation.

Unlike industrializing European nations, therefore, the United States did not rely primarily on its own population to produce its industrial work force. Instead, large numbers of immigrants manned the factories. The "pull" of job opportunities combined with factors "pushing" Euro-peans out of their native countries to produce a virtual flood of immigration (see Chapter 18). These large numbers facilitated industrialization but eventually produced a backlash from native-born Americans.

An Expanding Railroad Network

Americans developed a love/hate relationship with the railroads. The same locomotive that inspired Walt Whitman's rhapsody to its "fierce throated beauty" was described as "the leviathan, with tentacles of steel clutching into the soil" by Frank Norris in 1901. Despite these differing visions, no one doubted the importance of the railroads.

The railroads provoked strong emotions because of their crucial role in forging a new society. More than anything else, railroads helped to cre-ate an interdependent national economy. Rails brought raw materials to population centers, making possible large factories that mass-produced goods. Those goods could then be shipped to national markets over the same rails. Changes were required, however, before railroads could meet the needs of an expanding economy.

The early railroads were strictly local affairs. By 1865 there were al-ready 35,000 miles of rails, but few linked up in any rational way. Eleven different gauges of rail caused both goods and passengers to be unloaded from one set of cars and reloaded on another set—sometimes at a depot on the opposite side of town. Between New York and Chicago, cargoes had to be unloaded and reloaded as many as six times. In some cases the inefficiency was intentional. Many small antebellum roads purposely adopted different gauges and conflicting schedules to prevent being swallowed up by larger, powerful competitors.

Unlike many European rail systems, American railroads grew with little advance planning or regulation by government, sprouting like weeds in areas where immediate profits could be made. Especially in the South, where too many small lines serviced the same places, four hundred companies sprang up, each with an average track length of a mere 40 miles.

While too many railroads served some sections in the East, prior to 1869 no transcontinental lines linked the East and West coasts. Financing their construction was the major problem. The construction of the railroads of the East required large amounts of capital, but a return on the investment came quickly. This was not true in the West, where railroads often preceded settlement and, therefore, demand for their lines. Because of the need for transcontinental routes, land grants became the solution. Many analysts have questioned the size of those grants, but they undoubtedly had the desired effect. By the turn of the century five transcontinental routes had been established.

At the same time, after some fierce competitive battles, a few eastern railroad companies gained control of many of the numerous local lines. When the dust settled, seven major groups controlled over two-thirds of the nation's railroad mileage; the average track length of a railroad grew from a mere 100 miles in 1865 to over 1,000 in two decades; gauges were standardized; and a more efficient rail system emerged.

A Favorable Climate: The Role of Ideology, Politics, and Finance

People, materials, and machinery were the "seeds" of industrialization. For an abundant harvest, however, good soil, favorable climatic conditions, and adequate fertilization were required. The bountiful economic harvest of the late nineteenth century depended on the "good soil" of popular support fostered by intellectual and cultural justifications. Favorable governmental policies created a desirable climate, while legal and financial developments provided the needed "fertilizer." This combination produced not only more industries but also larger industries.

Social Darwinism and the Gospel of Wealth

Expanding economic opportunities fostered cutthroat competition from which fewer and fewer winners emerged. The road to wealth taken by the new captains of industry was strewn with ruined competitors and broken labor movements. Ruthlessness not only became increasingly necessary, it was also transformed into a virtue by the twin ideologies of Social Darwinism and the Gospel of Wealth.

For men like Andrew Carnegie, the writings of Social Darwinists Herbert Spencer and William Graham Sumner helped to relieve any unwelcome guilt. Spencer and his followers applied the evolutionary concepts of Charles Darwin to society. A process of natural selection was said to cause the fittest individuals to survive and flourish in the marketplace. Survival of the fittest supposedly enriched not only the winners but also society as a whole, since human evolution would produce what Spencer called "the ultimate and inevitable development of the ideal man."

According to the Social Darwinists, poverty and slums were as inevitable as the concentration of wealth in the hands of the "fittest." Spencer and Sumner argued that governmental or charitable intervention to improve the conditions of the poor would only interfere with the functioning of natural law and prolong the life of "defective gene pools" to the detriment of society as a whole.

The so-called fittest naturally greeted "scientific" endorsement of their elite positions with eagerness. But even many businessmen found the ruthlessness of Social Darwinism an unpalatable justification for their actions. They sought their solace in religious rationales for the accumulation of great wealth. Since colonial times, the Protestant work ethic had denounced idleness and viewed success as evidence of being among the "elect"—God's chosen people. Building upon this base, apologists constructed the "Gospel of Wealth." John D. Rockefeller asserted, "God gave me my riches." Not surprisingly, Carnegie was the one to produce a written, logically argued rationale which asserted that the "fittest" at the top were better able to decide what people needed than the people themselves. In Carnegie's case, he took that responsibility seriously, distributing some $300 million to such philanthropic causes as founding libraries.

Among the most effective apologists for the wealthy, however, were religious leaders of the era. In 1901 Bishop William Lawrence proclaimed, "Godliness is in league with riches." Not only did the elite deserve their riches, but the poor also were responsible for their status. Perhaps the most popular evangelist for the Gospel of Wealth was Russell Conwell, who delivered his celebrated "Acres of Diamonds" speech, in which he declared that anyone could get rich, approximately 6,000 times between 1861 and 1925.

Thus the maldistribution of wealth was not only inevitable but also desirable according to both scientific and religious thought. Probably more important was the support provided by popular culture. *McGuffey Readers* continued to stress the virtue of hard work and its inevitable rewards in poems such as "Try, Try Again." Novelist Horatio Alger penned many stories whose heroes rose from poverty to comfortable middle-class status through a combination of diligence and good luck. Thus popular literature reinforced the idea that success always came to those who deserved it in America, the land of opportunity.

Laissez-Faire in Theory and Practice

Economic theory also lent respectability to greed and to the idea that government should not intervene in the economy. In 1776 Adam Smith's *The Wealth of Nations* presented arguments that would long be used to explain the workings of a free economy and to proscribe government's role in that economy. Smith asserted that the market was directed and controlled by an "invisible hand" composed of a multitude of individual choices. If government did not meddle, and everyone was left free to act according to self-interest, competition engendered by an unregulated market would naturally lead to the production of desired goods and services at reasonable prices—an economy best suited to meet the needs of society in general.

Acceptance of the "invisible hand" of supply-and-demand economic theory naturally led to a policy called "laissez-faire." Government's proper role was to leave the economy alone, so as not to disrupt the operation of the natural forces that ordered the economy. Business leaders naturally endorsed the theory's rejection of governmental regulation, yet saw no contradiction in asking for government aid and subsidies to foster industrialization. To a large extent the industrialists got what they wanted—a laissez-faire policy that left them alone, except when they needed help. Ironically, this distortion of theory helped to produce an economy in which business consolidation wreaked havoc upon the very competition needed for natural regulation of the economy.

Absolute free enterprise never really existed. There was plenty of governmental activity—just not in the area of regulation. No laws protected the consumer from adulterated foods, spurious claims for ineffective or even dangerous patent medicines, the sale of stock in nonexistent companies, or unsafe and overpriced transportation services. No national regulating agency existed prior to the establishment of the Interstate Commerce Commission in 1887.

While denying support and protection to consumers or workers, government at all levels aided businesspeople. Alexander Hamilton's vision of an industrializing nation fostered by favorable governmental action never entirely died and was rejuvenated by the Republican party. Among the party's many promises in 1860 were pledges to enact higher tariffs, to subsidize the completion of a transcontinental railroad, and to establish a stable national banking system. The victory of Republican ideology undoubtedly helped to create a favorable environment for rapid industrialization.

Tariffs had a long history. Two days before Lincoln took office, Democratic President Buchanan signed the Morrill Tariff, which marked the first tariff increase since 1842, and initiated an upward, practically uninterrupted, rise in tariff rates for the remainder of the century. At first, such American industries as steel needed to be protected from European competition to survive. Yet even after the cost of steel production was greatly reduced, the tariff remained—allowing higher profits at the expense of consumers. Without foreign competition, businesspeople were able to charge more for goods. Consumers came to resent these higher prices. Such bonanzas should not, however, obscure the fact that tariffs were widely viewed as serving the national interest by fostering economic independence from the British and other industrial competitors.

Additional forms of subsidy were also meant to serve the public good. Dwarfing all others were government land grants to railroads. Only the scale of these grants was new; prior to the war railroads had already received nearly 20 million acres of federal land. During the 1860s Congress granted 20 square miles of public land in alternating sections for each mile of track laid by the Union Pacific and Central Pacific railroads in order to speed the completion of a transcontinental route. By the time the grants ended, a total of 130 million acres of federal land and 51 million acres of state land went to various railroads. Nevertheless, even that incredible number of acres constituted less than 7 percent of the national domain in the West. Although the land grants were later subject to severe public criticism, the federal government did receive certain benefits, paying only half fare to move troops and supplies. In addition, the value of the remaining land increased, and the uniting of the East and West spurred the entire economy.

Business also benefited from favorable labor and financial legislation as well as low-interest loans. Individuals exploited these policies for personal gain, and the results were not uniformly positive. Aid to business, however, was never unlimited or unrestricted, and enjoyed wide public support at first. Indeed nationalism and patriotism accompanied the process of industrialization. Many Americans took pride in the nation's growing economic power. Only after the problems of industrialization became more apparent did the public begin to cry "foul."

Corporations and Capital Formation

Such governmental aid as high tariffs, land grants, low interest loans, and lack of regulation provided rich fertilizer for economic expansion, which brought both blessings and problems. The same was true for the rise of the modern corporation and decline of individual ownership and partnerships.

There were many advantages to incorporation for large-scale enterprises, including selling "shares" to a multitude of individual investors, so that the great sums of capital needed by modern industry could be amassed. Furthermore, corporations did not risk the disruption of operation due to death of a partner or arguments between partners, and individuals could hedge their bets by investing their capital in several ventures.

Although corporations had a long history, their postwar domination of the economy was due in part to legal changes that had taken place during the Jacksonian period. Businesspeople had once been required to apply to a state legislature for a charter; by the 1830s, however, they could incorporate on their own, provided they met certain standards. Following the Civil War, courts also began to affirm the principle of "limited liability." Previously, bankruptcy could bring not only the loss of one's investment but also seizure of personal property by creditors. A corporation's liability finally became limited to its assets, making investment a safer and more desirable venture.

In *Santa Clara County* v. *The Southern Pacific Railroad* (1886) the Supreme Court perverted the Fourteenth Amendment, ruling that a corporation was a legal "person" and therefore entitled to all the protections granted by the amendment. States could not deny corporations "equal protection of the law" or deprive them of their rights or property without "due process" of the law. Corporations were also later granted the "right" to "reasonable" profits—to be determined by the courts, not the government.

Instead of receiving "equal protection," corporations actually became privileged members of society. Real people whose rights were protected by the Constitution were held personally responsible for illegal activities, whereas corporate directors and corporations were not. Such advantages helped to spur the growth of corporations; by 1904 almost 70 percent of all manufacturing employees worked for corporations.

Perhaps the greatest advantage of corporations remained the ability to raise large amounts of capital. The expansion of industry in the late nineteenth century required big infusions of money. Every sector of the economy demanded capital: farmers needed new machinery to increase productivity; manufacturers needed new plants to utilize the latest technology; cities needed new construction to service the needs of the urban population.

From where was all this money to come? Some, of course, was generated by the rising gross national product—the total value of goods and services produced in one year—which grew from $225 per person in 1870 to nearly $500 in 1900. New technology increased productivity and put more money into the hands of people—"extra money" not required to meet physical needs. This disposable income was often reinvested rather than spent for personal consumption, thus laying the foundations of the modern American economy.

Increasing amounts of this capital were invested in manufacturing partly because investment bankers like J. P. Morgan marketed corporate stocks and bonds. Foreign investment was also important; by 1900 Europeans had invested approximately one-third of the almost $10 billion used to finance manufacturing in the United States.

The net result of the favorable conditions of the late nineteenth century was industrial supremacy. Americans reveled in their nation's transformation to a colossus outproducing the entire world. Vast mineral wealth, technological breakthroughs, population changes, railroads, popular support, beneficial government policies, liberal corporation laws, and the availability of capital fostered this transformation. At first, favorable conditions worked like overfertilized land—producing too many plants for the available space and resources. In this overgrown industrial garden competition created chaos until such entrepreneurs as Andrew Carnegie found ways to prune away their rivals.

The Rise of Big Business

"You might as well endeavor to stay the formation of clouds, the falling of rains, the flowing of streams, as to attempt . . . to prevent the organization of industry." These words of John D. Rockefeller's attorney described what he considered to be the inevitable domination of entire industries by large corporations. In industry after industry, men like Rockefeller, Morgan, and Carnegie eliminated competitors and controlled markets. The impact of this consolidation of industry was enormous. As companies grew larger, new management styles and more white-collar workers were needed. Mass production began to rise—profoundly changing the nature of work for industrial laborers. Also giant corporations amassed great power over production, people, and politics.

Controlling Competition

Most business leaders did not really advocate free enterprise fueled by competition. To them competition meant chaos, and they sought to eliminate it. Men like J. P. Morgan believed that too many companies glutted the markets—producing instability and cutthroat competition.

As America's first big business, the railroad industry was the first to confront the problems of competition. Railroads desperately sought to woo shippers to their lines by giving lower rates for bulk shipments and long hauls. To some preferred customers they also gave "rebates"—secret kickbacks below their published prices. They sought to make up for the lost revenue by overcharging smaller shippers. Such tactics did not really solve the railroads' problems, especially when rate wars broke out. In the 1870s some railroad managers tried cooperation as a cure for competition. They formed "pools," regional federations to divide traffic equitably and to raise rates to increase profits. However, pools were difficult to enforce, and greed frequently doomed many such agreements.

For the railroads, consolidation—accompanied by ruthless tactics—became the key to controlling competition. The former shipping magnate Cornelius Vanderbilt gained control of the New York Central Railroad in 1867 by buying two key lines that connected with it, and then refusing to accept any rail cars going to or from the Central. In response to criticism, Vanderbilt replied: "Can't I do what I want with my own?" Elsewhere buyouts and mergers eventually reduced the number of competitors, especially after depressions in the 1870s and 1890s.

After a period of intense competition in the railroad industry, a few rail barons consolidated lines by often using unscrupulous methods, seemingly carving up the nation at will.

Like the railroads, the oil industry also suffered from the proliferation of so many small companies and dramatically fluctuating prices. John D. Rockefeller, founder of the Standard Oil Company, first tried a combination of pooling and rebates to deal with these problems. In 1872 he organized the South Improvement Company. This venture represented a combination of oil refiners and railroad directors aimed at dividing the oil carriage trade among the railroads. In return for a guaranteed share of the shipments, Rockefeller convinced the railroads to give rebates. Eventually Rockefeller was able to obtain rebates not only on the oil he shipped but also on the shipments of his competitors. Thus Rockefeller could undersell his competitors, whom he often bought out during bad economic times.

Such techniques allowed Rockefeller to control 90 percent of the oil business, but legal problems arose from Standard Oil's far-flung holdings. His solution was the "trust." In 1882 he convinced the major stockholders in a number of refineries to surrender their stock to a board of nine trustees. In return they received trust certificates that entitled them to a share of the joint profits of all the refineries. The benefits of this device were readily apparent. Pools had no legal standing and could be manipulated by some members to the detriment of other members. In a trust, however, competitive actions were of no benefit. Everyone shared all losses and gains.

John D. Rockefeller used ruthless techniques to eliminate competition and consolidate the oil-refining industry.

Andrew Carnegie disliked pools and trusts, but found other ways to gain a competitive edge. One of these was "vertical integration." Buying the sources of his raw materials—iron ore and coke—he both lowered their cost to him and controlled his supplies. Carnegie also acquired many of the transportation facilities needed to distribute his steel. This vertical integration lowered final prices by cutting out profit-taking by suppliers and shippers.

The key to Carnegie's success was his ability to cut costs without lowering quality. He used such traditional measures as wage cuts and increased hours for workers, but he also constantly explored new methods to increase productivity. By not focusing on short-term profits, he was willing to invest in expensive new technology to lower long-term costs of production.

Carnegie often boasted that he knew almost nothing about steel. He hired experts to do that. What he did know was how to run a company and make money. Carnegie effectively used all the economies of scale available to large firms. Soon he was able to undersell and destroy most of the steel companies that had blossomed in response to the increased demand by railroads and industry. He also was a master at exploiting downturns in business cycles. Most of his acquisitions were made during depressions, when prices were lower. Competitors and labor movements suffered from Carnegie's actions, but the result was better steel at cheaper prices. Such cheap steel aided the expansion of the railroads and the rise of other industries.

The role of bankers was also an important factor in the trend toward greater consolidation. J. P. Morgan and other bankers often stepped in during economic panics to reorganize bankrupt companies, forming them into single supercorporations. The result was a more orderly economy, but at the price of centralizing vast economic power into the hands of a few unelected individuals.

Andrew Carnegie rose from an immigrant textile mill worker to control the U.S. steel industry.

New Managerial Styles and an Expanding Middle Class

The consolidation of companies into giant corporations created the need for new management techniques. Again, the railroads served as pioneers. As railroad companies grew larger, their activities covered hundreds of miles and employed thousands of workers. Safety and market conditions also required the entire system to operate as a single unit under a tight schedule. These conditions caused managerial problems, since railroad management required a level of coordination previously unknown in business.

To deal with these problems, railroads established sophisticated administrative structures, defining the responsibilities of all employees, from local train agents to the president and board of directors. Better accounting procedures were also needed to keep track of the monies collected and paid out. Management and accounting of funds became the function of controllers' offices, and a cost-accounting system was adopted to provide accurate data to judge the performance of their lines.

Other large-scale businesses began to adopt these accounting methods, hierarchical administrative structures, and divisions of responsibilities pioneered by the railroads. The result was the creation of "middle management," which coordinated the operations of far-flung local plants and reported to the top executives. Big businesses were now run by bureaucracies staffed by white-collar workers.

A profound consequence of the new economic order was the expansion of the middle class. Corporations needed accountants, middle managers, clerical workers, and sales representatives. The urban growth that accompanied industrialization also created demands for the services of professionals, shopkeepers, and government employees. The earnings of the middle class rose nearly 30 percent between the Civil War and the 1890s. By 1900 more than a third of urban families owned their homes. Although its members were sometimes dissatisfied, the middle class clearly derived benefits from and had a stake in the new economic order.

Mass Marketing, Assembly Lines, and Mass Production

Drastic transformations occurred in consumer industries as well as basic industry, as can be seen in the meat-packing business. There the interplay of new technology and new organization also ushered in new marketing techniques. Once again, the railroads played a key role by providing access to the grazing ranges of the Great Plains. Because of its rail network, Chicago quickly became the major funnel through which cattle were distributed from the Union Stock Yards to slaughterhouses on the outskirts of eastern cities. The meat was then distributed through local butchers to city residents.

There were several problems with such a distribution system, chief of which was the deterioration of the stock during long train journeys. Until the development of the refrigerated car, the only alternative was pickling or curing meat. Cattle dealer Gustavus Swift realized the possibilities opened up by refrigerated cars. Not only could fresh beef and pork be shipped more safely, but by centralizing slaughtering, waste products could be utilized. Profits were increased by making horns into buttons and hooves into glue. Eventually Swift formed glue, fertilizer, soap, and glycerine factories. People said that Swift used every part of a pig except the squeal.

Local butchers and wholesalers usually lacked refrigerated storage facilities, so Swift established his own warehouses, bypassing wholesale distributors and their cut of the profits. Swift overcame consumer resistance to the idea of buying meat weeks after the animal was slaughtered in a distant city with a major advertising campaign that stressed the superiority of Western beef. His mass-marketing tactics proved successful. By the late 1890s six packers supplied almost 90 percent of all meat shipped in interstate commerce. Swift was also a pioneer in mass production, employing assembly lines that subdivided the slaughtering and packing process into numerous distinct jobs.

Engineer Frederick W. Taylor laid the foundations of "scientific management" with his time-and-motion studies. Stopwatch in hand, Taylor observed the workers and then divided the manufacturing process into units that allowed for little wasted motion. He believed his ideas would benefit labor as well as management. Instead, his aim "to induce men to act as nearly like machines as possible" promoted monotony and displaced workers—especially higher-paid, skilled ones.

In meat packing, machinery did not replace workers; their work was merely subdivided to increase efficiency. In other industries, after the work had been broken down into simple, repetitive tasks, machines were created to replace hand labor. Mass production by machine worked best on products made from standardized, interchangeable parts. The ingredients were now in place to mass produce large numbers of standardized goods.

The Power of Bigness

The creation of the gigantic U.S. Steel Corporation was not an isolated occurrence. By 1904 a single firm in each of 50 different industries accounted for 60 percent or more of the total output. Such concentrations of economic power alarmed many Americans. Competition was never entirely eliminated, however, and consolidation did bring such benefits as lower prices and higher standards of living. Nevertheless, the transition from local, independently owned shops and factories to giant national corporations with impersonal boards of directors dramatically altered the work and leisure time of the American people. However, the transition was often painful for individuals. The economy experienced a frightening cycle of boom and bust, and periodic depressions caused widespread unemployment and business failures.

Big business also created a class of millionaires who flaunted ostentatious homes and lavish life-styles. When one realizes that in 1890 about 11 million of the 12.5 million families in the United States averaged less than $380 a year in income, it is obvious that all did not share equally in the economic expansion of the era. Wealth had always been concentrated and industrialization continued the trend.

Many people resented or envied the life-styles such wealth provided, but they feared the power it produced. Big business grew while government and organized labor remained relatively small. Thus business leaders wielded enormous power over many phases of American life. Some actions benefited the nation but were taken in a high-handed manner. For example, to simplify train schedules, in 1883 railroad owners established four time zones—without consulting any branch of government. Such arbitrary power alarmed the American public, and popular outcries would eventually force government action to curb the excesses that the new industrial order had produced.

This portrait of the family of William Astor illustrates the lavish life-style of the rich. Parties of the wealthy were especially ostentatious; at one, guests smoked cigarettes rolled in one hundred dollar bills after drinking coffee.

Economic Modernization in the South and West

Although most industrialization occurred in the industrial Northeast, farming regions also experienced profound changes as a national, interdependent economy emerged, and a world based on personal relationships was displaced by a more impersonal world based on contractual relationships. The largely self-sufficient farmer gave way to the cash-crop farmer whose produce went to feed urban masses hundreds of miles away. Rural population kept growing, although not as rapidly as urban population. While the benefits of economic modernization were not shared equally—the South lagged far behind other regions of the country—the demand by the urban masses for food sparked a farming revolution based on mechanization and scientific agriculture.

Western Expansion

The transcontinental railroads were not originally meant to "open up" the West. They were laid across what was called the "Great American Desert" in order to link the East and West coasts. The perceived worthlessness of the Great Plains was reflected in the willingness to give much of it away— to the Indians and later to the railroads. The mining frontier first altered perceptions of the region's value. In addition to mineral wealth, the region had two other plentiful resources: grass and cattle. Railroads provided the means to get the cattle to eastern cities, where urban residents wanted more meat to eat. The result was the birth of western ranching.

At first, ranching did not require much capital. Both the cattle and the grass were free. By 1860 some five million head of wild Texas longhorns had descended from cattle imported by Spanish colonists. Joseph G. McCoy realized the potential for profit and established the first "cow town" at Abilene, Kansas, where he built stock pens and loading chutes. Cowboys drove cattle there for shipment by rail to Chicago, where they sold for $30 to $50 a head. Other cow towns arose as some six million head of cattle endured the "long drive" to those sites between 1866 and 1888.

The heyday of the cowboy was rather brief, since ranching, like mining, soon became an organized business. Profits from a successful drive were very good—about 40 percent. This naturally attracted eastern investors, and soon the long drives gave way to more efficient methods. The rounding up of stray, lean, rangy longhorns ended as the rail network expanded into Texas and ranchers began raising and breeding the longhorns with superior imported stock to improve the quality of the beef.

The cattle breeders needed large tracts of grassland for grazing and usually just appropriated land from the public domain. During this open-range era, high profits attracted even more investors. Eventually the ranchers joined other segments of the economy that were outproducing demand. Beef prices dropped from $30 to $10 a head in 1885 and 1886. Poorer producers were driven out by these low prices, challenges to their land claims by sheepherders and farmers, and bad weather. A winter of terrible blizzards following the scorching summer in 1886 led to the death of 90 percent of western cattle.

After sometimes bloody battles for supremacy between these economic competitors, the "Wild West" was largely tamed by the 1890s. Ranchers who remained established legal title to their grazing lands, fenced them in with barbed wire, and practiced scientific breeding and feeding of their stock. The forces of economic consolidation had reached ranching—making it a business requiring large amounts of capital.

Land legislation of the era aided the monopolization of ranching by a relatively few "cattle barons." Large tracts of public lands were given away or sold cheaply through such acts as the Homestead Act of 1862, the Timber Culture Act of 1873, and the Desert Land Act of 1877. Enacted to promote socially desirable goals, all had large loopholes that were exploited by cattlemen and land speculators. To promote settlement, the Homestead Act offered 160 free acres to those who would cultivate it for five years. The Desert Land Act granted 640 acres at $1.25 an acre to anyone who would irrigate the land. The Timber Culture Act, based on the theory that the trees increased rainfall, awarded 160 acres to anyone who would plant trees on a quarter of the land. Cattlemen and speculators fraudulently claimed to have met the terms of the grants or hired dummy entrymen to stake claims for them. A bucket of water was sometimes the only basis for claims of irrigation. Lumber barons in the Pacific Northwest similarly utilized other land-granting laws. Thus much of the newly discovered wealth of the West ended up in the hands of a few winners in the great land lottery.

While the mining, cattle, and lumber frontiers offered some quick, easy riches before being transformed into capital-intensive businesses, the farming frontier required more patience to make profits. By the time farmers arrived in the new West, much of the best land had already been appropriated. Most of the 274 million acres distributed under the terms of the Homestead Act were eventually purchased by bona fide settlers from speculators and cattlemen. Other farmers bought land from the railroads, which promoted settlement to increase traffic in isolated areas. To lure settlers, railroad companies often provided easy credit terms and extolled western opportunities in flyers and speeches.

Many farming pioneers soon learned that railroad propaganda sometimes overstated the promise of the West. When they arrived, they discovered a shortage of wood and water but an overabundance of severe weather, insects, and social isolation. The houses they built of "bricks" cut from thick prairie sod were functional but bleak. At first, many farmers managed only to eke out a bare subsistence. Eventually, however, western farmers were caught up in the forces of change that transformed agriculture as dramatically as other sectors of the economy.

The Changing Nature of Farming

When Congress passed the Homestead Act in 1862, most of the arable land east of the Mississippi was already taken. The established farmers of the old Northeast adapted fairly well to the changing economy and were generally prosperous, supplying rapidly growing urban areas with vegetables, dairy products, poultry, and pigs. They also profited from rising land values by selling extra acres to residential and industrial developers at high prices.

The challenges of farming were much greater in the West, and when they were finally met, overproduction depressed prices. Cultivation of the West required new agricultural techniques and adaptations to the environment. The scarcity of trees not only dictated the building of sodhouses, but also made the cost of fencing prohibitive. Until the develop-

Because of the scarcity of trees on the Plains, settlers built homes from "bricks" of sod. With walls 2 to 3 feet thick, the houses were gloomy but provided cozy and solid protection from the elements.

ment of barbed wire in 1874, crops were not easily protected from the millions of roaming cattle.

A more serious problem was the lack of water. Farmers tried to alleviate water shortages by using new varieties of seed, pumping water from far below the ground surface with windmills, and using cultivation techniques known as "dry farming." During good times, optimism flourished; but then came the droughts. By 1900 two-thirds of the homesteaders had failed, and farmers returned east with signs saying, "In God We Trusted; in Kansas We Busted."

In the South, at the very time the rest of the economy was consolidating, agriculture was marching off in the opposite, less efficient direction. The devastation caused by the Civil War had destroyed half the region's farm equipment and killed one-third of its draft animals. Productivity declined as large plantations were subdivided for use by sharecroppers. Another problem was a shortage of cash, which forced Southern farmers to borrow against future crops. Crop liens and high credit costs kept both black and white farmers trapped in a cycle of debt and poverty.

Many Plains and Southern farmers became losers in the economic modernization of agriculture. Nevertheless, both the winners and the losers were playing essentially the same game, the commercialization of farming. Most of the rules were the same as those for manufacturers: specialization, new technology, mechanization, expanded markets, heavier capital investment, and reliance on interstate transportation. Many farmers of that generation wholeheartedly embraced these changes until they fell behind their industrial cousins in the expanding economy.

Specialization became apparent in the decline of subsistence farming and the growing importance of cash crops. Although general farming continued, most farmers planted more of their acreage in the single crop best suited for their land and market. Cash crops were usually supplemented by small gardens and stock raising, except in the South, where landowners often forced debt-ridden tenant farmers to plant all available acreage with cotton.

Technology and mechanization revolutionized agriculture and increased productivity dramatically. After the mechanization of wheat farming, the hours required to farm an acre dropped from 61 to 3, and the per acre cost of production fell from $3.65 to $0.66. Machines entered every phase of agriculture, and included such items as hay loaders, cord binders, seeders, rotary plows, mowers, and combines. Farmers began to learn "scientific agriculture" at land-grant colleges that Congress had provided for under the Morrill Land Grant Act of 1862. Agricultural researchers explored ways to increase production and found new uses for overabundant crops at agricultural experiment stations funded by the Hatch Act of 1887. Obviously, farmers were not opposed to all government aid to the economy.

Although the average farm remained about 150 acres, the farms of the West were usually much larger because dry-farming techniques produced low yields per acre. To succeed, a western farmer needed more acres and more machines; both cost money. Thus, like businesspeople, farmers needed access to capital. Most obtained personal loans using their land, machinery, and crops as collateral. Unfortunately, as production increased, prices fell, and to counteract lower profits farmers further expanded production in a self-defeating downward spiral.

One solution to overproduction was to expand markets, which required cheap and reliable transportation facilities. Railroads, therefore, had as much impact on agriculture as on industry.

Most farmers realized and, at first, even celebrated their status as businesspeople. Agricultural expansion was as dramatic as that of industry, yet farmers began to lose ground in terms of wealth, status, and percentage of the total population. When they discovered that they could not adapt as well as industrialists to the new economic order, they began to assert the superiority of rural culture. They stressed farmers' ties to the soil and heralded individualism and self-sufficiency as truly American characteristics.

The New South

Many Southerners wholeheartedly endorsed the new economic order at first. Some even saw the South's salvation in the destruction of slavery and proclaimed the emergence of "a New South." Henry W. Grady, the editor of the *Atlanta Constitution,* wrote and traveled extensively to promote the region's unlimited opportunities. Grady envisioned three major changes from the Old South: diversified farming, industrialization, and racial accommodation and cooperation.

Many shared Grady's vision. At the Cotton States Exposition of 1895 in Atlanta, a black spokesman for the New South emerged. Booker T. Washington, principal of Tuskegee Normal and Industrial Institute in Alabama, was asked by the exposition's white organizers to give an address. His speech, known as the "Atlanta Compromise," offered an optimistic appraisal of Southern potential and outlined a basis for racial cooperation. Washington urged blacks to make themselves economically indispensable to whites and forego agitation for political and social rights in return for educational and economic opportunities. Their economic importance would bring them white acceptance—and the rights they desired. Washington practiced what he preached. Tuskegee was a model New South institution, focusing on industrial education and promoting diversified farming.

The New South optimism was based on dramatic changes taking place in the region. Railroad development increased at a rate greater than in the nation at large. The textile, timber, and tobacco industries boomed. Birmingham, Alabama grew into a major producer of raw steel, and by 1890 Southern steel and iron made up almost 20 percent of the national total. At the same time Southern agriculture was recovering. Cotton production exceeded prewar records by the 1870s.

The tobacco and textile industries especially seemed to bring the dream to life. Both were based on major Southern crops. In the 1880s James B. Duke introduced the cigarette industry to the region. By 1890 he had created a trust through which he controlled 150 companies in an almost perfect monopoly until 1911 federal antitrust actions disbanded the trust.

Textile mills were seen as the key to Southern economic salvation. Although profitable, these mills were not run according to the New South guidelines advocated by Grady. Workers, often whole families of poor whites—by custom African Americans were denied employment—labored an average of 12 hours a day. Wages were as low as 50 cents a day and were usually not paid in cash, but in "trade checks." These trade checks were accepted to pay rent on company houses or buy goods in company stores. Elsewhere merchants and landlords would not accept the checks at face value. Thus some mill workers never saw any cash, merely turning their trade checks back over to the mill owners in return for supplies and housing. It is no wonder that profits were high for mill owners. Those high profits caused a textile boom in the South, and the number of mills grew from 161 in 1880 to 400 in 1900.

Despite all the signs of progress, major obstacles prevented the South's economy from keeping pace with the rest of the nation. Southern agriculture remained trapped in the inefficient sharecropping system and single-crop agriculture. Increased cotton production was accompanied by falling crop prices. By 1900 over half of the region's white farmers and three-quarters of black farmers were tenants. Most barely made enough to feed and clothe their families; few had the money to improve farming techniques or try new crops. By 1880 the South was not growing enough food to feed its people. Poor nutrition added bad health and disease to the region's problems.

The persistent ideology of white supremacy also helped keep the South mired in poverty. Race relations actually worsened in the 1890s as white Southerners struggled to keep black Southerners "in their place." In 1896 the Supreme Court ruled in the *Plessy* v. *Ferguson* decision that separate accommodations for African Americans did not violate the Fourteenth Amendment if the facilities were substantially equal in quality. The effect was to legalize segregation—a disaster for both black and white Southerners. Accommodations were never really equal, and African Americans suffered from inferior schools and services. At the same time, keeping most of the black third of the Southern population in ignorance and poverty depressed wage scales and the tax base needed to support public education and other services.

Another key to the South's relative poverty was its shortage of capital, which was rooted in the slave system and the Civil War. Reliance on slavery and cotton had enriched the Old South but helped to impoverish the New South. While the antebellum North employed its capital to build canals, railroads, cities, and factories, the South used its profits to buy more slaves. Emancipation meant that as much as $4 billion that had been invested in slaves was lost. In addition, the war was largely fought on Southern soil. Railroads had been torn up, factories and cities were burned down. Before the Civil War the South had seen little reason to use its capital to build factories and cities. After the war, the region no longer had the capital to do those things.

In the late nineteenth century Northern dollars did flow south. In the 1880s Northerners increased their investments in the cotton industry sevenfold. They also provided most of the capital to rebuild and expand Southern railroads and to start the region's steel industry. However, the use of Northern capital in most industries also meant that the profits went to Northerners as well. For the most part, the region supplied unfinished raw materials, such as lumber, for which prices were rather low. After these products were converted into manufactured goods in the North, the South had to buy those goods at higher prices than it had received for the raw materials.

For all these reasons the South remained at the bottom of the economic ladder. As happened in the West, the South's reliance on Northern capital kept the majority of profits going elsewhere. By the late 1880s farmers in both regions would unite to oppose the changes brought by industrial capitalism.

Conclusion

In one generation the United States became the economic colossus of the world. There were many positive benefits of this economic expansion and consolidation. In some cases people were able to buy superior goods at cheaper prices. Although some skilled artisans slipped downward on the social ladder, upward social mobility did increase for large segments of the population. Of course, not all shared equally in the nation's newfound

Chronology of Key Events

1856	Bessemer steelmaking process invented
1859	Edwin Drake drills first commercial oil well
1861	Morrill Tariff, first in series of high protective tariffs, passed
1862	Homestead Act gives 160 acres of public land to those who will cultivate it for five years; Morrill Land Grant Act establishes many technical and agricultural colleges
1866	First trans-Atlantic telegraph cable laid
1869	First transcontinental railroad completed
1870	John D. Rockefeller founds Standard Oil Company
1873	Timber Culture Act awards 160 acres of public land to those who would plant trees on a quarter of the land
1876	Alexander Graham Bell invents telephone
1877	Thomas Edison invents phonograph; Desert Land Act grants 640 acres to those who would irrigate the land
1879	Edison invents incandescent light bulb
1883	Country divided into time zones
1886	*Santa Clara County* v. *Southern Pacific Railroad* rules that a corporation is entitled to constitutional protection
1888	George Eastman produces the first hand-held camera
1895	Booker T. Washington's "Atlanta Compromise" speech
1896	*Plessy* v. *Ferguson* rules that "separate but equal" facilities are unconstitutional
1901	Carnegie Steel company sold to J. P. Morgan

wealth, and few made the transition from rags to riches that Carnegie accomplished. Most industrial leaders instead came from rather privileged backgrounds. The majority were relatively well educated Protestants of native birth. Average annual incomes rose steadily for almost all classes of workers. On the other hand, those wage increases rarely equaled the rising cost of living. Nevertheless, most families' standard of living improved because more members of the family worked for wages.

At the same time, individuals paid huge social costs for these advances. Some people paid a disproportionate share of these costs. Patterns of working and living dramatically changed. Many workers found themselves in a new status that imperiled their independence. Personal relationships were being replaced by impersonal, contractual arrangements. Shady corporate practices corrupted public morality. In short, all aspects of life underwent profound transformation, and the story of the late nineteenth century is the story of adaptation and adjustment to the new social and economic order.

Suggestions for Further Reading

Valuable overviews of industrialization and the rise of big business include Alfred D. Chandler, *The Visible Hand: The Managerial Revolution in American Business* (1977); Carl N. Degler, ed., *The Age of the Economic Revolution* (1977); Glenn Porter, *The Rise of Big Business, 1865–1920,* 2d ed. (1992).

For more on ideology, culture, and public opinion consult Robert Bannister, *Social Darwinism* (1979); Louis Galambos, *The Public Image of Big Business in America* (1975); T. Jackson Lears, *No Place of Grace: Antimodernism and the Transformation of American Culture* (1981); Alan Trachtenberg, *The Incorporation of America: Culture and Society in the Gilded Age* (1982).

Issues regarding the modernization of the West are examined in Gunther Barth, *Instant Cities: Urbanization and the Rise of San Francisco and Denver* (1975); Edward E. Dale, *The Range Cattle Industry, 1865 to 1925,* rev. ed. (1969); Robert V. Hine, *The American West,* 2d ed. (1984); Patricia Nelson Limerick, *Legacy of Conquest* (1987); Rodman W. Paul, *Mining Frontiers of the Far West, 1848–1880* (1963). On the New South see Peter Daniel, *Breaking the Land* (1985); Paul Gaston, *The New South Creed* (1964).

Good biographies on the captains of industry include Maury Klein, *The Life and Legend of Jay Gould* (1986); Harold C. Livesay, *Andrew Carnegie and the Rise of Big Business* (1975); Andrew Sinclair, *Corsair: The Life of J. Pierpont Morgan* (1981).

Chapter *18*

Immigrants and Workers in Industrial America

In 1862, while the nation was locked in the grip of a terrible Civil War, Congress authorized the most ambitious building project that the country had ever contemplated: construction of a transcontinental railroad. The price tag was staggering: $136 million, more than twice the federal budget of 1861. The challenge was enormous: 1,800 miles across arid plains and desert and the rugged granite walls of the Sierra Nevada and the Rocky Mountains.

Two companies undertook the actual construction. The Union Pacific began laying track westward from Omaha, Nebraska, and the Central Pacific commenced eastward from Sacramento, California. Of the two companies, the Central Pacific faced the more arduous task. It had to carve a rail bed through the high Sierra Nevada. It also faced the more severe labor shortages.

In early 1865 the Central Pacific decided to dip into a new labor pool: Chinese immigrants. Within two years, 12,000 of the Central Pacific's 13,500 employees were Chinese immigrants. Earning reputations as tireless and extraordinarily reliable employees, they labored high in the mountains and inside tunnels. Explosions, avalanches, and other accidents left an estimated 1,200 Chinese workers dead.

Despite their heroic labors, California's Chinese immigrants faced discrimination and racial violence. White Americans criticized their attachment to their homeland and questioned their loyalty to the United States.

Since most Chinese immigrants never intended to stay in the United States, many may not have developed any emotional attachment to America or its institutions. In America they sought the opportunity to work—not voting rights, education, or assimilation—and no form of labor was beneath them. They resignedly accepted the most menial jobs in the mines, on the railroad construction gangs, and in the booming western cities.

Because they only came to America to accumulate money, the Chinese immigrants lived as inexpensively as possible. Sleeping in huge halls on matted floors, and sometimes sharing one mat by sleeping in eight-hour shifts, they were able to reduce lodging expenses to ten cents a month. Chinese workers sent most of their earnings back to their families in China, to whom they intended to return someday.

Immigration, then, could in no way be interpreted as a rejection of China. In reality, it was a defense of the Chinese way of life, for the money sent home helped preserve the traditional order. America was not a sacred idea, but a means to an end and, of course, sometimes a very lonely country.

Americans failed to understand the mind of the Chinese immigrant. To them, the Chinese were just non-Western, non-Christian, and non-white aliens. Although railroad builders and mine owners regarded the Chinese as good, inexpensive laborers, native-born American workers believed they brought down wages for all workers. Every major American labor organizer of the period called for federal action to restrict Chinese immigration. Some leaders charged that the "coolies" so depressed wages that women in white working families had to resort to prostitution to avoid starvation.

Labor leaders were joined by Irish-American politicians, the Catholic church, eastern editorialists, and California workers in their crusade against Chinese laborers. All agreed, the Chinese should—*must*—be excluded from the United States as undesirable, unassimilable aliens. In 1882 Congress responded with the Chinese Exclusion Act, which suspended Chinese immigration. It was the first time that the United States closed its doors to any immigrants for ethnocultural reasons.

Later, other immigrant groups shared experiences similar to the Chinese. Native-born Americans saw other ethnic groups as beyond reform, as not having the "right stuff" to become Americans. Again and again labor leaders, religious authorities, and old-line Americans joined forces in opposition to certain groups of immigrants. The entire movement toward restriction culminated in 1924 with the passage of the National Origins Act.

Yet immigrants contributed greatly to the growth of industrial America. They and their fellow workers—native-born white and black Americans—built the railroads that crisscrossed the country; mined the gold and silver that made other men rich; and labored in the oilfields, steel mills, coal pits, packing plants, and factories that made such names as Rockefeller, Carnegie, Swift, and Westinghouse famous. Without these men and their companions, there would have been no industrialization. In the process they made the United States an ethnically rich nation.

Huddled Masses at the Golden Door

On October 28, 1886, President Grover Cleveland traveled to New York Harbor to watch the unveiling of the Statue of Liberty. A gift from France, Frederic Auguste Bartholdi's grand statue was meant to symbolize solidarity between the two republics, but that was not how Americans and incoming immigrants interpreted the sculpture. For them it was a simple symbol of welcome, with the statue's torch lighting the path to a better future. A poem, written by Emma Lazarus and eventually placed at the base of the statue, emphasized the promise of America:

Most of the miners from Pennsylvania to California were immigrants from
Europe and Asia. Anxious to improve their standard of living in their
homeland, these immigrants would accept dangerous, but high-paying jobs.

> Give me your tired, your poor,
> Your huddled masses yearning to breathe free,
> The wretched refuse of your teeming shore.
> Send these, the homeless, tempest-tossed to me,
> I lift my lamp beside the golden door!

In popular theory, the promise of America exerted a powerful pull on Europe and Asia. The United States stood for political freedom, social mobility, and economic opportunity. Since the first settlers landed in Jamestown,
millions of immigrants had responded to the American magnet. At no time
was immigration as great as in the late nineteenth and early twentieth centuries; between 1860 and 1920 more than 25 million more people arrived.

The United States was not the only country to lure immigrants from
Europe. Millions more immigrated to Australia, New Zealand, South
Africa, Canada, Brazil, Argentina, and other underpopulated areas of the
globe. In truth, seen in its worldwide context, the United States' pull was
less powerful than Europe's push. During the nineteenth century almost

every European country experienced a dramatic population increase due to advances in medicine and improved public health standards. Available land and food, however, could not increase sufficiently to meet the new population demands. Thus emigration increased sharply.

Historians have divided immigration to the United States into two categories: old and new. The source of the old immigration was northern and western Europe—England, Ireland, France, Germany, and Scandinavia. The immigrants were mostly Protestants (except for the Irish Catholics) and always white; a majority were literate and had lived under constitutional forms of government. Assimilation for them was a relatively easy process. The new immigration came from eastern and southern Europe. Greeks, Poles, Russians, Italians, Slavs, Turks—these people found assimilation more difficult. Politically, religiously, and culturally, they differed greatly from both the earlier immigrants and native-born Americans.

The shift from "old" to "new" occurred during the 1880s. For example, in 1882, 87 percent of the immigrants to the United States came from northern and western Europe. By 1907 this pattern had changed;

Immigration, 1880–1889 and 1900–1909

The source of old immigration was primarily northern and western Europe—England, Ireland, Germany, and Scandinavia. By the late 1890s a wave of new immigrants began to arrive from eastern and southern Europe.

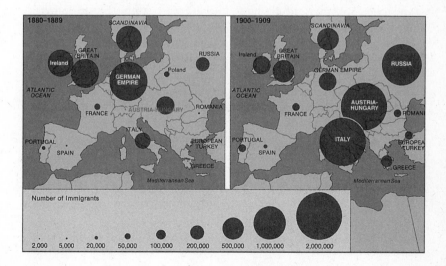

more than 80 percent were from southern and eastern Europe. Certainly, a geographic shift in origin of immigration to the United States took place, but more than geography differentiated the old and the new immigrants. Their reasons for leaving Europe, visions of America, settlement patterns, and occupational choices varied greatly.

By the late nineteenth century the motives and the opportunity to migrate to America were present in southern and eastern Europe. With the abolition of serfdom, peasants were free to emigrate; and with the rise in population, young men faced job, land, and food shortages. Finally, railroads and steamships made travel faster and less expensive. During the 1880s steamships carried immigrants across the Atlantic for as little as $8, and by the turn of the century the trip took only five and a half days. In short, the conditions were right for the push to America.

"Birds of Passage"

Essentially two types of immigrants came to America. Permanent immigrants formed one group; migrant workers comprised the other. The people in the second group, often called birds of passage, were like the Chinese. They never intended to make the United States their home, but simply came to America to work, save, and then returned to their homeland. Most were young men in their teens and twenties. They left behind their parents, young wives, and children, indications that their absence would not be too long. Before 1900 an estimated 78 percent of Italian immigrants and 95 percent of Greek immigrants were men. Some immigrants came to America fully intending to return home, but for one reason or another—love, hardship, early death—did not. Overall, 20 to 30 percent of all immigrants returned to their native land.

The activity of the birds of passage can be clearly seen in Italian immigration patterns of the late nineteenth century. Starting in the 1870s Italian birthrates began to rise and mortality rates fell. Heavily taxed and hurt by high protective tariffs on northern industrial goods, southern Italians sank deeper into poverty. Soon nature also joined the opposition. Natural disasters rocked southern Italy during the first decade of the twentieth century. Earthquakes and volcanic eruptions caused untold devastation. The most cruel blow came in 1908 when an earthquake and tidal wave swept through the Strait of Messina between Sicily and the Italian mainland. The disaster destroyed hundreds of villages and killed hundreds of thousands of people.

The kinds of jobs that Italian men sought reflected their attitude toward America. They did not look for careers. Occupations that provided opportunity for upward economic mobility were alien to them. Unlike most of the earlier immigrants to America, they did not want to farm or even own land, both of which implied a permanence that did not figure in their plans. Instead, Italians headed for the cities, where many found work in the construction industry. Few jobs were beneath them. Native-born Americans commented that the Italian birds of passage readily accepted "work no white man could stand." Expecting their stay in America to be short, they lived as inexpensively as possible under conditions that native-born families considered intolerable.

Italians were not the only birds of passage. The same forces—population pressure, unemployment, hunger, and the breakdown of agrarian societies—sent Greeks, Slavs, Chinese, Japanese, Mexicans, French Canadians, and inhabitants of scores of other nations to the United States. Seeking neither permanent homes nor citizenship, they desired only an opportunity to work for a living, hoping to save enough money to return to a better life in the country of their birth.

Slavs, and especially Poles, dramatized this pattern of temporary migration—the desire to use America as a means of improving their lot in their home country. Strong and determined, they preferred the work that paid the best, usually the most dangerous and physically exhausting. After disembarking at East Coast ports, Slavs generally headed directly to the mill and mining towns of Pennsylvania and the Midwest. Unlike the Italians who preferred to work in sociable gangs and above ground, Poles readily accepted the hard lonely labor of the mines and steel mills. The extra money was enough compensation for the danger of underground or indoor work. Employers quickly noted this Slavic inclination and solicited the labor of hardy Slavs in search of good wages and the fast route home.

In Search of a New Home

In contrast to the birds of passage, several million other immigrants came to America with no intention of ever returning to the land of their birth. These were the permanent immigrants, for whom America offered political and religious freedom as well as economic opportunity. The promise of America was especially appealing to members of ethnic and religious minorities who were persecuted, abused, and despised in their homelands.

The Jews were the prototypical true immigrants. Like the Irish Catholics a generation before, they fled nearly unbearable hardships. For millions of Russian Jews, for whom life was difficult in the best of times, conditions deteriorated rapidly following the assassination of the liberal

Czar Alexander II. Laws restricted Jewish businesses, prevented Jewish land ownership, and limited Jewish education. Pogroms, a form of legally sanctioned mob attack against Jews, killed and injured thousands of persons. Sometimes at the whim of authorities, Russian Cossacks burned Jewish houses and destroyed Jewish possessions.

Because they came to the United States to stay, the form of Jewish immigration differed substantially from that of the birds of passage. For them, immigration was not simply a young man's alternative. Jews, as all other permanent immigrants, tended to come to America in family units. Men and women, young and old—they were all represented. They brought their life savings and most valuable possessions with them, never expecting to see again what they left behind. As a result, the move to

In 1882 Congress passed the Chinese Exclusion Act, which barred Chinese laborers from entering the United States for ten years.

America was financially and physically taxing. And once in America, whole families had more expenses than the young male birds of passage.

Since America was now their home, Jewish men looked for jobs offering future opportunities rather than simply the opportunity to work for wages. They were not drawn to the steel mills and mines or even to jobs in construction. They desired skilled, not unskilled, labor. Many Jews were artisans, and in America they put these skills to use as tailors and seamstresses, cigar makers and toy makers, tanners and butchers, carpenters, joiners, roofers, and masons, coppersmiths and blacksmiths. They had the knowledge and ability to perform the thousands of skilled tasks needed in an urban environment.

Nativism: The Anti-Immigrant Reaction

Sometimes an isolated event, by itself not historically important, can illuminate like a flash of lightning the social landscape and beliefs of a particular time. Certainly this is true with the Hennessy case. In 1890 a feud between gangs on the New Orleans docks turned violent. The following year David Hennessy, the New Orleans superintendent of police, asserted that he had evidence that a secret Sicilian organization known as the Mafia was involved in the affair. Shortly after Hennessy made his bold charges, five armed men gunned him down.

The crime raised a hue and cry against Sicilians, and local police arrested scores, urged on by Mayor Joseph Shakespeare's instructions to "arrest every Italian you come across, if necessary." The mayor told the public, "We must teach these people a lesson that they will not forget for all time." Eleven Sicilians were brought to trial, but a jury failed to convict them. Undaunted, a local mob promptly took matters into its own hands and shot or clubbed to death nine and hanged two of the suspects. As far as most natives of New Orleans were concerned, justice had been done. Many Americans seemed to agree.

The Hennessy case soon faded from the front pages of American newspapers, but the emotions it revealed were very real. Native-born Americans harbored deep resentment toward immigrants, especially those from southern and eastern Europe. If American industrialists saw in the immigrants a bottomless pool of dependable inexpensive labor, American workers saw competition. Protestants saw Catholics and Jews. Educators saw illiterate hordes. Politicians saw peasants, unfamiliar with the workings of democracy. Social Darwinists saw a mass of dark-skinned people who were far "below" northern and western Europeans on the evolutionary ladder. In short, native-born Americans, heirs of a different culture, religion, and complexion, saw something alien and inferior, perhaps even dangerous.

This atmosphere of hostility often spilled over into open violence. In 1891 in a New Jersey mill town 500 tending boys in a glassworks rioted when the management hired 14 young Russian Jews. During an 1895 labor conflict in the southern Colorado coal fields, a group of American miners killed six Italians. When Slavic coal miners went on strike in 1897 in eastern Pennsylvania, local citizens massacred 21 Polish and Hungarian workers. On the West Coast, Chinese workers were subject to regular and vicious attacks. Especially during economic hard times, native-born Americans lashed out against the new immigrants.

Sources of Conflict

Nativism, as this anti-immigrant backlash was called, took many forms. Racial nativism decried the new immigrants as biologically less advanced than the Americans who traced their ancestry back to northern and western Europe. Some scholars gathered data on complexion, size of cranium, length of forehead, and slope of shoulders in an effort to demonstrate the inferiority of immigrants. Popular writers readily accepted these stereotypes. Jacob Riis, a Danish immigrant who became an urban reformer in America and wrote the popular book *How the Other Half Lives* (1890), characterized Italians as "born gamblers" who lived destitute and disorderly lives; Chinese as secretive and addicted to every vice; and Jews as "enslaved" by their pursuit of gold and living amid filth.

Religious differences reinforced ethnic variations. Overwhelmingly Catholic and Jewish, the new immigrants challenged the Protestant orthodoxy of the United States. Many Americans regarded the pope as the anti-Christ and Catholics as his evil minions. Native-born Americans viewed Jews with even greater suspicion. "Money is their God," wrote leading journalist and social critic Jacob Riis. Eventually many social clubs, country clubs, hotels, and universities excluded Jews, arguing that money alone could not purchase respectability.

The Leo Frank case painfully demonstrated the ubiquitous anti-Semitism in American society. Frank, the son of a wealthy New York merchant, managed an Atlanta pencil factory. In 1914 one of the factory hands, Mary Phagan, was found murdered on the premises. Frank was tried and convicted on flimsy evidence, but after reviewing the case the governor of Georgia commuted Frank's death sentence to life imprisonment. The decision outraged native Georgian whites. They boycotted Jewish merchants and clamored for Frank's blood. Finally, a group of citizens from Mary Phagan's hometown took Leo Frank from a state prison, transported him 175 miles across the state, and coldly hanged him. In the 1980s new evidence in the Phagan case proved Frank innocent, and Georgia's Board of Pardons granted him a posthumous pardon.

The wave of immigrants sparked political fears as well as racial and religious ones. Many Americans tended to equate immigration with radicalism and suspected that every boat that docked at Ellis Island contained a swarm of revolutionaries. As unfounded as their fears were, isolated cases of radicalism among immigrants did occur. They drew attention, for example, to Leon Czolgosz, born of eastern European immigrant parents and a convert to revolutionary anarchism. On September 6, 1901, Czolgosz shot and killed President William McKinley at the Pan-American Conference in Buffalo, New York. Such actions seemed to confirm the worst fears of antiradical nativists.

The strongest resentments against the new immigrants, however, were purely economic. American workers, particularly the unskilled, believed that the immigrants depressed wages by their willingness to "work cheap." Even skilled workers maintained that birds of passage were unwilling to support any union efforts to improve working conditions in America. Samuel Gompers, head of the American Federation of Labor, believed that the immigrants from eastern and southern Europe and from Asia were ignorant, unskilled, and unassimilable. Calling for strong restrictive legislation, he said, "Some way must be found to safeguard America."

In short, by the 1890s, when a terrible depression had disrupted the normal economic and social course of America, the new immigrants became a convenient scapegoat for the nation's ills. It was a time when people elevated racial prejudice and rumors to universal truths. Swept along by a wave of xenophobic fear, nativists claimed that the social ills of America's expanding cities—corruption, poor sanitation, violence, crime, disease, pollution—were the fault of the new immigrants. And they looked to the federal government for relief and protection.

Closing the Golden Door

The first immigrants attacked were those who were the most different from native-born Americans and the most unskilled—the Chinese. Between 1868 and 1882, more than 160,000 Chinese entered the United States. They laid down railroad tracks and mined for gold, silver, and coal. During the depression of the mid-1870s the Chinese came under increasingly bitter and violent attack. At the forefront of the nativistic onslaught were the Irish, themselves recent immigrants, who competed with the Chinese for unskilled jobs. Irish political leaders in America demanded an end to Chinese immigration into the United States.

Eventually Congress responded to the pressure for restriction. In 1880 China gave the United States the right "to regulate, limit, or suspend," though not to prohibit, the immigration of workers. Quickly the golden door slammed shut. In 1882 the Chinese Exclusion Act suspended Chinese immigration for ten years and drastically restricted the rights of the Chinese already in the United States. In 1892 Congress extended the act for another ten years, and then in 1902 extended it indefinitely. The legislation established a precedent for the future exclusion of other immigrants. By the 1890s most Americans agreed that the country should restrict "undesirable" immigrants.

In 1896 Congress passed a literacy test bill, which would have excluded any adult immigrant unable to read 40 words in his language. President Grover Cleveland vetoed the measure, arguing that it tested prior circumstances and America stood for open opportunities. The demand for restrictive legislation continued, however, and in 1917 Congress passed a literacy test bill, overriding the veto of Woodrow Wilson.

Hester Street, 1907, on New York City's Lower East Side was home to thousands of Jewish immigrants from Russia and eastern Europe. The immigrants crowded into the tenements lining the street, which bustled with peddlers and pedestrians.

World War I and the Bolshevik Revolution in Russia in 1917 chilled an already cold climate for immigrants from southern and eastern Europe. Once again American authorities regarded Jews from Russia as potential revolutionaries. Responding to this fear, in 1918 and 1920 Congress passed legislation to exclude or deport anarchists and other "dangerous radicals."

The generation-long battle over restriction ended with a clear victory for nativism, when Congress in 1921 passed the Emergency Quota Act, which limited immigration to a nation-based quota system. It provided that no more than 3 percent of any given nationality in America in 1910 could annually immigrate to the United States. In 1924 the National Origins Act lowered the quota to 2 percent of each nationality residing in America in 1890. The act was clearly aimed at restricting eastern and southern Europeans, and although modified in 1927 it achieved its desired result. The golden door was no longer fully open to eastern and southern Europeans, and it was completely closed to Asians. An important era in American history had ended.

Nativism and Native Americans

Immigrants were not the only people affected by nativist impulses. In a cruel irony, American Indians also felt the impact of nativist theories and prejudices. During the 1860s, 1870s, and 1880s Indians were forced onto reservations by the federal government. The process was not peaceful. At almost every step Indian tribes resisted, often clashing with federal troops.

The last major bloody confrontation occurred during the cold December of 1890 on the Pine Ridge Reservation (Sioux) in South Dakota. Poorly fed and supplied on the reservation and longing for the glories of their past, members of the Teton Sioux took up the "Ghost Dance," a ritual that promised the faithful the mystical disappearance of the whites and the return of their tribal lands. Troops were called in to suppress the Ghost Dance and arrest the Sioux leader Sitting Bull, who the government considered the focal point of Indian resistance. Sitting Bull was killed, and some Sioux took up arms and left the reservation. Near Wounded Knee Creek, U.S. soldiers, armed with rapid-fire Hotchkiss guns, attempted to disarm the Indians. When one Indian resisted, soldiers opened fire, killing more than 300 men, women, and children. The Battle of Wounded Knee, which resembled more a slaughter than a battle, ended the violent era of Indian and white relations.

By the time of Wounded Knee, however, the U.S. government had embarked on a new solution to the Indian problem. At the heart of this new policy was the destruction of the reservation system. Reservations encouraged tribal unity, and, as such, distinctiveness from white American society. Congress believed that the solution was to treat Indians less like members of individual tribes and more like autonomous individuals. In 1887 Congress passed the Dawes Severalty Act, which authorized the president to divide tribal lands and redistribute the lands among tribal members, giving 160 acres to each head of a family and lesser amounts to bachelors, women, and children. Although the plots would be held in trust for 25 years to prevent Indians from immediately selling the land, the object of the legislation was to make Indians individual landowners. In addition, all Indians receiving land grants were also made citizens of the United States.

Henry Dawes, a U.S. senator from Massachusetts, was motivated by what he believed were the best interests of the Indians. Like other reformers, he believed that the most effective solution to the Indian problem was to assimilate Indians into mainstream white American culture. Other reformers opened Indian schools to teach Indian children to be mechanics and farmers and to train them for citizenship. More than two dozen eastern boarding schools were established on the premise that the fastest and surest way to achieve assimilation was to remove children from their Indian way of life. Even more boarding schools were established on reservations to serve the same ends. However, the schools failed to break tribal loyalties or destroy Native-American culture.

While the reformers opened schools, Congress continued its efforts to break up the reservations. The Curtis Act of 1898 ended tribal sovereignty in Indian Territory, voiding tribal control of mineral rights, abolishing tribal laws and courts, and imposing the laws and courts of the United States on the Indians. Finally, in 1924 Congress enacted the Snyder Act, which granted all Indians born in the United States full citizenship. As far as Congress was concerned, the United States had now assimilated its true natives.

Reformers believed that these acts would end the tribal system and lead to assimilation. The legislation, however, served only the land interests of white Americans. By 1932 the allotment program had taken 90 million acres of land away from tribal control, and as late as 1981 a U.S. district court decision branded the program "probably one of the best-intended grievous errors in the history of American policy-making." Far from being assimilated, Indians saw their own culture attacked and partially destroyed, while at the same time they were never fully accepted into the dominant American culture.

Working in Industrial America

If during the 1920s advocates of immigration restrictions and Indian assimilation won an important battle, they lost their self-proclaimed war. They longed for a rural, white, Protestant, ethnically homogeneous

America, but the war they waged took the form more of a rearguard action than an offensive. Between 1870 and 1920 America had changed dramatically. It became a richly complex, ethnically diverse, industrial country. In 1880 more than 87 percent of the inhabitants of Chicago were immigrants and their children. In other major American cities the statistics were similar: Milwaukee and Detroit, 84 percent; New York and Cleveland, 80 percent; St. Louis and San Francisco, 78 percent.

These new immigrants provided the muscle for America's spectacular industrial growth. Indeed, without immigrant labor American industrialization would have moved forward at a far slower pace.

Wages, Hours, and Standard of Living

Was the price paid by native-born and immigrant labor for industrialization worth the benefits they received? This is not a simple question to answer; in fact, each laborer might have answered it differently, although their answers would have contained common themes. Unquestionably, industrialization extracted a heavy toll from the laborers, who suffered psychologically and emotionally in industrial America. It changed not only how, when, and where they worked but also how they regarded work and how they perceived themselves. Equally unquestionably, however, industrialization transformed the United States into the most prosperous country in the world. To some degree, laborers shared in that prosperity and increase in material comfort.

Wages played an important role in a laborer's attitude toward work. In general, wages rose and prices fell during the late nineteenth and early twentieth centuries. Exactly how much is a question of heated historical debate, but it is clear that the pace of wages and earnings lagged well behind the spectacular growth in the American economy. And even with modest improvements in wages, laborers fought a continual battle with poverty.

The most important factor in determining the economic well-being of a working-class family was how many members of the family had jobs. Fathers and sons, mothers and daughters, and often aunts, uncles, and grandparents—all contributed to the "family economy." To be sure, the nature of the family economy caused concern. Carroll D. Wright in the United States Census of 1880 warned, "the factory system necessitates the employment of women and children to an injurious extent, and consequently its tendency is to destroy family life and ties and domestic habits, and ultimately the home."

In truth, the opposite was probably true. Without the income earned by wives and children, families faced greater threats to their unity. Economically, families worked as a single entity; the desires of any particular individual often had to be sacrificed for the good of the family. This meant that women and children worked, families took in boarders, and all earnings were used for a common end. Far from destroying the family, the family economy often strengthened it.

During the first decade of the twentieth century social workers conducted numerous studies to determine how much a family or a single individual needed to sustain a typical working-class existence for a year. Estimates for New York City ranged between $800 and $876 for a family of four, $505 for a single man, and $466 for a working woman. Many of New York's laborers fell painfully below the recommended minimum. Single women lived particularly difficult lives. A New York study concluded that women earned about half as much as men, and that the majority made less than $300 per year. What was true for women was equally valid for blacks, Asians, and Mexicans in America. They were given the most exhausting and dangerous work, paid the least, and were fired first during economic hard times.

There were clear divisions even among workers. At the top ranks were the highly skilled laborers. Mostly English-speaking, generally Protestant, and almost exclusively white, they were paid well, had good job security, and considered themselves elite craftsmen. Below them were the semiskilled and unskilled workers. Most were immigrants from southern and eastern Europe, spoke halting if any English, and were Catholics or Jews. They lacked job security and had to struggle for a decent existence. At the bottom of the semiskilled and unskilled category were the nonwhite and women workers, for whom even a decent existence was normally out of reach.

Like wages, hours varied widely. Long hours were not a new phenomenon tied to industrial America. Farm workers and artisans often labored from sunup to sundown, but the tempo and quality of their labor was different. Farm work was governed by the season and the weather. The rhythms of the preindustrial workshop similarly mixed work with fellowship. If the work days were long, they were also sociable. Moreover, punctuality was not the golden virtue it became during industrialization. The idea of punching a time clock was alien to the preindustrial worker, who might think in terms of hours but not in terms of minutes.

Preindustrial labor, then, had a more relaxed atmosphere. Farm work and shop labor could be hard and dangerous, but there were not sharp lines between labor and leisure. Thrift, regularity, sobriety, orderliness, punctuality—hallmarks of an industrial society—were virtues not rigorously observed.

Given this new standard of work and time demanded by factory owners, laborers were reluctant to work the preindustrial dawn-to-dusk day. In 1889 hundreds of trade unionists paraded through the streets of

Worcester, Massachusetts, behind a banner which read: "Eight Hours for Work, Eight Hours for Rest, Eight Hours for What We Will." The reality, however, fell far short of the ideal. It is difficult to generalize about hours because they varied considerably from occupation to occupation. In 1890, for example, bakers averaged over 65 hours a week, steelworkers over 66, and canners nearly 77. Working in a steel mill blast furnace was a 12-hour-a-day, 7-day-a-week job, including one 24-hour continuous shift and one day off every two weeks.

For women, the new ideals of industrial America created even more work. The increased emphasis on cleanliness and greater demand for tidy homes resulted in more time devoted to cleaning, dusting, and scrubbing. In addition, the growing availability of washable cotton fabrics increased the amount of laundering housewives performed. Finally, more varied diets meant that women spent more time cooking meals. By 1900 the typical housewife worked six hours a day on just two tasks: meal preparation and cleaning. This was in addition to the time they spent on other household tasks.

The Lost Crafts

Although workers complained regularly about wages and hours, they were equally disturbed by several other results of industrialization. The late-nineteenth-century industries differed from the preindustrial workshop in four important areas: size, discipline, mechanization, and displacement of skill. The informality of the preindustrial workshop, with only a handful of employees, was an inevitable casualty. Huge plants demanded an organized, disciplined work force. Work became formalized and structured, and workers were carefully regulated to ensure maximum productivity.

Mechanization of work led to both the large factories and the incredible boom in productivity. It also caused an erosion of certain skilled trades. Imaginative inventors designed machines that performed tasks previously done by skilled artisans. Where once a single tailor took a piece of cloth, cut it, fashioned it, sewed it, and made it into a pair of pants, by 1859 a Cincinnati clothing factory had divided the process into 17 different semiskilled jobs. The replacement of highly skilled workers by semiskilled laborers was a characteristic of the factory system.

By the end of the century it appeared to many observers that all work was being mechanized and moving toward the factory mode. Even farmers followed the mechanization march. By the early 1880s one Dakota Territory wheat farm stretched over 30,000 acres, used 20 reapers and 30 steam-powered threshers, and employed 1,000 field hands.

Worker Discontent

In the long run, industrialization brought much to many. Between 1860 and 1920 the volume of manufactured goods increased almost 14-fold. Consumer goods, which once only the rich could afford, came into the purchasing range of the middle class. Newspapers and magazines advertised, and department stores displayed, a wide variety of factory products.

From a worker's perspective, however, industrialization was often an inhumane process. Factory labor tended to be monotonous, and machines made work more dangerous. Industrial accidents were alarmingly common, and careless or tired workers sacrificed their fingers, hands, arms, and sometimes even lives. Frequent speedups increased the chances of injury.

To make matters even worse, owners often assumed an uncaring attitude toward their laborers. Concerned with production quotas and cost efficiency, owners seemed insensitive to workers' needs; and in fact, many *were* insensitive. As one factory manager proclaimed, "I regard my people as I regard my machinery. So long as they can do my work for what I choose to pay them, I keep them, getting out of them all I can."

Workers did not passively accept industrialization and the changes caused by that enormous process. At almost every step they resisted change, and they had formidable weapons at their disposal. On one level, resistance entailed a simple, individual decision not to change completely. Factory managers demanded a steady, dependable work force, but they were plagued by chronic absenteeism. Immigrant workers refused to labor on religious holidays, and in some towns factories had to shut down on the day the circus arrived. Across America, heavy drinking on Sunday led to "blue Mondays," a term used to describe absenteeism.

Another form of individual protest was simply quitting. Most industrial workers changed jobs at least every three years, and in many industries the annual turnover rate was over 100 percent. Some quit because they were bored, "forced to work too hard," or because they were struck by spring wanderlust and simply wanted to move. Others quit because of severe discipline, unsafe working conditions, or low wages. Compulsive quitting was a clear indication that perhaps 20 percent of the work force never came to terms with industrialization.

Workers were similarly quick to take collective action. The late nineteenth century witnessed the most sustained and violent industrial conflict in the nation's history. Strikes were as common as political corruption during the period. Between 1881 and 1890 the Bureau of Labor Statistics estimated that 9,668 strikes and lockouts had occurred. Although most of the conflicts were relatively peaceful, some were so violent that citizens across the nation feared that America was moving toward another revolution.

Early Labor Violence

An examination of several conflicts indicates clearly the relative power of industrialists and workers. An early violent conflict occurred in the anthracite coal region of eastern Pennsylvania. The late 1860s and early 1870s were troubled times for this socially and ethnically divided area. Mine owners competed ruthlessly against each other, and they all distrusted the miners and their union, the Workingmen's Benevolent Association (WBA). Added to economic and class tensions, the area was torn by ethnic conflicts. American-born and Protestant Scots-Irishmen owned most of the mines, and Welshmen and Englishmen served as mine superintendents. Increasingly, however, the miners were Irish-Catholic immigrants. Old World prejudices thus mingled with New World economics.

Matters became worse during the depression of the mid-1870s, when the mine owners came together and agreed to cut wages and increase workloads. The Irish responded much as they had done in the old country. While the WBA battled the owners at the negotiation table, the Ancient Order of Hibernians, a secret fraternal society of Irish immigrants, and its inner circle, the Molly Maguires, waged a violent guerrilla war. They disrupted the operation of several mines and attacked a handful of mining officials.

The mine owners managed to infiltrate the Molly Maguires with a secret agent, Irish-born James McParlan, who agreed to inform on his fellow Irishmen for the Pinkerton agency. While McParlan was gathering information, the WBA went on strike. Disorder and violence followed. The public blamed the WBA for the violence, and the strike was broken. Shortly thereafter, McParlan's testimony was used to destroy both the Mollies and the WBA. Altogether, 20 Mollies were convicted and executed.

In eastern Pennsylvania and elsewhere, the greatest weapon against strikers was the community's fear of violence. If industrialists could convince the public that unions promoted violence, then they could characterize their own union-busting tactics as a sincere defense of law and order.

The same depression that convulsed the Pennsylvania coal fields shook the rest of the country as well. To keep from going under, many businessmen cut rates and attempted to recoup their losses by reducing labor costs. This was true especially in the highly competitive railroad business. Repeatedly, workers suffered wage cuts, and usually unskilled wages were slashed more than the skilled.

During mid-July 1877 the Baltimore and Ohio Railroad (B&O) announced its third consecutive 10 percent wage cut. Angry, frustrated, and led by the new Trainmen's Union, railroad workers along the line went on strike. When trouble followed, B&O workers seized an important junction at Martinsburg, West Virginia. The state militia and local sheriffs sympathized with the workers and could not end the strike. As a result, President Rutherford B. Hayes sent in federal troops to protect an army of strikebreakers.

From Martinsburg the strike spread. Railroad workers walked off their jobs, and trains sat unused and deserted. The strike paralyzed transportation in the Midwest and much of the industrial Northeast. In Baltimore the state militia shot into a mob and killed ten persons; in Pittsburgh rioters burned 2,000 freight cars, looted stores, and torched railroad buildings; in Buffalo, Chicago, and Indianapolis workers and police engaged in bloody battles.

When local police and state militiamen failed to quell the problems, President Hayes ordered more federal troops to do the job. Eventually, superior force restored peace and the trains started rolling again, but not before more than a hundred strikers were killed.

Like most spontaneous strikes, the Great Strike of 1877 failed. But the anger it revealed frightened America. Although some authorities labeled the disturbances as the work of communist agitators, more thoughtful observers realized it was caused by legitimate grievances. For owners and workers alike, the strike was a lesson. Owners learned that workers were not merely passive partners in the industrial process. Labor learned that when pressed, the federal government was not neutral—it would side with capital.

Employers Gain Power

Between 1877 and 1886 industrialists grew in organizational and economic power. In the steel, oil, coal, railroad, and meat industries ruthless competition and consolidation produced industrial giants. Workers could not match the power of Rockefeller, Carnegie, and Swift, who controlled their industries and were the victors in the competitive industrial wars.

The power of industrialists can be seen in the famous Haymarket Square riot of 1886. In 1885 skilled molders won a 15 percent pay increase after a strike at McCormick Harvester Machine Company in Chicago. Reacting angrily to the union's activities, McCormick introduced pneumatic molders that could be run by unskilled workers. Again in 1886, the skilled workers went on strike, but this time the result was different. The combined forces of McCormick and local police ensured the safety of an army of strikebreakers and the plant's output continued until the strike was broken.

Tempers, however, remained high, and violence resulted. In May, after the strike ended, police and workers clashed once again, and a handful of laborers were killed and wounded. Disturbed by the violent force used by police in defense of industrialists' positions, August Spies, a Chicago anarchist and labor agitator, called for a protest meeting in Haymarket Square. The meeting took place on May 4 before a generally unenthusiastic crowd of about 3,000 labor supporters. But as the peaceful meeting was breaking up, local police unexpectedly charged the crowd. Then somebody—to this day no one knows who—threw a bomb into the melee, killing police and protesters alike. The police opened fire, shooting protesters and even, accidentally, each other.

Industrialists, city officials, ministers, and the local press convinced the public that the bombing was a prelude to anarchistic revolution. Despite a lack of evidence, police arrested eight local radicals, including Spies, and charged them with conspiracy. The eight were tried and convicted, and seven were sentenced to be hanged. One man committed suicide in his cell and three were eventually pardoned, but Spies and three others were

The famous Haymarket Square riot of 1886 began as a peaceful protest meeting but ended in violence. The arrest of eight local radicals without real evidence sent a message to workers that the police and public opinion sided with the industrialists.

executed. For radicals, labor agitators, and unionists, the message was clear: police and public opinion were on the side of the industrialists.

The excessive violence of the Molly Maguires, the great strike of 1877, and the Haymarket Square riot was not necessarily typical of disputes between labor and management. Although labor violence continued unabated in the 1890s, late-nineteenth-century labor disputes were often settled peacefully. In most cases, however, management won the conflicts. Only in small towns, where prolabor and anti-industrial sentiment knew no class lines, did labor battle management on anything approaching even terms.

Unorganized and Organized Labor

Historians have used the term "robber barons" to characterize late-nineteenth-century industrialists. Whether "robber" is accurate or not is debatable, but "baron" is a fitting description. They controlled their industries as medieval barons ruled their fiefs. Their word was usually final, and such a modern concept as democracy found an unsympathetic environment inside factory walls.

Unfortunately, during the last third of the nineteenth century, labor was unable to form organizations powerful enough to deal with capital on equal terms. Before 1900 most unions were weak, and their goals were often out of touch with the changing American economy. In addition, the labor force itself was divided along ethnic, racial, gender, and craft lines. It was during this period, then, that labor attempted to overcome its own divisions and fumbled its way toward a clearer vision of what were its own best interests.

Before the 1870s most American unions were locally rooted, craft-based organizations. They were geared to the small Jacksonian workshop, not to the large modern factory. The first union to attempt to organize all workers was the short-lived National Labor Union (NLU). Founded in Baltimore in 1866, the NLU was a consciously national organization. In addition to shorter hours and higher wages, its ambitious program included women's and blacks' rights, monetary reform, and worker-owned industries. Rich in ideas and solutions, the NLU was poor in organization and finances. The NLU, whose reach exceeded its grasp, died during the depression of the mid-1870s.

The vision of the NLU was carried on by the Noble and Holy Order of the Knights of Labor. Begun in 1869 as a secret fraternal order as well as a union, the Knights remained small and unimportant until 1878 when they went public. Led by Terence V. Powderly, in 1881 the Knights opened their membership to all wage earners. The Knights excluded only bankers, lawyers, liquor dealers, speculators, and stockbrokers, whom they viewed as money manipulators and exploiters.

Complete worker solidarity was the Knights' goal. They welcomed and spoke for all laborers—women and men, black and white, immigrant and native, unskilled and skilled. Like the NLU, the Knights rejected industrial capitalism and favored cooperatively owned industries. Although critics labeled the Knights "wild-eyed, utopian visionaries," they are best understood in the context of exploited workers searching for a less exploitive alternative to industrial capitalism. If their rhetoric was extreme, their suffering was real.

An able leader, Powderly called for reforms of the currency system, the abolition of child labor, regulation of trusts and monopolies, an end to alien contract labor networks, and government ownership of public utilities. He favored peaceful arbitration of labor disputes, opposed strikes, and also opposed the formation of narrow trade unions, instead advocating that skilled workers should assist the unskilled. Harmony and fellowship ultimately dominated his vision of America's future. Consensus, not conflict, was his goal.

The Knights' rhetoric found sympathetic listeners among American workers. During the early 1880s membership rolls grew. Then came 1884, the beginning of what labor historians have called "the great upheaval." Strikes erupted in the coal fields of Pennsylvania and Ohio and the railroad yards of Missouri and Illinois. The labor conflicts continued into 1885 and 1886. Labor won some, but by no means all, of the strikes. Although their role was small, the Knights had a part in several important labor victories. By mid-1886 perhaps 750,000 workers had joined the Knights.

From that high point, however, the decline was rapid. From the start, the Knights could not weld together their diverse rank and file. Administrative and organizational problems surfaced, and Powderly's relatively conservative leadership was opposed by more radical members, who fully accepted strikes and conflict. In 1886 the Haymarket Square bombing branded all unions as un-American and violent in the public mind. By 1893, when Powderly was driven from office, the Knights' membership had declined precipitously. Weakened and divided, they failed to survive the depression of the mid-1890s.

Unlike the Knights and the NLU, the American Federation of Labor (AFL) did not aspire to remake society. Its leaders accepted industrial capitalism and rejected partisan politics and the dreams of radical visionaries. Instead the AFL concentrated on practical, reachable goals: higher wages, shorter workdays, and improved working conditions. Most important, it only recruited skilled laborers, recognizing that easily replaceable unskilled workers were in a poor position to negotiate with employers.

Formed in 1886 by the coming together of skilled trade unions, the AFL was ably led by Samuel Gompers, a Jewish immigrant who had been the president of a New York cigar makers' union. As the head of the AFL for almost 40 years, Gompers used his considerable "moral power" and organizational ability to fight for achievable goals. American laborers were divided over religious, racial, ethnic, gender, and political issues, but they all desired higher wages, more leisure time, and greater liberty. Gompers battled for those unifying issues, focusing on the real world, not the best of all possible worlds. For this reason, he opposed "theorizers" and "intellectuals" in the labor movement. Once effectively organized, he maintained, labor could deal with capital on equal terms.

Gompers's approach toward working with capital and organizing labor proved successful in the long run. Before 1900, however, the AFL was not more successful than the Knights or the NLU. In fact, workers benefited little from unions before the turn of the century. All together fewer than 5 percent of American workers joined trade unions, and the major areas of industrial growth were the least unionized. Nevertheless,

As head of the American Federation of Labor (AFL), Samuel Gompers worked for higher wages, shorter hours, industrial safety, and the right of skilled workers to organize.

the experimentation during the late nineteenth century taught workers valuable lessons. To combat the power of capital, labor needed equal power. During the twentieth century labor would finally gain that power.

Conclusion

In 1986 the Statue of Liberty was given a good cleaning. Its copper was shined as much as copper turned green can be shined, and its structure was refortified. America celebrated, and television newscasters recited once again Emma Lazarus's poem on the base of the statue. Few asked the question, "What are we celebrating?"

What the United States celebrated was nothing less than the emergence of modern America. In 1876 when France shipped the Statue of Liberty to the United States, the country, despite a recent civil war, was remarkably uniform. Most Americans traced their ancestry to Great Britain

Chronology of Key Events

1866	National Labor Union founded in Baltimore
1871	Knights of Labor founded
1877	Great railroad strike; 20 Molly Maguires convicted and executed for terrorism
1882	Chinese Exclusion Act suspends Chinese immigration for ten years
1886	Statue of Liberty unveiled; Haymarket Square riot in Chicago; American Federation of Labor founded
1887	Dawes Severalty Act
1890	U. S. soldiers kill more than 300 Sioux at Battle of Wounded Knee
1892	Homestead strike
1894	Pullman strike
1896	President Cleveland vetoes literacy requirement for adult immigrants
1915	Leo Frank lynched
1921	Emergency Quota Act restricts immigration
1924	National Origins Act lowers imigration quotas; Snyder Act grants citizenship to all U. S.-born Indians

and northern Europe, worshiped in a Protestant church, and lived on farms or in small villages. If they were divided, it was along political and economic lines, not along ethnic and religious ones. The United States was not a world leader. Its navy was small, its diplomats uninfluential, and its industry still largely underdeveloped.

By 1900 America had changed radically. Unprecedented immigration had transformed the country into the most diverse nation in the world as a host of immigrants crowded into American cities. For some it was an exciting, hopeful time; for others a painful, disillusioning one. Old America gave way to a New America with startling speed. In fact, most Americans in 1900 had not yet adjusted to the massive changes. What role would the new immigrants play in American life? What rights did workers have in the large industries? These and other questions would be answered in the next century.

Suggestions for Further Reading

For in-depth examinations of American immigration see John Bodnar, *The Transplanted* (1985); Roger Daniels, *Coming to America* (1990); Alan M. Kraut, *The Huddled Masses* (1982); Philip Taylor, *The Distant Magnet* (1971).

Experiences of specific ethnic groups are analyzed in John Duff, *The Irish in the United States* (1971); Yuji Ichioka, *The Issei: The World of the First Generation Japanese Americans* (1988); Helen Znaniecka Lopata, *Polish Americans* (1976); Joseph Lopreato, *Italian Americans* (1970); Kerby A. Miller, *Emigrants and Exiles: Ireland and the Irish Exodus to North America* (1985); Charles C. Moskos, Jr., *Greek Americans,* 2d ed. (1989); Moses Rischin, *The Promised City: New York's Jews, 1870–1914* (1962).

To gain additional insight into the lives of women immigrants see Cecyle S. Neidle, *America's Immigrant Women* (1975); Sydney Weinberg, *The World of Our Mothers: Lives of Jewish Immigrant Women* (1988). For nativist reaction to the immigrant exodus see David H. Bennett, *The Party of Fear* (1988); Robert Carlson, *The Quest for Conformity* (1975).

Issues facing industrial workers are examined in Melvyn Dubofsky, *Industrialism and the American Worker,* 2d ed. (1985); Herbert Gutman, *Work, Culture, and Society in Industrializing America* (1976); Alice Kessler-Harris, *Out to Work: A History of Wage-Earning Women in the United States* (1982); S. J. Kleinberg, *The Shadow of the Mills* (1989).

Chapter *19*

The Rise of an Urban Society and City People

A ndrew Borden had, as the old Scottish saying goes, short arms and long pockets. He was cheap, not because he had to be frugal but because he hated to spend money. He had dedicated his entire life to making and saving money, and tales of his unethical and parsimonious business behavior were legendary in his hometown of Fall River, Massachusetts. Andrew, however, was not interested in rumors or the opinions of other people; he was concerned with his own rising fortunes. By 1892 he had amassed over half a million dollars, and he controlled the Fall River Union Savings Bank as well as serving as the director of several companies.

Andrew was rich, but he did not live like a wealthy man. Instead of living alongside the other prosperous Fall River citizens in the elite neighborhood known as The Hill, Andrew resided in an area near the business district called the flats. He liked to save time as well as money, and from the flats he could conveniently walk to work. For his daughters, Lizzie and Emma, whose eyes and dreams focused on The Hill, life in the flats was an intolerable embarrassment. Their house was grim, lacking both comfort and privacy. The only washing facilities were a cold-water faucet in the kitchen and a laundry room water tap in the cellar, where the only toilet in the house was located. To make matters worse, the house was not connected to the Fall River gas main. Andrew preferred to use kerosene to light his house because it was less expensive. To save even more money, he and his family frequently sat in the dark.

The Borden home was far from happy. Lizzie and Emma, ages 32 and 42 in 1892, strongly disliked their stepmother Abby and resented Andrew's penny-pinching ways. Lizzie especially felt alienated from the world around her. Although Fall River was the largest cotton-manufacturing town in America, it offered few opportunities for the unmarried daughter of a prosperous man. Society expected a woman of Lizzie's social position to marry, and while she waited for a proper suitor, her only respectable social outlets were church and community service. She kept herself busy by teaching Sunday School classes and participating in the Woman's Christian Temperance Union and other organizations, but she was not happy.

In August 1892 strange things started to happen in the Borden home. They began after Lizzie and Emma learned that Andrew had secretly changed his will. Abby became violently ill. In time so did the Borden maid Bridget Sullivan and Andrew himself. Shortly thereafter Lizzie went shopping for prussic acid, a deadly poison she said she needed to clean her sealskin cape. When a Fall River druggist refused her request, she left the store in an agitated state. Later in the day she told a friend that she feared an unknown enemy of her father's was after him.

On August 4, 1892, Bridget awoke early and ill, but she still managed to prepare a large breakfast. After a hearty meal, Andrew left for work.

Bridget also left to do some work outside. This left Abby and Lizzie in the house alone. Then somebody did something very specific and very grisly. As Abby was bent over making the bed in the guest room, someone moved into the room unobserved and killed her with an ax.

Andrew came home for lunch earlier than usual. He asked Lizzie where Abby was, and she said she did not know. Unconcerned, Andrew, who was not feeling well, lay down on the parlor sofa for a nap. He never awoke. Like Abby, he was slaughtered by someone with an ax. Lizzie "discovered" his body, still lying on the sofa.

Experts have examined and reexamined the crime, and most have reached the same conclusion: Lizzie killed her father and stepmother. In fact, Lizzie was tried for the gruesome murders. Despite a preponderance of evidence, however, an all-male jury found her not guilty. They arrived at their verdict without debate or disagreement. A woman of Lizzie's social position, they affirmed, simply could not have committed such a terrible crime.

Even before the trial began, newspaper and magazine writers had judged Lizzie innocent for the same reasons. As one historian has noted, "Americans were certain that well-brought up daughters could not commit murder with a hatchet on sunny summer mornings." Criminal women, they believed, originated in the lower classes and even looked evil. They did not look like round-faced Lizzie Borden.

Jurors and editorialists alike judged Lizzie according to their preconceived notions of Victorian womanhood. They believed that such a woman was gentle, docile, and physically frail, short on analytical ability but long on nurturing instincts. Too uncoordinated and weak to accurately swing an ax and too gentle and unintelligent to coldly plan a double murder, women of Lizzie's background simply had to be innocent because of their basic virtue.

Preconceived notions of Victorian femininity saved Lizzie Borden from being convicted of murdering her father and stepmother.

While Lizzie was being tried and found innocent, Victorian notions were being challenged. In the larger cities of America a new culture was taking form, one based on freedoms, not restraints. Immigrants could become millionaires, and women could vote and hold office. Rigid Victorian concepts crumbled under the weight of new ideas; but the new freedoms came with a high price. In both the cities and the culture that flourished within them, a new order had to be constructed out of the chaos of freedom.

New Cities and New Problems

Transforming the Walking City

In an age before reliable mass transportation, when only the rich could afford a carriage, the majority of city dwellers had to walk to and from work. This simple fact dictated the type of cities that emerged in America. They were compact and crowded, their sizes normally limited to about two miles radius from center city or the distance a person could walk in half an hour. Even America's largest cities—New York, Philadelphia, and Boston—conformed to these standards.

Inside these cities, houses, businesses, and factories sat side by side. Tightly packed near the waterfront were shops, banks, warehouses, and business offices, and not far away were the residences of the people who owned or worked in those enterprises. There was little residential segregation. If the rich occupied the finest houses in the center city, the poor lived in the alleys and dirty streets close by. Rich and poor, native-born and immigrant, black and white—they all walked along the same streets and worked in the same area.

Booming industrialization during the last third of the century shattered this arrangement. As industrialists built their new plants in or near existing cities, urban growth accelerated at an alarming rate. Like twin children, factories and cities grew and matured together, each helping the other to reach its physical potentials. In 1860, before America's industrial surge, 20 percent of the population lived in cities. By 1900 almost 40 percent of the population lived in cities or towns, and that figure climbed to more than 50 percent in 1920. At the same time, the numbers of large cities (those with a population of over 100,000) increased at an even faster rate. In 1860 America had only nine large cities. The numbers rose to 38 in 1900 and 68 in 1920.

Immigrant as well as native sources fueled the urban explosion. Although most of the late-nineteenth-century immigrants came from rural communities, they settled in America's industrial heartland. Added to these were the native-born migrants who moved from poor rural areas to the cities. As in Europe and Asia, rural opportunities in the United States were dwindling at the same time that the rural population was growing. Thus ten farm sons moved to the cities for each son who became a farm owner.

Black migration from the rural South to the urban North further expanded the labor pool in the industrial cities. Slow at first, it increased each decade, as blacks left the land of their bondage determined to forge a better life for themselves and their families in the northern cities. Between 1897 and 1920 almost one million blacks left the South, and of those, 85 percent settled in the urban North.

City Technology

Even the largest of the walking cities was unprepared to meet the demands the newcomers placed on it. Cities were already crowded, and construction technology was not yet sufficiently advanced to accommodate the recent arrivals. But in time, engineers and scientists discovered ways to expand cities. During the half century after 1870 horizontal and vertical growth changed the skyline and living conditions of urban America.

Better transportation facilities, constructed and owned by entrepreneurs, solved the basic limitation of the walking city. As early as the 1830s, the horse-drawn omnibus, which carried 12 to 20 passengers along a fixed route, permitted a handful of wealthier urbanites to escape life in the crowded center city. Faster than walking, it was too expensive for unskilled laborers. Similarly the commuter railroads, which also dated back to the 1830s and 1840s, served only the wealthier classes.

The horse railway expanded the city for the middle-class urbanites, white-collar workers, and skilled workers. For 5 cents, these horse-drawn omnibuses carried passengers over steel rails at a speed of 6 to 8 miles per hour. By the 1880s over 300 American cities and towns had constructed horsecar lines, and they significantly expanded the size of cities. Now a person could live 5 miles from his or her place of work and still travel there in less than an hour. The age of walking was almost over.

The cable car, introduced during the 1870s, proved a blessing for urban dwellers in hillier cities like San Francisco and Pittsburgh. Utilizing steam power, cable cars were faster and cleaner than horse-drawn transportation. Even relatively flat cities such as Kansas City and Chicago installed cable cars. Pulled by a moving underground cable, these cars, engineers believed, would be the public transportation of the future—but the system's problems were considerable. Expensive to install and quick to break down, the cable car soon became outmoded, a victim of the electric trolley, which was cheaper to run and more dependable.

Employing the electrical current in overhead wires, trolleys could operate in stop-and-go traffic and travel at average speeds of 10 to 12 miles

This watercolor of New York City's Bowery at night by W. Louis Sonntag, Jr., shows how steam, steel, and electricity played a major part in transforming cities.

per hour. By 1902, 97 percent of urban transit mileage had been electrified. Trolleys connected not only city with suburb, but also city with city. By 1920 a person could travel from Boston to New York entirely by trolleys known as interurbans.

Trolleys were not without their problems, either. The overhead wires gave cities a weblike appearance, and in the winter the electric wires snapped from the cold and created serious dangers. In addition, they sometimes frightened horses and thus worsened traffic problems. Altogether, by the 1890s, the mixture of horsecars, cable cars, and trolleys jostling each other and pedestrians on city streets created immense traffic jams.

Clogged streets inspired engineers to search for other transportation solutions. Looking above and below ground, they designed elevated railway lines and subways, such as the Chicago "el" (elevated railway) and the New York City subway. Electricity powered both, and each helped to ease transportation for the masses.

While mass transportation allowed cities to spread miles beyond their cores, steel and glass permitted cities to reach for the sky. At midcentury, few buildings were higher than five stories. Church spires still dominated the urban skyline. Buildings, like cities themselves, were personal; they did not dwarf the individual. That, however, soon changed.

In 1885 New York architect William LeBaron Jenney, using light masonry over an iron and steel skeleton, built the Home Insurance Building in Chicago. Although only ten stories high, it was the first true skyscraper in history. Steel, light masonry, and eventually glass revolutionized building construction, and the use of electric elevators made skyscrapers functional.

Louis Henri Sullivan demonstrated the architectural possibilities of the skyscraper. Working in Chicago, Sullivan became the leading exponent of skyscraper technology. Turning his back on classical models, he preached the doctrine that "form follows function," and designed many of the most beautiful and practical skyscrapers in America, including the Wainwright Building in St. Louis and the Transportation Building in Chicago. By the turn of the century, skyscrapers had changed the profile of American cities as surely as industrialism had altered the American landscape.

The Segregated City

The outward and upward growth of cities brought an end to the more personal walking city. Mass transportation freed the upper and middle classes to move to the "streetcar suburbs." They commuted to work and no longer mixed on a daily basis with their economic inferiors.

The working class moved into areas and even houses deserted by wealthier families. Brownstone homes that had served the upper classes were divided into small apartments that satisfied the new demand for inexpensive housing. Since architects had not designed the houses to be used as multiunit apartments, numerous problems resulted. Heatless, sunless, and poorly ventilated rooms became increasingly common.

Ethnic groups and races, like economic classes, tended to stake out neighborhoods in the new, larger cities. In addition, real estate brokers and landlords restricted blacks and immigrants to particular areas. For the first time black ghettos emerged in the major northern cities. In Chicago, New York, Boston, and Philadelphia, English became a foreign language in ethnic neighborhoods. These neighborhoods reproduced in their finer details Old World communities. Familiar faces, foods, churches, and speech patterns comforted lonely immigrants.

Since members of the ethnic working class were too poor for even moderately priced mass transit, they tended to settle close to their places of work. In New York City Jews and Italians lived within walking distance of the Lower East Side garment factories. In Chicago Poles and Lithuanians who worked in the meat-packing industry lived near the stockyards.

Just as new residential trends separated rich and poor, the central business district underwent important changes. Prices for central city real estate shot up at an incredible rate, which only businesses and industries could afford. The central cities were turned over to high-income businesses, banks, warehouses, railroad terminals, and the recently developed department stores. It became an area where money was made, not where people lived.

The Problems of Growth

By the 1890s British observers despaired over what had become of the once small American cities. The uncontrolled growth, they suggested, had created ugliness on an almost unprecedented scale. Although English author Rudyard Kipling had seen the suffering and overcrowded conditions of Bombay and Cairo, he was appalled by Chicago: "This place is the first American city I have encountered . . . Having seen it, I urgently desire never to see it again."

Kipling's opinion was not that of an anti-American foreigner. Numerous American observers echoed this view. American cities were unprepared for the incredible growth they experienced during the late nineteenth century. Housing, clean water, competent police, and adequate public services were all in short supply. Finally, health standards were low everywhere, and scientists had barely begun to study the problems and diseases created by crowded urban conditions.

High crime rates plagued rich and poor. Pickpockets, robbers, con artists, and violent gangs roamed the streets and alleyways of American cities. Urban officials had established police forces in the 1830s and 1840s. In the 1850s police were outfitted with uniforms and badges and allowed to carry clubs and revolvers, but they still could not control or seriously curtail urban crime. Police corruption was common. Officers took bribes from saloon keepers and streetwalkers to overlook illegal activities, and owed their loyalty to the political boss who hired them. Not until the end of the century would there be successful attempts to bring professionalism and civil service reform to police departments.

Housing presented an even more pressing problem. The immigrants disembarking at the ports of entry and the farmers arriving at the train depots had to have some place to live. The situation created opportunities as well as problems. The building industry was one of the great urban boom industries, and its leaders largely determined the shape and profile of the modern city. Like the other businesspeople, they worked in an essentially unregulated economic world, bent on maximizing their profits and equipped with a lofty disregard of public opinion.

In urban housing, money talked. The rich built opulent mansions on New York's Fifth Avenue along Central Park. The "homes" of the leaders of New York's—and often the nation's—society, business, commerce, and industry shouldered each other for their place in the sun. High ceilings, European furnishings, and spacious rooms were commonplace, and even the new apartments of the upper classes were designed and constructed by gifted architects and artisans.

Tenements, built to minimal codes but overcrowded and undermaintained, greeted urban newcomers without money. They were designed to cram the largest number of people into the smallest amount of space. Like skyscrapers, tenements made use of vertical space by piling family upon family into small, poorly lighted, badly ventilated apartments. By 1900 portions of the Jewish Tenth Ward in New York's Lower East Side had reached population density levels of 500,000 persons to one square mile and as many as one person per square foot of land in the most crowded areas.

Dumbbell tenements were the most notorious examples of exploitative urban housing. Each building had an indentation in the middle—thus giving it a dumbbell shape—that allowed for better ventilation. Although they conformed to the Tenement Reform Law of 1879, which required all rooms to have access to light and air, they made maximum use of standard 25- by 100-feet urban lots. The problems inherent in dumbbell tenements were obvious from the first, but the design was not outlawed in New York until 1901.

Street conditions, unlike housing, were more democratic in that they plagued rich and poor alike. Well into the 1870s, pigs rooted for food amid trash and thousands of pounds of horse manure. Spring rains turned thoroughfares into fetid quagmires, and winter freezes left them with hard deep ruts. Waste not dumped onto the streets often found its way into the rivers that flowed through the major cities or the harbors that bordered them. By the turn of the century, 13 million gallons of sewage were emptied each day into the Delaware River, the major source for Philadelphia's drinking water. In Baltimore, according to Satirist H. L. Mencken, the bay smelled like a "billion polecats." Pittsburgh's rivers were blackened by the industrial waste poured into them.

Overcrowded housing, polluted streets and rivers, uncollected garbage—these problems and others contributed to the notoriously unhealthy urban environment. Unfortunately, advances in medicine and public health lagged behind technological and industrial progress. Diseases ranging from yellow fever and smallpox to diphtheria and typhoid claimed victims by the thousands. In 1878 a yellow fever epidemic, known as the American Plague, killed more than 9,000 people. Physician Walter Reed's discovery in 1900 that the disease was carried by the *Aedes aegypti* mosquito led to a cure for the dreaded scourge.

Smallpox proved a more persistent problem. Although not as deadly as yellow fever, it struck more people and left millions of faces scarred by pockmarks. Like diphtheria and scarlet fever, smallpox flourished in the overcrowded and garbage-strewn cities.

Tenement life on the Lower East Side of New York was overcrowded, filthy, and dangerous.

Death, suffering, and massive inconvenience prodded city officials to move toward a more systematic approach to their problems. It was a slow transition, involving the replacement of political appointees with trained experts. Yet during the late nineteenth century remarkable progress was made, particularly after the discovery of the germ theory in the 1880s, which linked contagious diseases to environmental conditions.

Health officials and urban engineers vigorously attacked the sewage and water problems. Without good sewers and clean drinking water, urban civilization was almost a contradiction of terms. To improve conditions, cities replaced cesspools and backyard privies with modern sewer systems. Most large cities turned to filtration and chlorination to assure pure water supplies.

From Private City to Public City

In housing, pure water, and clean streets, the battle lines in most cities were drawn between individual profits and public need. Individual entre-

For the wealthy, city life could be quite luxurious, as the rooms of Alexander T. Stewart's Fifth Avenue mansion show.

preneurs shaped the modern American city with horsecar and trolley lines, skyscrapers, apartments, and tenements. Motivated by profit like their industrial counterparts, they worked, planned, and invested, putting their pocketbooks before their civic responsibilities. The result was that they provided good housing and services for only those city dwellers who could pay.

Historians have termed this type of city the "private city." Allowing the profit motive to determine urban growth created numerous problems. It led to such waste and inefficiency as competing trolley lines and such inconveniences as poorly cleaned streets. Most important, it stood contrary to planned urban growth. Urban entrepreneurs were generally unconcerned about the city as a whole, regarding parks as uneconomic use of real estate and battling against the idea of zoning. In the end, they contributed to the ugliness and problems of Pittsburgh, New York, Chicago, and other American cities.

By the turn of the century, urban engineers and other experts began calling for planned urban growth and more concern for city services. Advocates of the "public city," they wanted efficient, clean, healthy cities where rich and poor alike could enjoy a decent standard of life. College educated, these professionals brought knowledge and administrative expertise to government service. After 1900 they would increasingly dominate the quest for better services and public responsibility, but in many cities their voices were heard too late. The scars of the private city remained on the urban landscape.

City Culture

Nightlife

At 3:00 P.M. on September 4, 1882, Thomas Edison's chief electrician threw the switch on the inventor's Pearl Street station in New York City. Four hundred electric lights went on. Wall Street buildings were for the first time illuminated by the clearest of all artificial lighting. Just as trolleys spelled the end for the horse car, electric lights eventually replaced gaslights, candles, kerosene, and oil lamps.

Electricity soon bathed America's leading cities in light. In the rural regions life revolved around the sun. Farmers awoke with the sun, labored during the daylight hours, and went to sleep soon after the sun disappeared over the horizon. Although one's labor changed depending on the season, the order of one's day was changeless. In cities and industries, however, night became more than just a time to rest. Labor and leisure claimed their share of the night.

This new nightlife fired the imaginations of urbanites. If nighttime labor proved a plague for the working class, nighttime leisure animated the lives of the wealthy. For New York's "fast set" the real fun began after the theaters closed. They moved down Broadway, stopping for a late-night dinner at one of the exclusive restaurants where eating became a refined pleasure and not just a physical necessity. The variety of dishes available at city eateries was but another example of the yawning gap between the values of an older rural America and those of the emerging urban society. The American diet expanded along with the nation's cities.

The middle and upper classes not only consumed different types of food, they consumed more of everything. Like the new diet, this shift in consumption patterns signaled a break with the past. The traditional Victorian ethos emphasized production and values—thrift, self-control, delayed gratification, and hard work—that encouraged production. But with industrial success came a general fear of overproduction, and increasingly advertisers and economic advisers attempted to transform Americans from "savers" to "spenders." In various ways, they told people to give in to their desire for luxury.

In large American cities not only restaurants but also department stores and hotels fostered this new attitude. John Wanamaker in Philadelphia, Marshall Field in Chicago, and Rowland H. Macy in New York opened department stores that catered to and pampered the middle and upper classes by offering an unequaled range of products and quality service. The architecture and plush interiors of the department stores inspired extravagant spending. Grand hotels, like the Waldorf Astoria in New York, trafficked in the same luxury. Inside the giant hotels and department stores the austerity doctrines of the early nineteenth century were easily forgotten.

It is difficult to imagine the impression electric lights, department stores, and grand hotels made on the people who lived in or visited American cities. They underscored a style of life clearly different from what existed in rural America. City life presented a strange new world that inspired American writers, painters, and musicians with feelings of excitement and revulsion. This ambivalent reaction formed the basis of a new urban culture which combined the energies and experiences of all city people—black and white, male and female, immigrant and native-born.

From the Genteel Tradition to Realism and Naturalism

Frank Norris was born in Chicago, grew up in San Francisco, and lived for a time in Paris. He restlessly moved about the world looking for action. As a newspaper reporter he traveled to Cuba to cover the Spanish-American War, and to South Africa to chronicle the Boer War. In his journalism and in his novels he fed his readers bloody slices of the real world. Shortly before he died at 32 of appendicitis in 1902, he boasted, "I never truckled. I never took off the hat to fashion and held it out for pennies. I told them the truth. They liked it or they didn't like it. What had that to do with me?"

How literature had changed during the previous generation! At the end of the Civil War the American literary tradition had little to do with harsh truth. Conforming to a "genteel tradition," great writers endeavored to reinforce morality, not portray reality. Real life was too sordid, corrupt, and mean; it was far too coarse, violent, and vulgar. Literature, these arbiters decided, should transcend the real and anchor to the ideal. Sex, violence, and passion were taboo.

Out of rural America came the first challenge to the genteel tradition. Such local colorists as Bret Harte, who set his stories in the rough mining camps of the West, emphasized regional differences and used regional dialects to capture the flavor of rural America. In their own way, the local colorists were as confined by their approaches to writing as the defenders of the genteel tradition. Although their characters used real American speech, they were hardly realistically presented. Humor and innocence were the hallmarks of local colorists.

Only Mark Twain, whose real name was Samuel Langhorne Clemens, transcended the genre. Like a local colorist, he used regional dialects, humor, and sentimentality in all his novels, but he also explored the darker impulses of human nature. *The Adventures of Huckleberry Finn* (1884), his classic work, exposes the greed, violence, and corruption in American society. Nowhere is Twain more insightful than when he deals with American racism. In one scene, Huck invents a story about a riverboat explosion. A woman asks if anyone was injured. "No'm," Huck responds. "Killed a nigger." Relieved, she replies, "Well, it's lucky; because sometimes people do get hurt."

Although Twain never outgrew his obsession with life on the Mississippi River, the impact of industrialism and city life on the American character fascinated most of the other great writers of his generation. They wanted to show American life in all its harsh and sordid reality. Realism, the name of their movement, soon replaced the genteel sentimentality of the previous generation. Defined as "the truthful treatment of material" by its leader William Dean Howells, realism centered on average individuals dealing with concrete ethical choices in realistic circumstances.

As realism matured in the largely unregulated and highly competitive cities, it turned into naturalism. A more pessimistic movement, naturalism portrayed the individual as a helpless victim, battered defenseless by natural forces beyond a person's control. Influenced by the writings of Charles Darwin, Karl Marx, and eventually Sigmund Freud, naturalists described a world in which biological, social, and psychological forces determined a person's fate. They were particularly interested in how the uncaring forces of industrialization and urbanization determined the course of individual lives. Even when they wrote about the problems of rural America, the power of factory and city worked in the shadows.

Describing the Urban Jungle

The premier naturalistic writer was Theodore Dreiser. Unlike most earlier American novelists, he was not the product of Protestant, Anglo-Saxon, middle-class respectability. His German-Catholic immigrant father's life was the flip side of the American success story. After a promising beginning, he and his family slid deeper and deeper into poverty and despair. Throughout his life, Dreiser remained sympathetic to those who had suffered.

Unlike better-educated writers, Dreiser had no genteel tradition to shed or rebel against. His first novel, *Sister Carrie* (1900), unflinchingly describes the effect of modern urban society on the lives of one woman and one man. Carrie travels to Chicago from the countryside in search of happiness, which she equates with material possessions, but she discovers only poverty, exploitation, and hardship. Like the course of Dreiser's own family, the likeable, friendly Carrie sinks ever deeper into physical and moral despair. The novel shocked most readers, and as a result Dreiser's genius was generally unappreciated during his lifetime.

Like Dreiser, Stephen Crane was also interested in the effects poverty and urban life had on individual character. His first novel, *Maggie: A Girl of the Streets* (1893), traces the life of a girl raised in a New York City slum. In rapid order, she loses her innocence, her virginity, and her life. It was not a story of a character being rewarded or punished; issues of personal good or evil were irrelevant. A victim of her environment, poverty determined Maggie's fate.

Taken together, naturalistic writers challenged the traditional idea that individuals had the power to control their own destinies. Rugged individualism, that cherished frontier ideal, seemed poor protection against the forces of urban poverty and industrial exploitation. Although neither *Maggie* nor *Sister Carrie* was a blueprint for reform, both suggested a pressing need for change. The same private city that offered opportunity for the wealthy held little promise for the poor.

Painting Urban Reality

American artists shared with American writers and social critics a general aesthetic and philosophical dislike of the city. As Americans moved west, artists like Albert Bierstadt focused on the dramatic landscape. Even the great, late-nineteenth-century realists—Winslow Homer, Thomas Eakins, and John LaFarge—harbored a suspicion, if not an outright fear, of the city.

By the end of the century, however, the varied urban landscape began to intrigue artists. Steel bridges, colorful immigrant costumes, smoke-filled, congested streets, clashing boxers, washed clothes hanging between tenements, pigeons soaring over flat apartment roofs—each demonstrated the everyday beauty of the city. The energy, conflict, and power of the city seemed to explode with artistic possibilities.

Appropriately enough, the center of this new movement was New York City. The leader of the school—often described as "ashcan" because of its urban orientation—was Robert Henri, an artistic and political radical. Skyscrapers thrilled him, and he saw beauty in the most squalid slum. He was joined by such other artists who shared his love of city life and political radicalism as John Sloan, George Luks, Maurice Prendergast,

Everett Shinn, W. J. Glackens, and Ernest Lawson. Their paintings were generally in the impressionistic style, but they were more concerned with content than technique. Like Theodore Dreiser, who admired the ashcan school, Henri and his followers used their talent to depict problems in the growing cities such as overcrowded tenement conditions and urban traffic.

Maturing along with the ashcan painters was a second school of artists that also gained inspiration from the urban landscape. Labeled modernists, they championed the pure freedom of nonrepresentational abstract painting. Their intellectual leader was Alfred Stieglitz, who used his studio at 291 Fifth Avenue in New York to exhibit the modernist paintings of Georgia O'Keeffe, Marsden Hartley, John Marin, Max Weber, and Arthur Dove. Like the ashcanners, the modernists chose the city—rife with conflict and power—as the prevalent theme for abstract art.

In 1913 the ashcanners and the modernists participated in the most important art exhibition in American history. Held at the Sixty-ninth Regiment Armory in New York, the show also included works by Cézanne, Van Gogh, Picasso, and other leaders of the European Postimpressionists. The Armory Show drew some sharp criticism; Marcel Duchamp's cubist *Nude Descending a Staircase* was called "an explosion in a shingle factory." Other critics and collectors maintained that the exhibition marked a new age for American art. Its more important result was to fuse European and American art movements. It further signaled the ascendancy of the modernists, who dominated the next generation of American art.

The Sounds of the City

Modern American music began in the nation's large cities, and from the very first was the language of the oppressed. Before the late nineteenth century critics regarded American music as decidedly inferior to European music. America had produced no great classical composers in the European tradition, and what music it did create was largely the sounds of work and worship. Uninfluenced by European traditions, American blacks adapted the rhythms and melodies of Africa to meet American conditions. African music centered on rhythmical complexity and used notes that did not conform to the standard scale. Repetition, call and response, and strong beat became the hallmarks of black American music.

The two traditions, African and European, existed independently in the United States until the 1890s, when they were suddenly thrown together in New Orleans. As in most southern cities, Jim Crow laws passed during the 1890s legally and forcefully separated the races in New Orleans. For the history of American music this process had unexpected results. Before the 1890s wealthy mulatto Creoles had lived in the affluent downtown section of New Orleans and followed European musical traditions. Segregation, however, forced them uptown, where poorer blacks who followed African musical traditions lived. Although Creoles and poor blacks did not mix socially, they did forge new musical styles.

The result was jazz, a musical form based on improvisation within a structured band format, which used both African and European traditions. Storyville, the New Orleans red-light district, provided employment for the jazz musicians, who could earn far more than even skilled laborers. Ragtime and the blues also flourished in Storyville. Ragtime, a syncopated piano style, needed only one performer and was therefore popular as café and bordello entertainment. Scott Joplin, a Texas-born black who had formal musical training, wrote several scores of popular rags, and his "Maple Leaf Rag" (1899) probably sold a million copies in sheet music form. Blues musicians, mostly from the Mississippi Delta region, performed in cheap saloons and expressed the pain of life in a hostile world.

During World War I, government officials closed Storyville, charging it was a health hazard. The talented black musicians headed north—to St. Louis, Chicago, Memphis, Kansas City, and New York. They continued

Jazz combined European and African-American music styles into a new musical form. Here King Oliver's Creole Jazz Band poses for a rare picture.

to play jazz and the form continued to evolve. White musicians, trained in the European tradition, soon put their imprint on the American musical form. Although larger jazz bands dominated music during the next generation, they were an outgrowth of the New Orleans sound.

Jazz was the result of the mixture of European and African traditions, and could only have happened in the fertile atmosphere of the cities, where old and new, black and white, immigrant and native-born combined to create new literary, artistic, and musical forms.

Entertaining the Multitudes

City sports, like city music, were loud and raucous. Before the urbanization of the late nineteenth century, the sports and games that Americans played tended to be informal and participant oriented. Rules varied from region to region, and few people even considered the standardization of rules desirable. By 1900 this cozy informality had changed dramatically. Entertainment became a major industry, and specialized performers competed for the right to entertain the multitudes.

The emergence of commercialized entertainment was the result of changes in both American technology and values. Transportation improvements allowed professional entertainers and sports teams to move across America more easily and cheaply, and technological advances in communications allowed the results of games and entertainment news to be spread quickly throughout the country. Added to this was the decline in the Victorian notion that associated popular entertainment with immorality, swearing, and drinking.

In the second half of the nineteenth century a new outlook challenged Victorian values. Immigrants brought with them to America a culture that was at odds with Victorian notions of work and play. In addition, immigrants tended to marry later than native-born Americans; even at midcentury 40 percent of men between the ages of 25 and 35 were unmarried. These men formed a "bachelor subculture" that centered around saloons, gambling halls, race tracks, boxing rings, billiard rooms, and cockpits. Toward the end of the century as the Victorian economic and social order began to crumble, upper-class and then middle-class Americans became interested in the activities of the bachelor subculture. The result was a new attitude toward sport and leisure.

Of Fields and Cities

"Baseball," wrote Mark Twain, "is the very symbol, the outward and visible expression of the drive and push and struggle of the raging, tearing, booming nineteenth century." It captured the bustle and hustle of city life. More than any other sport of the period, baseball was an urban game. All of the early professional teams were located in cities, and most of the paid players were products of the cities.

Ironically, the symbols of the game also recalled America's rural past. Unlike most modern sports, no clock governed the pace of a baseball game. In crowded, dirty cities, baseball was played on open, grassy fields with such bucolic names as Sportsman Park, Ebbets Field, and the Polo Grounds. The field even had fences and bullpens, and the game was played during the planting and harvesting seasons of spring, summer, and fall.

If the symbols and mythology of baseball were rural, the game itself was very urban. Team managers, like their industrialist counterparts, preached the values of hard work, punctuality, thrift, sobriety, and self-control to their players. Baseball, they emphasized, was like modern life, ruthlessly competitive and demanding sacrifice for the "good of the team." Like modern corporate society, modern sports reinforced the ideal of teamwork.

During the last third of the nineteenth century, as men like Rockefeller and Carnegie struggled to bring order to their industrial empires,

Baseball was the leading sport of the late nineteenth century. It brought a sense of America's rural past into the country's urban present.

modern baseball took form. Rules were standardized, and owners attempted to make the sport suitable for the urban middle class. They banned the spitball, arranged games to fit the urban professionals' schedules, fined players for using profanity, and encouraged women to attend the games.

Most important, they formed competitive professional leagues centered in the industrial cities of America. In 1869 Harry Wright took his all-professional Cincinnati Red Stockings on a barnstorming tour, traveling on the recently completed Transcontinental Railroad. During the year the team traveled 11,877 miles by rail, stage, and boat, and entertained more than 200,000 spectators.

The Cincinnati club impressed Americans with its professionalism, and demonstrated to entrepreneurs that there was money to be made in sports. In 1876 William A. Hulbert and several associates formed the National League. In business terms, the league was a loosely organized cartel designed to eliminate competition among franchises for players. Poorly paid and restricted in their ability to negotiate for higher salaries, the players revolted in 1890 and formed their own league. The Players' League was an experiment in workers' control of an industry that players felt was dominated by owners who were only concerned with profits. Lofty in ideals, the Players' League was badly managed and lasted only one year.

With the failure of the Players' League, the National League increased its control over professional baseball. It either crushed rival leagues or absorbed them. In 1903, for example, after a short business war the National League entered into a partnership with the American League. The only losers were the players, whose salaries decreased with the absence of competition. Nevertheless, the popularity of the sport soared. By 1909, when William Howard Taft established the practice of the president opening each season by throwing out the first ball, baseball had become the national pastime.

Bloody Knuckles

Only boxing rivaled baseball in popularity during the late nineteenth century. Like baseball, boxing began the period as a largely unstructured sport, but by 1900 entrepreneurs had reorganized the activity into a profitable business. Although boxing remained illegal in most parts of America, it produced some of the first national sports heroes.

Bare-knuckle boxing, the forerunner of modern boxing, was a brutal, bloody sport. It involved two men fighting bare-fisted until one could not continue. A round lasted until one of the men knocked or threw down his opponent. At that point both men rested for 30 seconds and then started to fight again. Fights could and often did last over 100 rounds and as long as seven or eight hours. After such a fight it took months for the men to recover.

Boxers, unlike baseball players, often emerged from poor immigrant families. Irish-Americans dominated the sport during the late nineteenth century, and they used boxing as a means of social mobility. John L. Sullivan, who won the bare-knuckle world heavyweight title in 1882, became the greatest known American athlete during the nineteenth century. Born in Boston of Irish immigrant parents, Sullivan was a loud boastful man who loved to fight. Politicians, actors, writers, and merchants avidly followed his exploits, but Sullivan never lost touch with his immigrant, working-class origins.

During the 1880s the sport gained greater respectability and, like baseball, underwent a series of reforms. The traditional challenge system for arranging fights was replaced by modern promotional techniques. Fighters started wearing gloves and adopted the Marquis of Queensberry Rules, which standardized a round at three minutes, allowed a one-minute rest period between rounds, and outlawed all wrestling throws and holds. The new rules also replaced the fight to the finish with a fight to a decision over a specified number of rounds. Although the new rules did not reduce the violence of the sport, they did provide for more orderly bouts.

The Excluded Americans

Although promoters talked about the democratic nature of sports, this was far from the case. To be sure, a number of Irish and German men—often immigrants or sons of immigrants—prospered in professional sports. Far more Americans were excluded from the world of sports.

In large cities the lines between social classes tended to blur, much to the discomfort of the wealthy who struggled to separate themselves from the masses. The rich moved to the suburbs and employed other methods of residential segregation to isolate themselves. Another tactic to protect their exclusive status was to allow their children to marry only within their narrow group of acquaintances.

One way to exclude the masses was to engage in sports that only the very rich could play. Yachting and polo demanded nearly unlimited free time, expensive equipment, and a retinue of hired helpers. The New York Yacht Club was founded in 1884, and by the 1890s every major eastern seaboard city had its exclusive yacht club. Each summer the richest yacht owners sailed their splendid vessels to Newport, Rhode Island, the most exclusive of the summer colonies.

Athletic clubs devoted to track and field, golf, and tennis were similarly exclusive, and catered to more than the members' athletic concerns. Each club had an elaborate social calendar filled with dress balls and formal dinners. When they did schedule sporting events, participation and the privilege of watching were normally on an invitation-only basis.

To prevent the various social classes from mixing too freely in athletics, wealthy patrons advocated the code of amateurism, which separated the professionals—who often came from the poorer classes—from the more prosperous athletes who participated in a sport simply for the love of the game. The revival of the Olympic Games in 1896 strengthened the amateur code. Thus when it was discovered that Jim Thorpe, an Oklahoma Indian who had attended the Carlisle Indian School and who won the decathlon and the pentathlon in the 1912 Stockholm Games, had briefly played baseball for a minor league professional team, the International Olympic Committee stripped him of his medals.

Although amateurism was a subtle attack on the working class, sports leaders moved more forcefully against blacks. During the 1870s and 1880s blacks and whites competed in sports against each other on a fairly regular basis. A number of blacks even rose to become world champions. With the advent of the Jim Crow laws, however, most sports became segregated. In 1892 John L. Sullivan issued his famous challenge to fight all contenders: "In this challenge I include all fighters—first come, first served—who are white. I will not fight a Negro. I never have and I never shall." By the 1890s major league baseball also excluded blacks, and it would remain so until Jackie Robinson broke the "color barrier" in 1946.

Cultural expectations and stereotypes also limited the development of women athletes. Compared to men, they were considered weak and uncoordinated. Although women might ride a bicycle or gently swing a croquet mallet, men ridiculed women who were interested in serious competitive athletics. The cult of domesticity, which idealized women as nurturers and maintained that women's proper sphere was the home, also militated against female participation in competitive sports.

Even during the 1890s, when women became more interested in sports and exercise, women's athletics developed along different lines than men's. Male and female physical educators considered women to be uncompetitive and decided that women's sports should serve a utilitarian function. Sports, they emphasized, should promote a woman's physical and mental qualities and thus make her more attractive to men. They also believed that sports and exercise would sublimate female sexual drives. As one physical educator noted, "There is a time in the life of a girl when it is better for her and for the community to be something of a boy rather than too much of a girl." Not until 1924 were women allowed to compete in Olympic track and field events, and even then on a limited basis.

From Central Park to Coney Island

Like sports, parks changed to satisfy new urban demands. Mid-nineteenth-century park designers felt uneasy about the urban environment.

In parks they saw an antidote for the tensions and anxieties caused by living in cities. Frederick Law Olmsted, the most famous park architect, believed cities destroyed community ties and fostered ruthless competition. He designed Central Park to serve as a rural retreat in the midst of New York. Surrounded by rolling hills and quiet lakes, city dwellers would be moved toward greater sociability.

Olmsted's vision of a quiet, orderly park was shared by other leaders of Victorian culture. They believed that culture and leisure activities should serve society by smoothing the rough edges of the urban masses. Instead of supporting baseball and boxing, they built parks, libraries, and museums. In 1870, for example, both the Metropolitan Museum of Art in New York and the Museum of Fine Arts in Boston were opened. Visitors to these repositories of culture were expected to behave in an orderly, quiet, respectful manner.

The quiet world offered by Central Park and the new museums, however, was too tame for many urbanites. They wanted entertainment and excitement, desires that entrepreneurs were quick to satisfy. During the 1890s a series of popular amusement parks opened in Coney Island. Unlike Central Park, which was constructed as a rural retreat, the Coney Island parks glorified the sense of adventure and excitement of the cities. They offered exotic, dreamland landscapes; wonderful, novel machines; and a free, loose social environment. At Coney Island men could remove their coats and ties, and both sexes could enjoy a rare personal freedom.

Coney Island also encouraged new values. If, as Olmsted believed, Central Park reinforced self-control, sobriety, and delayed gratification, Coney Island stressed the emerging consumer-oriented values of extravagance, gaiety, abandon, revelry, and instant gratification. It attracted working-class Americans who longed for at least a taste of the "good life."

The Magic of the Flickering Image

Coney Island showed workers that machines could liberate as well as enslave. It offered an escape from an oppressive urban landscape to an exotic one. The motion picture industry, however, offered a less expensive, more convenient escape. During the early twentieth century it developed into a major popular culture form, one that reflected the hopes and ambitions, fears and anxieties of an urban people.

The first "movies," as the new form was soon called, presented brief vaudeville turns or glimpses of everyday life. Still the movies attracted considerable interest, and filmmakers began to experiment with such new techniques as editing and intercutting separate "shots" to form a dramatic narrative. In 1903 the release of Edwin S. Porter's *The Great Train Robbery*, the first "western" and the first film to exploit the violence of armed robbery, fully demonstrated the commercial possibilities of the invention. Although *The Great Train Robbery* ran only 12 minutes, it mesmerized audiences.

During the early twentieth century movies developed a strong following in ethnic, working-class neighborhoods. Local entrepreneurs converted stores and saloons into nickelodeons and introduced immigrants to a silent world of promise. Movies provided inexpensive and short escapes from the grimmer realities of urban life. In addition, since the movies were silent, they required no knowledge of English to be enjoyed.

Ministers, politicians, and other guardians of traditional Victorian morality criticized the new form of entertainment for encouraging idleness, careless spending, and sexual temptation at the expense of work. Soon local boards of censorship formed to protect innocent boys and girls, and perhaps not so innocent men and women, from being corrupted by movies.

In the cities censorship movements ultimately failed. Furthermore, attempts by white, native-born American entrepreneurs to control the new industry similarly failed. Ironically, while films were beginning to attract middle-class audiences, control of the industry shifted to immigrant entrepreneurs, most of whom were Jewish and had come to America from eastern Europe. They proved better able than native-born businessmen to develop the possibilities of the medium. They emerged from a culture that valued laughter, cooperation, and entertainment. Committed to giving the people what they wanted, they were less constrained by the traditional Victorian code of morality.

To better entertain the public, film moguls started producing feature-length films and moved the industry from the East Coast to sunny Hollywood, where they could shoot outdoors and, not incidentally, escape union difficulties. While such "stars" as Charlie Chaplin, Douglas Fairbanks, and Mary Pickford captured the hearts of America, producers such as Adolph Zukor, William Fox, Louis B. Mayer, and Harry Warner forged a multimillion-dollar industry.

The Agony of Painless Escape

Coney Island and movie theaters provided one form of escape, and the criticism of both was fairly uniform. At the same time as popular culture was exploring the theme of mechanized instant gratification, however, Americans were seeking escape in other, more ominous forms, such as narcotics.

Like the whirring machines at Coney Island and the flickering images on the silent, silver screen, the mindless escape of narcotics attracted millions of Americans. During the late nineteenth and early twentieth centuries, as the nation underwent the trauma of industrialization and urbanization, Americans took drugs in unprecedented amounts. Apologists blamed this development on the Civil War. They claimed that soldiers became addicted to morphine after using the drug as a painkiller. Yet France, Germany, Great Britain, Russia, and Italy also fought wars in the second half of the nineteenth century, and their drug addiction rates were far below those of the United States.

Part of the problem was that before 1915 there were few restrictions on the importation and use of opium, its derivatives, and cocaine. Physicians prescribed opiates for a wide range of ailments, and patent medicine manufacturers used morphine, laudanum, cocaine, or heroin in their concoctions. Coca-Cola used cocaine as one of its secret ingredients, and the Parke Davis Company produced coca-leaf cigarettes, cheroots, and a Coca Cordial.

Cocaine in particular was regarded as a wonder drug. By the late 1890s, however, its harmful effects had become obvious. Eventually, angry citizens and the federal and state governments launched the first great American crusade against cocaine. It culminated with the Harrison Anti-Narcotic Act in 1914, which controlled the distribution of opiates and cocaine; but drug addiction remained a problem in American cities.

Robert Louis Stevenson's *Dr. Jekyll and Mr. Hyde,* which he wrote under the influence of cocaine, described the dangers of challenging society's standards and altering one's personality, but in America's cities a new culture had taken shape. It opposed Victorian restraints, glorified the freedoms of urban life, and at the same time worried about the implications of a liberated life-style. Social, as well as economic, freedom came with a price. By the 1890s many Americans believed some new regulations were needed to check the social and economic freedom unleashed in urban America.

Conclusion

On January 17, 1906, Marshall Field, the dry-goods merchant and founder of the large Chicago department store that bears his name, died. "The first as well as the richest citizen" in Chicago, noted the *New York Sun,* Field left his children over $140 million. Americans questioned how one man could accumulate such a fortune. "No man could earn a million dollars honestly," said politician William Jennings Bryan. Another critic suggested that Field's fortune was made at the expense of his more than 10,000 employees, 95 percent of whom earned $12 dollars a week or less.

Most Americans, however, focused on what Field offered shoppers more than what he paid his employees. Department stores brought order to shopping and emphasized standardization of products. Serving urban markets and satisfying urban desires, they enabled customers to buy a

*C*hronology of Key Events

1869	Cincinnati Red Stockings begin barnstorming tour of America
1870	Metropolitan Museum of Art in New York and Museum of Fine Arts in Boston open
1873	Cable car introduced
1878	Yellow fever epidemic
1879	New York City adopts Tenement Reform Law
1882	Electric lighting comes into widespread use for the first time in New York City
1884	Mark Twain's *The Adventures of Huckleberry Finn* published
1885	William LeBaron Jenney erects the Home Insurance Building in Chicago
1888	Electric-power trolley introduced
1892	Stephen Crane publishes his first novel, *Maggie: A Girl of the Streets*
1899	Scott Joplin composes "Maple Leaf Rag"
1900	Theodore Dreiser publishes *Sister Carrie*
1903	Edwin S. Porter's *The Great Train Robbery* released
1912	Jim Thorpe wins the decathlon and pentathlon at Olympic Games in Stockholm
1913	Armory Show in New York City includes works from artists of ashcan and modernist schools
1914	Harrison Anti-Narcotic Act controls distribution of opiates and cocaine

wide range of products hitherto unavailable under one roof. Inside one of the great department stores, consumers isolated themselves from the garbage in the streets, the filth in the air, and the sounds of traffic and commerce that dominated the outside world. They chose not to think about the workers who made the goods they purchased.

Both the orderly world of the department store and the chaotic one of the streets were the products of urban entrepreneurs who fashioned the modern cities. In pursuit of profits they were capable of producing dazzling monuments to commerce and terrible tributes to greed. By 1900 their days of absolute dominance were numbered. Although they would remain a vital part of American capitalism, in the future they would be rivaled by governmental planners—people who wanted to extend the smooth, efficient order of the department store to the outside streets.

The emergence of the great cities changed American life. They dominated not only the nation's economy but the American imagination. In the cities the clash of ideas and beliefs, of peoples and traditions created an exciting, new heterogeneous culture. The result was evident at places such as Coney Island and the Armory Show, it was visible in many of the movies, and it was audible at a New Orleans jazz café. As the nineteenth century drew to a close, a new culture was clearly emerging. It would add a new element to the new century.

Suggestions for Further Reading

Valuable overviews of the urbanization of America include Sean D. Cashman, *America in the Gilded Age* (1984); Howard P. Chudacoff, *The Evolution of American Urban Society* (1975); Raymond A. Mohl, *The New City* (1985); John Stilgoe, *Borderland: Origins of the American Suburb* (1988).

Aspects of urban culture and society are examined in Gunther Barth, *City People* (1980); Burton J. Bledstein, *The Culture of Professionalism* (1976); Lawrence W. Levine, *Highbrow/Lowbrow: the Emergence of Cultural Hierarchy in America* (1988); Martin V. Melosi, *Garbage in the Cities* (1982); Lewis O. Saum, *The Popular Mood of America* (1990).

The role of professional sports is analyzed in Melvin L. Adelman, *A Sporting Time* (1986); Warren Goldstein, *Playing for Keeps: A History of Early Baseball* (1989); Allen Guttmann, *A Whole New Ball Game: An Interpretation of American Sports* (1988); Donald J. Mrozek, *Sport and American Mentality* (1983); Randy Roberts, *Papa Jack: Jack Johnson and the Era of White Hopes* (1983), and *Jack Dempsey: The Manassa Mauler* (1979).

On the development of the arts consult Robert Crunden, *American Salons* (1992); Neil Leonard, *Jazz and the White Americans* (1962); Russell Lynes, *The Lively Audience* (1985); Richard J. Powell, *The Blues Aesthetic* (1989).

Chapter 20

End of the Century Crisis

On July 9, 1896, thirty-six-year-old William Jennings Bryan rose to speak to the delegates at the Democratic National Convention in Chicago. A congressman from Nebraska, Bryan had become the champion of the "free silver" movement. In the 1890s many American farmers favored expanding the amount of money in circulation by coining more silver dollars. Such an inflationary policy, they believed, would raise crop prices and alleviate their heavy debt burdens. Many rural residents felt the national government had not been responsive to their needs—that both political parties had been captured by industrialists, railroad owners, and bankers. In 1896 silver was a symbol for popular grievances. Among other things, silver represented rural values, the common people, and a growing discontent with northeastern political domination.

By the time of the 1896 Democratic convention the Republicans had nominated William McKinley and adopted a platform calling for the gold standard—or currency backed entirely by gold supplies in the federal treasury. The Democrats were divided between the "silverites" and the "Gold Democrats," monetary conservatives who supported President Grover Cleveland. Control of the party by the Northeast was being challenged by southern and western delegates when Bryan finally rose to speak.

Called "the Great Commoner," Bryan voiced the frustrations of farmers with the failure of traditional politicians to meet their needs. A compelling orator, he enthralled the crowd from the beginning, but his closing words created pandemonium. "We will answer the demand for a gold standard," he roared, "by saying to them: 'You shall not press down upon the brow of labor this crown of thorns, you shall not crucify mankind upon a cross of gold.' " As Bryan spoke his fingers first traced the course of imaginary trickles of blood from his temples. He closed with his arms outstretched as if he were nailed to a cross.

Bryan's "Cross of Gold" speech won him the Democratic nomination and clinched the victory of the party's silverites. President Cleveland's supporters, however, refused to support him, and nearly half the Democratic newspapers opposed his candidacy. As a result, Bryan was only able to raise the meager sum of $500,000.

Taking his campaign directly to the people, Bryan relied on his oratorical genius and electrifying charisma. He crisscrossed the country, railing against big business and corporate financiers and appealing to the sectional and class animosities of his listeners. He made his own travel arrangements, bought his own tickets, carried his own bags, altogether logging more than 18,000 miles and giving 600 speeches before election day.

In the 1896 election, Republicans sought to convince voters that Bryan (at right and below in the campaign poster) was a radical who threatened American values and institutions, while McKinley would guarantee stability, order, and integrity.

With a Republican campaign fund of more than $3.5 million, McKinley wisely refused to follow Bryan's course. Between June and November, McKinley conducted a "front porch" campaign, leaving his home in Canton, Ohio, for only three days. Huge crowds were brought in by railroad to McKinley's lawn for special events organized by the candidate's staff. McKinley stressed national unity rather than division in a calm and dispassionate style that contrasted sharply with the frenzied oratory of his opponent.

On election day Bryan and his wife rose at 6:30 A.M. and voted at a local fire station in Omaha, Nebraska. He then gave seven speeches in his hometown before collapsing, exhausted, in bed that evening. McKinley walked to his polling place and stood in line to vote. He then returned home to wait for the returns—his lawn and porch in worse shape than he was. All over the nation people waited to find out which man and party would preside over the dawning of the twentieth century.

The election came in a decade of turbulence that saw an increasingly militant labor movement, rising racial tensions, and agrarian unrest—all of which intensified after a major depression began in 1893. The social fabric seemed to be unraveling rapidly, which is why the election of 1896 was considered so important. For the first time since the 1870s voters were given a clear choice between two very different candidates and platforms.

Following Reconstruction, national politics were colorful but not very significant. No important policy differences separated the two major parties; the campaigns revolved around personalities, gimmicks, emotional slogans, and local issues. As elections were trivialized, they also became a major source of entertainment, and voters turned out in record numbers. This triumph of style over substance in politics, as well as culture, caused the era to be labeled the "Gilded Age." By 1890 both the Democratic and Republican parties were out of touch with the sentiments of large blocks of voters. The losers in the great national drive toward economic modernization were unable to unite around a viable progam. The issues they raised, however, appeared regularly on political agendas in the twentieth century.

Equilibrium and Inertia: The National Political Scene

In the late nineteenth century patronage, or the granting of political favors and offices, had become more important than issues to the two major parties. Close elections caused the parties to be careful not to alienate potential supporters. Most people also believed in limited government. Political parties were therefore organized more to win offices than to govern.

The result was a failure by government to deal effectively with the enormous changes wrought by industrialization and urbanization.

Divided Power: Republicans and Democrats

After Reconstruction both the Democratic and Republican parties emerged with sizable and stable constituencies. For the 20 years between 1876 and 1896 they shared a rare equality of political power. Elections were so close that until 1896 no president won office with a majority of the popular vote. Two (Hayes and Harrison) even entered the presidency without a plurality. Most of the time Congress itself was split, with Democrats generally taking the House and the Republicans the Senate. Very few seats shifted parties in any given election.

The party division of Congress inevitably weakened the presidents of the era. None was elected to consecutive terms; none was noteworthy in his accomplishments. To be fair, all were competent men, most with considerable public service. One reason they were so forgettable was the era's concept of the presidency. Presidents were only supposed to implement laws passed by Congress—occasionally vetoing ill-advised legislation. None considered it his duty to propose legislation. Congress was also hampered by outdated, complex rules and lax party discipline. Thus there was little possibility of formulating and enacting any coherent legislative program.

The lack of legislative action did not seem to be a serious problem at the start of the Gilded Age, since most people rejected the idea of an activist government. Widely accepted doctrines of laissez-faire and Social Darwinism limited what people expected of government. Both parties basically accepted a narrow vision of federal responsibility. When vetoing a small appropriation for drought relief in Texas, Democrat Cleveland asserted that "though the people support the Government, the Government should not support the people."

Such antigovernment sentiment tended to increase the power of the judicial branch. Many saw the courts as a bastion against governmental interference in the economy, and the courts certainly fulfilled that role. On the basis of the Fourteenth Amendment, judges were especially active in striking down state laws to regulate business. The courts narrowly interpreted the Constitution on federal authority—ruling that the power to tax did not extend to personal incomes and that the power to regulate interstate commerce applied only to trade, not manufacturing. Congress also indirectly gave judges more power by enacting vague laws that relied upon the courts for both definition and enforcement.

The Bases of Party Loyalty

One consequence of the equal power shared by the Democrats and Republicans was the reluctance of either party to chance losing voters by taking clear positions on the issues. Perhaps this reluctance was also based on the memories of the divisive 1860 election and its devastating impact on party and national unity. In addition, few Americans criticized industrialization and modernization during the early stages, and there was widespread agreement on many issues.

Until 1896 the parties shared numerous similarities. Both were led by wealthy men but still tried to appeal to wage earners and farmers as well as merchants and manufacturers. Most members of both parties believed in protective tariffs and "sound currency." Both rejected economic radicalism and positive programs to aid workers. Presidents of both parties sent federal troops to break up strikes. Business leaders had so little to fear from either party that they contributed generously to both.

Ironically, for all their similarities the parties evoked fierce loyalty from a heterogeneous mix of people, which was one reason party platforms were so innocuous. Because of its antislavery past, the Republican party retained the support of activist reformers, idealists, and African Americans. Yet most Republicans came from established, "old stock" families. The more wealth a man had, the more likely he was to vote Republican. The Democrats were even more mixed. The party's constituency, comprised of such disparate elements as Southern whites, immigrants, Catholics, and Jews, sometimes seemed united mainly by opposition to the Republicans.

For historical and cultural reasons, party loyalty was frequently determined by three factors: region, religion, and ethnic origin. The regional factor was most evident in the support white Southerners gave to the Democratic party. To vote for the party of abolition and Reconstruction was considered treason and a threat to white supremacy. On the other hand, the Republicans could count on heavy support from New Englanders, who saw the Democrats as members of the party of traitorous rebellion against the Union. The Republicans frequently "waved the bloody shirt," reminding Northerners of the Democrats' role in causing the Civil War.

For various reasons immigrants had long gravitated toward the Democratic party. Many were members of the poorest classes, which traditionally voted Democratic. Most of the "new immigrants" of the Gilded Age settled in cities controlled by Democratic political machines that won their loyalty by meeting the immigrants' needs. As immigration swelled, increasing Democratic strength, Republicans became more and more restrictionist. In fact, immigration policy was one of the very few substantive issues on which the parties took clearly different stands.

Religious affiliations also helped determine party loyalty, partly because of the positions on immigration. Many of the late-nineteenth-century immigrants were Catholics and Jews who were suspicious of the Protestant-dominated Republican party. There were also fundamental differences in the religious orientation of most Republicans and Democrats. Republicans frequently sought to legislate morality, supporting prohibition of alcohol and enforcement of Sunday blue laws, which barred various activities on the sabbath—including baseball. By contrast, many Democrats did not believe that personal morality could or should be a matter of state concern. Thus, the Republicans became known as the "party of morality," the Democrats the "party of personal liberty." Democrats not only rejected government interference in their personal life; in the nineteenth century they were also more suspicious of government action of any sort.

Because of their mixed constituencies, the differences and divisions *within* parties were often as great as those between them. Democrats could count on the South for all of that region's electoral votes, but conservative southern Democrats frequently broke party ranks when voting on legislation favorable to farmers, on financial and economic issues, as well as on immigration restriction.

The Republicans were even more deeply divided into factions. One group, led by Roscoe Conkling of New York, was labeled the "Stalwarts." Followers of James G. Blaine of Maine were called "Half-breeds." The only significant item of dispute between the two was who would receive the numerous jobs appointed by the president. Since the distribution of patronage was a prime function of both parties of the era, the rivalry was a bitter one.

There was one faction of the Republican party that did have some ideological basis. Composed of reformers whose primary concern was honest and effective government, they had bolted the party in 1872 because of the corruption of the Grant regime, and they bolted again in 1884. Party regulars ridiculed them, calling them "Mugwumps," asserting that they had their "mugs" on one side of the fence and their "wumps" on the other.

The divisions within the Democratic and Republican parties reflected the fact that the politicians of the day were less concerned with issues and ideology than with winning office and distributing patronage. Rather than confront the problems facing the nation, they put their energies into electioneering and party management.

The Business of Politics: Party Organization

The Gilded Age saw the largest voter turnouts in the nation's history, a phenomenon that had more to do with the ability of sophisticated party organizations to get out the vote than with compelling political issues. In the elections from 1860 to 1900 an average of 78 percent of eligible voters cast ballots. Outside of the South (where African Americans were increasingly prevented from voting and where the Democratic nomination determined the general election), the turnout sometimes reached 90 percent.

There was one main difference in Republican and Democratic party organization. Republicans generally depended on strong state organizations, and Democrats tended to rely on urban political machines to win and control votes. Since city governmental structures did not keep pace with the huge population increases, the political machines provided many of the social services for which government would later be held responsible. In return, the politicians were paid in votes from the people, bribes from legal and illegal businesses, and graft from contractors. The system worked so well that the Democrats usually carried the big cities.

Dominated by skilled professionals, Gilded Age politics was a rough and frequently corrupt business. In 1888 when Benjamin Harrison won the presidency, a Republican party boss noted that Harrison "would never know how close a number of men were impelled to approach the gates of a penitentiary to make him president." Electoral corruption was not limited to one party. In the same year a Mississippi Democrat admitted that "we have been stuffing ballot boxes, committing perjury, and . . . carrying the elections by fraud and violence."

Gilded Age politics was undoubtedly the prime form of mass entertainment. The drama of emotional tent meetings rivaled circuses. The pageantry of parades also provided excitement. Almost everyone got caught up in the elections, displaying such paraphernalia as buttons, handkerchiefs, hats, banners, and posters emblazoned with their party's symbol or slogan.

Many politicians surely must have enjoyed their status as "media stars" and folk heroes. For some, whose ethnic or class backgrounds closed conventional doors of opportunity, politics provided a vehicle of upward social mobility, similar to professional entertainment, athletics, or trade union leadership. Yet politics as a vocation offered other rewards. Elected and appointed officials not only received salaries but also openly accepted gifts from lobbyists and free passes from railroads, and sometimes used their governmental status to promote their private interests. One quip claimed that the United States had the best Congress money could buy.

Women and Politics

Politics during the Gilded Age remained a pastime enjoyed almost exclusively by males. In 1874 the Supreme Court ruled that citizenship did not automatically confer the vote and that suffrage could be denied specific groups, such as criminals, the insane, and women. Under the leadership of Elizabeth Cady Stanton and Susan B. Anthony, the National Woman Suffrage Association (NWSA) in 1878 succeeded in getting a constitutional amendment introduced into the Senate that stated that "the right to vote shall not be denied or abridged by the United States or by any state on account of sex." It continued to be submitted for the next 18 years but was usually killed in committee and only rarely reached the floor of the Senate.

At the state level, the American Woman Suffrage Association (AWSA) enjoyed somewhat more success. By 1890, 19 states allowed women to vote on school issues, and three states extended women the franchise on tax and bond issues; yet only the territory of Wyoming had granted women full political equality.

In 1890 the groups merged to form the National American Woman Suffrage Association (NAWSA). As male resistance mounted, the movement seemed to lose steam. No other state acted to grant full suffrage rights to women until 1910. Many men agreed with a Texas senator that "equal suffrage is a repudiation of manhood."

Style over Substance: Government in the Gilded Age

Politics provided great entertainment, but governmental inertia in Washington left many Americans dissatisfied. As discontent rose, many problems were first tackled by city, county, and state governments before becoming a part of the national agenda. Such issues as the currency and tariffs, however, could only be solved at the national level. Others, such as demands for honest government, were undertaken at all levels. On the whole, the states responded more vigorously than the national government to the problems created by economic changes—only to have the Supreme Court sometimes tie their hands. People began to look to Washington for solutions. The presidents and Congress responded timidly. National elections still focused mainly on trivial issues. When backed to the wall, Congress would enact laws to quiet popular cries for action, but such laws were limited in scope and often unenforceable. Style triumphed over substance, and most problems remained unsolved.

Hayes and the "Money Question"

Rutherford B. Hayes is probably best remembered for removing the remaining federal troops from the South in 1877, thus marking the end of Reconstruction. Hayes was honest, competent, and did much to establish the Republican party as the "party of morality" after the corruption of the Grant regime.

When Hayes came into office, the country was still in the throes of an economic depression that began with the Panic of 1873. As a result of hard times, a complex and heated political debate arose over federal monetary policy. At its root was a long period of deflation following the Civil War. Prices fell because the production of goods was growing faster than the supply of money. Farmers were particularly hard hit. Wheat, corn, and cotton prices declined more than other prices in the late nineteenth century. Farmers had also borrowed heavily to expand production, and they were caught in a debt squeeze with their mortgage payments remaining high while the prices they received for their goods fell.

Farmers and debtors of all occupations saw inflation as the cure to their problems. They advocated increasing the amount of "greenbacks"— paper money not backed by gold or silver—which had first been issued during the Civil War. Advocates of that solution organized the Greenback party in 1874. A conservative Congress, however, steadfastly supported a "hard money" policy, and one year later passed the Specie Resumption Act, gradually withdrawing the greenbacks then in circulation.

Some inflationists then turned their attention to silver. Since the 1790s the nation had been on a bimetallic standard. The value of a dollar was based on both gold and silver, and for years dollars were coined at a 16 to 1 mint ratio. In other words, a dollar contained 16 times as much silver as gold. By the 1870s this ratio did not reflect the market prices of the metals. Silver prices were so high that producers sold it on the open market rather than take it to the mint to be coined. Unable to buy silver at that ratio, Congress had passed the Coinage Act of 1873 that halted the minting of silver dollars.

Soon thereafter, the discovery of large deposits of silver drove prices down. Then it was in the interest of both silver miners and inflationists to return to the coining of silver at 16 to 1. Together they formed a large lobby that wrested minor concessions from Congress. The Bland-Allison Act of 1878 required the government to buy between $2 and $4 million worth of silver each month. However, the act proved ineffective; it neither raised silver prices nor inflated the currency significantly. Like much of the legislation of the Gilded Age, the Bland-Allison Act was a cosmetic answer to popular demands.

Garfield, Arthur, and the Patronage Issue

In the 1880 election neither of the two major parties focused on substantial issues but instead relied on slogans and gimmicks to win votes. The battle for the Republican nomination was between the Half-Breed and Stalwart factions since Hayes refused to run for a second term. On the thirty-sixth ballot the party picked James A. Garfield, a Civil War veteran but relatively unknown Ohio congressman. Chester A. Arthur, a Conkling henchman, became the vice-presidential nominee.

The Democrats nominated an even more obscure figure, General Winfield Scott Hancock, a hero of the Battle of Gettysburg. He was described as "a good man weighing 250 pounds." Despite the blandness of both candidates, the 1880 election was one of the closest of the century in popular vote. Garfield received a mere 39,000 vote plurality out of almost ten million ballots cast.

Once the election was over, the currency question was overshadowed by the issue of patronage because of returning prosperity and a tragic event. Only four months after Garfield's inauguration he was shot by a deranged office seeker named Charles Guiteau. His successor, Chester A. Arthur, was considered by many to be a party hack, but Arthur surprised them by becoming a champion of governmental reform.

During the 1870s the Mugwumps and other reformers had become increasingly concerned with the "spoils system" of patronage. Since the early 1800s government jobs had been considered the "spoils" of political victory to be awarded to party workers regardless of their qualifications. The problem had worsened as the federal government grew, and after the Civil War presidents spent much of their time appointing party loyalists to some 100,000 federal jobs.

Revulsion at Garfield's assassination finally prompted Congress to take action. With the support of President Arthur, Congress enacted the Pendleton Act in 1883. It outlawed political contributions by appointed officeholders and established competitive examinations for federal positions to be given by the Civil Service Commission. The act was rather timid—only applying to about ten percent of government employees. Moreover, since it was to apply only to future appointees, the act served to protect incumbents. The political system was becoming modernized, but some questioned whether it was being improved.

Cleveland, the Railroads, and Tariffs

Arthur's actions won him more favor from the public than from his party, and in 1884 the Republicans bypassed him and nominated James G. Blaine. Handsome and charismatic, Blaine was nonetheless a tainted political commodity. While in Congress he had become very rich without any visible means of outside income. Copies of letters were circulated that seemed to indicate Blaine was up for sale to the railroads. This revelation was more than the Mugwumps could stomach, and they refused to support him.

Realizing the potential advantage of a Mugwump defection, the Democrats selected Grover Cleveland, a reform governor of New York. Although he was neither physically attractive nor charismatic, he was honest. Because Cleveland and Blaine did not disagree on the major issues, their campaign revolved around personalities and became one of the most scurrilous in the nation's history.

Blaine's tainted past was obvious fodder for the Democrats' campaign. Unable to find a shred of evidence to challenge Cleveland's honesty, Republicans publicized a more personal scandal. As a bachelor, Cleveland had supported an illegitimate child since 1874, even though his paternity was questionable. Thus Republicans countered Democratic chants with "Ma! Ma! Where's my pa? Going to the White House? Ha! Ha! Ha!" In the end Cleveland won, in part because Republican efforts to portray the Democrats as the party of Roman Catholicism backfired, enabling the Democrats to rally Catholic voters to win key states.

The major legislation of Cleveland's first presidency came as the result of public pressure and actions of the courts. The power and discriminatory rates of the railroads scared and angered many Americans, and actions to regulate the railroads had started at the state level. By 1880, 14 states had established railroad commissions. The most active advocate of regulation was the Patrons of Husbandry, a farmers' group organized into local chapters called "granges." The Grangers and their allies, especially in the Midwest, got stronger legislation enacted that set maximum rates and charges within their states.

The railroad companies naturally attacked the so-called Granger laws through the courts. At first the railroads lost. In the 1877 *Munn* v. *Illinois* decision, the Supreme Court ruled that when "private property is affected with a public interest it . . . must submit to be controlled by the public for the common good." Nevertheless, it was difficult for states to regulate railroads chartered by other states and doing business across state lines. Then in a resounding defeat for the Grangers, the Supreme Court ruled in 1886 in *Wabash* v. *Illinois* that only Congress had the right to regulate interstate commerce.

Pressure began to build for federal action, and Congress responded with the 1887 Interstate Commerce Act. It prohibited pools, rebates, and rate discriminations; provided that all charges by the railroads should be "reasonable and just"; and established the Interstate Commerce Commission (ICC).

The commission was significant as the first federal regulatory agency, but its power was woefully limited. It could investigate charges against the railroads and issue "cease and desist" orders, which could only be enforced by the courts. Conservative courts soon nullified 90 percent of the commission's orders, and between 1887 and 1905 the Supreme Court ruled against the ICC in 15 of 16 cases.

The Interstate Commerce Act temporarily satisfied the "popular clamor" for reform without alienating railroad owners. It therefore did

Public anger over railroad power finally pushed Congress to pass the Interstate Commerce Act in 1887.

not become a partisan issue for either party. However, during Cleveland's term, a major issue on which Democrats and Republicans actually differed emerged: the tariff. Both parties supported these taxes on imports in order to raise revenue and to protect American products from being undersold by foreign competitors. The question was merely how high these tariffs should be. Supporters of protectionism were those who sold on the domestic markets; opponents depended on foreign markets. Both groups included some farmers and manufacturers from every region.

Like most Democrats, Cleveland had long been less enthusiastic about high tariffs. While in office he found that existing tariff rates were producing treasury surpluses that tempted congressmen to propose programs and appropriations that he considered a dangerous expansion of federal activities. Thus he became an advocate of tariff reduction, and made the tariff a focus of his reelection bid in 1888.

Harrison and Big Business

In 1888 the Democrats renominated Cleveland and wrote tariff reduction into their platform. The Republicans chose Benjamin Harrison and cheerfully picked up the gauntlet—denouncing Cleveland's "free trade" as unpatriotic. They also promised generous pensions to veterans. Voters at last were given a choice on a real issue. When Cleveland lost, Republicans erroneously interpreted his narrow defeat as a mandate for protectionism. Congress then enacted the McKinley Tariff, which raised the average duties to the highest level yet. A wave of public resentment followed. No longer able to afford foreign-made goods, many Americans saw the act as evidence of the tremendous power wielded by manufacturing interests in the nation's capital.

Growing hostility toward big business was also seen in the popular demand for legislative action against monopolistic trusts. Again action started on the state level; 15 southern and western states had passed antitrust legislation by the mid-1880s. Companies responded by incorporating in more sympathetic states. The laws were both ineffective and likely to be overturned by federal courts, but they did reflect popular outrage. Congress responded by enacting the Sherman Antitrust Act in 1890. On the surface it seemed to doom the trusts, prohibiting any "contract, combination in the form of trust or otherwise, or conspiracy in restraint of trade or commerce." But, as with the Interstate Commerce Act, appearances were deceiving.

The Supreme Court emasculated the law in *United States* v. *E. C. Knight Co.* (1895), ruling that it applied to commerce but not manufacturing. Thus the E. C. Knight Co., a sugar trust controlling 98 percent of the industry, was not in violation. Until 1901 the antitrust law was virtually unenforced; the Justice Department instituted only 14 suits and failed to get convictions in most of them. Indeed, the only effective use made of the act in its first decade was as a tool to break up labor strikes by court injunctions.

The currency issue continued to serve as a lightning rod for public protest against the new economic order. Following the Bland-Allison Act of 1878, the money supply continued to grow too slowly for the expanding economy, leading to increased pressure to coin more silver. In 1890 Congress responded with the Sherman Silver Purchase Act. It required the government to buy 4.5 million ounces of silver each month at the unrealistic ratio of 16 to 1. Paper money to pay for the purchases was redeemable in gold or silver, keeping the inflationary impact minimal. The act was a compromise that satisfied no one; consequently, the silver issue would grow more heated in the 1890s.

During Harrison's presidency Congress was more active than previously—passing the McKinley Tariff, the Sherman Antitrust Act, the Sherman Silver Purchase Act, and the first billion-dollar budget. At the same time the Republican party was becoming alienated from its abolitionist past and more closely tied to big business.

Minority Rights and Social Issues

To African Americans the Republicans remained the party of black rights, but following the election of 1876 the party did less and less to earn that label. By 1890, however, conditions finally moved some Republicans to action. Dismayed by increasing southern assaults on the black vote, Senator Henry Cabot Lodge and others drafted a federal elections bill which sought to protect voter registration and guarantee fair congressional elections by establishing mechanisms to investigate charges of voting fraud and to deal with disputed elections.

Outraged white Southerners and Northern Democrats joined to defeat the measure. Although in 1890 Republicans controlled both houses of Congress, they finally bartered away the Lodge Election Bill to gain support for the McKinley Tariff. Protection of manufacturers was more important to them than the protection of African Americans.

Other measures of the era affected minorities—but usually in a negative way. Southern white Democrats enacted discriminatory legislation against blacks at the local and state level. A movement for immigration restriction, usually initiated by Republicans, led to the Chinese Exclusion Act of 1882 and other legislation banning certain categories of immigrants and giving the federal government control of overseas immigration. In 1887 the Dawes Act attacked the tribal roots of American Indian culture by trying to make Native Americans homesteading farmers, and resulted unintentionally in making them dependent wards of the state.

Although most social issues received short shrift at the federal level, at the local and state level some—especially education and prohibition—received passionate attention. Alarmed by the seeming increase in alcohol consumption, Republicans moved beyond the educative temperance movement to attempt to make drinking alcohol a crime. They also sought to increase compulsory school attendance, but their efforts were often linked to moves to undermine parochial schools and schools that taught immigrants in their native tongues. In most areas these Republican actions backfired, losing more voters than they gained.

By 1890 very little effective legislation had been adopted to deal with the problems arising from a pluralistic society experiencing rapid social and economic change. This pattern resulted partly from a political equilibrium that bred inertia, as well as from traditional, widely held views regarding the limited nature of government. Nevertheless, public demands for change were growing. No group challenged the status quo more than the nation's farmers.

The Farmers Revolt

Cries for change naturally came from the losers in the new economic order. The declining prosperity of American farmers led many to the conclusion that the cards had been stacked against them. By the 1890s, many desperate farmers agreed with Populist leader Mary E. Lease that it was time "to raise less corn and more hell." Their success was limited, but they led the first American mass movement to reject Social Darwinism and laissez-faire principles. They also promoted the "radical" idea that "it is the duty of government to protect the weak, because the strong are able to protect themselves." Some even questioned basic tenets of industrial capitalism.

Grievances: Real and Imagined

The basic cause of the farmers' problems was the decline of agricultural prices—primarily because of overproduction. Farmers had a hard time believing, however, that they could produce too much, especially since there were still poorly clad and fed Americans.

Overproduction was an abstract, invisible enemy; many farmers sought more tangible, personal villains—the railroads, bankers, and monopolists. Farmers believed they were being robbed by high freight and credit costs, an unfair burden of taxation, middlemen who exploited their marketing problems, and an inadequate currency.

Although there was no conspiracy by the "monopolists" to fleece the farmers, their grievances did contain a germ of truth. Freight rates were higher for farmers in the West because of the long distances to markets and the scattered and seasonal nature of grain shipments. Although western farmers generally paid the same interest rates as easterners, they were more dependent on mortgages to finance their operations than the corporations. Southern farmers also paid dearly through higher credit prices for goods obtained by crop liens. Their large debts increased farmers' marketing problems. All the crops in a region were usually harvested at the same time, and farmers had to sell them immediately to pay off loans. Middlemen took advantage of the glutted markets, buying the crops at low prices and selling them after the prices rose.

Governmental policy also seemed to hurt more than help. Property taxes hit farmers hard because they had lots of land but little income. The tariffs generally hurt most farmers by both raising the prices they paid for

By the late 1880s many farmers were already suffering from severe economic
dislocation. This 1889 cartoon shows a poor, hungry farmer gazing at a banquet
for tariff-gorged industrialists while Congressman McKinley pours whiskey.

goods and making it harder for them to sell their crops on the international market. The deflationary policy of the federal government especially hurt the farmers because of their great indebtedness. Every economic downturn brought a wave of farm foreclosures and frustration.
Thousands of dreams died slowly, as one Kansas farmer's letter reveals.

> At the age of 52 years, after a long life of toil, economy and self-
> denial, I find myself and family virtually paupers. With hundreds
> of cattle, hundreds of hogs, scores of good horses, and a farm that
> rewarded the toil of our hands with 16,000 bushels of golden
> corn, we are poorer by many dollars than we were years ago.
> What once seemed a neat little fortune and a house of refuge for
> our declining years . . . has been rendered valueless.

The Farmers Organize

In the age of economic consolidation farmers realized early the need to
unite and cooperate. They were never able, however, to do so as effectively
as the industrialists and railroad magnates, due to their greater geographic
separation as well as a frontier-bred individualism. The first national farm
organization was the Patrons of Husbandry, founded in 1867. Organized

into local granges that sponsored lectures, dances, and picnics, the group met a deep hunger for social interaction, and the membership grew to more than one million by 1874.

The Grangers soon moved beyond their social functions to address the economic grievances of the farmers. In addition to their efforts to regulate the railroads, the Grangers established buying cooperatives, which were formed to purchase in bulk directly from manufacturers, thus eliminating retail markups. In some places granges established cooperative banks, grain elevators, cotton gins, insurance companies, processing plants, and even plants to manufacture farm implements. However, most of the cooperatives were short on capital and skilled management, and in the late 1870s the granges began to decline.

Economic grievances remained, however, and the farmers' organizational response shifted to the Farmers' Alliance movement. Although never very effective, a northwestern Alliance was formed in 1880. In the South the Alliance movement was more radical and more successful. By 1890 the southern Alliance was a national organization with about 1.5 million members, with an additional 1 million members in the Colored Alliance, its African-American affiliate.

Like the Grangers, Alliance members sought to establish cooperatives, mostly without long-term success. They also conducted wider social and educational programs and boasted about 1,000 newspapers. Self-help, however, proved inadequate. In 1890 they turned to political action to redress farmers' grievances, either by seeking to capture their state Democratic organizations or by establishing independent third parties.

The Agrarian Agenda

The demands of the farmers mixed rhetoric, radicalism, and realism. Their words expressed an anger that had flared white-hot after years of smouldering resentment. Rejecting certain aspects of capitalism, they spoke in a language that divided the nation into "haves" and "have-nots." They saw a division between the toiling masses who produced wealth and the parasitic capitalists who expropriated it. In response they proclaimed that "wealth belongs to him who creates it."

Scorned by critics, the movement did have its unsavory aspects. A few agrarians espoused simplistic and often anti–Semitic conspiracy theories. Other flamboyant demagogues such as "Pitchfork Ben" Tillman of South Carolina exploited rural anger for their personal political ambitions. Thus, with a mixture of contempt and fear, critics called the rural reformers "crackpot radicals" and "hayseed socialists."

By Gilded Age standards, agrarian demands were indeed radical, even though most have since been adopted. Many farmers called for government ownership and operation of the railroads and telegraph and telephone lines. As landowners they rejected socialism, but some did believe that transportation and communication facilities were "natural monopolies" that could only be run efficiently under centralized management and were too important to the public welfare to be in the hands of private monopolies.

The remainder of the agrarian political agenda reflected a rather realistic and moderate response to the farmers' problems. To ease their credit crisis farmers advocated an inflated, more flexible currency and the subtreasury plan. Considered by the Alliance members to be the keystone of their program, subtreasuries (federal warehouses) were to be constructed as places where farmers could store their crops until prices rose to relieve them of the pressure to sell immediately. To finance government programs farmers also called for a graduated income tax.

Believing that many of their problems could be relieved by a more responsive government, farmers called for greater popular participation in the political process. They advocated the direct election of senators, which would allow the people to elect senators instead of having state legislatures select them. They also called for initiative and referendum procedures, which would enable voters to propose legislation through petitions and enact laws by popular vote, thereby bypassing the state legislatures that seemed unwilling to act on their grievances.

Although the farmers failed to address the fundamental problem of overproduction, adoption of the agrarian demands could have relieved somewhat the agricultural distress fueling their anger. Thus the farmers became increasingly involved in political organization.

Emergence of the Populist Party

In 1890 Alliance members entered politics in the West and the South with remarkable success. Under independent party banners, western Alliance members elected a governor in Kansas, gained control of four state legislatures, and sent U.S. senators from Kansas and Nebraska. Working through the existing Democratic state parties, southern Alliance members elected four governors, 44 congressmen, and several senators.

Western Alliance farmers interpreted this success as a mandate to establish a national third party. Although at first Southerners were apprehensive, the Alliances joined hands in St. Louis to create the People's or Populist party. In July 1892 the Populist party's national convention in Omaha drafted a platform and gave its presidential nomination to James B. Weaver of Iowa, formerly a Union general and Greenback presidential candidate.

The Populist platform included all the agrarian demands: the subtreasury plan; an income tax; free coinage of silver to inflate the currency; government ownership of railroads, telephone, and telegraph; and the political reforms intended to restore government to "the hands of the people."

Most Populists were small-scale farmers in the South and West whose farms were minimally mechanized. Many relied on a single cash crop, had unsatisfactory access to credit, and lived in social isolation some distance from towns and railroads. The majority owned some land, but sizable numbers of sharecroppers and tenant farmers joined the party. Prosperous, large-scale, diversified farmers found little appeal in the party's platforms or activities.

The Populists realized the need to broaden the base of their constituency. Therefore, the Omaha platform included planks to appeal to urban workers. They advocated an eight-hour day, urged immigration restriction, opposed strikebreaking, and favored "fair and liberal" pensions to veterans. In the South some Populist leaders, such as Tom Watson of Georgia, sought to woo black voters. He told audiences of black and white farmers: "You are made to hate each other because upon that hatred is rested the keystone of the arch of financial despotism which enslaves you both."

The Populists conducted colorful campaigns, which one Nebraska Democrat called a blend of "the French Revolution and a western religious revival." Their anger fostered a revolutionary spirit that appealed to large numbers of farmers. In 1892 Weaver won more than one million popular votes—the first third-party candidate to do so—and 22 electoral votes. Although the Populists failed to carry a single southern state, it was a remarkable showing for a new party, revealing the extent of popular discontent. The next year brought the panic of 1893, which produced more discontent and gave the Populists great hopes for the election of 1896.

Depression and Turbulence in the 1890s

While the Populists made their bid for office in the election of 1892, the two major parties featured a rerun of the election of 1888. Once again Cleveland and Harrison faced each other over the issue of the tariff. The unpopular McKinley Tariff helped create a different outcome, and Cleveland entered the White House, the only president to serve two nonconsecutive terms.

The Panic of 1893

No sooner had Cleveland been inaugurated than the nation plunged into the worst depression it had yet experienced. A downturn in the European economy had caused overseas buyers to reduce their purchases of American goods, while at the same time foreign investors began to withdraw from American markets. These factors led to a serious shortage of currency, which in turn led to rapidly falling prices. There had also been serious overexpansion of the economy, especially in railroad construction. The collapse of several important railroads sent shock waves through the American economy. Confidence faltered, the stock market crashed, and banks failed.

The panic ushered in a depression in which unemployment reached 20 percent of the work force. Farm prices plummeted, and farm foreclosures reached new highs. Sharp wage cuts and massive layoffs took place in virtually every industry. Still opposed to direct federal aid, President Cleveland's only response was repeal of the Sherman Silver Purchase Act and the sale of lucrative federal bonds to a banking syndicate, headed by J. P. Morgan, aimed at protecting the nation's gold reserves.

The Democrats did pass the Wilson-Gorman Tariff in 1894, which reduced rates by 10 percent. Disappointed with the moderate cuts, reformers were appeased by a provision placing a 2 percent tax on incomes (ruled unconstitutional a year later). In the face of massive suffering, many people wanted the government to do more.

Expressions of Worker Discontent

Even before the Panic of 1893 violence in labor-management relations was on the rise. In 1892, for example, Andrew Carnegie and the Amalgamated Association of Iron and Steel Workers clashed at Carnegie's Homestead plant near Pittsburgh. In an effort to crush the union, Carnegie slashed wages, and, expecting a confrontation, he fortified his steel mills, hired strikebreakers, and employed the Pinkerton Agency to protect them.

On July 5 strikers and Pinkerton agents clashed in a battle that left ten men killed and another 70 wounded. Carnegie's manager and partner Henry Frick appealed for help to the governor of Pennsylvania, who dispatched 8,000 militiamen to Homestead to reopen the plant. In late July an anarchist named Alexander Berkman, who had no connections with the steel union, tried to assassinate Frick but only wounded him. The local and national press linked unionism with radicalism, as public support for the steel workers quickly subsided. The powerful forces of capital, government, and press had combined to defeat the strike and destroy the union.

During the depression employers frequently cut wages to preserve profits. In 1894 the workers in the Pullman plant at Chicago found their wages reduced several times while their rent for company-owned housing remained the same. When management refused to negotiate with the union, members of the American Railway Union (ARU) refused to handle any cars made in the Pullman plant. The boycott totally disrupted railroad traffic in the Midwest. When the liberal governor of Illinois, John P. Altgeld, refused to interfere, railroad executives turned to U.S. Attorney General Richard Olney, a former railroad corporation lawyer. Olney and Cleveland responded quickly, using the excuse of protecting the mails to send 2,000 troops to the Chicago area. When ARU president Eugene V. Debs defied a court injunction ordering union leaders to discontinue the strike, he was imprisoned. Federal troops managed to crush the strike, but only after bitter fighting and extensive damage to railroad property.

Such repressive force drove some workers to the political left. Prior to 1894, the Socialist Labor party had been able to muster only a small following. After the Pullman strike Eugene V. Debs emerged from prison a socialist and made socialism more respectable. Born in Indiana in 1855, Debs delivered with a Hoosier twang a version of socialism based upon distinctly American values. The movement thus acquired a fiery and effective orator. Under Debs's leadership the larger and stronger Socialist party of America began to form and directly challenge unrestrained capitalism.

The mass suffering during the depression also provoked some to urge the federal government to provide work for the unemployed. One such person was Jacob S. Coxey, an Ohio businessman who advocated putting men to work on the roads. To demand action and dramatize the plight of the unemployed, he staged a march on Washington that gained nation-wide attention. Federal authorities, however, took a dim view of such expressions of popular protest. When some of the marchers straggled into the capital on May 1, 1894, they were forcibly dispersed; their leader was arrested for walking on the grass. Once again the national government seemed out of touch with a large segment of the electorate and insensitive to its grievances.

Deteriorating Race Relations

The turbulent 1890s was also one of the worst decades of racial violence in the nation's history. The Republican party and all three branches of government deserted African Americans, and Populists failed to unite blacks and whites on the basis of class interests. Lynching increasingly became a tool for controlling both black votes and actions. Under the pretext of "maintaining law and order" vigilante mobs hanged, mutilated, and burned African Americans in increasing numbers. During the decade of the 1890s an average of two to three black southerners were lynched each week.

Attempts to limit black voting began in 1890 when Mississippi established poll taxes, literacy tests, and residency requirements. The Supreme Court displayed its disregard for black rights by upholding the so-called Mississippi Plan. Other states soon adopted similar measures. Later, to woo lower-class white voters, "grandfather" clauses were added—providing exemptions to the sons and grandsons of those who had voted prior to the Reconstruction Acts, a requirement that blacks, of course, could not meet.

Once whites stripped away black political power, discriminatory social legislation soon followed. Although segregation had long existed in a haphazard, informal way, it now became a legalized system of repression. Constitutional obstacles to this new means of racial control, such as the Fourteenth Amendment, were removed by the Supreme Court, which ruled in its 1896 *Plessy* v. *Ferguson* decision that public accommodations for blacks could be "separate but equal." With segregation legalized, southern states passed "Jim Crow" laws to require the separation of the races. Some states even passed laws prohibiting interracial checker playing and requiring textbooks used in black schools to be stored separately from those used in white schools.

The Tide Is Turned: The Election of 1896

As a new century approached, the United States seemed to be a nation torn by racial, class and regional antagonisms. The turbulence prompted one of the major parties to respond in 1896 to the popular clamor for reform, and in so doing brought the political equilibrium that had characterized the Gilded Age to an end.

The Populists had hoped to ride silver to power because of the growing popularity of the issue, but the Democrats stole their thunder by choosing William Jennings Bryan, an advocate of free silver. To nominate someone else would split the silver votes and ensure a victory for McKinley. Yet to nominate Bryan meant the loss of their identity and momentum.

Many Populists argued fervently against a union with the Democrats, who focused almost exclusively on silver at the expense of the rest of the Populist demands. In the end the Populists bit the bullet and nominated Bryan for president but chose Tom Watson for vice president rather than the Democratic choice, Arthur Sewall.

McKinley carried the popular vote 7.1 million to 6.5 million and the electoral college votes 271 to 176. The defeat of Bryan and the silver forces marked the beginning of an era of Republican dominance. Millions of disaffected Democrats joined the ranks of the Republicans, who won the presidency in seven of the nine contests between 1896 and 1928, and controlled both houses of Congress 17 of the next 20 sessions.

The Populists suffered the most from the election results: their party disappeared. Their attempt to unite farmers and laborers, blacks and whites, had failed. Like the Socialists and other radicals, the Populists were never able to recruit organized labor to forge a broadly based working-class movement because labor leaders argued that farmers' goals were not compatible with labor's interests. In the South, race proved to be more important than class, and many disillusioned white Populists such as Tom Watson became antiblack activists following their defeat.

Chronology of Key Events

1867	The Grangers, first national farmers' organization, founded
1873	Coinage Act declares that gold alone will back paper money
1875	Specie Resumption Act
1877	Southern Farmers' Alliance founded; *Munn* v. *Illinois* upholds constitutionality of state regulation of railroads
1878	Bland–Allison Act
1881	President James A. Garfield assassinated; Chester Arthur becomes twenty-first president
1883	Pendleton Act authorizes competitive examination for civil service positions
1886	*Wabash* case reverses *Munn* v. *Illinois* decision
1887	Congress establishes the Interstate Commerce Commission
1890	Founding of the National American Woman Suffrage Association; Congress passes Sherman Antitrust Act; Sherman Silver Purchase Act allows U. S. to issue paper money based on silver; Mississippi Plan to restrict black voting through poll taxes, literacy tests, and residency requirements
1892	Populist party formed; Homestead strike
1893	Panic of 1893; severe economic depression
1894	Pullman strike; Coxey's Army marches on Washington to protest unemployment
1895	*United States* v. *E. C. Knight Co.* weakens Sherman Antitrust Act
1896	*Plessy* v. *Ferguson;* William McKinley elected twenty-fifth president

Americans had come to a turning point in 1896 and chose the conservative path. The Republican administration quickly raised duties with the Dingley Tariff of 1897, and three years later officially put the nation on the gold standard by requiring all money to be redeemable in gold. Ironically, new discoveries of gold and more efficient extracting methods brought the inflation that farmers had sought from silver. Prosperity began to return, which undermined the agrarian movement as rising prices eased farmers' economic distress.

Conclusion

After Reconstruction, national politics entertained the masses rather than solved the emerging problems of industrialization. The two major parties differed little in their laissez-faire support of business and seemed more concerned with the spoils of office than with the suffering of farmers, workers, and minorities. Finally, a challenge to unrestrained capitalism arose from the losers in the race toward economic modernization. Led by disgruntled farmers, the Populists sought to unite large segments of the American population on the basis of class interest. As a result, the election of 1896 provided a real choice for American voters.

The conservative victory brought about the death of Populism, but many of the problems the farmers addressed in the 1890s continued into the twentieth century. Time vindicated their demands. A large number of their rejected solutions were adopted in the first two decades of the new century; most of their remaining agenda was enacted in modified form during the New Deal of the 1930s.

Suggestions for Further Reading

For general overviews of America during the Gilded Age see Sean Dennis Cashman, *America in the Gilded Age* (1984); John A. Garraty, *The New Commonwealth* (1968); Alan Trachtenberg, *The Incorporation of America* (1982).

Books that focus on political developments during the late nineteenth century include John M. Dobson, *Politics in the Gilded Age* (1972); Michael E. McGerr, *The Decline of Popular Politics* (1986); H. Wayne Morgan, *From Hayes to McKinley* (1969); Leonard D. White, *The Republican Era* (1958); R. Hal Williams, *Years of Decision* (1978).

For studies of women's issues consult Eleanor Flexner, *Century of Struggle,* rev. ed. (1975); Margaret Forster, *Significant Sisters* (1984); Aileen Kraditor, *The Ideas of the Woman's Suffrage Movement* (1965).

The currency debate is the focus of Walter T. K. Nugent, *Money and American Society* (1968); Allen Weinstein, *Prelude to Populism* (1970). For more on the spoils system and corruption in government see Ari Hoogenboom, *Outlawing the Spoils* (1961); Gerald McFarland, *Mugwumps, Morals and Politics* (1975); John C. Sproat, *The Best Men* (1968).

The Populist movement is analyzed in Lawrence Goodwyn, *Democratic Promise: The Populist Moment in America* (1976). Other valuable studies of the agrarian revolt include Steven Hahn, *The Roots of Southern Populism* (1983); Robert McMath, Jr., *Populist Vanguard* (1975); Norman Pollack, *The Populist Response to Industrial America* (1962).

Race relations during the Gilded Age are covered in Howard N. Rabinowitz, *Race Relations in the Urban South* (1978); C. Vann Woodward, *The Strange Career of Jim Crow,* rev. ed. (1974).

Chapter *21*

Imperial America, 1870–1900

D reams of expansion came easily to Americans during the 1800s. For most of the century they expanded westward, moving into Texas and Kansas, pushing across the Great Plains, and occupying California and the Pacific Northwest. But they did not restrict their dreams to the millions of acres between Mexico and Canada. They cast covetous eyes toward Central America and the islands of the Caribbean and the Pacific. Plans to annex Nicaragua, Cuba, Santo Domingo, the Virgin Islands, Hawaii, and Samoa fired politicians' imaginations. Before the Civil War the debate over slavery blocked these larger expansionist efforts. Once the Union was preserved, however, expansionists returned to their plans with revived energy and enthusiasm.

President Ulysses S. Grant had a pet expansionist project of his own. He eyed the Dominican Republic, the eastern two-thirds of the Caribbean island of Santo Domingo. Annexation, he maintained, would benefit America in a number of ways. The island was rich in mineral resources, possessed an important natural harbor, and its inhabitants were eager to buy American products. Most important for Grant, who was ever mindful of America's race problem, the Dominicans were black. The island could serve as a haven for black Americans, a retreat from Ku Klux Klan harassment.

With so much to gain, Grant put his full political weight behind annexation. His conduct was less than presidential. First, he sent his personal secretary and close friend Orville Babcock to Santo Domingo on a "fact-finding" mission. Unimpressed by the islanders, Babcock found them "indolent and ignorant." Nonetheless, he concluded that the Dominican Republic was a commercial and strategic prize worthy of annexation. Moreover, Buenaventura Baez, the unscrupulous president of the republic, was anxious to sell his country so he could afford to move to Paris or Madrid because, as Babcock noted, the Dominican Republic was "a dull country." The promise of American dollars had convinced Baez that his country should belong to the United States.

Unrest at home added fuel to Baez's willingness to sell. His government was threatened both by neighboring Haiti and a strong force of Dominican rebels. So difficult was Baez's position that Babcock had to order a United States Navy ship to protect the Baez government during the annexation negotiations, which were completed in the late fall of 1869.

The treaty of annexation, however, would have to be ratified by the Senate, a body more difficult to satisfy than Baez's government. Deciding to forego presidential protocol, Grant made a personal visit to the home of Charles Sumner, the chairman of the Senate Foreign Relations Committee. After listening to the president's arguments in favor of annexation,

Sumner promised his "most careful and candid consideration." Grant departed for his short walk back to the White House believing he had won Sumner's full support.

After consideration and considerable investigation, Sumner decided that the entire annexation scheme was distasteful. He was disturbed by Babcock's and Baez's unethical financial dealings and was enraged that the United States Navy had been used to keep the Dominican president in power. Not a person to mince words, Sumner accused Grant of being "a colossus of ignorance." By a vote of five to two, the Foreign Relations Committee voiced its disapproval of the treaty of annexation.

Grant was furious, and refused to concede defeat. He hinted that if the United States did not take the Dominican Republic, one of the European powers would, and he reported the results of a rigged plebiscite in which the Dominicans supposedly supported annexation by the suspiciously lopsided vote of 15,169 to 11. Grant's efforts to gain support failed, however, and on June 30, 1870, the Senate rejected the treaty.

The failed attempt to annex the Dominican Republic is important for the themes it underscored. It demonstrated both the desire for expansion by the president and his advisers and the power of Congress in foreign affairs. During the remainder of the century the scenario would be repeated again and again, often with different results. Gradually, presidents wrested more control over foreign affairs from Congress, which for its part came to accept a more expansionist foreign policy. As presidents and Congress found common ground, America expanded outward into the Caribbean and the Pacific. The expansion took different forms. Sometimes the United States annexed countries outright. Other times America remained content to exercise less forceful control over nominally independent countries. The results were the same. The United States ultimately acquired an overseas empire and expanded its influence over the Western Hemisphere.

Congressional Control and the Reduction of American Power

Foreign Service

In 1869 when Grant took office, congressmen and other Americans held the State Department and the diplomatic service in low esteem. Once regarded as a stepping-stone to the presidency, politicians increasingly viewed the post of secretary of state as a reward for outstanding party men or the refuge for defeated presidential aspirants. Even the diplomats themselves did not escape criticism. Some politicians considered the foreign service "a nursery of snobs" and viewed diplomats as an expensive, nearly useless luxury. A few reformers even advocated the abolition of the foreign service, arguing that international lawyers could be hired to handle really serious international crises.

The irreverent treatment of the State Department reflected the national mood. Concerns over the currency, civil service reform, Reconstruction, the tariff, the Indian problem, and railroad building dwarfed interest in foreign affairs. During the 1870s and 1880s, when a powerful Congress largely dictated foreign policy, the spirit of Washington's Farewell Address, which advised America to steer clear of foreign entanglements, and the Monroe Doctrine, which elevated isolationism to a national obsession, guided the country. Separated from a powerful Europe by the Atlantic, Congress saw no reason to spend time or money on the State Department or foreign affairs.

Using its control over the budget as a sword, Congress trimmed the State Department to the bone. In 1869 Congress allowed the State Department a paltry 31 clerks; by 1881 presidential efforts had succeeded in raising that number to a still inadequate 50.

Reduction of the Military

The sword that trimmed the State Department was also used on America's army and navy once the Civil War had ended. In 1865 the United States had the largest and perhaps the most powerful navy in the world. To be sure, it was a ragtag navy, but it numbered 971 vessels, ranging from the powerful *Monitor*-class ironclads to modest yachts. Within nine months of Appomattox, the fleet was reduced to 29. While the world's best navies converted to steel and steam, American naval leaders remained tied to wood and sails.

As Congress watched unconcerned, the navy declined intellectually as well as physically. The men appointed as the secretaries of the navy were mostly political appointees who knew little and cared less about ships. There were far too many officers, and with promotions based strictly upon length of service, any officer who lived long enough could become an admiral. Thus the system almost guaranteed poor leadership.

The power and effectiveness of the army were similarly reduced. Demobilization after the Civil War occurred quickly and haphazardly. In May 1865 the army contained 1,034,064 volunteers; by November 1866 only 11,043 remained in uniform. Eventually even the number of regular troops was reduced until, by the end of Reconstruction, the army was a skeleton of its former self. In 1876 the maximum strength stood at 27,442 troops.

Certainly in 1876 the United States did not need an active foreign service and a powerful army and navy to secure its borders. No countries threatened America. Geography defended the United States, and the European balance of power discouraged foolish European designs on any part of the Western Hemisphere. At the same time, the relative weakness of its foreign service, army, and navy discouraged the United States from attempting to extend its influence beyond its own borders. All in all, most congressmen were entirely happy with the situation.

Seward's Dreams

Not everyone in government agreed with congressional leadership in foreign affairs. William Henry Seward was among those who called for a more forceful, expansionist policy. While serving as secretary of state under Lincoln and Johnson, Seward advocated vigorous expansionism and dreamed of an American empire that would dominate the Pacific and Caribbean basins. He negotiated with Denmark to purchase the Danish West Indies (Virgin Islands), with Russia to buy Alaska, and with Santo Domingo for the Dominican harbor of Samana Bay. In addition, his plan for an American empire encompassed Haiti, Cuba, Iceland, Greenland, Honduras's Tigre Island, and Hawaii.

Congress, which did not share Seward's vision, balked. During Seward's term, America did acquire the Midway Islands in the middle of the Pacific Ocean, but few Americans even noticed. The purchase of Alaska in 1867 drew more comments, most of which were negative. Some senators claimed that $7.2 million was too much money for a frozen wasteland that only Eskimos and seals could love. But in the end the Senate, influenced by a few well-placed bribes, reluctantly ratified the treaty.

Articulate and aggressive anti-imperialists blocked the remainder of Seward's dreams during the late 1860s and the 1870s, when congressional power was at a high tide. Seward and President Andrew Johnson were no match for Congress, which consistently found other issues more pressing than foreign affairs. Some congressmen pushed for money to enact a fair Reconstruction policy. Others freely gave money to railroad construction companies and Union veterans to bolster their own reelection chances. But they drew America's purse strings tight when confronted with most expansionist schemes.

The Spirit of American Greatness

Although Congress was reluctant to endorse expansionist schemes, during the last third of the nineteenth century many citizens had become convinced that the United States had to adopt a more aggressive and forceful

During the turn of the century, the United States increasingly tried to influence world affairs. Here, Uncle Sam assumes a forceful attitude.

foreign policy. Their reasons varied. Some believed expansion would be good for American business. Others felt the United States had a duty to spread its way of life to less fortunate countries. Still others maintained that economic and strategic security required that the country acquire overseas bases. Behind all these arguments, however, rested a common assumption: the United States was a great country, and it should start acting the part.

American Exceptionalism

The idea of American exceptionalism—that the nation houses God's chosen people—has deep roots in the country's history. Puritan concepts of "a city upon a hill" mixed easily with talk of the greatness of republicanism and democracy and the manifest destiny of America. The teachings of

Social Darwinists added "scientific proof" to the concept of American exceptionalism. With such Darwinian phrases as "natural selection" and "survival of the fittest," American intellectuals praised the course of American history.

There was, however, a dark side to American exceptionalism, and this too many Americans were quick to endorse: if white Anglo-Saxon Americans were biologically superior, then other races and other nations had to be inferior. During the late nineteenth century such Social Darwinists as Herbert Spencer in England and John Fiske in the United States helped to make racism intellectually acceptable. Catering to white audiences, Social Darwinists advanced one pseudoscientific theory after another to "prove" the superiority of Anglo-Saxons.

From the idea of superiority to the acceptance of domination was a short step. If Americans were God's chosen people, why shouldn't they dominate and uplift less fortunate countries and peoples? This was the question posed by advocates of a more aggressive American foreign policy.

Sense of Duty

Religious leaders noted the duty that American exceptionalism implied. Talk of the "white man's burden" was rife during the period. Protestant missionaries carried their faith and beliefs to the far corners of the world. In addition to preaching salvation and saving souls, they also extolled the virtues of American civilization, which included everything from democracy and rule by law to sanitation, material progress, sewing machines, and cotton underwear. Defining good and bad, progress and savagery by American standards, they attempted to alter native customs and beliefs to conform to a single American model.

Popular writer and religious leader Reverend Josiah Strong voiced what other missionaries and true believers acted upon when he wrote: "The Anglo-Saxon is the representative of two great ideas . . . civil liberty [and] a pure *spiritual* Christianity." These two ideas, he added, are destined to elevate all humankind, and "the Anglo-Saxon . . . is divinely commissioned to be . . . his brother's keeper."

Search for Markets

Strong's message was not lost on the business leaders of America. They fully agreed that missionaries should preach the benefits of American material progress as well as the glories of the Protestant faith. Looking south toward Latin America and west toward Asia, American businesspeople and farmers

Many foreign missionaries sought to unite the people of the world by extolling the virtues of Western civilization.

saw vast virgin markets for their industrial and agricultural surpluses as well as endless sources of raw materials. Sensing that American markets, filled with low-paid workers, offered few new opportunities, they entertained fabulous visions of hungry Latin Americans and shoeless Chinese.

Although the United States had become the leading industrial and agricultural country in the world, domestic consumption did not keep pace with galloping production. In addition, throughout the period the government pursued tight-money policies, and the real income of laborers made only modest gains. The result was a boom and bust economy that witnessed spectacular growth as well as severe depressions.

In part, the United States was a victim of its own spectacular success. Increased production without increased consumption led only to glutted markets and falling prices. Increasingly, farmers and industrialists looked toward foreign markets. Too often, export trade spelled the difference between prosperity and bankruptcy. Although American businesspeople and bankers had yet to develop overseas marketing networks and foreign branch banks to market their goods and finance sales, they clearly saw the need for such additions. The future of America, many economic leaders believed, would be determined by the ability of the government to find and secure overseas markets.

During the depression years the lure of foreign trade proved particularly strong. Depressions meant farm foreclosures and industrial unemployment, problems that led to social unrest. The Grange and Populist movements, the two largest agrarian revolts, and such labor confrontations as the violent railroad strikes of 1877, the Haymarket riot of 1886, and the Pullman strike of 1894 occurred during lean economic times. For many Americans the issue was simple: the United States must acquire foreign markets or face economic hardship and revolution at home.

The State Department was in full agreement. Both William Henry Seward and his successor as secretary of state during the Grant administration, Hamilton Fish, believed firmly that the United States needed new markets. Seward especially coveted the lucrative markets of Asia, and he wanted the United States to acquire islands in the Pacific as stepping-stones toward that prize. Furthermore, American economic control, he believed, should be extended to include Canada and Latin America. Although both Seward and Fish had to contend with a cautious, isolationist Congress, several important strides toward the Asian markets were made during their terms in office.

During the late 1870s and 1880s economic hard times quickened the search for new markets. The United States successfully negotiated bilateral reciprocity treaties with many Latin American countries. These treaties lowered tariffs and thus stimulated trade between the United States and Latin America.

By the mid-1880s efforts in favor of expansion combined with economic and social problems at home convinced Congress to reevaluate its isolationist policies. The time had come to look at our oceans not as defensive barriers but as paths toward new markets and increased prosperity. A final problem, however, remained. America's navy and merchant marine seemed woefully unfit for the challenge.

The New Navy

If the United States hoped to compete for world markets, it had to upgrade its navy. During the 1880s advocates of a new navy moved Congress to action, and by 1890 great gains had been made. But serious problems remained. While England and Germany were building large, heavily armored battleships, the ships built by the United States were lightly armored, fast cruisers, inadequate for any major naval engagement. In 1890 Congress appropriated money for the construction of three first-class battleships and a heavy cruiser. It was the beginning of a new, offensive navy for the United States.

Talk of empire, navy, trade, and national greatness came together in 1890 in the publication of a monumentally important book, *The Influence of Sea Power upon History,* by Captain Alfred Thayer Mahan. According to Mahan, naval power was the key to national greatness. He attempted to demonstrate that countries rise to world dominance by expanding their foreign commerce and protecting that commerce with a strong navy. Without a powerful navy, Mahan emphasized, a nation could never enjoy full prosperity and security; in short, no nation could ever hope to be a world power.

Shaping Public Opinion

Mahan's writings were applauded by American politicians and business-people who felt it was time for the United States to assume the rights and responsibilities of world power status. These men of wealth, education, and influence like Henry Cabot Lodge, Theodore Roosevelt, Albert J. Beveridge, and John Hay were powerful politicians and administrators. They believed that the United States was destined to be the greatest of world powers. Increasingly after 1890, these and other men of like mind dominated and shaped America's foreign policy.

The expansionists often shared common experiences and beliefs. Most were prosperous Republicans from old-line American families, and most had traveled abroad widely. Anglo-Saxon by heritage, they tended to be ardent Anglophiles, full of praise for Great Britain's imperial efforts. They believed that the United States should join "Mother England" in administering to the "uncivilized" corners of the globe.

Lodge and other expansionists called for a bold foreign policy. They advocated the construction of a canal through Central America to allow American ships to move between the Atlantic and Pacific oceans more rapidly. To protect the canal, the United States would have to exert control over Cuba and the other strategically located Caribbean islands. The United States, they believed, also needed coaling stations and naval bases across the Pacific. Secure bases in Hawaii, Guam, Wake Island, and the Philippines would allow the United States to exploit the seemingly limitless China market. Finally, a powerful navy would have to protect the entire American empire.

The Emergence of Aggression in American Foreign Policy

Expansionists talked loudly about peace, but their rhetoric was couched in aggressive language. "To be prepared for war is the most effectual means to promote peace," said Theodore Roosevelt. The more they talked about peace, the closer war seemed. It is not surprising that the United States launched a more belligerent foreign policy at the same time it was building and launching more powerful ships. The two developments originated from the same source: a ready acceptance of force as the final arbiter of international disputes. This acceptance of force almost led to several wars in the late nineteenth century and culminated in the Spanish-American War in 1898. The Spanish-American War was not an aberrant event. Rather, it was the result of a more aggressive American foreign policy, one aimed at acquiring both world respect and an empire.

Confronting the Germans in Samoa

Changing American attitudes toward foreign policy were first seen in Samoa, a group of 14 volcanic islands lying 4,000 miles from San Francisco along the trade route to Australia. Throughout the nineteenth century American whalers stopped in Samoa, the harbors of which had often provided refuge for ships caught in Pacific storms. If the natives were quarrelsome among themselves, they were exceptionally friendly with Americans.

The U.S. government's interest was decidedly more mercenary. In 1878 the Senate ratified a treaty granting the United States rights to a naval station at the harbor of Pago Pago. Unfortunately for American interests, England and especially Germany were also determined to influence events on the islands.

Like the United States, Germany was just beginning to think in terms of empire. German Chancellor Otto von Bismarck decided that Samoa should belong to Germany. England sided with the "iron chancellor." President Cleveland firmly disagreed. Germany and the United States were set on a collision course.

When a conference between the three countries held in Washington in 1887 failed to solve the problem, war seemed inevitable. Neither Germany nor the United States had much money invested in the islands, but both felt their national pride was at stake. "We must show sharp teeth," remarked Bismarck. Nature, however, had the most powerful weapon. On the morning of March 16, 1889, a typhoon swept across Samoa, destroying the American and German warships anchored in Apia harbor.

The violent winds seemed to calm the ruffled emotions of the United States and Germany. That same year, Germany, the United States, and England met for a conference in Berlin, and without consulting the Samoans, they decided to partition the islands. Everyone seemed satisfied—except the Samoans who were deprived of their independence and saddled with an unpopular king. The plan lasted until 1899, when Germany and the United States ended the facade of Samoan independence and officially made colonies of the islands. The United States gained Tutuila, with the harbor of Pago Pago, and several smaller islands. Many expansionists believed that America's aggressive stand against Germany had paid handsome dividends.

Teaching Chile a Lesson

American expansionists had something to show for their confrontation with Germany over Samoa. Pago Pago was, after all, an ideal coaling station for ships running between San Francisco and Australia. American troubles with Chile, however, are more difficult to understand, since trade and strategic policy played small roles. More than anything else, touchy pride and jingoism pushed the United States toward war with Chile.

Had people not died, the background to the confrontation would have been amusing. In 1891 a revolutionary faction, which the United States had opposed, gained control of the Chilean government and initiated a foreign policy that was unfriendly toward America. Shortly thereafter, on October 16, 1891, an American cruiser, the *Baltimore,* anchored off the coast of Chile, sent about 100 members of its crew ashore on leave at Valparaiso. Many of the sailors did what sailors normally do on leave: they retired to a local saloon and drank. As the men left the saloon, a riot broke out. An angry, anti-American mob attacked the sailors, killing two and injuring 16. To make matters worse, the Chilean police, who had done nothing to halt the fighting, carried the surviving Americans off to jail.

It was an unfortunate affair, and the United States loudly protested, demanding a formal apology and "prompt and full reparation." The Chilean government refused. Incensed, President Benjamin Harrison threatened to break off diplomatic relations—a serious step toward war—unless the United States received an immediate apology. The American public supported Harrison's tough stand. Finally the Chilean government backed down. It apologized for the attack on the sailors and paid an indemnity of $75,000. The threat of force had again carried the day. Advocates of the new navy, a jingoistic press, and aggressively nationalistic Americans cheered.

The Hawaiian Pear

Throughout the late nineteenth century Hawaii figured prominently in American foreign policy planning. Earlier in the century, the islands had been a favorite place for many American missionaries, who went to Hawaii to spread Christianity and ended up settling and raising their families in the tropical paradise. More important still was the location of the islands. Not only were they ideally situated along the trade routes to Asia, but they offered a perfect site for protecting the Pacific sea lanes to the American

West Coast and the potential locations of an isthmus canal. In Hawaii, religious, economic, and strategic concerns met in complete harmony

By the mid-1880s expansionists who dreamed of Hawaii found willing allies in Congress. In 1884 a treaty between Hawaii and the United States set aside Pearl Harbor for the exclusive use of the American navy. After some debate the Senate ratified the treaty in 1887, and Hawaii officially became part of American strategic planning. By that time the islands were already tied economically to the United States. An 1875 treaty had allowed Hawaiians to sell their sugar in the United States duty-free, giving them a two cents per pound advantage over other foreign producers. The legislation encouraged American speculators to invest in Hawaiian sugar and to import Chinese and Japanese laborers to the islands to work on the large plantations. The investments returned incredibly high dividends, and for a time business boomed.

Problems arose suddenly in 1890. The McKinley Tariff Act removed all tariffs on foreign sugar and protected domestic sugar producers by awarding American sugar a bounty of two cents per pound. Hawaiian sugar prices plummeted, costing island producers about $12 million. U.S.-Hawaiian relations worsened when Queen Liliuokalani acceded to the throne in 1891. Adopting a strong anti-American policy, she wanted to purge American influences in Hawaii and disenfranchise all white men except those married to native women.

The white population in Hawaii reacted quickly. On January 17, 1893, white islanders overthrew her government. Supported by the American minister in Honolulu and aided by American sailors and marines, the revolution was fast, almost bloodless, and successful. The U.S. minister proclaimed Hawaii an American protectorate and wired his superiors in Washington that "the Hawaiian pear is now fully ripe, and this is the golden hour for the United States to pluck it."

The revolutionaries in Hawaii favored prompt American annexation of the islands. In Washington the Harrison administration, which was due to leave office on March 4, agreed. It negotiated a treaty of annexation with "indecent haste" and sent it to the Senate for ratification.

Before the Senate could ratify the treaty, Cleveland took office. An anti–imperialist, Cleveland had grave misgivings about the revolution, America's reaction, and the treaty. Five days after his inauguration, he recalled the treaty from the Senate and sent a special agent to Hawaii to investigate the entire affair. Upon learning that the majority of native Hawaiians opposed annexation, Cleveland killed the treaty.

This did not end the controversy. A white American minority continued to govern Hawaii. To correct the situation, Cleveland sent another representative to Hawaii to convince the new government to step down and allow Queen Liliuokalani to return to the throne, but Sanford B. Dole, president of a large Hawaiian pineapple corporation, refused. "Queen Lil" did not help matters by refusing to promise full amnesty for the revolutionaries if she were returned to power, vowing instead to behead those involved in the affair. In the end, Cleveland washed his hands of the entire matter, and the revolutionaries proclaimed an independent Hawaiian republic on July 4, 1894. Four years later, during the Spanish-American War, the United States finally annexed Hawaii.

Facing Down the British

Potentially the most serious conflict the United States faced during the 1890s originated in a border dispute between Venezuela and British Guiana. For almost 50 years this dispute remained peacefully unsettled, but the discovery of gold in the jungle region in the 1880s increased the importance of the issue. It was a rich deposit, and both Britain and Venezuela wanted it for their own. In response to Venezuelan requests for help, several times the United States offered to arbitrate the matter, and each time Britain refused the offer.

By June 1895 Cleveland and his new secretary of state, Richard Olney, had decided that Britain's actions were in violation of the spirit, if not the letter, of the Monroe Doctrine. In a strongly worded message to Great Britain, Olney affirmed U.S. sovereignty in the Western Hemisphere, and demanded that Britain submit the dispute to arbitration, hinting that the United States might intervene militarily if its wishes were not honored.

Britain waited four months to reply to Olney's note, and then answered, in effect, that the dispute did not involve either the United States or the Monroe Doctrine. Olney and the president were furious. In a special message to Congress, Cleveland asked for funds to establish a commission to determine the actual Venezuelan boundary, and he insisted that he would use force if necessary to maintain that boundary against any aggressors. Both houses of Congress unanimously approved Cleveland's request. The excitement of war was in the air.

America's bellicose reaction surprised British officials. England certainly did not want war, particularly at that time when it was becoming involved in a conflict in South Africa. It allowed a commission to arbitrate the dispute. In the end, the tribunal gave Britain most of the land it claimed.

America, however, felt it was the real winner. Cleveland had faced the British lion and won. The Monroe Doctrine and American prestige soared to new heights. More important for the future, Cleveland's actions, coupled with his handling of the Hawaiian revolution, significantly increased the power of the president over foreign affairs. Relations between the United States and Britain would quickly improve, and relations between America and Venezuela would rapidly deteriorate, but future presidents would not soon relinquish their control over foreign policy.

The War for Empire

During the Venezuela crisis and throughout the 1890s many Americans seemed openly to invite and look forward to the prospect of war. Viewed as a whole, it was a decade of strident nationalism and aggressive posturing. It was also a troubled and violent decade. Racked by the depression of 1893, frustrated by the problems created by monopolies and overproduction, and plagued by internal strife, Americans turned on each other, often with violent results. Strikes in Pullman, Illinois, and Homestead, Pennsylvania, saw laborers battle federal and state authorities. Populist protest dramatized the widening gulf between city and country, rich and poor. Anarchists and socialists talked about the need for violent solutions to complex problems.

Popular culture in America reflected this aggressive mood. Americans looked to arenas of conflict for their heroes. They glorified boxers like the great John L. Sullivan, and they cheered as violence increased on the Ivy League football fields. They admired body-builders like Bernard Macfadden, who declared, "Weakness Is a Crime." And in the parlors of the wealthy, Teddy Roosevelt stressed, "Cowardice in a race, as in an individual, is the unpardonable sin." Between Sullivan and Roosevelt, and the Americans that admired both men, was a bond forged by the love of violence and power.

This attitude led to the glorification of war and jingoistic nationalism. In public schools throughout the country administrators instituted daily flag salutes and made the recitation of the new pledge of allegiance mandatory. Even the popular music of the day, such as John Philip Sousa's "Stars and Stripes Forever" (1897), had a particularly martial quality and captured the aggressive, patriotic, and boisterous mood of the country.

As the disputes with Germany, Chile, and Great Britain demonstrated, neither the American people nor its leaders feared war. The horrors of the Civil War were dying with the generation that had known them. A younger generation of men, filled with romantic and idealized conceptions of battle and heroism, now openly sought a war of its own. In Washington some politicians even began to view war as a way to unite the country, to quell the protests of angry farmers and laborers.

The Cuban Revolution

In 1895 an independence revolt broke out in Cuba. Indirectly the United States had contributed to the turmoil that gripped the island; one year earlier Congress had passed the Wilson-Gorman Tariff, which raised the duty on foreign sugar, thus crippling the island's most important industry and causing great economic hardship. From the start, Americans expressed far more than casual interest in the rebellion. American businesses had invested over $50 million in Cuba, and the annual trade between the two countries totaled almost $100 million. Overall, however, economics played a relatively unimportant role in forming America's attitude toward the revolution.

Humanitarianism was a far more important factor. Americans cheered the underdog. In Cuba's valiant fight they saw a reenactment of their own war for independence. And the resourceful Cubans made sure that Americans stayed well supplied with stories of Spanish atrocities and Cuban heroism. The Cuban junta (central revolutionary committee) established bases in New York City and Tampa, Florida, and daily provided American newspapers with stories aimed at sympathetic American hearts.

Not all the stories were false. The Cuban—and Spanish—suffering was real enough. Unable to defeat the Spanish army in the field, Cuban revolutionaries resorted to guerrilla tactics. They burned sugarcane fields and blew up mills. They destroyed railroad tracks and bridges. They vowed to win their independence or destroy Cuba in the process. Supported by the populace, the guerrillas succeeded in turning Cuba into an economic and military nightmare for Spanish officials.

In 1896 Spain sent Governor-General Valeriano Weyler y Nicolau to Cuba to crush the rebellion. A man of ruthless clarity, he understood the nature of guerrilla warfare. Guerrillas could not be defeated by conventional engagements; their weapons were patience and endurance and popular support. Weyler knew this, and he decided to fight the guerrillas on their own terms.

His first plan was to rob the guerrillas of their base of support, the rural villages and the sympathetic peasants. He divided the island into military districts and relocated Cubans into guarded camps. He forced more than a half million Cubans from their homes and crowded them into shabbily constructed and unsanitary camps. The food was bad, the water worse. Disease spread with frightful speed and horrifying results. Perhaps 200,000 Cubans died in the camps as Weyler earned the sobriquet "the Butcher."

The Yellow Press

In the United States reports of the suffering Cuban masses filled the front pages of newspapers. In New York City William Randolph Hearst's *New*

York Journal and Joseph Pulitzer's *New York World* used the junta's lurid stories as ammunition in a newspaper war for increased circulation. Reporters freely engaged in "yellow journalism," exaggerating conditions and sensationalizing stories that were in truth depressingly sad and inhumane. Such coverage not only biased American opinion against Spain; it also sold newspapers. When Hearst bought the *Journal* in 1895 it had a daily circulation of 77,000 copies; by the summer of 1898 sales had increased to more than 1.5 million daily.

"Yellow journalism" persuaded many Americans to call for U.S. intervention in the Cuban Revolution. Grover Cleveland, however, was not easily moved by newspaper reports. His administration wanted to protect American interests in Cuba, but was dead set against any sort of military intervention in the conflict, and tried instead to convince Spain to grant "home rule." Unprepared to move beyond vague warnings, Cleveland passed the Cuban problems in 1897 to his successor William McKinley. Like Cleveland, McKinley deplored war. Before he would even consider military intervention, McKinley was determined to exhaust every peaceful alternative.

As many influential Americans called for U.S. intervention, McKinley worked diplomatically to end the fighting. Rather than inflame public opinion, he attempted to remove the issue from public debate. In his inaugural address, for example, he did not even mention Cuba. For a time it appeared that his efforts would succeed. In October 1897 a new government in Spain moved toward granting more autonomy to Cuba. It removed Weyler and promised to end his hated reconcentration program.

Spain moved with glacial slowness, only halfheartedly committed to reform. In Cuba the bloodshed continued, and pressure on McKinley to take stronger action mounted. In May 1897 he dispatched a trusted adviser, William J. Calhoun, to Cuba to provide him with an independent report of conditions on the island. The report confirmed the grim picture presented in American newspapers. "The country was wrapped in the stillness of death and the silence of desolation," Calhoun observed.

In early February 1898, William Randolph Hearst acquired with the help of the Cuban junta a private letter from Enrique Dupuy de Lôme, the Spanish minister in the United States, to a Spanish friend in Cuba. Reprinted on the front page of the *Journal,* the letter contained de Lôme's unguarded and undiplomatic opinion of McKinley. De Lôme called McKinley "weak and a bidder for the admiration of the crowd." Even worse, De Lôme suggested that Spain's new peace policy was mere sham and propaganda.

The letter hit the American public like a bombshell. Although de Lôme resigned, America was in no mood to forget and forgive. Less than one week later a second event rocked America. On the still evening of February 15 an explosion ripped apart the *Maine,* a U.S. battleship anchored in Havana harbor. The ship quickly sank, killing over 250 officers and men. An investigation in 1898 ruled that an external explosion had sunk the *Maine.* Although a recent study blamed the sinking on an internal explosion, in truth, no one knows the definitive answer. At the time, however, Americans were not in an impartial or philosophical mood. Through the streets of American cities went the cry, "'Remember the *Maine!* To Hell with Spain!'"

War was in the air, and it is doubtful if McKinley or any other president could have long preserved peace. Congress was ready for war, and on March 8 approved McKinley's request for $50 million in defense appropriations without a single dissenting vote. Although McKinley continued to work for a diplomatic solution to the crisis, his efforts lacked his earlier energy and optimism. By early April diplomacy had reached its end.

The sinking of the *Maine* was one of the major events leading to the Spanish-American War. It is still uncertain who or what caused the explosion that sank the ship.

On April 11 an exhausted McKinley sent a virtual war message to Congress, asking for authority to use force to end the Cuban war. On April 19 Congress officially acted. It proclaimed Cuba's independence, called for Spain's evacuation, and authorized McKinley to use the army and navy to achieve those ends. In the Teller Amendment, Congress added that the United States had no intention of annexing Cuba for itself. For some Americans it was a great and noble decision. For the men and boys who would have to fight the battles, the war would soon seem considerably less noble.

The Spanish-American War

No simple explanation can account for the Spanish-American War. Economics and imperial ambitions certainly played a part, but no more so than did humanitarianism and selfless concern for the suffering of others. President McKinley tried to find a peaceful solution, but he failed. Some historians and many of his contemporaries have viewed McKinley as a weak, hollow president, a messenger boy for America's financial community. Such was not the case. McKinley did have a vision—a peaceful vision—of America's role in world affairs. But the unpredictability of events and the mood of the nation were more powerful than the president.

In theory the United States had prepared for war with Spain. In 1897 the Navy Department had drawn up contingency plans for a war against Spain for the liberation of Cuba. It had envisioned a war centered mainly in the Caribbean, but the navy had plans to attack the Philippine Islands, which belonged to Spain, and even the coast of Spain, if necessary. In the Caribbean the navy planned to blockade Cuba and assist an army invasion of the island.

In reality, however, the military was not ready for war. The process of mobilizing troops was chaotic and the training given volunteers was inadequate. In addition, the army faced severe supply shortages. Volunteers suffered the most. They were herded into camps, often without such basic equipment as tents and mess kits. Long before they ever faced enemy guns or even saw Cuba, they battled thick wool uniforms, bad food, and deadly sanitary conditions. Far more volunteers died in stateside camps than were killed by Spanish bullets.

For black troops, regulars and volunteers, racism exacerbated already difficult conditions. Since most of the large camps were located in the South—in places such as Tampa, New Orleans, Mobile, and Chickamauga Park, Tennessee—they also had to battle Jim Crow laws and other forms of racial hostility. Once in the camps, they were given the lowest military assignments.

While mobilization was taking place, the navy moved into action. During the tense weeks before the United States went to war against Spain, Theodore Roosevelt, then acting secretary of the navy, wired his friend Commodore George Dewey, leader of America's Asiatic Squadron, to prepare for offensive operations in the Philippine Islands in the event that war against Spain was declared.

Dewey had been anxiously waiting for just that order. At the break of light on the morning of May 1, 1898, Dewey's ships destroyed Spain's Asiatic fleet in Manila Bay. It was a stunning victory. Only one American died, and he of heat prostration.

Not every victory came so easily. Closer to home, the main Spanish forces in Cuba were in control of the strategically important Santiago Bay. To defeat the Spanish it would take the combined efforts of the army and the navy. With this in mind, McKinley ordered 17,000 American troops under the command of Major General William R. Shafter from Tampa to Santiago. Delays, confused orders, and other problems slowed the process, foreshadowing future difficulties. Finally, toward the end of June, American troops landed at the ports of Daiquiri and Siboney.

From there they moved toward Santiago, but the road was little more than a rutted, dirt trail. Slowly the army moved forward, more concerned with broken wagons mired in the mud and tropical diseases than Spanish soldiers.

On July 1 American soldiers learned firsthand the horrors of battle. Blocking the American advance, Spanish troops had dug in along the San Juan Heights and the hamlet of El Caney. From the first, American plans broke down in the face of stiff Spanish opposition. U.S. troops struggled up Kettle and San Juan hills, moving very slowly and suffering alarming casualties. Although outnumbered more than ten to one, Spanish soldiers made U.S. troops pay for every foot they advanced. After America finally secured the enemy positions, correspondent Richard H. Davis wrote, "Another such victory as that of July 1 and our troops must retreat."

Shafter had neither the disposition nor the ability to lead an energetic campaign. Fortunately for him, Spain's forces in Cuba were even less ready to fight. In Santiago, Spanish soldiers faced shortages of food, water, and ammunition. On July 3 the Spanish squadron tried to break an American blockade and force its way out of Santiago Bay. The act was a suicidal move. American guns destroyed the Spanish fleet and killed some 500 Spanish sailors. Only one American died in the decisive engagement.

Little fighting remained. On July 17 the leading Spanish general in Cuba surrendered to Shafter. Timid in war, Shafter was petty in victory. He refused to permit any naval officers to sign the capitulation document, nor would he allow any Cubans to participate in the surrender negotiations and ceremonies. The Cubans who had fought so long and bravely for their independence were denied the glory of their success.

Before the full Spanish surrender, the United States extended its influence in the Caribbean. In late July, General Nelson A. Miles invaded Puerto Rico, Spain's other Caribbean colony. Without any serious resistance U.S. forces took the island. Finally, on August 12, Spain surrendered, granting Cuban independence and ceding Puerto Rico and Guam to the United States. Both countries agreed to settle the fate of the Philippines at a postwar peace conference to be held in Paris.

For America, it had been a short, successful war. Spanish bullets killed only 379 Americans, the smallest number in any of America's declared wars. Disease and other problems cost over 5,000 more lives. If the army's mobilization had been chaotic, its troops had performed heroically under fire. And the navy, which took most of the credit for winning the war, demonstrated the wisdom of its planners. Finally, the war served to bring the North and South closer together as the two sections fought alongside each other rather than against each other. All in all, many Americans agreed with U.S. Ambassador to England John Hay that it had been a "splendid little war."

There was nothing little about the consequences of the war. With the Spanish-American War the United States became an imperial power. The war increased America's appetite for overseas territories. The McKinley administration used the war to annex Hawaii and part of Samoa. In addition, at the Paris Peace Conference the United States wrested the Philippines, Puerto Rico, and Guam from Spain. Although the United States paid Spain $20 million for the Philippines, there was no question that Spain had to negotiate under duress. These new imperial possessions gave the United States strategic bases in the Caribbean and along the trade routes to Asia.

Freeing Cuba

Many Americans favored the annexation of Cuba. In the land grab that ended the war, the idealism of the Teller Amendment and the war's beginning was all but forgotten. When the war ended, U.S. troops stayed in Cuba, and the country was ruled by an American-run military government, which was to remain until "complete tranquility" and a "stable government" existed on the island. Under General Leonard Wood, the military government helped Cuba recover from its terrible conflict with Spain. Wood restored the Cuban economy and promoted reforms in the legal system, education, sanitation, and health care.

In 1903 the United States finally recognized Cuban independence—
but under certain conditions. According to the Platt Amendment of
1901, Cuba could exercise self-government, but it could sign no treaties
that might limit its independence. Should Cuban independence ever be
threatened, the Platt Amendment authorized the United States to intervene in the island's internal and external affairs. The amendment was also
written into the 1901 Cuban constitution. In short, for Cuba, independence had the look and feel of an American protectorate.

The Imperial Debate

Compared to the Philippines, Cuba was a minor problem. McKinley's decision to annex the Philippines pleased some Americans and angered
many more. Businessmen who dreamed of the rich China markets applauded McKinley's decision. Naval strategists similarly believed it was a
wise move. They argued that if the United States failed to take the Philippines, then one of the other major powers—Germany, Japan, or England—probably would. Finally, Protestant missionaries favored annexation to facilitate their evangelical efforts among the Filipinos, undeterred
by the knowledge that the Filipinos already favored Roman Catholicism.

Opposed to the annexation of the Philippines was a heterogeneous
group of Americans that included such notables as agrarian leader William
Jennings Bryan, steel magnate Andrew Carnegie, labor organizer Samuel
Gompers, and writer Mark Twain. Their reasons for being anti–imperialists were as varied as their occupations and backgrounds. Some were high-
minded idealists who believed that the Filipinos had the right to govern
themselves. Others had more selfish reasons for opposing annexation.
Samuel Gompers, for example, feared that annexation would lead to an
influx of Filipino workers into the United States and hurt the American
labor movement. Still others opposed annexation on racial grounds. The
annexation of "dependencies inhabited by ignorant and inferior races,"
noted the *Nation* editor E. L. Godkin, could only lead to trouble.

During early 1899 the imperial debate raged. Even Andrew
Carnegie's offer to write a personal check for $20 million to buy the inde-
pendence of the Philippines failed to end the debate. Ultimately, imperialists and anti–imperialists had different visions for America, and no
bridge could span the gulf between these two groups.

The issue was settled on February 6, 1899, when the Senate voted on
the Treaty of Paris. Strained tempers were evident in the tense atmosphere. For a time it appeared that the imperialists would not be able to
muster the two-thirds majority needed to ratify the treaty. Anti–imperialist William Jennings Bryan ironically saved the imperialist cause. Not

wanting to prolong the war by rejecting the treaty, he urged fellow Democrats to vote for ratification. In the close vote of 57 to 27 the Senate ratified the treaty. Undoubtedly Bryan hoped to use the issue of Philippine independence to capture the presidency in 1900, but such was not the case. With ratification of the treaty, the issue lost its sense of urgency and Americans grew tired of the debate.

The War to Crush Filipino Independence

Filipino independence, however, was not an abstract debate in the Philippines. Led by Emilio Aguinaldo, Filipinos had fought bravely against the Spanish both before and after Dewey arrived in Manila. They had no intention of allowing one colonial master to replace another. When it was clear that the United States did not have Filipino interests at heart, Aguinaldo and his followers resumed their fight for independence.

Between 1899 and 1902 American troops and Filipino revolutionaries fought an ugly and destructive colonial war. American soldiers faced a difficult task. Some did not know what they were fighting for, whose interests they were defending, or what rights they were protecting. Others regarded the Filipinos as subhuman. Black American troops fighting to destroy Filipino freedom faced an even greater and more painful

American Empire, 1900

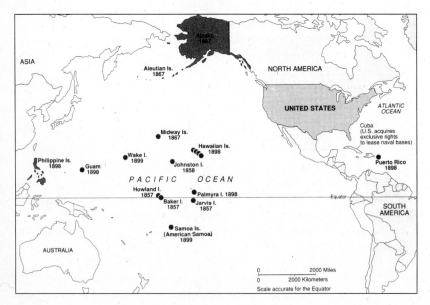

dilemma. Many black soldiers readily identified with Filipino aspirations. Although the majority of black troops professionally followed the orders of their white officers, an unusually large number deserted.

For black and white soldiers alike, however, the actual fighting was bloody and frustrating. Aguinaldo's men were efficient guerrilla warriors. They fought only when victory was certain, usually ambushing small patrols. They burned bridges, destroyed railroads, sniped, and sabotaged. They filled pits with sharpened stakes and tortured prisoners. Some American captives had their ears cut off, and many Filipinos who supported the United States were hacked to death with bolos or buried alive. Aguinaldo's hope was that eventually the game would not be worth the prize and that the American president would call his troops home.

McKinley was not about to do any such thing, and American troops proved just as vicious as the Filipino insurgents. The "water cure," used to obtain information, entailed forcing a prisoner to drink gallons of water and then emptying his stomach quickly with a kick or a punch. In one especially violent campaign U.S. troops were ordered to kill all males ten years old or older who were capable of bearing arms against the United States. Using tactics reminiscent of General Weyler's in Cuba, U.S. troops herded more than 300,000 civilians into concentration centers, where many died of disease and starvation.

Aguinaldo hoped that anti–imperialist Bryan would defeat McKinley for the presidency in 1900, but the November election dashed his hopes. Five months later American troops captured the Filipino leader. That same year McKinley sent a commission under the leadership of William Howard Taft, a federal judge, to the Philippines to improve the country's transportation, education, and public health systems. Aguinaldo's capture and the efforts of the Taft Commission doomed the Philippine independence movement. Approximately 4,200 Americans and over 20,000 Filipino soldiers had died in the struggle. Perhaps another 200,000 Filipino civilians died of famine, disease, and war-related incidents.

Keeping the Doors Open

The war against the Filipinos led to congressional investigations and shocked many Americans. Political and business leaders, however, continued to believe that the Philippines had been worth the fight because the islands were of strategic importance both as a military base and a stepping-stone toward the Asian markets. Yet policymakers understood the popular mood; they knew that the American public would be hostile to any U.S. military venture into China *just* to support trade.

To prevent other countries from carving up China, in 1899 Secretary of State John Hay issued an "open door" note. Hay believed that imperial competition in China was dangerous and economically inefficient. It stimulated costly anticolonial resistance and rebellion and gave no incentive to European countries to improve their economic efficiency. Hay's "open door" note was an attempt to prevent further European partitioning of the Manchu empire and to protect the principle of open trade in China. Under the terms of the Open Door policy, all countries active in China would respect each other's trading rights by imposing no discriminating duties and closing no ports within their spheres of influence. Although most European countries expressed little interest in Hay's Open Door policy—which, after all, benefited the United States the most—in 1900 Hay announced that the European powers had accepted his proposal.

The Chinese themselves had other plans. In the late spring of 1900 a group of Chinese nationalists, known as the Boxers, besieged the Legation Quarter in Peking, calling for the expulsion or death of all westerners in China. By late summer, 1900, a western expeditionary force had crushed the Boxer Rebellion.

These additional troops in China threatened Hay's Open Door policy. On July 3, 1900, during the tensest moment of the Boxer Rebellion, he issued a second "open door" note, calling on all western powers to preserve Chinese independence and uphold "the principle of equal and impartial trade with all parts of the Chinese Empire." Once again, few European countries paid attention to Hay's Open Door policy. Mutual distrust and the fear of provoking a general European war—more than any American plan—prevented the major European powers from dismembering China. Out of Hay's Open Door policy came the idea, held mostly in America, that the United States was China's protector. It was another example of the increasingly active role the United States had taken in world affairs.

Conclusion

Thirty-two years separated the inauguration of Ulysses S. Grant and the assassination of William McKinley, but during that generation America and the presidency changed radically. Part of the change can be attributed to growth—industry boomed, the population swelled, agricultural production increased. The growth was also psychological. During those years many Americans achieved a new sense of confidence. After 250 years of looking westward across America's seemingly limitless acres of land, they

Chronology of Key Events

1867   Russia sells Alaska to the United States

1870   Annexation of the Dominican Republic rejected by U.S. Senate

1889   Britain, Germany, and the United States agree to share control of Samoa

1890   Captain Alfred Thayer Mahan's *The Influence of Sea Power upon History* published

1893   Queen Liliuokalani of Hawaii deposed

1895   Venezuela border dispute; Cuban revolt against Spain begins

1898   *Maine* explodes in Havana harbor; Spanish-American War begins; Hawaii is annexed

1899   Filipino rebellion begins; Open Door note issued to prevent further partitioning

1900   Boxer Rebellion; Second Open Door note issued

1901   Platt Amendment

1902   Philippine revolt ends

began to look toward the oceans and consider the possibilities of a new form of expansion. They also began to follow the imperial examples of England, France, Italy, and Germany. Talk of world power, world outlook, and world responsibilities colored their rhetoric.

This outward thrust was accompanied and enhanced by the growth of presidential power. Grant worked hard for the annexation of the Dominican Republic, but Congress blocked his efforts. By the turn of the century, however, Congress clearly expected the president to lead the nation in the area of foreign affairs. Although the presidents pursued different policies, they agreed that the United States should have a greater influence in world affairs. None questioned the fundamental fact that the United States was and should be a world power.

Many questions, nevertheless, remained unanswered. What were the rights of a world power? What were its responsibilities? What were its duties? The limits and possibilities of American power had yet to be defined

and explored. The next three presidents—Roosevelt, Taft, and Wilson—
would help to define how the United States would use its new found power.

Suggestions for Further Reading

Overviews of American imperialism include Charles S. Campbell, Jr., *Transfor-*
mation of American Foreign Relations (1976); David F. Healy, *U.S. Expansionism:*
Imperialist Urge in the 1890s (1970), and *Drive to Hegemony: The United States in*
the Caribbean (1988); Walter LaFeber, *The New Empire* (1963); Thomas G. Paterson and Stephen C. Rabe, *Imperial Surge: The United States Abroad* (1992).

For studies focusing on the Spanish-American War see Philip Foner, *The*
Spanish-American-Cuban War and the Birth of American Imperialism, 2 vols.
(1972); Frank Freidel, *The Splendid Little War* (1958); Stuart C. Miller, *"Benev-*
olent Assimilation": The American Conquest of the Philippines (1982); David F.
Trask, *The War with Spain in 1898* (1981).

For information on the anti-imperialists consult Robert L. Beisner, *Twelve*
Against Empire (1968). Concerning the home front during the war see Gerald F.
Linderman, *The Mirror of War: American Society and the Spanish-American War*
(1974). Issues confronting black Americans during the age of imperialism are examined in Willard B. Gatewood, Jr., *Black Americans and the White Man's Bur-*
den (1975).

Chapter 22

The Progressive Struggle

Times had changed by 1902 when George F. Baer declared "anthracite mining is business and not a religious, sentimental or academic proposition." Those tough-minded words might have won public approval at an earlier time, but many believed that Baer, spokesperson for mine owners in Pennsylvania, was merely being pig-headed in his response to a request by John Mitchell of the United Mine Workers (UMW) for arbitration of a labor dispute. There was an unusual amount of support for the coal miners' position. Exposés had increased popular awareness of miserable working conditions, and the union's demands seemed reasonable: a nine-hour day, recognition of the union, a 10 to 20 percent increase in wages, and a fair weighing of the coal mined. Mitchell repeatedly stated the miners' willingness to accept arbitration, both before and after 50,000 miners walked out of the pits in May 1902.

Skillfully led, the coal miners stood firm month after month. By September, the nation's coal reserves were running short and prices were rising. With winter approaching, newspaper after newspaper expressed disgust with the mine owners, and some tentatively suggested government ownership of the mines.

On October 3 President Theodore Roosevelt presided over a conference in the White House attended by Mitchell, Baer, Attorney General Philander C. Knox, and other labor leaders and mine operators. Baer was still not in a mood to be cooperative. Refusing to speak directly to Mitchell, Baer urged Roosevelt to prosecute UMW leaders under the Sherman Antitrust Act and to use federal troops to break the strike, just as Cleveland had done in the 1894 Pullman strike. While Mitchell "behaved like a gentleman" according to Roosevelt, Baer remained obstinate.

When the mine owners returned to Pennsylvania, they took actions that indicated they might use force to break the strike. Roosevelt's response was to begin preparations to send 10,000 federal troops to take over and operate the mines. A compromise was soon reached, under which the miners returned to work and Roosevelt appointed a commission to arbitrate the dispute.

Decidedly pro-business, the commission's findings were essentially conservative: a 10 percent wage increase, reduction of working hours to eight hours a day for a handful of miners and to nine for most, no recognition for the union, and continuation of the traditional manner of weighing coal. The commission also suggested a 10 percent increase in the price of coal.

Nevertheless, for the first time, a president did not give knee-jerk support to business. The federal government became not merely a champion of the status quo, but also an arbiter of change. This retreat from laissez-faire principles was motivated by the demands of the middle class and

President Roosevelt, surrounded here by coal miners after their 1902 strike, set a precedent by threatening the use of force against management rather than labor.

workers. By 1902 many middle-class citizens had rejected the heavy-handed tactics of management, and sought instead a more orderly, stable, and just society through government intervention. Workers began flexing their political muscles at the ballot box, and Americans of all classes were learning the limits of individualism and joining together in organizations to accomplish their goals. National leaders such as Roosevelt began to recognize the need for change in order to preserve stable government and the capitalist system. For a variety of motives, a plethora of legislation was enacted—sometimes with unintended results.

The Progressive Impulse

Americans exalted progress as a basic characteristic of their nation's distinctiveness. Technology was reshaping the human environment in dramatic ways. In the late 1890s, as people seemed to stop and look around at their new world, much filled them with pride. Some of what they saw seemed outmoded or disruptive, but these problems appeared eminently solvable. Modern minds were explaining and harnessing natural forces. Could they not also understand and control human behavior? Could they not eliminate conflict and bring harmony to competing interests through some simple adjustments in the system? Americans increasingly answered "yes" and called themselves "progressives."

America in 1901

The twentieth century opened with a rerun of the 1896 election between William Jennings Bryan and William McKinley. Although the outcome was the same, much was different. By 1900 the crises of the 1890s had largely passed. Prosperity had returned and was shared by many. The nation also reveled in its newfound international power following the Spanish-American War. The social fabric seemed to be on the mend, but memories of the depression of the 1890s still haunted Americans, and society's blemishes appeared more and more intolerable.

Unequal distribution of wealth and income persisted. Four-fifths of Americans lived on a subsistence level, while a handful lived in incredible opulence. In 1900 Andrew Carnegie's income was $23 million; the average working man earned $500. The wealth of a few was increased by the exploitation of women and children. One out of five women worked, earning wages as low as $6 a week, while the sacrifice of the country's young to the god of economic growth was alarming.

Factory working conditions were horrifying, and for many Americans housing conditions were as bad or worse. One investigator described a Chicago neighborhood, remarking on the "filthy and rotten tenements . . . dilapidated outhouses, the broken sewer pipes, the piles of garbage fairly alive with diseased odors." At the same time the Vanderbilts summered in a "cottage" of 70 rooms.

The middle class experienced neither extreme. Its members did have their economic grievances, however. Prosperity increased the cost of living by 35 percent in less than a decade, while many middle-class incomes remained the same. Many blamed the monopolies and watched with alarm as trusts, proving to be immune to the Sherman Act, proliferated rapidly, thereby decreasing competition and opportunity. People came to believe that they had to find political solutions to wrestle government from the hands of a few and return it to the "people" in order to solve the nation's problems. The great democratic experiment seemed to have run afoul of wealthy industrialists, corrupt state and federal legislators, and urban political machines.

Most of these problems were not new; neither were the proposed solutions. Progressivism was rooted in the Gilded Age, but while reform had been a sideshow earlier, it now became a national preoccupation. Progressivism was more broadly based and enjoyed greater appeal than any previous reform movement. One reason it did so was the diversity and pervasiveness of the voices calling for change.

Voices for Change

By 1900 Americans had done nothing less than reinterpret their understanding of their world. Under the old, classical interpretation, the universe was governed by absolute, natural laws. There was divine logic to all and truth was universal—the same at all times. According to this vision, public policy should not attempt to change the course of those laws through human-made ones. Such logic justified the concentration of wealth as well as the lack of governmental regulation of business and assistance to the poor and weak.

Social Darwinism, laissez-faire economics, and the Gospel of Wealth never enjoyed total acceptance. Throughout the Gilded Age, challenges and alternative visions had chipped away at their bases of support. In 1879 Henry George wrote *Progress and Poverty* which addressed the unequal distribution of wealth. His solution was a "single tax" on land to control speculative profits. In *Looking Backward* (1888) Edward Bellamy provided a glimpse of a utopian society based upon a state-controlled economy propelled by cooperation rather than competition. These writings profoundly influenced the Populists, the Socialists, and many who called themselves progressive.

In literary circles, realist writers dethroned romanticism, describing the world as it was, not as it should be. The naturalists portrayed the powerlessness of the individual against the uncaring forces of urbanization and industrialization. Artists of the "ashcan" school painted urban scenes teeming with problems as well as life. Thus art and literature became mirrors of social concerns.

A revolution was also taking place in the academic world. One of the most important changes was the democratization of higher education. From 1870 to 1910 the number of colleges and universities nearly doubled. Higher education became less elitist, white, religious, and male, as female and black enrollment increased. Professors at these institutions became increasingly middle-class, and therefore had less interest in supporting the status quo.

Another academic change was the revolt against formalism. Intellectuals had once sought to explain the world by formulating abstract, universal theories. The new scholars, especially in the emerging social sciences, began by collecting concrete data which did not support the so-called natural laws propounded by their predecessors.

Whereas theories had prescribed limits to human action, facts now became weapons for change. A new breed of economists conducted field research to gather data, and their findings challenged traditional laissez-faire doctrines. To continue policies based on competition seemed absurd in an economy dominated by monopolies. A group of sociologists calling themselves "Reform Darwinists" rejected Spencer's Social Darwinism as another tool of exploitation. They accepted evolutionary principles and the influence of environment, but denied that people were merely pawns manipulated by natural forces. Human intelligence was an active factor that could control and change the environment, especially when people worked together. The goal of many social scientists was a more orderly society, based on rational planning and social engineering to do away with strife and unregulated growth.

Legal scholars also joined the assault on formalism. During the Gilded Age courts had read laissez-faire principles into their interpretation of the Constitution. Decisions striking down regulatory and reform legislation invoked such abstract principles as the sanctity of property rights and contracts. Challenging laissez-faire jurisprudence, Supreme Court Justice Oliver Wendell Holmes, Jr. rejected the idea that laws had ever been the logical result of pure, universal principles, arguing instead that laws had been and should be based on "the felt necessities of the time." Lawyer Louis D. Brandeis successfully argued these ideas in 1908. That year the Supreme Court upheld a ten-hour law for women working in Oregon laundries in *Muller* v. *Oregon,* primarily because of social research documenting the damage done to women's health by long working hours.

As Americans began to reject absolute truths and universal principles, the remaining question was how to determine right from wrong and good from bad. The answer came from philosopher William James with his doctrine of pragmatism. Ideas, he argued, were to be judged by their results. An idea that produced a socially desirable end was right and good. Philosophical thought was useless unless it focused on solving problems. Pragmatism was a distinctly American philosophy and found many adherents. One of them, John Dewey, applied its principles to education. Arguing against rote memorization of a static body of facts, he advocated that education should be based on experience and directed toward creativity and personal growth.

The literary and intellectual currents of the era helped to set the stage for reform, but the impact of organized religion on progressivism was even more profound. Embracing what became known as the Social Gospel movement, theology schools added courses in Christian sociology to teach "the application of our common Christianity to . . . social conditions." The Social Gospelers used the tools of scientific inquiry to root out and solve human problems in order to usher in the "Kingdom of God on Earth." Many settlement-house workers, such as Jane Addams, sought to use their Christian faith to solve social problems.

A final spark that ignited public interest in reform was popular journalism. The expansion of education and the growth of cities provided a mass audience for low-priced magazines such as *Collier's* and *McClure's.* Their editors quickly discovered people's fascination with evil and launched a series of exposés by investigative reporters. Labeled "muckrakers" by Teddy Roosevelt, they brought to light corruption in almost every facet of society.

Whether published serially in magazines or published as books, the exposés of the muckrakers shocked the public with their indictments of child labor, unscrupulous industrialists, or corrupt politicians. Ida Tarbell called Standard Oil "one of the most gigantic and dangerous conspiracies ever attempted." Lincoln Steffens denounced urban politics in *The Shame of the Cities,* and the socialist Upton Sinclair described the horrifying conditions in the meat-packing industry in *The Jungle.*

Progressives in Action

Voices of change echoed a genuine transformation of popular sentiment. Americans of all classes began calling themselves "progressives" and sought to reform whichever social evil captured their attention. Most believed problems could be legislated away, and that human progress would come through cooperation rather than competition. Thus they organized themselves into diverse groups that shared their own particular vision of a better world.

So varied were the aims of people calling themselves progressive that to think of progressivism as a movement is a mistake. There was little unity except in the idea that people could improve society. Most progressives, however, were middle-class moderates who abhorred radical solutions. Motivated by a fear and hatred of class conflict, such progressives sought to save the capitalists from their own excesses and thereby salvage the system. Their goal was an orderly and harmonious society.

The Drive to Organize

Organizing was a major activity at the turn of the century. Such professional groups as the American Medical Association (AMA) began to emerge in modern form. These groups reflected the rise of a new professionalism that helped to create a body of "experts" to be tapped by progressives wanting to impose order and efficiency on social institutions.

The organizations themselves also acted to effect change. The AMA's major goal was to improve professional standards. The government assisted by enacting laws that required licenses to practice medicine. Minimum standards for medical education were adopted, closing the doors of dozens of marginal medical schools, several of which trained minority doctors. The result of the new professionalism in most fields was to limit the number of practitioners. This helped weed out incompetents, but it also increased the incomes of the remaining practitioners and often reduced minority participation. In other words, order, stability, and improved standards often came at the cost of decreased opportunity.

To a large extent, middle-class women led in the organization of reform. Technology and domestic help lessened the burdens of running a home for these women, but a stigma remained on paid employment. Women's clubs provided an outlet for the energies and abilities of many competent and educated women. Local organizations flourished and reform groups founded and led mainly by women sprang up. The majority of activist, middle-class women became involved in movements closely linked to their assigned social roles as guardians of morality and nurturers of the family. One movement dominated by women's groups that enjoyed a strong resurgence in the late nineteenth century was prohibition.

By 1898 the Woman's Christian Temperance Union had 10,000 local branches. It was assisted by the Anti-Saloon League and such church organizations as the Temperance Society of the Methodist Episcopal church. Some of the prohibitionists were Protestant fundamentalists who considered the consumption of alcohol a sin; others saw it as the root cause of many social problems. While the AMA reported the physically devastating effects of alcoholism, urban reformers saw the consequences of alcohol abuse in domestic violence, accidents, and pauperism.

Many middle-class women came to believe that aid to the poor was an inadequate response to society's ills. By attacking the causes of poverty, they sought to improve wages and working conditions, especially for women, and to protect children from exploitation. The National Consumers League lobbied for protective legislation for women and children as well as better working and living conditions for all. Like most progressives, child labor reformers gathered data and photographs to document horrors for legislators at the local, state, and finally federal level.

Some reformers were not content to be merely advocates for the poor and the weak; they wanted to become directly involved with such people in an effort to educate them and organize them to help themselves. Here again middle-class women played a key role. Foremost among such activities was the settlement house movement. Following the lead of Jane Addams of Hull House in Chicago, many young college-educated women moved into slum neighborhoods to live and work with those they sought to help.

More than unselfishness motivated such women, some of whom wanted more freedom than marriage and part-time volunteer work seemed to offer. One appeal of settlement work was that men did not control it. The result was a growing social feminism that cut across class lines.

At first, such activity seemed to draw attention away from the suffrage movement. Women's roles in progressive reforms, however, convinced many people that women not only deserved the right to vote but also that their political participation would be socially beneficial. Arguments based on women's "special role," however, cut both ways. Some male writers charged that voting was so "unnatural" for women that pregnant women would miscarry and nursing mothers' milk would cease to flow.

Convinced that only national action could be effective, the National American Woman Suffrage Association, led by Carrie Chapman Catt after 1915, began a broad-based campaign for a federal amendment to the Constitution. More militant women who followed Alice Paul, founder of the National Woman's party in 1914, preferred the tactics of British suffragists who had picketed, gone on hunger strikes, and actively confronted both politicians and police.

Another group in the social justice movement worked to protect the rights of African Americans. White Southerners had continued to devise

Women employed a variety of tactics in their fight for the vote. Here Dr. Anne Shaw and Carrie Chapman Catt lead 20,000 marchers down Fifth Avenue in New York City.

forms of racial control to replace slavery, using legal segregation, disfranchisement, and violence. From the beginning, blacks resisted white efforts to suppress them. In city after city, African Americans utilized almost every tool and tactic that would prove successful in the 1960s—marching, lobbying, petitioning, challenging court decisions, and boycotting. Under the leadership of Booker T. Washington, they also tried conciliation. But nothing stemmed the rising tide of racism.

As conditions grew worse, educated African Americans became increasingly disenchanted with Booker T. Washington's conciliatory approach, his suppression of dissent by his fellow blacks, his influence with white politicians and philanthropists, and his control of much of the black press. The so-called anti–Bookerite radicals found their spokesperson in W. E. B. Du Bois. Unlike Washington, who had been born into slavery and educated at an industrial school, Du Bois was born to free parents in Massachusetts and became the first African American to receive a doctorate from Harvard.

Du Bois expressed the frustrations and dreams of his fellow blacks and criticized Washington's leadership in *The Souls of Black Folk* (1903). Du Bois took exception to Washington's refusal to recognize the importance of the vote, his emphasis on industrial education at the expense of higher education, his reluctance to criticize as well as praise white actions, and his willingness to give up previously won rights. Rejecting Washington's gradualist approach, Du Bois believed the key to black advancement was in cultivating what he called the "Talented Tenth." To him, more of the limited education funds should go to train the ablest ten percent of African Americans for leadership through liberal arts and professional schooling.

Relations between Washington and Du Bois deteriorated steadily. By 1905 their differences were so great that Du Bois joined William Monroe Trotter in forming the Niagara Movement, an organization devoted to two main objectives: opposition to Washington's leadership of the black community and the demand for "full manhood rights." Although only about 50 educated African Americans—mainly northerners—joined, it played an important role in convincing northern white progressives that an alternative to Washington was desirable. When a white mob in Springfield, Illinois, went on a rampage against African Americans, concerned whites joined with Du Bois to found the National Association for the Advancement of Colored People (NAACP) in 1909. At first the group was led and dominated by whites; Du Bois was the only African American to hold a responsible position. The organization became more black over time, but the focus of its activities remained essentially the same: education and propaganda, court challenges to discrimination, and lobbying for such legislation as a federal antilynching law.

Immigration policy became another source of organizational activity. The American Protective Association (1887) sought to control and limit the access of immigrants by lobbying for literacy tests and quotas. Some progressive Americans, however, welcomed the nation's new pluralism, and formed the North American League for Immigrants to "protect the newcomers from unscrupulous bankers, steamship captains and fellow countrymen."

Even if most were middle-class citizens, progressives obviously came from all classes, and within classes there was a diversity of responses to the modernization of society and the economy. Many businesspeople organized to fight regulatory and labor legislation in such groups as the National Association of Manufacturers. Others joined moderate reformist groups such as the Chamber of Commerce. Even more liberal was the National Civic Federation, which sought to bring together employers and employees to discuss industrial problems.

The drive to organize pervaded American society, creating such diverse groups as the Boy Scouts of America (1910), the Rotary Club (1915), the National Collegiate Athletic Association (1906), and the National Birth Control League (1915). As Americans came to believe in cooperative efforts to achieve goals, they also began to look to government for answers—starting at the local level and moving up to Washington.

Urban Beginnings

Progressivism was largely a response to modernization. It first confronted the most visible problems, most of which were found in the cities. Incredibly rapid increases in urban populations outpaced the ability of "small-town" governments to meet the challenges. Political machines provided needed services but came under attack in the 1890s as inefficient and corrupt.

Reformers demanded that governments be run "not by partisans, either Republican nor Democratic, but by men who are skilled in business management and social service." In their struggle for efficient, nonpartisan government, urban reformers fought for the secret ballot and voter registration. In an effort to do away entirely with "boss rule," many municipalities hired city managers or appointed commissioners to conduct city business.

Middle-class progressives sometimes found their will thwarted by lower-class voters. Breaking up urban machines often destroyed the informal welfare networks that met the needs of the poor. In 1901 the Tammany Hall machine recaptured New York with the campaign slogan "To hell with reform." Poor immigrants did not accept that their ignorance and "foreign ways" were at the root of urban problems.

In a number of cities voters elected mayors who sympathized with working-class objectives. Tom L. Johnson, elected mayor of Cleveland in 1901, expanded social services and brought about the public ownership of the waterworks, gas and electric utilities, and public transportation, thereby reducing their costs to the poor. After his election in 1899, Mayor Samuel "Golden Rule" Jones of Toledo, Ohio, reformed the police department and worked to provide free kindergartens, playgrounds, golf courses, and concerts. Advocating public ownership of utilities, many Socialists also showed growing strength at the local level. In 1910 Milwaukee elected a Socialist mayor, and by 1912 about 1,000 held offices in 33 states and 160 cities and towns.

Urban progressivism was obviously not a coherent, unified movement. Different groups succeeded at different times in different cities. Social services were cut to lower business taxes in some cities and expanded in others. In most cities the progressives attacked unhealthy living conditions with varying degrees of success. By the turn of the century, however, more and more people began to look to the states to solve problems.

Reform Reaches the State Level

Because cities had little power and the federal government seemed too remote, the states became major battlegrounds for reform. Leadership of state progressivism was as diverse and complex as urban progressivism, and drew its support from equally diverse constituencies.

State progressives pursued four major goals: establishing "direct democracy," protecting the public by regulating the economy, increasing state services, and social control. By World War I many states had adopted political procedures designed to give the people a more direct say in running the government, such as initiative, referendum, and recall. An initiative allowed voters to propose legislative changes, usually by petition; a referendum gave the public a mechanism for voting directly on controversial legislation; recall provided a way to remove elected officials. Many states also established direct primaries, the secret ballot, voter registration, and corrupt practices legislation. The drive for direct democracy culminated in the Seventeenth Amendment to the Constitution (1913), which substituted the popular election of senators for their election by state legislatures.

The victories of women suffragists at the state level also expanded democracy. Washington became the fifth state to give women the vote in 1910. California acted the next year, and four other western states followed suit by 1916. That year Jeannette Rankin was elected to Congress from Montana. These victories encouraged the efforts to obtain a constitutional amendment allowing women to vote.

Clearly, progressive actions to protect the public and regulate the economy took many forms. In the West, especially, the emphasis was on regulating railroads and utilities, and legislatures created commissions to regulate the rates charged by both.

In the industrialized states workmen's compensation became a major goal. Then in 1911 a major tragedy chilled the hearts of Americans when a fire broke out at the Triangle Shirtwaist Company in New York City. Because the doors were locked and many fire escape ladders were either broken or missing, 147 workers, mostly women and girls, lost their lives in the blaze. The relatives of many victims sued the company, and some received large settlements. After the Triangle fire, the idea of mandatory insurance grew in popularity with the support of many factory owners, who did not want the expense of lawsuits filed by workers. Between 1910 and 1916, 32 states enacted workmen's compensation laws.

The work of the National Child Labor Committee and other organizations moved states to legislate protection for women and children. Progressives gathered evidence of the harm done by long working hours and unsafe, unhealthy conditions, and demanded state action. By 1916, 32 states had laws regulating the hours women and children could work. Eleven had specified minimum wages for women, and every state regulated child labor in some manner. Other protective legislation included building and sanitary codes.

A number of states also expanded social services. Because of lobbying by settlement house workers, by 1914 some 20 states had provided mother's pensions to widows or abandoned wives with dependent children. Funding for education also increased, with the expansion of compulsory education to the high school level. Support often came from businesses, which saw public education as a means of preparing individuals for life in an industrial society. As a result, very few public schools were modeled on John Dewey's progressive educational doctrines, and instead promoted discipline and punctuality.

In the South progressivism was for whites only. Increased school funding was common, but the bulk went to educating white children, the *Plessy* v. *Ferguson* formula of "separate but equal" facilities notwithstanding. In 1919 southern states spent an average of $12.16 per white student and $3.29 per black student. More interested in social control than in social justice, southern whites trumpeted segregation as a reform, and often had the tacit approval of many northern progressives.

Other forms of social control, such as prohibition, also enjoyed considerable success at the state level. Prohibitionists won many victories in the states, especially in the South, where Protestant fundamentalism and the race question figured prominently in the debate. One southern prohibitionist argued that "whiskey must be taken out of the Negro's hands," and that it was the duty "of the stronger race to forego its own personal liberty for the protection of the weaker race." By 1916 nineteen states had adopted prohibition.

The legacy of progressivism in the states was mixed, as were the motives of state reformers. Regardless of their goals, most eventually turned to the federal government for help. They had little choice. As one reformer stated: "When I was in the city council . . . fighting for a shorter work day, [my opponents] told me to go to the legislature; now [my fellow legislators] tell me to go to Congress for a national law. When I get there and demand it, they will tell me to go to hell."

Progressivism Moves to the National Level

When McKinley was reelected in 1900, few expected a national reform leader; but for a quirk of fate they would have been right. On September 6, 1901, anarchist Leon Czolgosz shot McKinley, and eight days later Vice President Theodore Roosevelt became president. Many remembered that during the Pullman strike Roosevelt had suggested shooting the strikers. Most therefore did not expect the action he took in the 1902 coal strike. Nor did they think Roosevelt would help usher in an era of reform that would span almost two decades, resulting in a massive amount of legislation and four constitutional amendments by 1920.

Roosevelt and New Attitudes Toward Government Power

Roosevelt became the most forceful president since Lincoln, but few men have looked or sounded less presidential. He was short, nearsighted, beaver-toothed, and talked in a high-pitched voice. A frail, asthmatic child, he seemed intent on proving his manliness. Thus his life became a robust adventure of sports, hunting, and camping. His exuberance, vitality, and wit captivated most Americans. To understand him, an observer declared, one had to remember "the president is really only six years old." He was not a simple man, however. His hobbies included writing history books, and he displayed a keen intellect that he had honed as a student at Harvard.

Born into an aristocratic Dutch family in New York, Roosevelt rejected a leisurely life for the rough and tumble world of politics. His privileged background made him an unlikely candidate for a reformer, yet he ended up making reform both fun and respectable. He saw himself as a conservative, but felt that in in order to preserve what was vital, one had to reform.

Roosevelt shared two progressive sentiments. One was that government should be efficiently run by able, competent people. The other was that industrialization had created the need for expanded governmental action. Roosevelt reorganized and revitalized the executive branch, modernized the army command structure and the consular service, and pursued the federal regulation of the economy that has characterized twentieth-century America.

Although he was later remembered more for his "trust-busting" and "Square Deal," Roosevelt considered conservation his greatest domestic accomplishment. In 1902 he backed the Newlands Reclamation Act, which set aside the proceeds from public land sales for irrigation and reclamation projects. He also used presidential power to add almost 150 million acres to national forests and to preserve valuable coal and water sites for national development. With his chief forester, Gifford Pinchot, he sponsored a National Conservation Congress in 1908.

Some businesspeople already disliked Roosevelt for his conservation policies. He further alienated the business community by his handling of the coal strike, and again when the Justice Department filed a suit against the Northern Securities Company under the Sherman Antitrust Act. Northern Securities was a wise choice for action. It was a highly unpopular combination of northwestern railroad systems controlled by such heavyweights as James J. Hill and J. P. Morgan. In 1904 the Supreme Court ordered the company's dissolution. That same year, in a case against the major meat packers, the Court also reversed the *E. C. Knight* ruling of 1895 that exempted manufacturing from federal antitrust law.

The rulings pleased Roosevelt, who rejected the Court's earlier narrow, strict interpretations of the Constitution. Roosevelt's trust-busting was an answer to progressive prayers, since antimonopoly was a strong component of progressivism. Yet Roosevelt was not a true convert to trust-busting. He attacked trusts that abused their power and left alone trusts that acted responsibly. He preferred to negotiate differences, and to do so he established in 1904 a Bureau of Corporations within the recently formed Department of Commerce and Labor.

Campaigning on the promise to provide a "Square Deal" for all Americans, Roosevelt easily defeated the Democratic candidate Alton B. Parker in the 1904 presidential election. Now elected in his own right, he launched into expanding the regulatory power of the federal government. His top priority over the objection of conservative Republican senators was to control the railroads by expanding the power of the Interstate Commerce Commission (ICC). Although the Elkins Act, passed in 1903, had already eliminated rebates, Roosevelt wanted to give the ICC the power to set shipping rates. Through shrewd political maneuvering he got this with the Hepburn Act of 1906.

The publication of Upton Sinclair's *The Jungle* in that same year caused a consumer uproar for regulation of the food and drug industries. An investigation of the meat-packing industry ordered by Roosevelt proved the truth of Sinclair's charges of filth and contamination. As a result, Congress passed the Pure Food and Drug Act and the Meat Inspection Act on the same day in 1906. By 1908 Roosevelt had left his indelible mark on the nation and decided not to run for reelection. He cast his support to William Howard Taft, who easily defeated William Jennings Bryan, the Democratic nominee and loser for the third time. Roosevelt then retired and went off to hunt lions in Africa.

Taft and Quiet Progressivism

William Howard Taft brought to the presidency a distinguished record of public service. An Ohio lawyer, he had served as a federal judge, the first civil governor of the Philippines, and secretary of war. Weighing more than 350 pounds, Taft was far from charismatic and indeed quite shy. He was incapable of rallying public support for any cause, and reformers were especially skeptical about him.

Taft was essentially more conservative than Roosevelt, especially in his view of limited rather than expansive governmental power. On the other hand, Taft was far more the trust-buster than Roosevelt, initiating 43 antitrust indictments during his one term in office. He also supported the eight-hour day and favored legislation to improve mine safety. He urged passage of the Mann-Elkins Act of 1910, which increased the rate-setting power of the ICC and extended its jurisdiction to telephone and telegraph companies.

Nevertheless, Taft was not forceful enough to preside effectively over the growing divisions within the Republican party. The conservatives, led by the powerful Senator Nelson W. Aldrich, were determined to draw the line against further reform, while progressive Republicans such as Robert La Follette and George Norris were growing rebellious. Conflict came on several fronts. The first was the tariff. In his campaign Taft had promised a lower tariff, but in the end he accepted the much compromised Payne-Aldrich Tariff, which actually raised some key duties. It disappointed reformers immensely. Taft had suffered a defeat, but foolishly did not admit it; instead he called the tariff the "best" ever passed.

Caught in the middle of several conflicts, Taft eventually alienated the progressive wing of his party as well as Teddy Roosevelt. He first supported and then abandoned party insurgents who challenged the power of conservative Speaker of the House "Uncle Joe" Cannon. Later, when chief forester Gifford Pinchot protested a sale of public lands by Secretary of the Interior Richard A. Ballinger, Taft fired him, an action that infuriated both conservationists and Roosevelt.

By 1912 progressive Republicans were ready to bolt the party if Taft were renominated, and Roosevelt declared his intention to run. The fight for the nomination became bitter, but, as president, Taft was able to control the party convention. The defeated Roosevelt walked out with his supporters and formed a third party, known as the Progressive or Bull Moose party.

The Progressive Party's platform endorsed such wide-ranging reforms as abolition of child labor; federal old-age, accident, and unemployment insurance programs; an eight-hour day; and women's suffrage. At Roosevelt's request, however, a plank supporting black equality was deleted.

With the Republicans divided, Democratic chances of recapturing the White House increased. A hard fight for the Democratic nomination ensued, which New Jersey's progressive governor, Woodrow Wilson, won on the forty-sixth ballot. The Socialist party nominated Eugene V. Debs, making it a four-way race.

As soon became apparent, the real battle was between Wilson and Roosevelt. The campaign produced an unusually high level of debate over the proper role of government in a modern, industrialized society. Labeling his program the "New Freedom," Wilson aimed to restore competition by trust-busting. Roosevelt, on the other hand, believed that big business was not necessarily bad, but needed to be regulated. His answer was the "New Nationalism"—the expansion of federal power to control rather than dismantle the trusts. Big government would offset the power of big business. The rhetoric of the two candidates differed sharply, but in their presidencies each practiced a little of both the "New Freedom" and "New Nationalism."

The split in the Republican party enabled the Democrats to capture not only the White House but also the Senate. Democrats also consolidated their control of the House, so Wilson entered the presidency with his party solidly in power, even though he did not receive a majority of the popular vote. He got 6.3 million votes, Roosevelt 4.1 million, Taft 3.5 million, and Debs nearly 1 million. In the electoral college, however, Wilson won an impressive 435 votes to Roosevelt's 88 and a mere 8 for Taft.

Table 22.1

Election of 1912			
Candidate	Party	Popular Vote	Electoral Vote
Woodrow Wilson	Democratic	6,296,547	435
Theodore Roosevelt	Progressive (Bull Moose)	4,118,571	88
William H. Taft	Republican	3,486,720	8
	Minor Parties	1,135,697	—

Wilson and Moral Progressivism

The son and grandson of Presbyterian ministers, Woodrow Wilson grew up in the South and practiced law in Atlanta before receiving his doctorate from Johns Hopkins University. His book *Congressional Government* was published in 1895, and he became president of Princeton University in 1902 before being elected governor of New Jersey. His religion was an important factor in his personality, and he exuded a self-righteousness which was not endearing. Although much less charismatic, Wilson did resemble Roosevelt in his view of the role of the president. Roosevelt had called the presidency a "bully pulpit," and Wilson agreed that the president should be the "political leader of the nation."

Wilson's activism coincided with growing demands for further reform. Investigations and amendments launched earlier came to fruition during his presidency. The result was an outpouring of legislation. In 1913, his first year in office, Congress passed the Underwood Tariff, which significantly lowered duties for the first time since the Civil War. To recoup lost revenues, a graduated income tax was added to the act, and was ratified as the Sixteenth Amendment.

Congress passed banking reform the same year. Following the panic of 1907, Congress launched investigations into its causes. Everyone, including bankers, had come to believe the nation's banking system needed to be stabilized by governmental action. As a result, the Federal Reserve Act of 1913 was a compromise. It established the Federal Reserve System of 12 regional banks owned by bankers but under the control of a presidentially appointed Federal Reserve Board.

In 1914 Congress also took actions to deal with monopolies and to regulate business. In September it established the Federal Trade Commission to replace the Bureau of Corporations. The five-person body was charged with investigating alleged violations of antitrust law and could issue "cease and desist" orders against corporations found guilty of unfair trade practices. The next month the Clayton Antitrust Act sought to close some of the loopholes of the Sherman Act and prohibited a number of business practices such as price discrimination. One provision declared that labor unions were not to be considered illegal combinations in restraint of trade—a move designed to undermine the use of court injunctions against strikers.

At that point Wilson believed he had accomplished his agenda. A firm opponent of paternalistic government, he did not support further labor legislation or farm-credit plans. As the election of 1916 approached, however, progressives reminded him of the importance of the farm and labor vote. Legislation to win those votes soon followed. Farmers were

A distinguished professor, Woodrow Wilson brought both competence and a grim moral determination to the presidency.

given the Federal Farm Loan Act, which provided low-interest credit, and federal funding for agricultural specialists in each county. Labor got the Keating-Owen Child Labor Act, which barred goods made by children under 16 from interstate commerce; the Adamson Act, which established an eight-hour day for railroad workers; and the Workman's Compensation Act, which provided protection to federal employees. Progressives were also pleased by Wilson's appointment of Louis Brandeis to the Supreme Court. All of these actions helped to ensure victory over the Republican nominee Charles Evans Hughes in 1916.

Progressivism in the International Arena

Progressive victories on the home front, further bolstered by the nation's economic growth and victory in the Spanish-American War, expanded Americans' confidence in their ability to solve problems on the international level. Just as people differed over what alterations, if any, were required in domestic policies, various visions of a new American foreign policy also emerged. For some, progressivism simply redefined and reinvigorated the old ideas of America's manifest destiny. Other progressives believed that democratic principles required that all people, even foreigners, be free to determine their own destinies. Order and justice were two progressive goals that sometimes conflicted, both in the domestic and the international arenas.

Big Stick Diplomacy

Theodore Roosevelt's foreign policy reflected the same kind of vigor he displayed in everything else. Asserting that Congress was "not well fitted for the shaping of foreign policy," he expanded presidential power in the conduct of diplomacy. Order having been restored in Cuba and the Philippines by 1903, Roosevelt launched the United States into the role of policeman. His doctrine was to "speak softly and carry a big stick," but he really only lived up to the second half of the slogan.

Possession of the Philippines brought with it concern over turbulent Asian politics. Most alarming was the emergence of Japan after its unexpected victories in the Russo-Japanese War (1904–1905). Often playing the role of arbiter at home, Roosevelt now shifted his arena and mediated an end to the war at a conference held in Portsmouth, New Hampshire, in August 1905. Japan remained a formidable rival, however. In order to intimidate the Japanese, Roosevelt's "big stick" was displayed by conspicuous stops in the Pacific during a 1907–1909 tour of America's "Great White Fleet."

Within the Western Hemisphere Roosevelt was even less reluctant to threaten or use force. In 1906 he responded to Cuban demonstrations against the Platt Amendment by sending in marines, who stayed until 1909. "I am doing my best," he declared, "to persuade the Cubans that if only they will be good, they will be happy." The marines could be very persuasive.

Progress and strategic considerations also demanded that a canal in Central America link the Atlantic and Pacific oceans. Roosevelt was determined to make it happen. There were two possible routes: one through Nicaragua and one across the Panamanian isthmus, which belonged to Colombia. A start had been made in Panama by a French company, which ran out of funds and was reorganized as the New Panama Canal Company. The new company's major asset was its concession from Colombia that extended to 1904.

Deciding that the Panama route was preferable, the Roosevelt administration negotiated the Hay-Herrán Treaty, which provided the United States with rights to a six-mile-wide zone across the isthmus in return for a $10 million payment to Colombia and an annual rental fee of $250,000.

As in the United States, ratification required the consent of the Colombian senate, which in August 1903 rejected the treaty unanimously.

Roosevelt was furious. "The blackmailers of Bogota," he roared, should not be allowed "permanently to bar one of the future highways of civilization." He considered taking the canal zone by force, but a different solution presented itself when Philippe Bunau-Varilla, the chief engineer of the French canal company, incited a Panamanian revolt. Roosevelt promptly dispatched the USS *Nashville* to prevent Colombian troops from even getting to the so-called revolution. Three days after its start, Roosevelt recognized the independence of the Republic of Panama. Secretary of State John Hay and Bunau-Varilla then quickly drafted the Hay-Bunau-Varilla Treaty with essentially the same terms as the Hay-Herrán Treaty—only now the payment went to the rebels, not Colombia.

At first Roosevelt denied any part in the revolution, but he eventually admitted, "I took the Canal Zone and let Congress debate; and while the debate goes on the Canal does also." In 1914, the canal, a monument to both progress and Yankee imperialism, was completed.

At the same time, Latin American countries sometimes fell behind in debt payments to such European powers as Britain and Germany. As a result those two nations blockaded Venezuela in 1902–1903. A year later,

American Interventions in the Caribbean

Early in the twentieth century, the United States policed the Western Hemisphere and often took action when it judged Latin American countries were not managing.

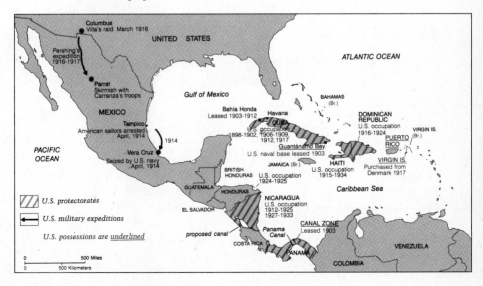

Roosevelt announced that the United States would assume the responsibility of seeing that the nations of the Caribbean behaved themselves and paid their debts in order to thwart European intervention and assure American dominance in the region. Known as the Roosevelt Corollary to the Monroe Doctrine, this policy justified U.S. intervention in such places as the Dominican Republic, Nicaragua, and Haiti. Roosevelt's "big stick" diplomacy established America as the "policeman of the Western Hemisphere"—a role that would last long into the twentieth century.

Dollar Diplomacy

By nature less aggressive than his predecessor, William Howard Taft believed in the need for order and stability as well as the limited capacity of armed force for solving problems. He also realized that the United States had a new source of power—its economic clout. From 1898 to 1909 American overseas investments had risen from about $800 million to more than $2.5 billion.

Called "dollar diplomacy," Taft's approach was to use dollars instead of bullets to ensure stability and order. He wanted American capital to replace European capital in Latin America in order to increase U.S. influence there. When British bondholders wanted to collect their debts from Honduras in 1909, Taft asked American financiers to assume the debt. In 1910 he convinced New York bankers to take over the assets of the National Bank of Haiti. When needed, however, Taft also wielded a big stick. He refused to recognize a revolution in Nicaragua until the leaders agreed to accept American credits to pay off British debts, and he sent in marines to punctuate his point.

Missionary Diplomacy

As in domestic policies, Woodrow Wilson's foreign policy differed more in style than substance from his predecessors. Wilson's moralism did not stop at national boundaries. Indeed his sermonistic foreign policy has sometimes been called "missionary diplomacy." His gospel was American-style democracy. "When properly directed," he declared, "there is no people not fitted for self-government."

The rhetoric was different from his predecessors', but the results were the same. Renouncing both big stick and dollar diplomacy, Wilson continued to maintain stability and order in the Caribbean by similar measures. He sent marines to the Dominican Republic and Haiti, and kept them in Nicaragua. His interventionism ran into more trouble in Mexico, where the overthrow of longtime dictator Porfirio Diaz in 1911 began a cycle of revolution. Just before Wilson entered office, General Victoriano Huerta seized power through assassination. To the surprise of many, the moralistic Wilson refused to extend diplomatic recognition to Huerta's government, which he called a "government of butchers."

American business interests were dismayed by Wilson's stand. They controlled 75 percent of Mexico's mines, 60 percent of its oil, and 70 percent of its rubber. Determined to unseat Huerta, Wilson persevered. His tactics escalated from diplomatic pressure to landing troops at Veracruz, a move that infuriated Mexicans more than Huerta's despotism. Even after Huerta was overthrown, civil war continued between the government forces of Venustiano Carranza and rebels led by Pancho Villa.

In an attempt to draw the United States into the fracas, Villa launched a raid into New Mexico in March 1916. The tactic worked, and Wilson sent an expedition to capture Villa. Led by General John Pershing, American troops failed to find him. Soon they were 300 miles deep into Mexican territory and, as a result, on the brink of war with Carranza's government. In January 1917, however, America was being drawn into World War I, and Wilson decided to withdraw the troops. In the end he got basically the kind of government he wanted for Mexico, but Mexicans continued to believe that their government was their business and deeply resented the American intervention.

American involvement in World War I diverted attention not only from the crisis with Mexico. Domestic reform took a backseat to "making the world safe for democracy." Yet progressivism did not entirely die. Indeed, prohibitionists, women suffragists, and immigration restrictionists won their greatest victories in the wake of war.

Progressive Accomplishments, Progressive Failures

Measured by direct results, most progressive reforms proved disappointing. In some cases unintended consequences actually worked against the intended goals of laws. Nevertheless, progressives established important precedents that opened doors to later, more effective reform.

The Impact of Legislation

Attempts to promote direct democracy were among the least effective. Direct election of senators did not seem to alter the kinds of people elected. Initiative, referendum, and recall were rarely used, since the expense and organization needed for petition drives were beyond the reach of any but well-financed pressure groups. An unintended result of democratization was to increase the power of urban machines, as the move toward popular voting increased the political power of the most populous cities and the machines that controlled them. Nevertheless, in some states, such as Wisconsin, government did become more responsive to public needs, and urban machines often adopted reform measures to maintain power.

Other kinds of urban reforms had varying results. City government did indeed become more efficiently and economically run. The competency and honesty of officials generally increased. Occasional consequences, however, were cuts in social services in less affluent neighborhoods.

Attempts to regulate the railroads on either the state or national level rarely produced dramatic benefits for the general public. The chief advocates and beneficiaries of railroad regulation were frequently large shipping interests that did not share lower costs with consumers. With the Hepburn Act, Roosevelt did accomplish his primary goal of giving the ICC the power to set rates, but the act was more significant as a precedent for expanded governmental power than as an immediate solution to problems, since the courts ruled in favor of the railroads in most rate disputes.

Antimonopoly actions also did not always produce the intended results. For example, the breakups of Standard Oil and the American Tobacco Company did not increase competition or lower prices. The Clayton Antitrust Act was considered too vague for effective enforcement. Perhaps the only legislation to fulfill the promise of the New Freedom was the Underwood Tariff, and it was reversed by tariff legislation in the 1920s.

The Federal Trade Commission (FTC) did not become an aggressive watchdog either. Wilson's appointments were fairly pro-business, and the appointments of the 1920s were even more so. In the end, the FTC proved most beneficial to big business by protecting firms from unexpected suits and by outlawing many "unfair trade practices," many of which had promoted competition at the expense of stability. On the other hand, the FTC was also an important precedent.

Proclaimed victories for labor frequently turned out to be more symbolic than real. In the arbitration of the 1902 coal strike, for example, the United Mine Workers did not win recognition. Yet the symbolism was important. The precedent that the government would not automatically support the demands of management was later built upon during the New Deal of the 1930s.

Some labor legislation brought benefits but also produced unintended results. Child labor laws in combination with compulsory education legislation decreased the number of children from ages 10 to 15 who worked for wages, while the number of students enrolled in secondary education increased. Both were desirable results, but in the short run at least the poor received a mixed blessing. The incomes of a family's children were often crucial to its welfare, and no alternatives were provided. Much the same can be said about limits imposed on women's working hours.

Laws establishing minimum wages for women helped somewhat to offset earning losses resulting from child labor legislation. In any event, laws such as the Child Labor Act were declared unconstitutional in the 1920s.

Workmen's compensation laws were an improvement over existing procedures but were not an unqualified victory of labor over management. Indeed, businesspeople eventually welcomed the relief from the growing number of suits instituted by lawyers on a contingency fee basis, which made it possible for poor workers to take legal action. For the industrialists, a predictable premium replaced the uncertainty of court actions, decreasing the risks and increasing stability in the cost of doing business.

The establishment of the Federal Reserve System also favored order and stability. Everyone benefited from the maintenance of cash reserves for emergencies, a more flexible currency, and national check-clearing facilities. The banking system became more resistant to panics but, as 1929 would prove, not immune to them. Wall Street was not a big loser; three of the five seats on the Federal Reserve Board went to important bankers. The new system was a significant improvement, but far from a radical change.

From the consumer's point of view, the Pure Food and Drug Act and the Meat Inspection Act were great victories. After the rise of mass production and mass marketing, only federal action could provide adequate protection from adulteration of the nation's foodstuffs. Unintended beneficiaries, however, were the large drug and meat-packing companies that could more easily afford the increased expenses of meeting required production standards. Thus the effect was anticompetitive. Like much progressive legislation, the final act did provide protection for consumers, but in a way agreeable to big business.

Other progressive legislation left mixed legacies. Roosevelt's conservation measures prevented the squandering of natural resources, but also aided the larger lumber companies. Prohibition proved to be a boon to organized crime and also fostered widespread disrespect for the law. With a maximum rate of six percent, the income tax did little to redistribute huge fortunes but did establish an important revenue raising precedent. Another significant precedent was set by the Adamson Act, through which the federal government first dabbled in wage and hour legislation. Many other progressive reforms were illusory or short-lived. In the 1920s lax enforcement and hostile court decisions reversed many of them. Nevertheless, laissez-faire had suffered an irreversible blow. That was a major accomplishment and perhaps as much as many progressives wanted.

Winners and Losers

Before the era ended, people from almost every class and occupation had sought to take advantage of the climate of change to promote their interests. Obviously not all were equally successful; some gained far more than others, and some lost more than they gained. Clearly, large corporations were among the biggest winners. Other winners included members of the growing body of middle-class technocrats. At all levels of government the search for orderly, efficient management created new job opportunities for engineers, health professionals, trained managers, and other experts. Reforms that diminished the influence of political parties also increased the power of special interest groups working for particular social and economic goals. Consumers of all classes shared benefits from government regulation.

In general, most of the winners were white, urban, Protestant, and middle-class. Working-class ethnics won a few victories in some cities and states. African Americans came closest to being unqualified losers. For them, the only lasting advances came from such organizations as the NAACP, which survived to become an important force later in the century. Other victories were mainly token; the defeats, however, were concrete.

Of the three presidents, Roosevelt was the most sympathetic to blacks. In 1901 he invited Booker T. Washington to dine at the White House, consulted with him on some southern appointments, and named a few African Americans to federal positions. His actions hardly reflected an acceptance of black equality, however.

Theodore Roosevelt gave the appearance of supporting African Americans when he invited Booker T. Washington to the White House, but like many white leaders, he did not promote equality between blacks and whites.

When Taft became president, he approved of southern disfranchisement and appointed white-supremacist Republicans to federal jobs. As a result, some African Americans, including W. E. B. Du Bois, supported Wilson in 1912. They made a mistake. The influence of Wilson's southern upbringing and advisers became apparent when he allowed his cabinet to segregate federal employees and to demote black officeholders, especially those "who boss white girls." Jim Crow moved to Washington, and Wilson's defense of these actions indicated the blindness and paternalism of many white progressives on ths subject of race.

Conclusion

At the start of the new century, Americans confronted the problems that had accompanied the forces of modernization and industrialization. They were determined to do something to achieve more social justice and stability. Numerous solutions were proposed and victories won. In the end, however, Americans rejected radicalism and ignored major problems.

Once again the nation resolutely refused to come to terms with its ethnic and cultural diversity. Rather than protect minorities, most actions infringed on their personal liberties and sought to control rather than accommodate their differences. Women won some victories, but the majority of Americans did not accept the radical feminists' vision of true equality. Socialists' dreams of a peaceful, democratic redistribution of the country's wealth fell on deaf ears. In the end, there was no significant change in the distribution of either wealth or power. Nonetheless, the vigor and diversity of progressive actions brought to light many problems and provided later generations with a body of experience in dealing with them.

Suggestions for Further Reading

Valuable overviews of progressivism include John W. Chambers, *The Tyranny of Change* (1980); Robert M. Crunden, *Ministers of Reform* (1982); Richard Hofstadter, *The Age of Reform* (1955); Gabriel Kolko, *The Triumph of Conservatism* (1963); Arthur S. Link and Richard L. McCormick, *Progressivism* (1983); Robert Wiebe, *The Search for Order* (1967).

For specific aspects of the Progressive agenda, consult Jerold S. Auerbach, *Unequal Justice* (1976); Harold U. Faulkner, *The Quest for Social Justice* (1931); Thomas Haskell, *The Emergence of Professional Social Science* (1977); David W. Marcell, *Progress and Pragmatism* (1974).

Chronology of Key Events

1879	Henry George's *Progress and Poverty* published
1888	Edward Bellamy's *Looking Backward* published
1889	Jane Addams founds Hull House
1901	President William McKinley assassinated; Theodore Roosevelt becomes twenty-sixth president
1902	Three states adopt initiative and recall; United Mine Workers' strike
1903	W. E. B. Du Bois's *The Souls of Black Folk* published; Elkins Act bars railroad rebates
1904	Northern Securities broken up; Lincoln Steffins's *Shame of the Cities* published; United States obtains right to build the Panama Canal; announcement of Roosevelt Corollary to the Monroe Doctrine, asserting the right of the United States to exercise international police power in the Caribbean
1905	Treaty of Portsmouth ends Russo-Japanese War
1906	Upton Sinclair's *The Jungle* published; Meat Inspection Act enforces standards; Pure Food and Drug Act; Hepburn Act
1908	First city manager hired; *Muller* v. *Oregon*
1909	National Association for the Advancement of Colored People (NAACP) founded; Mann-Elkins Act
1912–1917	Twelve states adopt minimum wage laws for women; 30 states adopt industrial accident insurance
1912	Progressive party created; Woodrow Wilson elected the twenty-eighth president
1913	Sixteenth Amendment; Underwood-Simmons Tariff; Seventeenth Amendment; Federal Reserve System created
1914	Federal Trade Commission established; Clayton Antitrust Act; U.S. Navy captures Veracruz
1915	U.S. marines dispatched to Haiti
1916	U.S. troops enter Mexico to search for Pancho Villa; U.S. marines sent to Dominican Republic; Adamson Act; Federal Workmen's Compensation Act; Keating-Owen Act
1919	Eighteenth Amendment prohibits liquor
1920	Nineteenth Amendment grants women voting rights

Social and intellectual currents are examined in David W. Noble, *The Progressive Mind,* rev. ed. (1981); Frank Tariello, *The Reconstruction of American Political Ideology* (1982); John L. Thomas, *Alternative America* (1983); Morton White, *Social Thought in America: The Revolt Against Formalism* (1975).

Studies of women's and children's issues include Nancy S. Dye, *As Equals and Sisters* (1980); Ellen Condliffe Lagemann, *A Generation of Women: Education in the Lives of Progressive Reformers* (1979); Ruth Rosen, *The Lost Sisterhood: Prostitution in America, 1900–1918* (1982).

The United States role in the international arena is the focus of P. Edward Haley, *Revolution and Intervention* (1970); Walter LaFeber, *The Panama Canal,* rev. ed. (1989); Lester Langley, *The United States and the Caribbean* (1980); Dana G. Munro, *Intervention and Dollar Diplomacy in the Caribbean* (1964); Whitney Perkins, *Constraints of Empire: The United States and Caribbean Interventions* (1981); Robert E. Quirk, *An Affair of Honor: Woodrow Wilson and the Occupation of Veracruz* (1962).

Chapter *23*

The United States and World War I

Disillusioned writers of the 1920s honored Randolph Bourne as "the intellectual hero of World War I," yet his appearance was anything but heroic. An unusually messy forceps delivery crushed one side of Bourne's skull at birth, leaving him with a misshapen ear, a partially paralyzed face, and a mouth permanently askew in a horrible grimace. Then, when he was four, an attack of spinal tuberculosis twisted his frame and left him a hunchback dwarf.

Bourne's brain, however, was razor sharp. A brilliant student, Bourne attended Columbia University, graduating on the eve of World War I. Determined to become a writer, he settled in New York's Greenwich Village, where self-styled literary radicals had declared war on the smugness and the optimism of American culture. While his interests ranged wide and far, he made his reputation as a critic of America's entrance into World War I.

Bourne loathed President Woodrow Wilson, but he directed his choicest barbs at fellow intellectuals who supported Wilson's policies. In effect, he accused them of not doing their job as thinkers. Instead of questioning Wilson's policies, they had betrayed their duty by "opening the sluices and flooding the public with the sewage of the war spirit."

Bourne refused to endow the war with lofty purposes. Hardly a knee-jerk pacifist, he knew that some wars were unavoidable, perhaps even necessary. In his judgment, however, World War I was not a struggle to make the world safe for democracy; it was nothing more than "frenzied mutual suicide." To those who argued that this war could somehow be converted into an instrument of progress and democracy, Bourne replied that World War I would unleash "all the evils that are organically bound up with it." America's allies would reject Wilson's call for a "peace without victory," and instead would try to win the war and "then grab what they can."

On the home front, warned Bourne, there would be the suppression of civil liberties and the growth of big government. "War is the health of the State," he declared in one of his most famous lines. "It automatically sets in motion throughout society those irresistible forces for uniformity, for passionate cooperation with the Government in coercing into obedience the minority groups and individuals which lack the larger herd sense."

Like many of his contemporaries, Bourne feared the state. During wartime the state's power grew exponentially, making it "the inexorable arbiter and determinant of men's businesses and attitudes and opinions." Most alarming of all, the war would kill reform by diverting public attention from the unfinished work of progressivism. It would "leave the country spiritually impoverished because of the draining away of sentiment into the channels of war."

A few days after the Armistice was signed in 1918, Bourne died, a victim of the influenza epidemic that killed 500,000 Americans that winter. Although he had no visible impact on Wilson's administration, Bourne raised important questions about the relationship between the individual and the state during wartime, and many of his fears proved prophetic. In the end, the United States had little choice but to enter the conflict on the side of the Allies. The war itself was a terrible human tragedy, and did not make "the world safe for democracy" or serve as the "war to end all wars" as President Wilson promised. Rather, World War I sowed the seeds of World War II.

The Road to War

On June 28, 1914, terrorists assassinated Archduke Franz Ferdinand, the heir to the Austro-Hungarian throne. A complicated system of alliances pitting the Triple Entente of France, Russia, and Great Britain against the Central Alliance of Germany, Austria-Hungary, Italy, and Turkey triggered a chain reaction that started World War I. In the Far East, Japan, England's ally since 1902, also declared war on Germany. A year after the war began, Italy switched sides and joined the fight against Germany.

World War I caught most people by surprise. Lulled by a century of peace that began with the defeat of Napoleon in 1815, many observers had come to regard armed conflict as a thing of the past. Convinced that the major powers had advanced too far morally and materially to fight, these optimists believed that nation states would settle disputes through diplomacy. World War I shattered these beliefs, demonstrating that death and destruction had not yet been banished from human affairs.

Both sides expected a swift victory; both sides miscalculated. After the Allies halted Germany's massive offensive through France and Belgium at the Marne River in September 1914, the Great War bogged down into trench warfare and a ghastly stalemate ensued, in which the two armies burrowed into the ground and fought pitched battles over narrow strips of blood-soaked earth.

Airplanes, tanks, hand grenades, and poison gases distinguished the Great War from earlier conflicts, but the machine gun did most of the killing. The grim cycle repeated itself countless times: Officers cried "Attack!"; men rose in waves; and the opposing forces opened fire with machine guns, spewing out death at the rate of eight bullets per second. In minutes, thousands of men lay wounded or dead, savage evidence of how efficiently military technology and insane tactics could slaughter a generation of young men. When the war ended, Germany had lost 1,800,000 men; Russia, 1,700,000; France, 1,385,000; Austria-Hungary, 1,200,000; and Great Britain, 947,000.

American Neutrality

Like the combatants, Americans did not see the war coming, and most felt relieved when President Woodrow Wilson issued an official declaration of neutrality on August 4. Mindful of the wisdom embodied in Washington's Farewell Address, steeped in a long tradition of isolation from Europe's wars, and shielded from the hostilities by the Atlantic Ocean, they hoped to avoid the conflict.

Two weeks after the official declaration of neutrality, Wilson asked his countrymen to remain impartial "in thought as well as in action." Yet the president himself could not meet this standard. Privately, his sympathies lay with the Allies, especially Great Britain, whose culture and government he had long admired. Moreover, with the notable exception of William Jennings Bryan, his secretary of state, Wilson's advisors all favored Great Britain, and pushed the president to side with the Allies. Yet Wilson saw the war's causes as complicated and obscure; simple prudence dictated that the United States must avoid taking sides.

Internal divisions underscored the wisdom of neutrality. Wilson knew his countrymen felt deeply divided over the war. Ties of language and culture prompted many Americans to side with the Allies, and, as the war progressed, the British adeptly exploited these bonds with anti-German propoaganda. Yet the Central Powers had their sympathizers, too, since more than ten million Americans were of German, Austrian, or Italian descent. Furthermore, millions of Irish-Americans sided with the Central Powers because they hated the English.

Domestic politics reinforced Wilson's determination to remain neutral. In 1914 the United States stood at the end of two decades of bitter social and political debate. Labor unrest, corporate growth, trust-busting, and the arrival of 12 million new immigrants since the turn of the century had opened deep fissures in American society. As Wilson struggled to correct these problems through legislation, he feared his domestic program would be endangered if neutrality failed.

Allied Violations of Neutrality

Because German armies held the edge in the land war, Great Britain had no choice but to press her naval superiority. During the early part of the war British efforts to control the seas posed repeated threats to Anglo-American relations. Immediately after war erupted, the British navy attempted to blockade Europe. In February 1915 British ships mined the North Sea and started seizing American vessels bound for neutral countries, often without offering compensation. The British captured not ony war matériel, but also noncontraband items, including food and cotton, bound for neutral nations such as Holland for reshipment to Germany. In 1916 Britain blacklisted some 87 American companies accused of trading with Germany and censored the mail coming from Europe to the United States.

These actions, coupled with England's ruthless suppression of the Irish Rebellion in 1916, infuriated Wilson. In retaliation, the State Department bombarded England with a flurry of protests. Although the British interpreted his ardent defense of neutral rights as petty, legalistic quibbling, they realized they could not push Wilson too far, since they needed American trade to survive.

Wilson could have ended the controversy over neutral rights by clamping an embargo on trade with the belligerents, but he refused to take this action because wartime trade was stimulating the American economy. The United States had been in a recession when Wilson entered office in 1913, and the war had quadrupled its exports to the Allied nations.

The huge volume of trade quickly exhausted the Allies' cash reserves, forcing them to ask the United States for credit. After hesitating several months, Wilson agreed in October 1915 to permit loans to belligerents, a decision that favored Great Britain and France far more than Germany. The United States became a creditor nation for the first time, giving Americans a strong economic interest in an Allied victory.

Submarine Warfare

Given Britain's overwhelming naval superiority, Germany decided to rely on a new weapon, the submarine, and on February 4, 1915 Germany proclaimed a "war zone" around the British Isles. Henceforth all enemy merchant ships that entered the zone would be torpedoed without warning, and neutral ships would not be guaranteed safe passage.

A new development in naval technology, the submarine posed serious challenges to international law. The law required ships that attacked other vessels on the high seas to warn their intended victims, allow time for passengers to reach lifeboats, and then rescue survivors after the sinking. By its very nature, the submarine could not abide by these regulations. A silent assassin whose effectiveness depended on the element of surprise, it had to strike from below the surface, in violation of international law.

Wilson's approach to foreign affairs was both legalistic and moralistic. He expected nation-states to behave like gentlemen; and, above all, that meant living up to the letter of international law and respecting the rights of every nation. To Wilson, German submarines were committing criminal acts. In contrast to British violations of American neutrality, which merely resulted in property losses, submarine warfare threatened to kill innocent civilians. In unusually blunt language, he warned Berlin that it would be held "strictly accountable" for American lives lost to submarine attacks. While international law did not guarantee the safety of neutrals who traveled on belligerents' ships, Wilson acted as though it did.

On March 28, 1915, a German submarine torpedoed the *Falaba,* a British liner, killing 104 passengers, including one American. Wilson was furious, but Secretary of State Bryan reminded the president of numerous British violations of American neutrality in her attempt to blockade Germany. "Why be shocked at the drowning of a few people," asked Bryan, "if there is no objection to the starving of a nation?"

On May 1 the German Embassy took out ads in New York newspapers warning Americans not to travel on Allied ships. Undeterred, 197 Americans sailed for the British Isles on board the British *Lusitania.* On May 7, 1915, a German submarine torpedoed the *Lusitania* off the coast of Ireland. She sank in 18 minutes, killing 1,198 persons, 128 of them Americans. The public was shocked and outraged. The *New York Nation* called the sinking "wholesale murder on the high seas," and a small minority of Americans demanded war. It did not matter that the *Lusitania* (like the *Falaba*) was transporting munitions in her hull and had secret orders to ram submarines on sight.

In a sharply worded dispatch, Wilson ordered Germany to apologize for the sinking, compensate the victims, and pledge to stop attacking merchant ships. When Berlin equivocated, Wilson sent a second *Lusitania* note repeating his demands. This time the Germans met him halfway, expressing regret over the *Lusitania* and agreeing to pay an indemnity. However, the Imperial Government refused to stop sinking merchant ships without warning, explaining that Germany's survival depended on full use of the submarine. Convinced that Wilson's policies would lead to war, Bryan resigned from the cabinet to protest what he saw as a dangerous tilt toward Great Britain.

On March 24, 1916, a submarine attacked the *Sussex,* an unarmed French passenger ship, killing more than 80 people in the attack and severely wounding seven Americans. Wilson threatened to sever diplomatic relations unless Germany promised to stop sinking all merchant and passenger ships without warning. Anxious to keep the United States neutral, Berlin agreed. The so-called *Sussex* pledge reduced tensions between the United States and Germany for the remainder of 1916, but the fragile peace depended solely on German restraint.

Preparedness Campaign

As the submarine threatened to draw the United States into the fighting, the American people and their leaders debated whether or not to make ready for war. Initially, Wilson's policy toward preparedness reflected cautious hostility.

Many Americans saw the issue differently. Wilson increasingly found himself assailed by prominent and highly vocal critics who insisted that the best way to preserve peace was to prepare for war. The pugnacious Theodore Roosevelt called the president "the popular pacifist hero," while Tin Pan Alley produced songs with titles such as "I Did Not Raise My Boy to Be a Coward."

Yet Wilson felt pressured by groups opposed to war. Socialists such as Eugene V. Debs dismissed the war as a struggle for assets among capitalist nations. Radicals such as anarchist Emma Goldman and "Big Bill" Haywood, head of the Industrial Workers of the World, shared this view. Liberal reformers feared that war would destroy the spirit of progressivism. Pacifists such as social worker Jane Addams opposed the war on moral grounds. Most troubling of all, Wilson had to worry about opposition from within his own party. Speaking for the peace Democrats, former Secretary of State Bryan warned that a preparedness campaign would transform the United States into "a vast armory with skull and crossbones above the door."

In the end, Wilson threw his support behind a moderate preparedness program. Throughout January and February 1916 he stumped the country pleading for a military force powerful enough to protect the nation's honor. In June Congress increased the army from 90,000 to 175,000 men, and a few months later appropriated more than $500 million for new ships. Though of small importance militarily, both acts drew fire from those who predicted that armaments would lead to war.

Despite his own support for military preparedness, Wilson decided to make peace the key issue in his bid for reelection in 1916. The Republicans chose Charles Evans Hughes, a former governor of New York and a Supreme Court justice who had earned a solid reputation as a liberal. Wilson charged that Hughes's election would plunge the United States into Europe's madness. "He kept us out of war" became the Democrats' rallying cry.

The race was extremely close. On election eve the *New York Times* and the *New York World* both awarded victory to Hughes, who went to bed believing he had won. However, Wilson won in the electoral college by a vote of 277 to 254, with a popular vote margin of 9.1 million to Hughes's 8.5 million.

The End of Neutrality

Interpreting his reelection as a vote for peace, Wilson attempted to mediate an end to the war. In January 1916 Wilson urged both sides to embrace his call for "peace without victory," but neither welcomed his overtures. Randolph Bourne was right. Above all else, the belligerents wanted victory.

Any hope for a negotiated settlement ended when Germany announced that after February 1, 1917, all vessels caught in the war zone, neutral or belligerent, armed or unarmed, would be sunk without warning. Driven to desperation by the British blockade and unable to break the impasse on land, Germany had decided to risk everything on a furious U-boat campaign designed to starve Britain into submission.

Members of his cabinet pressed Wilson to declare war, but he broke diplomatic relations instead, viewing war as the defeat of reason. For weeks he seemed indecisive and confused, unable to accept the fact that "strict accountability" demanded war once the Germans started sinking American ships.

The Zimmermann telegram snapped Wilson out of his daze. In January, British cryptographers intercepted a secret message from Arthur Zimmermann, the German foreign minister, to the German ambassador to Mexico, proposing an alliance between Germany and Mexico in the event Germany went to war with the United States. Germany promised to help Mexico recover the territory it had lost in the 1840s, roughly the present-day states of Texas, New Mexico, California, and Arizona. The British revealed the scheme to Wilson, hoping to draw the United States into the war.

The Zimmermann telegram convinced Wilson and millions of Americans that Germany would stop at nothing to satisfy her ambitions and that those ambitions posed a serious danger to America's rights and security. On March 12 Wilson issued an executive order arming merchant ships and instructing them to shoot submarines on sight.

At this critical juncture, with the United States and Germany virtually at war, the Russian Revolution erupted. Suddenly, the Czar's government was swept away, and in its place stood the provisional government of a Russian Republic, complete with a representative parliament. With the only autocratic regime among the Allies transformed overnight into a fledgling democracy, the war now truly seemed to pit the forces of democracy against the forces of despotism.

Pale and solemn, Wilson delivered his war message to Congress on April 2. The United States "had no quarrel with the German people," he insisted, but their "military masters" had to be defeated in order to make the world "safe for democracy." The next day the Senate approved the war resolution, 82 to 6; the House followed on April 6, 373 to 50. The president signed the declaration on April 7, 1917, and America was at war.

For more than two years Wilson had worked frantically to keep the United States at peace: Why did he now lead the nation to war? Cultural ties and economic motivations did not decide the issue. Wilson drew the sword, although reluctantly, because he concluded that German submarines had violated international law and made a mockery of America's long-standing commitment to freedom of the seas. His strong defense of neutral rights left him no choice but to declare war once Germany resumed its attacks on American ships.

One additional factor weighed heavily on Wilson—his desire to help shape the peace. By entering the war, the United States would be guaranteed a place at the peace table. "I hate this war," an anguished Wilson confided to an aide, "and the only thing I care about on earth is the peace I am going to make at the end of it."

Most Americans supported Wilson's call to arms. John Dewey, the famed educator, spoke for progressives when he described war as an ugly reality that had to be converted into an instrument for benefiting mankind. Randolph Bourne disagreed. "If the war is too strong for you to prevent," he asked pointedly, "how is it going to be weak enough for you to control and mould to your liberal purposes?"

American Industry Goes to War

The United States entered the Great War unprepared. The problems went far beyond the puny size of the military forces. Americans themselves had no idea of what the war would ask of them as a society. Decisions had to be made about mobilization, but the public had not formed a consensus on the proper role of government in society, especially during wartime. As a result, Wilson hesitated to mobilize by decree. Instead, he tried to create a system of economic incentives that would encourage Americans to support the war in a spirit of voluntary cooperation.

Voluntarism

It took nearly a year to organize an effective war administration. Wilson established a war cabinet with six key boards, each with broad powers to promote voluntarism. The War Industries Board (WIB), organized early in 1918 under the leadership of Bernard M. Baruch, a Wall Street financier, assumed the task of managing the economy by fixing prices, setting priorities, and reducing waste. To increase production, the WIB appealed to the profit motive, setting prices artificially high, permitting profits to triple during the war.

The Fuel Administration, the War Trade Board, the Shipping Board, and the U.S. Railroad Administration adopted similar policies. The Fuel Administration increased production by two-fifths and conserved supplies through voluntary "lightless nights" and "gasless Sundays." By offering large profits to railroads and high wages to workers, the Railroad Administration established an efficient rail system under national control.

Agricultural production came under the jurisdiction of the Food Administration, headed by Herbert Hoover, a self-made millionaire who had served with distinction as director of relief operations in Belgium. Appealing to the spirit of patriotism, he preached "the gospel of the clean plate." Americans "Hooverized" with wheatless Mondays and Wednesdays, meatless Tuesdays, and porkless Thursdays and Saturdays.

No foe of profits, Hoover set farm prices at high levels to encourage production, stabilized the grain market by guaranteeing farmers a minimum price, and purchased raw sugar and then sold it to refineries at a fixed rate. The policies worked. Overall, real farm incomes rose 30 percent during the war, food production increased by one-quarter, domestic food consumption fell, and America's food shipments to the Allies tripled.

Peace with Labor

The government also made concessions to labor. Gradually, Wilson recognized labor's right to organize and to engage in collective bargaining, and he sanctioned other key demands, including the eight-hour workday. To settle labor disputes, Wilson created the National War Labor Board (WLB). Though it lacked legal authority, the WLB had the president's backing and a commitment from industry and labor to accept its decisions.

While Wilson embraced moderate unions like the AFL, his administration opposed the militant Industrial Workers of the World (IWW or the "Wobblies"), which demanded higher wages and better working conditions, and went out on strike to win them. Because the Wobblies frequently employed the rhetoric of class warfare to dramatize their demands, their strikes frightened many Americans who feared social revolution. Businessmen played upon these fears to demand suppression of the radical unions. The Wobblies were "traitors," they sneered, and the IWW stood for "I Won't Work."

The AFL shrewdly separated itself from the militant workers, pledging not to strike for the duration of the war. The AFL supported the war and joined the administration's attack on socialist critics. In return, the AFL won a voice in home-front labor policy. Union men occupied seats in wartime agencies, where they pushed for the eight-hour day and staved off pressure from employers bent on preserving the open shop. Real income of manufacturing workers and coal miners rose, hours were reduced, and AFL membership jumped from 2.7 million in 1916 to 4 million in 1919.

Financing the War

By 1920 the war had cost $33.5 billion—33 times the federal government's revenues in 1916. Conservatives favored a regressive tax policy: consump-

Wilson's administration opposed militant labor unions like the Industrial Workers of the World (IWW), shown here striking against Oliver Steel in Pennsylvania. Such strikes did little to help the war effort at home. Samuel Gompers, who wanted to separate members of the American Federation of Labor (AFL) from more militant workers, pledged not to strike until the war was over.

tion taxes, borrowing, and, if necessary, a slight increase in income taxes. Reformers and radicals demanded a progressive tax policy: inheritance and excess profits taxes coupled with higher income taxes. Wilson walked the middle ground, but the heaviest burdens fell on the wealthy through taxes on large incomes, corporate profits, and estates. By 1919 the tax burden in the highest income brackets had risen to 77 percent.

World War I brought an important change in the sources of federal tax revenues. Before the war nearly three-quarters of federal revenues had come from excise and customs taxes. After the war, America's tax structure shifted from taxing consumption to taxing wealth, proof that progressives had won an important victory in the struggle to make upper-income groups pay a large share of the cost of government. On the tax issue Randolph Bourne was wrong.

The American Public Goes to War

Although Wilson preferred to rely on voluntary efforts rather than mandated government interference, federal powers were greatly expanded during World War I. Wilson's decision to substitute voluntarism for statutory controls on industry placed the burden of supporting the war on the profit motive and the public's sense of patriotism. This policy avoided the clash between Wilson and industry that would have resulted from strict government control over the economy, but it did so at a huge cost to civil liberties.

Selling the War

Throughout the war the government directed its coercion at people rather than industries, largely through the Committee on Public Information (CPI). Ably led by George W. Creel, the CPI became America's first propaganda agency. Creel immediately drafted a voluntary censorship agreement with newspapers to keep sensitive military information out of print. The CPI hired hundreds of musicians, writers, and artists to stage a patriotic campaign, sponsored 75,000 speakers to deliver war pep talks in vaudeville and movie theaters across the country, and got movie stars to sell war bonds.

Indeed, the CPI found a powerful ally in Hollywood. Quick to perceive the link between patriotism and profits, studio moguls cranked out scores of crude propaganda films with titles such as *The Prussian Cur, The*

Claws of the Hun, and *To Hell with the Kaiser,* which reduced World War I to a conflict between good and evil, heroes and villains.

Popular culture reflected the CPI's influence. Suddenly, dissent meant treason, Germans devolved into Huns, and German-Americans all spied for the fatherland. It did not matter that the vast majority of German-Americans supported the United States; the CPI consistently attacked their loyalty. At its best the CPI may have sold war bonds, discouraged

Hollywood and Tin Pan Alley did their parts to encourage patriotism by putting out scores of war films and a large number of music pieces like the one shown here.

war stoppages, and convinced the public to support the war; at its worst the CPI fostered a witch-hunt.

In the name of patriotism, musicians no longer played Bach and Beethoven, schools stopped teaching the German language, and Americans renamed sauerkraut "liberty cabbage." Cincinnati, with its large German-American population, even removed pretzels from the free lunch counters in saloons. More alarming, vigilante groups attacked anyone suspected of being unpatriotic. Many German-Americans became the victims of mob violence. Workers who refused to buy war bonds often suffered harsh retribution, and attacks on labor protesters were nothing short of brutal. The legal system backed the suppression. Juries routinely released defendants accused of violence against individuals or groups critical of the war.

Political Repression

The government fueled the hysteria. In June 1917 Congress passed the Espionage Act, which gave postal officials the authority to ban newspapers and magazines from the mails and threatened individuals convicted of obstructing the draft with $10,000 fines and 20 years in jail. Congress passed the Sedition Act in 1918, which made it a federal offense to use "disloyal, profane, scurrilous, or abusive language" about the Constitution, the government, the American uniform, or the flag. The government prosecuted over 2,100 people under these acts. Randolph Bourne's prediction that civil rights would fall victim to the power of the state rang true.

Political dissenters bore the brunt of the repression. Eugene V. Debs, who urged socialists to resist militarism, went to prison for nearly three years. In September 1917 the Justice Department staged massive raids on IWW officers, arresting 169 of its veteran leaders. Many observers thought the judicial system would protect dissenters, but the courts handed down stiff prison sentences to the Wobblies.

World War I did not cause repression; it merely intensified old fears, offering intolerant citizens a chance to lash out at those who had changed America. Immigrants, radical labor organizers, socialists, anarchists, Communists, and critics of any kind became victims of intolerance.

Wartime Reform

The war hysteria bred a curious alliance between superpatriots and old style reformers. Prohibitionists had little difficulty turning World War I to their advantage. In 1917 Congress prohibited the use of grain for the production of alcoholic beverages, insisting that foodstuffs must be used to feed America's soldiers and Allies. Prohibitionists joined the anti-German craze, warning that German-Americans controlled the nation's breweries. Congress passed the Eighteenth Amendment in 1917. The Volstead Act, which banned the manufacture, transportation, and sale of alcoholic beverages, took effect in 1920.

Like prohibition, women's suffrage benefited from the emergency atmosphere of World War I. Most women's organizations supported the war effort. As blue-collar female workers started pouring into defense industries, middle-class women showed their support by volunteering to help the sick and the wounded. Thousands of women joined the Red Cross and the American Women's Hospital Service, serving overseas as nurses, physicians, clerks, and ambulance drivers. Thousands more enlisted after the army established the Army Corps of Nurses in 1918.

Suffragists demanded the vote in return for their support of the war. Wilson had long opposed women's suffrage, but political reality ultimately forced his hand. Most western states had granted women the vote before he entered the White House. Alice Paul, head of the National Woman's Party, pressed the issue by organizing around-the-clock picketing in front of the White House. Determined to prevent women's suffrage from becoming a political issue in the congressional elections of 1918, Wilson told the Senate that the vote for women "is vital to the winning of the war." In 1919 Congress passed the Nineteenth Amendment, granting women the right to vote. Ratification followed in the summer of 1920.

Apart from voting rights, World War I brought few permanent changes for women. Women had hoped the war would open new jobs for them. Instead, employment opportunities proved meager and brief. Labor unions opposed hiring women and tolerated their presence solely as a wartime necessity, arguing that industrial jobs belonged to men and should be returned to them as soon as the war ended. As a result, the number of women who remained in the work force in 1920 dropped below the 1910 figures.

Blacks and the Great Migration

Like women, blacks wanted to use the war to improve their status. While the government had given blacks little reason to shed their blood, most black newspapers backed the war. W. E. B. Du Bois urged blacks to "close ranks" with whites, hoping that blacks, by demonstrating patriotism and bravery, could win public respect and earn better treatment after the war.

At first military leaders even denied blacks the right to fight for their country. The marines accepted no blacks; the navy used them only as mess boys; and the army planned to make them laborers and stevedores.

When the National Association for the Advancement of Colored People (NAACP) and other black organizations protested, however, the army agreed to compromise. Following the Civil War example, the army created black regiments commanded almost exclusively by white officers. Black regiments committed to battle fought bravely, but only one-fifth of the black troops ever saw combat. Instead, most were assigned to move supplies.

Back home the record was equally mixed. In the decades following the Civil War a steady trickle of blacks had left the South to search for jobs in northern cities. During World War I the trickle became a flood. When labor agents appeared in 1916 promising jobs in the North, blacks responded eagerly. By November 1918 the "Great Migration" had brought half a million southern blacks to the "Land of Hope." Many found jobs in northern factories and packinghouses. Still, regardless of the industry, discrimination forced blacks to the bottom of the ladder, where they took over the menial, backbreaking jobs that had been vacated by the most recent wave of immigrants.

The 369th Infantry Regiment returned from the war in February 1919. They were awarded the *Croix de Guerre* (war cross) for bravery in the Meuse-Argonne.

The Great Migration angered southern whites. The price of cotton tripled during the war; southern planters, fearing the loss of their labor force, resorted to intimidation and mob violence to stop the exodus. Northern whites opposed the Great Migration, too. Manufacturers welcomed cheap black labor (especially as strikebreakers), but most northerners felt threatened by the newcomers. Increasingly, they turned to segregation, discrimination, and violence; and blacks, hoping for a better life in the North, fought back. Race riots erupted in 26 cities in 1917, with the most serious violence occurring in East St. Louis, where at least 39 blacks died in the fighting.

Clearly, World War I meant different things to different groups: for the administration, a test of the limits of voluntarism; for businessmen and technocrats, a chance to pull the levers of government; for nativists and superpatriots, an excuse to lash out at "undesirable" elements; for radicals and dissenters, repression and hardship; for manufacturers and farmers, high profits; for reformers, victories on women's suffrage and prohibition; for trade unions, the right to organize for better pay; and for blacks, a chance to escape from southern poverty.

The War Front

The United States entered World War I without a large army or the ships to transport one to Europe. With the Allies ready to collapse due to huge casualties, low morale, and a dwindling supply of food, Wilson ordered the navy to act immediately. Six destroyers reached Ireland on May 4; 35 ships had arrived by July; and 343 ships patrolled the seas surrounding England by the war's end.

To cut down losses of merchant ships, which in April alone totaled 881,027 tons, the Americans proposed a convoy system—using warships to escort merchant ships to Great Britain. By December the convoy system had cut losses in half.

Raising an Army

Wilson's choice to lead the American Expeditionary Force (AEF) was Major General John J. "Black Jack" Pershing. Despite urgent requests from Allied commanders, Pershing refused to send raw recruits to the front, and he rejected demands that American units be integrated into British and French regiments. Instead, Pershing insisted on keeping American troops as independent units under his command. To bolster Allied morale, the War Department hurriedly dispatched the First Division to France, where it marched through Paris on July 4, 1917, to the cheers of thousands.

A bitter debate erupted over how to raise the troops. Despite heavy pressure from Theodore Roosevelt and others who favored a volunteer army, Wilson insisted on conscription. Congress passed the Selective Service Act on May 18, 1917.

To assign soldiers to the right military tasks, the army launched an ambitious program of psychological testing. Though the tests supposedly measured native intelligence, in reality they favored men with the most schooling, and thus reinforced the class structure of American society. Native-born whites achieved the highest scores, while blacks and recent immigrants consistently scored lower.

Apart from selecting officers, the army made little use of the test data. Ordinary soldiers were not assigned tasks on the basis of test scores. All the testing really accomplished was to sell the public on the idea of mental testing and lay the groundwork for a thriving peacetime industry. After the war, numerous businesses adopted mental tests to screen personnel, and many colleges began requiring them for admission. Few legacies of the war had a more lasting or widespread impact on American society.

The Defeat of Germany

As the American army trained, the situation in Europe deteriorated. Mutiny within the French army was spreading; the eastern front dissolved in March when the Bolsheviks, who had seized power in Russia in November, accepted Germany's peace terms; and German and Austrian forces had all but routed the Italian armies. In fact, by late 1917 the war had come down to a race between American mobilization and Germany's war machine.

On March 21, 1918, the Germans launched a massive offensive on the western front in the Valley of the Somme in France. For a time, it looked as though the Germans would succeed. Badly bloodied, the Allied forces lost ground. But with German troops barely 50 miles from Paris, Marshal Ferdinand Foch, the leader of the French army, assumed command of the Allied forces. Foch's troops, aided by 85,000 American soldiers, launched a furious counteroffensive, hitting the Germans hard in a series of bloody assaults. By the end of October the German army had been pushed back to the Belgian border.

During the final months of fighting, American troops hit Europe like a tidal wave. In June 279,000 American soldiers crossed the Atlantic; in July more than 300,000; in August, 286,000. All told, 1.5 million American troops arrived in Europe during the last six months of the war.

Fresh and battle ready, Pershing's forces made the crucial difference in the war. Buoyed by the fresh manpower, the Allies pressed their advantage. Their furious offensive in the summer of 1918 broke the opposition, and within a few months the Central Powers faced certain defeat. The Austro-Hungarian Empire asked for peace; Turkey and Bulgaria stopped fighting; and Germany requested an armistice. In a direct slap at the kaiser, Wilson announced he would negotiate only with a democratic regime in Germany. When the military leaders and the kaiser wavered, a brief revolution forced the kaiser to abdicate, and a civilian regime assumed control of the government.

Germany's new government immediately accepted the armistice and agreed to negotiate a treaty. At 11:00 A.M., November 11, 1918, the guns stopped. Throughout the Western world, crowds filled the streets to celebrate peace.

Social Unrest After the War

Peace did not restore stability to the United States. Race relations deteriorated, as tensions rose in the North because of competition between whites and blacks for jobs and housing. In the South whites felt threatened by the return of 400,000 black veterans, many of whom had been trained in the use of firearms, even if many had not seen actual combat. Moreover, many black veterans had served in France where they were treated as equals, and southern whites feared they would demand the same treatment at home. Determined to keep blacks repressed, southern whites instituted a reign of terror. About 70 lynchings occurred in the first year of peace.

As the heat of summer brought tensions to a boil, race riots broke out in 25 cities. The worst violence erupted on a Chicago beach where 17-year-old Eugene Williams strayed into waters claimed by whites. A rock-throwing mob kept him from reaching shore, and Williams drowned. Fighting broke out when police refused to arrest his killers. Thirteen days of street violence followed, leaving 38 dead, 578 injured, and 1,000 families homeless. Racial injustice remained a defining feature of American life throughout the Progressive Era, despite American efforts abroad to make the world "safe for democracy."

Labor Unrest and the Red Scare

Labor was another trouble spot. Most workers demonstrated their patriotism by not striking during the war, but the Armistice ended their truce with management. High inflation, job competition from returning veterans, and government policies all contributed to labor's discontent. Of the three, inflation hit workers the hardest. Food prices more than doubled between 1915 and 1920; clothing costs more than tripled. Wilson had made peace with trade unions only as a wartime necessity. After the fighting stopped, he removed controls on industry, and business leaders closed ranks to roll back concessions to workers.

The first strike came four days after the Armistice; many more occurred in the months that followed. Strikers ranged from clothing and textile workers to actors, miners, and telephone operators. In the steel industry 365,000 workers went on strike; even the Boston police force walked out. By the end of 1919 more than four million workers (20 percent of the work force) had staged over 3,600 strikes nationwide.

The strikes frightened middle- and upper-class Americans, who feared the country might be swept by revolution. The government made matters worse by blaming the strikes on Communists. In 1919 Russian Bolsheviks called for socialists and workers in Europe and the United States to seize their governments and join the worldwide revolution. When Communist revolts erupted in eastern Europe, Americans braced themselves for trouble at home.

A bomb scare brought public fears to a head. On the eve of May 1 (May Day), 1919, authorities discovered 20 bombs in the mail of prominent capitalists, including John D. Rockefeller and J. P. Morgan, Jr., as well as government officials like Justice Oliver Wendell Holmes. A month later bombs exploded in eight American cities. Anarchists were probably responsible, but the public blamed the Communists.

Fear sparked by the labor unrest, Communism, and the bombings plunged the United States into the "Red Scare." Every threat to national security, real or imagined, fed the public's anxiety. Vigilantism flourished as juries across the country acquitted individuals accused of violent acts against Communists. Federal authorities, breaking up the IWW, arrested 1,000 Wobblies and slapped the union's leaders with stiff prison sentences. The nation had lost confidence in its ability to survive without police-state tactics. Civil liberties became the first victim of the hysteria, for the Bill of Rights was all but suspended. Again, Randolph Bourne's warnings hit the mark.

Attorney General A. Mitchell Palmer led the attack on radicalism. Determined to become president in 1920, Palmer hoped to ride a wave of public hysteria against radicalism into the White House. To root out sedition, he created a General Intelligence Division (the precursor of the Federal Bureau of Investigation) in the Justice Department under the direction of J. Edgar Hoover. Hoover collected the names of thousands of known or suspected Communists and made plans for a coordinated government attack on their headquarters.

Within the course of three months, raids ordered by Palmer in 45 cities netted more than 4,000 arrests of alleged Communists, many of whom were jailed without bond, beaten, and denied food and water for days. Local authorities freed most of them in a few weeks, except for 600 aliens, who were deported. While Palmer insisted he was ridding the country of the "moral perverts," to cooler heads his tactics gave off the unmistakable odor of a police state. Suddenly on the defensive, Palmer tried to rally public support by predicting a second wave of terrorist attacks on May Day, 1920. Federal troops went on alert, and police braced themselves in cities across the country, but May Day came and went without incident. Palmer's bid for the White House fizzled, and the Red Scare faded into memory.

The Treaty of Versailles

Long before the war's military outcome became clear, the Allies started planning for peace, signing secret treaties plotting harsh peace terms for Germany. Their plans made a mockery of Wilson's call for "peace without victory." Wilson, however, felt a punitive treaty would sow the seeds of future wars. He repeatedly elaborated his ideas on the interdependence of democracy, free trade, and liberty, and on January 8, 1918, he unveiled the Fourteen Points, his personal peace formula.

The Fourteen Points

Among other things, Wilson called for "open covenants openly arrived at," freedom of the seas, free trade, arms reduction, and self-determination. Other points demanded partial or full independence for minorities and a recognition of the rise of nationalist sentiments. The fourteenth point, which Wilson considered the heart of his plan, called for a League of Nations, an international organization to promote world peace.

Economically, the Fourteen Points projected Wilson's vision of liberal capitalism onto a world stage. His call for freedom of the seas and free trade was designed to protect free market capitalism from monopolistic restrictions and open huge markets to booming American industries. Self-determination would offer independence to Europe's minorities and thereby delight millions of recent immigrants back in the United States, most of whom were drifting into the Democratic party. The League of

Nations would enable the world to police aggression and relieve the United States of that responsibility.

Wilson's personal prestige peaked with the Armistice. During the war Democrats and Republicans had closed ranks behind his leadership. Europeans saw Wilson as the moral leader of the Western democracies, and his authority rested not only on words but on might. Economically, the United States was now the most powerful nation on earth.

Yet Wilson proved to be his own worst enemy in marshaling support for his peace plans. His first mistake was in asking voters to support Democratic candidates at the polls in 1918. His request offended Republicans who had faithfully supported the administration throughout the war. When voters gave Republicans a narrow majority (primarily reflecting local issues), Wilson looked as if he had lost a national referendum on his leadership.

The American Peace Commission's composition further alienated Congress. Wilson elected to take personal responsibility for negotiating the peace, a role no previous president had assumed. In addition, he named only one Republican to the five-man commission; the other three men were loyal Democrats. The failure to include a prominent Republican senator, such as Henry Cabot Lodge, the newly elected chairman of the powerful Senate Committee on Foreign Relations, was a serious tactical error. The treaty had to be approved by two-thirds of the Senate, and Republicans picked up five new Senate seats in the congressional elections of 1918, giving them a two-vote majority.

Discord Among the Victors

The delegates, who arrived in Europe early in January 1919, confronted three basic issues: territory, reparations, and future security. On each of these issues, Wilson and the Allies disagreed. Early in the war the Allies decided to divide Germany's territorial possessions among themselves, but the Fourteen Points called for self-determination. Devastated by the war, the Allies (especially France) wanted to saddle Germany with huge reparations to pay for the war. The Fourteen Points rejected punishment, arguing it would only lead to future wars. On the issue of security, France wanted Germany dismembered while the other Allies favored treaties and alliances.

Only five nations played an important role in the proceedings (the Allies refused to allow Russia's Communist government a place at the peace table). Prime Minister David Lloyd George of Great Britain proved to be Wilson's staunchest ally, yet he also defended Britain's colonial ambitions and insisted on reparations. Premier Georges Clemenceau of

France was determined to break up the German empire and bleed the German people dry in order to rebuild France. Premier Vittorio Orlando of Italy was bent on pressing Italy's territorial ambitions in the Tyrol and on the Adriatic. When Wilson refused to sanction Italy's sovereignty over the largely Yugoslav population near Fiume, Orlando stormed out of the peace conference in disgust. The final important negotiator was Count Nobuaki Makino, the spokesman for Japan, who demanded control over German interests in the Far East.

To achieve any treaty at all, Wilson had to compromise. In the end he tried to scale down the Allied demands and pinned his hopes on the League of Nations. Under the territorial compromise, the Allies gained control of Germany's colonies as "mandates" under the League of Nation's supervision. Japan acquired Germany's Pacific islands under mandate and assumed Germany's economic interest in China's Shantung peninsula. In eastern Europe the delegates created the nation-states of Poland, Yugoslavia, Czechoslovakia, Estonia, Latvia, Lithuania, and Finland. Eu-

At the Versailles peace conference Wilson met with Prime Minister David Lloyd George, Premier Vittorio Orlando, and Premier Georges Clemenceau.

rope's political map for the first time roughly resembled its linguistic and cultural map.

Over the misgivings of most delegates, Wilson insisted on making the League of Nations an integral part of the final treaty. France remained dubious that any international organization could protect French borders and demanded a buffer zone. To satisfy Clemenceau, the delegates gave France a buffer zone to protect it from future German aggression. After Wilson and Lloyd George both signed security treaties guaranteeing these arrangements, France grudgingly agreed to join the League of Nations.

Despite promises of a just peace, the treaty imposed a harsh settlement on Germany, burdening the country with a $34 billion reparations bill, far more than Germany could pay. In addition, Germany lost territories that contained German people. Moreover, the war guilt clause in the reparations bill required Germany to accept the blame for World War I and dismantle its war machine. Germany felt betrayed. Clearly, this was not a peace based upon the Fourteen Points. Rather, it brought to life Bourne's prediction of victors who "grab what they can."

Wilson derived no joy from the Treaty of Versailles. He accepted the treaty's territorial and punitive provisions in order to ensure the adoption of the League of Nations, which he hoped would secure world peace and eventually redress the treaty's inequities. The League consisted of a general assembly, and an executive council composed of the United States, Great Britain, France, Italy, Japan, and four other states to be elected by the assembly. But the heart of the League was clearly Article 10, which pledged all members "to respect and uphold the territorial integrity and independence of all members of the League." It embodied Wilson's dream of an international organization that would keep the peace by giving all nations (large and small) equality and protection.

The Struggle for Ratification

Wilson knew the treaty faced stiff opposition back home. In February 1919, 39 Senate Republicans had signed a petition warning that they would not approve the League in its present form. To court domestic support, Wilson persuaded the delegates in Europe to acknowledge the Monroe Doctrine, omit domestic issues from the League's purview, and permit member states to withdraw after two years' notice. Though he worked to include provisions the Senate wanted, Wilson refused to separate the League from the treaty.

Senate opposition broke into three groups. The first, 14 "irreconcilables," were staunch isolationists who opposed the League of Nations in any form. Though their attack was broad-based, they concentrated their fire on Article 10, which called for the mutual protection of the territorial integrity of all member states. Critics charged that this article gave the League the authority to commit American troops to foreign military actions. Henry Cabot Lodge of Massachusetts spoke for the "strong reservationists." Lodge and his followers were basically in favor of the treaty and could have been won over if Wilson agreed to their modifications. Like the irreconcilables, they were also opposed to Article 10, insisting that only Congress had the right to commit American troops. The third group of opponents could have been won over by relatively minor alterations. They approached international affairs as cautious nationalists, favoring an independent foreign policy as the best tool for protecting American interests. With their backing and the support of Senate Democrats, the treaty would have passed easily.

As Wilson sailed back to the United States, polls suggested that most Americans favored the League in some form. All he had to do was compromise and the treaty would pass. Dismissing his opponents as "blind and little provincial people," he declared that the "Senate must take its medicine."

Fearing Senate debate had eroded popular support for the treaty, Wilson decided to take his case directly to the people. Although in poor health, he launched a nationwide tour in September 1919, covering 8,000 miles in 33 days and delivering 32 major addresses. He started in the Midwest where opposition to the treaty was strongest, gradually moving west where he met cheering crowds. Totally exhausted, Wilson collapsed on September 25 in Pueblo, Colorado. Four days after returning to Washington, he suffered a severe stroke that paralyzed the left side of his body.

Unable to work, the president did not meet his cabinet for more than six months. Since the law made no provision for removing an incapacitated president, Wilson's second wife, Edith, assisted by a few close aides, ran the government, operating under a cloak of silence about the president's condition.

As the Senate vote on the treaty drew near, Wilson, whose stroke may have impaired his judgment, remained intransigent. He ordered all Democrats to vote against the treaty if it contained any changes. On November 19 the Senate defeated the revised version of the treaty, 55 to 39; a few minutes later the Senate defeated the treaty without changes, 39 to 53.

The Senate's failure to reach a compromise must be blamed on Wilson. When the treaty's supporters tried again in March, many of the Democrats disobeyed the president and voted for a revised version. But 23 Democrats followed Wilson's orders, and the treaty fell seven votes short of adoption. It would be wrong to interpret the treaty's defeat as an endorsement of isolationism. In essence, the Senate rejected both isolationism and Wilsonian internationalism in favor of preserving a nationalistic foreign policy that would allow the United States to act independently.

The refusal of the Senate to ratify the Treaty of Versailles and join the League of Nations is satirized in this cartoon.

The Election of 1920

When the Democratic convention met in San Francisco, the delegates ignored Wilson's pathetic anglings for a third term and nominated Governor James M. Cox of Ohio. The Republicans nominated Senator Warren G. Harding of Ohio. A stalwart party regular on domestic issues, Harding had voted for the Treaty of Versailles with the Lodge reservations.

While Cox barnstormed the country, campaigning unequivocally for the League of Nations and the Treaty of Versailles, Harding waffled on the issue. Tired of foreign crusades, voters clearly wanted a change, giving Harding 61 percent of the popular vote. In the electoral college Harding trounced Cox 404 to 127.

Harding interpreted his victory as a mandate to reject the League. America never joined the League of Nations, opening the way for those who later blamed the United States for the rise of fascism in Italy and Nazism in Germany. Critics went so far as to claim that America's failure to join the League caused World War II. If the United States had only joined, they insisted, the League would have been able to deter German and Japanese aggression by presenting a united front. The war's main legacy, then, was not peace without victory, but bitterness and suspicion.

*C*hronology of Key Events

1914	World War I begins
1915	U.S. marines dispatched to Haiti; Germans sink *Lusitania,* British passenger ship
1916	*Sussex* pledge temporarily reduces tensions between U.S. and Germany
1917	Zimmermann telegram urges Mexico and Japan to join Central Powers; United States enters the war in Europe; Espionage Act passed; Russian Revolution begins; War Industries Board created to coordinate industrial production; Selective Service Act
1918	Wilson outlines plan for peace in his Fourteen Points; National War Labor Board created to arbitrate labor-management disputes; Sedition Act passed; Germany surrenders
1919	Treaty of Versailles ends World War I
1920	Red Scare; Senate rejects Treaty of Versailles; Nineteenth Amendment adopted; Warren Harding is elected twenty-ninth president

Conclusion

World War I made Randolph Bourne a prophet. The changes in American life between 1914 and 1919 bore out his fear that war obliterates idealism and brings out the dark side of the human spirit. World War I accelerated social and economic changes, expanded the power of the federal government, and unleashed extraordinary fears that led to attacks on labor unions, blacks, immigrants, and radicals. Similar confusion gripped America's foreign policy. The United States emerged from the Great War as the premier economic power on earth, with global interests requiring protection. Those responsibilities terrified a country that had been lulled into a sense of security by three centuries of geographic isolation. Tired and disillusioned, Americans attempted to flee their responsibilities rather than make global political commitments commensurate with their new economic interests.

The result was an upsurge in isolationist sentiment in the United States during the 1920s and 1930s that made it very difficult for America's leaders to respond strongly to the rise of despotic governments in Europe and the Far East. The Great War did not make the world "safe for democracy." It left humankind a legacy of bitterness, hatred, and suspicion, creating rich soil for the seeds of future conflicts.

In 1920, however, most Americans felt too numb to give much thought to the future. When President Harding promised a return to "normalcy," he struck a responsive chord. Millions of Americans thought he meant resurrecting rural villages and a small farm economy, restoring Anglo-Protestant culture, and forgetting about the rest of the world. The 1920s proved they were in for a surprise.

Suggestions for Further Reading

For excellent overviews of analyses of America and World War I, consult Ross Gregory, *The Origins of American Intervention in the First World War* (1971); Ellis W. Hawley, *The Great War and the Search for a Modern Order* (1979); Gordon Levin, Jr., *Woodrow Wilson and World Politics* (1968); Bernadotte Schmitt and Harold C. Vedeler, *The World in the Crucible* (1984).

Women during and after the war are examined in Maurine Weiner Greenwald, *Women, War, and Work* (1980); Christine A. Lunardini, *From Equal Suffrage to Equal Rights: Alice Paul and the National Woman's Party* (1986).

Other sociopolitical issues are examined in James R. Grossman, *Land of Hope: Chicago, Black Southerners, and the Great Migration* (1989); David M. Kennedy, *Over Here: The First World War and American Society* (1980);

Frederick C. Luebke, *Bonds of Loyalty: German-Americans and World War I* (1974); Carole Marks, *Farewell—We're Good and Gone: The Great Black Migration* (1989).

The contentious debates surrounding the Treaty of Versailles are discussed in Herbert F. Margulies, *The Mild Reservationists and the League of Nations Controversy in the Senate* (1989); Arno J. Mayer, *Politics and Diplomacy in Peacemaking: Containment and Counterrevolution at Versailles* (1967); Ralph A. Stone, *The Irreconcilables* (1970); William C. Widenor, *Henry Cabot Lodge and the Search for an American Foreign Policy* (1980).

The most in-depth biography of Woodrow Wilson remains Arthur S. Link, *Wilson,* (5 vols. (1947–1965). For a study of Randolph Bourne, see James R. Vitelli, *Randolph Bourne* (1981). Bourne's essays can be found in Randolph S. Bourne, *War and the Intellectuals: Collected Essays* (1915–1919) (1964).

Chapter *24*

Modern Times, the 1920s

In 1898 the Physicians Club of Chicago held a symposium on "sexual hygiene" to give its members some practical tips on marriage counseling. To those married women who wanted information on birth control, Chicago physicians offered this advice: "Get a divorce and vacate the position for some other woman, who is able and willing to fulfill all a wife's duties as well as to enjoy her privileges."

Most Americans shared this view. They did not believe sex should be separated from procreation. To the male custodians of morality, birth control challenged patriarchy. It would lead to sexual promiscuity and an epidemic of venereal diseases, they charged, and weaken the family by raising the divorce rate. Many women condemned birth control just as soundly. Taught from childhood to embrace the cult of domesticity, they accepted childbearing as their "biological duty" and rejected birth control as immoral and radical.

Yet by 1950 most Americans regarded birth control as a public virtue rather than a private vice. The person most responsible for this amazing transformation was Margaret Sanger, a tireless crusader who possessed an iron will and the soul of a firebrand. Sanger's mother, Margaret Higgins, bore 11 children, all ten-pounders or more; Michael Higgins, her father worked as a stonecutter. Her mother died of pulmonary tuberculosis at 43; her father lived to 84. For the rest of her life, Sanger blamed her mother's suffering on the absence of effective family planning.

An unhappy marriage also pushed Sanger toward reform work. While still in nursing school, she married William Sanger, an architect and would-be artist. After bearing three children in rapid succession, Sanger overcame her own struggle with tuberculosis, finished school, and began a nursing career. Feeling trapped by married life and determined to achieve her own identity, Margaret plunged into New York's labor movement. As her marriage to William slowly dissolved, she devoted herself to the working poor.

Convinced that large families placed a terrible economic burden on poor people, Sanger came to regard family planning as the most important issue of her day because birth control would make abortion, as well as unwanted babies, unnecessary. When male labor leaders refused to add contraception to their reform agenda, Sanger left the labor movement, resolving to make birth control her life's work.

From 1914 to 1937 Sanger campaigned to make birth control morally acceptable. She built a network of clinics where women could get accurate information about contraception and obtain inexpensive, reliable birth control devices. After World War II she helped organize the international planned parenthood movement and played a key role in the development of "the pill." Through her birth control work, Margaret Sanger probably had a greater influence on the world than any other American woman of her day.

Margaret Sanger, a nurse who had watched many women suffer from unwanted births and die from illegal abortions, was one of the founders of the modern American birth control movement. After spending a year studying medical literature and learning about contraceptives, Sanger began publishing the journal *The Woman Rebel.*

Sanger played a key role in the transition to modern times. Her career illustrates how the reform spirit of the Progressive Era survived the conservative climate of the 1920s to touch the lives of future generations. No legacy of progressivism was more far-reaching than the birth control movement, which reformed sexual mores, redefined women's role in society, and redistributed power within the family. But the birth control movement represented just one symptom of a society in flux, one in which urban growth, ethnic diversity, and economic development set the stage for controversy.

The Clash of Values

In the wake of the Great War's carnage and failed promises, many Americans disagreed on a host of issues. Wets battled drys, atheists ridiculed fundamentalists, nativists denounced the "new immigrants," whites lashed out against blacks. Rural folks debated the dubious morals of city dwellers, while farmers glowered at industrialists. Yet none of these disputes was new. Each was a continuing, if sharpening, controversy that had been building for decades. At bottom these conflicts were the unavoidable

growing pains of a nation struggling to come to grips with cultural pluralism and changing values.

The Growth of Cities

Cities underwent dramatic and visible changes. By 1920, more Americans
dwelled in cities than in the country for the first time in the nation's history. Most urbanites lived in small towns and cities, but a surprising number resided in large cities of 50,000 or more. During the 1920s nearly 15
million Americans moved to cities.

Urban growth drove up land values and reshaped the skyline of America's cities, especially in central business districts, where office space more
than doubled during the 1920s. Skyrocketing land prices forced architects
to build "up" instead of "out," launching the first great era of skyscrapers.

America's cities attracted large numbers of new immigrants from
southern and eastern Europe. These immigrants poured into the industrial cities of the Northeast and Midwest, filling them with new sights,
sounds, and smells that many old-stock Americans found offensive. World
War I briefly stopped the flow of immigrants, but between 1919 and
1926, more than 3.2 million immigrants poured into the United States.

Blacks contributed to the new urban growth. In 1910 three out of every
four black Americans lived on farms, and nine out of ten lived in the South.
World War I changed that profile. Hoping to escape the tenant farming,
sharecropping, and peonage of the South, 1.5 million blacks moved to cities
in the 1920s. Some went to southern cities, but most settled in major northern metropolises such as New York, Philadelphia, Cleveland, and Chicago.

Black migration intensified housing shortages, making competition for
limited housing a source of friction between blacks and whites. In city after
city, whites closed ranks against blacks, blocking access to white neighborhoods. Cities passed municipal residential segregation ordinances; white realtors refused to show blacks houses in white areas; and white property owners
formed "neighborhood improvement associations," largely in order to keep
blacks out. After the Supreme Court declared municipal residential segregation ordinances unconstitutional in 1917, whites resorted to the restrictive
convenant, a formal deed restriction binding white property owners in a
given neighborhood not to sell to blacks. Whites who broke these agreements
could be sued by "damaged" neighbors. Not until 1948 did the Supreme
Court strike down restrictive covenants. Zoning laws offered a more subtle
means of segregating blacks. Originally designed to keep businessmen and
industries out of residential neighborhoods, zoning restrictions had become
the tool of choice for segregating people on the basis of wealth by the 1930s.

Racial animosity, restrictive covenants, and zoning restrictions confined blacks to certain neighborhoods. Between World War I and World

War II scores of American cities developed cities within cities. These "black metropolises" resembled ethnic ghettos of the late nineteenth and early twentieth centuries, with one major difference: racial prejudice made it all but impossible for their residents to escape to the suburbs.

Black Protests

In the 1920s several black organizations stepped up their protests against discrimination, which heightened the fears of many old-stock Americans. Closely identified with Booker T. Washington's conciliatory approach to race relations, the National Urban League, organized in 1911 by social workers, white philanthropists, and conservative blacks, concentrated on finding jobs for urban African Americans. Despite the nation's postwar prosperity, blacks made scant progress on the job front during the 1920s.

Leaving economic issues to the Urban League, the National Association for the Advancement of Colored People (NAACP), formed in 1909, concentrated on civil rights and legal action. The NAACP won important Supreme Court decisions against the grandfather clause (1915) and restrictive covenants (1917). The NAACP also fought school segregation in northern cities during the 1920s, and lobbied hard, though unsuccessfully, for a federal antilynching bill. Though progress on these fronts did not come until after World War II, the NAACP became the nation's leading civil rights organization.

Black radicals dismissed the Urban League and the NAACP as too conservative. A. Philip Randolph, the editor of the Socialist monthly, the *Messenger,* called for a "New Negro" who would meet violence with violence to end discrimination and achieve racial equality. Randolph also urged blacks to seek admission into trade unions. Though Randolph addressed the black masses, he appealed to the college-educated, black elite. Most blacks neither read nor understood his theories.

Marcus Garvey spoke for the black masses. A flamboyant and charismatic figure from Jamaica, Garvey rejected integration and preached racial pride and black separatism, exhorting his followers to glorify their African heritage. In 1914 Garvey organized the Universal Negro Improvement Association (UNIA) to promote black migration to Africa. Under the slogan, "Africa for the Africans, at home and abroad," the UNIA's Black Star Steamship Line sold stock to thousands of members, promising to help blacks migrate to Africa. Garvey also advocated economic self-sufficiency for those who remained in the United States. To enable his followers to buy only from black-owned businesses, the UNIA opened a chain of laundries, groceries, restaurants, a hotel, a doll factory (whose products all had black bodies), and a printing plant.

The UNIA collapsed in the mid-1920s after the Black Star Line went bankrupt. Garvey was charged with mail fraud, jailed, and finally deported, but this "Black Moses" left behind a rich legacy. At a time when magazines and newspapers overflowed with advertisements for hair straighteners and skin-lightening cosmetics, Garvey's message of racial pride struck a responsive chord in many black Americans.

The Harlem Renaissance

The movement for black pride found its cultural expression in the Harlem Renaissance. Located in New York's upper Manhattan, Harlem attracted black intellectuals who migrated from small towns or rural areas where they had felt stifled and oppressed.

By the 1920s the Harlem Renaissance was in full bloom. Langston Hughes probed the past in his elegant poem, "The Negro Speaks of Rivers." In *Cane,* Jean Toomer, perhaps the most gifted prose writer of the renaissance, explored the lives of blacks who toiled in Georgia's sawmills in the 1880s. Yet for all its artistic promise, the Harlem Renaissance had little influence on the black masses, most of whom never knew it existed. Moreover, the Harlem Renaissance often reflected the cultural stereotypes of white liberals, who underwrote the renaissance by providing scholarships, prizes, and grants to aspiring young black artists. Leaders of the Harlem Renaissance shied away from controversial social issues and all but ignored jazz, one of the most important black contributions to American popular culture.

The New Woman and the Sex Debate

"If all girls at the Yale prom were laid end to end, I wouldn't be surprised," sighed Dorothy Parker, the official wit of New York's smart set. Parker's quip captured the public's perception that America's morals had taken a nosedive. Practically every newspaper featured articles on prostitution, venereal disease, sex education, birth control, and the rising divorce rate.

City life nurtured new sexual attitudes. With its crowded anonymity, urban culture eroded sexual inhibitions by relaxing community restraints on individual behavior. Cities also promoted secular, consumer values, and city people seemed to tolerate, if not welcome, many forms of diversity.

If cities spawned a new environment for sexual values, the new psychology of Sigmund Freud provided the ideas. A Vienna physician, Freud revolutionized academic and popular thinking about human behavior by arguing that unconscious sexual anxieties cause much of human behavior. Freud also explained how sexual desires and fears develop in infancy and stay with people throughout their lives. During the 1920s physicians, academics, advice columnists, women's magazines, and preachers debated Freud's theories.

The image of the "flapper"—the liberated woman who bobbed her hair, painted her lips, raised her hemline, and danced the Charleston—personified the public's anxiety about the decline of traditional morality. In the 1950s Alfred C. Kinsey, a researcher at Indiana University, found that women born after 1900 were twice as likely to have had premarital sex as their mothers, with the most pronounced changes occurring in the generation reaching maturity in the early 1920s.

Sexual permissiveness had eroded Victorian values, but the "new woman" posed less of a challenge to traditional morality than her critics

The image of the "flapper," who bobbed her hair, bared her knees, and smoked and drank in public, alarmed a public still clinging to Victorian codes of morality.

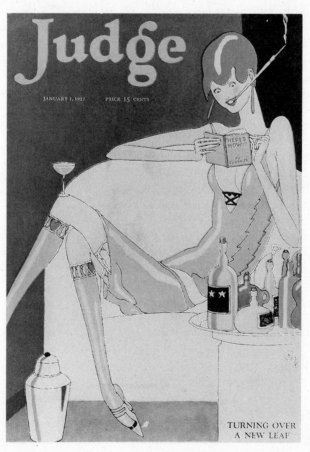

feared. Far from being promiscuous, her sexual experience before marriage was generally limited to one or two partners, one of whom she married. In practice, this narrowed the gap between men and women and moved society toward a single standard of morality. Instead of turning to prostitutes, men made love with their sweethearts, who in many instances became their wives.

Moreover, the sexual revolution did not redefine gender roles for women. The "new woman" embraced the traditional duties of wife and mother. In fact, the most striking theme of women's history in the 1920s was its continuity with the past. Nowhere was the absence of change more evident than in politics. Most feminists had viewed suffrage as the key to ending discrimination against women. After the Nineteenth Amendment passed, reformers talked about female voters uniting to clean up politics, improve society, and end discrimination in the marketplace.

None of these dreams came true during the 1920s. Women failed to organize into a bloc vote, and generally did not vote differently than men. Even more galling to feminists, substantial numbers of women during the 1920s failed to vote at all.

Nor did women win new opportunities in the marketplace. Although the American work force included eight million women in 1920, more than half were black or foreign-born. Domestic service remained the largest occupation, followed by secretaries, typists, and clerks—all low-paying jobs. The American Federation of Labor (AFL) remained openly hostile to women because it did not want females competing for male jobs. Female professionals, too, made little progress. They consistently received less pay than their male counterparts. Moreover, they were concentrated in traditionally "female" occupations—teaching and nursing.

Most Americans regarded working women as an anomaly. Young women could work during the interlude between leaving home and marriage, but they were expected to make homemaking their career after marriage. While economic necessity forced many poor women to continue working after marriage, most middle-class women of the 1920s abandoned any hope of combining careers with marriage.

Americans had not resolved the basic conflict between equal rights for women and the sexual division of labor that continued to confine women to the domestic sphere. Feminists had secured the vote, not true equality.

The Revolt of the Traditionalists

Teeming cities, crowded ghettos, unfamiliar immigrants, black migration, civil rights protests, and new sexual mores all proved deeply threatening to traditional white Protestants. During the 1920s old-stock Americans vented their fears and frustrations by attacking alcohol, smoking, evolution, immigrants, and radicals.

Prohibition

Like the sex debate, prohibition exposed deep fissures in American society. The issue turned on the class, ethnic, and religious makeup of individual communities, not merely on whether the community was rural or urban.

At first prohibition's apparent success muted its critics. Distilleries and breweries shut down, saloons locked their doors, arrests for drunkenness declined, and alcohol-related deaths all but disappeared. Compliance, however, had less to do with piety and public support than the law of supply and demand: since illegal liquor remained in short supply, its price rose beyond the average worker's means.

Private enterprise filled the void. Smugglers supplied wealthy imbibers, but the less affluent had to rely on small-time operators who produced for local consumption. Much of this booze ran the gamut from swill to poison. According to one story, a potential buyer who sent a liquor sample to a laboratory for analysis was shocked when the chemist replied: "Your horse has diabetes." For others the problem of "killer batches" was no laughing matter. Hundreds, perhaps thousands, died from drinking these illegal concoctions.

Neither federal nor state authorities had enough funds to enforce prohibition. Lax enforcement, coupled with huge profits, enticed organized crime to enter bootlegging. Long a fixture of urban life, with gambling and prostitution as its base, organized crime had operated on a small, local scale. Liquor, however, demanded production plants, distribution networks, and sales forces. Bootlegging turned into a gold mine for organized crime. By the late 1920s liquor sales generated revenue in excess of $2 billion annually. Chicago's Al Capone had a gross income of $60 million in 1927. A ruthless figure accused of ordering numerous gangland killings, he preferred to think of himself as a businessman.

From the outset, cynics insisted prohibition could not be enforced. They were right. Particularly in large cities, people openly defied the law. On more than one occasion journalists saw President Warren G. Harding's bootlegger deliver cases of liquor to the White House in broad daylight.

In 1923 New York became the first state to repeal its enforcement law, and by 1930 six more states had followed suit. Others remained firmly committed to prohibition. After a presidential commission reported prohibition could not be enforced, Congress finally repealed it in 1933, making liquor control a state and local matter.

The campaign to outlaw cigarette smoking was closely allied to the prohibition movement. Opposition to tobacco was not new. During the nineteenth century the antitobacco campaign remained an appendage of the temperance movement. After the introduction of machine-made cigarettes in the 1880s, however, opponents concentrated their fire specifically on the "little white slavers."

As early as the Civil War, a few cities had banned smoking in restaurants, theaters, public buildings, trolleys, and railway cars. After anti-smokers organized the National Anti-Cigarette League in 1903, scores of prominent leaders joined the crusade. By 1923, 14 states outlawed the sale of cigarettes, prompting calls for a constitutional amendment for national prohibition. By the end of the decade. however, every state had repealed its law against cigarette sales. A national consensus had not formed against tobacco, and the tobacco industry opposed every effort to restrict the sale of cigarettes, spending millions of dollars on advertisements. Thus smokers had no difficulty defending their right to smoke—at least for the present.

The Scopes Trial

Many custodians of small-town morality also fretted over the teaching of evolution in public schools, and they got their day in court in the celebrated "Monkey Trial." In 1925 the Tennessee legislature passed a bill that prohibited the teaching of evolution in public schools. Immediately afterwards, a 24-year-old science teacher, John Scopes, from Dayton, Tennessee, provoked a test case by declaring publicly he taught biology from an evolutionary standpoint.

Scopes was brought to trial in the summer of 1925. William Jennings Bryan, rural America's defender of the faith, agreed to join the team of prosecutors, and Clarence Darrow, the celebrated trial lawyer and self-proclaimed agnostic, volunteered his services to defend Scopes.

The trial opened on July 10, 1925. As Holy Rollers from the surrounding regions held revivals and religious zealots exhorted people to read their Bibles, huge crowds poured into Dayton to watch Bryan and Darrow do combat. Near the end of testimony the defense surprised everyone by asking Bryan to take the stand as an expert witness on the Bible. His simple, direct answers to Darrow's sarcastic questions revealed an unshakable faith in the literal truth of the Bible. Bryan insisted "it is better to trust in the Rock of Ages than to know the ages of rocks."

The outcome was never in doubt. Scopes admitted he had broken the law. He was convicted and fined $100. (Tennessee's supreme court later rescinded the fine on a technicality.) What gave the trial its drama was the clash between Bryan and Darrow and the opposite images of America they represented. Bryan, who died five days after the trial ended, left the courtroom believing he had carried the day. His opponents, however, thought he had been humiliated and proclaimed the Scopes trial a victory for academic freedom. In the end, the Scopes trial merely illustrated how little tolerance secular and fundamentalist groups had for each other.

Xenophobia and Restricting Immigration

Cultural fears unleashed a new wave of nativism in the 1920s. Organized labor, bent upon protecting high wages, resented competition from cheap labor; staunch nativists and superpatriots warned that foreign influences would corrupt the American character; and assorted businessmen denounced immigrants as dangerous radicals.

To protect the United States these groups demanded drastic changes in the nation's immigration policy. Congress passed the National Origins Act of 1924, establishing an annual immigration quota of two percent of each national group counted in the 1890 census, and barring Asians entirely. Since southern and eastern Europeans did not begin arriving in large numbers until the turn of the century, the law gave western and northern Europeans a big edge over the "new immigrants."

Hostility to immigrants also surfaced in the Sacco and Vanzetti case. On April 15, 1920, two unidentified gunmen robbed a payroll messenger from a shoe factory in South Braintree, Massachusetts, killing a paymaster and a guard. Two Italian immigrants, Nicola Sacco and Bartolomeo Vanzetti, both avowed anarchists, were arrested and charged with the crime. Although the state failed to prove its case, prosecutors succeeded in parading the radical political views of both men before the jury. On July 14, 1921, Sacco and Vanzetti were convicted and sentenced to death.

The trial brought a storm of protest from Italian-Americans, liberals, and civil rights advocates. Despite lengthy appeals, the conviction was upheld, and Sacco and Vanzetti, asserting their innocence to the end, went to the electric chair on August 23, 1927.

The Ku Klux Klan

Fear of political radicals and ethnic minorities found its most strident voice during the 1920s in the rebirth of the Ku Klux Klan. The secret organization, led by Colonel William Joseph Simmons, stood for "100 percent pure Americanism" and limited its membership to white, native-born Protestants. Membership remained small until Simmons hired two advertising specialists, Edward Young Clarke and Elizabeth Tyler, to market the Klan nationwide. Klan policy was set at the local level, varying from community to community to accommodate local prejudices, be they directed at blacks, Catholics, Jews, Mexicans, Orientals, foreigners, or "Reds."

Many people felt that Sacco and Vanzetti, Italian-born admitted anarchists, were persecuted for their immigrant status and radical views rather than for any real crime. Their trial, shown here in a painting by Ben Shahn, became an important symbol in the fight for civil liberties and brought about violent protest in America and abroad. Ben Shahn, *Bartholomeo Vanzetti and Nicola Sacco* (1931–32). Tempera on paper over composition board, 10 × 14; dp. Gift of Mrs. John D. Rockefeller, Jr./The Museum of Modern Art, New York.

Clarke and Tyler hired an army of organizers to canvas the country selling memberships in the Klan. (Membership cost $10; the sheet was $4 extra.) Working on commission and molding their pitch to match their clientele, they enjoyed astounding success. By 1921 the Klan had become a national organization with over 90,000 paying members; by 1925 it claimed a membership of five million. The Klan was strongest (and most violent) in the South, but it had a large following in the Southeast, the Far West, and the Midwest. Its natural habitat was not the countryside, but middling towns and small cities. Most members were not "poor white trash," but members of the lower middle class from old-stock, respectable families.

In the mid-1920s the Klan was a political force to reckon with. It influenced the election of several governors and state legislatures. In addition the Klan sought to intimidate individuals, using night ridings, cross

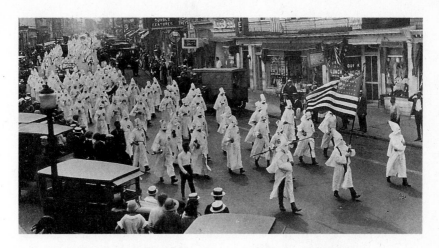

The Ku Klux Klan exploited postwar confusion and fear of anything "un-American." Although the Klan had flourished in small, rural towns across the South, during the 1920s it spread to working-class and middle-class neighborhoods of large cities, where people felt threatened by the influx of African-American and immigrant workers.

burnings, tar and featherings, public beatings, and lynchings as forms of coercion. The Klan did not limit its wrath to ethnic and religious offenders, but also lashed out against wife beaters, drunkards, bootleggers, gamblers—anyone who violated time-honored standards of morality.

In the end poor leadership and the absence of a political program destroyed the Klan. Once they attained office, Klan-supported officials offered no constructive legislation. Even more damaging, several Klan leaders became involved in sex scandals, and several more were indicted for corruption. By 1930 the white sheets and cross burnings vanished from public view, only to return again a few decades later when the civil rights movement challenged white supremacy.

The Rise of Urban Culture

Despite all the upheavals, a new force for social cohesion was drawing Americans together during the 1920s. The United States was rapidly evolving a consumer culture that blunted regional differences and imposed similar tastes and life-styles. Centered in the cities and propelled by revolutions in transportation, advertising, communications, and entertainment, a new consumer society emerged during the 1920s, enshrining materialism and self-indulgence as the dominant cultural motifs of prosperity's decade.

The Consumer Culture

In 1900 only 8,000 motor vehicles were registered in the United States and the automobile was little more than a rich man's toy; by 1920 Americans owned more than nine million automobiles. By 1925 Henry Ford had lowered the price of his sturdy Model T to less than $300, about three-months' pay for the average urban worker, and by 1930 automobile registrations had risen to 26,531,999. No previous form of transportation (except walking) had been so widely available. The great American love affair with the automobile had begun.

Enthusiasts claimed the automobile promoted family togetherness through evening rides, picnics, and weekend excursions. Critics decried squabbles between parents and teenagers over use of the automobile, and an apparent decline in church attendance resulting from Sunday outings. Worst of all, charged critics, automobiles gave young people freedom and privacy, "portable bedrooms" that couples could take anywhere. Critics also blamed the automobile for undermining the public's devotion to thrift. In the past, people had paid cash for consumer goods or done without. With auto manufacturers and banks encouraging the public to buy the car of their dreams on credit, this thrift ethic slowly eroded.

The increasing availability of electricity offered the key to another vast new market, appliances. As more and more of America's households received electricity, refrigerators, washing machines, vacuum cleaners, and toasters quickly took hold. Appliances eased the sheer physical drudgery of housework, but they did not shorten the average housewife's work week. Women had to do more because standards of cleanliness kept rising. Sheets had to be changed weekly; the house had to be vacuumed daily. In short, social pressure expanded household chores to keep pace with the new technology. Far from liberating women, appliances imposed new standards and pressures.

The Lost Generation

While most Americans embraced the consumer culture, others found it thoroughly disgusting. Disillusioned by the collapse of Wilsonian idealism, the hypocrisy of prohibition, and the upsurge of nativism, writers of this so-called Lost Generation felt alienated. To these cultural critics, America had become a nation of conspicuous consumption, awash in materialism and devoid of spiritual vitality.

No author captured these themes better than Sinclair Lewis, who in 1930 became the first American to win the Nobel Prize for literature. In *Main Street* (1920) he satirized small-town American life, with its narrow-minded complacency, while in *Babbitt* (1922) Lewis attacked the spiritual conformity that drove Americans to follow the crowd.

H. L. Mencken mounted a scathing attack on his countrymen. As editor of *Mercury* magazine, he wrote hundreds of essays mocking practically every aspect of American life. Calling the South a "gargantuan paradise of the fourth rate," and the middle class the "booboisie," Mencken directed his choicest barbs at reformers, whom he blamed for the bloodshed of World War I and the gangsters of the 1920s. "If I am convinced of anything," he snarled, "it is that Doing Good is in bad taste."

F. Scott Fitzgerald and Ernest Hemingway made the same points more obliquely. In novels such as *The Great Gatsby* (1925) and *Tender Is the Night* (1929) Fitzgerald exposed the decadence and materialism of American culture. Hemingway lionized toughness and "manly virtues" as a counterpoint to the softness of American life. In *The Sun Also Rises* (1926) and *A Farewell to Arms* (1929) he emphasized meaningless death and the importance of facing stoically the absurdities of the universe.

The Communication Revolution

In 1897 the United States had less than one telephone for every hundred residents; by 1930 the number stood at one in six. The telephone hastened the transition from the written to the electronically transmitted word, brought the home in closer contact with the outside world, and reduced household visiting among neighbors as friends picked up the phone instead of dropping in.

Radio had an even greater impact. It drew the nation together by bringing news, entertainment, and advertisements to more than ten million households by 1929. Radio not only offered something for everyone—news adventure shows, sports and "soaps"—but also helped create mass culture by blunting regional differences. Moreover, no other media had the power to create heroes and villains so quickly. When Charles Lindbergh became the first person to fly nonstop across the Atlantic from New York to Paris in 1927, the radio brought this incredible feat into American homes and made him a celebrity overnight.

In contrast, radio also brought the nation decidedly unheroic images. "Amos and Andy," one of the most popular shows of the depression, spread vicious racial stereotypes into homes whose white occupants knew little about black people. Other minorities fared no better. The Italian gangster, the bloodthirsty Indian, the Mexican with the singsong voice, the tightfisted Jew, and the Irish thug became stock characters in radio programming.

The Rise of Suburbs

Americans who bought the same products and listened to the same programs also shared new housing arrangements. New forms of transportation made the suburbs possible.

For much of the nation's history, cities could not grow larger because workers had to live within walking distance of their jobs. After the Civil War trolleys and streetcars permitted workers to move beyond the walking radius surrounding factories. In the twentieth century the automobile opened up vast new regions for housing, giving workers numerous options about where to live. Though suburbs had once been the exclusive domain of the well-to-do, the automobile enabled working-class families to move there, too.

Yet optimists who hoped to escape the city's congestion by moving to the suburbs got fooled. The sharp rise in road construction following the Federal Highway Act of 1916 produced complicated lateral traffic flows within cities and traffic congestion became worse. City planners counterattacked with traffic circles, synchronized stoplights, divided dual highways, and grade separation of highways from city streets, but nothing could free motorists from rush hour and holiday traffic jams.

Leisure Time

Thanks to the unprecedented prosperity of the 1920s, Americans had more money for leisure activities than ever before. Among the most popular were parlor games—mahjong sets, crossword puzzles, and the like. Contract bridge became the most durable of the new pastimes, followed closely by photography. Americans hit golf balls, played tennis, and bowled. Dance crazes like the fox trot, the Charleston, and the jitterbug swept the country.

While Lewis, Mencken, Fitzgerald, and Hemingway found a wide audience, millions of Americans preferred the new popular literature, largely because it resolved rather than explored cultural tensions. Edgar Rice Burroughs' *Tarzan of the Apes* became a runaway best-seller. For readers who felt concerned about urbanization and industrialization, the adventures of a lone white man in "dark Africa" revived the spirit of the frontier and individualism. Zane Grey's novels, such as *Riders of the Purple Sage,* enjoyed even greater popularity, using the tried but true formula of romance, action, and a moralistic struggle between good and evil, all put in a western setting. Between 1918 and 1934 Grey wrote 24 books and became the best-known writer of popular fiction in the country.

Other readers wanted to be titillated, as evidenced by the boom in "confession magazines." Urban values, liberated women, and Hollywood films had all relaxed Victorian standards. Confession magazines rushed to fill the vacuum, purveying stories of romantic success and failure, divorce, fantasy, and adultery. Writers survived the censors' cuts by placing moral tags at the end of their stories, advising readers to avoid similar mistakes in their own lives.

Spectator sports attracted vast audiences in the 1920s. The country yearned for heroes in an increasingly impersonal, organized society, and sports provided them. Prizefighters like Jack Dempsey became national idols. Team sports flourished, but Americans focused on individual superstars, people whose talents or personalities made them appear larger than life. Harold "Red" Grange, the "Galloping Ghost" halfback for the University of Illinois, raised professional football to new heights when he signed a contract with the Chicago Bears in 1926.

Baseball drew even bigger crowds than football. George Herman ("Babe") Ruth ruled as the sport's undisputed superstar. Up until the 1920s Ty Cobb's defensive brand of baseball, with its emphasis on base hits and stolen bases, dominated the sport. Ruth transformed baseball into the game of the home-run hitter. As a New York Yankee, Ruth set four home run records, hitting 60 in his best year, and led the team to four World Series. Between 1915 and 1930, the total number of home runs in major league baseball increased from 384 a year to 1,565. Baseball became the game of the big hitter, and none was bigger, literally or figuratively, than Babe Ruth.

Despite the mania for athletics, Americans shelled out ten times more money on movies than on spectator sports. By 1929, 90 million Americans—three fourths of the population—went to the movies every week to see Hollywood spectacles such as Cecil B. DeMille's *Ten Commandments* with its "cast of thousands" and dazzling special effects. Comedies, such as slapstick masterpieces starring Charlie Chaplin and Buster Keaton enjoyed great popularity as well. Like radio and sports, movies helped create a new popular culture, with common speech, dress, behavior, and heroes. And like radio, Hollywood did its share to reinforce racial stereotypes by denigrating minority groups. Mexicans appeared as sleepy-eyed peasants, while the only parts for blacks went to actors like Stepin Fetchit, who got rich playing superstitious, blithering idiots. The wooden box and the silver screen both molded and mirrored mass culture.

The Republican Restoration

The Republican party dominated American politics in the 1920s. When Republican leaders promised to restore prosperity, most Americans embraced the conservative rhetoric, hoping to find in politics the stability they found lacking in their culture. Talk about trust-busting and regulating big business gave way in New Era politics to calls for a partnership between government and industry, one that would promote the interests of American corporations at home and abroad.

Handsome Harding

By and large the presidents of the New Era were mediocre figures. Senator Warren G. Harding of Ohio, who led off the decade, suited the times perfectly. Handsome enough to be a movie star, he not only looked great, but promised voters what they wanted: a return to "normalcy." He appeared to be a moderate, responsible leader who would avoid extremes and guide the country into a decade of prosperity.

Harding, a fun-loving man who liked to play poker, drink whiskey, and shoot the breeze with old pals, left government to his cabinet members and the Supreme Court. Political conservatives all, they equated the people's interests with those of big business, championing American business interests abroad, denouncing government regulation, and slashing taxes on the rich.

Business leaders had contributed $8 million to the GOP's campaign chest in 1920; in return they expected the federal government to roll back the gains organized labor had made during World War I. They were not disappointed. Under the leadership of Chief Justice William Howard Taft, the Court took a narrow view of federal power, assigning the responsibility for protecting individual citizens to the states. During the 1920s the Court outlawed picketing, overturned national child labor laws, and abolished minimum wage laws for women.

The decade's most capable figure was Herbert Hoover, secretary of commerce under both Harding and his successor, Calvin Coolidge. A successful engineer, Hoover abhorred destructive competition and waste in the economy, which he proposed to eliminate through "associationism." Hoover called for voluntary trade associations to foster cooperation in industry and agriculture through commissions, trade practice controls, and ethical standards. By 1929 more than 2,000 trade associations were busily at work implementing Hoover's vision of a stable and prosperous economy. No other Harding appointment matched Hoover's talent and vision.

In fact, several of Harding's appointees proved to be disasters. Harding found it hard to say "no" to old friends and cronies, members of the so-called Ohio Gang, when they asked for government jobs. In the end this motley assortment of political hacks and hangers-on plunged his administration into disgrace, as major scandals involving bribes and kickbacks erupted in the Justice Department and in the Veterans Bureau. Shortly after these disclosures, Harding died of a cerebral embolism on August 2, 1923. Immediately after his death, more misdeeds came to light. In the infamous Teapot Dome oil scandal, Interior secretary Albert B. Fall was convicted of accepting $360,000 in bribes in exchange for leasing drilling rights on federal naval oil reserves, the first cabinet member in American history convicted for crimes in office. Attorney General Harry Daugherty, accused of accepting payoffs for selling German chemical patents controlled by the Alien Property Office, was forced to resign in disgrace.

Silent Cal

The election of 1924 symbolized, in a variety of ways, the tensions and concerns of the 1920s. Despite the Harding scandals, President Calvin Coolidge remained extremely popular, largely because of the nation's prosperity. Deeply divided over such issues as immigration, prohibition, and the Ku Klux Klan, the Democrats nominated a compromise candidate, John W. Davis, a Wall Street attorney.

A coalition of labor leaders, social workers, and former progressives bolted both major parties and formed the Progressive party, which nominated Wisconsin Senator Robert La Follette for president. Their platform called for government ownership of natural resources, abolition of child labor, elimination of monopolies, and increased taxes on the rich. In the end, no issue could match the GOP's prosperity crusade. Coolidge won the election by a comfortable margin.

Coolidge was a stern-faced, tight-lipped New Englander. Born in Plymouth Notch, Vermont, where five generations of Coolidges had worked the same family farm, he epitomized the rural values threatened by immigration, urbanization, and industrialization. As governor of Massachusetts, Coolidge had crushed a police strike in Boston in 1919 by calling out the National Guard, prompting the Republicans to give him the number two slot on their ticket in 1920.

Coolidge had no desire to be a strong president in the tradition of a Teddy Roosevelt or a Woodrow Wilson. A firm believer in the wisdom of inactivity, Coolidge slept ten hours a night, napped every afternoon, and seldom worked more than four hours a day. A staunch conservative,

Coolidge was positively consumed by his reverence for the corporate elite. "The man who builds a factory builds a temple," said Coolidge. "The man who works there, worships there." Government, he believed, should do everything in its power to promote business interests. While Coolidge set the tone for his administration, he left it to his cabinet members, the courts, and Congress to devise strategies for consummating the marriage between business and government.

The Twilight of Progressivism

The government's tilt toward business signaled a retreat from progressivism. With the Democrats in disarray and Teddy Roosevelt's wing of the GOP all but dead, conservative Republicans were riding high. Still, the reform impulse did not disappear entirely during the 1920s. A small band of beleaguered reformers, led by Robert La Follette of Wisconsin and George Norris of Nebraska, kept progressivism alive in Congress, where they worked for farm relief, child labor laws, and regulation of wages and working hours for women.

In keeping with their historic pattern, progressives had better luck at the state and local level than at the federal level, where they ran into stiff opposition from Congress or from Coolidge himself. Social workers and women's groups spearheaded campaigns which sponsored a broad range of welfare legislation. By 1930, 43 states had passed laws providing assistance to women with dependent children, and 34 states had adopted workers' compensation laws. Under the leadership of Governor Alfred Smith, New York granted women a 40-hour work week and instituted the nation's first public housing program.

Welfare opponents counterattacked, arguing labor reforms would increase production costs and leave states that passed welfare legislation at a competitive disadvantage with states without such laws. Asked to choose between social welfare programs and jobs, Congress, along with most states, opted for jobs.

The Election of 1928

After Coolidge announced his retirement from politics in 1928, the Republicans nominated Herbert Hoover, while the Democrats turned to Alfred E. Smith. Since both parties adopted nearly identical platforms, the election turned on personalities and images. Few elections have pitted opponents who better defined the two faces of America—one rural, the other urban.

A native of Iowa, Hoover depicted himself as a simple farmboy who, through hard work and pluck, had grown up to become wealthy and famous. Orphaned as a boy and cared for by a variety of relatives, Hoover worked his way through Stanford University, earning a degree in mining engineering. Brilliant and hard-working, he was a millionaire 12 years after landing his first engineering job. As a self-made man, Hoover presented a portrait of a safe, reassuring world.

Yet Hoover was also a spokesman for the future. He thought the federal government had a responsibility to coordinate the competing interests of a modern economy. He accepted the reality of industrialization, technology, governmental activism, and global markets, and in contrast to Harding and Coolidge, believed the president should lead the nation. According to Hoover, technology and expertise would make economic prosperity a permanent feature of American life.

The son of immigrants, Smith was an Irish Catholic from Hell's Kitchen in New York City who had started public life with nothing and had climbed the political ladder as a faithful son of the New York Democratic machine. Smith also represented the future, not so much in terms of science, technology, and organization, but in terms of cultural pluralism and urbanization. America's future lay with her cities, and the cities contained large groups of ethnic Americans struggling for acceptance and their share of the good life.

Aided by prosperity, Hoover coasted to an easy victory. Smith was hurt by his failure to bridge the North-South, urban-rural split in the Democratic party; by anti-Catholic sentiment; and by his opposition to prohibition. The Democrats were so divided that six states from Dixie abandoned the Solid South and defected to Hoover. Yet even in defeat, Smith's campaign revealed the most significant political change of the 1920s—the growing power of urban and ethnic voters and the shrinking influence of the rural element within the Democratic party.

Herbert Hoover's election marked the climax of New Era politics. As president he advocated total cooperation between government and business. Optimistic businesspeople, bankers, and stockbrokers applauded Hoover's promises, predicting a future of prosperity and progress. Ironically, the stock market crashed before their cheers had stopped echoing.

The Great Crash

Economic historians have been hard pressed to explain why "prosperity's decade" ended in financial disaster. Employment was high, prices were stable, and production was soaring. Manufacturing output nearly doubled between 1921 and 1929, and the real wages of industrial workers rose by about 17 percent. Not everyone prospered, to be sure. Strapped with long-term debts, high taxes, and a sharp drop in crop prices, farmers lost ground throughout the decade. Most blacks and Hispanics lived in poverty, large numbers of poor whites haunted southern Appalachia, and virtually every large American city had its ghetto. Still, more people were comfortable, well-to-do, or rich during the 1920s than ever before in American history.

Rampant speculation, in real estate and the stock market, was a by-product of the nation's newfound prosperity. Many speculators sought to make their fortunes in the Florida land boom of the mid1920s, until two devastating hurricanes brought land prices back down to earth. The Great Bull Market offered even more Americans the chance to vent their passion for speculation. Beginning in 1924 the price of securities began to rise steadily, until 1928 when the rate of increase switched from measured steps to vaulting leaps. In March of 1928 alone, the value of stocks shot up more than ten percent, with the price of individual stocks rising as much as 20 percent in a single day.

Credit provided the yeast for the Great Bull Market. Buying on margin—using a broker's loan to finance a large portion of the transaction—allowed the purchaser to buy securities at a fraction of their face value. Speculators could get all the benefits of ownership without paying the full purchase price. Investment borrowing transmuted itself into an orgy of speculation. Contrary to popular belief, the masses did not join in the fun. Most speculators were wealthy people or members of the upper middle class. Most working-class Americans did not own stocks, let alone play the market.

The Federal Reserve Board found itself in a real dilemma. If it raised interest rates to stifle speculation, it risked slowing down the economy and creating unemployment. If it lowered interest rates to stimulate the economy, it risked making securities speculation worse. Confused and uncertain, the Federal Reserve Board pursued contradictory policies. Between 1927 and 1929 the board raised and lowered interest rates several times in a futile attempt to slow Wall Street down without harming the economy. In the end, private greed and government impotence combined to create a catastrophe.

Financial analysts for the *New York Times* warned investors that the huge gap between stock prices and the rate of economic growth was bound to end in disaster. The bubble burst in September and October of 1929 when the market finally crashed. By November the value of the average stock had dropped 50 percent. The market continued its downward spiral for the next several years.

But the Great Crash did not cause the Great Depression. Whole segments of the American economy, including agriculture, banking, manufacturing, and foreign trade, were shaky long before the stock market collapsed. Farm prices had been depressed ever since the end of World War I,

York Times.

THE WEATHER
Cloudy and continued cold today;
tomorrow fair and warmer.

FRIDAY, OCTOBER 25, 1929.   TWO CENTS

WORST STOCK CRASH STEMMED BY BANKS; 12,894,650-SHARE DAY SWAMPS MARKET; LEADERS CONFER, FIND CONDITIONS SOUND

FINANCIERS EASE TENSION

Five Wall Street Bankers Hold Two Meetings at Morgan Office.

CALL BREAK 'TECHNICAL'

Lamont Lays It to 'Air Holes'
—Says Low Prices Do Not Depict Situation Fairly.

FINDS MARGINS BEING MET

Sees Market 'Susceptible to Betterment'—Mitchell, Potter, Wiggin, Prosser at Talks.

Wall Street Optimistic After Stormy Day; Clerical Work May Force Holiday Tomorrow

Confidence in the soundness of the stock market structure, notwithstanding the upheaval of the last few days, was voiced last night by bankers and other financial leaders. Sentiment as expressed by the heads of some of the largest banking institutions and by industrial executives as well was distinctly cheerful and the feeling was general that the worst had been seen. Wall Street ended the day in an optimistic frame of mind.

LOSSES RECOVERED IN PART

Upward Trend Start* With 200,000-Share Order for Steel.

TICKERS LAG FOUR HOURS

Thousands of Accounts Wiped Out, With Traders in Dark as to Events on Exchange.

SALES ON CURB 6,337,415

BIG DROP IN WHEAT; PIT IN A TURMOIL

Break of 12 Cents a Bushel to New Season Low and 8-Cent Rally Mark Wild Trading.

STOCKS TUMBLE IN CHICAGO

Selling Swamps Exchange in 1,200,000-Share Day—Part of Big Losses Recovered.

TREASURY OFFICIALS BLAME SPECULATION

Drastic Market Decline Found Not Due to Any Basic Business Weakness.

STILL PLAN TAX REDUCTION

Reserve Board Meets Twice in Day and Keeps in Constant Touch With Markets Here.

This newspaper headline from October 25, 1929, tried to reassure the public that the economy was fundamentally sound, but the downward spiral continued through 1932, when prices were 80 percent below their 1929 highs.

when European agriculture revived. Caught with declining incomes, farmers tried to recover their losses and make their debt payments by increasing production. The collective result of millions of farmers raising output was larger surpluses and lower prices, a vicious cycle that persisted throughout the decade. Moreover, the decline in farm income reverberated throughout the economy: Rural consumers stopped buying farm implements, tractors, automobiles, furniture, and appliances.

Millions of farmers defaulted on their debts, placing tremendous pressure on the banking system. Between 1920 and 1929 more than 5,000 of the country's 30,000 banks failed. Afraid to put their money in banks, large numbers of people began hoarding cash, which by 1930 removed more than $1 billion from circulation. Following the stock market crash in 1929 and the continued downward spiral through 1933, the banking system saw more of its assets destroyed. Between 1929 and 1933, when the entire banking system collapsed, another 5,000 banks went under.

Because of the banking crisis, thousands of small businesspeople failed because they could not secure working capital loans. Thousands more went bankrupt because they had lost their working capital in the stock market. Instead of plowing some of their profits during the 1920s back into their businesses and expanding capacity, many gambled on the securities markets instead. When the crash came, these small businesses shut their doors.

Labor formed another weak link in the chain. Like farmers, workers did not have enough purchasing power to sustain the economy. While business leaders promoted the consumer culture through advertising, they refused to give workers the wage increases needed to buy products. Drops in consumer spending led inevitably to reductions in production and worker layoffs. Unemployed workers then spent less and the cycle repeated itself.

Installment buying also weakened the economy. In the 1920s consumers went on a spending binge, encouraged by "buy now and pay later" advertising. Demand for automobiles and furniture, high in the early 1920s, ultimately reached a saturation point. By 1927 both industries found themselves with excess capacity and had to lay off workers.

Finally, Republican tariff policies damaged the economy by depressing foreign trade. Anxious to protect American industries from foreign competitors after World War I, Congress passed the Fordney-McCumber Tariff of 1922 and the Hawley-Smoot Tariff of 1930, raising tariff rates to unprecedented levels. Along with serious weaknesses in the European economies, American tariffs stifled international trade, making it difficult for European nations to pay off their debts.

All these factors sapped the economy, leaving it ripe for disaster. Yet the depression did not strike instantly; it infected the country gradually, like a slow-growing cancer. Measured in human terms, the Great Depression was the worst economic catastrophe in American history. It hit urban and rural areas, blue- and white-collar families alike. In the nation's cities, unemployed men took to the streets to sell apples or shine shoes. Thousands of others, many of whom deserted their wives and children, hopped freight trains and wandered from town to town looking for jobs or handouts.

Unlike most of Western Europe, the United States had no federal system of unemployment insurance. The relief burden fell on state and municipal governments working in cooperation with private charities, such as the Red Cross and the Community Chest. Created to handle temporary emergencies, these groups lacked the resources to alleviate the massive suffering created by the Great Depression. Poor southerners, whose states had virtually no relief funds, were particularly hard hit.

Urban centers in the North fared little better. Most city charters did not permit public funds to be spent on work relief. Adding insult to injury, several states disqualified relief clients from voting, while other cities forced them to surrender their automobile license plates. "Prosperity's decade" had ended in economic disaster.

Conclusion

Janus, the two-faced god of antiquity, offers an intriguing symbol for America in the 1920s. The nation's image was divided, with one profile looking optimistically to the future and the other staring longingly at the

Chronology of Key Events

1914	Marcus Garvey organizes the Universal Negro Improvement Association (UNIA)
1915	Ku Klux Klan revived
1917–1925	Approximately 600,000 black Americans migrate to northern industrial cities in the Great Black Migration
1920	Palmer raids arrest suspected Communists Sacco and Vanzetti tried on charges of murder and executed in 1927; Sinclair Lewis's *Main Street* published
1921	Warren Harding becomes twenty-ninth president
1922	Fordney-McCumber Tariff raises duties on imports
1923	President Harding dies; Calvin Coolidge becomes thirtieth president
1924	Teapot Dome oil-leasing scandal uncovered
1925	Scopes trial attacks teaching theory of evolution in public schools; F. Scott Fitzgerald's *The Great Gatsby* published
1929	Herbert Hoover becomes thirty-first president; stock market crashes
1930	Hawley-Smoot Tariff raises import duties

past. Caught between the disillusionment of World War I and the economic malaise of the Great Depression, the 1920s witnessed a gigantic struggle between an old and a new America.

No longer a nation of farms and villages, the United States had become a nation of factories and cities. The Protestant culture of rural America was being undermined by the secular values of urban society. Country against city, native against immigrant, worker against farmer, Protestant against Catholic and Jew, fundamentalist against liberal, conservative against progressive, wet against dry—all these confrontations reflected different images of the same battle: a colossal identity crisis that saw the United States struggling to come to terms with secular values and cultural pluralism. But what World War I started, the Great Depression interrupted. The intense cultural upheavals of the 1920s gave way to the equally intense economic debates of the 1930s as cultural politics took a backseat to the politics of survival.

Suggestions for Further Reading

Overviews of the 1920s include Frederick Lewis Allen, *Only Yesterday* (1931); William E. Leuchtenburg, *The Perils of Prosperity, 1914–32* (1958); Geoffrey Perrett, *America in the Twenties: A History* (1982).

Women's changing roles and the issues confronting women in the 1920s are examined in Dorothy Brown, *Setting a Course* (1987); William H. Chafe, *The American Woman* (1972); John D'Emilio and Estelle B. Freedman, *Intimate Matters* (1988); J. Stanley Lemons, *The Woman Citizen* (1973); Winifred D. Wandersee, *Women's Work and Family Values* (1981). On Margaret Sanger and the birth control movement see James Reed, *From Private Vice to Public Virtue* (1978).

On the Harlem Renaissance see Houston A. Baker, Jr., *Modernism and the Harlem Renaissance* (1987); Nathan Huggins, *Harlem Renaissance* (1971); Ira Katznelson, *Black Men, White Cities* (1973); David L. Lewis, *When Harlem Was in Vogue* (1981).

On the traditionalists and their opposition to modernization see David Chalmers, *Hooded Americans: The First Century of the Ku Klux Klan* (1965); Norman Furniss, *The Fundamentalist Controversy* (1954); Ray Ginger, *Six Days or Forever?* (1958); John Higham, *Strangers in the Land* (1955); Kenneth T. Jackson, *The Ku Klux Klan in the City* (1967); Don S. Kirshner, *City and Country* (1970).

Intellectual and cultural developments of the 1920s are examined in Loren Baritz, ed., *The Culture of the Twenties* (1970); Robert Crunden, *From Self to Society* (1972); Paula Fass, *The Damned and the Beautiful* (1977); Frederick Hoffman, *The Twenties: American Writing in the Postwar Decade*, rev. ed. (1962);

Roderick Nash, *The Nervous Generation* (1970); Robert Sklar, *Movie-Made America* (1975).

Good analyses of the stock market crash and the Great Depression include John Kenneth Galbraith, *The Great Crash, 1929* (1955); Jim Potter, *The American Economy Between the World Wars,* rev. ed. (1985); James Prothro, *The Dollar Decade: Business Ideas in the 1920s* (1954); Albert U. Romasco, *The Poverty of Abundance* (1965); Robert Sobel, *The Great Bull Market* (1968); George Soule, *Prosperity Decade* (1947).

Chapter *25*

The Age of Roosevelt

To fans of authentic folk music, Woodrow Wilson "Woody" Guthrie was a "Shakespeare in overalls," the finest American frontier balladeer of the twentieth century. His nasal, high-pitched singing voice was definitely an acquired taste, but Guthrie's lyrics were at once simple and penetrating. He sang of vagabonds who wandered in search of work, of union men who saw their comrades on the picket lines knocked to the ground by company goons, and of farmers who watched with horror as their land dried up and turned into a dust bowl. In short, he put to music the hardships and struggles of working-class Americans trapped in the Great Depression.

Guthrie drew his material from his life. Born in 1912, Woody grew up in Oklahoma and the Texas Panhandle in a family star-crossed by disasters. When he was still a boy his older sister died from setting herself on fire; his father, once a prosperous land speculator, sank into alcoholism; and his mother slipped slowly into madness and had to be committed to the state mental hospital.

In the face of these tragedies the Guthrie household simply dissolved, leaving Woody pretty much on his own. He passed the time by learning to play the guitar and harmonica. Eventually, he dropped out of school and became a drifter, driven by an internal restlessness that kept him on the road for the rest of his life.

Guthrie spent the Great Depression riding the rails, playing his music and visiting "his" people, along the boxcars, hobo jungles, and migrant camps from Oklahoma to California. He saw families sleeping on the ground and children with distended bellies who cried from hunger while guards hired to protect the orchards prevented them from eating fruit that lay rotting on the ground. Over time a quiet anger began to eat at him and he blamed the nation's "polli-Tish-uns" for not doing more to relieve the people's suffering. By 1940 Guthrie had recorded several albums of Dust Bowl ballads and union protest songs. His home-grown radicalism made him an instant hit with socialist and communist intellectuals and entertainment figures who saw his music as a powerful weapon in the class struggle. They saw Guthrie as an authentic folk hero, the very embodiment of the proletarian artist.

In truth, Guthrie held more radical political views than most Americans. Nevertheless, he aptly fulfilled his role as the "voice of the people" by putting to music the most important themes to emerge in American life during the 1930s—the common man's defiant pride, his will to survive in the face of adversity, and the extraordinary love Americans felt for their country.

In "God Blessed America" (which later generations of Americans would recognize by its first line, "This land is your land, this land is my land"), Guthrie sang of "endless skyways," "golden valleys," "diamond

Woody Guthrie often inscribed the phrase, "This machine surrounds hate and destroys it" on his guitars.

deserts," and "wheat fields waving," evoking the country's grandeur with a poet's sense of beauty. What gave the song its power, however, was the idea that America belonged to the people; every verse closed with the refrain, "God blessed America for me."

Even in the depths of the Great Depression, Guthrie found much of enduring value in America. In ballad after ballad, he celebrated the fortitude and dignity of the American people. They provided the glue that held things together while President Franklin D. Roosevelt experimented with policies and programs designed to promote relief, recovery, and reform.

Herbert Hoover and the Great Depression

When the Great Depression struck, most political and economic leaders regarded recessions as inevitable—a natural part of the business cycle. The prevailing economic theory held that government intervention was both unnecessary and unwise. Previous financial panics had failed to elicit much response from government; and many economists in 1929 continued to extol the virtues of inaction, arguing that the economy would recover by itself. President Hoover disagreed. Though Hoover saw the Great Crash as a temporary slump in a fundamentally healthy economy, he believed the president should try to facilitate economic recovery.

Conservative Responses

First, Hoover resorted to old-fashioned "jawboning." Shortly after the stock market crashed, he summoned business and labor leaders to the White House. Industrial leaders promised to maintain prices and wages, and labor spokesmen pledged not to strike or demand higher wages. While Hoover remained hopeful voluntary measures would suffice, business struggled to survive, forcing employers to lay off workers.

Next, the president tried cheerleading. The contrast between Hoover's speeches and conditions in the country was jarring. In 1930, according to Hoover, the economy was fundamentally sound, and recovery was just around the corner. His rosy pronouncements prompted critics to accuse Hoover of being insensitive to the unemployed and the dispossessed. Cynics called the shantytown slums on the edges of cities "Hoovervilles." Newspapers became "Hoover blankets" and empty pockets turned inside out, "Hoover flags."

Neither cruel nor insensitive, Hoover was tormented by poor people's suffering. Yet he could not bring himself to sanction large-scale federal public works programs because he honestly believed recovery depended on the private sector, because he wanted to maintain a balanced budget, and because he feared federal relief programs would undermine individual character by making the recipient dependent on the state.

Government Loans

When jawboning and cheerleading failed to revive the economy, Hoover reluctantly adopted other measures. In 1932 Congress created the Reconstruction Finance Corporation (RFC) and authorized it to loan $2 billion to banks, savings and loan associations, railroads, and life insurance companies. Blaming the depression on tight credit, Hoover believed federal loans would enable businesses to increase production and hire workers. The same principle applied to the Federal Home Loan Bank System (FHLBS), created by Congress in July 1932 to lend up to $500 million to savings and loan associations to revive the construction industry.

Yet by early 1933 Hoover's agencies had failed to make a dent in the Great Depression. The real problem was not tight credit but the soft demand for goods, a problem that flowed both from the chronic low wages paid to the bulk of American workers and the massive layoffs following the Great Crash. It was a vicious cycle. Unemployed workers could not buy goods, so businesspeople cut back production and laid off additional workers. Businesspeople did not ask banks for working capital loans, which the RFS and FHLBS were created to provide, because they had no interest in increasing production.

In the meantime, thousands of banks across the country went bankrupt, the unemployment rate climbed to 25 percent, and life got worse for millions of people.

Down to the bitter end, Hoover refused to admit people were starving in America, even though his opponents placed the responsibility squarely at the White House door.

Families in the Depression

The Great Depression did not affect everyone equally. Many rich people, insulated by their wealth, maintained opulent life-styles, and perhaps as many as 40 percent of Americans made it through these years without experiencing real hardships. Still, the majority of Americans saw the Great Depression as a wolf at the door. "Mass unemployment," as one journalist observed, "is both a statistic and an empty feeling in the stomach." Hunger pains were intense in 1933, the year Franklin D. Roosevelt took office, when one-quarter of the nation's families had no breadwinner.

For all but the most fortunate, the Great Depression reduced family income. In 1929 the average American family earned $2,300; by 1933 the figure had declined to $1,500, a 35 percent drop. Most of the loss resulted

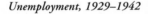

Unemployment, 1929–1942

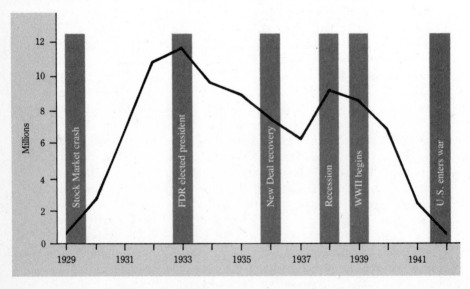

from unemployment, but it also reflected reduced wages for those who kept their jobs. By 1933 nine out of ten companies had cut wages (some by as much as 50 percent), and more than half of all employers had converted their work force from full- to part-time jobs, averaging roughly 60 percent of the normal work week.

The depression had a powerful impact on families. It forced couples to delay marriage, lowered the divorce rate (many couples could not afford to maintain separate households or pay legal fees to obtain divorces), and drove the birthrate below the replacement level for the first time in American history. Many unemployed fathers saw their status lowered by the Great Depression. With no wages to punctuate their authority, they lost power as primary decision makers. Large numbers of men lost self-respect, became immobilized, and stopped looking for work, while others turned to alcohol, became self-destructive or abusive to their families, or simply walked out the door, never to return.

In contrast to men, many women saw their status rise during the depression. To supplement the family income, married women entered the work force in large numbers. Although most women worked in menial occupations, the fact that they were employed and bringing home paychecks elevated their position within the family and gave them a say in family decisions.

Despite the hardships it inflicted, the Great Depression drew some families closer together. As one observer noted, "Many a family has lost its automobile and found its soul." Families had to devise strategies for getting through hard times because their survival depended on it. They pooled their incomes, moved in with relatives in order to cut expenses, bought day-old bread, ate in soup kitchens, and did without. Many families drew comfort from their religion, sustained by the hope things would turn out well in the end, while others placed their faith in themselves, in their own dogged determination to survive that so impressed observers like Woody Guthrie. But many Americans no longer believed the problems could be solved by people acting alone or through voluntary associations. Increasingly, they looked to the federal government for help.

Franklin Roosevelt and the First New Deal

Franklin D. Roosevelt won the Democratic nomination in June 1932. At first glance he did not look like a man who could relate to other peoples' suffering, for Roosevelt had spent his entire life in the lap of luxury. A fifth cousin of Teddy Roosevelt, he was born in 1882 to a wealthy New York family. Roosevelt enjoyed a privileged youth. He attended Groton, an exclusive private school, Harvard, and Columbia Law School. After three years in the New York state senate, Roosevelt was tapped by President Wilson to serve as assistant secretary of the navy in 1913. His status as the rising star of the Democratic party was confirmed when James Cox chose Roosevelt as his running mate in the presidential election of 1920.

The Election of 1932

Handsome and outgoing, Roosevelt seemed to have a bright political future. Then disaster struck. In 1921 he was stricken with polio. The disease left him paralyzed from the waist down and confined to a wheelchair for the rest of his life. Instead of retiring, however, Roosevelt labored diligently to return to public life. "If you had spent two years in bed trying to wiggle your toe," he later declared, "after that anything would seem easy."

Buoyed by an exuberant optimism and devoted political allies, Roosevelt won the governorship of New York in 1928, one of the few Democrats to survive the Republican landslide. Surrounding himself with able advisors, Roosevelt labored to convert New York into a laboratory for reform, involving conservation, old age pensions, public works projects, and unemployment insurance.

In his acceptance speech before the Democratic convention in Chicago, Roosevelt promised "a New Deal for the American people." Although his speech contained few concrete proposals, Roosevelt radiated confidence, giving many desperate voters hope. He even managed during the campaign to turn his lack of a blueprint into an asset, offering instead a policy of experimentation. "It is common sense to take a method and try it," he declared, "if it fails, admit it frankly and try another."

The Republicans stuck with Hoover. Dejected and embittered, he projected despair and failure. What little chance he had for reelection was dashed by his callous treatment of the "Bonus Army." A bedraggled collection of unemployed veterans and their families, the Bonus Army marched on Washington in the spring of 1932 to ask Congress for immediate payment of their war service bonuses, which did not come due until 1945. More than 15,000 strong, they erected a shantytown, camped out in vacant lots, and occupied empty government buildings. Though the House gave them what they wanted, the Senate killed the bill after Hoover lobbied against it.

Most of the veterans then left Washington, D.C., but a few thousand stayed behind because they had no place to go. At Hoover's request, Congress appropriated $100,000 to help pay their expenses home. When police tried to evict some of the marchers in late July, a riot broke out in which two policemen and two marchers died. Hoover then ordered General Douglas MacArthur to use federal troops to remove them from government buildings. Exceeding his orders, MacArthur used tanks and tear gas to drive the veterans from the city. Newsmen captured the melee in vivid photographs which papers carried the next day.

Although Hoover was appalled by what happened he publicly accepted the responsibility and endorsed MacArthur's charge that the bonus marchers included dangerous radicals who wanted to overthrow the government. Most Americans felt outraged by the government's harsh treatment of the Bonus Army, and Hoover encountered resentment everywhere he campaigned.

Upon learning of the Bonus Army incident, Franklin D. Roosevelt remarked: "Well, this will elect me." Roosevelt was correct; he buried Hoover in November, winning 22,809,638 votes to Hoover's 15,758,901, and 472 to 59 electoral votes. In addition, the Democrats won commanding majorities in both houses of Congress.

Roosevelt appealed to a wide range of voters, wooing southerners back into the Democrat fold, as well as new groups of voters, including young people, women, and ethnic Americans. Urban Catholics, Jews, and members of the Eastern Orthodox Church voted overwhelmingly for Roosevelt, the first of many elections to come in which the Democratic party's fortunes would be strongly affected by these groups.

The First 100 Days

The New Deal was a jumble of hastily improvised legislation and executive orders. Most of the legislation was economic and came in three spurts: one in 1933, during the first "100 days" of Roosevelt's administration, the second in 1935, and the last in 1938. From beginning to end, the New Deal represented an intensely personal enterprise unified only by Roosevelt's personality. In place of a well-defined political philosophy, he pursued a vague commitment to moderate reform, leavened with keen political instincts and a desire to help people.

Roosevelt's greatest asset was his ability to persuade, and no president has ever encountered a Congress so eager to follow. Promising decisive action, he called Congress into special session and demanded "broad executive power to wage a war against the emergency, as great as the power that would be given me if we were in fact invaded by a foreign foe." Across the nation people held their breaths waiting to see what the new president would do.

Roosevelt attacked the banking crisis first. In the months before he took office America's banking system had all but disintegrated. Hundreds of banks had collapsed, wiping out the life savings of nearly ten million people. On March 5 Roosevelt declared a national bank holiday, stopping all banking transactions. A few days later he sent Congress the Emergency Banking Relief Bill, which it immediately approved. The new law permitted solvent banks to reopen under government supervision, and allowed the RFC to buy the stock of troubled banks and keep them open until they could be reorganized. The law gave the president broad powers over the Federal Reserve System.

To generate support for his programs, Roosevelt appealed directly to the people. On March 12 he conducted the first of many radio "fireside chats." Using the radio the way later presidents exploited television, he explained what he had done in plain, simple terms and told the public to have "confidence and courage." When the banks reopened the following day, people demonstrated their faith by making more deposits than withdrawals. One of Roosevelt's key advisors did not exaggerate when he later boasted, "Capitalism was saved in eight days."

Three months later Congress passed the Glass-Steagall Banking Act of 1933. To protect depositors from risky projects, the law separated investment banking from commercial banking. It also established the Federal Deposit Insurance Corporation (FDIC), which guaranteed all deposits up to $2,500, to restore the public's confidence in banks.

Banking reform was just the beginning. During the "100 days," Congress rammed through 15 major bills, more legislation than any preceding session had passed in history. Most of the early bills were conservative and deflationary, reflecting Roosevelt's desire to pursue moderate reform within a balanced budget.

Within days after taking office, President Franklin Delano Roosevelt moved to restore the public's confidence in the banking system.

Table 25.1

Depression Shopping List: 1932–1934

Automobiles		Furniture	
Pontiac Coupe	$585.00	Dining room set, 8-piece	$ 46.50
Chrysler Sedan	995.00	Lounge chair	19.95
Dodge	595.00	Double bed and mattress	14.75
Studebaker	840.00	Mahogany coffee table	10.75
Packard	2150.00	Chippendale sofa	135.00
Chevrolet 1/2-ton pickup truck	650.00	Louis XV walnut dining table	124.00
		Wing chair	39.00
Clothing		Grand piano	395.00
Women's			
Mink coat	$585.00	**Toys**	
Leopard coat	92.00	Doll carriage	$ 4.98
Cloth coat	6.98	Sled	1.45
Wool dress	1.95	Tricycle	3.98
Wool suit	3.98	Bicycle	10.98
Wool sweater	1.69	Fielder's glove and ball	1.25
Silk stockings	.69		
Leather shoes	1.79	**Food**	
		Sirloin steak/lb	$ .29
Men's		Rib roast/lb	.22
Overcoat	$ 11.00	Bacon/lb	.22
Wool suit	10.50	Ham/lb	.31
Trousers	2.00	Chicken/lb	.22
Shirt	.47	Pork Chops/lb	.20
Pullover sweater	1.97	Salmon (16 oz can)	.19
Silk necktie	.55	Milk (quart)	.10
Stetson hat	5.00	Butter/lb	.28
Shoes	3.85	Eggs (dozen)	.29
		Bread (20 oz loaf)	.05
Household Items		Coffee/lb	.26
Silverplate flatware, 26 pieces	$ 4.98	Sugar/lb	.05
Double-bed sheets	.67	Rice/lb	.06
Bath towel	.24	Potatoes/lb	.02
Wool blanket	1.00	Tomatoes (16 oz can)	.09
Wool rug (9' × 12')	5.85	Oranges/dozen	.27
		Cornflakes (8 oz box)	.08
Appliances			
Electric iron	$ 2.00	**Air Travel**	
Electric coffee percolator	1.39	New York to Chicago,	
Electric mixer	9.95	round trip	$ 86.31
Vacuum cleaner	18.75	Chicago to Los Angeles,	
Electric washing machine	47.95	round trip	207.00
Gas stove	23.95		
Electric sewing machine	24.95		

The later bills of the "100 days" marked a change in direction. Distancing himself from Hoover's tight-money policies, Roosevelt provided relief to debtors and exporters by devaluing the dollar, abandoning the gold standard, and ordering the Federal Reserve System to ease credit. This shift reflected the declining clout within his administration of conservatives, and the growing influence of a group of economists and college professors who came to be known as the "brain trust." The "brain trust" supplied Roosevelt with economic ideas and oratorical ammunition. These advisors saw "bigness" as the natural product of a mature industrial economy. Instead of busting trusts, they believed government should accept consolidation and enforce regulations designed to promote open and fair competition. Acting on their advice, Roosevelt launched two major reforms, one directed at industry, the other at agriculture.

The National Recovery Administration

Roosevelt called the National Recovery Administration (NRA), established by the National Industrial Recovery Act (NIRA), "the most important and far-reaching legislation ever passed by the American Congress." The NRA, which sought to define a working relationship between government and industry, had much in common with Teddy Roosevelt's philosophy of "New Nationalism." The NRA proposed to resolve the major causes of economic instability (ruinous competition, overproduction, labor-management confrontations, and price fluctuations) through economic planning. Under the NRA, boards of industrial leaders, labor representatives, and government officials would draft codes of competition to limit production, assign quotas among individual producers, and impose strict price guidelines.

Participation in the NRA was purely voluntary, but businesses that joined were exempted from antitrust prosecution. In practice, this meant that the codes offered businesspeople the chance to fix prices. To attract labor's support, Section 7A of the NIRA guaranteed maximum hours, minimum wages, and collective bargaining. In short, the NRA proposed to restore economic health by letting industry regulate itself and by conferring the government's blessing on labor unions.

Led by General Hugh Johnson, the new agency got off to a promising start. By midsummer 1933, over 500 industries had signed codes covering 22 million workers. By the end of the summer the nation's ten largest industries had been won over, as well as hundreds of smaller businesses. All across the land businesses displayed the "Blue Eagle," the insignia of the NRA, in their windows.

The NRA's success was short-lived. Johnson proved to be an overzealous leader who alienated many businesspeople. Instead of creating a smooth-running corporate state, Johnson presided over a chorus of end-

less squabbling. The NRA boards, which were dominated by representatives of big business, drafted codes that favored their interests over those of small competitors. Moreover, even though they controlled the new agency from the outset, many leaders of big business resented the NRA for interfering in the private sector.

For labor the NRA was a mixed blessing. On the positive side, the codes abolished child labor and established the precedent of federal regulation of minimum wages and maximum hours. In addition, the NIRA boosted the labor movement by drawing large numbers of unskilled workers into unions. On the negative side, however, the NRA codes set wages in most industries well below what labor demanded, and large occupational groups, such as farm workers, fell outside the codes' coverage.

The NIRA also tried "pump priming," to promote industrial recovery, a favorite scheme of the "brain trusters." They advocated large public construction projects to stimulate the economy. The Public Works Administration (PWA), led by the overly cautious Harold Ickes, sponsored a variety of building projects, such as schools, hospitals, bridges and courthouses. The PWA eventually pumped $3 billion into the economy, but Ickes's prudence and fear of waste prevented the funds from being spent fast enough to have any measurable impact.

Other New Deal agencies followed the same pattern as the PWA. While the New Deal was remarkably scandal free, the government often worked at cross-purposes with itself, permitting concern for potential corruption to hamper prompt and decisive action.

Farm Policy

The Great Depression all but destroyed America's farmers. Between 1929 and 1933 farmers saw their income fall 60 percent, leaving them with crops they could not sell and mortgages they could not pay. To make matters worse, their current woes followed a decade of hard times in the 1920s. Small wonder farmers looked back wistfully to the brief period of prosperity they had enjoyed on the eve of World War I.

The New Deal attacked farm problems through a variety of programs. As late as 1935 more than six million of America's 6.8 million farms had no electricity. Unlike their sisters in the city, farm women had no washing machines, refrigerators, or vacuum cleaners. Nor did private utility companies intend to change things. Private companies insisted that it would be cost prohibitive to provide electrical service to rural areas.

Roosevelt disagreed. He wanted to break the private monopoly of electric power in rural areas, envisioning a future in which electric power would serve broader goals, including flood control, soil conservation, reforestation, diversification of industry, and a general improvement in the quality of life for rural Americans. Settling on the 40,000 square-mile valley of the Tennessee River as his test site, Roosevelt decided to put the government into the electric business.

Two months after he took office Congress passed a bill creating the Tennessee Valley Authority (TVA). The bill authorized the TVA to build 21 dams to generate electricity for tens of thousands of farm families. In 1935 Roosevelt signed an executive order creating the Rural Electrification Administration (REA) to bring electricity generated by government dams to America's hinterland. Between 1935 and 1942 the lights came on for 35 percent of America's farm families.

Nor was electricity the only benefit the New Deal bestowed on farmers. The Soil Conservation Service helped farmers battle erosion; the Farm Credit Administration provided some relief from farm foreclosures; and the Commodity Credit Corporation permitted farmers to use stored products as collateral for loans. Roosevelt's most ambitious farm program, however, was the Agriculture Adjustment Act (AAA).

Like the NRA, the AAA, led by Secretary of Agriculture Henry Wallace, sought a partnership between the government and major producers. Together the new allies would raise prices by reducing the supply of farm goods. Under the AAA, the large producers, acting through farm cooperatives, would agree upon a "domestic allotment" plan that would assign acreage quotas to each producer. Participation would be voluntary. Farmers who cut production to comply with the quotas would be paid for land left fallow.

Unfortunately for its backers, the AAA got off to a horrible start. Because the 1933 crops had already been planted by the time Congress established the AAA, the administration ordered farmers to plow their crops under, paying them over $100 million for mowing down ten million acres of cotton. The government also purchased and slaughtered several million pigs, salvaging only one million pounds for the needy. The public neither understood nor forgave the agency for destroying food while jobless people went hungry.

Overall, the AAA's record was mixed. Farm income doubled between 1933 and 1936, but large farmers reaped most of the profits. The AAA did little to help sharecroppers and tenant farmers, the groups hardest hit by the agricultural crisis. The problem of overproduction was never solved as technology and mechanization dramatically increased crop yields. As a result, between 1932 and 1935, three million Americans abandoned farming and moved to the city.

Job Programs

To provide short-term assistance for the unemployed, Roosevelt reluctantly turned to welfare programs. In March 1933 Congress created the

Civilian Conservation Corps (CCC) to offer young people jobs in national parks. By midsummer, the government had hired 300,000 young men between the ages of 18 and 25 who planted saplings, built fire towers, stocked depleted streams, and restored historic battlefields. By 1942, 2.5 million men had served in Roosevelt's "Tree Army."

No New Deal program enjoyed greater popularity. The CCC offered young men fresh air, exercise, healthy food, and educational programs. In addition to room and board, they received a modest wage, most of which went home to their families. Still, the CCC's economic impact was small. It excluded women, imposed rigid quotas on blacks, and offered employment to only a small number of the young people who needed work.

Much more ambitious was the Civil Works Administration (CWA), established in November 1933. Under the energetic leadership of Harry Hopkins, the CWA put 2.6 million men to work in its first month, and within two months it employed four million men building 250,000 miles of road, 40,000 schools, 150,000 privies, and 3,700 playgrounds.

In March 1934, however, Roosevelt scrapped the CWA because he (like Hoover) did not wish to create a permanent dependent class. Roosevelt badly underestimated the crisis. As government funding slowed

For $30 a month, workers in the Civilian Conservation Corps (CCC) planted trees and dug drainage ditches. Such federal work relief programs helped many retain their self-respect.

down and economic indicators leveled off, the depression deepened in 1934, triggering a series of violent strikes, which culminated on Labor Day, 1934, when garment workers launched the single largest strike in the nation's history. All across the land, critics attacked Roosevelt for not doing enough to combat the depression, charges that did not go unheeded in the White House.

Following the congressional elections of 1934, in which the Democrats won 13 new House seats and 9 new Senate seats, Roosevelt abandoned his hopes for a balanced budget, deciding that bolder action was required. He had lost faith in government planning and the proposed alliance with business, which left only one other road to recovery—government spending. Encouraged by the CCC's success, he decided to create more federal jobs for the unemployed.

In January 1935 Congress created the Works Progress Administration (WPA), Roosevelt's program to employ 3.5 million workers at a "security wage"—twice the level of welfare payments but well below union scales. To head the new agency, Roosevelt again turned to Harry Hopkins. Since the WPA's purpose was to employ men quickly, Hopkins opted for labor-intensive tasks, creating jobs that were often makeshift and inefficient. Jeering critics said the WPA stood for "We Piddle Along," but the agency built many worthwhile projects. In its first five years alone the WPA constructed or improved 2,500 hospitals, 5,900 schools, 1,000 airport fields,

Table 25.2

Legislation Enacted During the Hundred Days, March 9–June 16, 1933	
March 9	Emergency Banking Relief Act
March 20	Economy Act
March 22	Beer-Wine Revenue Act
March 31	Unemployment Relief Act
March 31	Civilian Conservation Corps Act
May 12	Agricultural Adjustment Act
May 12	Federal Emergency Relief Act
May 18	Tennessee Valley Authority Act
May 27	Securities Act of 1933
June 5	Gold Repeal Joint Resolution
June 13	Home Owners' Refinancing Act
June 16	Farm Credit Act
June 16	Banking Act of 1933
June 16	Emergency Railroad Transportation Act
June 16	National Industrial Recovery Act

and nearly 13,000 playgrounds. By 1941 it had provided jobs to 40 percent of the nation's unemployed, pumping $11 billion into the economy.

The WPA also sponsored several cultural programs. While folksingers like Woody Guthrie honored the nation in ballads, other artists were hired to catalog it, photograph it, paint it, record it, and write about it. In photojournalism, for example, the Farm Security Agency (FSA) employed scores of photographers to create a pictorial record of America and its people. Under the auspices of the WPA, the Federal Writers Project sponsored an impressive set of state guides and dispatched an army of folklorists into the backcountry in search of tall tales. Oral historians collected slave narratives, and musicologists compiled an amazing collection of folk music. Other WPA programs included the Theatre Project, which produced a live running commentary on everyday affairs, and the Art Project, which decorated the nation's libraries and post offices with murals of muscular workmen, bountiful wheat fields, and massive machinery.

Valuable in their own right, the WPA's cultural programs had the added benefit of providing work for thousands of writers, artists, actors, and other creative people. In addition, these programs established the precedent of federal support to the arts and the humanities, laying the groundwork for future federal programs to promote the life of the mind in America.

Protest from the Left

The WPA marked the zenith of Roosevelt's influence over Congress. Following its passage, Congress dallied for several months over the remainder of his program. Opposition came from both the right and the left, as the New Deal's failure to end the depression by 1935 led to growing frustration. Three figures stepped forward to challenge Roosevelt: Huey Long, a Louisiana senator; Father Charles Coughlin, a Catholic priest from Detroit; and Francis Townsend, a retired California physician.

Of the three, Huey Long attracted the widest following. Ambitious, endowed with supernatural energy, and totally devoid of scruples, Long was a fiery, spellbinding orator in the tradition of southern populism. As governor and then senator, he ruled Louisiana with an iron hand. Yet the people of Louisiana loved him because he attacked the big oil companies, increased state spending on public works, and improved public schools. Although he backed Roosevelt in 1932, Long quickly abandoned the president and opposed the New Deal as too conservative.

Early in 1934 Long announced his "Share Our Wealth" program. Vowing to make "Every Man a King," he promised to soak the rich by imposing a stiff tax on inheritances over $5 million and by levying a 100 percent tax on annual incomes over $1 million. The confiscated funds, in turn, would be distributed to the people, guaranteeing every American family an annual income of no less than $2,000, in Long's words more than enough to buy "a radio, a car, and a home." By February 1935 Long's followers had organized over 27,000 "Share Our Wealth" clubs. Roosevelt had to take him seriously, for a Democratic poll revealed Long could attract three to four million voters to an independent presidential ticket.

Like Long, Father Charles Coughlin was an early supporter who turned sour on the New Deal. Speaking on the radio to an estimated 30 million Americans from his Catholic parish in a Detroit suburb, Coughlin blamed the depression on greedy bankers and challenged Roosevelt to solve the crisis by nationalizing banks and inflating the currency. When Roosevelt refused to heed his advice, Coughlin broke with Roosevelt and formed the National Union for Social Justice.

Roosevelt's least strident opponent was Dr. Francis Townsend, a California public health officer who found himself unemployed at the age of 67, with only $100 in savings. Seeing many people in similar or worse straits, Townsend embraced old age relief as the key to ending the depression. In January 1934 Townsend announced his plan, demanding a $200 monthly pension for every citizen over the age of 60. In return, recipients had to retire and spend their entire pension every month within the United States. Younger Americans would inherit the jobs vacated by senior citizens, and the economy would be stimulated by the increased purchasing power of the elderly. Although critics lambasted the Townsend plan as ludicrous, several million Americans found his plan refreshingly simple.

The Second New Deal

Roosevelt could not afford to ignore his critics. In a close election Long, Coughlin, and Townsend commanded more than enough votes to tip the scales in favor of a Republican candidate. Thus, Roosevelt slowly abandoned his dream of building a coalition that would unite all Americans behind the New Deal. To remain in office, Roosevelt had to shift policies.

Roosevelt Moves Toward the Left

Alarmed by his critics, Roosevelt called for the further expansion of federal authority. Opposition from the Supreme Court also prodded Roosevelt in this direction. On May 26, 1935, the Court struck down the NRA in *Schechter* v. *United States*—the famous "sick chicken" case, in which the Court held unanimously that the federal government did not have the power to regulate the sale of poultry in Brooklyn. The ruling, a stinging rebuke to the president and his New Deal, infuriated Roosevelt. In June he refused to dismiss Congress until they passed his new legislative agenda. The result was the "Second Hundred Days."

The National Labor Relations Act (Wagner Act) came first. Senator Robert F. Wagner of New York, the bill's sponsor, seized the opportunity to replace Section 7A of the NIRA with what he called "labor's Magna Carta." Up to this point Roosevelt had resisted any drastic change in labor policy, but once the Wagner Act's passage seemed assured he gave it his belated blessing. The bill represented the government's most important concession to labor to date. It guaranteed labor's right to organize by creating the National Labor Relations Board (NLRB), which had the power to conduct labor elections, determine bargaining units, and restrain business from "unfair labor practices."

The Wagner Act inspired an unprecedented burst of labor organizing and increased union membership in many industries, giving labor the bargaining power to push its demands. In late 1936 Walter Reuther and the United Automobile Workers (UAW) launched "sit down" strikes in which workers occupied factories but refused to work. The automobile companies responded with violence, but the union prevailed. In February 1937 General Motors recognized the union, and UAW membership increased from 30,000 to more than 400,000 in less than a year. Under the effective leadership of John L. Lewis, the newly formed Congress of Industrial Organizations (CIO) enjoyed remarkable success in organizing the steel, automotive, and textile industries, and quickly became a powerful force in the labor struggle. The Wagner Act had put the full weight of the federal government behind labor's right to bargain collectively.

Social Security

A goal of reformers since the Progressive Era, the 1935 Social Security Act aimed to alleviate the plight of America's visible poor—dependent children, the elderly, and the handicapped. A major political victory for Roosevelt, the Social Security Act was a triumph of social legislation. It offered workers 65 or older monthly stipends based on previous earnings, and it gave the indigent elderly small relief payments, financed by the federal government and the states. In addition, it provided assistance to blind and handicapped Americans, and to dependent children who did not have a wage-earning parent. The act also established the nation's first federally sponsored system of unemployment insurance. Mandatory payroll deductions levied equally on employees and employers financed both the retirement system and the unemployment insurance.

While conservatives argued that the Social Security Act placed the United States on the road to socialism, the legislation was also profoundly disappointing to reformers, who demanded "cradle to grave" protection as the birthright of every American. The new system authorized pitifully small payments; its retirement system left huge groups of workers uncovered, such as migrant workers, civil servants, domestic servants, merchant seamen, day laborers; its budget came from a regressive tax scheme that placed a disproportionate tax burden on the poor; and it failed to provide health insurance.

Despite these criticisms, the Social Security Act introduced a new era in American history. It committed the government to a social welfare role by providing for elderly, disabled, dependent, and unemployed Americans. By doing so, the act greatly expanded the public's sense of entitlement, and the support people expected government to give to all citizens.

The remaining "must legislation" of the Second Hundred Days included utilities regulation, banking reform, and a new tax proposal. Yet none of these measures represented a drastic change in American politics or society. On the whole, the Second New Deal merely sought to make capitalism more humane. The majority of Americans did not want dramatic changes, and Roosevelt never contemplated, much less achieved, a social revolution. He made no attacks on private property; the well-to-do retained their privileges; wealth was not redistributed; and the poor remained poor.

To hear many wealthy conservatives tell it, however, Roosevelt was a wild-eyed radical who threatened the very foundation of capitalism. William Randolph Hearst ordered his newspapers to substitute the words "Raw Deal" for "New Deal." Firmly committed to a balanced budget, conservatives viewed heavy government spending as sacrilege, and they were appalled by the growth of the bureaucracy in Washington, D.C. By 1940 the number of federal employees in the nation's capital had risen to 139,770, nearly double what it had been in 1932. Conservatives feared government's growth would increase federal power at the expense of states' rights and individual liberties, and they believed Roosevelt would raise rich people's taxes to finance his relief programs. Viewing Roosevelt as a traitor to his class, many wealthy Americans saw the election of 1936 as their chance to save the country.

The Election of 1936

To carry its banner in 1936, the GOP picked Alfred M. Landon of Kansas, the only Republican governor who survived the 1934 elections. Landon was far more liberal than many of his backers. He had opposed the KKK, backed business regulation, and supported many New Deal programs. A poor public speaker, Landon offered few alternatives to Roosevelt's programs.

To win in 1936 the GOP needed help from a third party, but this assistance never arrived. Huey Long's organization fell apart following his assassination in 1935; Francis Townsend's campaign, already weakened by passage of the Social Security Act in 1935, collapsed in the spring of 1936 under charges of corruption; and by 1936 Father Coughlin had been reduced to an abusive name-caller who had been publicly rebuked by the Catholic church.

Roosevelt enjoyed the race, lashing out at "economic royalists" who opposed the New Deal. The Democrats were aided by positive economic indicators: In 1936 industrial output more than doubled its 1933 figures, and the national income rose half again as much. Roosevelt carried every state but Maine and Vermont. Democrats won an equally lopsided victory in the congressional races: 331 to 89 in the House and 76 to 16 in the Senate.

The Democratic victory rested on a broad base of support. Roosevelt's backers included poor people, organized labor, urban ethnics, the Democratic South, blacks, and many intellectuals. A formidable alliance of diverse groups, Roosevelt's New Deal coalition would shape the contours of American politics for decades to come.

The New Deal and Minorities

Until the New Deal, blacks had shown their traditional loyalty to the party of Lincoln by voting overwhelmingly Republican. By the end of Roosevelt's first administration, however, one of the most dramatic voter shifts in American history had occurred. In 1936, 75 percent of black voters supported the Democrats. Blacks turned to Roosevelt in part because his spending programs gave them a measure of relief from the depression and in part because the GOP had done little to repay their earlier support.

Still, Roosevelt's record on civil rights was modest at best. Instead of using New Deal programs to promote civil rights, the administration consistently bowed to discrimination. In order to pass major New Deal legislation, Roosevelt needed the support of southern Democrats. Time and time again, he backed away from equal rights to avoid antagonizing southern whites, although his wife, Eleanor, did take a public stand in support of civil rights.

Most New Deal programs discriminated against blacks. The NRA, for example, not only offered whites the first crack at jobs but authorized separate and lower pay scales for blacks. The Federal Housing Authority

(FHA) refused to guarantee mortgages for blacks who tried to buy in white neighborhoods, and the CCC maintained segregated camps. Furthermore, the Social Security Act excluded those job categories blacks traditionally filled.

The story in agriculture was particularly grim. Since 40 percent of all black workers made their living as sharecroppers and tenant farmers, the AAA acreage reduction hit blacks hard. White landlords could make more money by leaving land untilled than by putting land into production. As a result, the AAA's policies forced more than 100,000 blacks off the land in 1933 and 1934.

Even more galling to black leaders, the president failed to support an antilynching bill and a bill to abolish the poll tax. Roosevelt feared that conservative southern Democrats, who had seniority in Congress and controlled many committee chairmanships, would block his bills if he tried to fight them on the race question.

Yet the New Deal did record a few gains in civil rights. Roosevelt named Mary McLeod Bethune, a black educator, to the advisory committee of the National Youth Administration (NYA), and thanks to her efforts, blacks received a fair share of NYA funds. The WPA was colorblind, and blacks in northern cities benefited from its work relief programs. Harold Ickes, a strong supporter of civil rights who had several blacks on his staff, poured federal funds into black schools and hospitals in the South. Most blacks appointed to New Deal posts, however, served in token positions as advisors on black affairs. At best they achieved a new visibility in government.

Mexican Americans

Like blacks, most Mexican Americans reaped few benefits from the New Deal. Affected in much the same way as sharecroppers and tenant farmers, many Mexican-American migrant workers lost their jobs due to AAA acreage reductions or competition in the fields from unemployed whites.

Mexican Americans faced serious opposition from organized labor, which resented competition from Mexican workers as unemployment rose. Bowing to union pressure, federal, state and local authorities deported more than 400,000 people of Mexican descent during the 1930s to prevent them from applying for relief. Since this group included many who had been born in the United States, the deportations constituted a gross violation of civil liberties.

Still, the New Deal offered Mexican Americans a little help. The Farm Security Administration established camps for migrant farm workers in California, and the CCC and WPA hired unemployed Mexican

Americans on relief jobs. Many, however, did not qualify for relief assistance because as migrant workers they did not meet residency requirements. Furthermore, agricultural workers were not eligible for benefits under workers' compensation, Social Security, and the National Labor Relations Act.

Native Americans

The so-called "Indian New Deal" was the only bright spot in the administration's treatment of minorities. In 1933 Roosevelt appointed John Collier as commissioner of Indian affairs. At Collier's request, Congress created the Indian Emergency Conservation Program (IECP), a CCC-type project for the reservations which employed more than 85,000 Indians. Collier also made certain that the PWA, WPA, CCC, and NYA hired Native Americans.

Collier had long been an opponent of the 50-year-old government allotment program, in which tribal lands had been broken up and distributed to individual Native Americans and whites. In 1934 Congress passed the Indian Reorganization Act, which terminated the allotment program of the Dawes Severalty Act of 1887; provided funds for tribes to purchase new land; offered government recognition of tribal constitutions; and repealed prohibitions on Native American languages and customs. That same year, federal grants were provided to local school districts, hospitals, and social welfare agencies to assist Native Americans.

Women

Women achieved measured progress under the New Deal. Frances Perkins, the secretary of labor and the first woman cabinet member in American history, brought many women into government; Molly Dewson, the director of the Women's Division of the Democratic Committee, helped place women throughout the administration. By 1939 women held one-third of all positions in the independent agencies and almost one-fifth of the jobs in the executive departments.

Eleanor Roosevelt deserves much of the credit for the progress made by minorities. The first president's wife to stake out an independent public position, she provided the social conscience of the New Deal. The First Lady worked tirelessly to persuade her husband and the heads of government agencies to hire well-qualified women and blacks. More courageous than her husband and less restricted politically, she did not hesitate to take a public stand on civil rights.

The New Deal in Decline

As Roosevelt's first term drew to a close, the Supreme Court turned on the New Deal. In 1935 the Court ruled the NRA unconstitutional, and in 1936 it struck down the AAA. These decisions convinced Roosevelt the Supreme Court was at odds with the other two branches of government, and was threatening the success of his New Deal. In an effort to make his opponents on the Supreme Court resign so he could replace them with justices more sympathetic to his policies, Roosevelt announced a plan to add one new member to the Supreme Court for every judge who had reached the age of 70 without retiring (six justices were over 70). To offer a carrot with the stick, Roosevelt also outlined a generous new pension program for retiring federal judges.

The court-packing scheme was a political disaster. Conservatives and liberals alike denounced Roosevelt for attacking the separation of powers, and critics accused him of trying to become a dictator. Fortunately, the Court itself ended the crisis by shifting ground. In two separate cases the Court upheld the Wagner Act and approved a Washington state minimum wage law, furnishing proof that it had softened its opposition to the New Deal.

Yet Roosevelt remained too obsessed with the battle to realize he had won the war. He lobbied for the court-packing bill for several months, squandering his strength on a struggle that had long since become a political embarrassment. In the end, the only part of the president's plan to gain congressional approval was the pension program. Once it passed, Justice Willis Van Devanter, the most obstinate New Deal opponent on the Court, resigned. By 1941 Roosevelt had named five justices to the Supreme Court. Few legacies of the president's leadership proved more important, for the new "Roosevelt Court" significantly expanded the government's role in the economy and in civil liberties.

Roosevelt's second blunder involved fiscal policy. Secretary of the Treasury Henry Morganthau urged Roosevelt to cut federal spending in an effort to balance the federal budget and restore business confidence. Reassured by good economic news in 1936, Roosevelt slashed government spending the following year. The budget cuts knocked the economy into a tailspin. By early 1938 economic indicators dipped nearly as low as they had been in 1932, forcing Roosevelt to reverse himself and ask Congress to resume welfare spending.

By the end of 1938 the reform spirit was gone. A conservative alliance of southern Democrats and northern Republicans in Congress blocked all efforts to expand the New Deal. Yet if Roosevelt could not pass any new measures, neither could his opponents dismantle his programs. The New Deal ended in stalemate, but with several reforms ensconced as permanent features of American politics.

Conclusion

From a purely economic perspective, the New Deal barely made a dent in the Great Depression. Roosevelt's programs suffered from poor planning and moved with considerable caution. By 1939 national productivity had barely reached 1929 levels, and ten million men and women remained unemployed. Roosevelt simply could not bring himself to support huge federal budgets. As a result, government expenditures stayed below $10 billion a year, not nearly enough to fuel economic recovery. World War II, not the New Deal, snapped America out of the depression, for then and only then did unemployment disappear.

Yet whatever its shortcomings, the New Deal blunted the worst effects of the Great Depression. Through economic reforms and public works projects Roosevelt managed to preserve the public's faith in capitalism and in democratic government at a time when both seemed on the verge of collapse. Roosevelt accomplished this, in large measure, by reaching out to groups that Washington had largely neglected in the past. The Social Security program, while it ignored many, made the government responsible for old age pensions and welfare payments to citizens who could not support themselves. The NIRA and the Wagner Act encouraged the growth of unions; minimum wage laws benefited many workers; and child labor was finally abolished in industry (though it remained in agriculture). While the New Deal stopped far short of providing equal treatment under the law for minorities, it offered them a measure of relief from the depression.

The New Deal encouraged Americans to look to the White House for strong executive leadership. Roosevelt responded to the situation with decisive action. Increasingly, the public expected the other branches of government to support presidential initiatives. Roosevelt's administrative style, creating special agencies to handle specific problems and placing people in charge who answered directly to him, further enhanced presidential power. On a purely partisan level, the New Deal enabled Roosevelt to forge a Democratic coalition of diverse groups—labor, blacks, urban ethnics, intellectuals, and southern whites—that helped shape American politics for the next several decades.

Above all, the New Deal made the federal government responsible for safeguarding the nation's economic health. Prior to the 1930s, if people

Chronology of Key Events

1928   Herbert Hoover elected thirty-first president

1929   Stock market crashes

1930   Hawley-Smoot Tariff raises import duties

1932   Reconstruction Finance Corporation created to lend money to banks, railroads, and insurance companies; Federal Home Loan Bank System created to lend money to savings and loan associations; Bonus Army dispersed by federal troops in Washington, DC; Franklin Roosevelt elected thirty-second president

1933   Emergency Banking Relief Act addresses banking crisis; Civilian Conservation Corps created to employ young men in reforestation, road construction, and flood control projects; Federal Emergency Relief Act provides federal funds for state and local relief efforts; Civil Works Administration created to provide federal jobs for unemployed; Agricultural Adjustment Act sets up system of farm price supports and production limits; National Industrial Recovery Act (NIRA) created to revive business through a series of fair-competition codes; Tennessee Valley Authority constructs dams and hydroelectric plants in Tennessee River valley; Twenty-first Amendment repeals prohibition; Glass-Steagall Act creates Federal Deposit Insurance Corporation to insure savings accounts against bank failures; Farm Credit Administration and Home Owners' Loan Corporation provide low-interest loans to farmers and home owners

1934   Huey Long's "Share Our Wealth" program announced; Indian Reorganization Act repeals prohibitions on Native American customs

1935   *Schechter* v. *United States*; Emergency Relief Appropriation Act; National Labor Relations Act; Social Security Act creates federal system of old-age pensions

1937   Roosevelt proposes "court-packing" scheme

1938   Fair Labor Standards Act bans child labor, sets minimum wages and maximum hours were asked how the government affected them, they probably thought in terms of state or even local government. The New Deal, however, made the federal government such a daily presence in people's lives that they now expected Washington to involve itself in everything from farm subsidies to the sale of stocks and securities.

Suggestions for Further Reading

Good overviews of America during the Great Depression include Sean Dennis Cashman, *America in the Twenties and Thirties* (1989); William E. Leuchtenburg, *Franklin D. Roosevelt and the New Deal* (1963); Robert S. McElvaine, *The Great Depression: America* (1984).

Studies of the Hoover administration include William J. Barber, *From New Era to New Deal* (1985); Martin L. Fausold, *The Presidency of Herbert Hoover* (1985).

Good biographies of Franklin D. Roosevelt include James M. Burns, *Roosevelt: The Lion and the Fox* (1956); Frank Freidel, *Franklin D. Roosevelt,* 4 vols., (1952–1976); Arthur Schlesinger, Jr., *The Age of Roosevelt,* 3 vols. (1957–1960).

For specific New Deal policies, useful studies include Barbara Blumberg *The New Deal and the Unemployed* (1979); Bernard Bellush, *The Failure of the NRA* (1975); Ellis Hawley, *The New Deal and the Problem of Monopoly* (1966);

For opposition to Roosevelt's New Deal, consult Alan Brinkley, *Voices of Protest: Huey Long, Father Coughlin, and the Great Depression* (1982); T. Harry Williams, *Huey Long* (1969). Women's issues are examined in Susan Ware, *Beyond Suffrage: Women in the New Deal* (1981). Issues confronting minorities during the 1930s are dealt with in Abraham Hoffman, *Unwanted Mexican Americans in the Great Depression* (1974); James H. Jones, *Bad Blood: The Tuskegee Syphilis Experiment,* rev. ed. (1992); Lawrence C. Kelly, *The Assault on Assimilation* (1983); Kenneth Philp, *John Collier's Crusade for Indian Reform* (1977); Nancy J. Weiss, *Farewell to the Party of Lincoln: Black Politics in the Age of FDR* (1983); Raymond Wolters, *Negroes and the Great Depression* (1970).

Chapter 26

The End of Isolation: America Faces the World, 1920–1945

Allied armies won the decisive battles of World War II, but the Allied victory rested squarely on America's economic might. The gross national product rose from $91 billion in 1939 to $166 billion in 1945, and industrial production soared by an astonishing 96 percent. By 1943 America's productivity outstripped all its enemies combined; by 1944 it was twice as great.

No one symbolized this economic miracle better than Henry J. Kaiser. Before the war his Six Companies consortium built Boulder Dam and sank the piers for the Golden Gate Bridge. When World War II erupted, Kaiser immediately used his experience with government contracts and officials to become one of the leading industrial architects of the Allied victory.

Kaiser built ships—tankers, small aircraft carriers, troop ships, and Liberty ships, the basic cargo carrier of the war. He would not tolerate delays in production schedules. By 1945 his shipyards won more than $3 billion in government contracts and turned out a ship a day. With enemy submarines sinking everything in sight, Kaiser stressed speed and large-scale production, not efficiency, cost, or quality.

Kaiser's shipyards formed a microcosm of American society. Teeming with migrants from farms and small towns, they employed 125,000 men

One of the biggest producers of war goods was Henry Kaiser. Almost one quarter of America's entire wartime output of merchant shipping came from his shipyards.

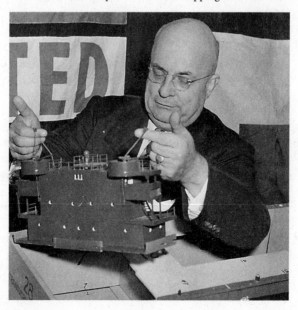

and women who faced problems ranging from overcrowded housing to nonexistent child care. Kaiser devised ingenious ways to attract workers. He paid good wages, built a modern hospital or clinic near every shipyard, enrolled workers and their families in an excellent health plan, and experimented with round-the-clock nurseries and child-care centers.

After the war Kaiser praised himself as the embodiment of rugged individualism, but in truth his success derived from "welfare capitalism." Government loans financed his shipyards, and cost-plus government contracts guaranteed his profits. Yet his concern for workers and their families tempered capitalism with compassion, creating a model of corporate management that survived long after the last of his ships went into mothballs.

Diplomacy Between the Wars

World War I's horrible casualties, disappointments over the Treaty of Versailles, the United States' failure to join the League of Nations, and the Red Scare left the public suspicious of foreign crusades. During the 1920s and much of the 1930s, the United States concentrated on improving its status in the Western Hemisphere and on avoiding European entanglements.

The Isolationist Mirage

Throughout the 1920s Republican leaders debated and ultimately refused to join the League of Nations or the World Court. Such commitments, they feared, might involve the United States too deeply in global politics. Yet Washington remained keenly interested in preserving international stability and tried to promote world peace through diplomatic means.

In December 1921 Secretary of State Charles Evans Hughes convened a disarmament conference in Washington, D.C., which produced the Five-Power Naval Treaty the following year. The treaty established a ten-year moratorium on the construction of battleships and set tonnage for battleships at a ratio of 525,000 tons for the United States and Great Britain, 300,000 tons for Japan, and 175,000 tons for France and Italy. In 1922 the United States also signed the Nine-Power Treaty, an agreement to preserve the "Open Door" in China, and the Four-Party Treaty, which committed the United States, Great Britain, France, and Japan to consult before going to war in Asia. None of these treaties, however, contained any provision for enforcement.

Several years later the United States and France launched an international crusade to banish war from world affairs. In 1928 the French foreign minister, Aristide Briand, and Secretary of State Frank B. Kellogg negotiated the Kellogg-Briand Pact, which renounced war as an instrument for resolving international disputes and symbolized the post-World War I era's disillusionment with naked power. If attacked, however, the signatories, 62 in all, could defend themselves by force. While it raised hopes for peace and earned Kellogg the Nobel Peace Prize, the Kellogg-Briand Pact had no chance of preventing future bloodshed, since it, too, lacked an enforcement mechanism.

The Good Neighbor Policy

During the 1920s Republican administrations inched away from gunboat diplomacy and tried to develop better relations with Latin America. Progress was uneven and Washington's policies occasionally reverted to heavy-handed interventions, but the thrust of Republican diplomacy during the 1920s—more trade and less military involvement—clearly anticipated the shift toward improved relations with Latin America, which the Democrats dubbed the "Good Neighbor Policy" in the 1930s.

In 1924, for example, the United States pulled the marines out of the Dominican Republic, and the following year American troops left Nicaragua, only to be sent back a few months later when a revolution broke out. President Herbert Hoover continued the diplomacy of reconciliation. He announced plans to withdraw marines from Nicaragua and Haiti, and he resisted pressure from Congress to establish a customs receivership in El Salvador when the government there defaulted on its bonds. In 1930 Hoover repudiated the Roosevelt Corollary to the Monroe Doctrine, which for 25 years had justified U.S. intervention in Latin America.

In his first inaugural address President Franklin D. Roosevelt dedicated the United States "to the policy of the good neighbor." Secretary of State Cordell Hull stunned Latin America in December 1933 by declaring, "no state has the right to intervene in the international or external affairs of another." The marines left Nicaragua in 1933 and Haiti in 1934. The United States also nullified the Platt Amendment, thereby surrendering the right to intervene in the affairs of Cuba, and gave Panama its political independence. Furthermore, when Mexico expropriated foreign oil properties in 1938, Roosevelt rejected calls to send in troops and let the action stand. The Good Neighbor Policy did not solve all the problems with Latin America, but it promoted better relations just when the United States needed hemispheric solidarity to meet the threat of global war.

The Coming of World War II

Conflict in the Pacific

The first major threat to international stability following World War I came in the Far East. Chronically short of raw materials, Japan was desperate to establish hegemony in Asia. In September 1931 the Japanese invaded Manchuria. President Hoover, a peaceful man, rejected military intervention. He also refused to impose economic sanctions against Japan, fearing such reprisals might hurt American exports or, worse yet, lead to war. Instead, Secretary of State Henry Stimson revived the Wilsonian policy of refusing to recognize governments based on force.

Expecting bolder measures, Japan ignored the Stimson Doctrine and concluded that the United States would not use military might to oppose its designs on the Far East. In 1937 Japan invaded China. In response, the League of Nations sponsored a conference at Brussels in November 1937. As the delegates debated whether or not to impose economic sanctions against Japan, the United States announced it would not support sanctions. The conference adjourned after passing a report mildly criticizing Japanese aggression.

Any doubts regarding the U.S. desire to avoid war vanished when a Japanese plane bombed the *Panay*, a U.S. gunboat stationed on the Yangtze Rivern in December 1937, killing three Americans. While the attack angered the public, few calls for war rang out similar to those following the sinking of the *Maine* or the *Lusitania*. Secretary Hull sent sharply worded protests to Tokyo, but the United States quickly accepted Japan's "profound apology," which included indemnities for the injured and relatives of the dead, promises against future attacks, and punishment of the pilots responsible for the bloodshed. In short, by the end of 1937, as one historian has noted, "America's Far Eastern Policy had retreated to inaction."

The Rome-Berlin Axis

The modern world had never known a leader like Adolf Hitler. Charismatic and a spellbinding orator, Hitler possessed a unique ability to articulate a nation's darkest fears and hatreds and then turn them to his own twisted purposes. Hitler found a receptive audience among many Germans, who were prepared to embrace any leader offering to restore the national honor which had been surrendered in the Treaty of Versailles in 1919. At that time, Germany had been forced to sign a "war guilt" clause, accepting full responsibility for the war. In addition, in 1921 the Allies presented Germany with a reparations bill of $34 billion to cover war damages. Unable to make the interest payments, let alone the principal, Germany staggered beneath the burden until its economy dissolved into severe unemployment and hyperinflation.

Confronted by Germany's imminent economic collapse, the United States offered a measure of relief. In 1924 Charles Dawes, a prominent American banker, worked out a proposal (the Dawes Plan) that reduced the reparations bill and provided Germany with an American loan. With prodding from the United States, Great Britain and France agreed to cut reparations to $2 billion in 1929, but even that proved too much when the Great Depression struck. Germany entered the 1930s with its economy in shambles.

Hitler came to power in 1933, vowing to reclaim Germany's position as a world leader. True to his word, he immediately pulled Germany out of the League of Nations. In 1935 he rearmed Germany and started a peacetime draft, clear violations of the Treaty of Versailles. Recognizing Germany's right to rearm, Great Britain and France did not oppose Hitler's actions.

Next Hitler concentrated on forging alliances with nations that shared Germany's taste for expansion and aggression. Germany and Japan signed the Anti-Comintern Pact (forerunner of a full-scale military alliance) in 1936. Shortly thereafter Hitler formed the Rome-Berlin Axis with Italy's fascist dictator, Benito Mussolini, who had recently attacked Ethiopia. Also in 1936, German troops reoccupied the Rhineland, the German-speaking region between the Rhine River and France. Once again, France and Great Britain did not oppose Hitler's bold advance, for they believed (or wanted to believe) the Rhineland would satisfy his ambitions.

But the Rhineland only whetted Hitler's appetite. Intent on reuniting all German-speaking peoples of Europe under the "Third Reich," Hitler annexed Austria in 1938. Once again, the British and the French acquiesced. Later that year he seized the Sudetenland, the German-speaking region of western Czechoslovakia.

This time France and Great Britain felt compelled to act. In September 1938 French and British leaders met with Hitler in Munich, Germany, to demand whether he had further designs on Europe. Fearing they could not count on each other to use force, they eagerly accepted Hitler's promises not to seek additional territory.

By 1938, then, Hitler had kept his promise to avenge the humiliations Germans had suffered at Versailles. Germany's frontiers were larger than they had been in 1914, Germany was rearmed, and German national pride had been restored. In addition, Germany had acquired powerful allies in Japan and in Italy. All this had transpired virtually unopposed by the victors of World War I. The League of Nations had failed to

Benito Mussolini and Adolf Hitler share their diplomatic triumph over France and England in Munich in 1938.

act and its member states had offered only feeble protests. Their caution reflected the mood of a war-weary world. Everyone hoped the Germans, Italians, and Japanese would be satisfied with their acquisitions and stop expanding. In retrospect, such hopes were clearly wrong, but at the time they did not appear unfounded. Western leaders assumed they were dealing with reasonable men; they had no way of knowing appeasement would only fuel the Axis dictators' appetites for expansion.

The United States responded to Europe's turmoil with caution. Preoccupied with the Great Depression, President Roosevelt had little time or energy to deal with foreign affairs. Yet America's timidity also reflected the strength of isolationist sentiment. Congress, not the president, played the dominant role in foreign affairs for much of the 1930s, and Congress was determined to keep the United States out of another European conflict.

Roosevelt's first diplomatic initiative involved the Soviet Union. Hoping to expand foreign trade and to use the Soviet Union to balance Japan in the Far East, he formally recognized the Soviet Union in 1933, provoking the wrath of isolationists and anti-Communists alike.

Meanwhile, isolationist forces were gaining strength. In 1934 Gerald P. Nye, a Republican senator from North Dakota, blamed international bankers and weapons manufacturers for involving the United States in World War I. While Nye's charges were never substantiated, they fed the public's fears that the United States had been suckered into the conflict by "merchants of death" who put profits above the national interest.

Privately, Roosevelt opposed the retreat into isolation. In his view, the United States had to play an important role in world affairs because it had become a major power. But Roosevelt's freedom to act was severely limited by isolationists in Congress. Between 1935 and 1937 Congress passed three separate neutrality laws that clamped an embargo on arms sales to belligerents, forbade American ships from entering war zones and prohibited them from being armed, and barred Americans from traveling on belligerents' ships. Clearly, Congress was determined to avoid what it regarded as the mistakes that had plunged the United States into World War I.

The neutrality laws troubled Roosevelt. Convinced that these laws posed a serious threat to presidential power, Roosevelt delivered a speech in October 1937 in which he spoke of the need to "quarantine the aggressors." But he immediately retreated into silence when it became clear that the public did not support vigorous action. This was where matters stood when Hitler decided to take advantage of the world's indecisiveness.

Conflict in Europe

On August 24, 1939, Germany and the Soviet Union signed the Nazi-Comintern Pact, a nonaggression treaty. In exchange for a sphere of influence over parts of Eastern Europe, Stalin approved Germany's designs on western Poland and Lithuania. His eastern flank protected, Hitler invaded Poland on September 1, 1939. Two days later, France and Great Britain honored their treaty obligations to defend Poland and declared war on Germany. World War II had formally begun.

Poland was no match for Germany. Though its people fought bravely, it fell in a few weeks. Land fighting in Europe then stopped for several months. The next "blitzkrieg" by Nazi forces came in April 1940, when German tanks swept through Denmark and Norway, then into the Netherlands, which fell in five days.

In May Nazi forces moved against France, which many observers expected to to be a more formidable opponent. But French leaders capitulated six weeks later; only the heroic boatlift at Dunkirk saved 300,000 British and French troops from capture.

Like Wilson before him, Roosevelt responded to Europe's war by declaring America's neutrality. Unlike the idealistic Wilson, however, he did not ask his countrymen to be "neutral in thought as well as in action." After France fell, Roosevelt feared a German victory would threaten America's future security, and he resolved to save England at all costs—including war.

Before he could rescue Britain, however, Roosevelt first had to regain control of American foreign policy. Soon after Germany invaded Poland, he pushed an act through Congress which modified earlier legislation by permitting belligerents to purchase war materials, provided they paid cash and carried the goods away in their own ships. This act was pro-British because England controlled the Atlantic. Acting on his own authority, Roosevelt then rushed thousands of planes and guns to Britain. In September 1940 he persuaded Congress to pass the first peacetime draft in American history and signed an executive agreement with Great Britain transferring 50 destroyers in exchange for 99-year leases on eight British bases in the Western Hemisphere. Most Americans, gravely concerned with events in Europe, supported the destroyers-for-bases deal.

Fearing Roosevelt was duplicating Wilson's mistakes, isolationists of both parties opposed the tilt toward Britain. Their most powerful argument was that Europe's war did not threaten "fortress America." Germany had no designs on the Western Hemisphere, they insisted. Therefore, the United States should sit this war out.

An "Arsenal of Democracy"

The war dominated the election of 1940. Running for an unprecedented third term, Roosevelt handily defeated Republican challenger Wendell Willkie 27 million votes to 22 million votes, and 449 electoral votes to 82. As New York City Mayor Fiorello La Guardia put it, Americans preferred "Roosevelt with his known faults to Willkie with his unknown virtues."

After the election, Churchill informed Roosevelt that England had run out of money and no longer could purchase war supplies. Consequently, the president replaced "cash and carry" with a "lend-lease" bill, which Congress passed after a bitter debate and Roosevelt signed in March 1941. With "this legislation," he declared, "our country has determined to do its full part in creating an adequate arsenal of democracy."

To cement the Anglo-American bond, Roosevelt met with Churchill in August 1941 on board the USS *Augusta* off the coast of Newfoundland. There they negotiated the Atlantic Charter, which pledged mutual support for democracy, freedom of the seas, arms reductions, and a just peace. In everything but name the United States and Great Britain were now allies.

While the public strongly supported aid for Great Britain, many Americans balked at helping the Russians, who had been invaded by Hitler in June 1941. Roosevelt, however, immediately offered lend-lease aid to the Soviet Union, and in November 1941 the United States allocated $1 billion in lend-lease to the Soviets. By 1945 America's allies had received $50 billion, four times the amount loaned to the allies in World War I.

In April 1941 the United States went beyond financial assistance by constructing bases in Greenland and escorting convoys as far as Iceland to protect them from German submarines. The American navy started tracking German submarines and signaling their locations to British destroyers. After a German submarine attacked an American destroyer in September, Roosevelt ordered the navy to "shoot on sight" any German ships in the waters around Iceland. Yet the president stopped short of asking Congress for a formal declaration of war; for a few more months the United States maintained the fiction of neutrality.

Pearl Harbor

Thanks to the public's preoccupation with Europe, Roosevelt had a relatively free hand in the Far East, where Japan was on the march to acquire an empire that would encompass large parts of China and the western Pacific. Yet Japan's dream of expansion clashed with the two main pillars of America's Far Eastern policy—preserving the "Open Door" for trade and protecting China's territorial integrity.

After Japan invaded China in 1937, relations between Washington and Tokyo deteriorated rapidly. The United States pressured Japan to withdraw, but Tokyo refused. In July 1939 Secretary of State Cordell Hull, aware that American exports fueled Japan's war machine, threatened to impose economic sanctions. Roosevelt, however, held back, fearing Japan would attack the Dutch East Indies to secure the oil it needed.

Events quickly forced Roosevelt's hand. In 1940 Japan occupied northern Indochina, an obvious step toward the Dutch East Indies. Late in September Roosevelt placed an embargo on scrap iron and steel, hoping economic sanctions would strengthen moderates in Japan who wished to avoid conflict with the United States.

When these actions failed to deter Japanese aggression, Roosevelt in July 1941 froze Japanese assets in the United States and cut off steel, oil, and aviation fuel exports to Japan. Hurt by these sanctions, Japan negotiated with the United States throughout 1941. Instead of compromising, however, the United States asked Japan to withdraw immediately from Indochina and China, concessions that would have ended Japan's dream of economic and military hegemony in Asia.

In a last-ditch effort to avoid war, Japan promised not to march further south, not to attack the Soviet Union, and not to declare war against the United States if Germany and America went to war. In return, Japan asked the United States to abandon the Chinese. Roosevelt refused. In

October 1941 the Japanese government fell and General Hideki Tojo, the leader of the militants, seized power. The new regime offered to compromise if Washington would soften its demands, but Secretary of State Hull refused to negotiate. War was imminent.

Most military experts expected Japan to attack the Dutch East Indies to secure oil and rubber. Before striking there, however, Japan moved to neutralize American power in the western Pacific. At 8:00 A.M. on Sunday morning, December 7, 1941, Japanese planes hit the U.S. naval base at Pearl Harbor, Hawaii, executing the most daring surprise attack in military history. In less than two hours Japan reduced the base to flames, sank two battleships, and heavily damaged six others. The remainder of the fleet was either damaged or destroyed. The United States lost more than 2,400 dead, while Japan sustained minimal losses.

Yet Japan had won a costly victory. Its planes failed to destroy America's aircraft carriers, and, more important, the attack united the American

In a little less than two hours, the surprise attack at Pearl Harbor had killed more than 2,400 American sailors and damaged or sunk eight battleships, including the USS *Arizona* pictured here.

public as nothing else could have. Opposition to Roosevelt simply evaporated. On December 8 Congress declared war on Japan with but one dissenting vote. Germany declared war on the United States on December 11.

America at War

Practically everyone agreed what had to be done: jump-start the economy, raise an army, and win the war. Yet the economic challenges facing the United States were truly mind-boggling. New plants had to be built and existing ones expanded; raw materials had to be procured and distributed where needed; labor had to be kept on the job; production had to be raised; and all this had to be accomplished without producing soaring inflation.

Economic Mobilization

Like Wilson before him, Roosevelt wished to make the transition to a wartime economy without government controls; he, too, would fail. Like Wilson, Roosevelt increased the size and power of the federal bureaucracy to meet the demands of the war effort. In January 1942 the president created the War Production Board (WPB) to "exercise general responsibility" over the economy.

Business leaders responded coolly to the call for economic conversion. With profits already booming because of the war in Europe, many industrialists did not wish to jeopardize their position in the domestic market by converting factories to military production. Others worried about getting stuck with inflated capacity after the war ended.

To gain their support, Washington offered even greater returns. The armed services suspended competitive bidding, offered cost-plus contracts, guaranteed low-cost loans for retooling, and paid huge subsidies for plant construction and equipment. Lured by huge profits, the automotive industry enthusiastically made the switch to military production. In 1940 6,000 planes rolled off Detroit's assembly lines; production jumped to 47,000 in 1942; and by the end of the war it exceeded 100,000, more than doubling Roosevelt's original goal.

Most military contracts went to big businesses because large-scale production simplified buying. At Roosevelt's insistence the Justice Department stopped prosecuting antitrust violators, a policy which accelerated business consolidations. Overall, industrial profits doubled, but small industries, lacking the capital to convert to war production, got crowded away from the federal trough.

Government-supported research became a major new industry during World War II. To counter Germany's scientific and technological superiority, especially in tanks and artillery, Roosevelt created the Office of Scientific Research and Development (OSRD) in 1942. Its most ambitious undertaking was the Manhattan Project, the code name for the atomic bomb, which cost more than $2 billion and employed 500,000 workers. Federal funds also supported the development of radar, flame throwers, antiaircraft artillery, and rockets. Thanks in large part to penicillin and new blood plasma techniques, the death rate of wounded soldiers who reached medical installations was half that of World War I. Moreover, antimalarial drugs and insecticides dramatically reduced the incidence of mosquito-carried diseases among troops in the Mediterranean and in the Pacific.

No less than industry, American agriculture performed impressively during World War II. To encourage production, Roosevelt allowed farmers to make large profits by setting crop prices. Good weather, mechanization, and a dramatic increase in the use of fertilizers did the rest. Cash income for farmers jumped from $2.3 billion in 1940 to $9.5 billion in 1945.

The distribution of profits in agriculture followed the same pattern as in industry: most went to large-scale operators who could afford expensive machinery and fertilizers. Many small farmers, saddled with huge debts from the depression, abandoned their farms for jobs in defense plants or the armed services. Over five million farm residents left rural areas during the war.

Overall, the war brought unprecedented prosperity to Americans. Workers never had it so good. The total income of families increased dramatically as large numbers of women joined the work force, creating millions of two-income families. In fact, World War II brought Americans more money than they could spend, for the production of consumer goods could not keep pace with the new buying power. Everything from toasters to diapers was in short supply.

Controlling Inflation

The shortages led to inflation. Prices rose 18 percent between 1941. Fearing inflation would destroy the economy, Congress created the Office of Price Administration (OPA) in January 1942, which quickly instituted price controls as well as rationing programs on such items as food, gasoline, and clothing. Relying on voluntarism and patriotism, the OPA extolled the virtues of self-sacrifice, telling people to "Use it up, wear it out, make it do, or do without."

In addition to rationing, Washington attacked inflation by reducing the public's purchasing power. The government encouraged the sale of war bonds, which not only helped finance the war but also absorbed more than 7 percent of the real personal income of Americans. Tax reforms were also used to combat inflation. To cool off consumer purchasing power, Congress passed the Revenue Act of 1942, which raised corporate taxes, increased the excess profits tax, and levied a 5 percent withholding tax on anyone who earned more than $642 a year. Tax reforms forced citizens to pay more than 40 percent of the war's total cost as the war progressed, and laid the foundation for postwar tax policies. Wage controls offered another tool for controlling inflation. The War Labor Board (WLB), established in 1942, had the power to set wages, hours, and working conditions. Thanks to overtime, however, the weekly paychecks of some workers rose 70 percent.

Working together, these programs brought inflation under control. Still, the administration's methods pleased no one. Everyone groused about taxes; manufacturers and farmers denounced price controls; and labor officials condemned wage freezes.

Yet American workers clearly reaped a bonanza from World War II, which created 17 million new civilian jobs. After Pearl Harbor, labor soared to an absolute premium, drawing into the work force previously unemployed and underemployed groups such as women, teenagers, blacks, senior citizens, and the handicapped. The war also gave labor unions a lift. Under the benevolent hand of government protection, unions rebounded from their sharp decline of the 1920s and early 1930s.

Despite these gains, labor unrest increased throughout the war. increased throughout the war. After Pearl Harbor, union officials pledged not to strike until the war ended, but inflation and wage restrictions quickly eroded their goodwill. Work stoppages rose, though most ended quickly and did not harm the war effort. Although most Americans condemned strikes as unpatriotic, Roosevelt remained a model of restraint with labor leaders. After all, labor formed a vital element of the New Deal coalition.

In contrast to Roosevelt, Congress took a hostile stand toward labor. Over the president's veto, it passed the Smith-Connally Act, which banned strikes in war industries, authorized the president to seize plants useful to the war effort, and limited political activity by unions. The Smith-Connally Act reflected a resurgence of conservatism, both in Congress and in the country at large. Though the Democrats continued to maintain a thin majority in both houses of Congress throughout the war, a coalition of Republicans and conservative Democrats after 1942 could defeat any measure.

Election of 1944

With reform in retreat, the Republicans expected to win the election of 1944. Thomas E. Dewey, the dapper, 42-year-old governor of New York, won his party's nomination on the first ballot. While Dewey accepted the New Deal as part of American life, he opposed its expansion. No distance separated the two major candidates on foreign affairs.

Despite his declining health, Roosevelt easily captured his party's nomination for a fourth term. To counter the resurgence of conservatism, he selected Senator Harry S Truman, a moderate from Missouri, as vice president. The campaign revitalized Roosevelt. He unveiled plans for a "GI Bill of Rights," promising liberal unemployment benefits, educational support, medical care, and housing loans for veterans, which Congress approved overwhelmingly in 1944. The president easily won reelection. Unwilling to switch leaders while at war, the public stuck with Roosevelt to see the crisis through.

Molding Public Opinion

Having witnessed the mistakes of World War I, Roosevelt did not want government propaganda to arouse hatreds or fuel false hopes. Shortly before Pearl Harbor, he created the Office of Facts and Figures, which soon became embroiled in bureaucratic struggles with government agencies, the armed services, and the Office of Strategic Services. By 1944 the government had all but abandoned its efforts to shape public opinion about the war.

Private enterprise filled the void. Movies, comic strips, newspapers, books, and advertisements reduced the war to a struggle between good and evil as the Allies engaged in mortal combat with Japan and Germany. The Japanese bore the brunt of the propaganda, especially during the first two years of fighting. Caricatured with thick glasses and huge buck teeth, public portraits of the Japanese grew more ugly and vicious as deeply ingrained racism fed the stereotypes, reviving old fears of the "yellow peril."

Germans, by contrast, elicited more complex attitudes in Americans, largely because racism did not inflame passions. At first, Americans blamed Hitler for the war. As eyewitness accounts of German atrocities began to filter back from the front, however, the public's views shifted. Gradually, Americans came to blame not just the Nazis, but all Germans for the war.

Motion pictures emerged as the most important instrument of propaganda during World War II, but Hollywood made little effort to confront the war's complexities. Instead, the industry churned out a series of simple morality plays, aimed at inspiring the public's patriotism. Movies such as *Back to Bataan* and *Guadalcanal Diary* showed a few Americans outfighting Japanese hordes. Hollywood produced 982 movies during the war, enough for three new movies each week at the neighborhood theater.

Social Changes During the War

World War II produced important changes in American life, some subtle, others profound. Above all, it set families in motion, pulling them off farms, out of small towns, and packing them into large urban areas. Urbanization had virtually stopped during the depression, but the war saw the number of city dwellers leap from 46 to 53 percent of the population.

Women

The war had a dramatic impact on women. Easily the most visible change involved the sudden appearance of large numbers of women in uniform. The military organized women into auxiliary units with special uniforms, their own officers, and, amazingly, equal pay. By 1945 more than 250,000 women had joined the Women's Army Corps (WAC), the Army Nurses Corps, the Women Accepted for Voluntary Emergency Service (WAVES), the Navy Nurses Corps, the marines, and the Coast Guard. Most women who joined the armed services either filled traditional women's roles, such as nursing, or replaced men in noncombat jobs.

Women also substituted for men on the home front. For the first time in American history the majority of married women worked outside the home. The war challenged the conventional image of female behavior, as "Rosie the Riveter" became the popular symbol of women who abandoned traditional female occupations to work in defense industries.

Women paid a price for their economic independence. Outside employment did not free wives from domestic duties. They had not one job now, but two, and the only way they could fill both was to sacrifice relaxation, recreation, and sleep. Outside employment also raised the problem of child care. A few industries, such as Kaiser Steel, offered day-care facilities, but most women had to make their own arrangements.

Many women, however, elected to cling to the familiar by embracing the traditional roles of housewives and mothers. From 1941 to 1945 the marriage rate rose, as did the birthrate, rebounding sharply from the all-time low during the depression. Overall, the "baby boom" did not signal a return to large families; rather, the birthrate rose because women married at younger ages and had their families earlier in life.

Hasty marriages between young partners often proved brittle. Wartime separations forced newlyweds to develop new roles and become self-reliant. Although the divorce rate rose, Americans had not soured on marriage. The divorce rate had been climbing steadily (except during the depression years) since 1900. Most Americans who divorced during the 1940s promptly remarried; they had rejected their mates, not marriage.

Minorities

World War II accelerated long-developing social trends for blacks. More than one million migrated to the North during the war (twice the number who did so in World War I), and more than two million found work in defense industries. Yet blacks continued to be the last hired and the first fired, and other forms of discrimination remained blatant, especially in housing and in employment.

Black leaders fought discrimination vigorously. In the spring of 1941 black labor leaders, backed by the NAACP, threatened to stage a march on Washington to protest discrimination in defense industries. Embarrassed and concerned, Roosevelt issued an executive order prohibiting discrimination in defense industries and creating the Fair Employment Practices Commission (FEPC). But the FEPC's tiny staff lacked the power and resources to enforce its decisions. During the war the FEPC did not even process most complaints, and contractors ignored 35 of the 45 compliance orders it issued.

Blacks fared no better in the public sector. Most blacks in the federal bureaucracy worked as janitors, and the armed services treated blacks as second-class citizens. The marines excluded blacks; the navy used them as servants; and the army created separate black regiments commanded mostly by white officers. The Red Cross even segregated blood plasma.

Not surprisingly, racial tensions deepened during the war. Many blacks joined the armed services hoping to find social mobility. Instead, they encountered segregation and discrimination. They resented white officials who denounced Nazi racism but remained silent about discrimination against blacks. On the home front, as urban areas swelled with defense workers, housing and transportation shortages exacerbated racial tensions. In 1943 a riot broke out in Detroit in a federally sponsored housing project. White soldiers from a nearby base joined the fighting, and other federal troops had to be brought in to disperse the mobs. The violence left 35 blacks and 9 whites dead.

Similar conflicts erupted across the nation, exposing in each instance the same jarring contradiction: white Americans espoused equality abroad but practiced discrimination at home. Many blacks responded to the rising tensions by joining such civil rights organizations as the NAACP, which intensified its legal campaign against discrimination. Some blacks, however, considered the NAACP too slow and too conciliatory. Rejecting legal action, the Congress of Racial Equality (CORE), founded in 1942, organized a series of "sit-ins." While black activists won few gains during World War II, they forged new demands and tactics that shaped the civil rights movement after the war.

World War II affected Mexican Americans no less than blacks. Almost 400,000 Mexican Americans served in the armed forces. As soldiers, they expanded their contacts with Anglo society, visiting new parts of the country and meeting for the first time large groups of people who held few prejudices against them. For Mexican Americans in the civilian sector, jobs in industry provided an escape hatch from the desperate poverty of migratory farm labor.

The need for farm workers rose dramatically after Pearl Harbor, prompting several hundred thousand Mexican workers to immigrate to the Southwest. Commercial farmers welcomed them, but labor unions resented the competition, leading to animosity and discrimination against Mexicans and Mexican Americans alike.

In Los Angeles, Anglo society both feared and resented newly formed Mexican-American youth gangs, whose members celebrated their ethnicity by wearing flamboyant "zoot suits." In June 1943 riots broke out between Anglo sailors on shore leave and Mexican-American youths. The local press blamed Mexican-American gangs, and the riots did not end until military police ordered sailors back to their ships.

Despite the outbursts of violence and discrimination, World War II benefited the poor of all races. Thanks to full employment and progressive taxation, people at the bottom saw income redistributed in their favor. Still, the gains made by poor people came from the state of the economy (the need for soldiers and workers), not from federal policies or the efforts of organized labor.

Fear of Enemy Aliens

On December 8, 1941, Roosevelt issued an executive order regarding enemy aliens. It suspended naturalization proceedings for Italians, Germans, and Japanese immigrants, required them to register, restricted their mobility, and prohibited them from owning items that might be used for sabotage, such as cameras and shortwave radios. In practice, however, the government did not accord enemy aliens the same treatment: Italian and German aliens received lenient treatment, while Japanese aliens suffered gross injustices.

Jewish refugees complicated the German question. Reflecting a nasty strain of anti-Semitism, Congress in 1939 refused to raise immigration quotas to admit 20,000 Jewish children fleeing Nazi oppression. Instead of relaxing quotas, American officials worked in vain to persuade Latin American countries and Great Britain to admit Jewish refugees.

While Hitler's death camps killed millions, American officials who knew the ghastly truth publicly downplayed press reports of genocide. Air reconnaissance missions had taken scores of photographs of the death camp at Auschwitz, and military intelligence officers had learned the locations of several other concentration camps. Not until January 1944 did Roosevelt create the War Refugee Board, which set up refugee camps in Italy, North Africa, and the United States. But America's response offered too little, too late. During the 18 months of the War Refugee Board's existence, Hitler killed far more Jews than the War Refugee Board saved.

Like Jews, Japanese Americans got a bitter taste of discrimination during World War II. They comprised a tiny portion of the population in 1941, totaling no more than 260,000 people, most of whom lived in Hawaii and on the West Coast. After Pearl Harbor, military authorities moved against Japanese Americans. In Hawaii, where the local economy depended on their labor, the military did not force Japanese Americans to relocate. On the West Coast, however, authorities ordered the Japanese to leave, drawing no distinction between aliens and citizens. Forced to sell their property for pennies on the dollar, most Japanese Americans suffered severe financial losses. Relocation proved next to impossible, as no other states would take them.

When voluntary measures failed, Roosevelt created the War Relocation Authority. It resettled 100,000 Japanese Americans in ten relocation camps, resembling minimum security prisons, in seven western states. In these camps American citizens who had committed no crimes were locked behind barbed wire, crowded into ramshackle barracks, and forced to endure bad food, inadequate medical care, and poorly equipped schools. Nearly 18,000 Japanese-American men won release from those camps to fight for the United States Army. In one of the most painful scenes in American history, Japanese-American parents, still locked inside concentration camps, received posthumous Purple Hearts for their sons.

Japanese Americans protested their treatment, claiming numerous civil rights violations. Finally, in December 1944, the Supreme Court ruled that the War Relocation Authority had no right to incarcerate law-abiding citizens. Two weeks later the federal government began closing down the camps, ending one of the most shameful chapters in American history.

Japanese Americans of all ages, tagged like pieces of luggage, awaited their relocation to one of ten detention camps in seven western states. This family was from Hayward, California.

The War in Europe

The Grand Alliance

Following Pearl Harbor, the Axis Powers of Germany, Japan, and Italy faced the Grand Alliance, composed of the United States, Great Britain, the Soviet Union and, later, the French government-in-exile. Yet from the beginning the Grand Alliance was an uneasy coalition, born of necessity and filled with tension. Apart from the need to defeat the enemy, the Allies found it difficult to agree on anything.

Winston Churchill, Great Britain's prime minister, approached international affairs in spheres-of-influence, balance-of-power terms. He wanted to block Soviet expansion, and was determined that Britain play a major role in postwar Europe. Furthermore, he wanted Britain to emerge from the war with its colonial empire intact.

France's goals reflected the vision of one man—General Charles de Gaulle, who after the fall of France in 1940 had established in London a French government-in-exile. Above all, de Gaulle wanted to restore France

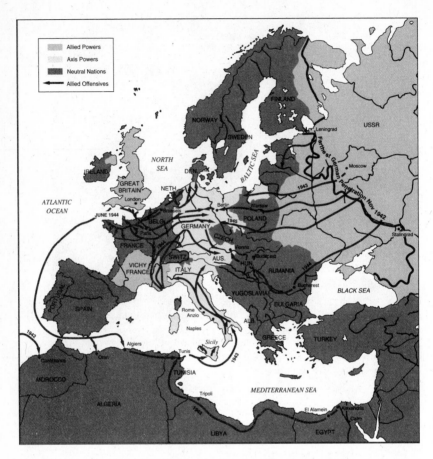

World War II, European Theater

to greatness. By nature aloof and suspicious, like Churchill he fought to retain his country's empire, and as the war progressed American officials came to regard de Gaulle as a political extremist. In policy disputes he often sided with Britain to oppose American and Soviet demands.

Joseph Stalin spoke for the Soviet Union. Iron-willed and deeply paranoid, Stalin rose to power by crushing all rivals during the turbulent years following the Bolshevik revolution. A formidable negotiator, he pressed for a postwar settlement that would guarantee the Soviet Union's future security and open new lands for communism. To protect the Soviet Union from future attacks, Stalin insisted upon Germany's total destruction. As additional insurance, he demanded parts of Poland and Finland and all of the Baltic states. Eastern Europe would then form a buffer against future aggression from the West, provide colonies for rebuilding the Soviet economy, and add new territory to the communist world map.

Roosevelt had his own ideas about how the world should look after the war. In broad terms, he opposed colonialism and the spread of communism; and he supported open markets, democratic elections to counter spheres of influence, and a new League of Nations to promote world peace. Among these objectives, anticolonialism and support for free markets were his top priorities, and both goals reflected Roosevelt's remarkable ability to join political principle with economic advantage.

No less than his counterparts, Roosevelt's personality shaped his policies. Because he disliked the rough and tumble of hard bargaining, he tried to avoid clashes with other leaders by postponing difficult decisions and by relying too heavily on his personal charm. In addition, Roosevelt's pragmatic approach to problem solving made him seek compromises whenever possible, which meant that he often sacrificed principles in order to preserve Allied cooperation.

From the outset, then, dissent riddled the Grand Alliance. In pursuit of its own national interest, each ally had a separate agenda, its own set of demands, and its own vision of the how the world map should look when the war ended. Given these conflicts, the Allies could look forward not to harmony but to clashes over military strategy throughout the war, bitter debates over peace terms at the war's end, and decades of international strife in the postwar era.

Stemming the Tide

For six months after Pearl Harbor, Japan looked unbeatable. Japanese forces captured Guam, Wake Island, the Philippines, Hong Kong, and Malaya and slashed deep into Burma. General Douglas MacArthur was driven from the Philippines in March 1942. In a matter of months Japanese troops had conquered a vast expanse extending from the Gilbert Islands through the Solomons and from New Guinea to Burma, leaving India and Australia vulnerable to attack.

Nor did the Allied cause look any brighter in Europe. During the first ten months of 1942, German submarines sank over 500 American merchant ships. With its lend-lease supplies threatened, Great Britain stood in danger of collapsing before the United States could mobilize. On the Russian front, German troops pressed toward Stalingrad, and in North Africa, where German Field Marshal Erwin Rommel, the famous "Desert Fox," was sweeping toward the Suez Canal, the situation seemed equally bleak. In short, World War II opened badly for the Allies. Axis victories in the Pacific, Europe, and Africa served notice that the war would be long and costly.

Roosevelt decided to assign Germany top priority for two reasons: first, he doubted Hitler could be defeated if Britain fell; and, second, Roosevelt wanted to placate Stalin, whose troops were bearing the brunt of the German war machine. As the Germans drove deep into Soviet territory in 1942, Stalin demanded a second front in France to force Germany to divide her armies, thereby relieving some of the pressure on the Soviet Union.

By the autumn of 1942 the tide was beginning to turn on the eastern front. In September the Red Army won a key victory at Stalingrad, then launched a furious counterattack, beginning the long drive to push the Germans back across the Ukraine. Despite Soviet victories and Stalin's repeated pleas for a second front, the Allies, at Churchill's insistence, decided to attack the Germans in North Africa instead of France. Stalin saw this as a betrayal and his suspicions deepened.

Allied victories in Africa seemed to confirm Churchill's wisdom. British Field Marshal Sir Bernard Montgomery drove the Germans back to Tunis in October, and in November 1942 General Dwight David Eisenhower led a force of 400,000 Allied soldiers in a full-scale invasion of North Africa. Complete victory came on May 12, 1943, when the remnants of the Axis armies surrendered. Germany and Italy had suffered a major defeat and Allied shipping could now cross the Mediterranean in safety.

Cheered by the North African victory, Churchill and Roosevelt met in Casablanca, French Morocco, in January 1943. Stalin did not attend, explaining he could not leave the Soviet Union at this critical juncture of the war. Churchill pushed hard for an attack on Sicily and then Italy. The United States initially opposed the plan, arguing it would delay the invasion of France, but Churchill prevailed. Vowing publicly to make peace with the Axis powers only on the basis of unconditional surrender, the two leaders also renewed their pledge to open a second front, although they kept Stalin in the dark about the decision for several months.

Sicily fell in August 1943 after a campaign of slightly more than a month. In Italy, however, victory did not come cheaply for the Allies. The terrain was mountainous, and the Germans offered fierce resistance. Stalin deeply resented the commitment of Allied troops there, which further postponed the long-promised second front. Moreover, since Soviet troops had not fought in the Italian campaign, Roosevelt and Churchill refused to permit Stalin to participate in organizing an occupation government there. The next time Stalin wanted a voice in a region he made certain to have his armies on site.

Liberating Europe

In November 1943 Roosevelt, Churchill, and Stalin held their first face-to-face meeting in Teheran, the capital of Iran. Buoyed by military success, Stalin sounded conciliatory as the three leaders discussed a second front. The leaders set May 1944 as the target date for Operation Overlord, the code name for the invasion of France. To increase the odds for success, Stalin promised to coordinate Russia's spring offensive with the invasion.

Once the leaders turned to postwar issues, however, the conference dissolved into bitter controversy. Stalin demanded Soviet control over Eastern Europe and insisted Germany be divided into several weak states. Opposing both demands, Churchill proposed democratic governments for Eastern Europe, especially in Poland, for which England had gone to war, and argued that the balance of power in postwar Europe required a united Germany. Roosevelt, on the other hand, knew Stalin had the inside track in Eastern Europe. Convinced he could handle "Uncle Joe," Roosevelt decided to leave territorial questions to a postwar international organization dominated by the victors. Apart from reaching agreement on the second front, the Teheran Conference merely aired the leaders' conflicting demands.

In preparation for the invasion, the Allies instituted saturation bombing, dropping more than two and a half million tons of bombs on German territory, killing 305,000 civilians. While these air raids were supposed to wipe out the German war machine and break the people's will to resist, missions such as the firebombing of Dresden, which killed 100,000 people, made many Germans believe Hitler's ravings about the evil Allies and stiffened their will to fight.

As the bombers pounded Germany, the Allies prepared for the invasion of France, massing more than three million soldiers in England under the command of General Dwight D. Eisenhower. D-Day came on June 6, 1944. After two weeks of desperate fighting on the beaches of Normandy, the Allies began to push inland. A month later Allied troops were sweeping across Europe in a race for Berlin. They liberated Paris in August, and by mid-September Allied forces had crossed the German border. True to his word, Stalin synchronized his spring offensive with the invasion. Soviet troops engaged the Germans in furious combat all across Eastern Europe, tying up men and materials that otherwise could have been hurled against the Allies.

On December 16, 1944, German troops launched a massive western counteroffensive. In the Battle of the Bulge German armored divisions slashed 60 miles to the Franco-Belgian border before being defeated by General George Patton's Third Army. Meanwhile, the eastern front had turned into a rout. By January 1945 Soviet troops had captured Warsaw, and by February they were within 45 miles of Berlin.

The Yalta Conference

With victory in Europe at hand, Roosevelt, Churchill, and Stalin met in February 1945 at Yalta, on the Black Sea, to settle the shape of the postwar world. They concurred on the partition of Germany, but there the agreement stopped. Stalin demanded $20 billion in reparations payments from Germany, half of which would go to Russia. Churchill opposed him, rejecting any plan that would leave Germany financially prostrate after the war.

Eastern Europe was the most divisive issue at Yalta. Stalin had long insisted on Soviet control over the Baltic states, as well as portions of Finland, Poland, and Romania as the price of Russian participation in an anti-German alliance. Moreover, in October 1944, Stalin and Churchill had met secretly in Moscow, where they agreed to divide Eastern Europe into British and Russian spheres of influence for the duration of the war. Consistent with these earlier demands, Stalin laid claim to eastern Poland at the Yalta Conference, reminding Churchill and Roosevelt that since he had not opposed their political decisions in Italy, he would not tolerate any interference in Eastern Europe. Under pressure from Roosevelt and Churchill, however, Stalin grudgingly agreed to hold free elections in

Stalin, Roosevelt, and Churchill met at Yalta in February 1945 to discuss the state of the postwar world.

Poland itself, and promised that any new government formed there would include democratic elements. Yet as one of Roosevelt's chief military advisors warned the president, Stalin tacked so many amendments onto the Polish agreement that the Soviets "could stretch it all the way from Yalta to Washington without technically breaking it."

The remaining issues at Yalta proved less troublesome. Stalin promised to enter the war against Japan within three months after Germany surrendered, and he renewed his pledge to join the United Nations. Roosevelt considered both concessions important victories because he wanted Soviet help in defeating Japan and because he remained hopeful that the United Nations could negotiate peaceful solutions to the disputes between the United States and the Soviet Union after the war.

Critics have denounced Roosevelt for his role at Yalta, insisting Stalin would have surrendered Eastern Europe had the president held firm. Yet this argument seriously discounts Stalin's obsession with protecting his homeland from future attacks. The Soviet Union had paid a staggeringly high price for victory in World War II. When the war finally ended, the country had suffered approximately 18 million military and civilian deaths. More Soviets died at Stalingrad than the United States lost in all theaters of the war combined. Stalin's determination to maintain Soviet control of Eastern Europe was also bolstered by the fact that the Red Army occupied Eastern Europe in the spring of 1945. Stalin was not about to lose at the conference table what he had won on the battlefield.

Allied victories came rapidly after the Battle of the Bulge. On March 4, American troops reached the Rhine River, and in April they joined forces with the Soviet army 60 miles south of Berlin. After Roosevelt's death on April 12, however, Stalin immediately tested the new president, Harry S Truman. Stalin ordered the execution of democratic leaders in Eastern Europe and replaced them with Communist governments. Truman deplored Stalin's disregard for the Yalta agreements, but like Roosevelt he refused to fight the Soviets to save Eastern Europe. Instead, he followed General Eisenhower's advice about finishing off Germany. On April 22 Soviet troops reached Berlin and occupied the city after house-to-house fighting. On April 30 Hitler committed suicide, and Germany surrendered one week later. On May 8, 1945, the Allies celebrated V-E (Victory in Europe) Day.

The War in the Pacific

Though Europe received top priority, American forces managed to halt Japanese advances in the Pacific by late summer 1942. In May a Japanese troop convoy was intercepted and destroyed by the U.S. Navy at Coral

Sea, preventing a Japanese attack on Australia. In early June, at Midway Island in the Central Pacific, the Japanese launched an aircraft carrier offensive to cut American communications and isolate Hawaii to the east. In a three-day naval battle the Japanese lost three destroyers, a heavy cruiser, and four carriers. The Battle of Midway broke the back of Japan's navy.

Island-Hopping

On August 7, 1942, American forces attacked Guadalcanal in the Solomon Islands, and after six months of hard fighting drove the Japanese troops into the sea, securing the Allied supply line to Australia. The victory also protected the Allies' eastern flank, enabling General Douglas MacArthur, commander of southwest Pacific forces, to seize the northern coast of nearby New Guinea in September 1943. Instead of assaulting Japanese strong points on the island, MacArthur leapfrogged up the coast. By capturing isolated positions, MacArthur cut Japanese supply lines and forced Japanese troops to abandon their fortifications. By July 1944 MacArthur's forces controlled all of New Guinea.

Meanwhile, Admiral Chester Nimitz's naval and marine forces in the Central Pacific were "island-hopping" toward Japan, capturing important positions, building airstrips, and then moving on to the next island. After securing the Gilbert Islands and the Marshall Islands, Nimitz attacked

World War II, Pacific Theater

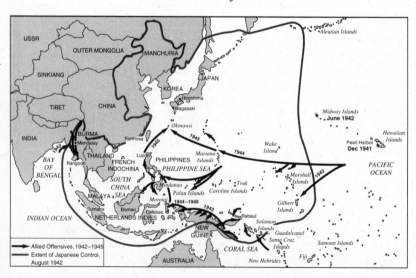

Saipan, Tinian, and Guam, from which the Americans could strike the main Japanese islands with B-29 bombers. Determined to protect their homeland against air raids, Japanese commanders resolved to fight to the last man. In the battle for Saipan, 30,000 of the island's 32,000 Japanese defenders died, and 6,000 of the island's 12,000 Japanese civilians committed suicide rather than surrender. Tinian and Guam fell to the Americans in early August, and B-29s began regular bombing raids over Japan in November 1944.

On October 21, 1944, General MacArthur invaded the Philippines. That same month the navy won a stunning victory at the Battle of Leyte Gulf, where the Japanese lost virtually their entire remaining battle fleet. American submarines now controlled Pacific shipping lanes, sealing the Japanese Islands off from military and food supplies. In January, Allied forces invaded Luzon, the main island of the Philippines, and Allied troops claimed victory five months later.

While MacArthur was reclaiming the Philippines, the American island-hopping strategy was entering its final phase. By early March the island of Iwo Jima fell to U. S. marines. Its capture enabled fighter planes to link up with B-29s heading out of Saipan, providing escorts for their raids on Japan. On April 1, 1945, American troops attacked Okinawa, 350 miles southwest of Japan. Japanese resistance was fierce. Kamikaze attacks (suicide flights by Japanese pilots) rose dramatically. Okinawa fell in June, after 70,000 Japanese soldiers had died defending it. In the meantime, B-29s firebombed Japan, killing more than 330,000 civilians and cutting deeply into its war production.

Confronted with certain defeat, many moderate leaders in Japan wanted to avoid an invasion, but strong factions within the military vowed to keep fighting. In an effort to save Japan, the emperor switched his support to the peace party in February 1945. He then sent out peace feelers to Stalin, who in turn conveyed them to Truman at the Potsdam Conference in July 1945.

Truman and the Dawn of the Atomic Age

Few presidents have been asked to conduct diplomacy with less preparation than Harry S Truman. He had risen to power as a loyal machine politician in Kansas City. As vice president and former senator from Missouri he knew next to nothing about foreign affairs, especially since Roosevelt had kept him largely in the dark. Yet Truman brought certain assets to the challenge. A man who possessed the courage of his convictions, he fully intended to be a strong president and to make decisions resolutely.

Truman's first test came at Potsdam, a suburb of Berlin, where the Allied leaders convened in July 1945 for their last wartime meeting. Though new to the job, Truman had been in office long enough to believe Roosevelt had been too soft on Stalin, whom he viewed as a liar and a bully. Deadlocked on Eastern Europe, Truman and Stalin turned their attention to Japan. The Potsdam Declaration of July 26 demanded immediate "unconditional surrender," warning that any other action would lead to "prompt and utter destruction."

During the Potsdam negotiations Truman learned that American scientists had successfully tested the first atomic bomb. However, many scientists who had worked on the Manhattan Project, as well as several key political figures, pleaded with Truman not to use the bomb because they foresaw its implications for a postwar arms race with the Soviet Union. Others, arguing from a moral position, wanted the United States to warn the Japanese about the bomb's terrifying power, giving them a chance to surrender.

Truman rejected these alternatives and decided to drop the bomb. Military considerations played a large role in his decision. According to the best intelligence reports, an invasion of the Japanese Islands might cost one million Allied casualties, with the Japanese suffering several times that figure. Ironically, the bomb had the potential to save countless lives on both sides by ending the war immediately. Yet Truman's decision also reflected his growing frustration with the Soviet Union. He wanted to

This photo of the remains of the Nagasaki Medical College shows the almost total destruction by the atomic blast. The buildings that remained standing were made of reinforced concrete.

demonstrate the bomb's awesome power to impress Stalin so that the Soviets would be easier to deal with after the war.

Following Japan's rejection of the Potsdam Declaration, Truman gave the final order. On August 6 three B-29s flew over Hiroshima and the lead bomber, the *Enola Gay,* dropped an atomic bomb that destroyed 4.4 square miles and killed 100,000 people instantly. Two days later the Soviets entered the war against Japan, making good on Stalin's promise at Yalta. Because Japan failed to surrender immediately, Truman ordered a second atomic strike. On August 9 Nagasaki was obliterated, killing another 35,000 Japanese instantly. The following day Japan asked for peace.

V-J Day (Victory in Japan) came on September 2, 1945, when Japanese officials surrendered unconditionally to General MacArthur aboard the battleship *Missouri* in Tokyo Bay. Truman refused to permit the Soviets to attend the ceremony or to play any role in creating an occupation government for Japan.

World War II was over. The fascist governments had been destroyed, their military machines crushed, their economies shattered, their major cities reduced to rubble, and their people ravaged by disease and starvation. Yet the war left the Allies hardly less devastated, except for the United States, which emerged from the fighting stronger than ever. Much of the world had to be reordered and rebuilt, but the conflicts between the United States and the Soviet Union that festered throughout the war raised grave doubts about the prospects for future cooperation.

Conclusion

World War II cost America one million casualties, and over 300,000 deaths. In both domestic and foreign affairs, its consequences were far-reaching. It had an immediate and spectacular impact on the economy by ending the Great Depression. Fueled by government contracts, the economy expanded dramatically, soaring to full employment and astounding the world with its productivity. The war accelerated corporate mergers and the trend toward large-scale agriculture. Labor unions also grew during the war as the government adopted pro-union policies, continuing the New Deal's sympathetic treatment of organized labor.

Presidential power expanded enormously during World War II, anticipating the rise of what postwar critics termed the "imperial presidency." The Democrats reaped a political windfall from the war. Roosevelt rode the wartime emergency to unprecedented third and fourth terms. Despite these victories, however, the reform spirit waned, a victim, it seemed, of the country's unmistakable swing to the right in politics.

Chronology of Key Events

1921	Washington Naval Conference places limits on construction of large warships
1922	Mussolini seizes power in Italy
1924	Dawes Plan to help Germany pay reparations
1928	Kellogg-Briand Pact renounces war "as an instrument of national policy"
1931	Japan invades Manchuria
1932	Stimson Doctrine declares that U.S. would not recognize Japanese territorial gains in China.
1933	Adolf Hitler appointed chancellor of Germany; Roosevelt announces Good Neighbor Policy, withdraws marines from Haiti, and nullifies Platt Amendment
1935–37	Neutrality Acts bar arm sales, loans to belligerents, and shipments of nonmilitary goods
1936	German troops reoccupy the Rhineland
1937	Japan invades China
1938	Germany annexes Austria; Munich Pact hands over a third of Czechoslovakia to Germany
1939	Soviet Union and Germany sign a nonaggression pact; World War II begins
1940	Destroyers for bases deal; United States institutes military draft; Roosevelt elected to third term
1941	Lend-Lease Act lets U.S. lend war material to Britain; Germany invades USSR; Japan attacks Pearl Harbor
1942	Office of Price Administration created to control prices and ration scarce goods; Japanese-Americans interned; Philippine Islands surrender; U.S. naval victory at Battle of Midway
1943	British and U.S. forces defeat Axis forces in North Africa; U.S. marines secure control of Guadalcanal in the Solomon Islands; Allies invade Italy; Soviets halt German advance into Soviet Union
1943–1944	U.S. forces seize Guam and New Guinea
1944	D-Day—Allied amphibious invasion of northern France; U.S. forces begin an invasion of Philippine Islands, launch aerial attacks on Japan; Allies victorious in Battle of the Bulge; both sides suffer heavy casualties
1945	Roosevelt, Churchill, and Stalin meet at Yalta to discuss Soviet entry into war against Japan, postwar division of Europe, and plans for United Nations; Roosevelt dies; Harry S Truman becomes thirty-third president; Germany surrenders; Potsdam conference plans postwar settlement in Europe and final attack on Japan; United States drops atomic bombs on Hiroshima and Nagasaki; Japan surrenders

The war's social effects varied from group to group. For most people, it had a disruptive influence—separating families, overcrowding housing, and creating a shortage of consumer goods. The war also accelerated the movement from the countryside to the cities; and it challenged gender and racial roles, opening new opportunities for women and minority groups. Yet sexual and racial barriers remained, highlighting reforms left unfinished at home even as American troops fought totalitarian forces abroad.

In foreign policy, the many disagreements between the Allies regarding military strategy and peace terms foreshadowed major conflicts which dominated the postwar era. Gone forever was the notion of fortress America, isolated and removed from world affairs. In its place stood a strong internationalist state, determined to exercise power on a global scale. Second only to the victory the Allies won for freedom, the war's most important legacy was the end of isolation and the rise of America's commitment to international security.

Suggestions for Further Reading

Excellent analyses of World War II include Martha Hoyle, *A World in Flames* (1970); Donald Watt, *How War Came* (1989); Gordon Wright, *The Ordeal of Total War* (1968).

The American reaction to the outbreak of war in Europe is examined in Selig Adler, *The Uncertain Giant* (1969); Wayne S. Cole, *Roosevelt and the Isolationists* (1983); Robert Divine, *The Reluctant Belligerent*, 2d ed. (1979). The attack on Pearl Harbor is the focus of Herbert Feis, *The Road to Pearl Harbor* (1950); Gordon W. Prange, *At Dawn We Slept* (1981). For Roosevelt's handling of the war, see Eric Larrabee, *Commander in Chief: Franklin Delano Roosevelt, His Lieutenants, and Their War* (1987).

Social and cultural aspects of the American home front are the focus of John Morton Blum, *V Was for Victory* (1976); Richard Lingeman, *Don't You Know There's a War On?* (1970); Richard Polenberg, *The War and Society* (1972). For information on the issues facing women and minorities, consult Karen Anderson, *Wartime Women* (1981); A. Russell Buchanan, *Black Americans in World War II* (1977); Sherna B. Gluck, *Rosie the Riveter Revisited* (1987); Susan M. Hartmann, *The Home Front and Beyond: American Women in the 1940s* (1982); Peter H. Irons, *Justice at War: The Story of the Japanese American Internment Cases* (1983); Mauricio Mazón, *The Zoot-Suit Riots* (1984).

Studies of American diplomacy include Diane Shaver Clemens, *Yalta* (1970); Gaddis Smith, *American Diplomacy During the Second World War* (1965). The decision to drop the atomic bomb is discussed in Gar Alperovitz, *Atomic Diplomacy*, rev. ed. (1985); Herbert Feis, *The Atomic Bomb and the End of World War II* (1966); Dan Kurzman, *Day of the Bomb*.

Chapter *27*

Waging Peace and War

It was Sunday, August 27, 1948. Whittaker Chambers appeared calm as he answered questions on "Meet the Press," a weekly radio news show. He knew he was on enemy ground and that questions were the ammunition of the war. The question he had been waiting for soon came. Edward T. Folliard, a reporter for the *Washington Post,* asked, "Are you willing to say now that Alger Hiss is or ever was a Communist?" Chambers paused a second before answering, for the answer could open him up to a slander or libel suit. Then came his terse, important reply: "Alger Hiss was a Communist and may be now."

The road to "Meet the Press" began for Chambers with an unhappy childhood that left him rebellious and feeling unwanted. Forced to withdraw from Columbia University for writing a mildly sacrilegious play, Chambers then flirted with radical political philosophies, moved through a succession of love affairs, and kicked about Europe. In 1926 his brother Richard committed suicide. Grief-stricken and needing a new direction and purpose in his life, Chambers committed himself fully to the Communist party.

During the late 1920s and early 1930s, as the United States sank deeper and deeper into the Great Depression, other Americans joined Chambers in the Communist party. Feeling betrayed by capitalism, they looked toward the Soviet Union, which appeared less affected by the depression than the West, for political and economic inspiration. Still more Americans joined the party because only the Soviets seemed to be standing up against the Fascist threat posed by Hitler and Mussolini.

Chambers met Alger Hiss in 1934, when they both belonged to the same Communist "cell" in Washington, D.C. In appearance and personality they were complete opposites. Chambers was overweight and sloppy, and his face had a sleepy, slightly disinterested cast. Hiss, then a legal assistant for a Senate committee investigating the munitions industry, was handsome, thin, and aristocratic looking. Popular with influential superiors and coworkers, Hiss seemed marked for success. It was during that time, Chambers later testified, that Hiss began to give him secret government documents.

Like many of his American comrades, Chambers abandoned the ideology of communism during the late 1930s. By 1938 news of Stalin's purges, which would eventually lead to the death of millions of Soviets, had reached the West. Such gross disregard for humanity shook many American Communists. In addition, in 1939 Stalin signed a nonaggression pact with Hitler's Germany. Once seen as the bulwark against Nazi expansion, the Soviet Union now joined Germany in dividing Poland. Although the United States and the Soviet Union later became allies, Communist ideology ceased to attract many American followers.

Chambers not only quit the Communist party, he turned against it with a vengeance. As an editor for *Time* magazine, he openly criticized Communist tactics and warned about the evils of the Soviet Union. Finally, in 1948 he went before the House Un-American Activities Committee (HUAC) and told his life story, carefully naming all his former Communist party friends and associates, among them the brilliant New Dealer Alger Hiss. Now a well-known and well-respected career diplomat, Hiss had gone to the Yalta Conference with President Roosevelt, helped to organize the United Nations, and served as the president of the Carnegie Endowment for International Peace.

Hiss denied Chambers's allegations. He too appeared before HUAC. Well-dressed and relaxed, he testified, "I am not and never have been a member of the Communist Party. . . . I have never followed the Communist Party line, directly or indirectly." As he answered questions, he smiled and confidently stood on his record of public service. Unlike his nervous, rumpled accuser, Hiss was the picture of placid truthfulness. His testimony satisfied most of the committee members, but not all.

After hearing both Chambers and Hiss, Richard Nixon, a junior congressman from California, still was not sure Hiss was as innocent as he seemed. Nixon, whose struggling background contrasted sharply with Hiss's career, insisted that Hiss and Chambers be brought together before HUAC. At that meeting, Chambers demonstrated his encyclopedic knowledge about Hiss, his family, and his life. He discussed the furniture in Hiss's house and Hiss's hobbies. He showed beyond any doubt that he had been close to Hiss. For once, Hiss's confident equanimity vanished. He challenged Chambers to make his accusations in public, where he would not be protected against a libel suit.

Chambers accepted the challenge, and on "Meet the Press" he repeated his charges. In response, Hiss sued Chambers for defamation. During the involved trials that followed, Chambers proved his case. He even produced a series of classified, microfilmed documents he had stored in a hollowed-out pumpkin on his Maryland farm that incriminated Hiss. Hiss was indicted for perjury by a federal grand jury. The first trial ended in a hung jury, but in January 1950 he was found guilty of perjury and sentenced to five years in prison.

The Hiss-Chambers affair was one of the major episodes of the late 1940s. It was a time of momentous changes. The United States took an active and aggressive stand in world affairs and accepted the responsibilities of world leadership. Across the globe it clashed with the Soviet Union over a series of symbolic and real issues. Labeled the Cold War, these ideological battles affected American domestic and foreign policy. Americans attacked the Communist threat inside as well as outside the United States. In an atmosphere charged with fear, anxiety, paranoia, and hatred, the United States waged peace and war with equal emotional intensity.

Alger Hiss (left), accused of being a Communist spy by Whittaker Chambers (right), was convicted of perjury. This episode helped heighten American fear of communism at home.

Containing the Russian Bear

During World War II, when the United States and the Soviet Union were allies, Joseph Stalin was known as Uncle Joe. The media portrayed him as a stern but fair leader and pictured communism as strikingly like capitalism. Even Hollywood cooperated in this image-making process, producing films in which Stalin appeared as a gentle, pipe-smoking, sad-eyed friend of America.

In reality Stalin was a determined, ruthless leader who had over the years systematically eliminated his actual and suspected political rivals. Between 1933 and 1938 he violently eliminated over 850,000 members of the Communist party, and perhaps one million more died in labor camps. He was apparently suspicious of almost everyone. If his attitude was extreme, it was not totally irrational. Twice in his lifetime Russia had been invaded from the West. Twice Germans had pushed into his country, killing millions upon millions of Russians. For Stalin, the West stood unalterably opposed to communism and could not be trusted.

Stalin, however, was not the only suspicious world leader. The newest Western leader, President Harry Truman, was wary of Stalin, but assumed he could deal with him. Advisers told Truman that Stalin was a tough, no-nonsense leader, characteristics that the tough, no-nonsense Truman could appreciate. But their totally different backgrounds and philosophies separated the two leaders from the start, and the directions in which they led their countries drove them farther apart. The United States and the Soviet Union emerged from World War II as the two most powerful countries in the world, even though the Soviet Union had suffered tremendous industrial, agricultural, and human losses during the war. Both countries were inexperienced as world leaders, but both knew exactly what they wanted, and what they wanted guaranteed future conflicts. The Cold War was the result.

Origins of the Cold War

World War II had ended successfully for the Allies, but too many issues had been left unresolved at Yalta and Potsdam. Anxious to avoid straining their uneasy wartime alliance, the Soviet Union, Great Britain, and the United States decided to set aside thorny issues until after the war. One of the thorniest was the fate of Eastern Europe and Germany. The debate centered on the fate of Poland, which Stalin was determined to maintain as a buffer zone against future invasions. Although Truman conceded that the Soviets had the right to expect any Polish government to be friendly toward the Soviet Union, he insisted that the Soviets allow free and democratic elections in Poland.

In America Poland's fate was no abstract diplomatic issue. Millions of Americans of Eastern European origins pressed Truman to take a tough stand. Truman complied. He told Soviet Foreign Minister V. M. Molotov that the United States would not tolerate Poland being made into a Soviet puppet state. His speech was salted with profanity. Molotov remarked, "I have never been talked to like that in my life."

Truman's tough language, however, did not impress Stalin. He was not now about to give away Poland or any other territory the Red Army occupied simply because of Truman's colorful phrases. As he had bluntly stated at Yalta, "For the Russian people, the question of Poland is not only a question of honor but also a question of security . . . of life and death for the Soviet Union."

Confronted by an inflexible opponent, Truman played his trump card. He threatened to cut off economic aid to the Soviet Union. Devastated by World War II, the Soviet Union needed the aid, but Stalin would not back down and accepted the loss of American money. In the end, Truman was powerless. Americans would certainly not accept a war with the Soviet Union to liberate Poland, and in 1945 the Soviet Union was not about to leave Poland voluntarily. Relations between the United States and the Soviet Union were strained to the breaking point.

A World Divided

The most contentious issue in Soviet-American relations was the degree of control over other nations. America's control was based on its strong economy as much as its military muscle. Even as the country demobilized, American leaders were confident that they could use foreign aid to exert influence on the future development of the world. They were also confident that what was good for America would indeed be good for the world. The Soviet Union's control in all of Eastern Europe depended on the physical presence of the Red Army. Stalin freely granted America and England their spheres of influence, but he wanted the West to recognize his own.

Truman refused. A believer in free trade, national self-determination, and the virtues of democracy, he opposed Stalin's use of military force as a diplomatic weapon. Approaching issues from different perspectives, the Soviet Union and the United States arrived at different conclusions. The fate of Germany illustrates the basic conflict between the two powers. The Soviets wanted to punish Germany by stripping the country of its industry and imposing harsh reparation payments. Only a prostrate Germany, unarmed and unthreatening, would satisfy Stalin. As Truman lost confidence in the Soviet Union, he came to believe in the need for a strong Germany to act as a block against Soviet expansion. The result of these conflicting approaches was a divided Germany. Occupied by the Red Army, East Germany became a Soviet satellite state. West Germany fell under the American, British, and French spheres of influence and soon became part of the postwar democratic alliance.

Control over atomic weapons also divided the two powers. The United States developed and used the first atomic bomb—demonstrating to the world that it possessed not only the scientific knowledge to construct the bomb but also the will to use it—but realized that future world safety depended on some plan to control the awesome potential of the weapon. Publicly Truman seemed favorable to international control of the world's fissionable materials. Yet privately he used the threat of the bomb in his negotiations with the Soviet Union. Stalin reacted with suspicion and bitterness to this contradictory policy, distrusting any atomic control plan that originated in the United States. Rather than make Stalin more manageable, America's atomic diplomacy stiffened his resolve, heightened his suspicions, and made him cling even more firmly to Eastern Europe as a buffer. The result was an atomic arms race, not international cooperation.

In February 1946 Stalin warned all Soviet citizens not to expect a lasting peace with the capitalistic West. Economic sacrifices and perhaps more warfare lay ahead. The next month, in Fulton, Missouri, Winston Churchill announced that "from Stettin in the Baltic to Trieste in the

Adriatic, an iron curtain has descended across the continent." Fortunately, Churchill emphasized, "God has willed" the atomic bomb to America. Dramatic words and ominous warnings, threats and counterthreats—the Cold War had clearly begun.

Tough Talk

Although real issues divided the United States and the Soviet Union, the emotionally charged rhetoric and the emergence of Cold War myths hardened the battle lines. Truman lacked the skill and the language of a diplomat, and followed the advice of those who encouraged him to take a hard line toward the Soviet Union. Remembering how the British and the French had given in to Hitler at the Munich Conference of 1938, American foreign policymakers were determined not to allow history to repeat itself. Equating Stalin's goals with Hitler's, however, was a grave mistake. Stalin was concerned more with security than expansion; he wanted to protect his country from a future attack, not initiate World War III.

The Truman Doctrine

America's rise as a world power was paralleled by Britain's decline. England, like much of the rest of Europe, suffered terribly during World War II. The war shattered its economy, and burned-out buildings and miles of fresh graveyards gave silent testimony to the country's physical and human losses. By early 1947 Britain could no longer stand as the leader of the Western democracies. On Friday, February 21, 1947, England passed the torch to America, when the British ambassador announced that his nation could no longer economically support Greece and Turkey in their fight against Communist rebels. If these two vital countries, which stood between the Soviet Union and the Mediterranean and the Middle East, were to be kept as Western allies, the United States had to aid their cause.

Truman was prepared to assume the burden, but there were doubts whether the country was. Republicans had regained control of Congress in the November 1946 elections, and they were not anxious to shoulder expensive new foreign programs. In addition, rapid demobilization after World War II had drastically reduced the size and effectiveness of American military forces. Truman's advisers and congressional leaders recommended that he speak directly to the American people. But as Republican Senator Arthur Vandenberg warned, to win public support the president would have to "scare the hell out of the American people."

On March 12, 1947, Truman appeared before a joint session of Congress and described the Greek and Turkish situations as battles between the forces of light and the legions of darkness. Congress sounded its approval as Truman came to his climactic sentence: "I believe that it must be the policy of the United States to support free peoples who are resisting attempted subjugation by armed minorities or outside pressures." Labeled the Truman Doctrine, the statement set the course U.S. foreign policy would follow during the next generation.

Specifically, Truman called for economic and financial aid to "save" Greece and Turkey. Congress responded by appropriating $400 million. In the future, the United States would send billions of dollars in economic and military aid to countries fighting communism, even though the leaders of some of those nations were themselves dictators. In Truman's morality play, however, "anti-Communists" and "free peoples" became synonymous.

Although Truman succeeded in getting aid for Greece and Turkey and in arousing the American public, a few foreign policy experts believed that his scare tactics did more harm than good. George Kennan deplored the sweeping language of the Truman Doctrine, which placed U.S. aid to Greece "in the framework of a universal policy rather than in that of a specific decision addressed to a specific set of circumstances."

The Marshall Plan: "Saving Western Europe"

The millions of dollars sent to Greece and Turkey stabilized the pro-American governments of the two countries. But at the same time the United States was losing support in Western Europe, a far more vital region. Although the war had ended in the spring of 1945, Europe's problems continued. It lacked the money to rebuild its war-torn economies and scarred cities. To make matters worse, the winters of 1946 and 1947 were brutally cold. The winter hardships fueled the Communist party, which made marked gains. American leaders assumed that economic distress would continue to breed political extremism.

At the Harvard University commencement on June 5, 1947, Secretary of State George C. Marshall announced a plan to bolster the recovery of Europe. Marshall suggested that America could not afford to send a Band-Aid to cover the deep European wounds; a complete cure in the form of massive economic aid was in order. Although the cost might seem high, without America's help "economic, social, and political deterioration of a very grave character" would result. And from a more selfish point of view, the United States needed a strong democratic Europe to provide rich markets for American goods and to act as a check against Soviet westward expansion.

In early 1948 Congress appropriated $17 billion to be spent over the next four years for the Marshall Plan. The program put food in the mouths of hungry children, coal in empty furnaces, and money in near-empty banks. More important, it rebuilt the economic infrastructure of Western Europe and restored economic prosperity to the region. In the process it created stable markets for American goods. Americans were proud of the Marshall Plan, and Europeans were grateful for the help. All told, the Marshall Plan greatly restored America's prestige abroad, fueled Europe's recovery, and served America's Cold War strategy by diminishing the threat of Communist expansion.

The Containment Policy

Money, even billions of dollars, could not substitute for a concrete foreign policy to guide U.S. actions: an explicit policy that mixed the international idealism of the Truman Doctrine and the economic realism of the Marshall Plan with the will to meet the real or perceived Soviet threat. The policy was not long in coming; its author was George Kennan, the government's foremost authority on Russian history. Kennan had spent his adult life in the U.S. foreign service where he carefully studied the Soviet scene. During World War II he was stationed in Moscow and was able to observe Soviet political behavior. Although he believed Russians were a "great and appealing people," he distrusted the Soviet government. In a 1947 *Foreign Affairs* article, published anonymously, Kennan expressed his views of the Soviet Union. He believed that Soviet communism was driven by two engines: the need for a repressive dictatorship at home and the belief that there could never be any sense of true accord with the capitalist West. But, Kennan argued, Stalin and the leaders in the Kremlin were more interested in security than expansion, and would only expand when allowed by American weakness. In short, the Soviet Union could be *contained* within its present borders by a politically, economically, and militarily active United States.

Although Kennan later argued that he was talking about the political containment of communism, in 1947 his article was viewed as a military blueprint. Once implemented, the policy of containment involved confronting the spread of communism across the globe. As Americans soon learned, the policy came with a heavy price tag. It meant supporting our allies around the world with billions of dollars in military and economic aid, and it meant thousands of Americans dying in foreign lands. Since containment was a defensive policy, it involved a permanent Cold War without any hope of ultimate victory. Unlike World War I and World War II, the Cold War emphasized the doctrine of limited wars fought for limited goals. It was a policy bound to breed frustration and anxiety—certain to influence domestic as well as foreign policy.

Berlin Test

During the late 1940s containment seemed to fit American needs. American-Soviet tensions centered particularly on the future of Germany. The United States maintained that the economic revival of Western Europe depended on a prosperous Germany. The Soviets believed that a reindustrialized Germany was a dangerous Germany. An early test of the two different viewpoints came in Berlin, a divided city located in the heart of East Germany, deep within the Soviet zone. In June 1948, Stalin decided to stop all road and rail traffic between West Germany and Berlin. It was a crisis tailor-made for the containment policy.

Stalin could close highways and railways, but he could not effectively close the skyways. For almost one year the United States and Britain kept West Berlin alive and democratic by a massive airlift. Food, coal, clothing, and all other essentials were flown daily into West Berlin. It was an heroic feat, a triumph of technology. Western pilots logged 277,264 flights into West Berlin; they hauled in 2,343,315 tons of food, fuel, medicine, and clothing. Finally, on May 12, 1949, Stalin lifted his blockade of West Berlin. In the West, containment had passed an important test.

Troubling Times

Truman scored a series of triumphs during 1947 and 1948. The Truman Doctrine, the Marshall Plan, and the Berlin Airlift strengthened his popularity at home and U.S. prestige abroad. In the election of 1948 Truman won a remarkable upset victory over Republican challenger Thomas E. Dewey. Then in 1949 eleven western democracies joined the United States in signing the North Atlantic Treaty Organization (NATO), a mutual defense pact. But difficult times for Truman, containment, and the United States lay ahead. In late August 1949 American scientists detected traces of radioactive material in the Soviet atmosphere. The cause was as clear as a mushroom-shaped cloud. The Soviets had the bomb—a full decade before American intelligence had predicted.

Between 1945 and 1949 the threat of the bomb had given teeth to American foreign policy. It was the country's check to the Red Army, and U. S. policymakers seldom allowed Soviet leaders to forget it. Now that the Soviet Union had entered the atomic age, Truman responded by asking his scientists to accelerate the development of a hydrogen bomb; Congress responded by voting appropriations for Truman's latest defense requests.

On the heels of the Soviet bomb came more unwelcome news—the establishment of the Communist government in China after a bitter civil war between Mao Zedung's (Mao Tse-tung) Communists and Jiang Jieshi's (Chiang Kai-shek) Nationalists. Although the United States had provided Jiang with more than $3 billion in aid between 1945 and 1949, it was unable to prop up a government that was structurally unsound, inefficient, and corrupt. In May 1949, Jiang fled to Taiwan, and on September 21 Mao proclaimed Red China's sovereignty.

The Truman administration tried to put the best face possible on the turn of events. Secretary of State Dean Acheson issued a thousand-page White Paper explaining how Mao had won the civil war. It detailed the rampant corruption in the Nationalist government and Jiang's many mistakes. For the American public, however, that explanation was not good enough. Republicans and supporters of Jiang in America blamed Truman for "losing" China. Led by Henry Luce, the influential publisher of *Time* and *Life* who was the China-born son of American missionaries, an informal group known as the China Lobby blasted the Truman administration. They claimed "phony liberals" had "sold China into atheistic slavery." Millions of Americans took their loud cries seriously.

Facing intense political pressure at home, Truman refused to recognize the Communist People's Republic of China. Instead he insisted that Jiang's Nationalist government on Taiwan was the legitimate regime. It was an unrealistic policy, but one that future presidents found politically difficult to reverse. The United States and the People's Republic of China did not establish formal diplomatic relations until 1979.

The Korean War

The rhetoric of the Truman administration tended to simplify complex issues, intensify the Cold War rivalry, and tie foreign policy to domestic politics. Failure abroad could have calamitous consequences for politicians at home. After "China fell," Truman was more than ever determined to contain communism.

The mood of the Truman administration is clearly evident in National Security Council Paper Number 68 (NSC-68), one of the most important documents of the Cold War. Completed in April 1950, it expressed the view that communism was a monolithic world movement directed from the Kremlin. NSC-68 extended the Truman Doctrine and called for the Unied States to protect the world against the spread of communism. The cost would be great—NSC-68 estimated it at 20 percent of the gross national product or more than a 300 percent increase in military appropriations—but planners warned that without the commitment the United States faced the prospect of a world moving toward communism. Two months later, in June 1950, America went to war in Korea.

Korea, like Germany, was a divided country. When the Japanese surrendered its forces in Korea after World War II, Soviet troops accepted the surrender north of the 38th parallel, American troops south of that line.

With the deepening of the Cold War, the temporary division line became permanent. North of the 38th parallel, the Soviet-backed communist government forged a modern, disciplined army during the late 1940s. South Korea, which received strong aid and support from the United States, opposed any reconciliation with Communist North Korea.

In an unfortunate speech before the National Press Club on January 12, 1950, Secretary of State Dean Acheson stated that South Korea lay outside America's primary "defense perimeter." In late June North Korea attacked, sending 90,000 men across the 38th parallel into South Korea. A weak, disorderly South Korean army quickly retreated.

Truman assumed that North Korea was acting on orders from Moscow, although there is little evidence to support this contention. Since both Koreas were technically wards of the United Nations, the Truman administration decided to take the matter to the Security Council. With the Soviet Union absent, the Security Council by a 9 to 0 vote condemned the North Korean assault and demanded an immediate cease-fire. Encouraged by the United Nations' prompt action and without consulting Congress, Truman pledged American support to South Korea

Truman termed the conflict a "UN police action" and, in fact, a number of UN member nations sent troops, but for all practical purposes it was a war that initially matched the United States and South Korea against North Korea. When bombing the Communist supply line failed to slow the North Korean advance, Truman took the fateful step of ordering American troops to Korea. They soon joined their South Korean allies in a headlong retreat. For six weeks the allies fell steadily back until they stabilized a perimeter in southeast Korea around the port city of Pusan.

North Korean troops besieged the city for two months. Determined to reverse the stalemate, U.N. commander General Douglas MacArthur, a bold, even arrogant man, decided to split his forces and launch a surprise attack against the North Koreans' rear. On the morning of September 15, 1950, American marines began an amphibious attack on Inchon, a port city just below the 38th parallel. It was a bold, risky, but successful maneuver.

Faced with an enemy to their front and their rear, North Korean troops retreated above the 38th parallel. Truman had achieved his objective: to restore the 38th parallel as the border between the two Koreas. But MacArthur wanted more—he wanted victory on the battlefield. And he said so, loudly and publicly.

After receiving MacArthur's reassurances that Red China would not intervene, Truman decided to allow U.S. forces to "liberate" North Korea. This time boldness failed. North Korea was a difficult country to invade. The American army had no reliable maps, and mountainous terrain rendered traditional military tactics impossible. In addition, as MacArthur's forces moved recklessly north toward Manchuria, Chinese officials sent

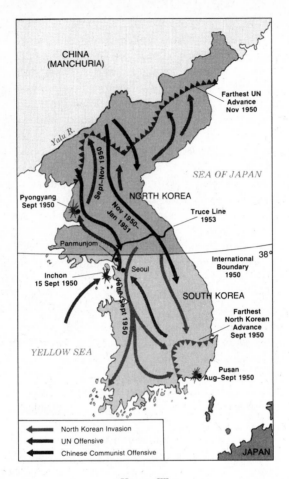

Korean War

informal warnings to the United States that unless the advance stopped, their country would enter the fray. MacArthur ignored Chinese warnings and kept moving. In late November Communist China struck, pouring more than 300,000 troops across the border and sending American forces reeling back across the 38th parallel.

Despite this stunning setback, McArthur continued to talk about absolute victory. If a nation was going to fight a war, he sermonized, it should fight to win. In Washington, however, the Truman administration was shifting back to the pre-Inchon policy of containment. When MacArthur publicly criticized the administration's newest approach, an angry Truman replaced him, a move that raised a firestorm of protest and contributed to the president's low public approval ratings.

The Korean War dragged on. Formal peace negotiations began on July 10, 1951, but they proved to be a long, difficult process. While diplomats talked, American soldiers fought and died. Altogether, 34,000 Americans were killed and 103,000 wounded during the Korean War. Finally, on July 26, 1953, the war ended as it began, with North Koreans above the 38th parallel and South Koreans below it. The war represented a victory for Truman's containment policy, but for millions of Americans it somehow tasted like defeat.

The Cold War at Home

As Truman waged the Cold War abroad, Cold War issues gradually came to dominate the American domestic scene. During the ensuing Red Scare, the fear of communism disrupted American life, and the freedoms that Americans took for granted came under attack. At home as well as abroad, Americans battled real and imagined Communist enemies.

Adjusting to Peace

Truman and his advisers approached the end of World War II with their eyes on the past. Memories of the Great Depression and the painful social and economic adjustment after World War I clouded their thinking. They knew that massive wartime spending, not the New Deal, had ended the decade of depression, and they worried that peace might bring more economic suffering. Peace with prosperity was their goal.

The solution to the problem of converting back to a peacetime economy, Truman believed, lay in the continuation, at least for a time, of wartime government economic controls. During the war the Office of Price Administration (OPA) had controlled prices and held inflation in check. To ensure prosperity, Truman asked Congress to continue price controls. He also advocated such economic measures as a 65-cents-an-hour minimum wage, nationalization of the housing industry, and stronger fair employment practices legislation.

Congress responded halfheartedly. It did pass the Employment Act of 1946 which, although less than Truman requested, provided the institutional framework for more government control over the economy. The act also created the Council of Economic Advisers, and in the decades after 1946 the council exerted a powerful influence over economic policy.

On the other hand, Republicans and southern Democrats balked at a return to more "New Dealism." Consequently, Congress destroyed the OPA by relaxing its controls, a policy that created immediate inflation, and refused to pass Truman's economic package. The American economy, however, was basically sound, and wartime employment and wartime saving had created a people whose money was burning holes in their pockets. Given the demand for consumer goods and the short supply, inflation was inevitable. But, as industries converted to peacetime production, consumer supplies rose to meet the new demands.

Confronting the Demands of Labor

During the war labor unions had taken "no strike" pledges, and through their efforts America became the "arsenal of democracy." Workers labored long and hard, agreeing to speedups and higher production quotas. As the war came to an end, however, workers demanded rewards for their wartime efforts and their loss of overtime pay. During 1946 more than 4.5 million laborers went on strike.

Truman was in no mood to coddle labor. When two national railway brotherhoods threatened to disrupt the transportation system, Truman proposed to draft the workers. Confronted by hostile public opinion and an unsympathetic president, the brotherhoods went back to work.

Labor was angry. As winter approached, United Mine Workers leader John L. Lewis took his men out on strike. The prospect of a cold winter created anxiety, and Truman reacted angrily. He threatened to take over the mines and lashed out publicly at the defiant Lewis. Finally, Truman appealed directly to the miners, asking them to go back to work for the good of the nation. It worked. Lewis called off the strike.

The congressional elections of 1946, which brought the conservative, Republican-controlled Eightieth Congress, added to labor's problems. Led by Robert Taft, Congress pushed through the Taft-Hartley Act in 1947 over Truman's veto, which outlawed the closed shop (a business or industry in which all the employees are required to join a union), gave presidents power to delay strikes by declaring a "cooling-off" period, and curtailed the political and economic power of organized labor. The act signified the conservative mood of the country.

It was a bad period for all industrial workers, but for female workers it was especially hard. During the war they had filled a wide range of industrial jobs, but returning soldiers quickly displaced them. What was worse, when new jobs opened employers hired and trained younger males rather than rehire the experienced females. Thus, while male workers complained about the antilabor mood of the country, many unemployed women laborers lamented the antifemale prejudices among employers.

Failure of the Fair Deal

Political experts expected America to vote Republican in the 1948 presidential elections. Truman's policies had angered liberals, labor, southerners, and most of Congress. Moreover, Democrats had occupied the White House since 1933. Republicans reasoned that it was time for a change. They nominated Thomas E. Dewey of New York, the GOP candidate in 1944. The Democrats stayed with Truman, even though large numbers of southerners and liberals deserted the party to follow third-party movements. Southerners, angered by Truman's support of civil rights, formed the States' Rights Democratic party—better known as the Dixiecrats—and nominated Governor J. Strom Thurmond of South Carolina for president. Liberals formed the Progressive party, which nominated FDR's former vice president Henry A. Wallace.

An underdog from the start, Truman rolled up his sleeves and took his cause to the people. Campaigning across the country by train, at each stop Truman blasted the "do-nothing" Eightieth Congress. "If you send another Republican Congressman to Washington, you're a bigger bunch of suckers than I think you are," he lectured. "Give 'em hell, Harry!" was the popular refrain. By contrast, Dewey's cold personality failed to move American voters.

By election day Truman had closed the gap. The old Roosevelt coalition—midwestern farmers, urban ethnics, organized labor, blacks, and southerners—remained sufficiently strong to send Truman back to the White House. Neither the Dixiecrats nor the Progressives hurt Truman in any substantial way. Most Democrats chose to remain in the center of the party with Truman rather than drift toward the radical fringes. The election was a testimony to the legacy of FDR as well as Truman's scrappiness, and to the often overlooked fact that Democrats outnumbered Republicans in the nation.

"Keep America Human With Truman," read one of his campaign posters. In 1949 the president announced a plan to do just that. Known as the Fair Deal, the legislative package included an expansion of Social Security, federal aid to education, a higher minimum wage, federal funding for public housing projects, a national plan for medical insurance, civil rights legislation for minorities, and other measures to foster social and economic justice.

Congress extended Social Security and raised the minimum wage to 75 cents an hour, but otherwise failed to enact Truman's plan. The more original proposals of the Fair Deal—civil rights legislation, a national health insurance program, an imaginative farm program, and federal aid to education—were rejected by a Congress that opposed anything defined as "creeping socialism."

Truman, as well as Congress, contributed to the ultimate failure of the Fair Deal to achieve its objectives. To be sure, Republicans and southerners joined forces in opposition to civil rights and government spending programs. But on domestic issues Truman demonstrated an almost total inability to work with Congress. In addition, by 1949 foreign policy dominated the president's attention and claimed an increasing share of the federal budget.

Searching for the Enemy Within

While Congress tampered with Truman's Fair Deal, Cold War winds were chilling the country's political landscape. The tough diplomatic rhetoric of Truman, Acheson, and other policymakers encouraged Americans to view the rivalry between the Soviet Union and the United States in simplistic terms. America became the "defender of free people," the Soviet Union the "atheistic enslaver of millions." Every time a world event did not go America's way, it was seen as a Soviet victory. The suspicion thus took shape that "enemies within" America were secretly aiding the Soviet cause and sabotaging U.S. foreign policy.

Were spies working against American interest to further the Soviet cause? Unquestionably, yes. In 1945 a Communist spy ring working in Canada and the United States was uncovered. The evidence led to the arrest of two British physicists who had worked on the Manhattan Project. The investigation led to a group of American radicals—among them Julius and Ethel Rosenberg—who had passed atomic secrets to the Soviets during the war. Whether this information helped the Soviet Union develop an atomic bomb remains largely conjecture.

The espionage issue soon became an instrument of partisan politics. Republicans accused Democrats of being "soft" on communism—in fact, of harboring spies in the State Department and other government agencies. California congressman Richard M. Nixon announced that Democrats were responsible for "the unimpeded growth of the communist conspiracy in the United States." As proof, Republicans pointed to the "fall" of China, the atomic bomb in the Soviet Union, and Alger Hiss in the State Department.

Truman reacted to such criticism as early as 1947 by issuing Executive Order 9835 establishing the Federal Employee Loyalty Program, which authorized the FBI to investigate all government employees. Although the search disclosed no espionage or treason, thousands of employees were forced to resign or were fired because their personal lives or past associations did not meet government inspection. Homosexuality, alcoholism, unpaid debts, contributions to left-wing causes, support of civil rights—all became grounds for dismissal.

Ethel and Julius Rosenberg paid the supreme price. They were Communists, and at least one—Julius—may have been a spy, but the death penalty was not mandatory for their crime. Judge Irving R. Kaufman, nevertheless, made an example of them, and ordered the couple's execution for treason. On June 19, 1953, the Rosenbergs, parents of two young sons, died in the electric chair.

The Rise and Fall of Joseph McCarthy

More than any other person, Wisconsin Senator Joseph McCarthy capitalized on the anticommunism issue. Although he did not start the crusade or even join it until 1950, the entire movement bears the name "McCarthyism." His career, which caused so much suffering for so many, illuminated the price the country had to pay for temporarily placing anticommunism above the Constitution.

First elected to the Senate in 1946, McCarthy spent four years in relative obscurity, all the while demonstrating his incompetency and angering his colleagues. Then on February 9, 1950, he gave a speech in Wheeling, West Virginia. Warning his audience about the threat of communism to America, he boldly announced, "While I cannot take the time to name all of the men in the State Department who have been named as members of the Communist Party and members of a spy ring, I have in my hand a list of 205 . . . a list of names that were known to the Secretary of State and who nevertheless are still working and shaping the policy of the State Department." McCarthy had no real list; he had no names. But within days he became a national sensation.

McCarthy dealt in simple solutions to complex problems. He told Americans that the United States could control the outcome of world affairs if it would get the Communists out of the State Department. It was those "State Department perverts," those "striped-pants diplomats" who "gave away" Poland, "lost" China, and allowed the Soviet Union to develop the bomb. It was the "bright young men who are born with silver spoons in their mouths" who were "selling the Nation out." His arguments found receptive ears among Catholics who had relatives in Eastern Europe, political outsiders who resented the power of the "Ivy League Eastern Establishment," and pragmatic Republicans who wanted to return to the White House in 1952. And with the outbreak of the Korean War in the early summer of 1950, Joseph McCarthy's support grew.

McCarthy's origins were humble; he worked his way through high school and a Catholic university. He was in all ways the opposite of Secretary of State Dean Acheson, whose Ivy League degrees, waxed mustache, and aristocratic accent were a red flag to McCarthy. Throughout the early 1950s McCarthy bitterly attacked "Red Dean" and the State Department. But in the end, McCarthy ferreted out no Communists, espionage agents, or traitors.

McCarthy's basic tactic was never defend. Caught in a lie, he told another; when one case dissolved, he created another. He attacked Truman and Eisenhower, Acheson and Marshall, the State Department and the U.S. Army. No authority or institution frightened him. In 1954 his campaign against the army became so bitter that the Senate arranged special hearings. Televised between April 22 and June 17, the Army-McCarthy hearings attracted a high audience rating. But for once McCarthy's attention-getting methods backfired badly. It was the first time that most Americans saw McCarthy in action—the bullying of witnesses, the cruel use of innuendo, the tasteless humor.

After the hearings, McCarthy's downfall was as rapid as his rise. When the polls showed that his popularity had swung sharply downward, his enemies mounted an offensive. On December 2, 1954, the Senate voted to censure McCarthy for his unsenatorial behavior. Newspapers stopped printing his outlandish charges. He sank back into relative obscurity, and died on May 2, 1957.

The end of the Korean War and McCarthy's downfall signaled the end of the Red Scare. The Cold War remained, but most Americans soon realized that there was no significant domestic Communist threat. They

Senator Joseph McCarthy's downfall came about as a result of his unsubstantiated charges of Communist infiltration in the U.S. Army.

learned that an occasional spy was part of the price that free societies pay for their personal freedom, and that "McCarthyism" can be the result of a curtailment of that freedom.

The Paranoid Style

The Cold War mentality left its imprint on politics and culture during the late 1940s and early 1950s, giving rise to a national mood that has been termed the "paranoid style." The nature of the fight against communism contributed to the paranoid style. Politicians warned Americans that communism was silently and secretly destroying the country from within. Although directed from Moscow, its aim was subversion through the slow destruction of a country's moral fiber. No one knew which institution it would next attack, or when. It might be the State Department or the YMCA; it might be the presidency, the army, the movie industry, or the Cub Scouts. Politicians counseled vigilance. They told Americans to watch for the unexpected, to suspect everyone and everything. As a result, between 1945 and 1955 a broad spectrum of institutions, organizations, and individuals came under suspicion. Whether it was the Mafia or the fluoridation of drinking water, Americans sought the answers to complex problems in the workings of conspiracies.

HUAC Goes to Hollywood

The House of Representatives established the Un-American Activities Committee (HUAC) in the late 1930s to combat subversive right-wing and left-wing movements. From the first it tended to see subversive Communists everywhere at work in American society. HUAC even announced that the Boy Scouts were Communist-infiltrated. During the late 1940s and the early 1950s HUAC picked up the tempo of its investigations, which it conducted in well-publicized sessions. Twice during this period HUAC traveled to Hollywood to investigate Communist infiltration in the film industry.

HUAC first went to Hollywood in 1947. A group of radical screenwriters and producers were called upon to testify. Asked if they were Communists, the "Hollywood Ten" refused to answer questions about their political views, believing that the First Amendment protected them. In the politically charged late 1940s, however, their rights were not protected. Those who refused to divulge their political affiliations were tried for contempt of Congress, sent to prison, and blacklisted.

HUAC went back to Hollywood in 1951. This time it called hundreds of witnesses from both the political right and the political left. Conservatives told HUAC that Hollywood was littered with "Commies." Walt Disney even recounted attempts to have Mickey Mouse follow the party line. Of the radicals, some talked but most remained silent. To cooperate with HUAC entailed "naming names"—that is, informing on one's friends and political acquaintances. Again, those who refused to name names found themselves unemployed and unemployable.

The HUAC hearings and blacklisting convinced Hollywood producers to make strongly anticommunist films. Between 1947 and 1954 they released more than 50 such films. Most were second-rate movies, starring third-rate actors. The films assured Americans that Communists were thoroughly bad people—they didn't have children, they exhaled cigarette smoke too slowly, they murdered their "friends," and they went berserk when arrested. If the films were bad civics lessons, they did have an impact. They seemed to confirm HUAC's position that Communists were everywhere, that subversives lurked in every shadow. They reaffirmed the paranoid style and helped to justify McCarthy's harangues and Truman's Cold War rhetoric.

"What's Wrong with Our Kids Today?"

At the same time that it turned out films about Communists, Hollywood produced movies that contributed to the fear that something was terribly wrong with the youth of America. Films such as *The Wild One* (1954), *Blackboard Jungle* (1955), and *Rebel Without a Cause* (1955) portrayed adolescents as budding criminals, emerging homosexuals, potential Fascists, and pathological misfits—everything but perfectly normal kids.

FBI reports and congressional investigations reinforced the theme of adolescent moral decline. J. Edgar Hoover, head of the FBI, linked the rise in juvenile delinquency to the decline in the influence of family, home, church, and local community institutions. Frederic Wertham, a psychiatrist who studied the problem extensively, agreed, emphasizing particularly the pernicious influence of comic books. He believed that crime and horror comic books fostered racism, fascism, sexism, and even homosexuality in their readers. Far from being an unheard voice, Wertham's attack generated congressional investigations of and local attacks against the comic book industry. In response, the comic book industry passed several self-regulatory codes designed to restrict the violent and sexual content of comic books.

For a number of critics, sports were an antidote to the ills of wayward youths. "Organized sport is one of our best weapons against juvenile

Movies like *Rebel Without a Cause,*
starring James Dean, depicted the
futility and hopelessness of American
youth in the 1950s.

delinquency," remarked J. Edgar Hoover. Youths who competed for championship trophies felt no inclination to steal cars. Nor would they turn to communism. As Senator Herman Welker of Idaho bluntly put it, "I never saw a ballplayer who was a Communist."

Given these widespread beliefs, the sports scandals of the early 1950s shocked the nation and raised fresh questions about the morality of American adolescents. In February 1951 New York authorities disclosed that players for the City College of New York (CCNY) basketball team had accepted money to fix games. By the time the investigations ended, seven other colleges were implicated in the scandal, which involved forging transcripts and paying players as well as fixing games. In August, a cheating scandal at the U.S. Military Academy at West Point resulted in he dismissal of 90 cadets, half of them football players.

The West Point scandal struck especially at the nation's heart, for half a world away in Korea American soldiers were battling to contain communism. What of their moral fiber? They too had read comics, watched films written by left-wing screenwriters, and been exposed to other "subversive" influences. Did they have the "right stuff"? These questions swirled around the Korean prisoner of war (POW) controversy. Early reports suggested the American POWs in Korea were different from, and inferior to, those of World War II. Journalists portrayed them as undisciplined, morally weak, susceptible to "brainwashing," uncommitted to traditional American values, and prone to collaborate with their communist guards.

What was wrong? Who was corrupting the youth of America? The Republican *Chicago Tribune* blamed the decline on the New Deal. The Communist *Daily Worker* said it was the fault of Wall Street, bankers, and greedy politicians. The paranoid style, after all, had no party affiliation. Other Americans, without being too specific, simply felt that there was some ominous force working within the United States against Americans.

Sociologists and historians have demonstrated that Korean POWs behaved in much the same way as POWs from earlier wars. During the late 1940s and 1950s juvenile delinquency was not on an upswing, nor were alien, subversive forces undermining American morality. But the rhetoric of the Cold War and McCarthyism created a political atmosphere that proved fertile for the paranoid style.

Conclusion

By 1953 and 1954 there were indications of a thaw in the Cold War. First came the death of Joseph Stalin in 1953. Shortly thereafter Georgi Malenkov told the Supreme Soviet, the highest legislative body of the Soviet Union: "At the present time there is no disputed or unresolved question that cannot be settled peacefully by mutual agreement. . . . This applies to our relations with all states, including the United States of America." That summer the Korean War ended in a stalemate that allowed both the United States and the Communist forces to save face. In America, 1954 saw the fall of McCarthy. Certainly these events did not end the paranoid style in either the United States or the Soviet Union, but they did ease the tension.

In addition, by 1954 both the United States and the Soviet Union had become more comfortable in their positions as world powers and had begun to realize that neither side could readily win the Cold War. Between 1945 and 1954 each had carved out spheres of influence. The Soviet Union and its sometime-ally China dominated most of Eastern Europe and the Asian mainland. America and its allies controlled Western Europe, North and South America, most of the Pacific, and to a lesser extent Africa, the Middle East, and Southeast Asia. Throughout much of the Third World, however, emerging nationalistic movements challenged both U.S. and Soviet influences.

In the United States the containment policy was seldom even debated. The Truman Doctrine governed foreign policy decisions, but economic and political questions lingered. How much would containment cost?

Chronology of Key Events

1938	House Un-American Activities Committee (HUAC) created to investigate Communist subversion
1945	United Nations is founded
1947	Truman Doctrine declared; Truman establishes Federal Employee Loyalty Oath Program; Marshall Plan provides economic aid for European recovery; Taft-Hartley Act bans closed shop; HUAC investigates Communist infiltration of the film industry
1948	West Germany founded; Soviet Union imposes Berlin blockade; ex-Communist Whittaker Chambers charges former State Department official Alger Hiss
1949	NATO founded; Berlin blockade ends; Mao Zedong's Communist forces win China's civil war; Soviet Union successfully tests atomic bomb
1950	Senator Joseph McCarthy claims to have names of State Department employees who are Communists; Korean War begins; UN forces invade North Korea; Chinese troops enter North Korea
1951	Ethel and Julius Rosenberg are sentenced to death for atomic espionage
1953	Joseph Stalin dies; Dwight D. Eisenhower inaugurated thirty-fourth president; cease-fire in Korean War
1954	Army-McCarthy hearings

Where would the money come from? Which Americans would pay the most? Would it mean the end of liberal reform? During the next decade American leaders would wrestle with these and other crucial questions.

Suggestions for Further Reading

Valuable studies of American foreign policy during the Cold War include Stephen E. Ambrose, *Rise to Globalism*, 5th ed. (1988); John L. Gaddis, *The United States and the Cold War* (1992); Walter LaFeber, *America, Russia, and the Cold War*, 5th ed. (1985); Thomas G. Paterson and Robert J. McMahon, *The Origins of the Cold War*, 3d ed. (1991).

Specific studies of Cold War foreign policy crises include Bruce Cumings, *The Origins of the Korean War,* 2 vols. (1981–1990); Michael Hogan, *The Marshall Plan* (1987); Howard Jones, *A New Kind of War* (1989); Akira Iriye, *The Cold War in Asia* (1974); Avi Shlaim, *The United States and the Berlin Blockade* (1983).

For American social, cultural, and political developments during this period see James Aronson, *The Press and the Cold War* (1970); William Leuchtenburg, *A Troubled Feast,* rev. ed. (1983); Larry Ceplair and Steven Englund, *The Inquisition in Hollywood* (1980); Nora Sayre, *Running Time: Films of the Cold War* (1982); Stephen J. Whitfield, *The Culture of the Cold War* (1991).

Examinations of McCarthy and McCarthyism include David M. Oshinsky, *A Conspiracy So Immense* (1983); Thomas C. Reeves, *The Life and Times of Joe McCarthy* (1982); Athan Theoharis, *Seeds of Repression: Harry S Truman and the Origins of McCarthyism* (1971). The Hiss-Chambers case is examined in Allen Weinstein, *Perjury* (1978), and in Hiss's own memoir, *Recollections of a Life* (1988).

Chapter 28

Ike's America

Mose Wright stood and surveyed the courtroom. Most of the faces he saw were white. The two accused men were white. The 12 jurors were white. The armed guards were white. Slowly, Wright, a 64-year-old black sharecropper, extended his right arm. "Thar he," Wright answered, pointing at J. W. Milam. He then pointed at Roy Bryant, the second defendant. In essence, Wright was accusing the two whites of murdering Emmett Till, his 14-year-old nephew—accusing them in a segregated courtroom in Sumner, Mississippi. As Wright later recalled: "It was the first time in my life I had the courage to accuse a white man of a crime, let alone something as terrible as killing a boy. I wasn't exactly brave and I wasn't scared. I just wanted to see justice done."

It was 1955, but the march of racial justice in the South had been painfully slow. In 1954 the Supreme Court of the United States in the landmark *Brown* v. *Board of Education of Topeka* decision had ruled that segregated schooling was "inherently unequal." News of the *Brown* decision drew angry comments and reactions from all corners of the Jim Crow South. Throughout Dixie, Klansmen burned crosses while other white leaders organized Citizens' Councils. These self-proclaimed protectors of white America vowed "to make it difficult, if not impossible, for any Negro who advocates desegregation to find and hold a job, get credit, or renew a mortgage."

Into this racially charged atmosphere came Emmett Till in August 1955. Taking a summer vacation from his home on the South Side of Chicago, he went to visit relatives living near Money, Mississippi. Emmett had known segregation in Chicago, but nothing like what he found in Money. Although his mother told him what to expect and how to act, Emmett had a mind and a mouth of his own. He told his cousins that he was friends with plenty of white people in Chicago; he even had a picture of a white girl, *his* white girl, he said. "Hey," challenged a listener, "there's a [white] girl in that store there. I bet you won't go in there and talk to her."

Emmett accepted the challenge. He entered Bryant's Grocery and Meat Market and browsed about. As he left, he said, "Bye, Baby" to Carolyn Bryant and gave a "wolf call" whistle. Outside an old black man told Emmett to scat before the woman got a pistol and blew "his brains out." Emmett beat a hasty retreat.

After midnight the following Saturday, Roy Bryant and his half-brother, J. W. Milam, drove to Mose Wright's unpainted cabin. They demanded the "boy who done the talkin'." Mose tried to explain that Emmett was from "up nawth," and was unfamiliar with southern ways.

The logic of the argument was lost on the two white men, who drove away with Emmett. What happened next is uncertain. According to Milam and Bryant's account, they had only meant to scare the northern youth. But Emmett did not beg for mercy. Therefore they *had* to kill him.

Mose Wright and his three boys, seated in the "colored" section of the courtroom, attended the trial of Bryant and Milam, accused of killing Emmett Till in Mississippi.

"What else could we do? " Milam asked. "He was hopeless. I'm no bully; I never hurt a nigger in my life. I like niggers in their place. I know how to work 'em. But I just decided it was time a few people got put on notice."

Three days later Emmett's badly beaten body was found in the Tallahatchie River. A gouged-out eye, crushed forehead, and bullet in his skull gave evidence to the beating he took. Around his neck, attached by barbed wire, was a 75-pound cotton gin fan. At the request of his mother, the local sheriff sent the decomposing body to Chicago for burial.

Mamie Bradley, Emmett's grieving mother insisted on an open casket funeral. Thousands of black Chicagoans attended, and the black press closely followed the episode. *Jet* magazine even published a picture of the mutilated corpse. In the black community the Till murder case became a cause célèbre.

In Money, white southerners rallied to Bryant and Milam's side. Supporters raised a $10,000 defense fund, and southern editorials labeled the entire affair a "Communist plot" to destroy southern society. Few people expected that Bryant and Milam would be judged guilty because few expected any blacks would testify against white men in Mississippi.

Mose Wright proved them wrong. He dramatically testified against the defendents, as did several other relatives of Emmett Till. But in his closing statement, John C. Whitten, one of the defense attorneys, told the all-white, all-male jury: "I'm sure that every last Anglo-Saxon one of you has the courage to free these men in the face of that [outside] pressure."

The jury returned a "not guilty" verdict in one hour and seven minutes. But if there was no fairness on that day in 1955, there were clear signs of change. A black man had demanded justice in white-controlled Mississippi. Soon other voices would join Mose Wright's. Their peaceful but insistent cries would be heard across America. They would force the United States to come to terms with its own ideology. After a heroic struggle against fascism and during a cold war against communism, Americans no longer could ignore racial injustice and inequality at home.

Slow, painful, poignant, occasionally uplifting—the march toward justice moved forward. It was part of other significant social and economic changes taking place in America. Against the backdrop of Dwight D. Eisenhower's calm assurances, a new country was taking shape.

Quiet Changes

Most white Americans during the late 1940s and the early 1950s were unconcerned about the struggles of their black compatriots. Other concerns seemed more urgent. In November 1952 the Korean War was dragging into its third year, and the chances for a satisfactory peace were fading. Joseph McCarthy was still warning Americans about the Communist infiltration of the U.S. government. At the polls Americans were ready to vote for change.

I Like Ike

The Democrats had occupied the White House for the previous 20 years. In 1952 they nominated Governor Adlai Stevenson of Illinois. A political moderate, the witty, sophisticated Stevenson was burdened by Truman's unpopularity.

Stevenson's Republican opponent was Dwight David Eisenhower. An aging war hero, Eisenhower promised to end the war in Korea and battle communism and corruption at home. His message and grandfatherly image appealed to many voters. "I like Ike" campaign buttons and posters captured the public sentiment. Eisenhower won a landslide victory, even carying several southern states and winning big in urban areas, traditional Democratic strongholds.

Few people had advanced so far while making so few enemies. An accomplished athlete and a good student, Ike earned an appointment to West Point, where he graduated in 1915. As an army officer, Eisenhower demonstrated rare organizational abilities and a capacity for complex detail work. With the outbreak of World War II, he was promoted with startling rapidity. General George C. Marshall passed over 366 more senior officers to promote Eisenhower to major general and appoint him commander of the European Theater of Operations. It was Ike who planned and oversaw America's invasions of North Africa, Sicily, and Italy, and who led the combined British-American D-Day invasion of France. By the end of the war, Ike was a four-star general and an international hero.

As president, Eisenhower practiced a brand of leadership that was strikingly different from Roosevelt and Truman. Preferring a behind-the-scenes approach to his executive duties, Eisenhower in public seemed friendly, outgoing, quick to please, but only slightly interested in being president. His "hidden hand" leadership relied upon a chain-of-command system that allowed him to delegate authority while keeping the major decisions of his administration in his own hands. Ike was in charge, but he left the detail work and the political battling to his subordinates.

Ike called himself a conservative, "but an extremely liberal conservative," one who was concerned with fiscal prudence but not at the expense of human beings. Throughout his eight years in office Eisenhower focused closely on two major priorities: U.S.–Soviet relations and a balanced budget. These issues, not civil or other important social concerns, occupied most of his attention. Ike termed his approach "modern Republicanism." In practice this approach led his administration to cut spending but not to attempt any rollback of New Deal social legislation.

During Ike's two terms the country made steady and at times spectacular economic progress. In 1955 the minimum wage was raised from 75 cents to $1 per hour, and during the 1950s the average family income rose 15 percent. Work was plentiful, and unemployment was extremely low. Stable prices, full employment, and steady growth were the economic hallmarks of the 1950s. Although the population increased by 28 million people, the country was on the whole better housed and fed than ever before. Especially for white Americans, "modern Republicanism" seemed a viable alternative to New Dealism.

A Country of Wheels

If Eisenhower labored to curtail the role of the federal government in some areas, he expanded it in others. As an expert on military logistics, Ike frequently expressed concern about the sad state of the American highway system. During World War II he had been impressed by Hitler's system of *Autobahnen,* which allowed the German dictator to deploy troops to different parts of Germany with incredible speed. From his first days in office Eisenhower worked for legislation to improve America's highway network.

A loose collection of pressure groups, including the automobile, trucking, bus, oil, rubber, asphalt, and construction industries, pushed for a new federally subsidized interstate highway system. Not only would such a project provide millions of new jobs, it would contribute to a safer America by making it easier to evacuate major cities in the event of a nuclear attack.

As a result of presidential and lobby pressure, in 1956 Congress passed the National System of Interstate and Defense Highways Act, the most significant piece of domestic legislation enacted under Eisenhower. As planned, the system would cover more than 40,000 miles, cost $26 billion, and take 13 years to construct. Although it took longer to complete and cost far more than Congress projected, it did create thousands of jobs and provided the United States with the world's most extensive superhighway system.

More than any other piece of legislation, the Highways Act also changed America, altering its culture and landscape. It accelerated the decline of the inner city and the flight to the suburbs. As downtown businesses, hotels, and theaters closed, suburban shopping malls with multiscreen cinemas and roadside motels began to dot the American highway landscape. Drive-in theaters, gasoline service stations, mobile homes, and multicar garages signified the birth of a new extended society, one without a clear center or focus.

America's commitment to highways and cars created numerous problems. Mass transportation suffered most conspicuously. Streetcars and commuter railroads languished, as did the country's major interstate railroads. In the years since the end of World War II, 75 percent of government expenditures for transportation have gone for highways as opposed to one percent for urban mass transit. As a result, those without the use of automobiles—the old, the very young, the poor, the handicapped—became victims of America's automobile obsession.

Ike, Dulles, and the World

For Eisenhower, "modern Republicanism" was more than simply a domestic economic credo. It also implied an internationalist foreign policy. As with domestic policy, in foreign policy Ike preferred to operate behind the scenes. But he did make all major foreign policy decisions.

The point man for Ike's foreign policy was Secretary of State John Foster Dulles. Rigid and moralistic, Dulles took himself, his Presbyterian religion, and the world seriously. One Washington correspondent described him as "a card-carrying Christian," and he frequently delivered lectures on the evils of "atheistic, materialistic Communism." Although Eisenhower and Dulles had strikingly different public styles, they shared a common vision of the world. Both were internationalists and cold warriors who believed that the Soviet Union was the enemy and that the United States was and should be the protector of the free world. Peace was their objective, but never a peace won by appeasement. To keep honorable peace, both were willing to consider the use of nuclear weapons and go to the brink of war.

Occasionally Dulles's impassioned anti-Communist rhetoric obscured the actual policies pursued by the Eisenhower administration. In public, Dulles rejected the containment doctrine as a "negative, futile and immoral policy" and advocated the "liberation" of Eastern Europe, using nuclear weapons if necessary to achieve America's objectives.

In reality, Eisenhower's objectives were far more limited and his approach toward foreign policy much more cautious. Ike supported containment, but he viewed Truman's approach as unorganized and far too expensive. Ike believed that the United States could not support every country that claimed to be fighting communism. If America continued Truman's policies, the costs would soon become higher than Americans would be willing to pay. A change, Ike maintained, was needed.

Eisenhower termed his adjustments of the containment doctrine the "New Look." In order to save money, he decided to emphasize nuclear weapons over conventional weapons, a "more bang for the buck" approach that drew angry criticism. Congressional hawks claimed that Eisenhower was "putting too many eggs in the nuclear basket," and liberals suggested that the program would inevitably lead to nuclear destruction.

Whatever the criticisms, the New Look did save money. While air and missile forces were expanded, the army's budget was greatly reduced. The results of Eisenhower's approach were dramatic. Between 1953 and 1956 the defense budget was cut by $14.6 billion, and troop levels were reduced by almost one-third.

The New Look took an unconventional approach to conventional warfare. Ike had learned from Truman's mistakes in Korea. America could not send weapons and men to all corners of the world to contain communism. Instead, the New Look emphasized the threat of massive retaliation to keep order, and reinforced America's position with a series of foreign alliances that encouraged indigenous troops and peoples to resist Communist expansion. Finally, Eisenhower used the Central Intelligence Agency as a covert foreign policy arm. Through assassinations and political coups engineered by the CIA, Eisenhower was able to prevent—or at least forestall—the emergence of anti-America regimes.

A New Face in Moscow

The world changed dramatically a few months after Eisenhower took office. In March 1953, Joseph Stalin died. Always fearful of rivals, Stalin did not groom a successor. The result was a power struggle within the Kremlin, from which Nikita Khrushchev emerged as the winner.

Short, rotund, and bald, Khrushchev, unlike Stalin, enjoyed meeting people, making speeches, and traveling abroad. If occasionally he lost his temper and uttered belligerent remarks (he once even took off his shoe and pounded it on a table at the United Nations), Khrushchev did try to lessen the tensions between the Soviet Union and the United States.

Ike shared Khrushchev's dream for peaceful coexistence between the two nations and used Stalin's death as an opportunity to extend an olive branch. The Soviet Union peacefully responded. During 1955 the nations resolved several thorny issues: The Soviets repatriated German prisoners of war held since World War II, established relations with Greece and Israel, gave up claims to Turkish territory, and withdrew from their occupation zone in Austria.

In July 1955 the two leaders met in Geneva, Switzerland, for a summit conference. During the meeting Eisenhower suggested that the United States and the Soviet Union allow aerial surveillance and photography of each other's nations to lessen the chance of a possible surprise attack. Although Khrushchev rejected this "open skies" proposal, the two leaders seemed to be working toward the same peaceful ends. "A new spirit of conciliation and cooperation" had been achieved, Ike announced. Unfortunately, "the Spirit of Geneva" would not survive the confrontations ahead.

1956: The Dangerous Year

While working toward peaceful coexistence, both Eisenhower and Khrushchev had to satisfy critics at home. In Washington, Dulles continued to call for the "liberation" of Eastern Europe and hinted that the United States would rally behind any Soviet-dominated country that rebelled. In reality, Eisenhower was not about to risk war with the Soviet Union over Eastern Europe.

At the same time, Khrushchev often promised more than he would or could deliver. On February 24, 1956, for example, Khrushchev delivered a four-hour speech before the Twentieth Party Congress, in which he condemned the former dictator's domestic crimes and foreign policy mistakes, endorsed "peaceful coexistence" with the West, and indicated that he was willing to allow greater freedom behind the "iron curtain." Although the speech was supposed to be secret, the CIA obtained copies and distributed them throughout Eastern Europe.

Poland took Khrushchev at his word and moved in a more liberal, anti-Stalinist direction. Since it did not attempt to withdraw from the Soviet bloc, Khrushchev allowed Poland to move along its more liberal course. What Poland had won, Hungary wanted—and more. In October 1956, an uprising in Budapest brought a more liberal government to power which the Soviets recognized. However, when the new government announced that it planned to pull out of the Warsaw Pact (the Soviet-dominated defense community that was created in response to NATO), Khrushchev sent Soviet tanks and soldiers into Budapest to crush what he now termed a "counterrevolution." Killing hundreds of demonstrators, the Soviets brutally restored their control over Hungary. All the while the Eisenhower administration watched, demonstrating that the notion of "liberation" was mere rhetoric, not policy.

At the time of the Soviet move into Budapest, Eisenhower was more concerned with problems in Egypt, whose nationalistic leader, President Gamal Abdel Nasser, was struggling to remain neutral in the Cold War. When Nasser recognized the People's Republic of China and pursued amicable relations with the Soviet Union, the Eisenhower administration withdrew a proposed loan to help build the Aswan Dam on the Nile. Nasser struck back by nationalizing the Suez Canal, the waterway linking the oil-rich Gulf of Suez and the Mediterranean. Half of Western Europe's oil came through the Suez Canal, which many considered essential to the security of Western Europe. British and French leaders were outraged, loudly claiming that the seizure threatened their Middle Eastern oil supplies. Eisenhower counseled caution, but Britain, France, and Israel resorted to "drastic actions." On October 29, 1956 Israel invaded Egypt, and Britain and France used the hostilities as a pretext to seize the Suez Canal.

Furious, Eisenhower refused to support the invasion. He interrupted his reelection campaign to return to Washington. Ike told Dulles to inform the Israelis that "we're going to apply sanctions, we're going to the United Nations, we're going to do everything that there is so we can stop this thing." Cut off from American support and faced with angry Soviet threats, Britain, France, and Israel halted their operations.

Sputnik *and Sputtering Rockets*

In foreign affairs, Eisenhower's second term was less successful than his first. Age and health may have contributed to this turn of events. During his first four years in office, Ike suffered a heart attack and a bout with ileitis, which entailed a serious operation. During his second term, he was more apt to take vacations and play golf and bridge with his close friends.

John Foster Dulles's health was also declining. During the Suez crisis doctors discovered that he had cancer. Acute physical pain punctuated his last years as secretary of state, and he died in 1959.

More than ill health plagued Ike's foreign policy. Soviet technological advances created a mood of edginess in American foreign policy and military circles. In 1957 the Soviet Union successfully launched *Sputnik,* the first artificial satellite to orbit the earth. Less than one month later, the Soviet Union launched its second *Sputnik,* this one built on a larger and grander scale, carrying a small dog which was wired with devices to gauge the effects of zero gravity on bodily functions. If the first *Sputnik* demonstrated that the Soviets had gained the high ground, the second indicated that they intended to go higher and to place men in space.

Before the year was out, the United States tried to respond with a satellite of its own. Code-named *Vanguard,* the satellite was placed on the top of a three-stage navy rocket that was launched on December 6. The rocket blew up only seconds after lift-off. It was the first of a series of highly publicized American rocket launches that ended with the sputtering sound of failure.

Sputnik forced Americans to question themselves and their own values. Had the country become soft and overly consumer-oriented? While Soviet students were studying calculus, physics, and chemistry, had American students spent too much time in shop, home economics, and driver education classes? More important, did *Sputnik* give the Soviet Union a military edge over the United States? If a Soviet rocket could put a thousand-pound ball in orbit, could the same rocket armed with a nuclear warhead hit a target in the United States? Such questions disturbed ordinary Americans and U.S. policymakers alike.

In truth, Americans overrated the importance of *Sputnik.* Launching a satellite was one thing; delivering a warhead to a specific target was quite another matter. That entailed sophisticated guidance systems, which the Soviet Union had not developed. Nonetheless American policymakers responded with more money for "defense-related" research and funneled more dollars into American higher education. In an attempt to improve science and mathematics skills, Congress passed the National Defense Education Act (1958) to help finance the undergraduate and graduate educations of promising students. Congress also organized the National Aeronautics and Space Administration (NASA) and allotted the agency huge sums of money in order to get ahead in the "space race."

Third-World Challenges

If *Sputnik* was largely an illusionary challenge, nationalist movements in the Third World created more serious problems. Eisenhower's response to

U.S. efforts to compete with the Soviet Union's space advances suffered a major setback when the *Vanguard* exploded two seconds after takeoff on December 6, 1957.

such movements varied from case to case. On the one hand, he opposed Britain and France's efforts to use aggression to whip Egypt into line. On the other hand, Ike employed covert CIA operations to achieve his foreign policy goals. In 1953 the CIA planned and executed a coup d'état that replaced a popularly elected government in Iran with a pro-American regime headed by Shah Mohammad Reza Pahlavi. The reason for the coup was that the elected government had taken over Iranian oil resources that the British had been exploiting. One year later the CIA master-minded the overthrow of a leftist government in Guatemala and replaced it with an unpopular but strongly pro-American government.

To keep order in what he believed were areas vital to American interests, Eisenhower would even resort to armed intervention. In 1958 Lebanese Moslems, backed by Egypt and Syria, threatened a revolt against the Beirut government dominated by the Christian minority. President Camille Chamoun appealed to Eisenhower for support. Concerned with Middle Eastern oil, Ike ordered marines from America's Sixth Fleet into Lebanon. Once order was restored and Lebanese politicians had agreed on a successor to Chamoun, Ike withdrew the troops.

In 1959 revolutionary Fidel Castro overthrew Fulgencio Batista, a right-wing dictator who had encouraged American investments in Cuba at the expense of the Cuban people. Castro quickly set about to change the situation. He confiscated land and properties in Cuba owned by Americans, executed former Batista officials, built hospitals and schools, ended racial segregation, improved workers' wages, and moved leftward. Before long, Castro had begun to jail writers and critics, hold public executions, postpone elections, and condemn the United States.

Instead of waiting for Cuba's anti-American feelings to subside, Eisenhower decided to move against Castro. He gave the CIA permission to plan an attack on Cuba by a group of anti-Castro exiles, a plan that would culminate with the disastrous Bay of Pigs invasion (see Chapter 29). As one of his last acts as president, in 1961 Eisenhower severed diplomatic relations with Cuba. Such actions only increased Castro's anti-American resolve and further drove him into the arms of the Soviet Union.

Ultimately, the Truman and Eisenhower brands of containment were unsuccessful in dealing with nationalistic independence movements. Such movements dominated the postwar world. Between 1944 and 1974, for example, 78 countries won their independence. These included more than one billion people, or close to one-third of the world's population. As the CIA activities in Guatemala, Iran, and Cuba indicated, short-term benefits came with long-term costs. Increasingly, the United States became identified with unpopular, undemocratic, and intolerant right-wing regimes. Such actions tarnished America's image in the Third World.

Not with a Bang, But a Whimper

Going into his last year in office, Eisenhower hoped to improve on the foreign policy record of his second term. Since his last meeting with Khrushchev in Geneva, the Cold War had intensified. In particular, the Soviets were once again threatening to cut off Western access to West

Berlin, an action Eisenhower feared might lead to a nuclear war. To solve the problem—or at least to neutralize it—Khrushchev visited the United States and agreed to a formal summit meeting set for May 1960 in Paris.

The two world leaders never again had serious talks. Just before the meeting the Soviets shot down an American U-2 spy plane over their territory. During the previous few years, U-2 missions had kept Eisenhower abreast of Soviet military developments and convinced him that *Sputnik* posed no military threat to the United States. Nevertheless, the existence of such planes was a military secret, and U-2 pilots had strict orders to self-destruct their planes rather than be forced down in enemy territory.

Assuming that the pilot had followed orders, Eisenhower responded to the Soviet charges of spying by publicly announcing that the Soviets had shot down a weather plane that had blown off course. Unfortunately for Ike, the pilot, Francis Gary Powers, had not followed orders, and the Soviets had him and the wreckage of his plane. Trying to save the summit, Khrushchev offered Eisenhower a way to save face. The Soviet leader indicated that he was sure that Eisenhower had not known about the flights. Eisenhower, however, accepted full personal responsibility and refused to apologize for actions he deemed were in defense of America. Rather than appear soft himself, Khrushchev refused to engage in the Paris summit.

Eisenhower's presidency ended on this note of failure. A chance to improve Soviet-American relations had been lost. But the end of his presidency should not obscure his positive accomplishments. He had concluded one war, kept America out of several others, limited military spending, and presided over seven and a half years of relative peace. Like George Washington, when Eisenhower left office he issued warnings to America about possible future problems. In particular, he noted, the "military-industrial complex"—an alliance between government and business—could threaten the nation's democratic processes.

We Shall Overcome

When Dwight Eisenhower took office in early 1953, racism—often institutionalized, sometimes less formal—was the order of the day. Below the Mason-Dixon line it reached its most virulent form in the Jim Crow laws that governed the everyday existence of southern blacks, and subjected them to daily bouts of degradation and soul-destroying humiliation. Whites framed these laws to separate the races and to demonstrate white superiority and black inferiority. Jim Crow dictated that whites and blacks eat in separate restaurants, drink from separate water fountains, sleep in separate hotels, and learn in separate schools. Jim Crow etiquette dictated that blacks give way on sidewalks to whites, speak respectfully to whites of all ages (whites addressed blacks of all ages by their first names), and give up their seats to whites when buses were full. Although the underpinning of the Jim Crow laws was the "separate but equal" doctrine enunciated in *Plessy* v. *Ferguson* (1896), both blacks and whites realized that subjugation, not equality, was the object of the laws.

North of Dixie the situation was not much better. To be sure, rigid Jim Crow laws did not exist, but blacks were informally excluded from the better schools, neighborhoods, and jobs. Whites argued that the development of ghettos was a natural process, not some sort of racist agreement between white realtors. Such, however, was not the case. William Levitt, the most famous post-World War II builder of suburban housing, attempted to keep blacks out of his developments by drafting neighborhood covenants that denied occupancy to blacks. Even after the courts struck down such restrictions, Levitt instructed his realtors not to sell to blacks. Indeed, *Shelley* v. *Kraemer* (1948), the case that stated that state courts could not uphold housing restrictions, only declared such restrictions legally unenforceable; it did not outlaw such practices per se.

When Ike left office in 1961, segregation remained largely unchanged. During his years in office, however, African Americans did make significant strides in their quest for civil rights. In particular, during the decade after 1954 blacks won a series of legal victories that in theory if not always in practice buried Jim Crow. These were years of joy and years of sadness, when the best as well as the worst aspects of the American character were clearly visible.

Taking Jim Crow to Court

World War II underscored the yawning gap between the promise and reality of life in America. Fighting against Nazi racist theories helped to draw attention to real racial problems at home. After the war, conditions improved, but at a snail's pace. With an eye on black Democratic northern voters, Truman established the President's Committee on Civil Rights, which issued a report that most white politicians ignored. While Truman called for "fair employment throughout the federal establishment" and ordered the racial desegregation of the armed services, southern politicians railed against these moderate reforms.

By the late 1940s African Americans realized that they would have to lead the fight against racial injustice themselves. In the early years of the battle the NAACP spearheaded the struggle. But the organization faced a number of problems, both within and outside the black community. For example, many blacks believed the NAACP was racist and elitist, since the organization was staffed by educated middle-class blacks who seemed out of touch with the majority of their race.

Mindful of white hostility, the NAACP moved cautiously. Instead of attacking segregation head-on and demanding full equality, the organization chose to chip away at the legal edges of Jim Crow. The separate but equal doctrine was particularly vulnerable, as NAACP lawyers demonstrated the impossibility, even the absurdity, of applying the yardstick to graduate education and law schools. The Supreme Court agreed. If, the court implied, separate but equal educational systems were to be continued, then states had to pay more than lip service to equality.

In grade school and high school education, just as in higher education, the South translated separate but equal to read "separate and highly unequal." In South Carolina's Clarendon County, for example, the county spent $179 per year on each white student and $43 per year on each black student. Intellectual and financial considerations were not the only factors that precluded equality. Psychologists argued that segregation instilled feelings of inferiority among black children, causing grave psychological damage.

In 1952 the NAACP consolidated a series of cases under the name of the first case—*Brown* v. *Board of Education of Topeka*—which challenged the very existence of the separate but equal doctrine. After months of deliberation, Chief Justice Earl Warren read the Supreme Court's unanimous decision on May 17, 1954: "Separate educational facilities are inherently unequal."

The *Chicago Defender* labeled the *Brown* decision "a second emancipation proclamation," and the *Washington Post* called it "a new birth of freedom." But such court decisions have to be enforced. As Charles Houston, an NAACP lawyer, remarked, "Nobody needs to explain to a Negro the difference between the law in the books and the law in action."

A Failure of Leadership

A year after the *Brown* decision the Supreme Court ruled that schools should desegregate "with all deliberate speed." This second decision placed the burden of desegregation in the hands of local, state, and national leaders. If the process was to be accomplished with the minimum amount of conflict, those leaders would have to be firm in their resolve to see justice done. Such, however, would not be the case.

On the national level, Eisenhower moved uncomfortably and cautiously on the issue of civil rights and desegregation. Having spent most of his life in a segregated army, Ike did not see racism as a great moral issue, and he was unresponsive to the black demand for equality. He believed that the *Brown* decision had been a mistake. When questioned about the case, he claimed, "I don't believe you can change the hearts of men with laws or decisions."

The brand of Ike's leadership and his ambitions for the Republican party further weakened his response. His behind-the-scenes approach led him to avoid speaking out clearly and forcefully on the subject. Moral outrage was not his style. In addition, he was popular in the South and harbored hopes of bringing that section of the country into the Republican party. Finally, his commitment to integration was lukewarm at best, and he placed controlling military spending above desegregating the South.

If Eisenhower had acted decisively in support of the *Brown* v. *Board of Education* decision—if he had placed the full weight of his office behind desegregation—there is some evidence that the South would have complied peacefully with the verdict. By not acting forcefully, however, Eisenhower strengthened the position of southern opponents of desegregation.

The Little Rock crisis demonstrated the failure of national and state leadership. In 1957 in Little Rock, Arkansas, school officials were ordered to desegregate their classrooms. As they prepared to do so, Governor Orval Faubus, locked in a reelection fight, intervened. He announced that any integration attempt would disrupt public order and sent in the National Guard to prevent black children from entering Central High. While Eisenhower quietly tried to maneuver behind the scenes, a crisis brewed. On the morning of September 23, 1957, when black children attempted to attend school, they were inhospitably greeted by an angry mob.

Television turned the ugly episode into a national drama. Millions of Americans witnessed violent racism for the first time. Television gave a face to racism, a concept that for many white Americans was still an abstraction. For the first but not last time, television aided the cause of civil rights by conveying the human suffering caused by racism.

To restore order, Eisenhower federalized the Arkansas National Guard and sent 1,000 paratroopers from the 101st Airborne Division to Little Rock. Although their presence desegregated Central High in 1957, the following year Faubus closed Little Rock's public schools. Taken together, Faubus's shortsighted political moves and Eisenhower's refusal to take action until public order had been disrupted created a crisis that more decisive leadership might have avoided.

The Word from Montgomery

The failure of white leaders convinced African Americans that court orders would not magically produce equal rights. Many blacks realized this

Paratroopers escorted black students to and from school in Little Rock, Arkansas, after violence erupted when the schools were instructed to desegregate.

even before the Little Rock crisis. On a cold afternoon in 1955 in Montgomery, Alabama, Rosa Parks, a well-respected black seamstress who was active in the NAACP, took a significant stride toward equality. She boarded a bus and sat in the first row of the "colored" section. The white section of the bus quickly filled, and, according to Jim Crow rules, blacks were expected to give up their seats rather than force whites to stand. Mrs. Parks, however, stayed seated. The bus stopped, the driver summoned the police, and Rosa Parks was arrested.

Black Montgomery rallied to Mrs. Parks's side. Like her, they were tired of riding in the back of the bus, tired of giving up their seats to whites, tired of having their lives restricted by Jim Crow. Local black leaders decided to organize a boycott of Montgomery's white-owned and white-operated bus system. They hoped that economic pressure would force changes that court decisions could not. For the next 381 days, more than 90 percent of Montgomery's black citizens participated in a heroic and successful demonstration against racial segregation.

To lead the boycott, Montgomery blacks turned to the new minister of the Dexter Avenue Baptist Church, a young man named Martin Luther King, Jr. Reared in Atlanta, the son of a respected minister, King had a doctorate in theology from Boston University. King believed in the power of nonviolent, direct action, and he possessed a gift for oratory that stirred people's souls. In King, the civil rights movement had found a genuine spokesperson, one who preached a doctrine of change guided by Christian love, not racial hatred. "In our protest," he observed, "there will be no cross burnings. No white person will be taken from his home by a hooded Negro mob and brutally murdered. There will be no threats and no intimidation."

The success of the Montgomery boycott inspired nonviolent black protests elsewhere in the South. Increasingly, young African Americans took the lead. Within a few months of the successful conclusion of the Montgomery boycott, demonstrations erupted in 54 cities in nine states. The protesters were arrested, jailed, beaten, and even knocked off their feet by high-pressure fire hoses, but still they challenged the traditional order.

The protests were widely reported in the country's newspapers and televised nightly on the news shows. They confronted Americans everywhere with the stark reality of segregation. As the violence continued, pressure mounted on white national politicians to take decisive action. By the early 1960s the time had come for freedom to become a reality.

The Sounds of Change

Beginning in the 1970s, American advertisers started to market a new commodity—the fifties. They marketed it as a Golden Decade, an age of innocence, tranquility, and static charm, a carefree time before the assassination of John F. Kennedy, the Vietnam War, and Watergate. According to the popular myth, kids in the 1950s thought "dope" referred to a dull-witted person, parents married for life, and major family problems revolved around whether or not "sis" had a date for the prom. In truth, however, that carefully packaged Golden Decade hardly existed. Instead, the decade was alive with dynamic, creative tensions.

Father Knows Best

The stock television situation comedy of the 1950s centered on a white family with a happily married husband and wife and two or three well-adjusted children. Most often, the family lived in a white, two-story suburban home, from which the father ventured daily to his white-collar job. The wife did not work outside the house—the husband made a comfortable living and, in any case, mothers were supposed to stay home and tend the children. "Father Knows Best," which ran from 1954 to 1962, was the classic example of this genre.

Television programs of the 1950s often centered around a happy, well-adjusted suburban family with two or three children.

The picture these sitcoms presented was generally correct. Starting after World War II, Americans moved steadily toward the suburbs, which during the 1950s grew six times faster than cities. Several factors contributed to this migration. The high price of urban real estate had driven industries out of the cities, and as always in American history, the population followed the jobs. In addition, developers built abundant, inexpensive homes, which newly married couples, aided by VA and FHA loans, purchased.

The television image of predominantly white suburban families was an accurate reflection of American demographic patterns. A far greater percentage of whites than blacks moved to the suburbs. Housing and job restrictions worked to keep blacks in the central cities while allowing whites to inhabit the suburban areas.

Even the sitcom image of the suburban housewife preoccupied with her husband and her family was correct. American women in the 1950s married younger, had children sooner, and raised larger families than they had in the previous two decades. The best-sellers list indicated America's concern with children and its glorification of motherhood. Between 1946 and 1976 the pocket edition of Dr. Benjamin Spock's *Baby and Child Care* sold over 23 million copies. The best-seller *Modern Woman: The Lost Sex* went so far as to say that an independent woman was "a contradiction in terms." The ideal woman, writers observed, was content being a wife and a mother or, in a word, a homemaker.

The Other Side of the Coin

"Father Knows Best" and other television shows portrayed an ideal world where serious problems seldom intruded and where life lacked complexity. In fact, the move to suburbia and the changes in family life forced Americans to reevaluate many of their beliefs.

Some observers claimed that life in suburbia fostered mindless conformity. Social critic Lewis Mumford described suburbs as "a multitude of uniform, unidentifiable houses, lined up inflexibly, at uniform distances, on uniform roads, in a treeless communal wasteland, inhabited by people of the same class, the same income, the same age group."

Some writers feared the United States had become a country of unthinking consumers driven by advertisers to desire only the latest gadget. Americans bought automobiles, houses, and electrical appliances as never before. While this enormous buying spree fueled the tremendous economic growth between 1945 and 1970, was it beneficial to the individuals who spent more and more of their time in their cars and watching their televisions? Cultural observers despaired.

Some women also expressed frustration about their roles as wives and mothers. Although many women worked, cultural stereotyping prevented most of them from rising to the higher paying, more prestigious positions. In addition, Betty Friedan, a leader in the women's rights movement, noted that those women who did place a career above marriage or family were regarded as abnormal.

Numerous films, novels, and articles explored the problems of suburban life. The film *Invasion of the Body Snatchers* (1956) was an outstanding example of the fear that suburbia had created a nation of conformists. In the movie, the inhabitants of the town Santa Mira are turned into emotionless shells by giant pods from outer space. Utterly lacking individuality, the pod people, as one explains, had been "reborn into an untroubled world, where everyone's the same." In that world, "there is no need for love or emotion." For such cultural critics as David Riesman, author of *The Lonely Crowd* (1955), America's acceptance of conformity threatened to make podism a form of reality.

The critics, however, overreacted to the "suburban threat." If the houses looked the same, the people were individuals. In the suburbs, white working-class families could afford for the first time to purchase homes and live middle-class lives. This was a real accomplishment. The problems that critics observed in the suburbs—the tendency toward conformity, cultural homogeneity, materialism, and anxiety over gender roles—were urban problems as well.

The Meaning of Elvis

The harshest critics of "suburban values" were American youths. Their criticism took different forms. Some of it was thoughtful and formalized, the result of the best efforts of young intellectuals. At other times it took a more visceral form, a protest that came from the gut rather than the mind. Of the second type of protest, none was more widely embraced by youths—or roundly attacked by adults—than rock and roll.

Rock and roll was the product of a heterogeneous American culture. It combined black rhythm and blues with white country music. It was made possible by the post–World War II demographic changes. The movement of southern blacks and whites to the cities of the upper South and North threw together different musical traditions and forged an entirely new sound.

Confronting conventional morality, rock and roll was openly vulgar. Its lyrics and heavy beat challenged the accepted standards of "good taste" in music. The very term—"rock 'n' roll"—had long been used in blues songs to describe lovemaking, and early black rock-and-roll singers, such as Little Richard and Bo Diddley, glorified physical relationships.

From its emergence in the early 1950s, rock and roll generated angry criticism. In the South white church groups attacked it as part of a plot to corrupt the morals of southern youths and foster integration. Between 1954 and 1958 there were numerous crusades to ban rock and roll from the airwaves.

Much of the criticism of rock and roll focused on Elvis Presley, who more than any other artist most successfully fused country music with rhythm and blues. Presley exuded sexuality. When he appeared on the Ed Sullivan Show, network executives instructed cameramen to avoid shots of Elvis's suggestive physical movements. Presley upset segregationists by performing the music of black artists. The head of Sun Records, Sam Phillips, had once claimed, "If I could find a white man who had the

Negro sound and the Negro feel, I could make a million dollars." Presley was that white man.

In the end, however, the protests implicit in Elvis Presley and rock and roll were largely co-opted by middle-class American culture. Record producers, most of whom were white, smoothed the jagged edges of rock and roll. Sexually explicit black recordings were rewritten and rere-corded—a process known as "covering"—by white performers and then sold to white youths. By 1959 rock and roll had become an accepted part of mainstream American popular culture.

A Different Beat

Rock-and-roll artists never rejected the idea of success in America. If they challenged conventional sexual mores and tried to create a unique sound, they accepted the rewards of success in a capitalistic society. Not all youth protests, however, were so easily absorbed into middle-class culture. The Beat movement, for example, questioned the values at the heart of that culture.

The Beat Generation extolled the very things that conventional Amer-icans abhorred, and they rejected what the others prized. Beats scorned

Elvis Presley, one of the great pioneers of rock-and-roll music, was the target of much controversy throughout his life.

materialism, traditional family life, religion, sexuality, and politics. Instead, they valued spontaneity and intuition, searching for truth through Eastern mysticism and drugs. Allen Ginsberg, the leading poet of the Beat Generation, preached a life based on experimentation and developed an authentic poetic voice. In 1955 he wrote "Howl," the prototypical Beat poem. Written under the influence of drugs, "Howl" is a literary kaleidoscope, a breathless succession of stark images and passionate beliefs.

Ginsberg and Jack Kerouac, the leading Beat novelist, outraged adults but discovered followers on college campuses and in cities across America. They tapped an underground dissatisfaction with the prevailing blandness of conventional culture. In this their appeal was similar to that of rock and roll. Both were scattering seeds that would bear fruit during the next decade.

Chronology of Key Events

1944	GI Bill of Rights grants veterans aid for education, loans for homes and businesses
1948	President Truman bans segregation in armed forces
1953	Dwight D. Eisenhower becomes thirty-fourth president; Stalin dies; Nikita Khrushchev emerges as leader of Soviet Union; CIA helps bring Shah Mohammad Reza Pahlavi to power in Iran
1954	CIA masterminds overthrow of leftist government of Guatemala; *Brown* v. *Board of Education of Topeka* holds that "separate educational facilities are inherently unequal"
1955	Emmett Till murder; Montgomery, Alabama, bus boycott; Eisenhower and Khrushchev hold summit in Geneva, Switzerland
1956	Hungarian uprising crushed; Suez crisis
1957	Troops sent to Little Rock, Arkansas; *Sputnik* launched
1958	U.S. marines intervene in Lebanon; Congress passes the National Defense Education Act to provide federal aid to schools and colleges
1959	Cuban Revolution
1960	U-2 spy plane is shot down over the Soviet Union

Conclusion

Ike's America was both more and less than what it seemed. In foreign and domestic affairs Eisenhower appeared to allow his subordinates to run the country, when in reality he made the important decisions. Whether it was national highways or the Middle East, Eisenhower's vision of order helped shape American policy. He was more influential than most Americans during the 1950s realized.

If Eisenhower was more active than he appeared, then the country was more dynamic than it seemed on the surface. Although critics railed against the conformity of suburban America, everywhere there were signs of change. During the 1950s African Americans quickened the pace of their struggle for equality and youths experimented with alternatives to traditional behavior. And increasingly these two rebellions merged to form a distinct subculture. During the 1960s the war in Vietnam would give a political edge to that subculture.

Suggestions for Further Reading

Good overviews of social, cultural, and political developments in postwar America can be found in William H. Chafe, *The Unfinished Journey*, 2d ed. (1991); William Leuchtenburg, *A Troubled Feast*, rev. ed. (1983); Richard Polenberg, *One Nation Divisible* (1980); Emily and Norman Rosenberg, *In Our Times*, 4th ed. (1991); Howard Zinn, *Postwar America* (1973).

Important studies of the Eisenhower presidency include Stephen E. Ambrose, *Eisenhower*, 2 vols. (1983–1984); Fred I. Greenstein, *The Hidden-Hand Presidency* (1982). Foreign policy during the Eisenhower years is dealt with in Robert A. Divine, *Eisenhower and the Cold War* (1981); Townsend Hoopes, *The Devil and John Foster Dulles* (1973); Richard Immerman, *The CIA in Guatemala* (1982); Richard Melanson and David Mayers, eds., *Reevaluating Eisenhower* (1987); Richard Welch, Jr., *Response to Revolution: The United States and the Cuban Revolution* (1985).

The postwar civil rights movement is examined in William Berman, *The Politics of Civil Rights in the Truman Administration* (1970); Richard Dalfiume, *Desegregation of the U.S. Armed Forces* (1969); David Garrow, *Bearing the Cross* (1986); David L. Lewis, *King*, 2d ed. (1978); Richard Kluger, *Simple Justice* (1976); Manning Marable, *Race, Reform, and Rebellion* (1991); Stephen B. Oates, *Let the Trumpet Sound: The Life of Martin Luther King, Jr.* (1982); Harvard Sitkoff, *The Struggle for Black Equality* (1981).

For studies of specific social and cultural trends, see Erik Barnauw *Tube of Plenty*, 2d ed. (1990); Carl Belz, *The Story of Rock*, 2d ed. (1972); Bruce Cook,

The Beat Generation (1971); David Marc, *Demographic Vistas: Television in American Culture* (1984); Douglas Miller and Marion Nowak, *The Fifties* (1977); David Riesman, *The Lonely Crowd* (1950); Lynn Spigel, *Make Room for TV* (1992).

The suburbanization of America is examined in Scott Donaldson, *The Suburban Myth* (1969); James Flink, *The Car Culture* (1975); John Kenneth Galbraith, *The Affluent Society,* 4th ed. (1984); Herbert Gans, *The Levittowners* (1967); Kenneth Jackson, *The Crabgrass Frontier* (1985).

Chapter 29

Vietnam and the Crisis of Authority

Ho Chi Minh was a tiny, frail, splinter of a man. He was gentle, and in public always deferential. Even after he had come to sole power in North Vietnam, he steadfastly avoided all the trappings of authority, favoring the simple shorts and sandals worn by the Vietnamese peasants. He was sure of who he was, certain of his place in Vietnamese history, and he had no desire to impress others with his position. To his followers, he was "Uncle Ho," who treated all Vietnamese citizens like the children he never had. But in the pursuit of Vietnamese independence and the realization of a Communist nation, Ho could be cold-blooded and ruthless.

Born around 1890 in a village in a central province of Vietnam, Ho left Vietnam in 1912 and began a generation-long world odyssey. Signing aboard a French freighter, he moved from one port to the next, including Boston, New York City, and San Francisco. He was amazed not only by America's skyscrapers but also by the fact that immigrants in the United States enjoyed the same legal rights as American citizens. He was also struck by the impatience of the American people, their expectations of immediate results. (Later, during the Vietnam War, Ho would say to his military leaders, "Don't worry, Americans are an impatient people. When things begin to go wrong, they'll leave.")

After three years of almost constant travel, Ho settled in London, where he lived in squalid quarters and learned that poverty existed even in the wealthiest, most powerful countries. Then it was on to Paris, where he came in contact with the French Left. There he studied, and his nationalist ambitions became tinged with revolutionary teachings. He was still in Paris when World War I ended and the world leaders came to Versailles

Ho Chi Minh was influenced by French socialism and Soviet communism in his goal to liberate Vietnam from the French.

for the Peace Conference. Inspired by Woodrow Wilson's call for national self-determination, Ho wanted to meet Wilson to plead for his country's independence from France. Wilson ignored his request. Ho moved on— farther east and further Left.

He traveled to Moscow, where Lenin had denounced capitalist imperialism. In the Soviet Union Ho embraced communism. In the ideology he saw a road to his ultimate goal, the liberation of Vietnam. By the early 1920s he was actively organizing Vietnamese exiles into a revolutionary force. He lived a life of secrecy, moving from place to place, changing his name, renouncing anything even remotely resembling a personal life.

In 1941 Ho returned to his homeland. The time was right, he believed, to free Vietnam from colonial domination. During the early part of World War II the Japanese had won control of the country from the French; now Ho and his followers would force out the Japanese. Ho allied himself with the United States. Working alongside American Office of Strategic Services (OSS) agents, Ho impressed them with his bravery, intelligence, and unflagging devotion to his cause. On September 2, 1945, borrowing passages from the American Declaration of Independence, Ho declared Vietnamese independence.

The French reasserted their control over Vietnam after the war, but Ho's struggle continued. Although he did not expect to live to see Vietnam free of French domination, he believed that the struggle of others would eventually secure independence. Ho's patience was only one of many qualities that the West found difficult to understand.

A deep intellectual chasm divided Vietnam and the West. The West viewed history as a straight line in which progress was the governing principle. Emphasizing technological advancements and material improvements, westerners glorified change and prized individualism. The Vietnamese were products of different beliefs. Notions of competition, individualism, and technological change were anathema to tradition-bound Vietnamese. For a thousand years they had survived using the same rice-cultivating methods. To survive, the Vietnamese organized life around villages and practiced cooperative existence. Rich people were considered selfish because they gained wealth at the expense of others.

Like wealth, individualism threatened the corporate nature of village life, which was based on social harmony, not individual rights. Nor did the Vietnamese believe in intellectual freedom, which fostered debate and discord, rather than community stability. Americans considered Soviet communism evil in part because it discouraged the exchange of free ideas; Ho Chi Minh was drawn to the doctrine because it provided a set of answers not subject to question.

Motivated by the Cold War, during the period between 1954 and 1973, U.S. officials became convinced that they had to "save" Vietnam from Ho Chi Minh and his Communist brand of nationalism. Given Vietnamese leadership, traditions, and desire for independence, the American intervention in Vietnam was almost certain to fail.

The Illusion of Greatness

Television's President

John Fitzgerald Kennedy was made for television. His tall, thin body gave him the strong vertical line that cameras love, and his tanned looks appealed to women without intimidating men. His public persona, too, was tailor-made for television—wit, irony, and understatement, all delivered with a studied nonchalance.

In the 1960 presidential race Kennedy challenged his Republican opponent Richard M. Nixon to a series of television debates. At the time, Kennedy faced an uphill battle. Kennedy was considered by many to be too young, too handsome, and too wealthy to make an effective president. His undistinguished political record stood in stark contrast to Nixon's work in Congress and eight years as Eisenhower's vice president. In addition, Kennedy was Catholic, and Americans had never elected a Catholic president. Behind in the polls, Kennedy needed a dramatic boost. Against the advice of his campaign manager, Nixon accepted Kennedy's challenge.

The first debate was held in Chicago on September 26, 1960, only a little more than a month before the election. Nixon arrived looking ill and weak. Still recuperating from an infected kneecap, he appeared pale and haggard. Makeup experts offered to hide his heavy beard and soften his jowls, but Nixon accepted only a thin coat of pancake makeup. Kennedy looked very much better, needing neither makeup nor special lighting. He did, however, change suits from gray to dark blue, a color he thought would look better under the bright television lights.

Kennedy spoke first. Although he was nervous, he exuded confidence. Disregarding prearranged ground rules, Kennedy shifted what was supposed to be a debate on domestic issues to one on foreign policy. Nixon fought back. He perspired, scored debating points, produced memorized facts, and struggled to win. But while they heard a knowledgeable candidate, viewers saw an uncertain man, one whose clothes did not fit and whose face looked pasty and white. Kennedy was the clear winner. Only later did Nixon realize that the telecast had been a production, not a debate.

The polls registered the results. Most of the people who were undecided before watching the debate voted for Kennedy. That proved to be the margin of victory. Only one tenth of one percent separated the two candidates. Perhaps the most important result of the election, however, was not Kennedy's victory but the demonstration of the power of television. It came into its own in 1960.

The "Macho" Presidency

John F. Kennedy was the first American president born in the twentieth century, the torchbearer for "a new generation." Competition and an aggressively masculine view of the world ran through his life. He was the son of a multimillionaire who demanded excellence of all his sons and who believed that as Boston Irish Catholics they had to try harder and be tougher than their Protestant neighbors. This was particularly difficult for John Kennedy, who suffered throughout his life from a series of illnesses and chronic physical problems.

During the Kennedy-Nixon debates, John F. Kennedy demonstrated that for television politics, style was as important as substance.

But Kennedy never used—and his father never accepted—pain as an excuse for inactivity. At Harvard University he played football and other sports; during vacations at the family home in Hyannis Port he rough-housed with his brothers and sisters. Throughout his life, Kennedy maintained this physical view of life.

Kennedy's macho ethos extended to his attitude toward women, whom he viewed first and foremost as sexual objects. During his Washington years as a U.S. senator, he moved from one affair to the next, a habit that continued after he was married and elected president. When he wanted companionship and conversation he turned to his male friends.

Kennedy brought this masculine attitude to his presidency. He surrounded himself with advisers who shared his energetic approach to work and play. He seemed charged with a sense of urgency and often expressed the belief that America was entering a period of crisis. Without crisis, Kennedy believed, no person could achieve greatness, and he desired greatness.

Something Short of Camelot

From the very first, journalists associated the Kennedy administration with Camelot. According to the popular legend, King Arthur established in the realm of Camelot a period of unparalleled peace and prosperity. Although Kennedy himself encouraged the Camelot comparisons, the record of his administration fell short of the ideal.

Several factors worked to limit the success of Kennedy's domestic programs. To begin with, Kennedy lacked both political support in Congress and a firm commitment to push for liberal reforms. Ideologically, he was a centrist Democrat. In addition, although his party held a solid majority in the House, 101 of 261 Democratic representatives came from southern and border states, and they normally voted with conservative Republicans. Added to this problem was Kennedy's distaste for legislative infighting and his poor working relations with many senators. He limited his domestic agenda, which he named the "New Frontier," to such traditional Democratic proposals as a higher minimum wage, increased Social Security benefits, and modest housing and educational programs. In the final analysis, Kennedy was so concerned with the "crises abroad" that he risked little of his political capital on unpopular domestic reforms.

There were small successes. Congress raised the minimum wage, expanded Social Security, and appropriated a few billion dollars for public housing and aid to economically depressed areas. However, these gains were offset by the setbacks, which Kennedy accepted perhaps too stoically. Congress defeated the president's plan for federal aid to education, a health insurance plan for the aged, and programs to help migrant workers, unemployed youths, and urban commuters.

African Americans were especially disappointed with Kennedy's performance. For blacks, the early 1960s were difficult, violent years that tested their resolve. White segregationists confronted blacks' nonviolent desegregation efforts with unprovoked ferocity. In city after city violence erupted.

Through his first two years in office Kennedy remained largely silent on the issue of civil rights. Although his brother, Attorney General Robert Kennedy, aided protesters when federal laws were violated, JFK and the FBI staked out a conservative position. As one historian noted, "Civil rights workers were assaulted and shot at—systematically, often openly, frequently by law enforcement officials themselves. And through it all, in virtually every case, federal authorities did nothing."

In 1963 Kennedy changed his position. In part this about-face was the result of Robert Kennedy's prodding. In part it was the result of television, which daily showed shocking examples of brutality in the South and accelerated the demand for change. In late May 1963, Kennedy eloquently announced his new position.

Perhaps Kennedy was convinced that the time had come for "the nation to fulfill its promise." Perhaps, as his supporters claim, Kennedy was beginning to fulfill his own promise. His death in November 1963 left questions unanswered, potential unrealized. Judged by his accomplishments, however, Kennedy's Camelot, like King Arthur's, existed largely in the realm of myth. Although he could inspire people to follow, too often on domestic issues he chose not to lead.

Cuba Libre *Revisited*

Foreign affairs consumed Kennedy's interest. Kennedy generally continued the essentially Cold War policies of Truman and Eisenhower. He accepted the strategy of containment and the notion that the Soviet Union would take advantage of any sign of weakness by the United States. Unlike domestic politics, international conflicts were more clear-cut, and the divisions between "us" and "them" more certain.

Kennedy's handling of Cuban relations revealed his bellicose tendencies. Like Eisenhower, Kennedy was dismayed by the success of Fidel Castro. Just as Americans during the 1890s had cried "*Cuba Libre,*" on taking office Kennedy began to search for a way to "free" Cuba, this time from Castro's communism rather than Spain's colonialism. His desire to strike a blow against communism led him to embrace a CIA plot to overthrow Castro.

Hatched during the Eisenhower administration, the CIA plan entailed the assassination of Castro and the training and transporting of a force of Cuban exiles to Cuba, where they would launch a counterrevolution. It was a plan that even the joint chiefs of staff believed would probably fail. Making matters worse, the plan was a poorly kept secret, known even to Cuban authorities.

The invasion on April 17, 1961, at the Bay of Pigs was an unmitigated disaster. The Cuban people did not rise up to join the invaders, who were trapped on the beaches. Nor would Kennedy authorize U.S. air support for the anti-Castro forces. As a result, all but 300 of the 1,500 invaders were killed or captured. If anything, the Bay of Pigs fiasco strengthened Castro's position in Cuba.

In the fall of 1962 a more serious Cuban crisis arose when the Soviet Union began to install intermediate-range ballistic missiles (IRBMs) on the island. Instead of trying to work through proper diplomatic avenues—a process that would have taken time and might have hurt the Democrats in the upcoming election—Kennedy announced the alarming news on television. After showing the public the American cities that the missiles could destroy, Kennedy said he would not permit Soviet ships transporting the weapons to enter Cuban waters.

Behind the scenes, Kennedy and Soviet Premier Nikita Khrushchev searched for a way to defuse the crisis. In the end, the world leaders achieved a solution. Khrushchev agreed to remove the missiles under United Nations inspection in return for an American pledge not to invade Cuba. The two "superpowers" had stood at the brink, gazed into the abyss, and stepped back.

The Kennedy administration interpreted the result as a victory. "We're eyeball to eyeball and I think the other fellow just blinked," Secretary of State Dean Rusk observed during the episode. And, indeed, the Soviet Union could hardly disagree. The missile crisis provided the ammunition to force Khrushchev out of power.

Friends of Kennedy claimed that he reached maturity during the crisis and that it motivated him to move toward détente—an easing of tensions— with the Soviet Union. In several 1963 speeches he called for "not merely peace in our time but peace for all time" and a "world safe for diversity." And he did support a treaty banning all atmospheric testing of nuclear weapons.

On November 22, 1963, Lee Harvey Oswald assassinated Kennedy in Dallas, Texas. (Later investigations, however, questioned whether Oswald acted alone.) The tragedy moved the nation. Once again, television gave the event a mythical quality. Americans mourned together, eyes fixed on their television sets; and immediately commentators began to evaluate Kennedy's presidency in terms of not what was but what might have been.

Vietnam: America's Longest War

How did the war start? And when? Even in the 1960s most Americans, including some foreign policy experts, were not exactly sure of the answers to such basic questions. Lyndon B. Johnson said he was continuing Kennedy's policy, who had continued Eisenhower's, who had continued Truman's, who had acted as he believed Roosevelt would have acted. The answers stretch back into time.

A Small Corner of a Bigger Picture

For almost 2,000 years Vietnam had battled China for its own independence. The French came next. During the seventeenth, eighteenth, and nineteenth centuries French traders and missionaries established their control over Vietnam. The Japanese took over the country during World War II.

In 1945 the Vietnamese declared their independence, but the same year the French returned, bent on the resubjugation of the country. The struggle continued, with the Communist Vietminh under Ho Chi Minh controlling the north of the country and the French the south. Between 1945 and 1954 both sides suffered terrible losses in the bitter guerrilla warfare.

The United States faced a difficult decision. During World War II Franklin Roosevelt had favored Vietnamese independence and aided Ho's fight against the Japanese. Roosevelt recognized that the age of colonialism was doomed, but he also believed that a strong postwar Western Europe was essential to American security, and he did not want to alienate Britain or France by pressing too hard for an end to empires.

Harry Truman inherited FDR's problems. Even more than his former boss, he advocated a strong Western Europe, even if that strength had to be based on the continuation of empires. In the game of Cold War politics Vietnam became a pawn. Truman wanted French support against the Soviet Union; in return, he willingly agreed to aid France's ambitions in Vietnam.

The success of Mao Zedong's Communist revolution in China strengthened America's support of the French in Vietnam. Obsessed with the idea of an international Communist conspiracy, Truman and his advisers contended that Stalin, Mao, and Ho were united by the single ambition of world domination. They overlooked the historical rivalries that pulled Russia, China, and Vietnam apart.

By the late 1940s the United States had assumed a large part of the cost of France's effort to regain its control over Vietnam. The price escalated during the early 1950s. By 1952 the United States was shouldering roughly one-third of the cost of the war, and between 1950 and 1954 America contributed $2.6 billion to France's war effort. But it was not enough. France was unable to defeat Ho's Vietminh forces.

In 1954 the war reached a crisis stage. In an effort to lure the Vietminh into a major engagement, the ranking French commander moved more than 13,000 soldiers to Dien Bien Phu, a remote outpost in a river valley in northwest Vietnam. The Vietminh surrounded the fort and moved artillery pieces to the hills above the French airstrip. From there they mounted a siege of Dien Bien Phu. As the months passed, French troop strength and prestige suffered punishing blows. Finally, on May 7, 1954, the French surrendered.

At the peace talks in Geneva the countries involved agreed to temporarily divide Vietnam at the 17th parallel into two countries and hold elections in the summer of 1956 to reunify Vietnam. Eisenhower supported the independent government established in South Vietnam under the leadership of Ngo Dinh Diem, a staunch anti-Communist. As a popular leader, however, he had no appeal. A Roman Catholic in an overwhelmingly Buddhist nation, Diem successfully alienated almost everyone who came into contact with him. Even United States intelligence sources rated his chances of establishing order in South Vietnam as "poor."

Diem, nevertheless, was America's man. Vietnam had become a test case, an opportunity for the United States to battle communism in Asia with dollars instead of U. S. troops. When the time came to hold the unification election, Diem, with American backing, refused. Instead, he held "free" elections in South Vietnam, where he received an improbable 98.2 percent of the popular vote. In Saigon, where there were only 405,000 registered voters, Diem received 605,000 votes.

By the end of 1957 Vietminh guerrillas in South Vietnam—often called the Vietcong—were in open revolt. Two years later North and South Vietnam resumed hostilities. The United States increased its aid, most of which went toward improving the South Vietnamese military or into the pockets of corrupt officials. The United States spent little money on improving the quality of life of the peasants. Nor did the United States object strongly to Diem's dictatorial methods.

By the end of Eisenhower's second term the United States had become fully committed to Diem and South Vietnam. To be sure, problems in Vietnam were not America's major concern. In fact, most Americans were unaware of their country's involvement there. More than anything, Vietnam was a small corner of a bigger picture. U.S. policy there was determined by larger Cold War concerns. America's presence in Vietnam, however, would soon be expanded.

Kennedy's Testing Ground

On taking office, John Kennedy reaffirmed his country's commitment to Diem and South Vietnam. The president announced his intention to be even more aggressive than Truman or Eisenhower. In Vietnam, Kennedy saw an opportunity to "prove" his nation's resolve and strength. In the end, South Vietnam as a country was less important to Kennedy than the challenge it presented.

Kennedy believed that the United States needed a fresh military approach. Eisenhower's "massive retaliation" was too rigid. It was of no use in a guerrilla war like Vietnam. Kennedy labeled his approach "flexible response," which entailed the development of conventional and counterinsurgency (antiguerrilla) forces as well as nuclear weapons. Vietnam rapidly became the laboratory for counterinsurgency activities, a place for Special Forces (Green Berets) units to develop their own tactics.

To "win" in Vietnam, Kennedy realized that he would have to strengthen America's presence there. In November of 1961 he decided to deploy American troops to South Vietnam. By the end of 1961, 3,205 American "advisers" were in Vietnam. Kennedy increased this force to 11,300 in 1962 and 16,300 in 1963.

As U.S. involvement deepened, Diem's control over South Vietnam declined. He alienated peasants by refusing to enact meaningful land reforms and Buddhists by passing laws to restrict their activities. Responding to Diem's pro-Catholic policies, Buddhists conducted hunger strikes and nonviolent protests, and one Buddhist monk, in full view of American reporters and cameras, burned himself to death on a busy, downtown Saigon intersection.

More fiery suicides followed. Protests mounted. Outside of Saigon, Diem exerted little influence. The Kennedy administration soon reached the conclusion that Diem had to go. Behind the scenes, Kennedy encouraged Vietnamese generals to overthrow Diem. On November 1, 1963, Vietnamese army officers arrested and murdered Diem and his brother. Although Kennedy did not approve of the assassination, the United States quickly aided the new government.

Three weeks later Kennedy was assassinated in Dallas. Several friends of the slain president have suggested that he had begun to reevaluate his Vietnam policy and that after the 1964 election he would have started the process of American disengagement. But whatever his future plans, Kennedy had increased U.S. involvement in Vietnam.

Unfortunately for Kennedy's successor, the prospects for South Vietnam's survival were less than they had been in 1961. By 1963 South Vietnam had lost the fertile Mekong Delta to the Vietcong and with it most of the country's rural population. From the peasants' perspective, the

Saigon government stood for heavy taxes, no services, and military destruction; and increasingly they identified the United States with Saigon. Such was the situation Lyndon B. Johnson inherited.

Texas Tough in the Gulf of Tonkin

Lyndon Baines Johnson was a complex man—shrewd, arrogant, intelligent, sensitive, vulgar, and occasionally cruel. He loved power, and he knew where it was, how to get it, and how to use it. Everything about Johnson seemed to emphasize or enhance his power. He was physically large, and seemed even bigger than he was. He used both his size and the famous "Johnson treatment"—a backslapping, hugging sort of camaraderie—as tools of persuasion.

A legislative genius, Johnson had little experience in foreign affairs. Reared in the poverty of the Texas hill country, educated at a state teachers' college, and concerned politically with domestic issues, before becoming president LBJ had expressed little interest in foreign affairs. "Foreigners are not like the folks I am used to," he often said, and whether it was a joke or not he meant it.

Yet to say Johnson had little experience in foreign affairs is not to suggest that he did not have strong opinions on the subject. Like most politicians of the period, Johnson was an unquestioning Cold Warrior. In addition, along with accepting the domino theory (the idea that if Vietnam fell, other nations would also fall to communism) and a monolithic view of communism, Johnson cherished a traditionally southern notion of honor and masculinity. It was his duty, he maintained, to honor commitments made by earlier presidents. Leaving Vietnam, Johnson believed, would be a dishonorable act, dangerous for the nation's future. To show weakness and back down was worse than cowardly—it was unmanly. Furthermore, Johnson believed that any retreat from Vietnam would destroy him politically. He had not forgotten that Truman had been blamed by the Republicans for the collapse of China. He was determined not to "lose" Vietnam.

Before winning in Vietnam, however, Johnson had to win in the United States. The presidential election in 1964 was his top priority. He was pitted against Barry Goldwater, the powerful Arizona senator from the Republican Right. "Extremism in the defense of liberty is no vice," Goldwater said, and if elected he promised to defend South Vietnam at any cost. He also preached against the welfare state, Social Security, the Nuclear Test Ban Treaty of 1963, and any rapprochement with the Soviet Union or China. Democrats suggested that Goldwater might start a nuclear war, a view that Goldwater did little to discourage, even going so far as to coin the uncomfortably comforting phrase "conventional nuclear weapon."

Johnson's campaign strategy was to appear as the thoughtful, strong moderate. He would not lose Vietnam, he told voters, but neither would he use nuclear weapons or send American troops "to do what Asian boys ought to be doing themselves." Johnson promised that, if elected, he would create a "Great Society" at home and honor American commitments abroad. Voters rewarded him with a landslide victory in the November election.

Behind the scenes, however, the Johnson administration was maneuvering to obtain a free hand for conducting a more aggressive war in Vietnam. He did not want a formal declaration of war, which might frighten voters. Rather he desired a quietly passed resolution giving him the authority to deploy American forces. Such a resolution would allow him to act without the consent of Congress. Johnson and his advisers were planning to escalate American involvement in the Vietnam War, but they hoped it would go unnoticed.

Johnson used two reported North Vietnamese attacks on the American destroyer *Maddox* as a pretext for going before Congress to ask for the resolution. Actually, he was less than truthful about the circumstances of the attack. The first incident occurred in the Gulf of Tonkin in early August 1964 when the North Vietnamese suspected the *Maddox* of aiding a South Vietnamese commando raid into North Vietnam. The American ship and supporting navy jets opened fire, sinking one of the North Vietnamese ships and crippling two others; the *Maddox* was not hit and suffered only superficial machine gun damage. The second of the Gulf of Tonkin incidents probably never occurred. Assaulted by high waves, thunderstorms, and freak atmospheric conditions, the *Maddox's* sonar equipment apparently malfunctioned, registering 22 invisible enemy torpedoes. Soon after the incident the commander of the *Maddox* reached the conclusion that no attack had ever taken place.

Johnson realized the dubious nature of the second attack. Nevertheless, he went on national television and announced, "Aggression by terror against the peaceful villages of South Vietnam has now been joined by open aggression on the high seas against the United States of America." A few days later Johnson pressed Congress for a resolution authorizing him to "take all necessary measures" to prevent aggression, and protect American security. Almost without debate, the Senate passed the Tonkin Gulf resolution on August 7 with only two dissenting votes, and the House of Representatives endorsed it unanimously. In the years that followed Johnson used his new powers to escalate the war.

Lyndon's War

Lyndon Johnson liked to personalize things. Once a military aide tried to direct him to the correct helicopter, saying "Mr. President, that's not your

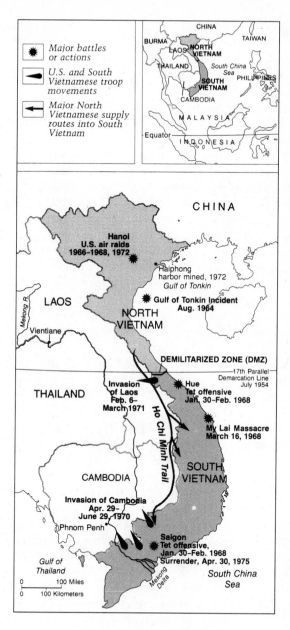

Major battles or actions

U.S. and South Vietnamese troop movements

Major North Vietnamese supply routes into South Vietnam

CHINA

BURMA
LAOS
NORTH VIETNAM
TAIWAN
THAILAND
South China Sea
SOUTH VIETNAM
PHILIPPINES
CAMBODIA
MALAYSIA
Equator
INDONESIA

CHINA

Hanoi
U.S. air raids
1966–1968, 1972

Haiphong
harbor mined, 1972
Gulf of Tonkin

Gulf of Tonkin Incident
Aug. 1964

LAOS

Mekong R.

Vientiane

NORTH VIETNAM

DEMILITARIZED ZONE (DMZ)

17th Parallel
Demarcation Line
July 1954

Invasion
of Laos
Feb. 6–
March 1971

THAILAND

Hue
Tet offensive
Jan. 30–Feb. 1968

Ho Chi Minh Trail

My Lai Massacre
March 16, 1968

CAMBODIA

SOUTH VIETNAM

Invasion of Cambodia
Apr. 29–
June 29, 1970

Phnom Penh

Saigon
Tet offensive,
Jan. 30–Feb. 1968
Surrender, Apr. 30, 1975

*Gulf of
Thailand*

Mekong Delta

South China
Sea

0   100 Miles
0   100 Kilometers

Vietnam Conflict, 1964–1975

helicopter." "Son, they're all my helicopters," Johnson replied. So it was with the Vietnam War. He did not start the war, but once reelected he quickly made it "his war," exercising complete control.

When he became president it was still a relatively obscure conflict for most Americans. By the end of 1964 there were 23,300 military personnel in Vietnam, most of whom were volunteers. Only a few people strongly opposed America's involvement. All this would change dramatically during the next four years.

With the election behind him, Johnson in early 1965 started to reevaluate the position of the United States. In Saigon crisis followed crisis as one unpopular government gave way to the next. Something had to be done, and Johnson's advisers suggested two courses. The military and most of LBJ's foreign policy experts called for a more aggressive military presence in Vietnam, including bombing raids into North Vietnam and more ground troops. Other advisers, notably Under Secretary of State George Ball, believed that a land war in Indochina was not in America's best strategic interests and that bombing North Vietnam would only stiffen the Communists' resolve.

Johnson chose the first course, claiming it would be dishonorable not to come to South Vietnam's aid. In February 1965 Vietcong troops attacked the American base in Pleiku, killing several soldiers. Johnson used the assault as a pretext to commence air raids into the North. Code-named Rolling Thunder, the operation was designed to use American technological superiority to defeat North Vietnam. At first, Johnson limited U.S. air strikes to enemy radar and bridges, but as the war dragged on, he ordered pilots to hit military targets in metropolitan areas. Between 1965 and 1973 American pilots flew more than 526,000 sorties and dropped 6,162,000 tons of bombs on enemy targets, almost three times more than were dropped in World War II.

However, the bombs did not lead to victory. Ironically, as Ball had predicted, the bombing missions actually strengthened the Communist government in North Vietnam. As a U.S. intelligence report noted, the bombing had enabled Ho's regime "to increase its control of the populace and perhaps even to break through the political apathy and indifference which have characterized the outlook of the average North Vietnamese in recent years." The massive use of air power also undermined U.S. counterinsurgency efforts. By using bombing raids against the enemy in both the North and South, U.S. forces inevitably killed large numbers of civilians, the very people they were there to help.

A larger air war also led to more ground troops; between 1965 and 1968 the escalation of American forces was dramatic. Needless to say, escalation of American troops and deaths went hand in hand. The year-end totals for the United States between 1965 and 1968 were:

1965: 184,300 troops; 636 killed.
1966: 385,300 troops; 6,644 killed.
1967: 485,600 troops; 16,021 killed.
1968: 536,000 troops; 30,610 killed.

But still there was no victory.

To Tet and Beyond

Throughout the escalation Johnson was less than candid with the American people. He argued that there had been no real change in American policy and that victory was in sight. Anyone who said otherwise, he roundly criticized. Increasingly he demanded unquestioning loyalty from his close advisers. Such demands led to an administration "party line." As the war ground on, the "party line" bore less and less similarity to reality.

In late 1967 General William Westmoreland, commander of U.S. forces in Vietnam, returned to America briefly to assure the public that he could now see the "light at the end of the tunnel," and that the enemy was "increasingly resorting to desperation tactics." At the time, the American press focused most of its attention on the battle of Khe Sanh, and Westmoreland assured everyone that victory there was certain.

Then with a suddenness that caught all America by surprise, North Vietnam struck into the very heart of South Vietnam. On the morning of January 30, 1968, North Vietnam launched the Tet offensive. A Vietcong suicide squad broke into the U.S. embassy in Saigon, and Vietnamese Communists attacked cities, towns, and hamlets in South Vietnam.

For a few weeks the fighting was ferocious and bloody. In order to retake Hue, an ancient city close to the border between North and South Vietnam, U.S. troops had to destroy part of the city. Before they evacuated, North Vietnamese and Vietcong soldiers killed several thousand political leaders, teachers, and other civilians, many of whom were buried alive in one mass grave. In another village, where victory came at a high price, the liberating American general reported, "We had to destroy the town to save it."

Technically, the Tet offensive was a military defeat for North Vietnam, but it was also a profound psychological victory. Johnson, his advisers, and his generals had been proclaiming that the enemy was on the run and almost defeated. Tet demonstrated that the contrary was true. The Tet offensive, more than any other single event, turned the media against the war and exposed the widening "credibility gap" between official pronouncements and public beliefs.

After Tet, Americans stopped thinking about victory and turned toward thoughts of how best to get out of Vietnam. In the polls Johnson's popularity plummeted, and in the New Hampshire primary Democratic peace candidate Eugene McCarthy received surprisingly solid support. On the night of March 31, 1968, LBJ went on television and made two important announcements. First, he said that the United States would limit its bombing of North Vietnam and would enter into peace talks any time and at any place. And second, Johnson surprised the nation by announcing his decision not to seek another term as president.

A major turning point had been reached. The gradual escalation of the war was over. The period of de-escalation had started. Even in official government circles, peace had replaced victory as America's objective in Vietnam.

The Politics of a Divided Nation

As Johnson himself realized, his policies had deeply divided the nation. Instead of fully committing the United States by calling up the reserves and National Guard and by pushing for higher taxes to pay for the war, Johnson had gambled that a slow, steady escalation would be enough to force North Vietnam to accept a negotiated peace. During the buildup, LBJ told the American people that he was not drastically changing policy and that victory was in sight. After Tet, many Americans refused to believe such assurances.

Dissatisfaction with Johnson's policy surfaced first among the young, the very people who were being asked to fight and die for the cause. In the early years of "Lyndon's war," many soldiers sincerely believed that they were fighting—and dying—to preserve freedom and nourish democracy in Southeast Asia. As the war lengthened, however, an ever-growing number of soldiers expressed disillusionment. Some turned to drugs to relieve the constant stress and fear that the war engendered. A 1969 Pentagon study estimated that nearly two of every three American soldiers in Vietnam were using marijuana and that one of every three or four had tried heroin.

Other soldiers reacted by viewing all Vietnamese as the enemy. In part the nature of the war against the Vietcong caused this attitude. In a village of "civilians" any man, woman, or child *might* be the enemy. Tension and anxiety were ever present.

Empty government phrases, however, also contributed to the problem. How could soldiers win the "hearts and minds" of villagers one day and rain napalm on them the next? Reacting to the surface idealism of U.S. policy, one experienced soldier commented, "All that is just a *load* man. We're here to kill gooks, period." The My Lai massacre, which saw American soldiers kill more than 100 (the official figure was 122 but it was probably many more) South Vietnamese civilians, was the sad extension of this attitude.

As the war lengthened, the morale of American soldiers plummeted. Desertion and absent-without-leave (AWOL) rates skyrocketed. Even worse, "fragging"—the term soldiers used to describe the assassination of overzealous officers and noncommissioned officers (NCOs) by their own troops—increased at an alarming rate. The army claimed that at least 1,011 officers and NCOs were killed or wounded by their own troops during the Vietnam War.

At home, thousands of university students, most of whom had draft exemptions, also reacted to the war and Johnson's policies. They were the earliest and most vocal critics of the Vietnam War. If they lacked a coherent ideology, they were strong in numbers and energy. Not all students demonstrated against the war; most protesters were from upper middle-class families and could afford the intellectual luxury of being political idealists. Led by such leftist groups as Students for a Democratic Society (SDS), they called for a more just society in which political life was governed by morality, not greed. During the early 1960s they focused on the civil rights movement, participating in freedom rides and voter registration drives. By the mid-1960s, however, they were increasingly shifting their attention to America's "unjust and immoral" war in Southeast Asia; and with the shift their numbers swelled. By 1968 the SDS boasted more than 100,000 members. By then, too, older voices had joined the student chorus of condemnation.

It was the older voices, energized by the idealism of youth, that led to Johnson's decision not to seek reelection in 1968. For many, it seemed as if the future of American politics belonged to the proponents of peace and morality. Students initially flocked to presidential candidate Eugene McCarthy's peace cause. After Johnson pulled his hat out of the ring, Robert Kennedy announced his candidacy. Although RFK had started in political life as an aggressive cold warrior, by 1968 he had radically reevaluated these beliefs. An eloquent spokesman for the cause of humanity and peace, Kennedy exhibited the passion and commitment that McCarthy lacked.

By the conclusion of the primaries Kennedy had become the Democratic front-runner. But the hopes of American liberals for a candidate who spoke their language and addressed their concerns abruptly ended when, moments after giving a speech at a party celebrating his victory in the California primary, Kennedy was shot in the head by a Palestinian fanatic, Sirhan B. Sirhan.

The Democratic party went to the Chicago convention without a candidate. There party leaders battled among themselves—young and old; radical, liberal, and conservative. In the streets, outside the convention hall, police beat protesters in full view of television cameras. An official commission later termed it a "police riot." Inside the convention hall the fighting was largely verbal, but it was just as intense and bitter. In the end, the Democratic party chose Hubert Humphrey, Johnson's liberal vice president. Instead of change, the Democratic party chose a representative of the "old politics."

In a more tranquil convention in Miami the Republican party endorsed Richard M. Nixon, who promised when elected to end the Vietnam War honorably, move against forced busing of black children to white schools, and restore "law and order." Nixon claimed to speak for the great majority of Americans who obeyed the nation's laws, paid their taxes, regularly attended church, and loved their country.

In a similar vein, Alabama's governor George Wallace, running in 1968 on the American Independent ticket, spoke for millions of working-class white Americans, young and old alike, who opposed forced integration of schools and neighborhoods, radical college students, and what they believed was the country's drift toward the Left. Although Humphrey finished the campaign strong, Nixon's and Wallace's appeal to traditional values had an undeniable attraction. And on election day Nixon received 43.4 percent of the popular vote, Humphrey 42.7 percent, and Wallace 13.5 percent. Given the combined votes for Nixon and Wallace—57 percent—it was clear that the country was moving Right rather than Left.

The Tortuous Path Toward Peace

During the presidential campaign of 1968 Richard Nixon sported a new public image, which the press often referred to as the "new Nixon"—experienced, statesmanlike, mature, and well adjusted. But in many respects the new Nixon was not very different from the old. He still considered himself something of an outsider, a battler against an entrenched political establishment. Reared on the West Coast in humble circumstances, he had to overcome considerable obstacles in his rise to power. In the process certain character traits emerged. He was a hard worker—careful, studious with a tendency toward perfectionism. He was also a loner—shy, introverted, humorless, uncomfortable in social situations.

As a restless outsider, Nixon harbored a heightened suspicion of political insiders. On taking office he therefore surrounded himself with close advisers who held noncabinet titles. Cabinet appointees, and particularly his secretary of state, William Rogers, had almost no voice in key decisions. Personal aides H. R. Haldeman and John Ehrlichman advised Nixon on domestic political issues. Vice President Spiro Agnew assumed the role of the administration's hatchet man, attacking liberals with the ferocity of a professional wrestler verbally abusing an archrival. For foreign affairs, Nixon relied on his national security adviser, Henry Kissinger. Vain, articulate, and intellectual, Kissinger shared Nixon's desire to alter the very nature of the country's foreign relations and to make history. Both men were attracted by the diplomacy of secrecy and intrigue.

Vietnamization

During his campaign Nixon had promised "peace with honor" in Vietnam. One thing was certain: Nixon knew that he could not continue Johnson's policy. Whatever else he did, Nixon realized that to ensure some semblance of domestic tranquillity he would have to begin to remove American troops from Vietnam. In May 1969, the president announced that henceforth South Vietnamese soldiers would carry more of the combat burden. Certainly the United States would continue to aid materially any anticommunist struggle, but the aid would not include the wholesale use of American troops.

Nixon's Vietnamization policy was based on the questionable premise that the South Vietnamese government of Nguyen Van Thieu was stable and prepared to assume greater responsibility for fighting the war, Nixon announced that he planned gradually to de-escalate American military involvement. Increasingly U.S. aid would be limited to war matériel, military advice, and air support. He coupled Vietnamization with a more strenuous effort to move along the peace talks.

Actually, the idea of Vietnamization was hardly new. Advisers for Eisenhower, Kennedy, and Johnson had suggested one variation or another of the plan as the solution to the war. The major problem was that the South Vietnamese could not successfully fight the war on their own. But faced with angry criticism at home, Nixon had no choice but to implement the policy.

At the same time as he extended the olive branch, he expanded the nature of the conflict. Hoping to slow down the flow of North Vietnamese supplies and soldiers into South Vietnam, Nixon ordered American B-52 pilots to bomb the Ho Chi Minh Trail both in Vietnam and Cambodia. He kept this violation of Cambodian neutrality secret from the American public. It was a bold move, but the bombs only reduced the flow of men and supplies by approximately 10 percent.

When both increased bombings of North Vietnam and Kissinger's peace talks with North Vietnamese officials failed to end the war, Nixon decided to send American ground forces into Cambodia to destroy Communist supply bases. On April 30, 1970, he went on television to announce a joint American and South Vietnamese "incursion" into Cambodia's border regions to be limited to 60 days.

Militarily the "incursion" fell far short of success. Although American forces captured large stockpiles of weapons and supplies, the operation did not end the war. But the "incursion" had dangerously enlarged the battlefield.

More important, the invasion of Cambodia reignited the fires of the peace movement at home, as colleges and universities shut down in protest. At Kent State University in Ohio a volley of gunshots fired by National Guardsmen broke up a peaceful demonstration, killing 4 students and wounding 11 others. Less than two weeks later, policemen shot two more innocent students at Jackson State University in Mississippi. Instead of victory or even peace, Nixon's efforts had further divided America.

In the spring of 1970, Ohio National Guardsmen fired into a group of protesting students at Kent State University, killing four.

As an effective policy for ending the war, Vietnamization was a failure. To be sure, the policy allowed Nixon to bring home American combat troops. When Nixon took office, 540,000 American troops were in Vietnam; four years later only 70,000 remained. But American reductions were not accompanied by a marked improvement in the South Vietnamese army. If anything, South Vietnam became more dependent on the United States during the years of Vietnamization.

A *"Decent Interval"*

By 1972 Nixon simply wanted to end the war with as little embarrassment as possible. Without an active U.S. military presence, Vietnam's demise was a foregone conclusion. Negotiations presented the only way out. Nixon and Kissinger hoped to arrange for a peace that would permit the United States and South Vietnam to save face and allow a "decent interval" of time to ensue between the American departure and the collapse of the government in Saigon. In pursuit of this goal, Nixon changed the character of American foreign policy.

The Soviet Union and the People's Republic of China aided and advised North Vietnam. Yet the two large Communist nations were hardly allies themselves. In fact, the Sino-Soviet split demonstrated to American

U.S. troop levels in Vietnam

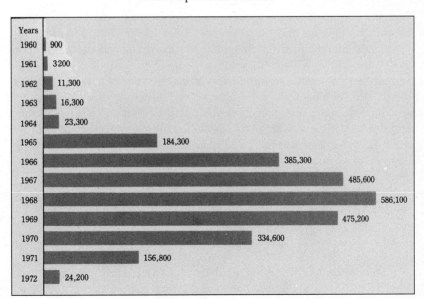

Years	
1960	900
1961	3200
1962	11,300
1963	16,300
1964	23,300
1965	184,300
1966	385,300
1967	485,600
1968	586,100
1969	475,200
1970	334,600
1971	156,800
1972	24,200

leaders the fallacy of the old Cold War theme of a monolithic Communist movement. Nixon and Kissinger were astute enough to use the Sino-Soviet rift to improve U.S. relations with both countries. Improved relations, they believed, would move the United States several steps closer to an "honorable" peace in Vietnam. Unfortunately, Nixon and Kissinger greatly overestimated the influence of the Soviet Union and China on North Vietnam.

From his first days in office Nixon had his eyes on the People's Republic of China, a nation that the United States had refused to recognize. Nixon's Cold War record—his opposition to any concession to the Communists—was well known. But he understood that his very record would protect him from public cries of being soft on communism.

In the summer of 1971 Kissinger made a very secret trip to China, which paved the way for Nixon's own very public trip to China in February 1972. American television cameras recorded Nixon's every move as he toured the Great Wall, the Imperial Palace, and the other sites of historic China. Nixon thoroughly enjoyed the event, going so far as quoting Chairman Mao at an official toast and learning to eat with chopsticks. Although full diplomatic relations would not be established until 1979, Nixon's trip to China was the single most important event in the history of the relations between the United States and the People's Republic of China. It bridged, as Chinese foreign minister Chou En-lai remarked, "the vastest ocean in the world, twenty-five years of no communication."

Concerned about the growing rapprochement between China and America, the Soviet Union sought to move closer to the United States. Once again, Nixon and Kissinger were pleased to oblige. In late May 1972, after many months of preparatory talks, Nixon traveled to Moscow to sign the Strategic Arms Limitation Treaty (SALT I) with Soviet leader Leonid Brezhnev. Although the treaty froze intercontinental ballistic missile (ICBM) deployment, it did not alter the buildup of the more dangerous multiple independent reentry vehicles (MIRVs). As so often was the case during the Cold War, SALT I provided more a warm breeze than the real heat wave necessary for a complete thaw of the Cold War. Both the United States and the Soviet Union hoped that SALT I would lead to other, more comprehensive, arms reductions treaties.

In other areas the United States and the Soviet Union made more substantial progress. American businesspeople forged inroads into the Soviet market place, and some farmers also reaped significant rewards when disastrous harvests at home led the Soviet Union to purchase several billion dollars worth of American wheat, corn, and soybeans.

Thus, although Nixon had not been able to end the Vietnam War, his 1972 triumphs in the Soviet Union and China gave him more influence with North Vietnam's major allies and dazzled voters at home. In 1972 Nixon easily defeated Democratic candidate George McGovern, capturing 61 percent of the popular vote and 521 of the 538 votes of the electoral college. Nixon's success with blue-collar workers, conservative Roman Catholics, and southerners signified the end of the New Deal coalition.

Once reelected, Nixon again focused on Vietnam. A month before the election, Kissinger had announced, "Peace is at hand," but no sooner was Nixon safely reelected than the peace talks broke down once again. Nixon's response was more and heavier bombing of North Vietnam. Starting on December 18, 1972 and continuing for the next ten days, the Christmas bombings—code-named Operation Linebacker II—attacked military targets in Hanoi and Haiphong and killed more than 1,500 civilians. When the bombings concluded, the warring nations resumed peace talks.

In a week North Vietnam and the United States hammered out a peace strikingly similar to the October proposal. On January 27, 1973, America ended its active participation in the Vietnam War. The peace treaty provided for the release of all prisoners of war and U.S.'s military withdrawal from Vietnam. It also established a monitored cease-fire between North and South Vietnam and set up procedures aimed at solving the differences between the two countries. Nixon quickly claimed that he had won an honorable peace. The war had claimed the lives of 58,000 American, 107,000 South Vietnamese, more than 500,000 North Vietnamese soldiers and, of course, the lives of many thousands of Vietnamese civilians.

But the war was not yet over. All the peace provided for was a "decent interval" between America's withdrawal and North Vietnam's complete victory. Almost as soon as the ink on the treaty was dry, North Vietnam and the Vietcong were once again engaged in a war with the government in South Vietnam. Finally, in the spring of 1975 South Vietnamese forces collapsed. On April 30 South Vietnam formally announced its unconditional surrender. Vietnam was finally unified. Free elections in 1956 might have accomplished the same results.

The Legacy of the War

At home, the controversy engendered by the war raged on long after the American withdrawal. Much of the controversy centered on the returning veterans. Reports of drug use and "fragging" shocked many Americans who had come no closer to the war than their television sets. And veterans—most of whom had served their country faithfully and to the best of their abilities—were angered by the cold, hostile reception they received when they returned to the United States.

During the 1970s and 1980s the returning Vietnam War veteran loomed large in American popular culture. He was first portrayed as a dangerous killer, a deranged time bomb that could explode at any time and in any place. He was Travis Bickle in *Taxi Driver* (1976), a veteran wound so tight that he seemed perpetually on the verge of snapping, or he was Colonel Kurtz in *Apocalypse Now* (1979), who adjusted to a mad war by going mad himself. Not until the late 1970s did popular culture begin to treat the Vietnam War veteran as a victim of the war or even as a hero, rather than a madman produced by the war.

The transformation of the veteran that took place in the late 1970s and 1980s indicated a fundamental shift in America's attitude toward the war. Millions of Americans began once again to see the war in terms of a noble crusade that could have been won. As John Rambo said in *Rambo: First Blood II,* "Do we get to win this time?" His former commander replied: "This time it's up to you." This message fit well with the political message of Ronald Reagan's America.

Conclusion

The Vietnam War confused and divided the nation. Tim O'Brien captured something of this confusion in his acclaimed novel *Going after Cacciato* (1978). After fighting in the war, his protagonist "didn't know who was right, or what was right; he didn't know if it was a war of self-determination or self-destruction, outright aggression or national liberation; he didn't know which speeches to believe, which books, which politicians; he didn't know if nations would topple like dominos or stand separate like trees; he didn't know who started the war, or why, or when, or with what motives; he didn't know if it mattered."

Vietnam destroyed Lyndon Johnson's presidency, and it helped to undermine Nixon's. Both men had injured their cause by using conscious deception in dealing with the American people. It was a war that left scars—on the people who fought in it and on the people who opposed and supported it; on Americans and on Vietnamese; and on America's position in the world.

The most constructive outcome of the war was the lessons it taught. Congress learned that it had to take a more active role in foreign affairs. The War Powers Act (1973), which requires the president to account for his actions within 48 hours of committing troops in a foreign conflict,

Chronology of Key Events

1954	Dien Bien Phu falls to Vietnamese nationalists; Geneva conference divides Vietnam
1961	John F. Kennedy inaugurated thirty-fifth president; Alliance for Progress pledges aid to Latin America; Cuban exiles stage abortive invasion of Cuba at Bay of Pigs; Berlin Wall erected
1962	Cuban missile crisis; American advisers in South Vietnam increased to approximately 16,000
1963	Limited test ban treaty; President Diem murdered; President Kennedy assassinated; Lyndon Johnson becomes thirty-sixth president
1964	Gulf of Tonkin Resolution gives president authority to retaliate against North Vietnamese aggression
1965	Operation Rolling Thunder; first American ground combat troops sent to South Vietnam
1968	Tet offensive: bombing of North Vietnam suspended; Johnson decides not to run for reelection; Robert F. Kennedy assassinated; Richard M. Nixon elected thirty-seventh president
1969	Nixon Doctrine announced
1970	Invasion of Cambodia; antiwar protests at Kent State University and Jackson State University; Congress repeals Gulf of Tonkin Resolution
1972	Nixon travels to China; Strategic Arms Limitation Treaty freezes intercontinental ballistic missile deployment
1973	United States ends active participation in the Vietnam War
1975	Fall of Saigon

demonstrated that the Gulf of Tonkin Resolution had taught Congress a painful lesson. Ho Chi Minh's nationalism taught policymakers that communism was not a monolithic movement and that not all small nations are dominos. Perhaps politicians, policymakers, and citizens alike even learned that national policy should be based on the realities of specific situations and not the kind of stereotypes generated by the Cold War.

Suggestions for Further Reading

For information on Kennedy and his presidency see David Burner, *John F. Kennedy and a New Generation* (1988); Henry Fairlie, *The Kennedy Promise* (1973); Bruce Miroff, *Pragmatic Illusions: The Presidential Politics of JFK* (1976); Herbert S. Parmet, *JFK: The Presidency of John F. Kennedy* (1983); Thomas C. Reeves, *A Question of Character* (1991).

The Kennedy administration's Cuban crises are examined in James G. Blight and David A. Welch, *On the Brink* (1989); Herbert S. Dinerstein, *The Making of a Missile Crisis* (1976); Louise FitzSimons, *The Kennedy Doctrine* (1972); Trumbull Higgins, *The Perfect Failure* (1987); Richard Walton, *Cold War and Counterrevolution* (1972); Peter Wyden, *Bay of Pigs* (1979).

Studies of American involvement in Vietnam include Larry Berman, *Planning a Tragedy* (1989); Larry E. Cable, *Unholy Grail: The War in Vietnam* (1991); Philip Caputo, *A Rumor of War* (1977); Frances FitzGerald, *Fire in the Lake* (1972); David Halberstam, *The Making of a Quagmire,* rev. ed. (1988); George C. Herring, *America's Longest War,* 2nd ed. (1986); Stanley Karnow, *Vietnam, A History* (1983); David Levy, *The Debate over Vietnam* (1991); James S. Olson and Randy Roberts, *Where the Domino Fell* (1991); Marilyn Young, *The Vietnam Wars: 1945–1990* (1991).

A thorough study of Lyndon Johnson's early career is Robert Dallek, *Lone Star Rising* (1991). For a more critical analysis, see Robert Caro, *Means of Ascent* (1990). For Johnson's presidential years, see Doris Kearns, *Lyndon Johnson and the American Dream* (1976). Studies of Richard Nixon and his administration include Stephen E. Ambrose, *Nixon, the Education of a Politician;* William Shawcross, *Sideshow: Kissinger, Nixon, and the Destruction of Cambodia,* rev. ed. (1987). See also Richard Nixon's autobiography, *RN,* 2 vols. (1978).

Chapter *30*

The Struggle for a Just Society

He has been called the nation's nag. He has denounced soft drinks for containing excessive amounts of sugar; and warned Americans about the health hazards of red dyes used as food colorings and of nitrates as preservatives in hot dogs. He has even denounced high heels: "It is part of the whole tyranny of fashion, where women will inflict pain on themselves . . . for what, to please men." His name is Ralph Nader and since the mid-1960s he has been the nation's leading consumer advocate.

An extraordinarily frugal and committed crusader on behalf of the nation's consumers, Nader credits his parents with instilling the sense of justice and civic duty that has inspired his career. Born in 1934, Nader received his bachelor's degree from Princeton and earned a law degree at Harvard, where he found his initial cause: automobile safety. After learning that auto accidents were the fourth leading cause of death (behind

Ralph Nader is the best-known advocate of consumer protection laws in the United States. His group of attorneys, nicknamed "Nader's Raiders," have investigated such wide-ranging problems as automobile safety, the rights of the handicapped, tax reform, the environment, and public health. Here, Nader looks on during a demonstration showing the operation of an automobile air bag safety restraint.

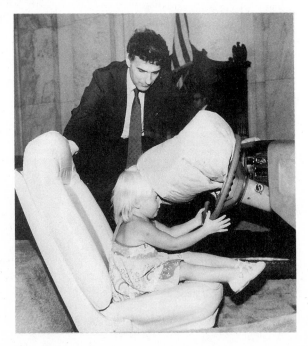

heart disease, cancer, and strokes), he launched a study of auto injury cases. His research convinced him that the law placed too much emphasis on driver mistakes and not enough on the unsafe design of cars.

In 1963 Nader decided to devote his life to consumer protection. Two years later he published a best-seller, *Unsafe at Any Speed,* which charged that automakers stressed styling, comfort, speed, power, and a desire to cut costs at the expense of safety. General Motors Corporation was so unhappy with the book it hired a detective to investigate Nader's politics, religion, and sex life. GM was forced to apologize for this invasion of privacy and eventually paid Nader a $425,000 settlement. Nader used the money to establish more than two dozen public interest groups. The people who work for these groups are known as "Nader's Raiders."

During the 1960s and 1970s Nader was the driving force behind the passage of more than two dozen landmark consumer protection laws, including the National Traffic and Motor Vehicle Safety Act (which set up a federal agency to establish auto-safety standards and order recalls of cars that failed to meet them), the Occupational Safety and Health Act (which established another agency to set standards for on-the-job safety), the Consumer Products Safety Act, and the Freedom of Information Act (which allows citizens to request and see government records). His efforts have been instrumental in obtaining job protection for employees who expose corrupt or abusive business practices, federal financing of presidential elections, and the creation of the Environmental Protection Agency. Few Americans have ever compiled such a long and impressive list of legislative accomplishment.

But Nader's ultimate goal was not simply to protect consumers from shoddy or dangerous products. It was to reinvigorate the nation's ideal of democracy by encouraging active grass-roots citizen participation in politics. The best answer to society's problems, he believed, was for ordinary citizens to campaign for safer consumer products, better schools, a cleaner environment, and safer workplaces.

During the late 1970s and 1980s, Nader's influence seemed to wane. In 1978, Congress defeated his proposal for a Consumer Protection Agency. Critics dismissed him as a "scold." In a decade of deregulation, his call for greater regulations seemed out of step with the times.

As the 1980s ended and the 1990s began, however, it was clear that Nader remained a major force in American politics. He played a central role in passing a California initiative that rolled back the cost of auto insurance. He led a bitter fight against a proposed 51 percent congressional pay raise. And his long campaign for auto safety achieved an important breakthrough when the major automobile manufacturers agreed to install air bags in most of their cars.

Ralph Nader illustrates in vivid terms the difference that one person's life can make. His life also epitomizes the idealism and activism of the 1960s—a decade when hundreds of thousands of Americans gave new life to the nation's democratic ideals. African Americans used sit-ins, freedom rides, and protest marches to fight segregation, poverty, and unemployment. Feminists demanded equal employment opportunities and an end to sexual discrimination. Mexican Americans protested discrimination in voting, education, and employment. Native Americans demanded that the government recognize their land claims and the right of tribes to govern themselves.

Although these and other grass-roots activists seemed to fade from public view during the 1980s, they—like Ralph Nader—never abandoned their causes and today remain a significant force in American life. Indeed, the success of their efforts has led to a conservative grass-roots reaction, one in which equally committed Americans have denounced busing, affirmative action, quotas, and abortion.

The Struggle for Racial Justice

For African Americans in 1960 the statistics were grim. Their average life span in 1960 was seven years less than that of white Americans. Their children had only half the chance of completing high school, only a third the chance of completing college, and a third the chance of entering a profession when they grew up. On average, black Americans earned half as much as white Americans and were twice as likely to be unemployed.

Despite a string of court victories during the late 1950s, many blacks were still second-class citizens, due to lax enforcement of civil rights laws. Six years after the landmark *Brown* v. *Board of Education* decision, only one percent of black schoolchildren in the 11 states of the old Confederacy attended public school with white classmates. Less than a quarter of the South's voting-age black population could vote, and in certain southern counties blacks could not serve on grand juries and trial juries, or frequent all-white beaches, restaurants, and hotels.

In the North, too, African Americans suffered humiliation, insult, embarrassment, and discrimination. Many neighborhoods, businesses, and unions almost totally excluded blacks. Unemployment soared as laborsaving technology eliminated many semiskilled and unskilled jobs that historically provided many blacks with work. Black families experienced severe strain; the proportion of black families headed by women jumped from 8 percent in 1950 to 21 percent in 1960.

During the 1960s, however, a growing hunger for full equality arose among African Americans. The Rev. Dr. Martin Luther King, Jr., gave voice to the new mood when he said: "We can't wait any longer. Now is the time."

Freedom Now

"Now is the time." These words became the credo and rallying cry for a generation. On Monday, February 1, 1960, four black freshmen at North Carolina Agricultural and Technical College walked into the F.W. Woolworth store in Greensboro, North Carolina, and sat down at the lunch counter. Each asked for a cup of coffee. A waitress told them that she would only serve them if they stood.

Instead of walking away, the four college freshmen stayed in their seats until the lunch counter closed, giving birth to the "sit-in." The next morning, the four college students reappeared at Woolworth's, accompanied by 25 fellow students. By the end of the week protesters filled Woolworth's and other lunch counters in town. Although the student protesters subscribed to King's doctrine of nonviolence, their opponents did not—assaulting the students both verbally and physically. When the police were called, they often arrested black protesters, not the whites who tormented them.

By the end of February lunch counter sit-ins had spread through 30 cities in seven southern states. This form of protest was also used against segregated libraries and other facilities. In April, 142 student sit-in leaders from 11 states met in Raleigh, North Carolina, and voted to set up a new group to coordinate the sit-ins, the Student Nonviolent Coordinating Committee (SNCC). The Rev. Dr. Martin Luther King, Jr., told the students that their willingness to go to jail would "be the thing to awaken the dozing conscience of many of our white brothers."

In the summer of 1960 sit-ins gave way to "wade-ins" at segregated public beaches. In Atlanta, Charlotte, Greensboro, and Nashville, black students lined up at white-only box offices of segregated movie theaters. By the end of 1960, 70,000 people had taken part in sit-ins in over 100 cities in 20 states. Police arrested and jailed more than 3,600 protesters. Nevertheless, the new tactic worked. By August 1 lunch counters in 15 states had been integrated. By the end of the year protesters had succeeded in integrating eating establishments in 108 cities.

The Greensboro sit-in initiated a new, activist phase in black America's struggle for equal rights. Fed up with the slow, legalistic approach that characterized the civil rights movement in the past, southern black college students began to attack the Jim Crow laws directly. In the upper South, federal court orders and student sit-ins successfully desegregated lunch counters, theaters, hotels, public parks, churches, libraries, and beaches. But in three states—Alabama, Mississippi, and South Carolina—segregation remained intact. In those states young civil rights activists launched new assaults against segregation.

To the Heart of Dixie

In early May 1961, 13 men and women, black and white, set out from Washington, D.C., on two buses. They called themselves "freedom riders," and they wanted to demonstrate that despite a federal ban on segregated travel on interstate buses, segregation prevailed throughout much of the South. The freedom riders' trip was sponsored by the Congress of Racial Equality (CORE), a civil rights group dedicated to breaking down racial barriers through nonviolent protest.

In Virginia and North Carolina the freedom riders met little trouble. But in Winnsboro, South Carolina, police arrested two black freedom riders, and outside Anniston, Alabama, a white hurled a bomb through one of the bus's windows, setting the vehicle on fire. Waiting white thugs beat the freedom riders as they tried to escape the smoke and flames. Eight other whites boarded the second bus and assaulted the freedom riders before police restrained the attackers.

In Birmingham and Montgomery, Alabama, another mob of whites attacked the freedom riders with clubs, blackjacks, and pipes. Local law enforcement agencies were slow in aiding the protesters. Explained Montgomery's police commissioner: "We have no intention of standing police guard for a bunch of troublemakers coming into our city."

President Kennedy was appalled by the violence. He hastily deputized 400 federal marshals and Treasury agents and flew them to Alabama to protect the freedom riders' rights. The president publicly called for a "cooling-off period," but conflict continued. When the freedom riders arrived in Jackson, Mississippi, 27 were arrested for entering a "white-only" washroom and were sentenced to 60 days on the state prison farm.

The threat of racial violence in the South led the Kennedy administration to pressure the Interstate Commerce Commission to desegregate air, bus, and train terminals. In more than 300 southern terminals signs saying "white" and "colored" were taken down from waiting room entrances and lavatory doors.

Civil rights activists next aimed to open state universities to black students. Many southern states opened their universities to black students without incident. Other states were stiff-backed in their opposition to integration. A major breakthrough occurred in September 1962, when a federal court ordered the state of Mississippi to admit James Meredith to the University of Mississippi in Oxford. Governor Ross Barnett vowed that he would go to jail rather than permit Meredith to register for classes. Barnett flew into Oxford, named himself special registrar of the university, and ordered the arrest of federal officials who tried to enforce the court order.

James Meredith refused to back down. He arrived at the Ole Miss campus in the company of police officers, federal marshals, and lawyers. Angry white students waited, chanting, "Two, four, six, eight—we don't want to integrate."

Four times James Meredith tried unsuccessfully to register at Ole Miss. He finally succeeded on the fifth attempt, escorted by several hundred federal marshals. The ensuing riot left two people dead and 375 injured, including 166 marshals. Ultimately, President Kennedy sent 16,000 troops to put down the violence.

"Bombingham"

By the end of 1961, protests against segregation, job discrimination, and police brutality had erupted from Georgia to Mississippi and Tennessee to Alabama. Staunch segregationists responded by vowing to defend the Jim Crow laws. The symbol of unyielding resistance to integration was Alabama governor George C. Wallace. Elected on an extreme segregationist platform, Wallace declared at his inauguration in January 1963: "I draw the line in the dust and toss the gauntlet before the feet of tyranny, and I say segregation now, segregation tomorrow, segregation forever."

It was in Birmingham, Alabama, that civil rights activists faced the most determined resistance. A sprawling steel town of 340,000 people, Birmingham had a long history of racial acrimony. In open defiance of Supreme Court rulings Birmingham had closed its public playgrounds, swimming pools, and golf courses rather than integrate them. Calling Birmingham "the most thoroughly segregated city in the United States," Martin Luther King announced in early 1963 that he would lead demonstrations in the city until demands for fair hiring practices, desegregation, and amnesty for previously arrested civil rights demonstrators were met.

Day after day, well-dressed men, women, and children marched against segregation—only to be jailed for demonstrating without a permit. On April 12 King himself was arrested—and while in jail wrote his now-famous "Letter from Birmingham City Jail," a scathing response to a group of white clergymen who had publicly criticized King for staging the demonstrations.

For two weeks all was quiet, but in early May demonstrations resumed with renewed vigor. On May 2 and again on May 3 more than a thousand of Birmingham's black youths marched for equal rights. In response, the local police chief, Eugene "Bull" Connor, unleashed police dogs and sprayed the marchers with high-pressure fire hoses. Watching the willful brutality on television, millions of Americans, white and black, were shocked by the face of segregation.

Tension mounted as police arrested 2,543 blacks and whites between May 2 and May 7, 1963. Under intense pressure, the Birmingham Chamber of Commerce reached an agreement on May 9 with black leaders to desegregate public facilities, hire blacks as clerks and salespersons, and release demonstrators without bail in return for an end to the protests.

King's goal was nonviolent social change—but the short-term result of protest was violence and confrontation. On May 11 white extremists firebombed an integrated motel. That same night a bomb destroyed the

Police used dogs, high-pressure water hoses, clubs, and electric cattle prods to break up the nonviolent civil rights demonstration in Birmingham, Alabama, in May 1963. Scenes such as this one, broadcast on television to millions of viewers, aroused public indignation and sympathy for the civil rights movement.

home of King's brother. Shooting incidents and racial confrontations quickly spread across the South. In June a gunman killed Medgar Evers, the NAACP field representative in Mississippi. In September an explosion destroyed Birmingham's Sixteenth Street Baptist Church, killing four black girls and injuring 14 others. All told, ten people died during racial protests in 1963, 35 black homes and churches were firebombed, and 20,000 people were arrested during civil rights protests.

Kennedy Finally Acts

The eruption of violence forced the Kennedy administration to introduce legislation to guarantee black civil rights. Twice before, in 1957 and 1960, the federal government had adopted weak civil rights acts designed to provide federal protection for African American voting rights. Now Kennedy responded to the racial violence by proposing a new stronger civil rights bill that required the desegregation of public facilities, outlawed discrimination in employment and voting, and allowed the attorney general to initiate school desegregation suits.

Kennedy's record on civil rights inspired little confidence. He had voted against the 1957 Civil Rights Act, and in the 1960 campaign many African American leaders backed Richard Nixon, even though Kennedy worked hard to court the black vote by promising new civil rights legislation and declaring that as president he would end housing discrimination. A few weeks before the 1960 election, Kennedy broadened his black support by helping to secure the release of Martin Luther King from an Atlanta jail, where he had been imprisoned for leading an antisegregation demonstration.

Once in office, however, Kennedy moved slowly on civil rights issues, both because he feared alienating white southern Democrats and because he had no deep commitment to the cause. Although Kennedy's administration filed 28 suits to protect black voting rights (compared to ten suits filed during the Eisenhower years), it was not until November 1963 that Kennedy took steps to fulfill his campaign promise to end housing discrimination.

The violence that erupted in Birmingham and elsewhere in 1961 and 1962 alarmed many veteran civil rights leaders. Eager to rededicate the movement to the principle of nonviolence, African American leaders decided that a massive march for civil rights and jobs might provide the necessary pressure to prompt Kennedy and Congress to act.

On August 28, 1963, over 200,000 people gathered around the Washington Monument and marched to the Lincoln Memorial. Ten speakers addressed the crowd, but the event's highlight was an address by Martin Luther King. After he finished his prepared text King launched into his legendary closing words. "I have a dream," he declared, "that one day on the red hills of Georgia the sons of former slaves and the sons of former slaveowners will be able to sit down together at the table of brotherhood. . . . I have a dream that one day even the state of Mississippi, a state sweltering with people's injustices, sweltering with the heat of oppression, will be transformed into an oasis of freedom and justice." As the audience roared its approval, King continued: "I have a dream that one day this nation will rise up and live out the true meaning of its creed: 'We hold these truths to be self-evident; that all men are created equal.'"

For seven months, debate raged in the halls of Congress. In a futile effort to delay the Civil Rights Bill's passage, opponents proposed over 500 amendments and staged a protracted filibuster in the Senate. On July 2, 1964—a little over a year after President Kennedy had sent it to Congress—the Civil Rights Act was enacted into law, skillfully pushed through Congress by President Lyndon Johnson. The act prohibited discrimination in voting, employment, and public facilities such as hotels and restaurants, and it established the Equal Employment Opportunity Commission to prevent discrimination in employment on the basis of race, religion, or gender.

Although most white southerners accepted the new federal law without resistance, many violent incidents occurred as angry whites vented their rage. Even so, the Civil Rights Act was a success. In the first weeks under the 1964 civil rights law segregated restaurants and hotels across the South opened their doors to black patrons. Over the next ten years the Justice Department would bring hundreds of suits against school districts, hotels, restaurants, taverns, gas stations, and truck stops charged with racial discrimination.

The 1964 Civil Rights Act prohibited discrimination in employment and public accommodations. But many African Americans were denied an equally fundamental constitutional right, the right to vote. The most effective barriers to black voting were state laws requiring prospective voters to read and interpret sections of the state constitution. In Alabama, voters had to provide written answers to a 20-page test on the Constitution and state and local government.

In an effort to bring the issue of voting rights to national attention, Martin Luther King in early 1965 launched a voter registration drive in Selma, Alabama. Even though blacks slightly outnumbered whites in the city of 25,000, Selma's voting rolls were 99 percent white and one percent black. For seven weeks King led hundreds of black residents to the county courthouse to register to vote. Nearly 2,000 black demonstrators, including King, were jailed by County Sheriff James Clark for contempt of court and parading without a permit. After a federal court ordered Clark not to interfere with orderly registration, the sheriff forced black applicants to stand in line for up to five hours before being permitted to take a "literacy" test. Not a single black voter was added to the registration rolls.

When a young black man was killed during a riot in nearby Marion, King responded by calling for a march from Selma to the state capital of Montgomery, 50 miles away. On March 7, 1965, black voting-rights demonstrators began their march, but were attacked by 200 mounted state police as they crossed a bridge spanning the Alabama River. The march resumed on March 21 with federal protection. The marchers chanted: "Segregation's got to fall . . . you never can jail us all." On March 25 a crowd of 25,000 gathered at the state capitol to celebrate the march's completion.

Two measures adopted in 1965 helped safeguard the voting rights of black Americans. On January 23 the states completed ratification of the Twenty-fourth Amendment to the Constitution barring a poll tax in federal elections. At the time, five southern states still had a poll tax. On August 6 President Johnson signed the Voting Rights Act, which prohibited literacy tests and sent federal examiners to seven southern states to register black voters. Within a year, 450,000 southern blacks registered to vote.

Black Nationalism and Black Power

At the same time that such civil rights leaders as Dr. Martin Luther King fought for racial integration, other black leaders emphasized separatism and identification with Africa. One of the most important expressions of the separatist impulse during the 1960s was the rise of the Black Muslims, which attracted 100,000 members. Founded in 1931, the Nation of Islam drew its appeal from among the growing numbers of urban blacks living in poverty.

The Black Muslims, led by Elijah Muhammad, elevated racial separatism into a religious doctrine and declared that whites were doomed to destruction unless they acceded to the Muslim separatist demands. The Black Muslims did more than vent anger and frustration. The organization was also a vehicle of black uplift and self-help. The Black Muslims called upon black Americans to "wake up, clean up, and stand up" in order to achieve true freedom and independence. To root out any behavior that conformed to racist stereotypes, the Muslims forbade eating pork and cornbread, drinking alcohol, and smoking cigarettes. Muslims also emphasized the creation of black businesses.

The most controversial exponent of black nationalism was Malcolm X. The son of a Baptist minister who had been an organizer for Marcus Garvey's United Negro Improvement Association, he was born Malcolm

Little in Omaha, Nebraska, and grew up in Lansing, Michigan. A re-formed drug addict and criminal, Malcolm X learned about the Black Muslims in prison. After his release in 1952, he adopted the name Malcolm X to replace "the white slave-master name which had been imposed upon my paternal forebears by some blue-eyed devil."

He quickly became one of the Black Muslims' most eloquent speakers. His main message was that discrimination led many black Americans to despise themselves. Self-hatred, he argued, caused black Americans to lose their identity, straighten their hair, and become involved in crime, drug addiction, and alcoholism. Condemned by some whites as a demagogue for such statements as "If ballots won't work, bullets will," Malcolm X gained widespread public notoriety by attacking Martin Luther King as a "chump" and an Uncle Tom, by advocating self-defense against white violence, and by emphasizing black political power.

In March 1964 Malcolm X withdrew from Elijah Muhammad's organization and set up his own Organization of Afro-Americans. Less than a year later, his life ended in bloodshed. On February 21, 1965, in front of

Malcolm X, frustrated with moderate civil rights advocates, spoke sharply against racism and called for African-American self-defense against white violence. In 1964, he founded the Organization of Afro-American Unity.

400 followers, he was shot and killed, apparently by followers of Black Muslim leader Elijah Muhammad.

Inspired by Malcolm X's example, young black activists embraced the new spirit of radicalism and increasingly challenged the traditional leadership of the civil rights movement and its philosophy of nonviolence. The single greatest contributor to the growth of militancy was the continued violence perpetrated by white racists. One of the most publicized incidents took place in the summer of 1964, when three civil rights workers—two whites, Andrew Goodman and Michael Schwerner, and one black, James Chaney—disappeared near Philadelphia, Mississippi. Six weeks after they were reported missing, the bodies of the men were found buried under a dam; all three had been beaten, then shot. David Dennis, a black civil rights leader, spoke at James Chaney's funeral. He angrily declared: "I'm sick and tired of going to the funerals of black men who have been murdered by white men. . . . I've got vengeance in my heart."

In 1966 two key civil rights organizations—SNCC and CORE (the Congress of Racial Equality)–embraced black nationalism. In May, Stokely Carmichael was elected chairman of SNCC and proceeded to transform the group from an interracial organization committed to nonviolence and integration into an all-black organization committed to "black power." "Integration is irrelevant," declared Carmichael. "Political and economic power is what the black people have to have." Although Carmichael initially denied that "black power" implied racial separatism, he eventually called on blacks to form their own separate political organizations. In July 1966 CORE also endorsed black power and repudiated nonviolence.

Of all the groups advocating racial separatism and black power, the one that received the widest publicity was the Black Panther party. Formed in October 1966 in Oakland, California, the Black Panthers were an armed revolutionary socialist organization advocating self-determination for black ghettoes. The Black Panthers gained public notoriety by entering the gallery of the California State Assembly brandishing guns and by following police to prevent brutality toward blacks.

Separatism and black nationalism attracted no more than a small minority of African Americans, and public opinion polls indicated that the overwhelming majority of blacks considered Martin Luther King their favored spokesperson. The older civil rights organizations such as the NAACP rejected black power, viewing it as an abandonment of the goals of nonviolence and integration.

Yet despite their relatively small following, black power advocates exerted a powerful and positive influence upon the civil rights movement. In addition to giving birth to a host of community self-help organizations, supporters of black power spurred the formation of black studies programs in universities and encouraged black Americans to take pride in their racial background. A growing number of African Americans began to wear "Afro" hairstyles and take African or Islamic surnames. Singer James Brown captured the new spirit: "Say it loud—I'm black and I'm proud."

In an effort to maintain support among more militant blacks, civil rights leaders began to address the problems of the poor blacks who lived in the cities. By the mid-1960s Martin Luther King had begun to move toward the political Left. King denounced the Vietnam War as "an enemy of the poor," and urged a radical redistribution of wealth and political power in the United States to provide medical care, jobs, and education for all of the nation's people.

The Civil Rights Movement Moves North

On August 11, 1965, five days after President Lyndon Johnson signed the Voting Rights Act, the arrest of a 21-year-old for drunk driving ignited a

A major achievement of the black power movement was to increase educational opportunities for minorities in universities across the country.

riot in Watts, a predominantly black section of Los Angeles. The violence lasted five days and resulted in 34 deaths, 3,900 arrests, and the destruction of over 744 buildings in a 20-square-mile area. Rioters smashed windows, hurled bricks and bottles from rooftops, and looters stripped store shelves.

Over the next four summers the nation's inner cities experienced a wave of violence and rioting. The last major wave occurred following the assassination of Martin Luther King in Memphis, Tennessee, on April 4, 1968. Violence erupted in 168 cities, leaving 46 dead, 3,500 injured, and $40 million worth of damage. In Washington, D.C., fires burned within three blocks of the White House.

In 1968 President Johnson appointed a commission to examine the causes of the race riots of the preceding three summers. The commission attributed racial violence to "white racism" and its heritage of discrimination and exclusion. Joblessness, poverty, a lack of political power, decaying and dilapidated housing, police brutality, and poor schools bred a sense of frustration and rage that had exploded into violence. The commission warned that unless major steps were taken, the United States would inevitably become "two societies, one black, one white—separate and unequal."

Until 1964 most white northerners regarded race as a peculiarly southern problem that could be solved by extending political and civil rights to southern blacks. Beginning in early 1964, however, thousands of blacks throughout the North staged sit-ins, boycotts, and demonstrations to protest school segregation as well as job, housing, and employment discrimination. Americans learned that discrimination and racial prejudice were nationwide problems.

In the North African Americans suffered from de facto discrimination in housing, schooling, and employment—discrimination that lacked the overt sanction of law. The most obvious example of de facto segregation related to schooling. An overwhelming majority of northern black children attended predominantly black inner-city schools while most white children attended schools with an overwhelming majority of whites. In 1968—fourteen years after the *Brown* v. *Board of Education* decision—federal courts began to order busing as a way to deal with de facto segregation brought about by housing patterns. In April 1971 in the case of *Swann* v. *Charlotte-Mecklenburg Board of Education* the Supreme Court upheld "bus transportation as a tool of school desegregation."

The Great Society

Lyndon B. Johnson had a vision for America. Believing that problems of housing, income, employment, and health were ultimately a federal responsibility, Johnson used the weight of the presidency and his formidable political skills to enact the most impressive array of reform legislation since the days of Franklin Roosevelt, a figure Johnson greatly admired. He envisioned a society without poverty or discrimination, in which all Americans enjoyed equal educational and job opportunities. He called this vision the "Great Society."

A major feature of Johnson's Great society program was the "War on Poverty." The federal government raised the minimum wage and enacted programs to train poorer Americans for new and better jobs, including the 1964 Manpower Development and Training Act and the Economic Opportunity Act, which established such programs as the Job Corps and the Neighborhood Youth Corps. To assure adequate housing, Congress in 1966 adopted the Model Cities Act to attack urban blight, set up a cabinet-level Department of Housing and Urban Development, and began a program of rent supplements.

To promote education, Congress passed the Higher Education Act in 1965 providing student loans and scholarships, the Elementary and Secondary Schools Act of 1965 to pay for textbooks, and the Educational Opportunity Act of 1968 to help the poor finance college educations. To address the nation's health needs, the Child Health Improvement and Protection Act of 1968 provided for prenatal and postnatal care, the Medicaid Act of 1968 paid for the medical expenses of the poor, and Medicare, established in 1965, extended medical insurance to older Americans under the Social Security system.

Johnson also prodded Congress to pass a broad spectrum of civil rights laws, ranging from the Civil Rights Act of 1964 and the Voting Rights Act of 1965 to the 1968 Fair Housing Act barring discrimination in the sale or rental of housing. In 1965 LBJ issued an executive order requiring government contracts to ensure that job applicants and employees were not discriminated against. It required all contractors to prepare an "affirmative action plan" to achieve these goals.

Johnson broke many other color barriers. In 1966 he named the first black cabinet member and appointed the first black woman to the federal bench. In 1967 he appointed Thurgood Marshall to become the first black American to serve on the Supreme Court. The first southerner to reside in the White House in half a century, Johnson showed a stronger commitment to improving the position of black Americans than any previous president.

When President Johnson announced his Great Society program in 1964, he promised substantial reductions in the number of Americans living in poverty. When he left office, he could legitimately argue that he had delivered on his promise. In 1960, 40 million Americans, 20 percent of the population, were classified as poor. By 1969, their number had fallen to 24 million, 12 percent of the population. Johnson also pledged to qualify the poor for new and better jobs, to extend health insurance to the poor and elderly to cover hospital and doctor costs, and to provide better housing for low-income families. Here too Johnson could say he had delivered. Infant mortality among the poor, for example, fell by one-third in the decade after 1965 as a result of expanded federal medical and nutritional programs.

Although critics argued that Johnson took a shotgun approach to reform and pushed poorly thought-out bills through Congress, supporters responded that at least Johnson tried to move toward a more compassionate society. During the 1960s median black family income rose by 53 percent, while black employment in professional, technical, and clerical occupations doubled. The proportion of blacks below the poverty line fell from 55 percent in 1960 to 27 percent in 1968. The black unemployment rate fell 34 percent. The country had taken major strides toward extending equality of opportunity to African Americans. In addition, the number of whites below the poverty line dropped dramatically, and such poverty-plagued regions as Appalachia made significant economic strides.

White Backlash

Ghetto rioting, the rise of black militancy, and resentment over Great Society social legislation combined to produce a backlash among many whites. Commitment to bringing black Americans into full equality declined. In the wake of the riots, many whites fled the nation's cities. The Census Bureau estimated that 900,000 whites moved each year from central cities to the suburbs between 1965 and 1970.

The 1968 Republican candidate Richard Nixon promised to eliminate "wasteful" federal antipoverty programs and to name conservatives to the Supreme Court. As presidnet, Nixon moved quickly to keep his commitments. In an effort to curb Great Society social programs, Nixon did away with the Model Cities program and the Office of Economic Opportunity. The administration urged Congress not to extend the Voting Rights Act of 1965 and to end a fair housing enforcement program.

Nixon also made a series of Supreme Court appointments that brought to an end the liberal activist era of the court. During the 1960s the Supreme Court greatly increased the ability of criminal defendants to defend themselves. In *Mapp* v. *Ohio* (1961) the high court ruled that evidence secured by the police through unreasonable searches must be excluded from trials. In *Gideon* v. *Wainwright* (1963) it declared that indigent defendants have a right to a court-appointed attorney. In *Escobedo* v. *Illinois* (1964) it ruled that suspects being interrogated by police have a right to legal counsel.

As president, Nixon promised to alter the balance between the rights of criminal defendants and society's rights. He selected Warren Burger, a moderate conservative, to replace Earl Warren as chief justice of the Supreme Court and then nominated two conservative white southerners for a second court vacancy, only to have both nominees rejected (one for financial improprieties, the other for alleged insensitivities to civil rights). He eventually named four justices to the high court: Burger, Harry Blackmun, Lewis Powell, and William Rehnquist.

Under Chief Justice Burger and his successor William Rehnquist, the Supreme Court defined the remedies that can be used to clarify past discrimination. In 1974 the court limited the use of school busing for purposes of racial desegregation. In 1978 in the landmark *Bakke* case, the court held that educational institutions could take race into account when screening applicants, but could not use rigid racial quotas. The following year, however, the court ruled that employers could legally establish voluntary programs, including the use of quotas, to aid minorities and women in employment.

The Struggle Continues

Over the past quarter century African Americans have made impressive social and economic gains, yet full equality remains an elusive dream. State-sanctioned segregation was eliminated, and many barriers to equal opportunity were shattered. In political representation, educational attainment, and representation in white-collar and professional occupations, black Americans have made striking gains. Between 1960 and 1988 the number of black political officeholders rose from just 300 to nearly 6,600. Black mayors have governed many of the nation's largest cities, including Chicago, Detroit, Los Angeles, Philadelphia, and Washington, D.C.

Nevertheless, millions of African Americans still do not share fully in the promise of American life, and separation of the races in housing and schooling remains widespread. According to census figures, blacks still suffer twice the unemployment rate of whites and earn only about half as much. The poverty rate among black families is three times that of whites, the same ratio as in the 1950s. Forty percent of black children are raised in fatherless homes and almost half of all black children are born into families earning less than the poverty level.

Although the United States has eliminated many obstacles to black progress, reformers maintain that much remains to be done before the country attains the equality Martin Luther King and Lyndon Johnson envisioned.

The Youth Revolt

During the 1960s one age group of Americans loomed larger than any other: youth. As a result of the depressed birthrates during the 1930s and the postwar baby boom, there was a sudden explosion in the number of teenagers and young adults. Unlike their parents, whose values had been shaped by the depression and World War II, young people of the 1960s grew up during a period of prosperity. This sense of economic security allowed them to seek personal fulfillment and to dismiss the older generation's success-oriented lives. Their skepticism of corporate and bureaucratic authority, their strong emotional identification with the underprivileged, and their intense desire for stimulation and instant gratification shaped the nation's politics, dress, music, and film.

At no earlier time in American history had the gulf between the generations seemed so wide. Blue jeans, long hair, psychedelic drugs, casual sex, hippie communes, campus demonstrations, and rock and roll all became symbols of the distance separating youth from the world of conventional adulthood.

The New Left

Late in the spring of 1962 five dozen college students gathered at a lakeside camp near Port Huron, Michigan, to discuss politics. For four days and nights the members of an obscure student group known as Students for a Democratic Society (SDS) talked passionately about such topics as civil rights, foreign policy, and the quality of American life. The gathering ended with the participants agreeing on a political platform. This manifesto, one of the pivotal political documents of the 1960s, became known as the Port Huron Statement. Its chief author was Tom Hayden, who had spent much of 1961 in the South, working with SNCC in the civil rights movement. Hayden would become a key figure in the student movement.

The goal set forward in the Port Huron Statement was the creation of a radically democratic political movement in the United States that rejected hierarchy and bureaucracy. In its most important paragraphs the document called for "participatory democracy"—direct individual involvement in the decisions that affected their lives. This notion would become the battle cry of the student movement of the 1960s—a movement that came to be known as the New Left.

During the 1960s thousands of young college students became politically active. The first issue to spark student radicalism was the modern university, which many students criticized for being too bureaucratic and impersonal. Students questioned university requirements, restrictions on student political activities, and dormitory rules. Restrictions on students handing out political pamphlets on university property led to the first campus demonstrations that broke out at the University of California at Berkeley, led by Mario Savio and the Berkeley Free Speech Movement. The protests soon spread to other campuses.

Involvement in the civil rights movement in the South initiated many students into radical politics. In the early 1960s many white students from northern universities began to participate in voter registration drives, freedom schools, sit-ins, and freedom rides to help desegregate the South.

Student radicalism also drew inspiration from a literature of social criticism that flourished in the 1950s. During that decade, many of the most popular films, novels, and writings aimed at young people criticized conventional middle-class life. Popular films, like *Rebel Without a Cause* (1955), and popular novels, like J. D. Salinger's *Catcher in the Rye* (1951), celebrated sensitive, directionless, alienated youths unable to conform to the conventional adult values of suburban and corporate America. Sophisticated works of social criticism, by such maverick sociologists, psychologists, and economists as Herbert Marcuse, Norman O. Brown, Paul Goodman, Michael Harrington, and C. Wright Mills, documented the growing concentration of power in the hands of social elites, the persistence of poverty in a land of plenty, and the stresses and injustices in America's social order.

Above all, student radicalism owed its support to student opposition to the Vietnam War. SDS held its first antiwar march in 1965, which attracted at least 15,000 protestors to Washington, and commanded wide press attention. Over the next three years opposition to the war brought thousands of new members to SDS. In addition to its antiwar activities, members of SDS also tried to organize a democratic "interracial movement of the poor" in northern city neighborhoods.

Many members of SDS quickly grew frustrated by the slow pace of social change and began to embrace violence as a tool to transform society. After 1968, SDS rapidly tore itself apart as an effective political force, and its final convention in 1969 degenerated into a shouting match between radicals and moderates. That same year the Weathermen, a surviving faction of SDS, attempted to launch a guerrilla war in the streets of Chicago—an incident known as the "Days of Rage." Finally, in 1970 three members of the Weathermen blew themselves up in a Greenwich Village brownstone trying to make a bomb out of a stick of dynamite and an alarm clock.

Throughout the 1960s the SDS and other radical student organizations claimed to speak for the nation's youth, and in thousands of editorials and magazine articles journalists accepted this claim. In reality, SDS represented only a small minority of college students, who themselves composed a minority of the country's youth. Far more young Americans voted for George Wallace in 1968 than joined SDS, and most college students during the decade spent more time studying and enjoying the college experience than protesting. Nevertheless, radical students did help to draw the nation's attention to the problem of racism in American society and the moral issues involved in the Vietnam War. In that sense, their impact far exceeded their numbers.

The Making of a Counterculture

The New Left had a series of heroes, ranging from Marx, Lenin, and Ho, to Mao, Fidel, and other revolutionaries. It also had its own uniforms, rituals, and music. Faded blue work shirts and jeans, wire-rimmed glasses, and work shoes were *de rigueur;* so was the political protest folk music of Greenwich Village—of Phil Ochs, Bob Dylan, and Joan Baez.

But the New Left was only one part of youth protest during the 1960s. While the New Left labored to change the world and remake American society, other youths attempted to alter themselves and reorder consciousness. Variously labeled the counterculture, hippies, or flower children, they had their own heroes, music, dress, and approach to life.

In theory, supporters of the counterculture rejected individualism, competition, and capitalism, and challenged prevailing middle-class standards of behavior. Adopting rather unsystematic ideas from oriental religions, they sought to become one with the universe. Rejection of monogamy and the traditional nuclear family gave way to the tribal or communal ideal, where members renounced individualism and private property and shared food, work, and sex. In such a community, love was a general abstract ideal rather than a focused emotion.

The quest for oneness with the universe led many youths to experiment with hallucinogenic drugs. LSD had a particularly powerful allure. Under its influence, poets, musicians, politicians, and thousands of other Americans claimed to have tapped into an all-powerful spiritual force. Timothy Leary, the Harvard professor who became the leading prophet of LSD, asserted that the drug would unlock the mysteries of the universe.

Although LSD was outlawed in 1966, the drug continued to spread. Perhaps some takers discovered profound truths, but by the late 1960s drugs had done more harm than good. The history of the Haight-Ashbury section of San Francisco illustrated the problems caused by drugs. In 1967 Haight was the center of the "counterculture," the home of the "flower children." In the "city of love" hippies ingested LSD, smoked pot, listened to "acid rock," and proclaimed the dawning of a new age. Yet the area was suffering from severe problems. High levels of racial violence, venereal disease, rape, drug overdoses, and poverty ensured more bad trips than good.

Even music, which along with drugs and sex formed the counterculture trinity, failed to alter human behavior. In 1969 journalists hailed the Woodstock Music Festival as a symbol of love. But a few months later a group of Hell's Angels violently interrupted the Altamont Raceway music festival. As Mick Jagger sang "Sympathy for the Devil" an Angel stabbed a black man to death.

Like the New Left, the counterculture fell victim to its own excesses. Sex, drugs, and rock and roll did not solve the problems facing the United States. And by the early 1970s the counterculture had lost its force.

Liberation Movements

The struggle of African Americans for racial justice inspired a host of other groups to seek full equality. Women, Mexican Americans, Native Americans, and many other deprived groups protested against discrimination and organized to promote social change.

Women's Liberation

One of the most popular daytime television shows of the 1950s was "Queen for a Day." Five times a week, three women, each with a hard luck story, recited their tales of woe—diseases, difficult children, poverty—and the studio audience, with the aid of an applause meter, decided which woman was the most miserable. She became "Queen for a Day." Gifts for the winner included cosmetics, a makeover, and kitchen appliances— everything a woman needed to be a prettier and better housewife.

One woman in the television audience was Betty Friedan. A 1942 honors graduate of Smith College and former psychology Ph.D. candidate at the University of California at Berkeley, Friedan had quit graduate school, married, moved to the New York suburbs, and bore three children. American culture told her that husband, house, children, and electric appliances were true happiness. But Friedan was not happy. And she was not alone.

In 1957 Friedan sent out questionnaires to fellow members of her college graduating class. The replies amazed her. Again and again, she found women suffering from "a sense of dissatisfaction." Over the next five years Friedan interviewed hundreds of other women, and she repeatedly found an unexplainable sense of melancholy and incompleteness. Friedan was not the only observer to detect a widespread sense of discontent among American women. Doctors identified a new female malady, the housewife's syndrome, characterized by a mixture of frustration and exhaustion. When *Redbook* magazine asked for examples of this problem, in an article entitled "Why Young Mothers Feel Trapped," it received 24,000 replies.

Why, Friedan asked, were American women so discontented? In 1963 she published her answer in a book entitled *The Feminine Mystique*. Friedan analyzed and criticized the role of educators, psychologists, sociologists, and the mass media in conditioning women to believe that they could only find fulfillment as housewives and mothers. By requiring women to subordinate their own individual aspirations to the welfare of their husbands and children, the "feminine mystique" prevented women from achieving self-fulfillment and inevitably left women unhappy.

One of the most influential books ever written by an American, *The Feminine Mystique* helped launch a new movement for women's liberation. The book touched a nerve, but the origins of the movement lay much deeper—in the traditional role of females in American society.

During the 1950s many American women reacted against the poverty of the depression and the upheavals of World War II by placing renewed emphasis on family life. Young women married earlier than had their mothers, and had more children and bore them faster—producing a population growth rate approaching that of India. Growing numbers of women decided to forsake higher education or a full-time career and achieve emotional fulfillment as wives and mothers.

Politicians, educators, psychologists, and the mass media all echoed the view that women would find their highest fulfillment managing a house and caring for children. Women's magazines pictured housewives as happy with their tasks and depicted career women as neurotic, unhappy, and dissatisfied.

Already, however, a series of important social changes was underway that would contribute to a rebirth of feminism. A dramatic upsurge took place during the 1950s in women's employment and education, as more and more married women entered the labor force; the number of women receiving college degrees also rose. Meanwhile, beginning in 1957 the birthrate began to drop as women elected to have fewer children. A growing discrepancy had begun to appear between the popular image of happy women as full-time housewives and mothers and the actual realities of many women's lives.

Women in 1960 played a limited role in American government. Although women comprised about half of the nation's voters, there were no female Supreme Court justices, federal appeals court justices, governors, cabinet officers, or ambassadors. Only two of 100 U.S. senators and 15 of 435 representatives were women.

Economically, women workers were concentrated in low-paying service and factory jobs. The overwhelming majority worked as secretaries, waitresses, beauticians, teachers, nurses, and librarians. Lower pay for women doing the same work as men was commonplace. One out of every three companies had separate pay scales for male and female workers. Altogether, the earnings of women working full-time averaged only about 60 percent of those of men.

In many parts of the country the law discriminated against women. In three states—Alabama, Mississippi, and South Carolina—women could not sit on juries. Many states restricted married women's right to make contracts, sell property, engage in business, control their own earnings, and make wills. In practically every state men had a legal right to have intercourse with their wives and to administer an unspecified amount of physical punishment.

Women were often portrayed in the mass media in unrealistic ways. Magazines like *Reader's Digest* and television shows like "I Love Lucy" often stereotyped women as stupid or foolish, jealous of other women, irresponsible about money, and overanxious to marry.

In December 1961 President Kennedy placed the issue of women's rights on the national political agenda by establishing a President's Commission on the Status of Women. Chaired by Eleanor Roosevelt, the commission issued its report in 1963, the year that Betty Friedan published *The Feminine Mystique.* The report's recommendations included a call for an end to all legal restrictions on married women's right to own property, to enter into business, and to make contracts; equal opportunity in employment; and greater availability of child-care services. The most important reform to grow out of the commission's investigations was the 1963 Equal Pay Act, which required equal pay for men and women who performed the same jobs under equal conditions. The Equal Pay Act was the first federal law to prohibit discrimination on the basis of gender.

The next year Congress developed a new weapon in the fight against sex discrimination. Title VII of the 1964 Civil Rights Act prohibited discrimination in hiring or promotion based on race, color, religion, national origin, or gender by private employers and unions. The act made it illegal for employers to discriminate against women in hiring and promotion unless the employer could show that gender was a "bona fide occupational qualification" (for example, hiring a man as an attendant for a men's restroom). To investigate complaints of employment discrimination, the act set up the Equal Employment Opportunity Commission (EEOC).

At first, the EEOC focused its enforcement efforts on racial discrimination and largely ignored sex discrimination. To pressure the EEOC to enforce the law prohibiting such discrimination, Betty Friedan and 300 other women formed the National Organization for Women (NOW) in 1966. With Friedan as president, NOW filed suit against the EEOC "to force it to comply with its own government rules." It also sued the country's 1,300 largest corporations for sex discrimination and lobbied President Johnson to issue an executive order that would include women within federal affirmative action requirements.

At its second national conference in November 1967 NOW drew up an eight-point bill of rights for women. It called for adoption of an Equal Rights Amendment (ERA) to the Constitution, prohibiting sex discrimination; equal educational, job training, and housing opportunities for women; and repeal of laws limiting access to contraceptive devices and abortion.

Two proposals produced fierce dissension within the new organization. One source of disagreement was the Equal Rights Amendment, which stated: "Equality of rights under the law shall not be denied or abridged by the United States or by any state on account of sex." It had originally been proposed in 1923 and was submitted to Congress at almost every session for the next 40 years. The other issue that generated controversy was the call for reform of laws that made abortion a criminal offense.

Despite internal disagreements, NOW's membership grew rapidly, reaching 40,000 by 1974 and 175,000 by 1988. The group broadened its attention to include such issues as the plight of poor and nonwhite women, domestic violence, rape, sexual harrassment, the role of women in sport, and the rights of lesbians. At the same time, the organization claimed a number of achievements. Two victories were particularly important. In 1967 NOW persuaded President Johnson to issue Executive Order 11375, which prohibited government contractors from discriminating on the basis of gender and required them to take "affirmative action" to ensure that women were properly represented in their work force. The next year the EEOC ruled that separate want ads for men and women were a violation of Title VII of the 1964 Civil Rights Act.

Radical Feminism

Alongside NOW, other more radical feminist groups emerged during the 1960s. In cities across the country, independent women's groups sprouted up, establishing the first feminist bookstores, battered women's shelters, rape crisis centers, and abortion counseling centers. Women within these organizations resented their status as "second class citizens" in a male-dominated culture. In 1968 radical women's groups staged a protest of the Miss America pageant, concluding their rally by crowning a sheep Miss America.

In 1971 Gloria Steinem and others published *Ms.,* the first national feminist magazine. The first 300,000 copies were sold out in eight days. Meanwhile, radical new ideas began to fill the air, and a host of new words and phrases entered the language, such as "consciousness raising," "bra burning," "sexism," and "male chauvinist pig."

In the years following the publication of *The Feminine Mystique* feminists developed a large body of literature analyzing the economic, psychological, and social roots of female subordination. It was not until 1970, however, that the more radical feminist writings reached the broader reading public with the publication of Shulamith Firestone's *The Dialectic of Sex,* Germaine Greer's *The Female Eunuch,* and Kate Millett's *Sexual Politics.* These books argued that gender distinctions structure virtually every aspect of individual lives, not only in such areas as law and employment, but also in personal relationships, language, literature, religion, and an individual's internalized self-perceptions. Even more controversially, these works attributed female oppression to men and an ideology of male supremacy. "Women have very little idea how much men hate them," declared Greer. As examples of misogyny, these authors cited pornography, grotesque portrayals of women in literature, sexual harrassment, wife abuse, and rape.

Sex Discrimination

Despite its conservative image, the Supreme Court under chief justices Warren Burger and William Rehnquist were active in the area of sex discrimination and women's rights. The Burger Court issued its first important discrimination decision in 1971. In its landmark decision, *Griggs* v. *Duke Power Company,* the Court established the principle that regardless of an employer's intentions, any employment practice is illegal if it has a "disparate" impact on women or minorities and "if it cannot be shown to be related to job performance."

The court's most controversial decision involving women's rights was delivered in 1973 in the case of *Roe* v. *Wade.* The court struck down a nineteenth-century Texas law prohibiting abortion and all similar laws in other states. In its ruling, the court declared that the decision to have an abortion is a private matter of concern only to a woman and her physician, and that only in the last three months of pregnancy could the government limit the right to abortion.

Many Americans—including many Roman Catholic lay and clerical organizations—bitterly opposed the Supreme Court's *Roe* v. *Wade* decision and banded together to form the "right to life" movement. The major legislative success of the right-to-life movement was adoption by Congress of the so-called Hyde Amendment, which permitted states to refuse to fund abortions for indigent women.

In March 1972 Congress passed an Equal Rights Amendment (ERA) to the United States Constitution, prohibiting gender discrimination. Before the year was over, 22 state legislatures ratified the ERA, only 16 short of the 38 states required before the amendment would be added to the Constitution. Over the next five years, only 13 more states ratified the amendment—and five states rescinded their ratification. In 1978 Congress gave proponents of the amendment 39 more months to obtain ratification, but no other state gave its approval.

The ERA was defeated in part by organized labor, which feared that the amendment would eliminate state "protective legislation" that established minimum wages and maximum hours for women workers. Increasingly, however, resistance to the amendment came from conservative activists such as Phyllis Schlafly, a Radcliffe-educated mother of six. Schlafly argued that the ERA was unnecessary because women were already protected by the Equal Pay Act of 1963 and the Civil Rights Act of

Women have been involved in protest movements throughout the years. Here women march in support of the Equal Rights Amendment. Failure to achieve ratification by the required three-fourths of states sent the amendment to its final defeat in 1982.

1964, which barred sex discrimination, and that the amendment would outlaw separate public rest rooms and deny wives the right to financial support. She also raised the "women in combat" issue by suggesting that the passage of the ERA would mean that women would have to fight alongside men in wartime.

Impact of the Women's Liberation Movement

Since 1960 women have made impressive social gains. Advances in employment have been particularly noteworthy. During the 1970s the number of working women climbed 42 percent and much of the increase was in what traditionally was considered "men's" work and professional work—lawyers, professors, doctors, managers, and administrators.

Striking gains have been made in undergraduate and graduate education. Today, for the first time in American history, women constitute a majority of the nation's college students and nearly as many women as men receive master's degrees. In addition, the number of women students receiving degrees from professional schools—including dentistry, law, and medicine—has shot upward, from just 1,425 in 1966 to over 20,000 by the early 1990s. Women comprise nearly a third of the students attending law school and medical school.

Women have also made substantial political gains. In 1988 more than two dozen women served in Congress, and 80 served as mayors of large cities. In 1981 Sandra Day O'Connor became the first woman to sit on the Supreme Court, and in 1984 a major political party nominated a woman, Geraldine Ferraro, as its vice presidential candidate.

In spite of all that has been achieved, however, problems remain. Most women today continue to work in a relatively small number of traditional "women's" jobs, and a full-time female worker earns only 68 cents for every $1 paid to men. Even more troubling is the fact that large numbers of women live in poverty. Today, nearly half of all marriages end in divorce and many others end in legal separation and desertion—and the economic plight of these women is often grave. Although female-headed familes constitute only 15 percent of the U.S. population, they account for over 50 percent of the poor population.

Mexican-American Liberation

On election day, 1963, hundreds of Mexican Americans in Crystal City, Texas, did something that many had never done before: vote. Although Mexican Americans outnumbered Anglos two to one, Anglos controlled all five seats on the Crystal City council. For three years, organizers struggled to register Mexican-American voters. When the election was over, Mexican Americans had won control of the city council. "We have done the impossible," declared Albert Fuentes, who led the voter registration campaign. "If we can do it in Crystal City, we can do it all over Texas."

As the 1960s began, Mexican Americans shared problems of poverty and discrimination with other minority groups. The median income of a Mexican-American family was just 62 percent of the median income of the general population. Unemployment was twice that of non-Hispanic whites, and four-fifths of employed Mexican Americans were concentrated in semiskilled and unskilled jobs, a third in agriculture.

Educational attainment lagged behind other groups (Mexican Americans averaged less than nine years of schooling as recently as 1970), and Mexican-American pupils were concentrated in predominantly Mexican-American schools, less well staffed and supplied than non-Mexican-American schools, with few Hispanic or Spanish-speaking teachers. Gerrymandered election districts and restrictive voting legislation resulted in the political underrepresentation of Mexican Americans. They were underrepresented or excluded from juries by requirements that jurors be able to speak and understand English.

During the 1960s a new Mexican-American militancy arose. In 1962 César Chávez began to organize California farm workers, and three years later, in Delano, California, he led his first strike. At the same time that Chávez launched his struggle for higher wages and union recognition, Reies Lopez Tijerina fought to restore the legal rights of heirs to Spanish and Mexican land grants that had been guaranteed under the treaty ending the Mexican War.

In Denver, Rodolfo "Corky" Gonzales formed the Crusade for Justice in 1965 to protest school discrimination; provide legal, medical, and financial services and jobs for Chicanos; and foster the Mexican-American cultural heritage. La Raza Unida political parties arose in a number of small towns with large Mexican-American populations. On college campuses across the Southwest, Mexican Americans formed political organizations.

In 1968 Congress responded to the demand among Mexican Americans for equal educational opportunity by enacting legislation encouraging school districts to adopt bilingual education programs to instruct non-English speakers in both English and their native language. In a more recent action, Congress moved in 1986 to legalize the status of many immigrants, including many Mexicans, who entered the United States illegally. The Immigration Reform and Control Act of 1986 provided permanent legal residency to undocumented workers who had lived in the United States since before 1982 and prohibits employment of illegal aliens.

Since 1960 Mexican Americans have made important political gains. During the 1960s four Mexican Americans were elected to Congress. In

1974 two Chicanos were elected governors, becoming the first Mexican-American governors since early in this century. In 1981 Henry Cisneros of San Antonio became the first Mexican-American mayor of a large city.

Today, the 10.5 million Mexican Americans, the nation's second largest minority group, continue to struggle to expand their political influence, improve their economic position, and preserve their distinctive culture.

The Native American Power Movement

In November 1969, 200 Native Americans seized the abandoned federal penitentiary on Alcatraz Island in San Francisco Bay. For 19 months Indian activists occupied the island in order to draw attention to conditions on the nation's Indian reservations. Alcatraz, the Native Americans said, symbolized conditions on reservations: "It has no running water; it has inadequate sanitation facilities; there is no industry, and so unemployment is very great; there are no health care facilities; the soil is rocky and unproductive."

On Thanksgiving Day, 1970, 350 years after the Pilgrims' arrival, Wampanoag Indians, who had taken part at the first Thanksgiving, held a National Day of Mourning at Plymouth, Massachusetts. A tribal representative declared, "We forfeited our country. Our lands have fallen into the hands of the aggressor. We have allowed the white man to keep us on our knees." Meanwhile, another group of Native Americans established a settlement at Mount Rushmore, to demonstrate Indian claims to the Black Hills.

During the late 1960s and early 1970s a new spirit of political militancy arose among Native Americans, just as it had among black Americans and women. No other group, however, faced problems more severe than Native Americans. Throughout the 1960s Indians were the nation's poorest minority group, worse off than any other group according to virtually every socioeconomic measure. In 1970 the Native American unemployment rate was 10 times the national average, and 40 percent of the Indian population lived below the poverty line. In that year, Native-American life expectancy was just 44 years, a third less than that of the average American. Half a million Indian families lived in unsanitary, dilapidated dwellings that lacked indoor plumbing.

During World War II Native Americans began to revolt against such conditions. In 1944 they formed the National Congress of American Indians (NCAI), the first modern intertribal association. Among the group's primary concerns were protection of Indian land rights and improved educational opportunities. When Congress voted in 1953 to allow states to assert legal jurisdiction over Indian reservations without tribal consent and the federal government sought to transfer federal Indian responsibilities for a dozen tribes to the states (a policy known as "termination") and to relocate Indians into urban areas, the NCAI rallied opposition to these measures.

By the 1960s a new spirit of Indian nationalism had arisen. In 1961 a militant new Indian organization appeared, the National Indian Youth Council, which began to use the phrase "Red Power" and sponsored demonstrations and protest marches. Native Americans in the San Francisco Bay area in 1964 established the Indian Historical Society to present history from the Indian point of view, while the Native American Rights Fund brought legal suits against states that had taken Indian land and abolished Indian hunting, fishing, and water rights in violation of federal treaties. Many tribes also took legal action to prevent strip-mining or spraying of pesticides on their lands.

The best known of the Native-American groups was AIM, the American Indian Movement, formed by a group of Chippewas in 1966 to protest alleged police brutality. In the fall of 1972 AIM seized the offices of the Bureau of Indian Affairs in Washington, D.C., and occupied them for a week to dramatize Indian grievances. In the spring of 1973, 200 heavily armed Indians took over the town of Wounded Knee, South Dakota, site of an 1890 massacre of 300 Sioux by the U.S. army cavalry, and occupied the town for 71 days.

Indians are no longer a vanishing group of Americans. The 1980 census recorded an Indian population of 1.38 million in the United States, 72 percent over the figure reported in 1970 and four times the number recorded in 1950. About half live on reservations. The largest Native-American populations are located in Alaska, Arizona, California, New Mexico, and Oklahoma.

Although Native Americans continue to face severe problems of employment, income, and education, they have demonstrated that they will not abandon their Indian identity and culture or be treated as dependent wards of the federal government.

Conclusion

In the early 1960s black college students and religious groups, impatient with the slow pace of change, staged protests to challenge legal segregation in the South. Their efforts led the federal government to pass the Civil Rights Act of 1964, prohibiting discrimination in public facilities and employment, and the Twenty-fourth Amendment to the Constitution and the Voting Rights Act in 1965, guaranteeing black voting rights.

Despite significant legal gains, and the far-reaching effort of Lyndon Johnson's Great Society program, many African Americans felt a growing sense of frustration and anger. The violence perpetrated by white racists and

*C*hronology of Key Events

1960   First sit-ins held to protest segregation; Student Nonviolent Coordinating Committee (SNCC) founded

1961   Congress of Racial Equality (CORE) stages freedom rides; *Mapp* v. *Ohio* rules that evidence obtained by unreasonable search must be excluded

1962   James Meredith enrolls at University of Mississippi; SDS issues Port Huron Statement; César Chávez organizes California farm workers

1963   Martin Luther King, Jr., leads Birmingham, Alabama, demonstrations; racial violence sweeps the South; Betty Friedan's *The Feminine Mystique* published; Equal Pay Act requires equal pay for equal work; *Gideon* v. *Wainright;* Civil rights march on Washington, D.C.; John F. Kennedy assassinated; Lyndon Johnson becomes thirty-sixth president

1964   War on Poverty announced; Manpower Development and Training Act and Economic Opportunity Act establish the Job Corps and Neighborhood Youth Corps; *Escobedo* v. *Illinois;* Civil Rights Act prohibits discrimination in employment; Twenty-fourth Amendment prohibits poll taxes in federal elections

1965   Malcolm X assassinated; Martin Luther King, Jr., leads demonstrations in Selma, Alabama; Voting Rights Act prohibits literacy tests; Watts riot; Medicare extended to older Americans; Ralph Nader publishes *Unsafe at Any Speed*

1966   SNCC and CORE embrace black nationalism; Black Panther party organized; National Organization for Women formed; Model Cities Act passed to attack urban blight

1967   Riots in 127 cities

1968   Medicaid expanded to cover the poor; Martin Luther King, Jr. assassinated; riots in 168 cities

1971   *Swann* v. *Charlotte-Mecklenburg Board of Education* upholds busing as tool to achieve racial integration

1973   *Roe* v. *Wade* legalizes abortion

1986   Immigration Reform and Control Act provides permanent legal residency to undocumented workers who have lived in United States since 1982

a growing white backlash against civil rights led black nationalists to downplay the goal of integration and instead emphasize black power and black pride. Frustration was particularly evident in urban ghettoes, where the black poor faced problems that were not addressed by civil rights legislation.

The example of the civil rights movement inspired other groups to press for equal opportunity. The women's movement fought for passage of antidiscrimination laws, equal educational and employment opportunities, and a transformation of traditional views about women's place in society. Mexican Americans battled for bilingual education programs in schools, unionization of farm workers, improved job opportunities, and increased political power. Native Americans pressed for control over Indian lands and resources, the preservation of Indian cultures, and tribal self-government.

Suggestions for Further Reading

For insight into America during the 1960s consult Taylor Branch, *Parting the Waters* (1988); William H. Chafe, *Unfinished Journey,* 2d ed. (1991); Richard N. Goodwin, *Remembering America* (1988); Allen Matusow, *The Unraveling of America* (1984); William O'Neill, *Coming Apart* (1971).

The literature on the civil rights movement is voluminous. Besides those mentioned in the bibliography in Chapter 28, valuable analyses include Michel Belknap, *Federal Law and Southern Order* (1987); Derrick Bell, *And We Are Not Saved* (1987); David R. Goldfield, *Black, White, and Southern* (1990); Vincent Harding, *There is a River* (1981); Richard Kluger, *Simple Justice* (1975); Steven Lawson, *Running for Freedom* (1991); Nicholas Lemann, *The Promised Land* (1991); Doug McAdam, *Freedom Summer* (1988); Harvard Sitkoff, *The Struggle for Black Equality* (1981); Juan Williams, *Eyes on the Prize* (1987).

Useful books on feminism include Mary Frances Berry, *Why ERA Failed* (1986); William H. Chafe, *Women and Equality* (1977); Sara Evans, *Personal Politics* (1979); Leila Rupp and Verta Taylor, *Survival in the Doldrums* (1987).

The Mexican American struggle for equal rights is discussed in Rodolfo Acuña, *Occupied America,* 3d ed. (1988); Albert Camarillo, *Hispanics in a Changing Society* (1979); Mario T. García, *Mexican Americans* (1989); and Juan Gómez-Quiñones, *Chicano Politics* (1990). Books on Native Americans include Peter Iverson, *The Navajo Nation* (1981); Roger Nichols, *The American Indian: Past and Present,* 3d ed. (1985).

The youth movement and the rise of the New Left are examined in Paul Buhle, *History and the New Left* (1990); Morris Dickstein, *Gates of Eden* (1977); Todd Gitlin, *The Sixties* (1987); Maurice Isserman, . . . *If I Had a Hammer* (1987); W. J. Rorabaugh, *Berkeley at War* (1989); Theodore Roszak, *The Making of a Counter Culture* (1969); Kirkpatrick Sale, *SDS* (1973); Irwin Unger, *The Movement.*

America in Our Time

S hortly after 1 A.M. on the morning of June 17, 1972, a security guard at the Washington, D.C., Watergate office complex spotted a strip of masking tape covering the lock of a basement door. He removed it. A short while later, he found the door taped open again. He called the police, who found two more taped locks and a jammed door leading into the offices of the Democratic National Committee. Inside they discovered five men carrying cameras and electronic eavesdropping equipment.

At first, the Watergate break-in seemed like a minor incident. The identities of the burglars, however, suggested something more serious. One, James McCord, was chief security coordinator of the Committee for the Reelection of the President (CREEP). Others had links to the CIA.

Over the course of the next year, it became clear that the break-in was one of a series of secret operations coordinated by the White House. Financed by illegal campaign contributions, these operations posed a threat to America's constitutional system of government and eventually forced Richard Nixon to resign the presidency.

The Watergate break-in had its roots in Richard Nixon's obsession with secrecy and political intelligence. To stop "leaks" of information to the press, in 1971 the Nixon White House assembled a team of "plumbers," consisting of former CIA operatives. This private police force, paid for in part by illegal campaign contributions, engaged in a wide range of criminal acts, including phone tapping and burglary, against those on its "enemies list."

In 1972 when President Nixon was running for reelection, CREEP authorized another series of illegal activities. It hired Donald Segretti to stage "dirty tricks" against potential Democratic nominees, which included mailing letters that falsely accused one candidate of homosexuality and fathering an illegitimate child. It considered a plan to use call girls to blackmail Democrats at their national convention and to kidnap anti-Nixon radical leaders. The committee also authorized $250,000 for intelligence-gathering operations. Four times the committee sent burglars to break into Democratic headquarters.

Precisely what the campaign committee hoped to learn from these intelligence-gathering activities remains a mystery. It seems likely that it was seeking information about the Democratic party's campaign strategies and any information the Democrats had about illegal campaign contributions to the Republican party.

On June 23—six days after the botched break-in—President Nixon ordered aides to block an FBI investigation of White House involvement in the break-in on grounds that an investigation would endanger national security. He also counseled his aides to lie under oath, if necessary.

The Watergate break-in did not hurt Nixon's reelection campaign. Between the activities of the burglars and the president were layers of deception that had to be carefully peeled away. *Washington Post* reporters Bob Woodward and Carl Bernstein, sensing that the break-in was only part of a larger scandal, slowly pieced together part of the story. Facing long jail terms, some of the burglars began to tell the truth, and the truth illuminated a path leading to the White House.

If Nixon had few political friends, he had legions of enemies. Over the years he had offended or attacked many Democrats—and a number of prominent Republicans. His detractors latched onto the Watergate issue with the tenacity of bulldogs.

The Senate appointed a special committee to investigate the Watergate scandal. Most of Nixon's top aides continued the cover-up. John Dean, the president's counsel, did not. Throughout the episode he had kept careful notes, and in a quiet precise voice he told the Senate Watergate Committee that the president was deeply involved in the cover-up. The matter was still not solved. All the committee had was Dean's word against the other White House aides.

On July 16, 1973, a former White House employee dropped a bombshell by testifying that Nixon had recorded all Oval Office conversations. Whatever Nixon and his aides had said about Watergate in the Oval Office, therefore, was faithfully recorded on tape.

Nixon tried to keep the tapes from the committee by invoking executive privilege, insisting that a president had a right to keep confidential any White House communication, whether or not it involved sensitive diplomatic or national security matters. When Archibald Cox, a special prosecutor investigating the Watergate affair, persisted in demanding the tapes, Nixon ordered his attorney general, Elliot Richardson, to fire him; Richardson refused and resigned; Richardson's assistant, William Ruckelshaus, also resigned. Ruckelshaus's assistant, Robert Bork, finally fired Cox, but Congress forced Nixon to name a new special prosecutor, Leon Jaworski.

In the midst of the Watergate investigations another scandal broke. Federal prosecutors accused Vice President Spiro Agnew of extorting payoffs from building contractors while he was Maryland's governor and Baltimore County executive. In a plea bargain, Agnew pleaded no contest to a relatively minor charge—that he had falsified his income tax in 1967—in exchange for a $10,000 fine. Agnew was succeeded as vice president by Gerald Ford, whom Nixon appointed.

The Watergate scandal gradually came to encompass not just the cover-up but a wide range of presidential wrongdoings, including political favors to powerful business groups in exchange for campaign contributions; misuse of public funds; deceiving Congress and the public about the secret bombing of Cambodia; authorization of illegal domestic political surveillance and espionage against dissidents, political opponents, and journalists; and attempts to use FBI investigations and income tax audits by the IRS to harass political enemies.

On July 24, 1974, the House Judiciary Committee recommended that the House of Representatives impeach Nixon for obstruction of justice, abuse of power, and refusal to relinquish the tapes. On August 5 Nixon obeyed a Supreme Court order to release the tapes, which confirmed Dean's detailed testimony. Nixon had indeed been involved in a cover-up. On August 9 he became the first American president to resign from office. The following day Gerald Ford became the new president. "Our long national nightmare," he said, "is over."

Crisis of Political Leadership

The Vietnam War and the Watergate scandal had a profound effect on the presidency. The office suffered a dramatic decline in public respect, and Congress became increasingly unwilling to defer to presidential leadership. Congress enacted a series of reforms that would make future abuses

On August 9, 1974, Richard Nixon resigned the presidency after the release of secret tapes revealed that he had been involved in a cover-up of the Watergate affair.

of presidential authority less likely. In the process Congress recaptured constitutional powers that had been ceded to an increasingly dominant executive branch.

Restraining the Imperial Presidency

Over the course of the twentieth century the presidency gradually supplanted Congress as the center of federal power. Presidential authority increased, presidential staffs grew in size, and the executive branch gradually acquired a dominant relationship over Congress.

Beginning with Theodore Roosevelt, the president, and not Congress, established the nation's legislative agenda. Increasingly, Congress ceded its budget-making authority to the president. Presidents even found a way to make agreements with foreign nations without congressional approval. After World War II presidents substituted executive agreements for treaties requiring approval of the Senate. Even more important, presidents gained the power to take military action, despite the fact that Congress is the sole branch of government empowered by the Constitution to declare war.

No president went further than Richard Nixon in concentrating powers in the presidency. He refused to spend funds that Congress had appropriated; he claimed executive privilege against disclosure of information on administration decisions; he refused to allow key decision makers to be questioned before congressional committees; he reorganized the executive branch and broadened the authority of new cabinet positions without congressional approval; and during the Vietnam War, he ordered harbors mined and bombing raids launched without consulting Congress.

Watergate brought a halt to the "imperial presidency" and the growth of presidential power. Over the president's veto, Congress enacted the War Powers Act (1973), which required future presidents to obtain authorization from Congress to engage U.S. forces in foreign combat for more than 90 days. Under the law, a president who orders troops into action abroad must report the reason for this action to Congress within 48 hours.

In the wake of the Watergate scandal Congress passed a series of laws designed to reform the political process. Disclosures during the Watergate investigations of money-laundering led Congress to provide public financing of presidential elections, public disclosure of sources of funding, limits on private campaign contributions and spending, and enforcement of campaign finance laws by an independent Federal Election Commission. To make it easier for the Justice Department to investigate crimes in the executive branch, Congress now requires the attorney general to appoint a special prosecutor to investigate accusations of illegal activities. To reassert its budget-making authority, Congress created a Congressional Budget Office and specifically forbade a president to impound funds without its approval. To open government to public scrutiny, Congress opened more committee deliberations and enacted the Freedom of Information Act, which allows the public and press to request the declassification of government documents.

Some of the post-Watergate reforms have not been as effective as reformers anticipated. The War Powers Act has never been invoked. Campaign financing reform has not curbed the ability of special interests to curry favor with politicians or the capacity of the very rich to outspend opponents.

On the other hand, Congress has had somewhat more success in reining in the FBI and the CIA. During the 1970s congressional investigators discovered that these organizations had, in defiance of federal law, broken into the homes, tapped the phones, and opened the mail of American citizens; illegally infiltrated antiwar groups and black radical organizations; and accumulated dossiers on dissidents; which had been used by presidents for political purposes. Investigators also found that the CIA had been involved in assassination plots against foreign leaders, among them Fidel Castro, and had tested the effects of radiation, electric shock, and drugs (such as LSD) on unsuspecting citizens. In the wake of these investigations, the government severely limited CIA operations in the United States and laid down strict guidelines for FBI activities. To tighten congressional control over the CIA, Congress established a joint committee to supervise its operations.

New Style Presidents

In contrast to Nixon's abuses of presidential power, the next two presidents, Gerald Ford and Jimmy Carter, cultivated reputations as honest, forthright leaders. Both were men of decency and integrity, but neither established reputations as strong, dynamic leaders. Although many Americans admired their honesty and sincerity, neither Ford nor Carter succeeded in winning the confidence of the American people. Moreover, neither administration had a clear sense of direction. Both Ford and Carter seemed to waffle on major issues of public policy. As a result, both came to be regarded as unsure, vacillating presidents.

A 13-term congressman from Grand Rapids, Michigan, Gerald Ford dismissed the possibility of pardoning Richard Nixon for his Watergate misdeeds, then changed his mind. In the realm of economic policy, he began by urging tax increases, but later called for a large tax cut. His energy policy was crippled by the same indecision. At first, he tried to raise prices by imposing import fees on imported oil and ending domestic price controls; then he abandoned that position in the face of severe political pressure.

Carter, too, suffered from the charge that he modified his stances in the face of political pressure. A two-term Democratic governor from Georgia who defeated Ford in the 1976 presidential election, Carter came to office determined to cut military spending, calling for the abolition of nuclear weapons and the withdrawal of American troops from South Korea. By the end of his term, however, Carter spoke of the need for sustained growth in defense spending, upgrading nuclear forces in Europe, and developing a new strategic bomber.

Both men were described as "passionless presidents" who failed to project a clear vision of where they wanted to lead the country. But in their defense, both faced serious problems, ranging from dealing with rising oil prices to confronting third-world terrorists.

Wrenching Economic Transformations

At one time, the car makers in Detroit produced automobiles that mirrored America's strength and power. They were big, heavy, powerful cars, with such expensive options as power windows, power brakes, and power steering. So what if they were not energy-efficient (most got 10 to 13 miles per gallon)? Gas was cheap; just 37 cents a gallon in 1973. The public kept buying big cars, Detroit kept producing them, and the automobile industry reaped big profits.

By the late 1970s the rising costs of Middle Eastern oil forced the American automotive industry to rethink its strategy. Emerging Arab nationalism and the solidarity of the Organization of Petroleum Exporting Countries (OPEC) drove the price of a gallon of gas toward the dollar mark. American drivers started purchasing smaller, better-engineered, fuel-efficient cars from Japan and Europe. By 1982 Japanese cars had captured 30 percent of the U.S. market.

Since 1973, the American economy has undergone a series of wrenching economic transformations. Economic growth slowed; productivity flagged; inflation rose; and major industries faltered in the face of foreign competition. Despite a massive influx of women into the work force, family wages stagnated. A quarter century of rapid post-World War II economic growth had come to an end.

The Age of Inflation

In 1967 the average price of a three-bedroom house was $17,000. A brand new Cadillac convertible went for $6,700 and a new Volkswagen

$1,497; a Hershey chocolate bar sold for a nickel; a pound of sirloin for 89 cents. Two decades later the prices of these products had quadrupled.

The upsurge in inflation started when Lyndon Johnson decided to fight the Vietnam War without raising taxes enough to pay for it. By 1968 the war was costing the United States $3 billion dollars a month, and the federal budget skyrocketed to $179 billion. With hundreds of thousands of Americans in the military service and even more working in defense-related industries, unemployment fell, wages rose, and government deficits increased. Inflation was further fueled by a series of crop failures and sharp rises in commodities, especially oil.

High inflation had many negative effects on the American economy. It wiped out many families' savings. It provoked labor turmoil, as workers went on strike for higher wages. It encouraged speculation in tangible assets—like art, precious metals, and real estate—rather than productive investment in new factories and technology. Above all, certain organized interest groups were able to keep up with inflation, while other less powerful groups, such as welfare recipients, saw the value of their benefits decline significantly.

Inflation reduced the purchasing power of most Americans. For over a decade, real family wages remained flat. By the end of the 1970s they had climbed just $36 over 1973 levels. Yet inflation raised the prices of virtually all goods and services. Health care and housing, in particular, experienced price rises far above the inflation rate. The consequences were a sharp increase in the number of Americans unable to afford health insurance, and a dramatic increase in the cost of housing, which resulted in an increase in homelessness.

Oil Embargo

Political unrest in the oil-rich Middle East contributed significantly to America's economic troubles. After suffering a humiliating defeat at the hands of Israel in the 1973 "Yom Kippur" war, Arab leaders unsheathed a new political weapon—oil. In order to pressure Israel out of territory conquered in the 1967 and 1973 wars, Arab nations cut oil production 25 percent and embargoed all oil exports to the United States. Leading the way was OPEC, which had been founded by Iran, Saudi Arabia, and Venezuela in 1960 to fight a reduction in prices by oil companies.

Because Arab nations controlled 60 percent of the oil reserves in the non-Communist world, they had the western nations over a barrel. Production cutbacks produced an immediate global shortage. The United States imported a third of its oil from Arab nations; Western Europe imported 72 percent from the Middle East; Japan, 82 percent. Gas prices rose, long lines formed at gas pumps, some factories shortened the work-week, and some shopping centers restricted business hours.

The oil crisis brought to an end an era of cheap energy. Americans had to learn to live with smaller cars and less heating and air conditioning. But the crisis did have a positive side effect. It increased public consciousness about the environment and stimulated awareness of the importance of conservation. For millions of Americans the lessons were painful to learn.

Foreign Competition

In 1947 the United States was truly the world's factory. Half of all the world's manufacturing took place in the United States. Americans made 57 percent of the world's steel and 80 percent of the world's cars. It was inevitable that other countries would eventually challenge the dominance that American manufacturers had enjoyed in the aftermath of World War II. During the early 1960s foreign manufacturers produced 6 percent of the cars purchased by Americans. That figure climbed to 20 percent in the late 1970s.

The foreign penetration extended far beyond the market for compact cars. Foreign countries began to dominate the highly profitable, techno-logically advanced fields such as consumer electronics, luxury automo-biles, and machine tools. Americans discovered that technologies their country had pioneered—such as semiconductors, color televisions, and videocassette recorders—were now produced almost exclusively by for-eign manufacturers. The decline in the American share of the market meant fewer jobs in the American automobile, steel, rubber, and electron-ics industries. In addition, American and even Japanese companies shifted low-skill production work to such places as South Korea, Taiwan, Hong Kong, Singapore, and Indonesia, where goods could be produced more cheaply because of lower wage scales.

Few economic developments aroused as much public concern during the 1970s as the loss of American jobs in basic industry. According to one estimate, 30 million jobs disappeared. Displaced workers saw their sav-ings depleted, mortgages foreclosed, and health and pension benefits lost. Even when they found new jobs, they typically had to settle for wages substantially below what they had earned before. Plant shutdowns and closings had profound effects on entire communities, which lost their tax bases at the time when they needed to fund health and welfare services.

Whipping Stagflation

During the 1960s the primary goal of economic policy was to encourage growth and keep unemployment low. But by the early 1970s the economy started to suffer from *stagflation*—high unemployment and inflation coupled with stagnant economic growth. This presented economic policymakers with a new and perplexing dilemma, since unemployment and inflation usually do not coexist.

The problem with stagflation was the pain of its options. To attack inflation by reducing consumer purchasing power only made unemployment worse. The other choice was no better. Stimulating purchasing power and creating jobs also drove prices higher. Not surprisingly, economic policy during the 1970s was a nightmare of confusion and contradiction.

By 1971 pressures produced by the Vietnam War and federal social spending, coupled with the increase in foreign competition, pushed the inflation rate to 5 percent and unemployment to 6 percent. President Richard Nixon responded by increasing federal budget deficits and devaluing the dollar in an attempt to stimulate the economy and to make American goods more competitive overseas. Nixon also imposed a 90-day wage and price freeze, followed by a mandatory set of wage-price guidelines, and then by voluntary controls. Inflation stayed at about 4 percent during the freeze, but once controls were lifted, inflation resumed its upward climb.

In 1974 during the first oil embargo, inflation hit 12 percent. Gerald Ford, the new president, initially attacked the problem in a traditional Republican fashion, tightening the money supply by raising interest rates and limiting government spending. In the end, his economic program proved to be no more than a series of ineffectual wage and price guidelines monitored by the federal government. In the subsequent recession unemployment reached 9 percent.

When Jimmy Carter took office in January 1977, 7.4 percent of the work force was unemployed. Carter responded with an ambitious spending program and called for the Federal Reserve (the Fed) to expand the money supply. Within two years inflation had climbed to 13.3 percent.

With inflation getting out of hand, the Federal Reserve Board announced in 1979 that it would fight inflation by restraining the growth of the money supply. Unemployment increased, and interest rates rose to their highest levels in the nation's history. By November 1982 unemployment hit 10.8 percent, the highest since 1940. One out of every five American workers went some time without a job.

Along with high interest rates, the Carter administration adopted another weapon in the battle against stagflation: deregulation. Convinced that regulators too often protected the industries they were supposed to oversee, the Carter administration deregulated air and surface transportation and the savings and loan industry.

The effects of deregulation are still hotly contested. Rural towns suffered cutbacks of bus, rail, and air service. Truckers and rail workers lost the economic benefits of regulation. Travelers complained about rising air fares and congested airports. Cable TV viewers resented rising rates. Champions of deregulation argued that the policy increased competition, stimulated new investment, and forced inefficient firms either to become more efficient or shut down.

A New American Role in the World

In his inaugural address in 1961 John Kennedy stated that America would "pay any price, bear any burden, meet any hardship, support any friend or oppose any foe to assure the survival and the success of liberty." But by 1973, in the wake of the Vietnam War, American foreign policymakers regarded Kennedy's stirring pledge as unrealistic.

The Vietnam War offered a lesson about the limits of American power. It underscored the need to distinguish between vital national interests and peripheral interests, and to balance America's military commitments with its available resources. Above all, the Vietnam War appeared to illustrate the dangers of obsessive anticommunism. Such a policy failed to recognize that the world was becoming more complex, that power blocs were shifting, and that the interests of Communist countries and the United States could sometimes overlap. Too often, American policy seemed to have driven nationalists and reformers into Communist hands and to have led the United States to support corrupt, unpopular authoritarian regimes. The great challenge facing American foreign policymakers was how to preserve the nation's international prestige and influence in the face of declining defense budgets and mounting congressional opposition to direct overseas intervention.

Détente

As president, Richard Nixon radically redefined America's relationship with its two foremost adversaries, China and the Soviet Union. In a remarkable turnabout from his record of staunch anticommunism, he opened relations with China and began strategic arms limitation talks with the Soviet Union. The goal of *détente* (the easing of tensions between nations), was to continue to resist and deter Soviet adventurism while striving for "more constructive relations" with the Communist world.

Nixon and Henry Kissinger believed that it was necessary to curb the arms race, improve great-power relationships, and learn to coexist with Communist regimes. The Nixon administration sought to use the Chinese and Soviet need for western trade and technology as a way to extract foreign policy concessions.

Recognizing that one of the legacies of Vietnam was a reluctance on the part of the American public to risk overseas interventions, Nixon and Kissinger also sought to build up regional powers that shared American strategic interests, most notably China, Iran, and Saudi Arabia.

By the late 1970s an increasing number of Americans believed that the Soviet hard-liners viewed détente as a mere tactic to lull the West into relaxing its vigilance. Soviet Communist party chief Leonid Brezhnev reinforced this view, boasting of gains that his country had made at the United States's expense—in Vietnam, Angola, Cambodia, Ethiopia, and Laos.

An alarming Soviet arms buildup contributed to the sense that détente was not working. By 1975, the Soviet Union had 50 percent more intercontinental ballistic missiles (ICBMs) than the United States, three times as many army personnel, three times as many attack submarines, and four times as many tanks. The United States continued to have a powerful strategic deterrent, holding a 9,000 to 3,200 advantage in deliverable nuclear bombs and warheads. But the arms gap between the countries was narrowing.

Foreign Policy Triumphs

In the Middle East Carter achieved his greatest diplomatic success by negotiating peace between Egypt and Israel. Since the founding of Israel in 1948, Egypt's foreign policy had been built around destroying the Jewish state. In 1977 Anwar el-Sadat, the practical and farsighted leader of Egypt, decided to seek peace with Israel. It was an act of rare political courage, for Sadat risked alienating Egypt from the rest of the Arab world without a firm commitment for a peace treaty with Israel.

Although both countries wanted peace, major obstacles had to be overcome. Sadat wanted Israel to retreat from the West Bank of the Jordan River and from the Golan Heights (which it had taken from Jordan in the 1967 war), recognize the Palestine Liberation Organization (PLO), provide a homeland for the Palestinians, relinquish its unilateral hold on the city of Jerusalem, and return the Sinai to Egypt. Such conditions were unacceptable to Israeli Prime Minister Menachem Begin, who refused to consider recognition of the PLO or the return of the West Bank. By the end of 1977 Sadat's peace mission had run aground.

Jimmy Carter broke the deadlock by inviting both men to Camp David, the presidential retreat in Maryland, for face-to-face talks. For two weeks in September 1978 they hammered out peace accords. Although several important issues were left unresolved, Begin did agree to return the

Sinai to Egypt. In return, Egypt promised to recognize Israel, and as a result became a staunch U.S. ally. For Carter it was a proud moment. Unfortunately, the Camp David accords were denounced by the rest of the Arab Middle East, and in 1981 Sadat paid for his vision with his life when anti-Israeli Egyptian soldiers assassinated him.

In 1978 Carter also pushed the Panama Canal Treaty through the Senate, which provided for the return of the Canal Zone to Panama and improved the image of the United States in Latin America. One year later he extended diplomatic recognition to the People's Republic of China. Carter's successes in the international arena, however, would soon be overshadowed by the greatest challenge of his presidency—the Iran hostage crisis.

No Islands of Stability

One of the tragic aspects of American foreign policy is that the United States historically has supported many countries that hold power through murder, torture, and other violations of human rights, practices which are an affront to basic American values. During the presidency of Jimmy Carter, the United States began to show a growing regard for the human rights practices of its allies. Carter was convinced that American foreign policy should embody the country's basic moral beliefs. In 1977 Congress began to require reports on human rights conditions in countries receiving American aid.

Of the nations accused of practicing torture, one of the most frequently cited was Iran. Estimates of the number of political prisoners in

Jimmy Carter's greatest triumph as president came with the signing of the Camp David accords between Egypt and Israel.

Iran ranged from 25,000 to 100,000. It was widely believed that most of them had been tortured by SAVAK, the secret police.

Since the end of World War II, Iran had been a valuable friend of the United States in the troubled Middle East. In 1953 the CIA had worked to ensure the power of the young shah, Mohammad Reza Pahlavi. During the next 25 years, the shah often repaid the debt. He allowed the United States to establish electronic listening posts in northern Iran along the border of the Soviet Union, and during the 1973–1974 Arab oil embargo the shah continued to sell oil to the United States. The shah also bought arms from the United States, which helped ease the American balance-of-payments problem. Few world leaders were more loyal to the United States.

Like his predecessors, Carter was willing to overlook the shah's violations of human rights. To demonstrate American support, Carter visited Iran in late December 1977. He applauded Iran as "an island of stability in one of the most troubled areas of the world" and praised the shah as a great leader who had won "the respect and the admiration and love" of his people.

The shah was indeed popular among wealthy Iranians, but in the slums of Teheran and in rural, poverty-stricken villages, there was little respect, admiration, or love for his regime. Led by a fundamentalist Islamic clergy and emboldened by want, the masses of Iranians turned against the shah and his westernization policies.

In the early fall of 1978 the revolutionary surge in Iran gained force. The shah, who had once seemed so powerful and secure, was paralyzed by indecision, alternating between ruthless suppression and attempts to liberalize his regime. In Washington, Carter also vacillated, uncertain whether to stand firmly behind the shah or to cut his losses and prepare to deal with a new government in Iran.

In January 1979, the shah fled to Egypt. Exiled religious leader Ayatollah Ruholla Khomeini returned to Iran, preaching the doctrine that the United States was the "Great Satan" behind the shah. Relations between the United States and the new Iranian government were terrible, but Iranian officials warned that they would become infinitely worse if the shah were granted asylum. Nevertheless, Carter permitted the shah to enter the United States for treatment of lymphoma. The reaction in Iran was severe.

On November 4, 1979, Iranian supporters of Khomeini invaded the American embassy in Teheran and captured 66 Americans, 13 of whom were freed several weeks later. The rest were held hostage for 444 days and were the objects of intense political interest and media coverage.

Carter was helpless. Because Iran was not a stable country in any recognizable sense, its government was not susceptible to pressure. Iran's demands—the return of the shah to Iran and admission of U.S. guilt in supporting the shah—were unacceptable. Carter devoted far too much attention to the almost insoluble problem. The hostages stayed in the public spotlight in part because Carter kept them there.

Carter's foreign policy problems mounted in December 1979, when the Soviet Union sent tanks into Afghanistan. In response, the Carter administration embargoed grain and high-technology exports to the Soviet Union and boycotted the 1980 Olympics in Moscow. (The Soviet Union gradually withdrew its troops a decade later.)

As public disapproval of the president's handling of the Iran crisis increased, some Carter advisers advocated the use of force to free the hostages. At first, Carter disagreed, but eventually he authorized a rescue attempt. It failed, and Carter's position became even worse. Negotiations finally brought the hostages' release, but in a final humiliation for Carter, the hostages were held until minutes after Ronald Reagan, Carter's successor, had taken the oath of office as president.

When Carter left office in January 1981 many Americans judged his presidency a failure. Instead of being remembered for the good he accom-

After 444 days the Iranian hostage crisis ended, but not before it had virtually paralyzed Carter's administration and destroyed his chances for reelection.

plished for the Middle East at Camp David, he was remembered for what he failed to accomplish. The Iranian hostage crisis had become emblematic of a perception that America's role in the world had declined.

The Reagan Revolution

The traumatic events of the 1970s—Watergate, stagflation, the energy crisis, the decline of American industy, the defeat of South Vietnam, and the Iranian hostage crisis—produced a severe loss of confidence among the American people. Americans were deeply troubled by the relative loss of American strength in the world; the decline of productivity and innovation in American industry; and the dramatic growth of lobbies and special-interest groups that seemed to have paralyzed the legislative process. Many worried that too much power had been stripped from the presidency, that political parties were so weakened and Congress so splintered that it was impossible to enact a coherent legislative program.

Ronald Reagan capitalized on the public's frustration. When he ran for the presidency against Carter in 1980, he asked Americans, "Are you better off than you were four years ago?" With annual inflation at 18 percent, the answer was a resounding "No." Reagan won a landslide victory, carrying 43 states and almost 51 percent of the popular vote compared to Carter's 41 percent. In addition, the Democrats lost the Senate for the first time since 1954.

The Gipper

When he was elected president in 1980, Ronald Reagan was already well known to the American people as a movie actor and television announcer. He had risen to celebrity status from extremely modest beginnings. Born in 1911, Reagan, the son of a shoe salesman, grew up in a succession of small Illinois towns. After a stint as a sportscaster at a radio station in Des Moines, Reagan landed a Hollywood screen test in 1937. He went on to make 50 films, most of them B movies. Often remembered for his performance in *Knute Rockne, All American* (1940), Reagan played George Gipp, the Notre Dame halfback, whose dying words were "win one for the gipper." After World War II he served as president of the Screen Actors Guild, and in 1954 he turned to television, hosting "GE Theater" and "Death Valley Days."

In politics, he started out as a liberal, staunchly supporting Franklin D. Roosevelt and the New Deal. As head of the Screen Actors Guild, however, he became concerned about Communist infiltration of the labor movement in Hollywood. Reagan was catapulted into the national political spotlight in 1964 when he gave an emotional speech in support of Republican nominee Barry Goldwater, denouncing big government, foreign aid, welfare, urban renewal, and high taxes. Two years later, he successfully ran for governor of California, promising to cut state spending and crack down on student protesters.

In the 1980 presidential campaign Reagan drew strong support from white southerners, suburban Roman Catholics, evangelical Christians, and particularly the New Right, a confederation of disparate political and religious groups bound together by their concern over what they considered the erosion of values in America.

Reaganomics

When President Reagan took office he promised to rebuild the nation's defenses, restore economic growth, and trim the size of the federal government by limiting its role in welfare, education, and housing. He pledged to end exorbitant union contracts to make American goods competitive again, to cut taxes drastically to stimulate investment and purchasing power, and to decontrol businesses strangled by federal regulation. Even though his policies trimmed little from the size of the federal government, failed to make American goods competitive in the world market, and led to increased consolidation rather than competition—many Americans believed that he had improved the country's economic situation.

Reagan blamed the nation's economic ills on declining capital investment and a tax structure biased against work and productive investment. To stimulate the economy, he persuaded Congress to slash tax rates. In 1981 he pushed a bill through Congress cutting taxes 5 percent in 1981 and 10 percent in 1982 and 1983. In 1986 the administration pushed through another tax bill, which substantially reduced tax rates on the wealthiest Americans to 28 percent, while closing a variety of tax loopholes.

In August 1981 Reagan dealt a devastating blow to organized labor by firing 15,000 striking air-traffic controllers. Union leaders condemned the firings, but in an antiunion atmosphere most Americans backed Reagan. His popularity ratings soared.

To strengthen the nation's defenses, the Reagan administration doubled the defense budget, to more than $330 billion by 1987. Reagan believed that a militarily strong America would not have been humiliated by Iran and would have discouraged Soviet adventurism.

Reagan expanded the Carter administration's efforts to decontrol and deregulate the economy. Congress deregulated the banking and natural gas industries and lifted ceilings on interest rates. Federal price controls on airfares were lifted as well. The Environmental Protection Agency relaxed its interpretation of the Clean Air Act; and the Department of the Interior opened up large areas of the federal domain, including offshore oil fields, to private development.

The results of deregulation were mixed. Bank interest rates became more competitive, but smaller banks found it difficult to hold their own against larger institutions. Natural gas prices increased, but so did production, easing some of the country's dependence on foreign fuel. Airfares on high-traffic routes between major cities dropped dramatically, but fares for short, low-traffic flights skyrocketed. Most critics agreed, however, that deregulation had restored some short-term competition to the marketplace. Yet in the long term, competition also led to increased business failures and consolidation.

Reagan's laissez-faire principles could also be seen in his administration's approach to social programs. Convinced that federal welfare programs promoted laziness, promiscuity, and moral decay, Reagan limited benefits to those he considered the "truly needy." His administration cut spending on a variety of social welfare programs, including Aid to Families with Dependent Children; food stamps; child nutrition; job training for young people; programs to prevent child abuse; and mental health services. The Reagan administration also eliminated welfare assistance for the working poor, and reduced federal subsidies for child-care services for low-income families. A symbol of Reagan social service cuts was an attempt by the Agriculture Department in 1981 to allow ketchup to be counted as a vegetable in school lunches.

Reagan left office with the economy in the midst of its longest post–World War II expansion. The economy was growing faster, with less inflation, than at any time since the mid-1960s. Adjusted for inflation, disposable personal income per person rose 20 percent after 1980. Inflation fell from 13 percent in 1981 to less than 4 percent annually. Unemployment was down to around 5 percent.

Critics, however, charged that Reagan had only created the illusion of prosperity. They denounced the massive federal budget deficit, which increased $1.5 trillion during the Reagan presidency, three times the debt accumulated by all 39 of Reagan's presidential predecessors. They decried the growing income gap between rich and poor, as well as the expensive consequences of reduced government regulation, such as cleaning up federal nuclear weapons facilities, and, especially, bailing out the nation's savings and loans industry.

The Celebration of Wealth

In 1981, the year Ronald Reagan was inaugurated as president, ABC television introduced the smash hit "Dynasty," a show celebrating glamour and greed. It was, in the eyes of many social commentators, an appropriate beginning for the 1980s—a decade of selfishness and an anything-goes attitude.

Wall Street enthusiastically took part in the new celebration of wealth, as the Reagan years witnessed a corporate merger and takeover boom of unprecedented proportions. By using low-grade, risky "junk bonds" to finance corporate acquisitions, corporate raiders such as Michael Milken of Drexel, Burnham, Lambert purchased and then dismantled companies for huge profits. In 1987, Milken earned $550 million by financing acquisitions.

During the 1980s, 100,000 Americans became millionaires every year. The average annual earnings of the bottom 20 percent, however, fell from $9,376 to $8,800. In addition, many of the new jobs created during the Reagan years were in the low-wage service industries.

By the early 1990s, there were signs that the time had come to pay for the financial excesses of the 1980s. Following a 508-point fall in the Dow Jones industrial average on October 19, 1987—a 22.6 percent plunge in stock values—many Wall Street stock brokerage firms began to lay off employees, cutbacks which continued despite the market's recovery. In 1989 Milken was indicted on charges of criminal racketeering and securities fraud. The next year Drexel, Burnham Lambert agreed to pay a fine of $650 million and filed for bankruptcy. Wall Street speculator Ivan Boesky was fined $100 million for insider trading and sentenced to jail. Those Americans who had fostered in the ambition, greed, and excesses of the eighties seemed to be getting their comeuppance.

The Reagan Doctrine

During the early years of the Reagan presidency, Cold War tensions between the Soviet Union and the United States intensified. Reagan entered office deeply suspicious of the Soviet Union. Reagan described the Soviet Union as "an evil empire" and called for a space-based missile defense system, derided by critics as "Star Wars."

Reagan and his advisers tended to view every regional conflict through a Cold War lens. Nowhere was this more true than in the Western Hemisphere, where he was determined to prevent Communist takeovers. In October 1983 Prime Minister Maurice Bishop of Grenada, a small island nation in the Caribbean, was assassinated and a more radical Marxist government took power. Soviet money and Cuban troops came to Grenada, and when they began constructing an airfield capable of landing large military aircraft, the Reagan administration decided to remove the Communists and restore a pro-American regime. On October 25 U.S. troops invaded Grenada, killed or captured 750 Cuban soldiers, and established a new government. The invasion sent a clear message throughout the region that the Reagan administration would not tolerate communism in its hemisphere.

In his 1985 state of the union address President Reagan pledged his support for anti-Communist revolutions in what would become known as the "Reagan Doctrine." In Afghanistan the United States was already providing aid to anti-Soviet freedom fighters, ultimately helping to force Soviet troops to withdraw. It was in Nicaragua, however, that the doctrine received its most controversial application.

In 1979 Nicaraguans revolted against the corrupt Somoza regime. A new junta took power, dominated by young Marxists known as Sandinistas. The Sandinistas insisted that they favored free elections, nonalign-

U.S. Involvement in Central America and the Caribbean

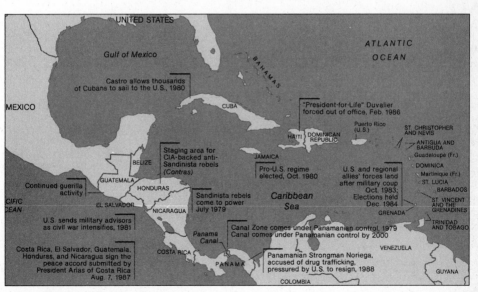

ment, and a mixed economy, but once in power they postponed elections, forced opposition leaders into exile, and turned to the Soviet bloc for arms and advisers. For the Reagan administration, Nicaragua looked "like another Cuba," a Communist state that threatened the security of its Central American neighbors.

In his first months in office President Reagan approved covert training of anti-Sandinista rebels (called "contras"). While the contras waged war on the Sandinistas from camps in Honduras, the CIA provided assistance. In 1984 Congress ordered an end to all covert aid to the contras.

The Reagan administration circumvented Congress by soliciting contributions for the contras from private individuals and from foreign governments seeking U.S. favor. The president also permitted the sale of arms to Iran, with profits diverted to the contras. The arms sale and transfer of funds to the contras were handled surreptitiously through the CIA intelligence network, apparently with the full support of CIA director William Casey. Exposure of the Iran-Contra affair in late 1986 provoked a major congressional investigation. The scandal seriously weakened the influence of the president.

The American preoccupation with Nicaragua began to subside in 1987, after President Oscar Arias Sanches of Costa Rica proposed a regional peace plan. In national elections in 1990 the Nicaraguan opposition routed the Sandinistas, bringing an end to ten turbulent years of Sandinista rule.

A Remarkable Ideological Turnaround

In 1982, 75-year-old Soviet party leader Leonid Brezhnev died. His regime had been marked by growing stagnation, corruption, and a huge military buildup. Initially, the post-Brezhnev era seemed to offer little change in U.S.- Soviet relations. KGB leader Yuri Andropov succeeded Brezhnev, but died after only 15 months in power. He was replaced by another Brezhnev loyalist, Konstantin Chernenko, who died just a year later. In 1985 Soviet party leadership passed to Mikhail S. Gorbachev, a 54-year-old agricultural specialist with little formal experience in foreign affairs who pledged to continue the policies of his predecessors.

Within weeks, however, Gorbachev called for sweeping political liberalization—*glasnost*—and economic reform—*perestroika*. He allowed wider freedom of press, assembly, travel, and religion. He persuaded the Communist party leadership to end its monopoly on power; created the Soviet Union's first working legislature; allowed the first nationwide competitive elections in 1989; and freed hundreds of political prisoners. In an effort to boost the sagging Soviet economy, he legalized small private business cooperatives, relaxed laws prohibiting land ownership, and approved foreign investment within the Soviet Union.

In foreign affairs Gorbachev completely reshaped world politics. He cut the Soviet defense budget, withdrew Soviet troops from Afghanistan and Eastern Europe, allowed a unified Germany to become a member of NATO, and agreed with the United States to destroy short-range and medium-range nuclear weapons. Most dramatically, Gorbachev actively promoted the democratization of former satellite nations in Eastern Europe. For his accomplishments in defusing Cold War tensions, he was awarded the 1990 Nobel Peace Prize.

The Reagan Revolution in Perspective

In the presidential election of 1984 Ronald Reagan and Vice President George Bush won in a landslide over Walter Mondale and Geraldine Ferraro, the first woman nominated for vice president on a major party ticket. Although Reagan's second term was plagued by the Iran-contra scandal, he left office after eight years more popular than he arrived. He could claim the distinction of being the first president to serve two full terms since Dwight Eisenhower.

Ronald Reagan could also point to an extraordinary string of accomplishments. He dampened inflation, restored public confidence in government, and presided over the beginning of the end of the Cold War. He doubled the defense budget, named the first woman to the Supreme Court, launched a strong economic boom, and created a heightened sense of national unity. In addition, his supporters said that he restored vigor to the national economy and psyche, rebuilt America's military might, regained the nation's place as the world's preeminent power, restored American patriotism, and championed traditional family values.

On the other hand, his detractors criticized him for a reckless use of military power, and for circumventing Congress in foreign affairs. They accused Reagan of fostering greed and intolerance, and they charged that his administration, in its zeal to cut waste from government, ripped the social safety net and skimped on the government's regulatory functions. The administration, they further charged, was insensitive on racial issues.

Reagan's detractors were particularly concerned about his economic legacy. During the Reagan years the national debt tripled, from $909 billion to almost $2.9 trillion (the interest alone amounted to 14 percent of the federal budget) soaking up savings, causing interest rates to rise, and forcing the federal government to shift more and more responsibilities onto the states. Corporate and individual debt also soared. During the early 1990s the American people consumed $1 trillion more goods and services than they produced. The United States also became the world's biggest debtor nation, as a result of a weak dollar, a low level of exports, and the need to borrow abroad to finance budget deficits.

The Bush Presidency

In the 1988 presidential campaign the Republican candidate, Vice President George Bush, was said to have the best résumé in Washington. Winning the Distinguished Service Cross during World War II, Bush had made a fortune in the Texas oil business, and then went to Washington where he served as a Congressman, ambassador to the United Nations, envoy to China, and director of the CIA. His Democratic opponent, Massachusetts governor Michael Dukakis, was a serious, hardworking son of Greek immigrants.

Mudslinging and personal invective are nothing new in American politics, but the 1988 campaign was unusually vacuous and cynical. Real differences between the candidates were submerged in a battle over character, abortion, prison furloughs, school prayer, and patriotism. The campaign dramatized a development that had been reshaping American politics since the late 1960s: the growing power of media consultants and pollsters, who marketed candidates by emphasizing imagery and symbolism. At the end of a race that saw both candidates use negative campaigning, Bush was elected the forty-first president of the United States, with 56 percent of the popular vote.

A Kinder, Gentler Nation

In his inaugural address, Bush signaled a departure from the avarice and greed of the Reagan era by calling for a "new engagement in the lives of others." He promised to be more of a "hands on" administrator than his predecessor, and he committed his presidency to creating a "kinder, gentler" nation, more sensitive and caring to the poor and disadvantaged.

During his first years in office President Bush and the Democratic-controlled Congress addressed many issues ignored during the Reagan years. For the first time in eight years, the minimum wage was raised from $3.35 to $4.25 an hour. Congress amended federal air pollution laws in order to reduce noxious emissions and acid rain. For the first time since 1971, Congress considered child-care legislation, and ultimately voted to provide subsidies to low-income families to defray the costs of child care. In other actions, Congress prohibited job discrimination against the disabled, required nutrition labeling on processed foods, and expanded immigration into the United States.

In two areas critics accused President Bush of reneging on his promise of a "kinder, gentler" nation. He vetoed a new civil rights bill bolstering protections for minorities and women against job discrimination, on the grounds that it would lead to quotas, and he also vetoed a bill that would have provided up to six months of unpaid family leave for workers with newly born or adopted children or emergencies. In November 1991, however, Bush signed a compromise Civil Rights Act, which made it easier for workers to win antidiscrimination lawsuits.

Economic Policy

Many Americans believed that the end of the Cold War would bring a huge peace dividend, which could be used to reduce the federal budget deficit and fund domestic social programs. Soon after Bush took office, however, Americans learned that much of the peace dividend would have to be spent to clean up nuclear wastes produced at federal facilities and to bail out the nation's troubled savings and loan industry.

The roots of the savings and loan crisis were planted during the presidency of Jimmy Carter, when high inflation and high interest rates threatened to bankrupt savings institutions, which could not compete with other financial institutions permitted to pay high interest rates. A 1980 law lifted limits on the interest rates that savings institutions could pay and allowed them to make a limited amount of investments in commercial real estate. In 1982 and 1983 Congress broadened the banking industry's capacity to make unsecured commercial loans and investments in commercial real estate.

The savings and loan industry's problems began in the mid-1980s, when falling oil prices led to a collapse of land values, especially in the Southwest, creating huge losses for institutions that had invested in real estate. By the end of the decade these institutions began to fail in large numbers. The mounting bills for the savings and loan bailout propelled President Bush in 1990 to violate his 1988 "no new taxes" campaign pledge.

Foreign Policy

The first important foreign policy act of the Bush administration was an invasion of Panama, which the Pentagon called Operation Just Cause. The origins of the conflict stretched back to 1987 when a high Panamanian military official accused strong-man General Manuel Antonio Noriega of committing fraud in the 1984 presidential election and of drug trafficking. Violent street demonstrations broke out in Panama, as angry Panamanians called for Noriega's overthrow. Noriega responded by declaring a state of emergency. The crisis escalated when two Florida grand juries indicted the general on charges that he protected and assisted the Colombian drug cartel.

U.S.-Panamanian relations deteriorated further when Noriega voided results of the 1989 presidential election and sent paramilitary forces into the streets of Panama City where they beat up opposition candidates. Conflict grew imminent when Noriega declared his country in a "state of war" against the United States. A day later four unarmed American military personnel were fired on at a roadblock by Panamanian troops, and one American was killed. Bush dispatched a force of 10,000 troops to safeguard the lives of Americans and protect the integrity of the Panama Canal treaties. Between 300 and 800 Panamanian civilians and military personnel died during the invasion; there were 23 American casualties. Noriega was forced out of power and deported to the United States to stand trial for drug trafficking.

Collapse of Communism

For 40 years Communist party leaders in Eastern Europe had ruled confidently. Although each year their countries fell further behind the West, they remained secure in the knowledge that the Soviet Union, backed by the Red Army, would always send in the tanks when the forces for change became too great. But they had not bargained on a liberal Soviet leader like Mikhail Gorbachev.

As Gorbachev moved toward reform within the Soviet Union and détente with the West, he pushed the conservative regimes of Eastern Europe outside his protective umbrella. By the end of 1989 the Berlin Wall had been smashed and across Eastern Europe citizens took to the streets, overthrowing 40 years of Communist rule. Like a series of falling dominos, Communist parties in Poland, East Germany, Hungary, Czechoslovakia, Romania, and Bulgaria fell from power.

Gorbachev, who had wanted to reform communism, may not have anticipated the swift swing toward democracy in Eastern Europe. Nor had he fully foreseen the impact that democracy in Eastern Europe would have on the Soviet Union. By 1990 leaders of several Soviet republics began to demand independence or greater autonomy within the Soviet Union.

Gorbachev had to balance the growing demand for radical political change within the Soviet Union with the demand by Communist hardliners that he contain the new democratic currents and turn back the clock. Faced with dangerous political opposition from the right and the left and with economic failure throughout the Soviet Union, Gorbachev tried to satisfy everyone and in the process satisfied no one.

For nearly three decades the Berlin Wall was the most visible symbol of the Cold War and of the division between East and West. The most dramatic incident marking the end of the Cold War was the destruction of the Wall in November 1989.

In 1990, following the example of eastern Europe, the three Baltic states of Lithuania, Latvia, and Estonia announced their independence and other Soviet republics demanded greater sovereigny. Nine of the 15 Soviet republics agreed to sign a new union treaty, granting far greater freedom and autonomy to individual republics. But in August 1991, before the treaty could be signed, conservative communists tried to oust Gorbachev in a coup d'etat. Boris Yeltsin, the President of the Russian Republic and his supporters defeated the coup, which undermined support for the Communist party. Gorbachev fell from power. The Soviet Union ended its existence in December 1991, when Russia and most other republics formed the Commonwealth of Independent States.

The Persian Gulf War

At 2 A.M., August 2, 1990, 80,000 Iraqi troops invaded and occupied Kuwait, a small, oil-rich emirate on the Persian Gulf, touching off the first major international crisis of the post-Cold War era. Iraq's leader, Saddam Hussein, justified the invasion on the grounds that Kuwait, which he accused of intentionally depressing world oil prices, was a historic part of Iraq.

Iraq's invasion caught the United States off guard. The Hussein regime was a brutal military dictatorship that ruled by secret police and used poison gas against Iranians, Kurds, and Shiite Moslems. During the 1970s and 1980s the United States—and Britain, France, the Soviet Union, West Germany—sold Iraq an awesome arsenal that included missiles, tanks, and the equipment needed to produce biological, chemical, and nuclear weapons. During Baghdad's eight-year-long war with Iran, the United States, which opposed the growth of Muslim fundamentalist extremism, tilted toward Iraq.

On August 6, 1990, President Bush dramatically declared, "This aggression will not stand." With Iraqi forces poised near the Saudi Arabian border, the Bush administration dispatched 180,000 troops to protect the Saudi kingdom. In a sharp departure from American foreign policy during the Reagan presidency, Bush also organized an international coalition against Iraq, convincing Turkey and Syria to close Iraqi oil pipelines, winning Soviet support for an arms embargo, and establishing a multinational army to protect Saudi Arabia. In the United Nations the administration succeeded in persuading the Security Council to adopt a series of resolutions condemning the Iraqi invasion, demanding restoration of the Kuwaiti government, and imposing an economic blockade.

Bush's decision to resist Iraqi aggression reflected the president's assessment of vital national interests. Iraq's invasion gave Saddam Hussein direct control over a significant portion of the world's oil supply. It disrupted the Middle East balance of power and placed Saudi Arabia and the Persian Gulf emirates in jeopardy. Iraq's 545,000-man army threatened the security of such valuable U.S. allies as Egypt and Israel.

In November 1990, the crisis took a dramatic turn. President Bush doubled the size of American forces deployed in the Persian Gulf, a sign that the administration was prepared to eject Iraq from Kuwait by force. The president went to the United Nations for a resolution permitting the use of force against Iraq if it did not withdraw by January 15, 1991. After a heated debate, Congress also gave the president authority to wage war.

President Bush's decision to liberate Kuwait was an enormous political and military gamble. The Iraqi army, the world's fourth largest, was equipped with Exocet missiles, top-of-the-line Soviet T-72 tanks, and long-range artillery capable of firing nerve gas. But after a month of allied bombing, the coalition forces had achieved air supremacy and destroyed thousands of Iraqi tanks and artillery pieces, supply routes and communications lines, command-and-control bunkers, and limited Iraq's ability to produce nuclear, chemical, and biological weapons. Iraqi troop morale suffered so badly under the bombing that an estimated 30 percent of Baghdad's forces deserted before the ground campaign started.

The allied ground campaign relied on deception, mobility, and overwhelming air superiority to defeat a larger Iraqi army. The allied strategy was to mislead the Iraqis into believing that the allied attack would occur along the Kuwaiti coastline and Kuwait's border with Saudi Arabia. Meanwhile, General H. Norman Schwarzkopf, American commander of the coalition forces, shifted more than 300,000 American, British, and French troops into western Saudia Arabia, allowing them to strike deep into Iraq. Only 100 hours after the ground campaign started, the war ended. Saddam Hussein remained in power, but his ability to control events in the region was dramatically curtailed.

Major Action in the Persian Gulf

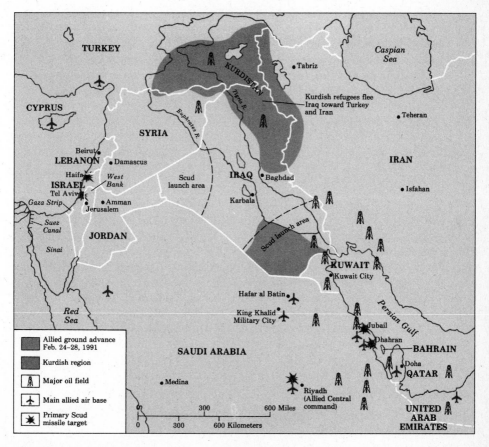

The Persian Gulf conflict was the most popular U.S. war since World War II, restoring American confidence in its position as the world's sole superpower and helping to exorcise the ghost of Vietnam that had haunted American foreign policy debates for nearly two decades. The doubt, drift, and demoralization that began with the Vietnam War and the Watergate scandal appeared to have ended.

Enter Bill Clinton

In the Persian Gulf War, Bush acted from clear, unequivocal principles. Convinced that it was necessary to humiliate Saddam Hussein and prove that America would resist aggression, Bush demonstrated that a determined and skillful president has the power to move a reluctant nation to support his policies.

In domestic affairs, on the other hand, Bush's leadership was less decisive. On such issues as taxes, abortion, and civil rights, he adopted a flexible, pragmatic approach that led some critics to describe him as a political chameleon. Unlike Ronald Reagan, who brought a series of fixed philosophical principles to domestic issues, Bush appeared less interested in domestic affairs and more willing to renege on his pledge not to raise taxes.

Bush's failure to alter the downward slide of the American economy played the crucial role in the 1992 presidential election. In a bitter three-way contest, marked by intense assaults on the candidates' records and characters, Arkansas Governor Bill Clinton defeated George Bush and Texas businessman Ross Perot to become the first Democratic president in 12 years. President Bush, whose popularity soared to 90 percent following the Persian Gulf War, received only 38 percent of the popular vote, to Clinton's 43 percent and Perot's 19 percent.

The central issue in the election was the nation's sluggish economy. During the Bush presidency fewer new jobs were created than in any other presidential term since World War II. Unemployment reached the highest level in eight years; personal incomes stagnated; businesses failed in record numbers; the federal debt surpassed $4 trillion; and medical care absorbed 15 percent of the nation's output, while a quarter of the population lacked health insurance. Poverty rose to the highest rate in over two decades—a fact dramatically underscored by the outbreak of the deadliest riot in America's history, in Los Angeles in April 1992.

President Clinton pledged a "new covenant" for America: a new approach to government between the unfettered free market championed by the Republicans and the welfare state economics that the Democratic party had represented in the past. Promising to focus like a laser beam on he economy, he strove to reduce the federal budget deficit by raising taxes on the wealthiest Americans and on gasoline and cutting government spending. To create jobs, he sought to stimulate world trade. In late 1993 he convinced Congress to pass the North American Free Trade Agreement (NAFTA), eliminating tariff barriers between Canada, Mexico, and the United States, and also completed negotiations on the General Agreement on Trade and Tariffs (GATT), reducing global trading barriers.

Clinton committed his administration to ending twelve years of "legislative gridlock" and "social neglect." To aid working parents, he signed parental leave legislation, allowing parents to take unpaid job leaves during family emergencies. To combat violent crime, he persuaded Congress to enact a waiting period for handgun purchases and a ban on the sale of assault weapons. He also revised policies that had excluded homosexuals from the military and pledged to eliminate "welfare as we know it," by replacing welfare dependency with programs emphasizing education and job training. The centerpiece of Clinton's legislative agenda was a program of universal health care coverage—the largest federal social welfare initiative since Social Security during the Great Depression—to guarantee lifelong care to the millions of Americans without health insurance.

In foreign policy, his administration witnessed the end of apartheid in South Africa and the replacement of white rule with a multiracial democracy, as well as the Israeli transfer of control over the Gaza Strip and portions of the West Bank to the Palestine Liberation Organization. The Clinton administration also ended a longstanding U.S. trade embargo with Vietnam.

Conclusion

As the twentieth century draws to a close, America's ideals of democracy and personal freedom are ascendant across the world. From Tiananmen Square—where Chinese students erected a goddess of liberty modeled on the Statue of Liberty—to the Philippines, popular protests and demonstrations have called for "government of the people, by the people, and for the people." In Eastern Europe, the former Soviet Union, and across Latin America, people demand free speech, freedom of religion, freedom of the press, and free markets.

Yet paradoxically, as American ideals and values flourish abroad, Americans are anxious about their economy and their country's future. Many are angry, expressing cynical contempt toward their government. Many fear that American competitiveness and inventiveness are declining. Other nations, such as Japan and Germany, save more and

*C*hronology of Key Events

1971   Nixon authorizes establishment of "plumbers" unit

1972   Watergate burglars arrested; President Nixon takes part in summit in China; President Nixon reelected

1973   Senate Watergate hearings begin; Spiro Agnew resigns

1974   House Judiciary Committee adopts three articles of impeachment against President Nixon; Nixon resigns; Ford becomes thirty-eighth president; Federal Campaign Reform Act

1976   Jimmy Carter elected thirty-ninth president

1978   President Carter mediates Egyptian-Israeli peace settlement; Iranian revolution begins

1979   United States recognizes China; Iranian militants seize American hostages; Soviet Union invades Afghanistan; Somoza regime in Nicaragua overthrown

1980   Ronald Reagan elected fortieth president

1981   American hostages released from Iran; Reagan approves covert training of anti-Sandinista contras; Reagan tax cuts are approved

1982   Congress deregulates banking industry and lifts controls on air fares

1983   Reagan proposes "Star Wars" missile defense system: United States topples Communist government of Grenada

1985   United States begins secret arms-for-hostages negotiations with Iran; Mikhail Gorbachev becomes Soviet leader

1986   Profits from Iranian arms sales are diverted to Nicaraguan contras

1987   Iran-Contra hearings; stock market plunges

1988   George Bush elected forty-first president

1989   Communist regimes collapse in Eastern Europe

1990   Iraqi troops invade Kuwait

1991   Persian Gulf War; independence for Soviet republics

1992   Bill Clinton elected forty-second president

invest more than the United States, and their economies have been growing faster. Except for a few areas of trade—such as high-tech products, financial services, and aircraft—foreign countries dominate the most technologically advanced fields, such as consumer electronics, luxury automobiles, and machine tools. No longer does the United States possess the world's highest level of per capita income. Particularly troubling are the national debt and federal deficit, which stand at record levels.

Americans also worry about crime, the state of their central cities, and the quality of health and education in their society. The level of crime and violence in the United States is the highest in the industrialized world, as are America's rates of drug use, juvenile delinquency, teenage pregnancy, and teen suicide.

At the end of World War II many commentators referred to the twentieth century as the "American century." Today the United States remains the mightiest, most productive nation in the world, a model of freedom and pluralism that people across the globe still strive to emulate. The great question to be asked as the century comes to an end is whether Americans have the will to solve the many problems that confront their cities, their schools, and their physical environment.

Suggestions for Further Reading

Informative surveys of recent American life include Michael Barone, *Our Country* (1990); Peter N. Carroll, *It Seemed Like Nothing Happened: The Tragedy and Promise of the 1970s* (1990); Kim McQuaid, *The Anxious Years* (1989).

On Watergate and its consequences, consult Stanley I. Kutler, *The Wars of Watergate* (1990); Theodore White, *Breach of Faith* (1975). For more on the Republican presidencies in the 1970s, see James Reichley, *Conservatives in an Age of Change* (1981); Edward L. and Frederick H. Schapsmeier, *Gerald R. Ford's Date with Destiny* (1989).

The Carter presidency is examined in James A. Bill, *The Eagle and the Lion* (1988); Charles O. Jones, *The Trustee Presidency* (1988); Gaddis Smith, *Morality, Reason and Power: American Diplomacy in the Carter Years* (1986). See also Carter's memoir, *Keeping Faith* (1982). For a study of the oil crisis, consult Daniel Yergin, *The Prize* (1990).

For analyses of Reagan and the Reagan years see Sidney Blumenthal, *Our Long National Daydream* (1988); Paul Boyer, ed., *Reagan as President* (1990);

Lou Cannon, *President Reagan: The Role of a Lifetime* (1991); Robert Dallek, *Ronald Reagan: The Politics of Symbolism* (1984); Theodore Draper, *A Very Thin Line: The Iran-Contra Affairs* (1991); Haynes Johnson, *Sleepwalking Through History: America in the Reagan Years* (1991); Garry Wills, *Reagan's America* (1987). Aspects of the post-Reagan era are examined in Kevin Buckley, *Panama: The Whole Story* (1991); Lawrence J. White, *The S&L Debacle* (1991); Bob Woodward, *The Commanders* (1991).

Appendix

The Declaration of Independence

When in the Course of human events, it becomes necessary for one people to dissolve the political bands which have connected them with another, and to assume among the Powers of the earth, the separate and equal station to which the Laws of Nature and of Nature's God entitle them, a decent respect to the opinions of mankind requires that they should declare the causes which impel them to the separation.

We hold these truths to be self-evident, that all men are created equal, that they are endowed by their Creator with certain unalienable Rights, that among these are Life, Liberty and the pursuit of Happiness. That to secure these rights, Governments are instituted among Men, deriving their just powers from the consent of the governed. That whenever any Form of Government becomes destructive of these ends, it is the Right of the People to alter or to abolish it, and to institute new Government, laying its foundation on such principles and organizing its powers in such form, as to them shall seem most likely to effect their Safety and Happiness. Prudence, indeed, will dictate that Governments long established should not be changed for light and transient causes; and accordingly all experience hath shown, that mankind are more disposed to suffer, while evils are sufferable, than to right themselves by abolishing the forms to which they are accustomed. But when a long train of abuses and usurpations, pursuing invariably the same Object evinces a design to reduce them under absolute Despotism, it is their right, it is their duty, to throw off such Government, and to provide new Guards for their future security.—Such has been the patient sufferance of these Colonies; and such is now the necessity which constrains them to alter their former Systems of Government. The history of the present King of Great Britain is a history of repeated injuries and usurpations, all having in direct object the establishment of an absolute Tyranny over these States. To prove this, let Facts be submitted to a candid world.

He has refused his Assent to Laws, the most wholesome and necessary for the public good.

He has forbidden his Governors to pass Laws of immediate and pressing importance, unless suspended in their operation till his Assent should be obtained; and when so suspended, he has utterly neglected to attend to them.

He has refused to pass other Laws for the accommodation of large districts of people, unless those people would relinquish the right of Representation in the Legislature, a right inestimable to them and formidable to tyrants only.

He has called together legislative bodies at places unusual, uncomfortable, and distant from the depository of their Public Records, for the sole purpose of fatiguing them into compliance with his measures.

He has dissolved Representative Houses repeatedly, for opposing with manly firmness his invasions on the rights of the people.

He has refused for a long time, after such dissolutions, to cause others to be elected; whereby the Legislative Powers, incapable of Annihilation, have returned to the People at large for their exercise; the State remaining in the mean time exposed to all the dangers of invasion from without, and convulsions within.

He has endeavoured to prevent the population of these States; for that purpose obstructing the Laws of Naturalization of Foreigners; refusing to pass others to encourage their migration hither, and raising the conditions of new Appropriations of Lands.

He has obstructed the Administration of Justice, by refusing his Assent to Laws for establishing Judiciary Powers.

He has made Judges dependent on his Will alone, for the tenure of their offices, and the amount and payment of their salaries.

He has erected a multitude of New Offices, and sent hither swarms of Officers to harass our People, and eat out their substance.

He has kept among us, in times of peace, Standing Armies without the Consent of our legislature.

He has affected to render the Military independent of and superior to the Civil Power.

He has combined with others to subject us to a jurisdiction foreign to our constitution, and unacknowledged by our laws; giving his Assent to their acts of pretended legislation:

For quartering large bodies of armed troops among us;

For protecting them, by a mock Trial, from Punishment for any Murders which they should commit on the Inhabitants of these States;

For cutting off our Trade with all parts of the world;

For imposing taxes on us without our Consent;

For depriving us in many cases, of the benefits of Trial by Jury;

For transporting us beyond Seas to be tried for pretended offences;

For abolishing the free System of English Laws in a neighbouring Province, establishing therein an Arbitrary government, and enlarging its Boundaries so as to render it at once an example and fit instrument for introducing the same absolute rule into these Colonies;

For taking away our Charters, abolishing our most valuable Laws, and altering fundamentally the Forms of our Governments;

For suspending our own Legislature, and declaring themselves invested with Power to legislate for us in all cases whatsoever.

He has abdicated Government here, by declaring us out of his Protection and waging War against us.

He has plundered our seas, ravaged our Coasts, burnt our towns, and destroyed the lives of our people.

He is at this time transporting large armies of foreign mercenaries to compleat the works of death, desolation and tyranny, already begun with circumstances of Cruelty & perfidy scarcely paralleled in the most barbarous ages, and totally unworthy the Head of a civilized nation.

He has constrained our fellow Citizens taken Captive on the high Seas to bear Arms against their Country, to become the executioners of their friends and Brethren, or to fall themselves by their Hands.

He has excited domestic insurrections amongst us, and has endeavoured to bring on the inhabitants of our frontiers, the merciless Indian Savages, whose known rule of warfare, is an undistinguished destruction of all ages, sexes and conditions.

In every stage of these Oppressions We have Petitioned for Redress in the most humble terms: Our repeated Petitions have been answered only by repeated injury. A Prince, whose character is thus marked by every act which may define a Tyrant, is unfit to be the ruler of a free People.

Nor have We been wanting in attention to our British brethren. We have warned them from time to time of attempts by their legislature to extend an unwarrantable jurisdiction over us. We have reminded them of the circumstances of our emigration and settlement here. We have appealed to their native justice and magnanimity, and we have conjured them by the ties of our common kindred to disavow these usurpations, which, would inevitably interrupt our connections and correspondence. They too have been deaf to the voice of justice and of consanguinity. We must, therefore, acquiesce in the necessity, which denounces our Separation, and hold them, as we hold the rest of mankind, Enemies in War, in Peace Friends.

We, therefore, the Representatives of the united States of America, in General Congress, Assembled, appealing to the Supreme Judge of the world for the rectitude of our intentions, do, in the Name, and by Authority of the good People of these Colonies, solemnly publish and declare, That these United Colonies are, and of Right ought to be Free and Independent States; that they are Absolved from all Allegiance to the British Crown, and that all political connection between them and the State of Great Britain, is and ought to be totally dissolved; and that as Free and Independent States, they have full Power to levy War, conclude Peace, contract Alliances, establish Commerce, and to do all other Acts and Things which Independent States may of right do. And for the support of this Declaration, with a firm reliance on the Protection of Divine

Providence, we mutually pledge to each other our Lives, our Fortunes and our sacred Honor.

John Hancock,
Josiah Bartlett, Wm Whipple, Saml Adams, John Adams, Robt Treat Paine, Elbridge Gerry, Steph. Hopkins, William Ellery, Roger Sherman, Samel Huntington, Wm Williams, Oliver Wolcott, Matthew Thornton, Wm Floyd, Phil Livingston, Frans Lewis, Lewis Morris, Richd Stockton, Jno Witherspoon, Fras Hopkinson, John Hart, Abra Clark, Robt Morris, Benjamin Rush, Benja Franklin, John Morton, Geo Clymer, Jas Smith, Geo. Taylor, James Wilson, Geo. Ross, Caesar Rodney, Geo Read, Thos M:Kean, Samuel Chase, Wm Paca, Thos Stone, Charles Carroll of Carrollton, George Wythe, Richard Henry Lee, Th. Jefferson, Benja Harrison, Thos Nelson, Jr., Francis Lightfoot Lee, Carter Braxton, Wm Hooper, Joseph Hewes, John Penn, Edward Rutledge, Thos Heyward, Junr., Thomas Lynch, Junor., Arthur Middleton, Button Gwinnett, Lyman Hall, Geo Walton.

The Constitution of the United States of America

W e the people of the United States, in Order to form a more perfect Union, establish Justice, insure domestic Tranquility, provide for the common defence, promote the general Welfare, and secure the Blessings of Liberty to ourselves and our Posterity, do ordain and establish this CONSTITUTION for the United States of America.

Article I

Section 1.

All legislative Powers herein granted shall be vested in a Congress of the United States, which shall consist of a Senate and House of Representatives.

Section 2.

The House of Representatives shall be composed of Members chosen every second Year by the People of the several States, and the Electors in each State shall have the Qualifications requisite for Electors of the most numerous Branch of the State Legislature.

No Person shall be a Representative who shall not have attained to the Age of twenty-five Years, and been seven Years a Citizen of the United States, and who shall not, when elected, be an Inhabitant of that State in which he shall be chosen.

Representatives and direct Taxes shall be apportioned among the several States which may be included within this Union, according to their respective Numbers, which shall be determined by adding to the whole Number of free

Persons, including those bound to Service for a Term of Years, and excluding Indians not taxed, three fifths of all other Persons. The actual Enumeration shall be made within three Years after the first Meeting of the Congress of the United States, and within every subsequent Term of ten Years, in such Manner as they shall by Law direct. The Number of Representatives shall not exceed one for every thirty Thousand, but each State shall have at Least one Representative; and until such enumeration shall be made, the State of New Hampshire shall be entitled to chuse three, Massachusetts eight, Rhode-Island and Providence Plantations one, Connecticut five, New-York six, New Jersey four, Pennsylvania eight, Delaware one, Maryland six, Virginia ten, North Carolina five, South Carolina five, and Georgia three.

When vacancies happen in the Representation from any State, the Executive Authority thereof shall issue Writs of Election to fill such Vacancies.

The House of Representatives shall chuse their Speaker and other Officers; and shall have the sole Power of Impeachment.

Section 3.

The Senate of the United States shall be composed of two Senators from each State, chosen by the Legislature thereof, for six Years; and each Senator shall have one Vote.

Immediately after they shall be assembled in Consequence of the first Election, they shall be divided as equally as may be into three Classes. The Seats of the Senators of the first Class shall be vacated at the Expiration of the second Year, of the second Class at the Expiration of the fourth Year, and of the third Class at the Expiration of the sixth Year, so that one-third may be chosen every second Year; and if Vacancies happen by Resignation, or otherwise, during the Recess of the Legislature of any State, the Executive thereof may make temporary Appointments until the next Meeting of the Legislature, which shall then fill such Vacancies.

No Person shall be a Senator who shall not have attained to the Age of thirty Years, and been nine Years a Citizen of the United States, and who shall not, when elected, be an Inhabitant of that State in which he shall be chosen.

The Vice President of the United States shall be President of the Senate, but shall have no vote, unless they be equally divided.

The Senate shall chuse their other Officers, and also a President pro tempore, in the absence of the Vice President, or when he shall exercise the Office of the President of the United States.

The Senate shall have the sole Power to try all Impeachments. When sitting for that purpose, they shall be on Oath or Affirmation. When the President of the United States is tried, the Chief Justice shall preside: And no person shall be convicted without the Concurrence of two thirds of the Members present.

Judgment in Cases of Impeachment shall not extend further than to removal from Office, and disqualification to hold and enjoy any Office of honor, Trust, or Profit under the United States: but the Party convicted shall nevertheless be liable and subject to Indictment, Trial, Judgment, and Punishment, according to Law.

Section 4.

The Times, Places and Manner of holding Elections for Senators and Representatives, shall be prescribed in each state by the Legislature thereof; but the Congress may at any time by Law make or alter such Regulations, except as to the Places of Chusing Senators.

The Congress shall assemble at least once in every Year, and such Meeting shall be on the first Monday in December, unless they shall by Law appoint a different Day.

Section 5.

Each House shall be the Judge of the Elections, Returns and Qualifications of its own Members, and a Majority of each shall constitute a Quorum to do Business; but a smaller number may adjourn from day to day, and may be authorized to compel the Attendance of absent Members, in such Manner, and under such Penalties, as each House may provide.

Each House may determine the Rules of its Proceedings, punish its Members for disorderly Behavior, and, with the Concurrence of two thirds, expel a Member.

Each House shall keep a Journal of its Proceedings, and from time to time publish the same, excepting such Parts as may in their Judgment require Secrecy; and the Yeas and Nays of the Members of either House on any question shall, at the Desire of one fifth of those Present, be entered on the Journal.

Neither House, during the Session of Congress, shall, without the Consent of the other, adjourn for more than three days, nor to any other Place than that in which the two Houses shall be sitting.

Section 6.

The Senators and Representatives shall receive a Compensation for their Services, to be ascertained by Law, and paid out of the Treasury of the United States. They shall in all Cases, except Treason, Felony, and Breach of the Peace, be privileged from arrest during their Attendance at the Session of their respective Houses, and in going to and returning from the same; and for any Speech or Debate in either House, they shall not be questioned in any other Place.

No Senator or Representative shall, during the Time for which he was elected, be appointed to any civil Office under the Authority of the United States, which shall have been created, or the Emoluments whereof shall have been increased, during such time; and no Person holding any Office under the United States shall be a Member of either House during his continuance in Office.

Section 7.

All Bills for raising Revenue shall originate in the House of Representatives; but the Senate may propose or concur with Amendments as on other bills.

Every Bill which shall have passed the House of Representatives and the Senate, shall, before it become a Law, be presented to the President of the United States; If he approve he shall sign it, but if not he shall return it, with his Objections, to that House in which it shall have originated, who shall enter the Objections at large on their Journal, and proceed to reconsider it. If after such Reconsideration two thirds of that House shall agree to pass the bill, it shall be sent, together with the objections, to the other House, by which it shall likewise be reconsidered, and if approved by two thirds of that House, it shall become a Law. But in all such Cases the Votes of both Houses shall be determined by Yeas and Nays, and the Names of the Persons voting for and against the Bill shall be entered on the Journal of each House respectively. If any Bill shall not be returned by the President within ten Days (Sundays excepted) after it shall have been presented to him, the Same shall be a Law, in like Manner as if he had signed it, unless the Congress by their Adjournment prevent its Return, in which Case it shall not be a Law.

Every Order, Resolution, or Vote to which the Concurrence of the Senate and House of Representatives may be necessary (except on a question of Adjournment) shall be presented to the President of the United States; and before the Same shall take Effect, shall be approved by him, or being disapproved by him, shall be repassed by two thirds of the Senate and House of Representatives, according to the Rules and Limitations prescribed in the Case of a Bill.

Section 8.

The Congress shall have Power To lay and collect Taxes, Duties, Imposts and Excises, to pay the Debts and provide for the common Defence and general Welfare of the United States; but all Duties, Imposts and Excises shall be uniform throughout the United States;

To borrow money on the credit of the United States;

To regulate Commerce with foreign Nations, and among the several States, and with the Indian Tribes;

To establish an uniform Rule of Naturalization, and uniform Laws on the subject of Bankruptcies throughout the United States;

To coin Money, regulate the Value thereof, and of foreign Coin, and fix the Standard of Weights and Measures;

To provide for the Punishment of counterfeiting the Securities and current Coin of the United States;

To establish Post Offices and post Roads;

To promote the Progress of Science and useful Arts, by securing for limited Times to Authors and Inventors the exclusive Right to their respective Writings and Discoveries;

To constitute Tribunals inferior to the Supreme Court;

To define and punish Piracies and Felonies committed on the high Seas, and Offences against the Law of Nations;

To declare War, grant Letters of Marque and Reprisal, and make Rules concerning Captures on Land and Water;

To raise and support Armies, but no Appropriation of Money to that Use shall be for a longer Term than two Years;

To provide and maintain a Navy:

To make Rules for the Government and Regulation of the land and naval forces;

To provide for calling forth the Militia to execute the Laws of the Union, suppress Insurrections and repel Invasions;

To provide for organizing, arming, and disciplining the Militia, and for governing such Part of them as may be employed in the Service of the United States, reserving to the States respectively, the Appointment of the Officers, and the Authority of training the Militia according to the discipline prescribed by Congress;

To exercise exclusive Legislation in all Cases whatsoever, over such District (not exceeding ten Miles square) as may, by Cession of particular States, and the acceptance of Congress, become the Seat of Government of the United States, and to exercise like Authority over all Places purchased by the Consent of the Legislature of the State in which the Same shall be, for the Erection of Forts, Magazines, Arsenals, dock-Yards, and other needful Buildings;—And

To make all Laws which shall be necessary and proper for carrying into Execution the foregoing Powers, and all other Powers vested by this Constitution in the government of the United States, or in any Department or Officer thereof.

Section 9.

The Migration or Importation of such Persons as any of the States now existing shall think proper to admit, shall not be prohibited by the Congress prior to the Year one thousand eight hundred and eight, but a tax or duty may be imposed on such Importation, not exceeding ten dollars for each Person.

The privilege of the Writ of Habeas Corpus shall not be suspended, unless when in Cases of Rebellion or Invasion the public Safety may require it.

No Bill of Attainder or ex post facto Law shall be passed.

No capitation, or other direct, Tax shall be laid unless in Proportion to the Census or Enumeration herein before directed to be taken.

No Tax or Duty shall be laid on Articles exported from any State.

No Preference shall be given by any Regulation of Revenue to the Ports of one State over those of another: nor shall Vessels bound to, or from, one State, be obliged to enter, clear, or pay Duties in another.

No Money shall be drawn from the Treasury, but in Consequence of Appropriations made by Law; and a regular Statement and Account of the Receipts and Expenditures of all public Money shall be published from time to time.

No Title of Nobility shall be granted by the United States: And no Person holding any Office of Profit or Trust under them, shall, without the Consent of the Congress, accept of any present, Emolument, Office, or Title, of any kind whatever, from any King, Prince, or foreign State.

Section 10.

No State shall enter into any Treaty, Alliance, or Confederation; grant Letters of Marque and Reprisal; coin Money; emit Bills of Credit; make any Thing but gold and silver Coin a Tender in Payment of Debts; pass any Bill of Attainder, ex post facto Law, or Law impairing the Obligation of Contracts, or grant any Title of Nobility.

No State shall, without the Consent of the Congress, lay any Imposts or Duties on Imports or Exports, except what may be absolutely necessary for executing its inspection Laws: and the net Produce of all Duties and Imposts, laid by any State on Imports or Exports, shall be for the Use of the Treasury of the United States; and all such Laws shall be subject to the Revision and Control of the Congress.

No State shall, without the Consent of Congress, lay any duty of Tonnage, keep Troops, or Ships of War in time of Peace, enter into any Agreement or Compact with another State, or with a foreign Power, or engage in War, unless actually invaded, or in such imminent Danger as will not admit of delay.

Article II

Section 1.

The executive Power shall be vested in a President of the United States of America. He shall hold his Office during the Term of four years, and, together with the Vice President, chosen for the same Term, be elected, as follows:

Each State shall appoint, in such Manner as the Legislature thereof may direct, a Number of Electors, equal to the whole Number of Senators and Representatives to which the State may be entitled in the Congress; but no Senator or Representative, or Person holding an Office of Trust or Profit under the United States, shall be appointed an Elector.

The Electors shall meet in their respective States, and vote by Ballot for two persons, of whom one at least shall not be an Inhabitant of the same State with themselves. And they shall make a List of all the Persons voted for, and of the Number of Votes for each; which List they shall sign and certify, and transmit sealed to the Seat of the Government of the United States, directed to the President of the Senate. The President of the Senate shall, in the Presence of the Senate and House of Representatives, open all the Certificates, and the Votes shall then be counted. The Person having the greatest Number of Votes shall be the President, if such Number be a Majority of the whole Number of Electors appointed; and if there be more than one who have such Majority, and have an equal Number of Votes, then the House of Representatives shall immediately chuse by Ballot one of them for President; and if no Person have a Majority, then from the five highest on the List the said House shall in like Manner chuse the President. But in chusing the President, the votes shall be taken by States, the Representation from each State having one Vote; a quorum for this Purpose shall consist of a Member or Members from two-thirds of the States, and a Majority of all the States shall be necessary to a Choice. In every Case, after the Choice of the President, the Person having the greatest Number of Votes of the Electors shall be the Vice President. But if there should remain two or more who have equal votes, the Senate shall chuse from them by Ballot the Vice President.

The Congress may determine the time of chusing the Electors, and the Day on which they shall give their Votes; which Day shall be the same throughout the United States.

No person except a natural-born Citizen, or a Citizen of the United States, at the time of the Adoption of this Constitution, shall be eligible to the Office of President; neither shall any Person be eligible to that Office who shall not have attained to the Age of thirty-five years, and been fourteen Years a Resident within the United States.

In Case of the Removal of the President from Office, or of his Death, Resignation, or Inability to discharge the Powers and Duties of the said Office, the same shall devolve on the Vice President, and the Congress may by Law provide for the Case of Removal, Death, Resignation, or Inability, both of the President and Vice President, declaring what Officer shall then act as President, and such Officer shall act accordingly, until the disability be removed, or a President shall be elected.

The President shall, at stated Times, receive for his Services a Compensation, which shall neither be increased nor diminished during the Period for which he shall have been elected, and he shall not receive within that Period any other Emolument from the United States, or any of them.

Before he enter on the execution of his Office, he shall take the following Oath or Affirmation:—"I do solemnly swear (or affirm) that I will faithfully execute the Office of President of the United States, and will, to the best of my Ability, preserve, protect, and defend the Constitution of the United States."

Section 2.

The President shall be Commander in Chief of the Army and Navy of the United States, and of the Militia of the several States, when called into the actual Service of the United States; he may require the Opinion, in writing, of the principal Officer in each of the executive Departments, upon any subject relating to the Duties of their respective Offices, and he shall have Power to Grant Reprieves and Pardons for Offences against the United States, except in Cases of Impeachment.

He shall have Power, by and with the Advice and Consent of the Senate, to make Treaties, provided two thirds of the Senators present concur; and he shall nominate, and by and with the Advice and Consent of the Senate, shall appoint Ambassadors, other public Ministers and Consuls, Judges of the supreme Court, and all other Officers of the United States, whose Appointments are not herein otherwise provided for, and which shall be established by Law: but the Congress may by Law vest the Appointment of such inferior Officers, as they think proper, in the President alone, in the Courts of Law, or in the Heads of Departments.

The President shall have Power to fill up all Vacancies that may happen during the Recess of the Senate, by granting Commissions which shall expire at the End of their next Session.

Section 3.

He shall from time to time give to the Congress Information of the State of the Union, and recommend to their Consideration such Measures as he shall judge necessary and expedient; he may, on extraordinary occasions, convene both Houses, or either of them, and in Case of Disagreement between them, with respect to the Time of Adjournment, he may adjourn them to such Time as he shall think proper; he shall receive Ambassadors and other public Ministers; he shall take Care that the Laws be faithfully executed, and shall Commission all the Officers of the United States.

Section 4.

The President, Vice President and all civil Officers of the United States, shall be removed from Office on Impeachment for, and Conviction of, Treason, Bribery, or other high Crimes and Misdemeanors.

Article III

Section 1.

The judicial Power of the United States, shall be vested in one supreme Court, and in such inferior Courts as the Congress may from time to time ordain and establish. The Judges, both of the supreme and inferior Courts, shall hold their Offices during good Behaviour, and shall, at stated Times, receive for their Services, a Compensation, which shall not be diminished during their Continuance in Office.

Section 2.

The judicial Power shall extend to all Cases, in Law and Equity, arising under this Constitution, the Laws of the United States, and treaties made, or which shall be made, under their Authority;—to all Cases affecting ambassadors, other public ministers and consuls;—to all cases of admiralty and maritime

Jurisdiction;—to Controversies to which the United States shall be a Party;—to Controversies between two or more States;—between a State and Citizens of another State;—between Citizens of different States,—between Citizens of the same State claiming Lands under Grants of different States, and between a State, or the Citizens thereof, and foreign States, Citizens or Subjects.

In all Cases affecting Ambassadors, other public Ministers and Consuls, and those in which a State shall be Party, the supreme Court shall have original Jurisdiction. In all the other Cases before mentioned, the supreme Court shall have appellate Jurisdiction, both as to Law and Fact, with such Exceptions, and under such Regulations as the Congress shall make.

The trial of all Crimes, except in Cases of Impeachment, shall be by Jury; and such Trial shall be held in the State where the said Crimes shall have been committed; but when not committed within any State, the Trial shall be at such Place or Places as the Congress may by Law have directed.

Section 3.

Treason against the United States, shall consist only in levying War against them, or in adhering to their Enemies, giving them Aid and Comfort. No Person shall be convicted of Treason unless on the testimony of two Witnesses to the same overt Act, or on Confession in open Court.

The Congress shall have power to declare the Punishment of Treason, but no Attainder of Treason shall work Corruption of Blood, or Forfeiture except during the Life of the Person attained.

Article IV

Section 1.

Full Faith and Credit shall be given in each State to the public Acts, Records, and judicial Proceedings of every other State. And the Congress may by general Laws prescribe the Manner in which such Acts, Records and Proceedings shall be proved, and the Effect thereof.

Section 2.

The Citizens of each State shall be entitled to all Privileges and Immunities of Citizens in the several States.

A Person charged in any State with Treason, Felony, or other Crime, who shall flee from Justice, and be found in another State, shall on demand of the executive Authority of the State from which he fled, be delivered up, to be removed to the State having Jurisdiction of the crime.

No Person held to Service or Labour in one State, under the Laws thereof, escaping into another, shall, in Consequence of any Law or Regulation therein, be discharged from such Service or Labour, but shall be delivered up on Claim of the Party to whom such Service or Labour may be due.

Section 3.

New States may be admitted by the Congress into this Union; but no new State shall be formed or erected within the Jurisdiction of any other State; nor any State be formed by the Junction of two or more States, or parts of States, without the Consent of the Legislatures of the States concerned as well as of the Congress.

The Congress shall have Power to dispose of and make all needful Rules and Regulations respecting the Territory or other Property belonging to the United States; and nothing in this Constitution shall be so construed as to Prejudice any Claims of the United States, or of any particular State.

Section 4.

The United States shall guarantee to every State in this Union a Republican Form of Government, and shall protect each of them against Invasion; and on Application of the Legislature, or the Executive (when the Legislature cannot be convened) against domestic Violence.

Article V

The Congress, whenever two-thirds of both Houses shall deem it necessary, shall propose Amendments to this Constitution, or, on the Application of the Legislatures of two-thirds of the several States, shall call a Convention for proposing Amendments, which, in either Case, shall be valid to all Intents and Purposes, as part of this Constitution, when ratified by the Legislatures of three-fourths of the several States, or by Conventions in three-fourths thereof, as the one or the other Mode of Ratification may be proposed by the Congress; Provided that no Amendment which may be made prior to the Year One thousand eight hundred and eight shall in any Manner affect the first and fourth Clauses in the Ninth Section of the first Article; and that no State, without its Consent, shall be deprived of its equal Suffrage in the Senate.

Article VI

All Debts contracted and Engagements entered into, before the Adoption of this Constitution, shall be as valid against the United States under this Constitution, as under the Confederation.

This Constitution, and the Laws of the United States which shall be made in Pursuance thereof; and all Treaties made, or which shall be made, under the

Authority of the United States, shall be the supreme Law of the Land; and the Judges in every State shall be bound thereby, any Thing in the Constitution or Laws of any State to the Contrary notwithstanding.

The Senators and Representatives before mentioned, and the Members of the several State Legislatures, and all executive and judicial Officers, both of the United States and of the several States, shall be bound by Oath or Affirmation to support this Constitution; but no religious Test shall ever be required as a qualification to any Office or public Trust under the United States.

Article VII

The ratification of the conventions of nine States shall be sufficient for the establishment of this Constitution between the States so ratifying the same.

Done in Convention by the unanimous consent of the States present, the seventeenth day of September in the year of our Lord one thousand seven hundred and eighty-seven and of the Independence of the United States of America the twelfth. In witness whereof we have hereunto subscribed our names.

George Washington,
President and Deputy from Virginia

New Hampshire
John Langdon
Nicholas Gilman

Massachusetts
Nathaniel Gorham
Rufus King

Connecticut
William S. Johnson
Roger Sherman

New York
Alexander Hamilton

New Jersey
William Livingston
David Brearley
William Paterson
Jonathan Dayton

Pennsylvania
Benjamin Franklin
Thomas Mifflin
Robert Morris
George Clymer
Thomas Fitzsimons
Jared Ingersoll
James Wilson
Gouverneur Morris

Delaware
George Read
Gunning Bedford, Jr.
John Dickinson
Richard Bassett
Jacob Broom

Maryland
James McHenry
Daniel of St. Thomas
  Jenifer
Daniel Carroll

Virginia
John Blair
James Madison, Jr.

North Carolina
William Blount
Richard Dobbs Spraight
Hu Williamson

South Carolina
J. Rutledge
Charles C. Pinckney
Pierce Butler

Georgia
William Few
Abraham Baldwin

Amendments to the Constitution

*A*rticles in Addition to, and Amendment of, the Constitution of the United States of America, Proposed by Congress, and Ratified by the Legislatures of the Several States, Pursuant to the Fifth Article of the Original Constitution.

Amendment I [1791]

Congress shall make no law respecting an establishment of religion, or prohibiting the free exercise thereof; or abridging the freedom of speech, or of the press; or the right of the people peaceably to assemble, and to petition the Government for a redress of grievances.

Amendment II [1791]

A well regulated Militia, being necessary to the security of a free State, the right of the people to keep and bear Arms shall not be infringed.

Amendment III [1791]

No Soldier shall, in time of peace, be quartered in any house, without the consent of the Owner, nor in time of war, but in a manner to be prescribed by law.

Amendment IV [1791]

The right of the people to be secure in their persons, houses, papers, and effects, against unreasonable searches and seizures, shall not be violated, and no Warrants shall issue, but upon probable cause, supported by Oath or affirmation, and particularly describing the place to be searched, and the persons or things to be seized.

Amendment V [1791]

No person shall be held to answer for a capital or otherwise infamous crime, unless on a presentment or indictment of a Grand Jury, except in cases arising in the land or naval forces, or in the Militia, when in actual service in time of War or public danger; nor shall any person be subject for the same offence to be twice put in jeopardy of life or limb; nor shall be compelled in any criminal case to be a witness against himself, nor be deprived of life, liberty, or property, without due process of law; nor shall private property be taken for public use, without just compensation.

Amendment VI [1791]

In all criminal prosecutions, the accused shall enjoy the right to a speedy and public trial, by an impartial jury of the State and district wherein the crime shall have been committed, which district shall have been previously ascertained by law, and to be informed of the nature and cause of the accusation; to be confronted with the witnesses against him; to have compulsory process for obtaining witnesses in his favor, and to have the Assistance of Counsel for his defence.

Amendment VII [1791]

In suits at common law, where the value in controversy shall exceed twenty dollars, the right of trial by jury shall be preserved, and no fact tried by a jury, shall be otherwise reexamined in any Court of the United States, than according to the rules of the common law.

Amendment VIII [1791]

Excessive bail shall not be required, nor excessive fines imposed, nor cruel and unusual punishments inflicted.

Amendment IX [1791]

The enumeration in the Constitution, of certain rights, shall not be construed to deny or disparage others retained by the people.

Amendment X [1791]

The powers not delegated to the United States by the Constitution, nor prohibited by it to the States, are reserved to the States respectively, or to the people.

Amendment XI [1798]

The Judicial power of the United States shall not be construed to extend to any suit in law or equity, commenced or prosecuted against one of the United States by Citizens of another State, or by Citizens or Subjects of any Foreign State.

Amendment XII [1804]

The Electors shall meet in their respective States and vote by ballot for President and Vice-President, one of whom, at least, shall not be an inhabitant of the same State with themselves; they shall name in their ballots the person voted for as President, and in distinct ballots the person voted for as Vice-President, and they shall make distinct lists of all persons voted for as President, and of all persons voted for as Vice-President, and of the number of votes for each, which lists they shall sign and certify, and transmit sealed to the seat of the government of the United States, directed to the President of the Senate;—The President of the Senate shall, in the presence of the Senate and House of Representatives, open all the certificates and the votes shall then be counted;—The person having the greatest number of votes for President, shall be the President, if such number be a majority of the whole number of Electors appointed; and if no person have such majority, then from the persons having the highest numbers not exceeding three on the list of those voted for as President, the House of Representatives shall choose immediately, by ballot, the President. But in choosing the President, the votes shall be taken by states, the representation from each state having one vote; a quorum for this purpose shall consist of a member or members from two-thirds of the states, and a majority of all the states shall be necessary to a choice. And if the House of Representatives shall not choose a President whenever the right of choice shall devolve upon them, before the fourth day of March next following, then the Vice-President shall act as President, as in the case of the death or other constitutional disability of the President.—The person having the greatest number of votes as Vice-President, shall be the Vice-President, if such number be a majority of the whole number of Electors appointed, and if no person have a majority, then from the two highest numbers on the list, the Senate shall choose the Vice-President; a quorum for the purpose shall consist of two-thirds of the whole number of Senators, and a majority of the whole number shall be necessary to a choice. But no person constitutionally ineligible to the office of President shall be eligible to that of Vice-President of the United States.

Amendment XIII [1865]

Section 1.

Neither slavery nor involuntary servitude, except as a punishment for crime whereof the party shall have been duly convicted, shall exist within the United States, or any place subject to their jurisdiction.

Section 2.

Congress shall have power to enforce this article by appropriate legislation.

Amendment XIV [1868]

Section 1.

All persons born or naturalized in the United States, and subject to the jurisdiction thereof, are citizens of the United States and of the State wherein they reside. No State shall make or enforce any law which shall abridge the privileges or immunities of citizens of the United States; nor shall any State deprive any person of life, liberty, or property, without due process of law; nor deny to any person within its jurisdiction the equal protection of the laws.

Section 2.

Representatives shall be apportioned among the several States according to their respective numbers, counting the whole number of persons in each State, excluding Indians not taxed. But when the right to vote at any election for the choice of electors for President and Vice-President of the United States, Representatives in Congress, the Executive and Judicial officers of a State, or the members of the Legislature thereof, is denied to any of the male inhabitants of such State, being twenty-one years of age, and citizens of the United States, or in any way abridged, except for participation in rebellion, or other crime, the basis of representation therein shall be reduced in the proportion which the number of such male citizens shall bear to the whole number of male citizens twenty-one years of age in such State.

Section 3.

No person shall be a Senator or Representative in Congress, or elector of President and Vice-President, or hold any office, civil or military, under the United States, or under any State, who, having previously taken an oath, as a member of Congress, or as an officer of the United States, or as a member of any State legislature, or as an executive or judicial officer of any State, to support the

Constitution of the United States, shall have engaged in insurrection or rebellion against the same, or given aid or comfort to the enemies thereof. But Congress may by a vote of two-thirds of each House, remove such disability.

Section 4.

The validity of the public debt of the United States, authorized by law, including debts incurred for payment of pensions and bounties for services in suppressing insurrection or rebellion, shall not be questioned. But neither the United States nor any State shall assume or pay any debt or obligation incurred in aid of insurrection or rebellion against the United States, or any claim for the loss or emancipation of any slave; but all such debts, obligations, and claims shall be held illegal and void.

Section 5.

The Congress shall have the power to enforce, by appropriate legislation, the provisions of this article.

Amendment XV [1870]

Section 1.

The right of citizens of the United States to vote shall not be denied or abridged by the United States or by any State on account of race, color, or previous condition of servitude—

Section 2.

The Congress shall have power to enforce this article by appropriate legislation.

Amendment XVI [1913]

The Congress shall have power to lay and collect taxes on incomes, from whatever source derived, without apportionment among the several States, and without regard to any census or enumeration.

Amendment XVII [1913]

The Senate of the United States shall be composed of two Senators from each State, elected by the people thereof, for six years; and each Senator shall have one vote. The electors in each State shall have the qualifications requisite for electors of the most numerous branch of the State legislatures.

When vacancies happen in the representation of any State in the Senate, the executive authority of such State shall issue writs of election to fill such vacancies: *Provided,* That the legislature of any State may empower the executive thereof to make temporary appointments until the people fill the vacancies by election as the legislature may direct.

This amendment shall not be so construed as to affect the election or term of any Senator chosen before it becomes valid as part of the Constitution.

Amendment XVIII [1919]

Section 1.

After one year from the ratification of this article the manufacture, sale, or transportation of intoxicating liquors within, the importation thereof into, or the exportation thereof from the United States and all territory subject to the jurisdiction thereof for beverage purposes is hereby prohibited.

Section 2.

The Congress and the several States shall have concurrent power to enforce this article by appropriate legislation.

Section 3.

This article shall be inoperative unless it shall have been ratified as an amendment to the Constitution by the legislatures of the several States, as provided in the Constitution, within seven years from the date of the submission hereof to the States by the Congress.

Amendment XIX [1920]

The right of citizens of the United States to vote shall not be denied or abridged by the United States or by any State on account of sex.

Congress shall have power to enforce this article by appropriate legislation.

Amendment XX [1933]

Section 1.

The terms of the President and Vice-President shall end at noon on the 20th day of January, and the terms of Senators and Representatives at noon on the 3d day of January, of the years in which such terms would have ended if this article had not been ratified; and the terms of their successors shall then begin.

Section 2.

The Congress shall assemble at least once in every year, and such meeting shall begin at noon on the 3d day of January, unless they shall by law appoint a different day.

Section 3.

If, at the time fixed for the beginning of the term of the President, the President elect shall have died, the Vice-President elect shall become President. If a President shall not have been chosen before the time fixed for the beginning of his term, or if the President elect shall have failed to qualify, then the Vice President elect shall act as President until a President shall have qualified; and the Congress may by law provide for the case wherein neither a President elect nor a Vice-President elect shall have qualified, declaring who shall then act as President, or the manner in which one who is to act shall be selected, and such person shall act accordingly until a President or Vice-President shall have qualified.

Section 4.

The Congress may by law provide for the case of the death of any of the persons from whom the House of Representatives may choose a President when ever the right of choice shall have devolved upon them and for the case of the death of any of the persons from whom the Senate may choose a Vice-President whenever the right of choice shall have devolved upon them.

Section 5.

Sections 1 and 2 shall take effect on 15th day of October following the ratification of article.

Section 6.

This article shall be inoperative unless it shall have been ratified as an amendment to the Constitution by the legislatures of three-fourths of the several States within seven years from the date of its submission.

Amendment XXI [1933]

Section 1.

The eighteenth article of amendment to the Constitution of the United States is hereby repealed.

Section 2.

The transportation or importation into any State, Territory, or possession of the United States for delivery or use therein of intoxicating liquors, in violation of the laws thereof, is hereby prohibited.

Section 3.

This article shall be inoperative unless it shall have been ratified as an amendment to the Constitution by conventions in the several States, as provided in the Constitution, within seven years from the date of the submission hereof to the States by the Congress.

Amendment XXII [1951]

No person shall be elected to the office of the President more than twice, and no person who has held the office of President, or acted as President, for more than two years of a term to which some other person was elected President shall be elected to the office of the President more than once.

But this Article shall not apply to any person holding the office of President when this Article was proposed by the Congress, and shall not prevent any person who may be holding the office of President, or acting as President, during the term within which this Article becomes operative from holding the office of President or acting as President during the remainder of such term.

Amendment XXIII [1961]

Section 1.

The District constituting the seat of Government of the United States shall appoint in such manner as the Congress may direct:

A number of electors of President and Vice President equal to the whole number of Senators and Representatives in Congress to which the District would be entitled if it were a State, but in no event more than the least populous State; they shall be in addition to those appointed by the States, but they shall be considered, for the purposes of the election of President and Vice President, to be electors appointed by a State; and they shall meet in the District and perform such duties as provided by the twelfth article of amendment.

Section 2.

The Congress shall have power to enforce this article by appropriate legislation.

Amendment XXIV [1964]

Section 1.

The right of citizens of the United States to vote in any primary or other election for President or Vice President, for electors for President or Vice President, or for Senator or Representative in Congress, shall not be denied or abridged by the United States or any State by reason of failure to pay any poll tax or other tax.

Section 2.

The Congress shall have the power to enforce this article by appropriate legislation.

Amendment XXV [1967]

Section 1.

In case of the removal of the President from office or his death or resignation, the Vice President shall become President.

Section 2.

Whenever there is a vacancy in the office of the Vice President, the President shall nominate a Vice President who shall take the office upon confirmation by a majority vote of both houses of Congress.

Section 3.

Whenever the President transmits to the President pro tempore of the Senate and the Speaker of the House of Representatives his written declaration that he is unable to discharge the powers and duties of his office, and until he transmits to them a written declaration to the contrary, such powers and duties shall be discharged by the Vice President as Acting President.

Section 4.

Whenever the Vice President and a majority of either the principal officers of the executive departments, or of such other body as Congress may by law provide, transmit to the President pro tempore of the Senate and the Speaker of the House of Representatives their written declaration that the President is unable to discharge the powers and duties of his office, the Vice President shall immediately assume the powers and duties of the office as Acting President.

Thereafter, when the President transmits to the President pro tempore of the Senate and the Speaker of the House of Representatives his written declaration that no inability exists, he shall resume the powers and duties of his office unless the Vice President and a majority of either the principal officers of the executive departments, or of such other body as Congress may by law provide, transmit within four days to the President pro tempore of the Senate and the Speaker of the House of Representatives their written declaration that the President is unable to discharge the powers and duties of his office. Thereupon Congress shall decide the issue, assembling within 48 hours for that purpose if not in session. If the Congress, within 21 days after receipt of the latter written declaration, or, if Congress is not in session, within 21 days after Congress is required to assemble, determines by two-thirds vote of both houses that the President is unable to discharge the powers and duties of his office, the Vice President shall continue to discharge the same as Acting President; otherwise, the President shall resume the powers and duties of his office.

Amendment XXVI [1971]

Section 1.

The right of citizens of the United States, who are 18 years of age or older, to vote shall not be denied or abridged by the United States or any state on account of age.

Section 2.

The Congress shall have the power to enforce this article by appropriate legislation.

[Amendment XXVII] [1992]

No law varying the compensation for the services of the Senators and Representatives shall take effect, until an election of Representatives shall have intervened.

Presidential Elections, 1789–1992

Year	Candidates	Party	Popular Vote*	Electoral Vote**
1789	**George Washington**			69
	John Adams			34
	Others			35
1792	**George Washington**			132
	John Adams			77
	George Clinton			50
	Others			5
1796	**John Adams**	Federalist		71
	Thomas Jefferson	Democratic Republican		68
	Thomas Pinckney	Federalist		59
	Aaron Burr	Democratic Republican		30
	Others			48
1800	**Thomas Jefferson**	Democratic Republican		73
	Aaron Burr	Democratic Republican		73
	John Adams	Federalist		65
	Charles C. Pinckney	Federalist		64
1804	**Thomas Jefferson**	Democratic Republican		162
	Charles C. Pinckney	Federalist		14

A-28

Year	Candidates	Party	Popular Vote*	Electoral Vote**
1808	**James Madison**	Democratic Republican		122
	Charles C. Pinckney	Federalist		47
	George Clinton	Independent Republican		6
1812	**James Madison**	Democratic Republican		128
	DeWitt Clinton	Federalist		89
1816	**James Monroe**	Democratic Republican		183
	Rufus King	Federalist		34
1820	**James Monroe**	Democratic Republican		231
	John Quincy Adams	Independent Republican		1
1824	**John Quincy Adams**	Democratic Republican	108,704 (30.5%)	84
	Andrew Jackson	Democratic Republican	153,544 (43.1%)	99
	Henry Clay	Democratic Republican	47,136 (13.2%)	37
	William H. Crawford	Democratic Republican	46,618 (13.1%)	41
1828	**Andrew Jackson**	Democratic	647,231 (56.0%)	178
	John Quincy Adams	National Republican	509,097 (44.0%)	83
1832	**Andrew Jackson**	Democratic	687,502 (55.0%)	219
	Henry Clay	National Republican	530,189 (42.4%)	49
	William Wirt	Anti-Masonic		7
	John Floyd	National Republican		11
1836	**Martin Van Buren**	Democratic	761,549 (50.9%)	170
	William H. Harrison	Whig	549,567 (36.7%)	73
	Hugh L. White	Whig	145,396 (9.7%)	26
	Daniel Webster	Whig	41,287 (2.7%)	14

* Because only the leading candidates are listed, popular vote percentages do not always total 100.

** The elections of 1800 and 1824, in which no candidate received an electoral vote majority, were decided in the House of Representatives.

(continues)

Year	Candidates	Party	Popular Vote*	Electoral Vote**
1840	**William H. Harrison** (**John Tyler,** 1841)	Whig	1,275,017 (53.1%)	234
	Martin Van Buren	Democratic	1,128,702 (46.9%)	60
1844	**James K. Polk**	Democratic	1,337,243 (49.6%)	170
	Henry Clay	Whig	1,299,068 (48.1%)	105
	James G. Birney	Liberty	62,300 (2.3%)	
1848	**Zachary Taylor** (**Millard Fillmore,** 1850)	Whig	1,360,101 (47.4%)	163
	Lewis Cass	Democratic	1,220,544 (42.5%)	127
	Martin Van Buren	Free Soil	291,263 (10.1%)	
1852	**Franklin Pierce**	Democratic	1,601,474 (50.9%)	254
	Winfield Scott	Whig	1,386,578 (44.1%)	42
1856	**James Buchanan**	Democratic	1,838,169 (45.4%)	174
	John C. Frémont	Republican	1,335,264 (33.0%)	114
	Millard Fillmore	American	874,534 (21.6%)	8
1860	**Abraham Lincoln**	Republican	1,865,593 (39.8%)	180
	Stephen A. Douglas	Democratic	1,382,713 (29.5%)	12
	John C. Breckinridge	Democratic	848,356 (18.1%)	72
	John Bell	Constitutional Union	592,906 (12.6%)	39
1864	**Abraham Lincoln** (**Andrew Johnson,** 1865)	Republican	2,206,938 (55.0%)	212
	George B. McClellan	Democratic	1,803,787 (45.0%)	21
1868	**Ulysses S. Grant**	Republican	3,013,421 (52.7%)	214
	Horatio Seymour	Democratic	2,706,829 (47.3%)	80

Year	Candidates	Party	Popular Vote*	Electoral Vote**
1872	**Ulysses S. Grant**	Republican	3,596,745 (55.6%)	286
	Horace Greeley	Democratic	2,843,446 (43.9%)	66
1876	**Rutherford B. Hayes**	Republican	4,036,572 (48.0%)	185
	Samuel J. Tilden	Democratic	4,284,020 (51.0%)	184
1880	**James A. Garfield**	Republican	4,449,053 (48.3%)	214
	(Chester A. Arthur, 1881)			
	Winfield S. Hancock	Democratic	4,442,035 (48.2%)	155
	James B. Weaver	Greenback Labor	308,578 (3.4%)	
1884	**Grover Cleveland**	Democratic	4,874,986 (48.5%)	219
	James G. Blaine	Republican	4,851,981 (48.2%)	182
	Benjamin F. Butler	Greenback Labor	175,370 (1.8%)	
1888	**Benjamin Harrison**	Republican	5,444,337 (47.8%)	233
	Grover Cleveland	Democratic	5,540,050 (48.6%)	168
1892	**Grover Cleveland**	Democratic	5,554,414 (46.0%)	277
	Benjamin Harrison	Republican	5,190,802 (43.0%)	145
	James B. Weaver	People's	1,027,329 (8.5%)	22
1896	**William McKinley**	Republican	7,035,638 (50.8%)	271
	William Jennings Bryan	Democratic; Populist	6,467,946 (46.7%)	176
1900	**William McKinley**	Republican	7,219,530 (51.7%)	292
	(Theodore Roosevelt, 1901)			
	William Jennings Bryan	Democratic; Populist	6,356,734 (45.5%)	155

*Because only the leading candidates are listed, popular vote percentages do not always total 100.

**The elections of 1800 and 1824, in which no candidate received an electoral vote majority, were decided in the House of Representatives.

(continues)

Year	Candidates	Party	Popular Vote*	Electoral Vote**
1904	**Theodore Roosevelt**	Republican	7,628,834 (56.4%)	336
	Alton B. Parker	Democratic	5,084,401 (37.6%)	140
	Eugene V. Debs	Socialist	402,460 (3.0%)	
1908	**William H. Taft**	Republican	7,679,006 (51.6%)	321
	William Jennings Bryan	Democratic	6,409,106 (43.1%)	162
	Eugene V. Debs	Socialist	420,820 (2.8%)	
1912	**Woodrow Wilson**	Democratic	6,286,820 (41.8%)	435
	Theodore Roosevelt	Progressive	4,126,020 (27.4%)	88
	William H. Taft	Republican	3,483,922 (23.2%)	8
	Eugene V. Debs	Socialist	897,011 (6.0%)	
1916	**Woodrow Wilson**	Democratic	9,129,606 (49.3%)	277
	Charles E. Hughes	Republican	8,538,221 (46.1%)	254
1920	**Warren G. Harding** (Calvin Coolidge, 1923)	Republican	16,152,200 (61.0%)	404
	James M. Cox	Democratic	9,147,353 (34.6%)	127
	Eugene V. Debs	Socialist	919,799 (3.5%)	
1924	**Calvin Coolidge**	Republican	15,725,016 (54.1%)	382
	John W. Davis	Democratic	8,385,586 (28.8%)	136
	Robert M. La Follette	Progressive	4,822,856 (16.6%)	13
1928	**Herbert C. Hoover**	Republican	21,392,190 (58.2%)	444
	Alfred E. Smith	Democratic	15,016,443 (40.8%)	87
1932	**Franklin D. Roosevelt**	Democratic	22,809,638 (57.3%)	472
	Herbert C. Hoover	Republican	15,758,901 (39.6%)	59
	Norman Thomas	Socialist	881,951 (2.2%)	

Year	Candidates	Party	Popular Vote*	Electoral Vote**
1936	**Franklin D. Roosevelt**	Democratic	27,751,612 (60.7%)	523
	Alfred M. Landon	Republican	16,681,913 (36.4%)	8
	William Lemke	Union	891,858 (1.9%)	
1940	**Franklin D. Roosevelt**	Democratic	27,243,466 (54.7%)	449
	Wendell L. Willkie	Republican	22,304,755 (44.8%)	82
1944	**Franklin D. Roosevelt**	Democratic	25,602,505 (52.8%)	432
	(Harry S Truman, 1945)			
	Thomas E. Dewey	Republican	22,006,278 (44.5%)	99
1948	**Harry S Truman**	Democratic	24,105,812 (49.5%)	303
	Thomas E. Dewey	Republican	21,970,065 (45.1%)	189
	J. Strom Thurmond	States' Rights	1,169,063 (2.4%)	39
	Henry A. Wallace	Progressive	1,157,172 (2.4%)	
1952	**Dwight D. Eisenhower**	Republican	33,936,234 (55.2%)	442
	Adlai E. Stevenson	Democratic	27,314,992 (44.5%)	89
1956	**Dwight D. Eisenhower**	Republican	35,590,472 (57.4%)	457
	Adlai E. Stevenson	Democratic	26,022,752 (42.0%)	73
1960	**John F. Kennedy**	Democratic	34,227,096 (49.9%)	303
	(Lyndon B. Johnson, 1963)			
	Richard M. Nixon	Republican	34,108,546 (49.6%)	219
1964	**Lyndon B. Johnson**	Democratic	43,126,233 (61.1%)	486
	Barry M. Goldwater	Republican	27,174,989 (38.5%)	52

(continues)

* Because only the leading candidates are listed, popular vote percentages do not always total 100.

** The elections of 1800 and 1824, in which no candidate received an electoral vote majority, were decided in the House of Representatives.

Year	Candidates	Party	Popular Vote*	Electoral Vote**
1968	**Richard M. Nixon**	Republican	31,783,783 (43.4%)	301
	Hubert H. Humphrey	Democratic	31,271,839 (42.7%)	191
	George C. Wallace	Amer. Independent	9,899,557 (13.5%)	46
1972	**Richard M. Nixon**	Republican	45,767,218 (60.6%)	520
	(Gerald R. Ford, 1974)			
	George S. McGovern	Democratic	28,357,668 (37.5%)	17
1976	**Jimmy Carter**	Democratic	40,828,657 (50.6%)	297
	Gerald R. Ford	Republican	39,145,520 (48.4%)	241
1980	**Ronald Reagan**	Republican	43,899,248 (51%)	489
	Jimmy Carter	Democratic	36,481,435 (41%)	49
	John B. Anderson	Independent	5,719,437 (6%)	
1984	**Ronald Reagan**	Republican	54,455,075 (59%)	525
	Walter F. Mondale	Democratic	37,577,185 (41%)	13
1988	**George Bush**	Republican	48,881,221 (54%)	426
	Michael Dukakis	Democratic	41,805,422 (46%)	111
1992	**Bill Clinton**	Democratic	43,728,375 (43%)	370
	George Bush	Republican	38,167,416 (38%)	168
	H. Ross Perot	Independent	19,237,247 (19%)	

* Because only the leading candidates are listed, popular vote percentages do not always total 100.

** The elections of 1800 and 1824, in which no candidate received an electoral vote majority, were decided in the House of Representatives.

Presidential Administrations

Washington, 1789–1797

Vice-President	John Adams	1789–1797
Secretary of State	Thomas Jefferson	1789–1793
	Edmund Randolph	1794–1795
	Timothy Pickering	1795–1797
Secretary of War	Henry Knox	1789–1794
	Timothy Pickering	1795–1796
	James McHenry	1796–1797
Secretary of Treasury	Alexander Hamilton	1789–1795
	Oliver Wolcott, Jr.	1795–1797
Postmaster General	Samuel Osgood	1789–1791
	Timothy Pickering	1791–1794
	Joseph Habersham	1795–1797
Attorney General	Edmund Randolph	1789–1793
	William Bradford	1794–1795
	Charles Lee	1795–1797

John Adams, 1797–1801

Vice-President	Thomas Jefferson	1797–1801
Secretary of State	Timothy Pickering	1797–1800
	John Marshall	1800–1801
Secretary of War	James McHenry	1797–1800
	Samuel Dexter	1800–1801
Secretary of Treasury	Oliver Wolcott, Jr.	1797–1800
	Samuel Dexter	1800–1801
Postmaster General	Joseph Habersham	1797–1801
Attorney General	Charles Lee	1797–1801
Secretary of Navy	Benjamin Stoddert	1798–1801

Jefferson, 1801–1809

Vice-President	Aaron Burr	1801–1805
	George Clinton	1805–1809

(continues)

Secretary of State	James Madison	1801–1809
Secretary of War	Henry Dearborn	1801–1809
Secretary of Treasury	Samuel Dexter	1801
	Albert Gallatin	1801–1809
Postmaster General	Joseph Habersham	1801
	Gideon Granger	1801–1809
Attorney General	Levi Lincoln	1801–1805
	Robert Smith	1805
	John C. Breckinridge	1805–1806
	Caesar A. Rodney	1807–1809
Secretary of Navy	Robert Smith	1801–1809

Madison, 1809–1817

Vice-President	George Clinton	1809–1813
	Elbridge Gerry	1813–1817
Secretary of State	Robert Smith	1809–1811
	James Monroe	1811–1817
Secretary of War	William Eustis	1809–1812
	John Armstrong	1813–1814
	James Monroe	1814–1815
	William H. Crawford	1815–1817
Secretary of Treasury	Albert Gallatin	1809–1813
	George W. Campbell	1814
	Alexander J. Dallas	1814–1816
	William H. Crawford	1816–1817
Postmaster General	Gideon Granger	1809–1814
	Return J. Meigs, Jr.	1814–1817
Attorney General	Caesar A. Rodney	1809–1811
	William Pinkney	1811–1814
	Richard Rush	1814–1817
Secretary of Navy	Paul Hamilton	1809–1813
	William Jones	1813–1814
	Benjamin W. Crowninshield	1814–1817

Monroe, 1817–1825

Vice-President	Daniel D. Tompkins	1817–1825
Secretary of State	John Quincy Adams	1817–1825
Secretary of War	George Graham	1817
	John C. Calhoun	1817–1825
Secretary of Treasury	William H. Crawford	1817–1825
Postmaster General	Return J. Meigs, Jr.	1817–1823
	John McLean	1823–1825
Attorney General	Richard Rush	1817
	William Wirt	1817–1825
Secretary of Navy	Benjamin W. Crowninshield	1817–1818
	Smith Thompson	1818–1823
	Samuel L. Southard	1823–1825

John Quincy Adams, 1825–1829

Vice-President	John C. Calhoun	1825–1829
Secretary of State	Henry Clay	1825–1829
Secretary of War	James Barbour	1825–1828
	Peter B. Porter	1828–1829
Secretary of Treasury	Richard Rush	1825–1829
Postmaster General	John McLean	1825–1829
Attorney General	William Wirt	1825–1829
Secretary of Navy	Samuel L. Southard	1825–1829

Jackson, 1829–1837

Vice-President	John C. Calhoun	1829–1832
	Martin Van Buren	1833–1837
Secretary of State	Martin Van Buren	1829–1831
	Edward Livingston	1831–1833
	Louis McLane	1833–1834
	John Forsyth	1834–1837
Secretary of War	John H. Eaton	1829–1831
	Lewis Cass	1831–1837
	Benjamin Butler	1837
Secretary of Treasury	Samuel D. Ingham	1829–1831
	Louis McLane	1831–1833
	William J. Duane	1833
	Roger B. Taney	1833–1834
	Levi Woodbury	1834–1837
Postmaster General	William T. Barry	1829–1835
	Amos Kendall	1835–1837
Attorney General	John M. Berrien	1829–1831
	Roger B. Taney	1831–1833
	Benjamin F. Butler	1833–1837
Secretary of Navy	John Branch	1829–1831
	Levi Woodbury	1831–1834
	Mahlon Dickerson	1834–1837

Van Buren, 1837–1841

Vice-President	Richard M. Johnson	1837–1841
Secretary of State	John Forsyth	1837–1841
Secretary of War	Joel R. Poinsett	1837–1841
Secretary of Treasury	Levi Woodbury	1837–1841
Postmaster General	Amos Kendall	1837–1840
	John M. Niles	1840–1841
Attorney General	Benjamin F. Butler	1837–1838
	Felix Grundy	1838–1840
	Henry D. Gilpin	1840–1841
Secretary of Navy	Mahlon Dickerson	1837–1838
	James K. Paulding	1838–1841

(continues)

William Harrison, 1841

Vice-President	John Tyler	1841
Secretary of State	Daniel Webster	1841
Secretary of War	John Bell	1841
Secretary of Treasury	Thomas Ewing	1841
Postmaster General	Francis Granger	1841
Attorney General	John J. Crittenden	1841
Secretary of Navy	George E. Badger	1841

Tyler, 1841–1845

Vice-President	None	
Secretary of State	Daniel Webster	1841–1843
	Hugh S. Legare	1843
	Abel P. Upshur	1843–1844
	John C. Calhoun	1844–1845
Secretary of War	John Bell	1841
	John C. Spencer	1841–1843
	John M. Porter	1843–1844
	William Wilkins	1844–1845
Secretary of Treasury	Thomas Ewing	1841
	Walter Forward	1841–1843
	John C. Spencer	1843–1844
	George M. Bibb	1844–1845
Postmaster General	Francis Granger	1841
	Charles A. Wickliffe	1841
Attorney General	John J. Crittenden	1841
	Hugh S. Legaré	1841–1843
	John Nelson	1843–1845
Secretary of Navy	George Badger	1841
	Abel P. Upshur	1841
	David Henshaw	1843–1844
	Thomas W. Gilmer	1844
	John Y. Mason	1844–1845

Polk, 1845–1849

Vice-President	George M. Dallas	1845–1849
Secretary of State	James Buchanan	1845–1849
Secretary of War	William L. Marcy	1845–1849
Secretary of Treasury	Robert J. Walker	1845–1849
Postmaster General	Cave Johnson	1845–1849
Attorney General	John Y. Mason	1845–1846
	Nathan Clifford	1846–1848
	Isaac Toucey	1848–1849
Secretary of Navy	George Bancroft	1845–1846
	John Y. Mason	1846–1849

Taylor, 1849–1850

Vice-President	Millard Fillmore	1849–1850
Secretary of State	John M. Clayton	1849–1850
Secretary of War	George W. Crawford	1849–1850
Secretary of Treasury	William M. Meredith	1849–1850
Postmaster General	Jacob Collamer	1849–1850
Attorney General	Reverdy Johnson	1849–1850
Secretary of Navy	William Preston	1849–1850
Secretary of Interior	Thomas Ewing	1849–1850

Fillmore, 1850–1853

Vice-President	None	
Secretary of State	Daniel Webster	1850–1852
	Edward Everett	1852–1853
Secretary of War	Charles M. Conrad	1850–1853
Secretary of Treasury	Thomas Corwin	1850–1853
Postmaster General	Nathan K. Hall	1850–1852
	Sam D. Hubbard	1852–1853
Attorney General	John J. Crittenden	1850–1853
Secretary of Navy	William A. Graham	1850–1852
	John P. Kennedy	1852–1853
Secretary of Interior	Thomas M. T. McKennan	1850
	Alexander H. H. Stuart	1850–1853

Pierce, 1853–1857

Vice-President	William R. King	1853
Secretary of State	William L. Marcy	1853–1857
Secretary of War	Jefferson Davis	1853–1857
Secretary of Treasury	James Guthrie	1853–1857
Postmaster General	James Campbell	1853–1857
Attorney General	Caleb Cushing	1853–1857
Secretary of Navy	James C. Dobbins	1853–1857
Secretary of Interior	Robert McClelland	1853–1857

Buchanan, 1857–1861

Vice-President	John C. Breckinridge	1857–1861
Secretary of State	Lewis Cass	1857–1860
	Jeremiah S. Black	1860–1861
Secretary of War	John B. Floyd	1857–1861
	Joseph Holt	1861
Secretary of Treasury	Howell Cobb	1857–1860
	Philip F. Thomas	1860–1861

(continues)

Postmaster General	John A. Dix	1861
	Aaron V. Brown	1857–1859
	Joseph Holt	1859–1861
	Horatio King	1861
Attorney General	Jeremiah S. Black	1857–1860
	Edwin M. Stanton	1860–1861
Secretary of Navy	Isaac Toucey	1857–1861
Secretary of Interior	Jacob Thompson	1857–1861

Lincoln, 1861–1865

Vice-President	Hannibal Hamlin	1861–1865
	Andrew Johnson	1865
Secretary of State	William H. Seward	1861–1865
Secretary of War	Simon Cameron	1861–1862
	Edwin M. Stanton	1862–1865
Secretary of Treasury	Samuel P. Chase	1861–1864
	William P. Fessenden	1864–1865
	Hugh McCulloch	1865
Postmaster General	Horatio King	1861
	Montgomery Blair	1861–1864
	William Dennison	1864–1865
Attorney General	Edward Bates	1861–1864
	James Speed	1864–1865
Secretary of Navy	Gideon Welles	1861–1865
Secretary of Interior	Caleb B. Smith	1861–1863
	John P. Usher	1863–1865

Andrew Johnson, 1865–1869

Vice-President	None	
Secretary of State	William H. Seward	1865–1869
Secretary of War	Edwin M. Stanton	1865–1867
	Ulysses S. Grant	1867–1868
	John M. Schofield	1868–1869
Secretary of Treasury	Hugh McCulloch	1865–1869
Postmaster General	William Dennison	1865–1866
	Alexander W. Randall	1866–1869
Attorney General	James Speed	1865–1866
	Henry Stanbery	1866–1868
	William M. Evarts	1868–1869
Secretary of Navy	Gideon Welles	1865–1869
Secretary of Interior	John P. Usher	1865
	James Harlan	1865–1866
	Orville H. Browning	1866–1869

Grant, 1869–1877

Vice-President	Schuyler Colfax	1869–1873
	Henry Wilson	1873–1875
Secretary of State	Elihu B. Washburne	1869
	Hamilton Fish	1869–1877

Secretary of War	John A. Rawlins	1869
	William T. Sherman	1869
	William W. Belknap	1869–1876
	Alphonso Taft	1876
	James D. Cameron	1876–1877
Secretary of Treasury	George S. Boutwell	1869–1873
	William A. Richardson	1873–1874
	Benjamin H. Bristow	1874–1876
	Lot M. Morrill	1876–1877
Postmaster General	John A. J. Creswell	1869–1874
	James W. Marshall	1874
	Marshall Jewell	1874–1876
	James N. Tyner	1876–1877
Attorney General	Ebenezer R. Hoar	1869–1870
	Amos T. Ackerman	1870–1871
	G. H. Williams	1871–1875
	Edwards Pierrepont	1875–1876
	Alphonso Taft	1876–1877
Secretary of Navy	Adolph E. Borie	1869
	George Robeson	1869–1877
Secretary of Interior	Jacob D. Cox	1869–1870
	Columbus Delano	1870–1875
	Zachariah Chandler	1875–1877

Hayes, 1877–1881

Vice-President	William A. Wheeler	1877–1881
Secretary of State	William B. Evarts	1877–1881
Secretary of War	George W. McCrary	1877–1879
	Alexander Ramsey	1879–1881
Secretary of Treasury	John Sherman	1877–1881
Postmaster General	David M. Key	1877–1880
	Horace Maynard	1880–1881
Attorney General	Charles Devens	1877–1881
Secretary of Navy	Richard W. Thompson	1877–1880
	Nathan Goff, Jr.	1881
Secretary of Interior	Carl Schurz	1877–1881

Garfield, 1881

Vice-President	Chester A. Arthur	1881
Secretary of State	James G. Blaine	1881
Secretary of War	Robert T. Lincoln	1881
Secretary of Treasury	William Windom	1881
Postmaster General	Thomas L. James	1881
Attorney General	Wayne MacVeagh	1881

(continues)

| Secretary of Navy | William H. Hunt | 1881 |
| Secretary of Interior | Samuel J. Kirkwood | 1881 |

Arthur, 1881–1885

Vice-President	None	
Secretary of State	Frederick T. Frelinghuysen	1881–1885
Secretary of War	Robert T. Lincoln	1881–1885
Secretary of Treasury	Charles J. Folger	1881–1884
	Walter Q. Gresham	1884
	Hugh McCulloch	1884–1885
Postmaster General	Timothy O. Howe	1881–1883
	Walter Q. Gresham	1883–1884
	Frank Hatton	1884–1885
Attorney General	Benjamin H. Brewster	1881–1885
Secretary of Navy	William H. Hunt	1881–1882
	William E. Chandler	1882–1885
Secretary of Interior	Samuel J. Kirkwood	1881–1882
	Henry M. Teller	1882–1885

Cleveland, 1885–1889

Vice-President	Thomas A. Hendricks	1885
Secretary of State	Thomas F. Bayard	1885–1889
Secretary of War	William C. Endicott	1885–1889
Secretary of Treasury	Daniel Manning	1885–1887
	Charles S. Fairchild	1887–1889
Postmaster General	William F. Vilas	1885–1888
	Don M. Dickinson	1888–1889
Attorney General	Augustus H. Garland	1885–1889
Secretary of Navy	William C. Whitney	1885–1889
Secretary of Interior	Lucius Q. C. Lamar	1885–1888
	William F. Vilas	1888–1889
Secretary of Agriculture	Norman J. Colman	1889

Benjamin Harrison, 1889–1893

Vice-President	Levi P. Morton	1889–1893
Secretary of State	James G. Blaine	1889–1892
	John W. Foster	1892–1893
Secretary of War	Redfield Proctor	1889–1891
	Stephen B. Elkins	1891–1893
Secretary of Treasury	William Windom	1889–1891
	Charles Foster	1891–1893
Postmaster General	John Wanamaker	1889–1893
Attorney General	William H. H. Miller	1889–1891
Secretary of Navy	Benjamin F. Tracy	1889–1893
Secretary of Interior	John W. Noble	1889–1893
Secretary of Agriculture	Jeremiah M. Rusk	1889–1893

Cleveland, 1893–1897

Vice-President	Adlai E. Stevenson	1893–1897
Secretary of State	Walter Q. Gresham	1893–1895
	Richard Olney	1895–1897
Secretary of War	Daniel S. Lamont	1893–1897
Secretary of Treasury	John G. Carlisle	1893–1897
Postmaster General	Wilson S. Bissell	1893–1895
	William L. Wilson	1895–1897
Attorney General	Richard Olney	1893–1895
	Judson Harmon	1895–1897
Secretary of Navy	Hilary A. Herbert	1893–1897
Secretary of Interior	Hoke Smith	1893–1896
	David R. Francis	1896–1897
Secretary of Agriculture	Julius Sterling Morton	1893–1897

McKinley, 1897–1901

Vice-President	Garret Hobart	1897–1899
	Theodore Roosevelt	1901
Secretary of State	John Sherman	1897–1898
	William R. Day	1898
	John M. Hay	1898–1901
Secretary of War	Russell A. Alger	1897–1899
	Elihu Root	1899–1901
Secretary of Treasury	Lyman J. Gage	1897–1901
Postmaster General	James A. Gary	1897–1898
	Charles E. Smith	1898–1901
Attorney General	Joseph McKenna	1897–1898
	John W. Griggs	1898–1901
	Philander C. Knox	1901
Secretary of Navy	John D. Long	1897–1901
Secretary of Interior	Cornelius N. Bliss	1897–1899
	Ethan A. Hitchcock	1899–1901
Secretary of Agriculture	James Wilson	1897–1901

Theodore Roosevelt, 1901–1909

Vice-President	Charles Warren Fairbanks	1905–1909
Secretary of State	John M. Hay	1901–1905
	Elihu Root	1905–1909
	Robert Bacon	1909
Secretary of War	Elihu Root	1901–1904
	William Howard Taft	1904–1908
	Luke E. Wright	1908–1909

(continues)

Secretary of Treasury	Lyman J. Gage	1901–1902
	Leslie M. Shaw	1902–1907
	George B. Cortelyou	1907–1909
Postmaster General	Charles Emory Smith	1901–1902
	Henry C. Payne	1902–1904
	Robert J. Wynne	1904–1905
	George B. Cortelyou	1905–1907
	George von L. Meyer	1907–1909
Attorney General	Philander C. Knox	1901–1904
	William H. Moody	1904–1906
	Charles J. Bonaparte	1906–1909
Secretary of Navy	John D. Long	1901–1902
	William H. Moody	1902–1904
	Paul Morton	1904–1905
	Charles J. Bonaparte	1905–1906
	Victor H. Metcalf	1906–1908
	Truman H. Newberry	1908–1909
Secretary of Interior	Ethan A. Hitchcock	1901–1907
	James R. Garfield	1907–1909
Secretary of Agriculture	James Wilson	1901–1909
Secretary of Labor and Commerce	George B. Cortelyou	1903–1904
	Victor H. Metcalf	1904–1906
	Oscar S. Straus	1906–1909

Taft, 1909–1913

Vice-President	James S. Sherman	1909–1912
Secretary of State	Philander C. Knox	1909–1913
Secretary of War	Jacob M. Dickinson	1909–1911
	Henry L. Stimson	1911–1913
Secretary of Treasury	Franklin MacVeagh	1909–1913
Postmaster General	Frank H. Hitchcock	1909–1913
Attorney General	George W. Wickersham	1909–1913
Secretary of Navy	George von L. Meyer	1909–1913
Secretary of Interior	Richard A. Ballinger	1909–1911
	Walter Lowrie Fisher	1911–1913
Secretary of Agriculture	James Wilson	1909–1913
Secretary of Labor and Commerce	Oscar S. Straus	1909
	Charles Nagel	1909–1913

Wilson, 1913–1921

Vice-President	Thomas R. Marshall	1913–1921
Secretary of State	William Jennings Bryan	1913–1915
	Robert Lansing	1915–1920
	Bainbridge Colby	1920–1921
Secretary of War	Lindley M. Garrison	1913–1916

	Newton D. Baker	1916–1921
Secretary of Treasury	William Gilbert McAdoo	1913–1918
	Carter Glass	1918–1920
	David F. Houston	1920–1921
Postmaster General	Albert Sidney Burleson	1913–1921
Attorney General	James Clark McReynolds	1913–1914
	Thomas Watt Gregory	1914–1919
	A. Mitchell Palmer	1919–1921
Secretary of Navy	Josephus Daniels	1913–1921
Secretary of Interior	Franklin Knight Lane	1913–1920
	John Barton Payne	1920–1921
Secretary of Agriculture	David F. Houston	1913–1920
	Edwin T. Meredith	1920–1921
Secretary of Commerce	William C. Redfield	1913–1919
Secretary of Labor	William Bauchop Wilson	1913–1921

Harding, 1921–1923

Vice-President	Calvin Coolidge	1921–1923
Secretary of State	Charles Evans Hughes	1921–1923
Secretary of War	John W. Weeks	1921–1923
Secretary of Treasury	Andrew W. Mellon	1921–1923
Postmaster General	Will H. Hays	1921–1922
	Hubert Work	1922–1923
	Harry S. New	1923
Attorney General	Harry M. Daugherty	1921–1923
Secretary of Navy	Edwin Denby	1921–1923
Secretary of Interior	Albert B. Fall	1921–1923
	Hubert Work	1923
Secretary of Agriculture	Henry C. Wallace	1921–1923
Secretary of Commerce	Herbert C. Hoover	1921–1923
Secretary of Labor	James J. Davis	1921–1923

Coolidge, 1923–1929

Vice-President	Charles G. Dawes	1925–1929
Secretary of State	Charles Evans Hughes	1923–1925
	Frank B. Kellogg	1925–1929
Secretary of War	John W. Weeks	1923–1925
	Dwight F. Davis	1925–1929
Secretary of Treasury	Andrew W. Mellon	1923–1929

(continues)

Postmaster General	Harry S. New	1923–1929
Attorney General	Harry M. Daugherty	1923–1924
	Harlan Fiske Stone	1924–1925
	John G. Sargent	1925–1929
Secretary of Navy	Edwin Denby	1923–1924
	Curtis D. Wilbur	1924–1929
Secretary of Interior	Hubert Work	1923–1928
	Roy O. West	1928–1929
Secretary of Agriculture	Henry C. Wallace	1923–1924
	Howard M. Gore	1924–1925
	William M. Jardine	1925–1929
Secretary of Commerce	Herbert C. Hoover	1923–1928
	William F. Whiting	1928–1929
Secretary of Labor	James J. Davis	1923–1929

Hoover, 1929–1933

Vice-President	Charles Curtis	1929–1933
Secretary of State	Henry L. Stimson	1929–1933
Secretary of War	James W. Good	1929
	Patrick J. Hurley	1929–1933
Secretary of Treasury	Andrew W. Mellon	1929–1932
	Ogden L. Mills	1932–1933
Postmaster General	Walter F. Brown	1929–1933
Attorney General	William D. Mitchell	1929–1933
Secretary of Navy	Charles F. Adams	1929–1933
Secretary of Interior	Ray L. Wilbur	1929–1933
Secretary of Agriculture	Arthur M. Hyde	1929–1933
Secretary of Commerce	Robert P. Lamont	1929–1932
	Roy D. Chapin	1932–1933
Secretary of Labor	James J. Davis	1929–1930
	William N. Doak	1930–1933

Franklin D. Roosevelt, 1933–1945

Vice-President	John Nance Garner	1933–1941
	Henry A. Wallace	1941–1945
	Harry S Truman	1945
Secretary of State	Cordell Hull	1933–1944
	Edward R. Stettinius, Jr.	1944–1945
Secretary of War	George H. Dern	1933–1936
	Henry A. Woodring	1936–1940
	Henry L. Stimson	1940–1945
Secretary of Treasury	William H. Woodin	1933–1934
	Henry Morgenthau, Jr.	1934–1945
Postmaster General	James A. Farley	1933–1940
	Frank C. Walker	1940–1945

Attorney General	Homer S. Cummings	1933–1939
	Frank Murphy	1939–1940
	Robert H. Jackson	1940–1941
	Francis Biddle	1941–1945
Secretary of Navy	Claude A. Swanson	1933–1940
	Charles Edison	1940
	Frank Knox	1940–1944
	James V. Forrestal	1944–1945
Secretary of Interior	Harold L. Ickes	1933–1945
Secretary of Agriculture	Henry A. Wallace	1933–1940
	Claude R. Wickard	1940–1945
Secretary of Commerce	Daniel C. Roper	1933–1939
	Harry L. Hopkins	1939–1940
	Jesse H. Jones	1940–1945
	Henry A. Wallace	1945
Secretary of Labor	Frances Perkins	1933–1945

Truman, 1945–1953

Vice-President	Alben W. Barkley	1949–1953
Secretary of State	Edward R. Stettinius, Jr.	1945
	James F. Byrnes	1945–1947
	George C. Marshall	1947–1949
	Dean G. Acheson	1949–1953
Secretary of War	Robert P. Patterson	1945–1947
	Kenneth C. Royall	1947
Secretary of Treasury	Fred M. Vinson	1945–1946
	John W. Snyder	1946–1953
Postmaster General	Frank C. Walker	1945
	Robert E. Hannegan	1945–1947
	Jesse M. Donaldson	1947–1953
Attorney General	Tom C. Clark	1945–1949
	J. Howard McGrath	1949–1952
	James P. McGranery	1952–1953
Secretary of Navy	James V. Forrestal	1945–1947
Secretary of Interior	Harold L. Ickes	1945–1946
	Julius A. Krug	1946–1949
	Oscar L. Chapman	1949–1953
Secretary of Agriculture	Clinton P. Anderson	1945–1948
	Charles F. Brannan	1948–1953
Secretary of Commerce	Henry A. Wallace	1945–1946
	W. Averell Harriman	1946–1948
	Charles W. Sawyer	1948–1953
Secretary of Labor	Lewis B. Schwellenbach	1945–1948
	Maurice J. Tobin	1948–1953
Secretary of Defense	James V. Forrestal	1947–1949
	Louis A. Johnson	1949–1950
	George C. Marshall	1950–1951
	Robert A. Lovett	1951–1953

(continues)

Eisenhower, 1953–1961

Vice-President	Richard M. Nixon	1953–1961
Secretary of State	John Foster Dulles	1953–1959
	Christian A. Herter	1959–1961
Secretary of Treasury	George M. Humphrey	1953–1957
	Robert B. Anderson	1957–1961
Postmaster General	Arthur E. Summerfield	1953–1961
Attorney General	Herbert Brownell, Jr.	1953–1958
	William P. Rogers	1958–1961
Secretary of Interior	Douglas McKay	1953–1956
	Fred A. Seaton	1956–1961
Secretary of Agriculture	Ezra Taft Benson	1953–1961
Secretary of Commerce	Sinclair Weeks	1953–1958
	Lewis L. Strauss	1958–1959
	Frederick H. Mueller	1959–1961
Secretary of Labor	Martin P. Durkin	1953
	James P. Mitchell	1953–1961
Secretary of Defense	Charles E. Wilson	1953–1957
	Neil H. McElroy	1957–1959
	Thomas S. Gates, Jr.	1959–1961
Secretary of Health, Education, and Welfare	Oveta Culp Hobby	1953–1955
	Marion B. Folsom	1955–1958
	Arthur S. Flemming	1958–1961

Kennedy, 1961–1963

Vice-President	Lyndon B. Johnson	1961–1963
Secretary of State	Dean Rusk	1961–1963
Secretary of Treasury	C. Douglas Dillon	1961–1963
Postmaster General	J. Edward Day	1961–1963
	John A. Gronouski	1963
Attorney General	Robert F. Kennedy	1961–1963
Secretary of Interior	Stewart L. Udall	1961–1963
Secretary of Agriculture	Orville L. Freeman	1961–1963
Secretary of Commerce	Luther H. Hodges	1961–1963
Secretary of Labor	Arthur J. Goldberg	1961–1962
	W. Willard Wirtz	1962–1963
Secretary of Defense	Robert S. McNamara	1961–1963
Secretary of Health, Education, and Welfare	Abraham A. Ribicoff	1961–1962
	Anthony J. Celebrezze	1962–1963

Lyndon Johnson, 1963–1969

Vice-President	Hubert H. Humphrey	1965–1969
Secretary of State	Dean Rusk	1963–1969
Secretary of Treasury	C. Douglas Dillon	1963–1965
	Henry H. Fowler	1965–1969

Postmaster General	John A. Gronouski	1963–1965
	Lawrence F. O'Brien	1965–1968
	Marvin Watson	1968–1969
Attorney General	Robert F. Kennedy	1963–1964
	Nicholas Katzenbach	1965–1966
	Ramsey Clark	1967–1969
Secretary of Interior	Stewart L. Udall	1963–1969
Secretary of Agriculture	Orville L. Freeman	1963–1969
Secretary of Commerce	Luther H. Hodges	1963–1964
	John T. Connor	1964–1967
	Alexander B. Trowbridge	1967–1968
	Cyrus R. Smith	1968–1969
Secretary of Labor	W. Willard Wirtz	1963–1969
Secretary of Defense	Robert F. McNamara	1963–1968
	Clark Clifford	1968–1969
Secretary of Health, Education, and Welfare	Anthony J. Celebrezze	1963–1965
	John W. Gardner	1965–1968
	Wilbur J. Cohen	1968–1969
Secretary of Housing and Urban Development	Robert C. Weaver	1966–1969
	Robert C. Wood	1969
Secretary of Transportation	Alan S. Boyd	1967–1969

Nixon, 1969–1974

Vice-President	Spiro T. Agnew	1969–1973
	Gerald R. Ford	1973–1974
Secretary of State	William P. Rogers	1969–1973
	Henry A. Kissinger	1973–1974
Secretary of Treasury	David M. Kennedy	1969–1970
	John B. Connally	1971–1972
	George P. Shultz	1972–1974
	William E. Simon	1974
Postmaster General	Winton M. Blount	1969–1971
Attorney General	John N. Mitchell	1969–1972
	Richard G. Kleindienst	1972–1973
	Elliot L. Richardson	1973
	William B. Saxbe	1973–1974
Secretary of Interior	Walter J. Hickel	1969–1970
	Rogers Morton	1971–1974
Secretary of Agriculture	Clifford M. Hardin	1969–1971
	Earl L. Butz	1971–1974
Secretary of Commerce	Maurice H. Stans	1969–1972
	Peter G. Peterson	1972–1973
	Frederick B. Dent	1973–1974
Secretary of Labor	George P. Shultz	1969–1970
	James D. Hodgson	1970–1973
	Peter J. Brennan	1973–1974

(continues)

Secretary of Defense	Melvin R. Laird	1969–1973
	Elliot L. Richardson	1973
	James R. Schlesinger	1973–1974
Secretary of Health, Education, and Welfare	Robert H. Finch	1969–1970
	Elliot L. Richardson	1970–1973
	Caspar W. Weinberger	1973–1974
Secretary of Housing and Urban Development	George W. Romney	1969–1973
	James T. Lynn	1973–1974
Secretary of Transportation	John A. Volpe	1969–1973
	Claude S. Brinegar	1973–1974

Ford, 1974–1977

Vice-President	Nelson A. Rockefeller	1974–1977
Secretary of State	Henry A. Kissinger	1974–1977
Secretary of Treasury	William E. Simon	1974–1977
Attorney General	William B. Saxbe	1974–1975
	Edward H. Levi	1975–1977
Secretary of Interior	Rogers C. B. Morton	1974–1975
	Stanley K. Hathaway	1975
	Thomas S. Kleppe	1975–1977
Secretary of Agriculture	Earl L. Butz	1974–1976
	John A. Knebel	1976–1977

Secretary of Commerce	Frederick B. Dent	1974–1975
	Rogers C. B. Morton	1975–1976
	Elliot L. Richardson	1976–1977
Secretary of Labor	Peter J. Brennan	1974–1975
	John T. Dunlop	1975–1976
	W. J. Usery, Jr.	1976–1977
Secretary of Defense	James R. Schlesinger	1974–1975
	Donald H. Rumsfeld	1975–1977
Secretary of Health, Education, and Welfare	Caspar W. Weinberger	1974–1975
	F. David Mathews	1975–1977
Secretary of Housing and Urban Development	James T. Lynn	1974–1975
	Carla Anderson Hills	1975–1977
Secretary of Transportation	Claude S. Brinegar	1974–1975
	William T. Coleman, Jr.	1974–1977

Carter, 1977–1981

Vice-President	Walter F. Mondale	1977–1981
Secretary of State	Cyrus R. Vance	1977–1980
	Edmund S. Muskie	1980–1981
Secretary of Treasury	W. Michael Blumenthal	1977–1979
	G. William Miller	1979–1981

Attorney General	Griffin B. Bell	1977–1979
	Benjamin R. Civiletti	1979–1981
Secretary of Interior	Cecil D. Andrus	1977–1981
Secretary of Agriculture	Robert Bergland	1977–1981
Secretary of Commerce	Juanita M. Kreps	1977–1979
	Philip M. Klutznick	1979–1981
Secretary of Labor	F. Ray Marshall	1977–1981
Secretary of Defense	Harold Brown	1977–1981
Secretary of Health, Education, and Welfare	Joseph A. Califano, Jr.	1977–1979
	Patricia Roberts Harris	1979
Secretary of Health and Human Services	Patricia Roberts Harris	1979–1981
Secretary of Housing and Urban Development	Patricia Roberts Harris	1977–1979
	Moon Landrieu	1979–1981
Secretary of Transportation	Brock Adams	1977–1979
	Neil E. Goldschmidt	1979–1981
Secretary of Energy	James R. Schlesinger, Jr.	1977–1979
	Charles W. Duncan, Jr.	1979–1981
Secretary of Education	Shirley M. Hufstedler	1979–1981

Reagan, 1981–1989

Vice-President	George Bush	1981–1989
Secretary of State	Alexander M. Haig, Jr.	1981–1982
	George P. Shultz	1982–1989
Secretary of Treasury	Donald T. Regan	1981–1985
	James A. Baker, III	1985–1988
	Nicholas F. Brady	1988–1989
Attorney General	William French Smith	1981–1985
	Edwin A. Meese, III	1985–1988
	Richard Thornburgh	1988–1989
Secretary of Interior	James C. Watt	1981–1983
	William P. Clarke, Jr.	1983–1985
	Donald P. Hodel	1985–1989
Secretary of Agriculture	John R. Block	1981–1986
	Richard Lyng	1986–1989
Secretary of Commerce	Malcolm Baldrige	1981–1987
	C. William Verity, Jr.	1987–1989
Secretary of Labor	Raymond J. Donovan	1981–1985
	William E. Brock	1985–1987
	Ann D. McLaughlin	1987–1989
Secretary of Defense	Caspar W. Weinberger	1981–1987
	Frank C. Carlucci	1987–1989

(continues)

Secretary of Health and Human Services	Richard S. Schweiker	1981–1983
	Margaret M. Heckler	1983–1985
	Otis R. Bowen	1985–1989
Secretary of Housing and Urban Development	Samuel R. Pierce, Jr.	1981–1989
Secretary of Transportation	Andrew L. Lewis, Jr.	1981–1983
	Elizabeth Hanford Dole	1983–1987
	James H. Burnley	1987–1989
Secretary of Energy	James B. Edwards	1981–1982
	Donald P. Hodel	1982–1985
	John S. Herrington	1985–1989
Secretary of Education	Terrel H. Bell	1981–1985
	William J. Bennett	1985–1988
	Lauro F. Cavazos	1988–1989

Bush, 1989–1993

Vice President	J. Danforth Quayle	1989–1993
Secretary of State	James A. Baker III	1989–1992
Secretary of Treasury	Nicholas Brady	1989–1993
Attorney General	Richard Thornburgh	1989–1991
	William P. Barr	1991–1993
Secretary of Interior	Manuel Lujan	1989–1993
Secretary of Agriculture	Clayton K. Yeutter	1989–1991
	Edward Madigan	1991–1993
Secretary of Commerce	Robert Mosbacher	1989–1992
	Barbara Franklin	1992–1993
Secretary of Labor	Elizabeth Hanford Dole	1989–1991
	Lynn Martin	1991–1993
Secretary of Defense	Richard Cheney	1989–1993
Secretary of Health and Human Services	Louis W. Sullivan	1989–1993
Secretary of Education	Lauro F. Cavazos	1989–1991
	Lamar Alexander	1991–1993
Secretary of Housing and Urban Development	Jack F. Kemp	1989–1993
Secretary of Transportation	Samuel K. Skinner	1989–1992
	Andrew H. Card Jr.	1992–1993
Secretary of Energy	James D. Watkins	1989–1993
Secretary of Veterans Affairs	Edward J. Derwinski	1989–1993

Clinton, 1993–

Vice President	Albert Gore	1993–
Secretary of State	Warren Christopher	1993–
Secretary of Treasury	Lloyd Bentsen	1993–
Attorney General	Janet Reno	1993–

Secretary of Interior	Bruce Babbitt	1993–
Secretary of Agriculture	Michael Espy	1993–
Secretary of Commerce	Ronald Brown	1993–
Secretary of Labor	Robert B. Reich	1993–
Secretary of Defense	Les Aspin	1993–1994
	William Perry	1994–
Secretary of Health and Human Services	Donna Shalala	1993–
Secretary of Housing and Urban Development	Henry G. Cisneros	1993–
Secretary of Education	Richard W. Riley	1993–
Secretary of Transportation	Federico Peña	1993–
Secretary of Energy	Hazel R. O'Leary	1993–
Secretary of Veterans Affairs	Edward J. Derwinski	1993–

Supreme Court Justices

Chief Justices in italics.

	Term of Service	Years of Service
John Jay	1789–1795	5
John Rutledge	1789–1791	1
William Cushing	1789–1810	20
James Wilson	1789–1798	8
John Blair	1789–1796	6
Robert H. Harrison	1789–1790	—
James Iredell	1790–1799	9
Thomas Johnson	1791–1793	1
William Paterson	1793–1806	13
*John Rutledge**	1795	—
Samuel Chase	1796–1811	15

	Term of Service	Years of Service
Oliver Ellsworth	1796–1800	4
Bushrod Washington	1798–1829	31
Alfred Moore	1799–1804	4
John Marshall	1801–1835	34
William Johnson	1804–1834	30
H. Brockholst Livingston	1806–1823	16
Thomas Todd	1807–1826	18
Joseph Story	1811–1845	33
Gabriel Duval	1811–1835	24
Smith Thompson	1823–1843	20
Robert Trimble	1826–1828	2

	Term of Service	Years of Service
John McLean	1829–1861	32
Henry Baldwin	1830–1844	14
James M. Wayne	1835–1867	32
Roger B. Taney	1836–1864	28
Philip P. Barbour	1836–1841	4
John Catron	1837–1865	28
John McKinley	1837–1852	15
Peter V. Daniel	1841–1860	19
Samuel Nelson	1845–1872	27
Levi Woodbury	1845–1851	5
Robert C. Grier	1846–1870	23
Benjamin R. Curtis	1851–1857	6
John A. Campbell	1853–1861	8
Nathan Clifford	1858–1881	23
Noah H. Swayne	1862–1881	18
Samuel F. Miller	1862–1890	28
David Davis	1862–1877	14
Stephen J. Field	1863–1897	34
Salmon P. Chase	1864–1873	8

*Never confirmed as Chief Justice

	Term of Service	Years of Service
William Strong	1870–1880	10
Joseph P. Bradley	1870–1892	22
Ward Hunt	1873–1882	9
Morrison R. Waite	1874–1888	14
John M. Harlan	1877–1911	34
William B. Woods	1880–1887	7
Stanley Matthews	1881–1889	7
Horace Gray	1882–1902	20
Samuel Blatchford	1882–1893	11
Lucius Q. C. Lamar	1888–1893	5
Melville W. Fuller	1888–1910	21
David J. Brewer	1890–1910	20
Henry B. Brown	1890–1906	16
George Shiras, Jr.	1892–1903	10
Howell E. Jackson	1893–1895	2
Edward D. White	1894–1910	16
Rufus W. Peckham	1895–1909	14
Joseph McKenna	1898–1925	26
Oliver W. Holmes, Jr.	1902–1932	30
William R. Day	1903–1922	19

(continues)

	Term of Service	Years of Service
William H. Moody	1906–1910	3
Horace H. Lurton	1910–1914	4
Charles E. Hughes	1910–1916	5
Willis Van Devanter	1911–1937	26
Joseph R. Lamar	1911–1916	5
Edward D. White	1910–1921	11
Mahlon Pitney	1912–1922	10
James C. McReynolds	1914–1941	26
Louis D. Brandeis	1916–1939	22
John H. Clarke	1916–1922	6
William H. Taft	1921–1930	8
George Sutherland	1922–1938	15
Pierce Butler	1922–1939	16
Edward T. Sanford	1923–1930	7
Harlan F. Stone	1925–1941	16
Charles E. Hughes	1930–1941	11
Owen J. Roberts	1930–1945	15
Benjamin N. Cardozo	1932–1938	6
Hugo L. Black	1937–1971	34
Stanley F. Reed	1938–1957	19

	Term of Service	Years of Service
Felix Frankfurter	1939–1962	23
William O. Douglas	1939–1975	36
Frank Murphy	1940–1949	9
Harlan F. Stone	1941–1946	5
James F. Byrnes	1941–1942	1
Robert H. Jackson	1941–1954	13
Wiley B. Rutledge	1943–1949	6
Harold H. Burton	1945–1958	13
Fred M. Vinson	1946–1953	7
Tom C. Clark	1949–1967	18
Sherman Minton	1949–1956	7
Earl Warren	1953–1969	16
John Marshall Harlan	1955–1971	16
William J. Brennan, Jr.	1956–1990	34
Charles E. Whittaker	1957–1962	5
Potter Stewart	1958–1981	23
Byron R. White	1962–	—
Arthur J. Goldberg	1962–1965	3
Abe Fortas	1965–1969	4
Thurgood Marshall	1967–1991	24

	Term of Service	Years of Service
Warren E. Burger	1969–1986	18
Harry A. Blackmun	1970–1994	24
Lewis F. Powell, Jr.	1971–1987	15
*William H. Rehnquist***	1971–	—
John P. Stevens III	1975–	—
Sandra Day O'Connor	1981–	—
Antonin Scalia	1986–	—
Anthony M. Kennedy	1988–	—
David H. Souter	1990–	—
Clarence Thomas	1991–	—
Ruth Bader Ginsburg	1993–	—
Stephen Breyer	1994–	—

*Never confirmed as Chief Justice.
**Chief Justice from 1986 on.

Admission of States to the Union

State	Date of Admission
1. Delaware	December 7, 1787
2. Pennsylvania	December 12, 1787
3. New Jersey	December 18, 1787
4. Georgia	January 2, 1788
5. Connecticut	January 9, 1788
6. Massachusetts	February 6, 1788
7. Maryland	April 28, 1788
8. South Carolina	May 23, 1788
9. New Hampshire	June 21, 1788
10. Virginia	June 25, 1788
11. New York	July 26, 1788
12. North Carolina	November 21, 1789
13. Rhode Island	May 29, 1790
14. Vermont	March 4, 1791
15. Kentucky	June 1, 1792
16. Tennessee	June 1, 1796
17. Ohio	March 1, 1803
18. Louisiana	April 30, 1812
19. Indiana	December 11, 1816
20. Mississippi	December 10, 1817
21. Illinois	December 3, 1818
22. Alabama	December 14, 1819
23. Maine	March 15, 1820

State	Date of Admission
24. Missouri	August 10, 1821
25. Arkansas	June 15, 1836
26. Michigan	January 26, 1837
27. Florida	March 3, 1845
28. Texas	December 29, 1845
29. Iowa	December 28, 1846
30. Wisconsin	May 29, 1848
31. California	September 9, 1850
32. Minnesota	May 11, 1858
33. Oregon	February 14, 1859
34. Kansas	January 29, 1861
35. West Virginia	June 20, 1863
36. Nevada	October 31, 1864
37. Nebraska	March 1, 1867
38. Colorado	August 1, 1876
39. North Dakota	November 2, 1889
40. South Dakota	November 2, 1889
41. Montana	November 8, 1889
42. Washington	November 11, 1889
43. Idaho	July 3, 1890
44. Wyoming	July 10, 1890
45. Utah	January 4, 1896
46. Oklahoma	November 16, 1907
47. New Mexico	January 6, 1912
48. Arizona	February 14, 1912
49. Alaska	January 3, 1959
50. Hawaii	August 21, 1959

Credits

Unless otherwise acknowledged, all photographs are the property of Scott, Foresman and Company. Page abbreviations are as follows: (T)top, (C)center, (B)bottom, (L)left, (R)right.

Page 3, Courtesy of the Plymouth Society, Plymouth, Mass.   **Page 13,** Rare Books and Manuscripts Division/New York Public Library, Astor, Lenox and Tilden Foundations   **Page 20,** Copyright the British Museum   **Page 35,** Courtesy American Antiquarian Society   **Page 41,** Peabody Essex Museum, Salem   **Page 46,** Collection of Tazwell Ellett III   **Page 59,** Library of Congress   **Page 81,** Spencer Collection/New York Public Library, Astor, Lenox and Tilden Foundations,   **Page 89,** Library of Congress   **Page 95,** Library of Congress   **Page 108,** Courtesy of the Valley Forge Historical Society   **Page 115,** Copyright Yale University Art Gallery   **Page 134,** Historical Society of Pennsylvania   **Page 135,** Library of Congress   **Page 152,** Bowdoin Museum of Fine Arts, Bowdoin College   **Page 164,** Library of Congress   **Page 166,** Library of Congress   **Page 171,** The Metropolitan Museum of Art, Gift of Colonel and Mrs. Edgar William Garbisch, 1963   **Page 182,** Copyright Yale University Art Gallery, Bequest of Oliver Burr Jennings, B.A. 1917 in memory of Miss Annie Burr Jennings,   **Page 186,** Washington and Lee University   **Page 195,** Library of Congress   **Page 205L,** In the Collection of the Corcoran Gallery of Art   **Page 213,** I.N. Phelps Stokes Collection/New York Public Library, Astor, Lenox and Tilden Foundations,   **Page 234,** Library of Congress   **Page 235,** Memphis Brooks Museum of Art   **Page 255,** The Museum of the City of New York   **Page 260,** Sophia Smith Collection, Smith College   **Page 261,** The Metropolitan Museum of Art   **Page 264T,** Library of Congress   **Page 278,** Copyright Yale University Art Gallery, Gift of George Hoadley   **Page 283,** Prints Division/New York Public Library, Astor, Lenox and Tilden Foundations   **Page 293,** Prints Division/New York Public Library, Astor, Lenox and Tilden Foundations   **Page 294,** Library of Congress   **Page 305,** California Department of Parks and Recreation   **Page 311,** The Bancroft Library, University of California   **Page 322,** National Academy of Design   **Page 348,** Prints Division/New York Public Library, Astor, Lenox and Tilden Foundations   **Page 360L,** Courtesy Georgia Department of Archives & History   **Page 360R,** John L. McGuire Collection   **Page 371,** Library of Congress   **Page 372,** Library of Congress   **Page 390,** Valentine Museum   **Page 401,** Library of Congress   **Page 402,** Library of Congress   **Page 421,** Edison National Historic Site/U.S. Dept. of the Interior   **Page 430,** Culver Pictures   **Page 431,** Culver Pictures   **Page 432,** Brown Brothers   **Page 435,** Mrs. Vincent Astor   **Page 438,** Nebraska State Historical Society   **Page 448,** Culver Pictures   **Page 452,** Culver Pictures   **Page 456,** From the Hultz Collection   **Page 465,** The Granger Collection   **Page 473,** Culver Pictures   **Page 476,** The Museum of the City of New York   **Page 480,** George Eastman House   **Page 481,** Brown Brothers   **Page 487,** Hogan Jazz Archives,   **Page**

489, Library of Congress   **Page 500,** Culver Pictures   **Page 500B,** Courtesy American Antiquarian Society   **Page 510,** Harper's Weekly   **Page 514,** Culver Pictures   **Page 529,** Bettmann Archive   **Page 531,** Library of Congress   **Page 541,** Library of Congress   **Page 553,** National Park Service/U.S. Dept. of the Interior   **Page 559,** AP/Wide World   **Page 569,** Brown Brothers   **Page 576,** Library of Congress   **Page 590,** The Archives of Labor and Urban Affairs, Wayne State Univ.   **Page 592,** Music Division/ New York Public Library, Astor, Lenox and Tilden Foundations   **Page 602,** Brown Brothers   **Page 605,** Chicago Tribune-NY News Syndicate   **Page 611,** Culver Pictures   **Page 615,** Culver Pictures   **Page 620,** Ben Shahn, BARTHOLOMEO VANZETTI AND NICOLA SACCO (1931–32). Tempera on paper over composition board, 10 x 14; dp. Gift of Mrs. John D. Rockefeller, Jr. Collection, The Museum of Modern Art, New York   **Page 621,** Brown Brothers   **Page 631,** New York Times, October 25, 1929   **Page 638,** Culver Pictures   **Page 644,** Brown Brothers   **Page 649,** AP/Wide World   **Page 663,** Culver Pictures   **Page 668,** United Press International Photo   **Page 672,** Official U.S. Navy Photograph   **Page 681,** The National Archives   **Page 686,** The Franklin D. Roosevelt Library   **Page 690,** United States Air Force photo   **Page 697L,** James Whitmore/Life Magazine/Time Warner Inc.   **Page 697R,** Thomas D. McAvoy   **Page 712,** Bettmann Archive   **Page 715,** Film Stills Archive Collection/ The Museum of Modern Art   **Page 721,** AP/Wide World   **Page 729,** Bettmann Archive   **Page 735,** AP/Wide World   **Page 737,** Life Magazine/Time Warner Inc.   **Page 740,** Don Wright/Life Magazine/Time Warner Inc.   **Page 745,** Bettmann Archive   **Page 748,** Bettmann Archive   **Page 764,** Kent State University News Service   **Page 772,** AP/Wide World   **Page 778,** Charles Moore/Black Star   **Page 782,** John Launois/Black Star   **Page 784,** Constantine Manos/Magnum Photos   **Page 797,** Arthur Grace/Sygma   **Page 807,** Alex Webb/Magnum Photos   **Page 816,** Bill Fitzpatrick/The White House   **Page 818,** Special Features/SIPA-Press   **Page 829R,** Bossu/Sygma

Index